Comparing Economic Systems in the Twenty-First Century

Comparing Economic Systems in the Twenty-First Century

Seventh Edition

Paul R. Gregory
University of Houston
German Institute for Economic Research (DIW Berlin)

Robert C. Stuart
Rutgers University

HOUGHTON MIFFLIN COMPANY   Boston   New York

We dedicate this book to our wives, Annemarie and Beverly.

V.P., Publisher: George Hoffman
Sponsoring Editor: Ann West
Editorial Associate: Tonya Lobato
Senior Project Editor: Maria Morelli
Senior Production/Design Coordinator: Jennifer Meyer Dare
Senior Manufacturing Coordinator: Priscilla Bailey
Executive Marketing Manager: Andy Fisher

Cover Image: "Fall 2000," gouache on paper, by Nancy Simonds

Printed in the U.S.A.

Library of Congress Catalog Card Number: 2002116643

ISBN: 0-618-26181-8

2 3 4 5 6 7 8 9-MP-07 06 05 04

Contents

Preface

This seventh edition of *Comparative Economic Systems* is unique by adopting a new title, and in many respects, a new approach to the study of different economic systems. This book has been organized to facilitate a tour through the contemporary field of comparative economic systems in a global setting. In earlier editions of *Comparative Economic Systems*, we dealt with the central issue of capitalism versus socialism during an era in which roughly one-third of the world's population lived under some form of a socialist economic system. During this era, differences among capitalist variants were not viewed as important, and the demise of the Soviet Union and its empire in Eastern Europe was viewed as a remote possibility. Transition was a theoretical concept and reform of the socialist systems was viewed as modest and ineffective. Systemic change, the cornerstone of transition in the 1990s, was largely nonexistent in an earlier era.

Today, in the early years of a new millennium, we live in a new and very different world. The Soviet-style "administrative command" economy exists only in limited variants such as Cuba and North Korea. The Soviet Union itself has disappeared to be replaced by fifteen independent nations. The two largest countries in the world, India and China, can now be counted as fast-growing economies. Europe is well on its way to creating a "United States of Europe," which in the summer of 2003 agreed to expand its boundaries to admit new entrants from Eastern and Southeastern Europe, events unthinkable only a few years ago. The transition from socialism to capitalism is no longer a theoretical exercise since more than twenty-five independent nations are currently engaged in the difficult task of institutional restructuring moving towards the creation of market economies. Indeed, even in economies not generally classified as transition economies (for example, China), the components of transition (for example, privatization) are of fundamental importance.

Economists have long argued that differing economic systems, or different organizational arrangements, matter as they influence resource allocation in various national (country) settings. In recent years, the national settings have changed, as have the economic systems themselves, to provide important new perspectives on the nature and impact of differing economic systems in a global setting. Economists have a new interest in these issues.

For much of the latter half of the twentieth century, the field of comparative economic systems was dominated by two important characteristics. First, there were, both in theory and in practice, clearly delineated (though not necessarily pure) variants of differing economics systems. The main variants were the administrative command economy of the Soviet Union, and the market capitalist economy of the United States. While at the same time there were interesting system variants such as Sweden,

Yugoslavia, and Japan, the era of the cold war was a dominant political paradigm for framing our analyses of differing economic systems with much of our attention inevitably devoted to the United States–Soviet Union comparison. Second, one of the most challenging aspects of comparing different economic systems was the need to characterize different systems, and to develop both a theoretical framework and the analytical tools necessary for careful comparative work in an era of limited systemic change and secrecy. The contemporary era is one in which there has been an explosion of interest in these issues, vastly improving our ability to understand and to compare different economic systems. Most important, economic systems have come to be recognized as organizational arrangements subject to change, a set of themes now substantially integrated into mainstream microeconomic theory. This presents observers with a setting fundamentally different in several ways from that which prevailed during most of the command era.

First, the stylized variants have largely disappeared following the collapse of the Soviet Union in December of 1991 as a political and economic entity, and the emergence of transition as a critical phase of system change. Second, with the end of the cold war era, globalization has accelerated, and most notably has influenced many countries and differing systems that were not formerly major participants in the global economy. Third, these dramatic changes have significantly enhanced our interest in differing economic systems both from a theoretical perspective and also from a practical perspective as we observe new and important alliances emerging in the global economy. Fourth, the new comparative economics of the twenty-first century must address a new set of issues. We are now learning that the capitalist world is itself operating according to different models, yielding quite different outcomes. Countries like the United States, Canada, Australia, New Zealand, and the United Kingdom follow an Anglo-Saxon model that uses flexible labor markets, a smaller role for the welfare state, and shareholder-oriented corporate governance. At the same time, the European model uses more structured labor markets and corporate governance arrangements that favor stakeholders over shareholders and that rely more on bank finance than on stock markets. Over the years, these models have produced remarkably different outcomes. The Asian Model, pioneered in Japan, mobilizes capital to create a high rate of capital formation disbursed by large banks, and uses family-owned conglomerates for production. This Asian model produced the Japanese economic miracle of the early post World War II era, and the subsequent rise of the Four Tigers of Southeast Asia. However, it also produced an Asian crisis in Southeast Asia in 1997 and more than a decade of stagnation in Japan. While the Anglo-Saxon model has produced relatively rapid economic growth in the United States since the early 1980s, the United States economy has continued to experience cyclical instability and an investment bubble that burst at the turn of the century.

Organization

Past and present users may wish to know how this Seventh Edition differs from previous editions. This edition is divided into six parts: Part I deals with the definition and measurement of economic systems and their change over time. Part II deals with the theory of economic systems, identifying the main models: planned and market socialism, and capitalism. The chapters in Part III, which occupy the bulk of the book, look at economic systems in practice. Part IV studies the transition of one economic system to another, namely the process of transition from planned socialism to a market economy. Part V discusses transition in practice and looks at common components of transition economies. Finally, Part VI concludes with an evaluation of transition performance since the 1980s and looks ahead to the future of economic systems in the twenty-first century.

Part I is perhaps the least changed because the pure theory of economic systems has not changed that much, but there are some notable updates. Chapter 1 examines transition with better historical perspective now that we have more than a decade of experience and some specialists are asking whether "transition has been completed." It presents a slightly less optimistic view of the institutions of market economies, given the troubling stagnation of the European and Japanese economies. Chapter 2 continues to use the classic threefold divisions of economic systems into capitalism, planned and market socialism, but introduces as well new models such as an Islamic model and the to-date poorly defined Latin American model. It also adds discussion of public choice, namely the organization of political decision making either by democracy or by dictatorship.

In Chapter 3, we look at how economic systems are established and maintained and what determines an economic outcome. Chapter 4 looks at the dynamics of economic systems and why they change, and now contains stronger elements of the new institutional economics, while providing an overview of transition for those readers who cannot delve into this topic deeply in the fourth part of this book.

Part II examines the theory of capitalism (Chapter 5), planned socialism (Chapter 6), and market socialism (Chapter 7). The material in these chapters has been updated but the format remains the same as in the previous edition.

Part III departs from the country emphasis of the previous edition by dividing capitalism into three basic variants: the Anglo-Saxon model, the European model, and the Asian model. Rather than discussing the peculiar features of specific market economies, we look for common features that bind them to a particular type of economic model. In each case, we examine the model's constitutional foundations, its corporate governance procedures, the functioning of its capital and labor markets, and how it provides for income and security.

Chapter 8, almost entirely rewritten, is no longer the "American Economy," but rather the "Anglo-Saxon Model of Capitalism," which begins with the constitutional foundations of the U.S. Constitution. We look at this broader model's corporate governance structures, oriented towards creating shareholder value, and its use of equity markets to raise capital. The role of government regulation (and deregulation) is also discussed, and the "flexible" Anglo-Saxon labor market is examined. The overall role of government in providing for income and security rounds out the chapter.

Chapter 9, a new chapter on the European model, examines first the political context of the European Union and then discusses the model's philosophical foundations in the theories of mercantilism, Marx, and the social market economy, which reflect themselves in its civil law legal foundations. European corporate governance, capital markets, labor markets and provisions for welfare are then contrasted with those of the Anglo-Saxon model. The European labor market is shown to be less flexible; its capital market relies more on bank lending, and its corporate governance is influenced by stakeholder interests and by worker participation. In the European model, the state provides a more generous welfare state, and state enterprise plays a greater role.

Chapter 10, largely rewritten from the former Chapter 12, presents the Asian model, pioneered in Japan and then exported to many parts of Asia including the Four Tigers of Southeast Asia—South Korea, Singapore, Taiwan, and Hong Kong. The Asian model's ideological foundations, largely uninfluenced by events in the Western world, are shown to be rooted in Confucianism; and economic policies are shown to be heavily influenced by relative backwardness, a theory formulated by Alexander Gerschenkron to explain the greater state role and the high capital formation proportions of the Asian economies. Asian labor markets, corporate governance, and state regulation are then contrasted with both the Anglo-Saxon and European models, and the limited role of the welfare state is discussed.

Chapter 11, heavily revised from former Chapter 9, discusses the Soviet administrative command economy in terms of its history, operations, and performance. Recent research on how this economy functioned from the formerly secret Soviet state and party archives is introduced, and the political economy of the dictatorship installed first by Stalin is discussed.

Chapter 12, also heavily revised (formerly Chapter 10), considers the Chinese economy as a possible model of market socialism but primarily from the perspective of its rapid growth since 1979 and its ability to organize rapid growth under the continued domination of the Communist party. China's initial successes are discussed as are the problems that could threaten its future growth, including the state-dominated capital market and the political protection of state-owned enterprises.

The second half of the book, encompassing Parts IV, V, and VI, is almost entirely new to the seventh edition and focuses on transition in theory and practice. The transition era, at the forefront of our study in the last three parts, represents change unthinkable only a few years ago, and has become integral to our understanding of economic systems today and moving forward.

In Part IV we turn to a discussion of transition and the experiences of the transition economies following the collapse of the administrative command economies during the late 1980s and their replacement with market economic systems during the 1990s.

As a lead-in to the beginnings of transition, the discussion of the collapse of the command economies is retained in Chapter 13. In Chapter 14, the emerging terminology and concepts of the transition are introduced along with a characterization of those economies typically classified as transition economies.

Chapter 15 focuses on issues of measurement and especially the characteristic pattern of output change during transition, specifically an initial collapse, in some cases of major proportions, followed by gradual economic recovery. Examining this pattern of output change is important not only for an ultimate assessment of the results of transition, but also for analyzing the patterns of change during the transition process.

Throughout the transition era, a great deal of attention has been paid to transition models, the "big push" compared to the gradualist approach. These models and their subsequent replacement with a more sophisticated analysis of emerging transition patterns, for example the sequencing and harmonizing of transition elements, is the focus of Chapter 16, setting the scene for a discussion of the components of transition.

In Part V we turn to the transition experience itself, characterized in terms of not only the performance of the transition economies, but also the major components of transition, namely privatization, macroeconomic change in a global perspective, and issues pertaining to the well-being of human populations, specifically the maintenance of a safety net. Chapter 17 is devoted to privatization, perhaps the core of transition as private property rights emerge to replace state ownership of the command era. Once again, timing is important as the early emphasis on mass privatization has been replaced by emphasis on restructuring or changes in corporate governance. Attention is paid to the empirical evidence on the effectiveness of privatization and changes in corporate governance in the transition economies, emerging market economies, and in the industrialized Western economies.

Chapter 18 is devoted to the development of new macroeconomic arrangements, perhaps one of the weakest components of the administrative command experience. In this chapter, the focus is the role of the government sector in the transition economy, the development of banking and financial arrangements, and the emergence of new policy issues in the transition setting.

Chapter 19 presents a discussion of transition economies in the global environment. Emerging from the peculiar trading arrangements, policies, and outcomes of the command era, the transition economies faced the immediate need to develop new trading arrangements and to move quickly toward the introduction of convertible currencies. For economies generally thought to be "closed" over a period of many years, the challenges of entering a rapidly expanding global trading system were significant.

Chapter 20 is devoted to more detailed discussion of the well-being of the population or the maintenance of the safety net. The safety net is a crucial component of the transition process and a major element of our assessment of successes and failures.

In the concluding part of the text, Chapters 21 and 22 provide a detailed overview of global economic systems characterized within the dimensions developed in earlier chapters. Although projections of future performance must be developed and assessed with caution, the recent critical patterns of change in both transition and non-transition economies, and indeed our changing perspectives on the evolution of different economic systems is a major focus of the concluding chapters.

A Note on Studying Economic Systems Today

It is perhaps ironic that defining the boundaries and the content of the field of comparative economic systems is more difficult today than it was twenty years ago. It is ironic because the events of recent years have sharply increased our interest in, and analysis of, differing economic systems. As we examine different economic systems in theory and in practice, we can now do so through a body of literature far richer than would have been the case just a few years ago. For example, in past times, it was difficult to understand the inner workings of the socialist enterprise, and even more difficult to characterize the impact of peculiar trading arrangements in what were effectively "closed" economies. Today, there is a burgeoning literature on privatization, a changing role for the state, and changes in corporate governance. Additionally, economic theory has paid increasing attention to institutions; the cornerstone of economic systems, and transition has provided us with a wealth of empirical literature on differing outcomes in different historical and geographical settings, using different policy perspectives with differing institutional arrangements. In these new settings, the potential for both theorizing and empirical analysis is great. Moreover, as the command economies have emerged into a global setting, a vast array of new trading arrangements and exchange rate regimes have been developed to handle special national and regional circumstances.

The sizable body of new literature requires us to pay careful attention to sources and definitions. Notes and references are critical for the presentation of key sources. Entering a significantly larger body of literature is a rewarding but challenging task. Moreover, the transition era has created a considerable amount of new terminology related especially to the transition experience. This terminology appears in bold face in the text and is defined in a glossary at the end of the book.

If the content of comparative economic systems was narrowly focused on stylized system variants during much of the twentieth century, nothing could be further from the truth in the twenty-first century. Indeed, the content of contemporary comparative economic systems is closer to the mainstream of economic and political thought than ever before, and there is no region of the world, whether Latin America, Asia, or Europe that escapes attention. It is this new content and new relevance of comparative economic systems that is the central theme of this book.

Acknowledgments

We are indebted to the large number of scholars who laid the groundwork for our ever-changing exploration of comparative economic systems. Finally, we greatly appreciate the help and guidance received from the staff at Houghton Mifflin. Special thanks go to Ann West, Senior Sponsoring Editor, Tonya Lobato, Editorial Associate, and Maria Morelli, Senior Project Editor.

Paul R. Gregory
Robert C. Stuart

PART I

Economic Systems: Issues, Definitions, Comparisons

1

World Economic Systems in the Twenty-First Century

Comparative economic systems studies economic systems and their impact on the allocation of resources. Comparative economic systems focuses on how an economy's organizational arrangements combine with economic policies in distinct natural and historical settings to influence economic outcomes. If the economic system itself or its system components influence resource allocation in identifiable ways, we can select an optimal set of organizational arrangements to achieve our economic objectives (for example, rapid economic growth).

The **economic system** *is the set of institutional arrangements used to allocate scarce resources.* The limits of productive resources (labor, land, and capital) dictate the scarcity of resources. As a result of scarcity, we must decide in an orderly way what is produced, how to produce it, and for whom it is produced. If orderly arrangements are absent, anarchy and chaos will result. Economic systems exist within countries both large and small, developed and less developed. Some countries are rich in human capital; others are rich in natural resources.

The World Economy, History, and Economic Systems

As we enter the third millennium, we should consider what we can learn for the present from the past. If we look back almost two centuries to 1820, we find that the world was populated by one billion people, most of whom were in Asia. These one billion people produced a world output well below one trillion in today's dollars. At the start of the third millennium, more than five billion people populate the globe, producing a GDP of thirty trillion dollars.[1] In 1820, the best single measure of the living standard, world per capita GDP, stood at less than $700; by 2000 it had increased to almost $6,000. In the past two centuries, population increased by more than seven times, production by more than thirty times, and the standard of living by almost nine times.

These dry statistics point to significant changes in the way we live. Two hundred years ago, most people worked in agriculture; few had traveled more than fifty miles from where they were born; most subsisted on bread and a few vegetables. The wealthy went to bed cold because of poor heating, and occupants of the most opulent house of Europe, the Versailles Palace, went for months without baths. In the year 2003, the average citizen of the United States or of a European country works in an well-heated office, enjoys a wide variety of affordable foods from all over the world, and has traveled to other continents.

This economic progress has not been evenly shared. If we go further back in time to 1500, we see that living standards were roughly equal throughout the world, with Asia, Africa, and Europe having about the same per capita GDP (Figure 1.1). We all started with approximately the same standard of living—presumably not much above that required for subsistence. Asia was the dominant producer in 1500, given its much larger population. Europe was relatively small, and North America had just been discovered. By 1820, Europe and the United States had already begun to pull ahead of the rest of the world, and by 1950, the difference between Europe and the United States and other regions was dramatic. At the end of World War II, Western Europe and the United States accounted for most of world output and had per capita GDPs that were large multiples of those of the rest of the world. Asia had been eclipsed, and Africa continued its relative downward spiral. The Soviet empire accounted for almost 15 percent of world output, thanks to the perceived industrial might of the Soviet Union itself (Figure 1.2). Between 1820 and 1950, Japan was the only Asian nation to achieve affluence.

The half-century from 1950 to the new millennium saw a resurgence of the long-dormant Asia and the dramatic decline of the republics that made up the former Soviet

FIGURE 1.1   Per Capita GDP, 1990 International Dollars

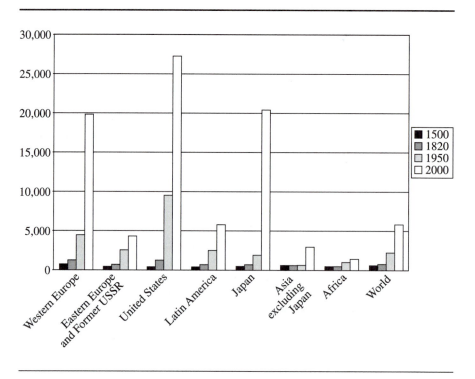

FIGURE 1.2   Shares of World GDP

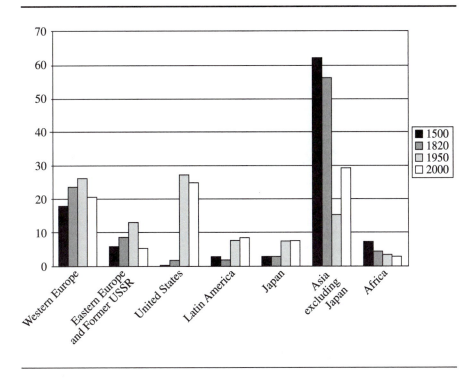

Union as they began their transformations to a market economy. Asia's resurgence was largely the consequence of exceptional economic growth in China since the late 1970s. Recently India began to grow rapidly, but it is too early to tell whether this rapid growth will be sustained. If the world's two most populous countries, China and India, continue on their path to economic development, the face of the world will be changed forever. China, despite three decades of rapid growth, remains today a relatively poor country. Asia's other economic giant, Japan, virtually ceased growing in the 1990s and shows no signs of recovering its earlier dynamism. Despite some promising starts, Latin America failed to make much progress over the past half-century, and Africa remains mired in economic and social stagnation.

Europe and the European offshoots in North America and Australasia produce more than half of the world's output but account for less than a quarter of its population. Less than 20 percent of the world's population lives in the affluent countries of Western Europe, North America, Australasia, and Japan (see Figure 1.3A). The affluence that most of us take for granted is actually quite rare in today's world. As we begin the third millennium, we still have a "third world" that has not shared in economic progress.

This economic progress of the past thousand years has given us the gift of a longer life. In the first year of the second millennium (1000), the average newborn could

FIGURE 1.3(A)   Changes in the Distribution of World Population
over the Last Two Centuries

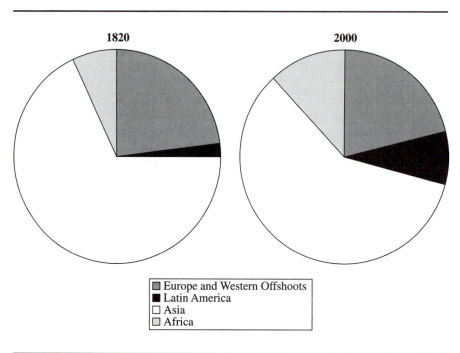

expect to live to the ripe old age of 24. Eight hundred years later, life expectancy had not increased much in Asia, Africa, or Latin America, but it had risen to 36 in the affluent world. By 1950, life expectancies had increased in both rich and poor countries. Newborns in the poor countries of Asia, Africa, and Latin America could expect to live to 44, and newborns in the most affluent countries had an expected lifespan of 66 years. Half a century later, newborns in affluent countries could expect to live to 78 years, 14 years longer than newborns in poor countries (see Figure 1.4). These advances were due to the better nutrition, science, and technology that accompany economic progress. Those who protest economic growth and yearn for the simpler life of yesteryear are unwittingly wishing for a life that is nearly over by the age of 50.

Since 1820, there has been a significant realignment of economic fortunes in favor of a select few countries located largely in Western Europe, North America, and parts of Asia. The dramatic economic rise of Europe and North America in the nineteenth century is called the **Industrial Revolution**, a phenomenon that began in England and then spread to the European continent and to North America. The Industrial Revolution was fueled by the rapid growth of science and technology (the steam engine, the cotton spindle, and electricity); the first transportation and communications revolution (steamships, railroads, and the telegraph); and the creation of institutions that favored economic progress, such as the limited-liability corporation, constitutions that limited

FIGURE 1.3(B)   Changes in the Distribution of World Output (GDP) over the Last Two Centuries

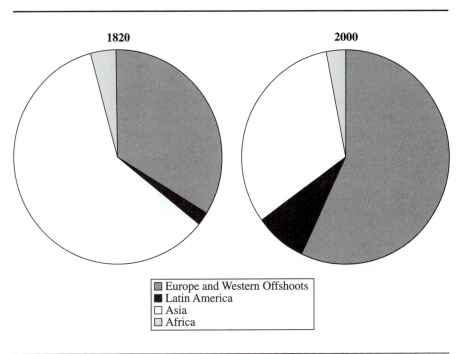

1820   2000

☐ Europe and Western Offshoots
■ Latin America
☐ Asia
☐ Africa

the reach of government and protected private property, and stock exchanges that raised capital. Asia was a latecomer to the Industrial Revolution. Japan experienced it in the first half of the nineteenth century, and the Four Southeast Asian Tigers (Hong Kong, Singapore, Taiwan, and South Korea) and the world's most populous country, China, began experiencing rapid growth in the 1970s and thereafter.

Other countries or empires had experienced economic progress in the remote past, but this progress was not sustained. The Greek, Roman, and early Chinese and Indian civilizations created high levels of wealth for their eras, but their achievements were later reversed. It was only with the Industrial Revolution that economic progress appeared to become irreversible, although, as we have noted, not evenly shared.

Economic progress occurs when at least one of the following four conditions is met:[2]

1. Opportunities arise to settle empty areas endowed with fertile land and resources.
2. Opportunities arise to increase trade and the movement of capital among countries.
3. Technological innovations occur.
4. Economic institutions improve.

The settlement of new areas was the source of growth for the Roman Empire and explains the relatively high level of Chinese living standards in the eighth century. The

FIGURE **1.4**   Life Expectancy in Years, from 1000 to 2000

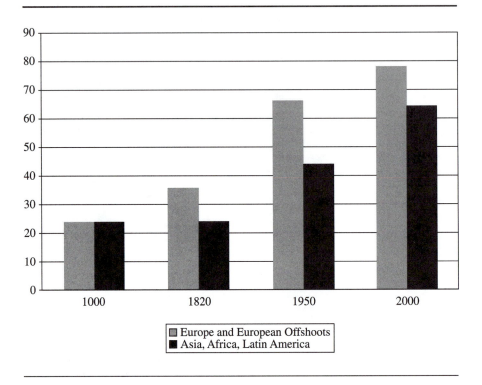

European settlement of North America after Columbus's discovery of the new world in 1492 explains the rising affluence of Western Europe and of North America itself.

The rising wealth of Venice between 1000 and 1500 is explained by the Venetian opening of land trade routes to China and India. Portugal's rise after 1500 is attributable to its opening of trade, navigation, and settlement of the Atlantic Islands, Africa, Japan, and China by sea routes. The rapid economic growth of the affluent world in the late nineteenth century and after World War II is largely due to the rapid growth of international trade as new transportation and communications systems emerged and barriers to trade fell.

Periods of economic prosperity also can often be explained by technological change. The Industrial Revolution that began in England in the eighteenth century was based on new sources of power and on mechanized factories—primitive technologies by today's standards. The rapid growth of the United States in the 1990s can be attributed to the revolution in computer and communications technologies. Future waves of economic growth will be spurred by technologies that we cannot even conceive of today.

This book is about the fourth source of economic growth and prosperity: the economic system that we use to take advantage of trading opportunities, to settle new areas, and to use new technologies to economic advantage. Economic history shows that economic progress depends on having the right constellation of economic institutions. **Economic institutions** are those bodies that reflect the way we organize our economic activities. They cover a broad range of economic, social, and political activities: how we govern ourselves, our laws concerning internal and external trade, how property is owned, how economic activity is organized into various business forms, and our formal and informal practices. We discuss these institutions and how they are measured in the next chapter.

Prior to the end of the 1990s, comparative economics focused on two distinct models: capitalism and socialism. Now we must examine different issues for the twenty-first century.

The Economy of the Twenty-First Century

If Rip Van Winkle woke in 2003 after a thirty-year sleep, he would be hard pressed to recognize the world he had last seen. In 1973, at the beginning of his sleep, life was more simple. About one-third of the world's population lived under Soviet-style or Chinese-style socialism dictated by the Communist party leadership. Although these economies were not prospering, they were muddling along without imminent threat of demise. The countries of Eastern Europe were held in the political and economic embrace of the Soviet Union. Although some reform of their Soviet-type economies had occurred, change was modest and often unsuccessful.

The Western world, in 1973, was experiencing energy shocks, recessions, and stagflation. How well it would deal with these problems remained to be seen. The rest of the world, with the exception of Japan, appeared stuck at a low level of economic development. Latin America, South America, and Africa were not progressing toward long-term economic growth and development.

Imagine Rip Van Winkle's shock upon awakening in 2003. The Soviet empire has disintegrated; Germany has reunited; the Communist party no longer exists as a centralized, controlling organization; China has been experiencing phenomenal growth; the Soviet Union has been broken up into fifteen separate countries, ranging from the large economies of Russia and Ukraine to the smaller Central Asian countries surrounding the Caspian Sea. After an extended depression, Russia is growing again and was officially declared a "market economy" in the spring of 2002. The "Four Asian Tigers"—Taiwan, Hong Kong, South Korea, and Singapore—have been growing at phenomenal rates since the 1970s, although their growth was interrupted by an "Asian Crisis" in 1998. Japan, a model of rapid growth in the 1950s and 1960s, remains mired in recessions that have undermined its efforts for nearly a decade. Although there are some bright spots in Latin America, such as Chile and Brazil, its economies are not progressing along a broad front. The whole region continues to be plagued by economic and political instability. Africa remains stagnant. A large number of its countries are controlled by oppressive dictators who have little or no interest in economic progress. Africa has experienced debilitating civil wars, and its suffering population has been struck by a massive AIDS epidemic.

The Collapse of Communism

The year 1985 marked the starting point for serious change in the communist bloc. In this year, the newly selected leader of the Soviet Communist party, Mikhail Gorbachev, announced his intention to initiate "radical" reform. Up until this point, the Soviet Union had been the prime example of a centrally planned economy. It had experienced serious problems in economic performance for decades but had limited interest in economic reform. Few in 1985 could anticipate that five years later, Mikhail Gorbachev would receive a Nobel Peace Prize for his bold reforms, especially those related to Eastern Europe and foreign policy.

As one reform after another was instituted, the terms *glasnost, democratization,* and *perestroika* entered the vocabulary. Indeed, the pace of political and social change was rapid. Most significant from a political and economic perspective, the constitutionally guaranteed "leading role" of the Communist party was ended in the summer of 1991. The international consequences were far-reaching. Soviet tanks would no longer be used to prop up unpopular dictatorships. Caught between the pincers of liberal reform in the Soviet Union and the attraction of consumer affluence in Western Europe, former communist dictatorships tumbled one after the other. The Berlin Wall was opened in November of 1989 and subsequently dismantled.

The overthrow of the East German communist regime was followed by a series of mostly bloodless revolutions in Eastern and central Europe. By the end of 1989, the Communist political structure in Czechoslovakia (the Czech and Slovak Federal Republic) was toppled, as Václav Havel was elected president. In Bulgaria, the communist regime was replaced in November of 1989. In Hungary, free elections were held in 1990. In the fall of 1989, Lech Walesa was elected president of Poland. Finally, the despotic dictator of Romania, Nicolae Ceausescu, was executed in a bloody uprising.

Political and economic change took a different course in the fifteen "newly independent states" formed from the ashes of the Soviet Union. Whereas in Eastern Europe the new leaders were largely drawn from the ranks of those who opposed communist power, in the former Soviet Union the old elite remained in charge. In Russia, the former communist Politburo member Boris Yeltsin became the first Russian president and introduced in 1993 the Yeltsin Constitution, creating a powerful Russian presidency. Yeltsin instituted reforms that put Russia on the path to creating a market economy, but the legislature continued to be dominated by the Communist party, which resisted reform. As Yeltsin's health deteriorated, his own commitment to reform faltered. He was replaced at the end of 1999 by his designated successor Vladimir Putin, a former KGB operative, and at long last, Russia had a relatively young leader prepared to oversee its economic development. The other former Soviet republics, with the exception of the three Baltic republics, continued to be led by leaders from the Soviet past, who established near dictatorships in a number of cases, such as in Belarus, Azerbaizhan, Uzbekistan, and Turkmenistan. Each of these newly independent states suffered severe declines in output that dwarfed the U.S. Great Depression of the 1930s. Although their growth resumed near the turn of the century, it remains unclear whether these countries will be able to create economic systems that will yield rising standards of living.

Events in China were equally dramatic, but they had quite different results. In the late 1970s the aging Chinese communist leadership determined to open the country to the West and to reform the Chinese planned economic system. The reintroduction of private incentives in agriculture and a large influx of foreign investment boosted economic growth and brought about substantial improvements in living standards. However, liberalization quickly spilled over into political and social life. When, in the spring of 1989, opposition groups began to demand fundamental changes—an end to the Communist party monopoly, free speech, and democratic elections—the communist regime cracked down with the Tiananmen Square massacre and the arrest of leading dissidents. In response, Western governments imposed sanctions against the Chinese regime. China's leaders continued economic reform, especially the freeing of private initiative and openness to the West, despite its rejection of political democracy. China assumed domestic rule of Hong Kong in 1998 in accordance with an international agreement long in place, and the future of Hong Kong's democracy remains unclear.

By the start of the new millennium, strict communist regimes remained only in Cuba, and North Korea. Vietnam and Cambodia took steps toward reform and reconciliation with their archenemies in the West, a course that resulted in Vietnam's restoration of diplomatic relations with the United States in 1994.

An Appraisal of Transition

The collapse of communist economies and of communist states dates back less than two decades—a short time for economic appraisal. The centrally planned economies of the communist countries of the Soviet Union, Eastern Europe, Asia (China, Cambodia, Mongolia, and Vietnam), and Latin America (Cuba) had long realized that their economic system was not producing the desired results of economic growth, technological progress, and rising living standards. They therefore attempted reform. **Reform** is an attempt to improve an economic system without changing its fundamental character. These reform efforts originated in the Soviet Union in the late 1950s and spread to Eastern Europe, but in no case was reform successful. In the late 1980s and early 1990s, the centrally planned economies turned from reform to transition. **Transition** is the process of change from one type of economic system to another. In the case of the planned socialist economies, the desired transition was from a planned to a market economy. Detailed definitions will be provided in the next chapter. For now, it is sufficient to consider the general course of this transition.

Of the twenty-five or more transition economies, fewer than ten are clear success stories. They are located in Central Europe (Poland, Hungary, the Czech and Slovak Republics), on the northern border of Europe (the three Baltic states of Estonia, Latvia, and Lithuania), and to the immediate south of Austria (Slovenia). We can hope that other transition economies, such as Russia, Bulgaria, and Romania, can soon be declared transition successes, but it is still too early to decide. Some transition countries remained stagnant, with few signs of progress.

The Industrialized World

Although change was less dramatic in the industrialized West, change has occurred. With few exceptions, the 1990s witnessed voter repudiation of the more extreme forms of social democracy. The 1980s had been dominated by Reaganism in the United States and by Thatcherism in England—both movements committed to replacing the ills of "big government" with the exercised benefits of the market. In Germany, the conservative Christian Democratic party exercised power over German politics at the expense of the Social Democratic Party until the late 1990s. Western conservatism set in motion policies to reduce the role of government in the economy and to shift existing government functions from federal to state and local levels. Tax reductions were used to improve incentives, welfare programs were cut, and privatization was encouraged in Great Britain, Germany, and France. Even Sweden, long a symbol of welfare statism, experienced a voter backlash against excessive social expenditures and high tax rates.

The 1990s held fewer surprises for the industrialized West. The major change was the shattering of the myth of Japanese invincibility. Japan's growth rates have tapered off, and Japan has been bogged down by recessions since the 1990s. Although Japan's trade performance has remained strong, doubt has begun to grow about the wisdom of Japan's touted industrial policy and its practice of lifetime employment.

The recessions of the late 1990s, which hit Western Europe, raised Europe's already high unemployment rates. Europe's hard times forced it to consider restructuring its social welfare policies and instituting policies to reestablish its competitive position in world markets.

The conservative economic policies that characterized the industrialized West in the 1980s spread into Latin America in the 1980s. In Latin America, programs were initiated to reestablish private enterprise, and experiments with socialism were largely aborted. In Southeast Asia, the remarkable rise of the "Four Tigers" (Singapore, South Korea, Taiwan, and Hong Kong) demonstrated that formerly poor Asian countries could industrialize rapidly and compete in world manufacturing markets using export-oriented economic policies. The strong economic performance of the Four Tigers contrasted sharply with the continued stagnation of Bangladesh and Pakistan, countries that continued to pursue economic policies of state interventionism and protection.

The 1980s and 1990s revealed the limits to conservative economic policies. United States political experience showed public unwillingness to alter fundamentally the social security system put in place in the 1930s. And the British experience under Thatcher revealed a general unwillingness to abandon the national health service or to support growth-oriented tax reform that appeared to favor upper-income groups.

The Third World

A striking feature of the world economy of the early twenty-first century is that prosperity remains limited to a small proportion of the world's population. More than three-quarters of the world's population continues to live in poverty. The average citizen of Asia, Africa, and Latin America remains largely untouched by the industrial–technological revolutions that have created enormous affluence in North America, Western Europe, and Australia. The twentieth century had offered few examples of countries that had made the transition from relative poverty to relative affluence, such as Japan.

In the last two decades of the twentieth century, a remarkable shift took place. Previously poor countries in Southeast Asia—Hong Kong, South Korea, Taiwan, and Singapore—underwent rapid growth that culminated in the achievement of living standards approaching those of the industrialized West. Other Asian countries, such as Indonesia, Thailand, and Malaysia, attempted to duplicate this feat. Moreover, Latin American countries, such as Chile and Brazil, have recorded rapid growth. The Asian miracle experienced setbacks in 1998 as currency crises and bank failures precipitated an "Asian Crisis." The election victories of Bill Clinton in the United States, Tony Blair in Great Britain, and Gerhart Schroeder in Germany in the 1990s were all achieved with promises of a "middle way" between conservatism and social democracy. The Clinton presidency, for example, was characterized by reform of the welfare system and by balanced budgets. The Blair government continued the basic policies of Thatcher, and the Schroeder government initially lowered taxes on business.

The early years of the first decade of the twenty-first century have again shown that fine balance between the right and the left. A Republican, George Bush, was elected president of the United States in 2000; Italy elected a conservative president in 2001, and the French socialists lost the presidential election of 2002 in a rout.

Multinationalism and Globalism

The 1980s and 1990s saw a strong expansion of economic internationalism and an expanding role for multinational corporations. Europe established a united European Union and now has one currency, the euro. The United States, Canada, and Mexico established a barrier-free North American market (NAFTA) in 1994. This decisive move toward economic integration has raised the issue of multinationalism versus national sovereignty—a divisive issue that must be resolved in the twenty-first century. Multinationalism threatens national identity and weakens sovereign control over economic destiny. How much autonomy should supranational European economic organizations enjoy? How will the European central bank administer its common monetary policy and a common European currency?

The movement toward economic multinationalism has been accompanied by a deeper and more gradual trend: the increased integration of the world economies. The major industrial firms of the West are no longer constrained by national boundaries. In fact, they are no longer national companies; rather, they have become multinational corporations. The IBMs, Siemens, and Sonys of the world are now equally at home in New York, Mexico City, Montreal, London, and Singapore. An oil venture in Indonesia may be carried out by a consortium of BP/Amoco, Royal Dutch Shell, and Exxon/Mobil and may be financed by the Bank of Tokyo and Deutsche Bank. A slight change in U.S. interest rates can cause billions of dollars to flow from Hong Kong, Zurich, and Toronto to New York. Transactions between Venezuela and Austria are conducted in U.S. dollars.

The Choice of Economic Systems in the Twenty-First Century

The dramatic events of the 1990s—the end of the cold war, German reunification, the fall of communist political systems in Eastern Europe, and the dissolution of the Soviet Union—surprised most observers. These changes, unimaginable a few years earlier, raised new and challenging issues.

Only a decade ago, we could frame the study of comparative economic systems as the choice between two quite different economic systems: market capitalism (or simply "market economies") and planned socialism. Market capitalism was practiced in North America, Western Europe, Australasia, and Japan. Planned socialism was practiced throughout the Soviet empire. Now, in the twenty-first century, planned socialism has become an endangered species practiced by two maverick countries, and most of the other countries of the world are striving to become market economies. In fact, in the summer of 2002, Russia, the most populous country of Europe, was officially declared a market economy by an international organization.

The fact that the struggle between capitalism and socialism is over for the time being does not mean that economic systems no longer matter. How a society organizes its economic institutions continues to matter a great deal, only now the differences are more subtle. The Four Tigers of Southeast Asia experienced phenomenal growth because they chose the proper institutional arrangements—export orientation, high saving rates, and heavy investments in education. India (at least until recently), Pakistan, and Bangladesh have stagnated because they have traditionally chosen institutions that do not create economic growth, such as protection from imports. The superior economic performance of the Untied States over Europe in the past two decades is attributed to its more efficient capital market and its more flexible labor market. Japan's economic decline is attributed to its inert political system, inflexible labor markets, and inefficient capital market.

In the twenty-first century, we must study a large number of differences in economic institutions—differences that affect economic performance in significant ways yet are not as significant as the differences between capitalism and socialism.

History shows that we do have a choice of economic systems. The former Soviet Union and the countries of Eastern Europe are actively searching for their economic systems. It is still unknown what answers they will find. The industrialized West has operated with fairly stable economic systems for decades if not centuries, but even these societies must make continuous and often subtle choices concerning the shape of their economic systems. The emerging worlds of Asia and Latin America must make crucial choices concerning the economic systems that will bring them to an appropriate level of affluence. Africa must develop institutions that can create economic progress.

If choosing among economic systems were not possible, the study of comparative economic systems would be less compelling. Insofar as people, through the ballot box and through their private and public lives, make choices that affect the economic system, it is important to stay informed about the strengths and weaknesses of alternative economic systems. We have made a number of such choices in the past.

The first full-fledged, conscious creation of an economic system began in the Soviet Union in the late 1920s, a decade after the October revolution of 1917. After World War II, the Soviet experiment expanded into Eastern Europe, China, North Korea, Cuba, and North Vietnam. At its peak, about one-third of the world's population lived in countries generally described as socialist economic systems dominated by Marxist–Leninist orthodoxy and communist political systems. The spread of Soviet-style communism stimulated a debate about which economic system is "better." In the 1930s, the contrast between the depression-ridden West and the industrializing Soviet Union cast doubt on the superiority of capitalism. The weaknesses of the capitalist system were all too evident, whereas the flaws of the Soviet system were hidden behind a veil of official secrecy and claims of extraordinary successes. The immediate postwar period of the 1950s saw the remarkable economic successes of West Germany and Japan, but slow growth elsewhere caused some again to question the vitality of the capitalist system. A confident Soviet Union launched the first piloted space vehicle and declared its intention to "bury" the West. Soviet leader Nikita Khrushchev boasted about Soviet economic performance. Soon, however, the 1970s and 1980s revealed to what degree the Soviet economy was unable to adjust to change.

The gap between the economic performance of the East and that of the West became more pronounced in the 1980s. The West experienced a sustained recovery from the oil shocks of the 1970s and began a long, uninterrupted business expansion. The East, on the other hand, continued its secular decline. In the Soviet Union, this decline came to be called the "period of stagnation." Promises that things would be better in the future lost their meaning to people who had made considerable sacrifices from the 1930s through World War II. The contrast between the affluence of the West and the stagnation of the East set the stage for the collapse of communism. The final victory of capitalism over socialism was declared, and Marxist–Leninist thought was proclaimed an historical dead end. The Soviet experiment may be dead, but its appeal could be resurrected. If an appropriate path to transition cannot be found and the end result is chaos, enthusiasm for the old system could be revived. Some could claim that although it did not work well, at least it worked.

In our personal and business lives, we copy success. The same is true of economic systems. In the years after World War II, many thought that the Soviet experiment was a success and sought to copy it. In the 1990s, the success of the "Four Tigers" prompted other Asian countries, such as Indonesia, Thailand, and the Philippines, to emulate them. Chile's rapid economic growth has served as an example for other countries in Latin America.

Just as individuals learn from the examples of others, countries learn from the successes and failures of other countries. The ultimate goal of the study of comparative economic systems is to learn what works and in what settings.

Key Terms

economic system	economic institutions	transition
Industrial Revolution	reform	

Notes

1. These figures are from Angus Maddison, *The World Economy: A Millennial Perspective* (Paris: OECD, 2001), pp. 31, 174.
2. *Ibid.,* p. 18.

Recommended Readings

F. A. Hayek, *Studies in Philosophy, Politics, and Economics* (New York: Norton, 1969).

Angus Maddison, *The World Economy: A Millennial Perspective* (Paris: OECD, 2001).

David Remnick, *Lenin's Tomb: The Last Days of the Soviet Empire* (New York: Random House, 1993).

Joseph E. Stiglitz, *Whither Socialism?* (Cambridge, Mass.: MIT Press, 1994).

Gale Stokes, *The Walls Came Tumbling Down: The Collapse of Communism in Eastern Europe* (New York: Oxford University Press, 1993).

World Bank, *From Market to Plan: World Development Report 1996* (Washington, D.C.; World Bank, 1996).

2

Definition and Classification of Economic Systems

Comparative economics has been described as "a field in search of a definition."[1] The definition has become more complex becomes we can no longer neatly divide the world into capitalist and socialist economies. *Comparative economic systems studies economic outcomes in different institutional, geographic, and political settings.* The economic system, along with the conventional inputs of land, labor, and capital, matters in observable and understandable ways. Beyond the economic system and traditional inputs, economic outcomes are also influenced by social, economic, cultural, geographic, and random forces. We must develop methods to understand and to control (hold constant) all these variables in order to isolate the influence of the economic system.

Economic Systems: Definition and Classification

Traditionally, economic systems were classified according to the "isms"—feudalism, capitalism, socialism, and communism. This classification identified a system in terms of one or two important characteristics, such as ownership of the means of production. Our approach is to classify economic systems in terms of their institutional features. **Institutions** exist in a large number of forms: corporations, legal systems, legislatures, unions, and economic customs. They vary in complexity. There is no universally accepted definition of the term *institutions,* but most definitions focus on their serving as the "rules of the game" under which economic decisions are made.[2] Nobel laureate Douglass North writes that "institutions are the rules of the game of a society or, more fundamentally, are the humanly devised constraints that shape human interaction. In consequence, they structure incentives in human exchange whether political, social, or economic."[3] According to this definition, institutions are broadly interpreted to include customs, voting procedures, legislation, organizations such as trade unions and corporations, or any other political, social, and economic rules that affect the way people deal with each other in the exchange of private or public goods. Whenever there are rules of behavior, there must be a means of enforcing these rules. Thus institutions consist not only of the rules themselves but also of the means of their enforcement. Voigt and Engerer cite the five types of **rules** and **enforcement mechanisms** given in Table 2.1.[4]

TABLE 2.1   Societal Institutions:
The Rules of the Game

Type of Rule	Means of Enforcement
Convention	Self-enforcing
Ethical rule	Self-commitment
Customs	Informal social control
Private rule	Organized private enforcement
State law	Organized state enforcement

Rules can be enforced by the state or by private institutions. Conventions are generally accepted practices, such as the unwritten rule that physicians not charge for referrals. Ethical rules, such as the practice of not selling customers defective or dangerous goods, are self-enforced, in this case by the commitment of merchants to accepted codes of behavior. Customs are enforced through informal social control. For example, the practice that officers of a corporation act in the interest of the corporation rather than in their own private interest—called a fiduciary responsibility—is enforced by the threat of firing or salary reduction by the owners of the corporation. Private rules, such as the rules that govern the behavior of dealers in stock exchanges, can be enforced by private enforcement bodies. Violators of these private rules are punished by private bodies, such as the NASDAQ stock exchange. We are more accustomed to rules issued by the state (by which we mean any governing body, state or federal), such as laws and regulations. The state may rule, for example, that two competitors may not formally agree on their prices. If they violate this rule, they can be investigated by a government enforcement agency, such as a justice department, and can then be punished through the court system by fines or imprisonment. State law can also regulate exchanges in which conventions or customs apply. For example, a state may pass consumer protection laws to protect buyers from shoddy or dangerous goods, thereby transferring enforcement from private actors to the state.

Exchanges can take place between two individuals, between an individual and an organization, or between two **organizations**. The organization of a giant multinational corporation is more complex than that of a small family business. Organizations are not only business organizations. They include churches, charitable bodies, governmental organizations, and clubs. In the study of comparative economies, we are primarily interested in how businesses are organized to conduct private economic activity and how governments are organized to conduct public economic activity. In particular, we are interested in how government makes **public choices** concerning how to tax citizens and to spend public resources. No matter how simple or complex, organizations can all be described in terms of certain characteristics, such as how they deal with information, behavior rules, decision-making arrangements, and their ownership arrangements.

In this book, we use institutions and organizations to define and classify economic systems. We can identify at least five different categories of institutions and an even larger number of categories of organizations; hence, societies can organize their economic institutions in a large number of ways. Differences in institutions and organizations may be great or subtle. The "isms" represent the great differences that can exist between economic systems, and they continue to serve as a useful way of thinking:

> Capitalism, communism, socialism, and kindred terms, whatever system traits they may in actuality represent, have a life of their own. They live as symbols or clusters of symbols in the minds of participants in all modern systems . . . , and they may have a profound influence on the way actual systems change or on the reasons why they fail to change.[5]

Definition

We use the definition of an economic system proposed by Assar Lindbeck, one that emphasizes the multidimensional aspect of an economic system.[6]

An **economic system** is a set of institutions for decision making and for the implementation of decisions concerning production, income, and consumption within a given geographic area.

According to this definition, the economic system consists of mechanisms, organizational arrangements, and decision-making rules. An economic system can vary in any of its dimensions, particularly in its structure, its operation, and its adaptability to change through time. It "includes all those institutions, organizations, laws and rules, traditions, beliefs, attitudes, values, taboos, and the resulting behavior patterns that directly or indirectly affect economic behavior and outcomes."[7]

Economic systems are *multidimensional,* a feature that can be formalized in the following manner:

$$ES = f(I_1, I_2, \ldots, I_n) \tag{2.1}$$

As equation 2.1 indicates, an economic system (ES) is defined by its institutions (I_i) or characteristics, where there are n such attributes. An economic system cannot be defined in terms of a single institution such as property ownership; rather, the full set of institutions must be known before ES is specified. We shall focus on five general types of institutions ($n = 5$) that are critical in differentiating economic systems:

1. Organization of decision-making arrangements: structure
2. Mechanisms (rules) for the provision of information and for coordination: market and plan
3. Property rights: control and income
4. Mechanisms for setting goals and for inducing people to act: incentives
5. Procedures for making public choices: the role of government

These five characteristics have been chosen because economic systems differ along these dimensions. They have also been chosen because they affect economic outcomes. We do not list features that are relatively uniform across systems—for example, the organization of production in factory units.

Characteristics of Economic Systems

We shall now examine each of the five characteristics and explain why economic outcomes differ with respect to them. Initially, the characteristics appear to have little in common with characterizations of economic systems as capitalist or socialist. But later in this chapter, we will bring them together to formulate definitions of capitalism and socialism based on the nature of organizational arrangements.

The Organization of Decision-Making Arrangements

Most economic activity is carried out in organizations. Nobel laureate Herbert Simon writes that "organization refers to the complex pattern of communications and other relations in a group of human beings."[8] According to J. M. Montias, "an organization consists of a set of participants (members) regularly interacting in the process of carrying on one or more activities. . . ."[9] Organized behavior has advantages over unorganized behavior. In an organization, goals exist, information is created, and assumptions and attitudes are formed, all of which play a part in the making of decisions.

According to organization theory, individuals participate in organized behavior, pursuing **self-interest** constrained by **bounded rationality.**[10] Economic theory usually assumes that we make perfectly rational decisions, armed with perfect information. If we lack perfect information and outcomes are uncertain, we cannot rationally weigh every decision to find the maximizing outcome. Rather, in such a situation, we turn to the use of rules as guidelines. Thus in an organization, such as a corporation, rules replace a complex series of profit-maximizing choices. The corporation may set general hiring rules, guidelines on minimum rate of return, or travel rules—standards that may not be optimal in all instances but that work under conditions of uncertainty. Self-interest may be construed as the maximization of some utility function constrained by a broad range of human limitations, such as the ability to generate, process, and utilize information. These characteristics lead to two major classes of organizational problems. **Technical–administrative problems** derive from individuals who are limited in their ability to make decisions because of, for example, incomplete information. If we knew everything, we would not have to use rules in organizations because every decision could be made in such a way as to yield optimal results. However, in the real world, information is costly. Organizations are faced with **transaction costs**—the costs associated with searching for information, bargaining, and policing and enforcement.[11] When such costs are high, the organization is inclined to use rules instead of making individual decisions in each case. **Agency–managerial problems** derive from individuals who, while pursuing self-interest, may pursue objectives differing from those established for the organization.

To handle these problems, an organization must establish rules concerned with setting up subgroups within the organization, assigning tasks, coordinating activities, monitoring activities, and describing the nature of incentive arrangements. These rules, along with such external factors as cultural and historical influences, largely determine the nature of the organization and lead to basic and important distinctions among economic systems.

The rules within an organization determine how the activities of the organization are carried out. The two extremes of organizational structure are **hierarchy** and **association**. In an organization based on hierarchy, superiors (principals) establish objectives and issue orders to subordinates (agents) who are supposed to carry out assigned tasks to achieve organizational objectives. In an association-based organization, by contrast, decision making occurs among individuals where there is no superior–subordinate relationship, but rather equality among the individuals.

Except in the case of very simple organizations (such as an owner-operated company with no employees), a hierarchy is present. There can be substantial differences in, for example, the number of levels in the hierarchy, the allocation of tasks among these levels, and the span of control or the number of subordinates directed by a superior.

Armen Alchian and Harold Demsetz[12] suggest one reason why hierarchy exists. Technology requires members of the organization (say, a firm) to work together in "team production." Because the team effort produces output, it is difficult to assess each individual's contribution. Such a setting may cause some to slacken work effort unless a superior monitors work and relates rewards to this effort.

There are other reasons for hierarchy in organizations.[13] Some individuals are risk takers, whereas others avoid risk. Employees agree to work for an owner and to obey the owner's instructions. The owner reaps the rewards of profits if the business succeeds but also risks sustaining losses if the business fails. Production is often carried out in a hierarchical setting because management problems are at times too complicated to organize production through markets.

Principal–Agent Problems   An organization is characterized by the levels at which resource-allocation decisions are made and executed. In a **decentralized** organization, decisions are made primarily at low levels of the organization, whereas in a **centralized** organization, most decisions are made at high levels. Decision-making levels reflect the organization's structure, the manner in which the organization generates and utilizes information, and finally, the way it allocates authority and responsibility for decision making among the levels of the organization.[14]

In most organizations, a superior–subordinate (or principal–agent) relationship implies that agents are organized as groups, subunits, or smaller organizations. For example, an enterprise may be a branch of a larger company that is itself owned by a conglomerate. A government enterprise may be subordinate to a government department that in turn is subordinate to a ministry.[15]

Organizations enter into relationships in which they can act either as a principal or as an agent. A **principal** is a party that has controlling authority and that engages an agent to act subject to the principal's control and instruction. An **agent** is a party that acts for, on behalf of, or as a representative of a principal.

Firm X is a principal when it enters into a contract with Firm Y whereby Firm Y (the agent) will supply Firm X with specified amounts of a product at specified prices over a specified period of time. Firm X is also a principal when it signs a contract with an employee (the agent) that calls for the employee to perform specific services at a specified wage for a specified period of time. Once an agency relationship is established, the principal is responsible for monitoring performance to ensure that the agent is providing the services specified in the agreement. When both the principal and the agent are motivated by achievement of the same goal, or when the performance of the agent can be easily monitored, conflicts between principal and agent are unlikely to arise. However, when the parties have different goals and when monitoring is difficult, conflicts between principal and agent are expected.

Figure 2.1 illustrates the principal–agent relationships in a planned economy. In such an economy, the political authority (such as the Communist party) works with planners to issue instructions to its agents, the industrial ministries. The industrial ministries then issue instructions to their agents, the enterprises subordinate to them.

Information Problems   In a perfectly centralized organization, the authority to make decisions rests in a single central command that issues orders to lower units in the organization. The perfectly decentralized case would be a structure wherein all decision-making authority rests with the lowest subunits (households and individual firms), independent of superior authorities. In the real world, authority is typically spread through various levels in the hierarchy.

The level of decision making depends on the handling of **information**. Perfect centralization of information means that a single decision maker possesses all information about all participants, their actions, and their environment. Decentralization

FIGURE 2.1   The Hierarchical Command Economy: Principals and Agents

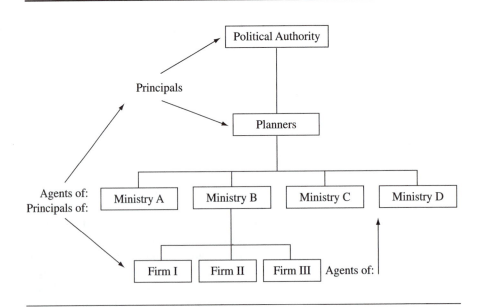

means that decision makers possess less than complete information. An "information-ally decentralized" system generates, processes, and utilizes information at the lowest level in the organization without exchanging information with higher levels in the or-ganization. In a decentralized system, information on prices is exchanged only among the lowest units. Conversely, an "informationally centralized" system involves the generation, processing, and utilization of information by superior agencies and the subsequent transmission of only limited pieces of information to lower subunits.

In reality, perfect centralization of information is not possible because of the mass of information on prices, locations, outputs, and technologies. Organizations must have some degree of information decentralization. Typically, lower-level units have an information advantage concerning their local circumstances compared with higher-level organizations. Information advantages offer agents the opportunity to engage in **opportunistic behavior** relative to their principals, using their informa-tion advantage against the interests of their superiors. For example, the ministries shown in Figure 2.1, may hide information from planners, and firms may conceal in-formation from the ministries.

Opportunistic behavior of this type can take two forms: moral hazard and ad-verse selection.[16] **Moral hazard** occurs when the lower-level unit exploits an infor-mation advantage to alter its behavior after entering into an agreement with the upper-level unit. For example, a buyer may promise a supplier steady purchases at fixed prices if that supplier acquires specialized equipment suited only to that buyer's product. Then, after the equipment has been installed, the buyer, as the sole buyer of that product, reduces its purchases or the price it will pay. In Figure 2.1, the enterprise may agree to produce 100,000 meters of high-quality cloth, but substan-tially reduces its quality. **Adverse selection** occurs when agents conceal information from principals, making it impossible for their superiors to distinguish among them. For example, all enterprises may claim that they cannot adopt a new technology pro-posed by the ministry. Some can and others cannot, but those that can adopt it con-ceal this fact from the ministry. The ministry therefore may be forced into inefficient decision making, such as requiring all firms to adopt the technology.

Market and Plan

The **market** and the **plan** are the two major mechanisms for providing information and for coordinating decisions in organizations. Centralization is commonly identi-fied with plan and decentralization with market, but there is no simple relationship between the level of decision making and the use of market or plan as a coordi-nating mechanism. In some economies, it is possible to combine a considerable con-centration of decision-making authority and information in a few large corporations with substantial state involvement and yet to have no system of planning as such. Planned economies can also vary substantially: Witness the centralized planning of the former Soviet Union, the "indicative" planning system of France, and the com-binations of plan and market that exist in other countries. To identify an economy as planned does not necessarily reveal the prevalent coordinating mechanism or, for that matter, the degree of centralization in decision making. Both depend on the *type* of planning mechanism.

Markets or Plan? Coase   Nobel laureate Ronald Coase posed the question of why some activities are carried out through markets, whereas others are carried out by directives (plan) within enterprises.[17] Coase concluded that activities will be carried out by directives whenever the transaction costs of using markets are too high.

The coordination of decision-making activities in markets has costs. The participants in market-coordinated activities must develop appropriate contracts based on market-generated information and must bear the legal and financial consequences of unfulfilled contracts. Business firms can limit the costs of market coordination. Consider, for example, the task of building a jet aircraft. Managerial coordination can reduce transaction costs and negotiations and can enforce a myriad of contracts through directing employees to fulfill required tasks, thus limiting the need for subcontractors. As long as the cost of organizing an activity inside the firm remains below the cost of organizing that activity using markets, the task is carried out within the firm.

Figure 2.2 illustrates the choice of market or plan by firms, government entities, and households. Firms can acquire goods through the product market or produce them within the firm. For example, an auto manufacturer can either produce tires or buy them from other producers. The firm can use its own employees or hire outside consultants through the factor market. Similarly, the government can produce its own weapons with its own employees or acquire them through markets.

Coase applied his theory of transaction costs to explaining why economies organize themselves into business organizations. His ideas could be applied on a grander

FIGURE 2.2   Market versus Plan

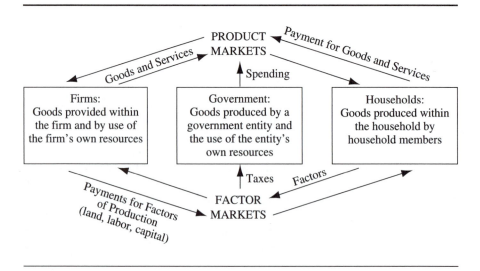

level to explain why some organizations, such as economic systems, may wish to carry out all their transactions by directive or command and not use markets at all. If the system's directors conclude that the transaction costs of using markets are everywhere too high, they may decide that a planned economy is better than a market economy.

Planned versus Market Economies   A **planned economy** is one wherein agents are coordinated by specific instructions or directives formulated by a superior agency (a planning board) and disseminated through a plan document (sometimes termed **directive planning**). The participants are induced to carry out the directives via appropriate incentives or threats, which are designed by the planning authorities. The specifics differ from one case to another, but in a planned economy, economic activity is guided by instructions or directives devised by higher units and subsequently transmitted to lower units. Rewards depend on the achievement of plan directives. A planned economy and a market economy are mutually exclusive: In the former, resources are allocated in accordance with the instructions of planners, who thereby usurp the role of the market as allocator of resources.

In the case of a **market economy**, the market—through the forces of supply and demand—provides signals that trigger organizations to make decisions on resource utilization. The market thereby coordinates the activities of decision-making units. Households earn income by providing land, labor, and capital, and with this income they buy the goods that firms supply. Firms and households respond to the market. Other mechanisms for information or coordination are not necessary, and decision-making authority is vested at the lowest level of the economic system.

In **indicative planning**, the market serves as the principal instrument for resource allocation, but a plan is prepared to guide decision making. An indicative plan is one in which planners seek to project aggregate or sectoral trends and to provide information beyond that normally supplied by the market. An indicative plan is *not* broken down into directives or instructions for individual production units; enterprises are free to apply the information in the indicative plan as they see fit, though indirect means are often used to influence economic activity.

The ultimate decision makers are different in planned and market economies. In a market economy, the consumer can "vote" in the marketplace and exercise **consumer sovereignty**. If consumer sovereignty prevails, then the basic decision of what to produce is dominated by consumers in the marketplace. In a planned economy, on the other hand, decisions are made by the planners, and hence **planners' preferences** prevail. Where planners' preferences dominate, the basic decision of what to produce is made by planners.

Figure 2.3 illustrates the differences between a planned and a market economy. It depicts the production and allocation of a particular industrial commodity such as pig iron, denoted by X. The demand curve D shows the quantity of X demanded by the various potential users at different "prices" of X. The price could be the official price or some more comprehensive price, which captures the resources costs that potential users must pay to acquire X. The supply curve S shows the various quantities of X supplied by its producers at different prices. If this were a market economy (diagram on the left), the market would determine how much of X is produced and which potential

FIGURE **2.3**   Market Economy versus Planned Economy

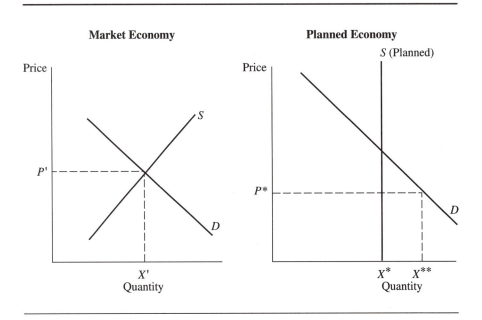

users would get the available supply. All those willing to pay the market price (P') would get X'. The basic feature of an administrative-command economy (diagram on the right) is that the dictator decides both how much X is produced and who gets X. The market (diagram on the left) is driven by an **invisible hand** that does not distinguish among buyers. Anyone who can pay the price will get the good. The planner, on the other hand, can use his "visible hand" of allocative power to reward and punish either buyers or producers for economic or political ends. In the diagram, the planner sets the production of X at X^* and its price at P^*. At this price, the producer is supposed to sell the entire output (X^*) to authorized buyers at the official price P^*. The planner decides who gets X^* among all those willing to pay the official price, P^*. Note that buyers wish to buy more than is available (X^{**}). Planners allocate the available supply among a larger number of willing buyers. If subordinates obey orders, only those designated to receive X will actually get it.

According to this diagram, there is a basic **equilibrium** in a market economy and a basic **disequilibrium** in a planned economy. In the market economy, all those willing to pay the market price will get the product. Buyers are prepared to buy the same amount as sellers are prepared to sell. All others who "want" the good are excluded from the market because they are not prepared to pay its market price. In the planned economy, buyers want to buy more of the good than is available at the price. It is the planner, not the price, that determines who gets the product. This contrast reveals potential sources of conflict between the principal (the planner) and agents (the buyers of the product). Those who are prepared to pay the going price but are excluded by the planner may seek to strike a side deal with the producer to get the good in place of those designated by the planner. We shall discuss this conflict in greater detail in a later chapter.

Property Rights: Control and Income

Institutions also differ in how property is owned. "**Ownership** is an amalgam of rights that individuals may have over objects or claims on objects or services" and "these rights may affect an object's disposition or its utilization."[18] **Property rights** may be divided into three broad types. First is the *disposition* of the object in question—the transfer of ownership rights to others, as in the selling of a privately owned automobile. Second, ownership may include the right to *utilization,* whereby the owner can use the object in question in a manner deemed appropriate. Third, ownership implies the *right to use the products and/or services generated by the object in question.*

Ownership rights may be temporary or permanent, and they may well rest with different individuals at any time. The individual who rents an automobile has the right to the utilization of that automobile but not to its disposition. The owners of a private firm have a claim over the profits of the firm, even though the operation may be significantly circumscribed by government rules and regulations. De jure ownership rights may differ significantly from de facto rights. For example, although members of Soviet collective farms (*kolkhoz*) "owned" the assets of the farm, departing members could not sell their share of these assets.

There are three broad forms of property ownership—**private, public,** and **collective** (cooperative). Under private ownership, each of the three ownership rights ultimately belongs to individuals, whereas under public ownership, these rights belong to the state.

Differences in ownership rights affect economic outcomes. Consider an economy in which all three ownership rights belong to individuals. As the owners seek to maximize their lifetime incomes, capital will be disbursed so as to yield the highest rate of return commensurate with the risk involved. If capital is owned by the state, the rules of capital allocation may be different. Greater attention may be paid to long-term social rates of return. Moreover, time preferences may differ according to whether individuals or the state owns the capital. The distribution of income will differ according to private or state ownership: Property income will accrue to private owners in the one case, to the state in the other. Finally, because the allocation of capital ultimately determines the direction of economic activity, the ownership of capital determines whether allocation is done by private individuals or by the state.

Clearly, ownership arrangements are important in the classification of economic systems. As previously noted, in the traditional classification in terms of the "isms," ownership arrangements are a distinguishing characteristic among the different arrangements. Most economic systems are, in fact, mixed. Even in economic systems that may be classified as market or capitalist systems, not only are there major differences in the nature of private ownership, but also major segments of the economy are dominated by what has been broadly termed public ownership, where traditional ownership rights are much less well established. We know much more about deci-sion making in the private sector.[19] The nature of decision making and of its impact on resource allocation in a state enterprise or a state bureaucracy is much less well understood in both theory and practice. An economic system must organize both pri-vate and public decisions. Identifying the nature of differing mixes of decision-making arrangements, especially the effect these differences have on resource allocation, is a major challenge for the field of comparative economic systems.

Incentives

An organization can also be characterized in terms of the incentives that motivate people. "Goals and incentives are . . . vital links in understanding the transformation of property rights and informational inputs into effective actions."[20]

An incentive mechanism should induce participants at lower levels (agents) to fulfill the directives of participants at higher levels (principals). An effective mech-anism must fulfill three conditions.[21] First, the agent who is to receive the reward must be able to influence the outcomes for which the reward will be given. Second, the agent's principal must be able to check on the subordinate to see whether tasks have been executed properly. Third, the potential rewards must matter to the agent.

In a hierarchy in which superiors issue binding directives to their subordinates, incentives would not be necessary if the principal had perfect information. Armed with perfect information, the principal would automatically know whether the agent was carrying out designated tasks properly. In complex organizations, however, principals typically lack such perfect information. The subordinate knows much more about local circumstances than the superior, and the superior cannot issue perfectly detailed instructions to the subordinate. Because of the imperfect information of the principal, the agent gains local decision-making authority in a number of realms. The principal needs to devise an incentive system that will induce the agent to act in the interests of the superior when the subordinate makes such local decisions. If the principal's incentive system is flawed, then the agent will not act in the interest of the superior.

The information disadvantage of superior organizations relative to their agents affects the way the system is organized. If it is not possible to devise incentive sys-tems that cause agents spontaneously to work in the interests of superior organiza-tions, a more centralized solution may be required. If incentive systems do not elicit information, the superior organization may impose decisions on the subordinate organization without consultation. If private insurance companies cannot elicit infor-mation on disabilities or on driving habits in a cost-effective way, then government agencies, rather than private markets, may have to provide disability or automobile insurance. Information disadvantages explain why governments instead of private markets handle unemployment and poverty insurance.

The superior can devise and use either material or moral incentives to motivate the subordinate. Material incentives have typically been dominant in modern eco-nomic systems, yet some systems have attempted to emphasize moral rewards. **Material incentives** promote desirable behavior by giving the recipient a greater claim over material goods. **Moral incentives** reward desirable behavior by appealing to the recipient's responsibility to society (or the company) and accordingly raising the recipient's social stature within the community. Moral incentives do not give recipients greater command over material goods. In simpler terms, the difference between material and moral incentives is the difference between giving an outstanding performer a cash bonus and bestowing a medal.

Modes of Public Choice

Societies must have arrangements for making public choices, the political decisions that societies make on taxation and government expenditures. The government must provide public goods: Roads must be built, children must be educated, and provision must be made for national defense and police protection. Even in market economies, public goods must be provided by the state because nonpayers, called free riders, cannot be prevented from using them, and one person's use does not prevent any other person from using them. Decisions on public choices can be made according to different political institutional arrangements. At one extreme, **dictatorship**, public choices are made by a person or small group of persons who make the significant political decisions of a society. At the other extreme stands a **pure democracy**, in which each and every public choice is put to a vote and the majority carries the issue. Pure democracy is rare, because it is difficult to subject every public choice to a vote. Therefore, most democracies are **representative democracies** in which the voters elect representatives to make their public choices for them. Elected representatives gather in legislatures or parliaments, and power is usually divided among executive, legislative, and judicial branches.

   Dictatorships are usually associated with planned economies. In fact, Nobel laureate Friedrich Hayek argued that planning inevitably leads to political dictatorship.[22] However, a large number of present and past dictators have presided over economies that are largely market economies. In fact, Augusto Pinochet, the military dictator of Chile in the 1970s and 1980s, set as his goal the establishment of a market economy.

A Threefold Classification

This chapter examined the attributes that characterize economic systems. Figure 2.4A summarizes the alternative options available for each attribute. Five criteria for distinguishing among economic systems have been selected. Although additional criteria could have been introduced, these five are especially useful. They result in a threefold classification of economic systems: *capitalism, market socialism,* and *planned socialism.* As Figure 2.4B shows, each system is characterized multidimensionally in terms of the five criteria we have established.

Capitalism is characterized by private ownership of the factors of production. Decision making is decentralized and rests with the owners of the factors of production. Their decision making is coordinated by the market mechanism, which provides the necessary information. Material incentives are used to motivate participants. Public choices are made by democratic political institutions.

FIGURE 2.4(A)   Attributes of Economic Systems

ATTRIBUTE	CONTINUUM OF OPTIONS
Organization of Decision Making	Centralization ←——→ Decentralization
Provision of Information and Coordination	Plan ←————————→ Market
Property Rights	Public ←——→ Cooperative ←——→ Private
Incentive System	Moral ←————————→ Material
Organization of Public Choices	Dictatorship ←————→ Democracy

Market socialism is characterized by public ownership of the factors of production. Decision making is decentralized and is coordinated by the market mechanism. Both material and moral incentives are used to motivate participants.

Planned socialism is characterized by public ownership of the factors of production. Decision making is centralized and is coordinated by a central plan, which issues binding directives to the system's participants. Both material and moral incentives are used to motivate participants. Public choices are made by a dictator.

These definitions raise as many questions as they answer. They merely state the most important characteristics of economic systems; they do not tell us how and how well each system solves the economic problem of resource allocation. Under capitalism, how do the owners of the factors of production actually allocate their resources, according to what rules, and with what results? Under market socialism, how can public ownership of the factors of production be made compatible with market coordination? In fact, is public ownership *ever* compatible with market coordination? Under planned socialism, how is information gathered and processed to allocate resources effectively? How is it possible to ensure that the system's participants will follow the center's directives?

Figure 2.4(B)   The Pure Systems

	CAPITALISM	MARKET SOCIALISM	PLANNED SOCIALISM
Decision-making Structure	Primarily Decentralized	Primarily Decentralized	Primarily Centralized
Mechanisms for Information and Coordination	Primarily Market	Primarily Market	Primarily Plan
Property Rights	Primarily Private Ownership	State and/or Collective Ownership	Primarily State Ownership
Incentives	Primarily Market	Material and Moral	Material and Moral
Public Choice	Democracy	?	Dictatorship

Alternative Economic Systems: Islamic Economics and the Latin American Model

This chapter focused on three basic models of economic systems: market capitalism, planned socialism, and market socialism. Planned socialism basically disappeared with the collapse of the Soviet empire in the former Soviet Union and in Eastern Europe and is practiced only by eccentric holdouts in Cuba and in North Korea. The Asian communist countries have long turned their back on this system. The most significant defection was that of the world's most populous country, China, starting in 1979. China's success created new interest in the third model of economic systems, market socialism, as China experimented with the combination of public ownership and market allocation.

Most of the world's economies operate as mixed economies, some with great success, others with relatively little. We will differentiate in subsequent chapters among the Anglo-Saxon model, as practiced in the United States and in a number of other countries dispersed around the globe (such as New Zealand, Ireland, and in part in Canada and Australia); the European model, as practiced in the European Union; and the Asian model, which originated in Japan and then spread throughout Southeast Asia in the postwar period. We shall also devote considerable attention to those economies of the former Soviet Union and Eastern Europe that are in transition and hence are still in process of choosing their economic system. The most successful have been those geographically closest to Western Europe. The least successful have been those remote from Europe that have sought to continue many of the practices of the earlier period.

An Islamic Model?

This chapter limited itself to the three major economic systems. Another economic system—the Islamic model—may rise in prominence in the twenty-first century. A substantial percentage of the world's population is Muslim, and a number of countries practice Islamic economics and call themselves Islamic republics. Hence it is important to identify the features of the Islamic model.

None of the economic systems we have discussed so far is strictly tied to religion, although the Asian model was influenced by Confucian thought, and the Anglo-Saxon model was probably influenced in some fashion by Protestantism. The term *Islamic economics* derives from the teachings of the Koran and from centuries-old practices, but it was coined by the Pakistan social thinker Sayyid Abdul A'la Maududi in the late 1940s. Islamic economics was practiced throughout the Muslim world in the Middle Ages, when Islamic merchants were active traders from the Mediterranean to the Baltic Sea, spreading instruments of Islamic finance throughout Europe. Two contemporary nations—Iran and Pakistan—have legislated that their economies should be run according to Islamic principles. Their state constitutions require their banking systems to be fully compatible with Islamic law. In Egypt, Indonesia, Malaysia, Sudan, and the Gulf Cooperation Council (GCC) countries, Islamic banking exists alongside conventional banking. There is no single Islamic financial center that is the equivalent of New York or London. The stock markets in Iran and Sudan come closest to operating in compliance with Islamic principles.

The three basic principles of Islamic economics are said to derive directly from the Koran. They are the *prohibition of interest;* the *zakat* system, which transfers income from the wealthy to the poor; and the use of *Islamic moral norms* in business.[23] Islamic economists disagree on other matters, such as private property and the role of state regulation, but there is agreement on these three points, especially on the prohibition of interest.

The prohibition of interest stems from the belief that it is unjust to earn money without risk. Insofar as the lender of money is presumed not to take on risk, it is therefore unjust to accept a reward in the form of a fixed rate of interest. Profit is legitimate only as a reward for assuming risk. Hence the lender of funds should accept some of the risk either by sharing of profit and loss or by more innovative risk-sharing methods. Interest payments are prohibited even when the lending market is competitive and the interest rate yields the lender a normal rate of return. Islam encourages the earning of profits, because profits symbolize successful entrepreneurship and creation of additional wealth. Interest, on the other hand, is a cost that is accrued irrespective of the business outcome and does not create wealth if there are business losses. Social justice demands that borrowers and lenders share rewards as well as losses in an equitable manner, although it remains unclear how this sharing is to proceed.

More than one hundred financial institutions in over sixty countries practice some form of Islamic finance today. The Islamic financial market's current annual turnover is in the neighborhood of $100 billion, compared with $5 billion in 1985.[24] In the late 1980s, the two largest Islamic banking groups had assets of $23 billion. Depositors in Islamic banks are said to earn not interest but "profit shares" that tend to fluctuate. Borrowers do not pay interest, but they are assessed markups and service charges that resemble interest payments. In fact, in Turkey, where Islamic banks coexist with conventional banks, depositors receive the same rates of interest from Islamic and conventional banks.[25] In practice, therefore, Islamic finance has proved flexible and has created financial instruments that allow profitable banking operations without being called interest charges.

The most prevalent instrument is trade with markup or cost-plus sale, whereby the bank supplies specific goods or commodities to customers (borrowers), which are delivered now but paid for in the future at an agreed-upon markup. For example, a bank customer may receive computers purchased by the bank for $100,000 under an agreement whereby it pay the bank $107,000 one year from the date of receipt. This $7,000 "markup" thus closely resembles an interest payment. Around 75 percent of Islamic financial transactions are for such markup sales. Another instrument is leasing, such as leasing of a house or an airplane, where a portion of the installment payment goes toward the final purchase (with the transfer of ownership to the lessee).

There is little uniformity in the religious principles applied in Islamic countries. In the absence of a universally accepted central religious authority, Islamic banks have formed their own religious boards for guidance. Islamic banks have to consult their respective religious boards, or *shariah* advisors, to seek approval for each new instrument. Differences in interpretation of Islamic principles by different schools of thought mean that identical financial instruments are rejected by one board but accepted by another. Thus the same instrument may not be acceptable in all countries.

The second feature of Islamic economics is the zakat system of redistributing wealth from the rich to the poor. In most cases, the zakat is voluntary, but in six countries (Yemen, Saudi Arabia, Malaysia, Libya, Pakistan, and Sudan), the zakat system is run by the government. The zakat system accumulates funds from wealthy donors, or taxpayers if the system is obligatory, and distributes these funds to widows and to religious or educational institutions. Zakat obligations can apply both to individuals and to businesses. The empirical evidence suggests that the obligatory zakat system has not put a dent in poverty in those nations with a government-run system. There is also evidence that it leads to corruption, with funds going to connected individuals, even to religious leaders, rather than to the poor.[26]

The third principle of Islamic economics is the substitution of Islamic norms for capitalist norms. Businesspeople are supposed to deal fairly with their business partners observing Islamic morality. They should charge fair prices, provide accurate information, and not engage in fraud or deceit. The principle of fairness is difficult to apply because people have different notions of fairness. In the Iranian Islamic Republic, morality committees attached to factories and institutions are supposed to enforce Islamic morality, and various religious leaders issue edicts on morality. But in general, each person, group, or country has its own notion of Islamic morality, and there is no central authority to define it.

A Latin American Model?

Latin America has been torn in the postwar period between political and economic extremes. Authoritarian political regimes and populist economic policies have alternated with movements toward political democracy and free-market reform. Most Latin American countries have had their share of military dictatorships and economic populist leaders, the best known being Juan Peron in Argentina, who favored nationalized industries, strict government control, and highly redistributive policies. Latin American economists, trained in free-market traditions in the United States, enacted liberalization reforms in a number of Latin American countries, beginning in Chile under the military dictatorship of Pinochet, which ruled Chile from September of 1973 to March of 1990.[27] Under this military dictatorship, a team of young economists trained at the University of Chicago opened up the Chilean economy, liberalized prices, eliminated state controls, and privatized state industries. After a rocky start, a Chilean "economic miracle" began in 1975, a period of rapid economic growth that was interrupted by a number of setbacks.[28] The Chilean economy began to grow rapidly, and its investment rate soared. Although the democratically elected governments that followed the military dictatorship have altered Chile's policies of the mid-1970s, the basic framework of the Chilean economy remains. Today, despite numerous setbacks, Chile is one of Latin America's "more successful economies."[29] Largely inspired by Chile's example, a number of Latin American economies embarked on free-market reforms, including Mexico, Brazil, Peru, and Argentina. Despite a number of financial crises, such as Argentina's default on its international debt in 2001, the people of Latin America now generally favor privatization and a reduced role of government.[30] The Latin America reform model of privatization, reduction of trade barriers, and deregulation is still too fragile to classify it as an alternative economic system. Vested interests that control large state enterprises, such as Mexico's national oil company and Chile's national copper company, resist change and continue to supply patronage and benefits to political allies and workers.

Summary

- The field of comparative economic systems identifies and studies the differences among economic systems and the effect of inputs (land, labor, and capital).
- Economic systems have traditionally been categorized as market capitalism, market socialism, and planned socialism.
- Institutional features occur in varying mixes and influence resource allocation in every economy.

- Institutions are the constraints that people impose to shape the interaction and incentives in various types of exchange (economic, political, or social).
- Institutions include customs, voting procedures, legislation, organizations, and other rules and enforcement mechanisms that affect the exchange of public and private goods.
- Organizations exist in many forms, including business, governmental bodies, and charitable organizations.
- Public choice is the process of making decisions about taxation and spending policies.

Key Terms

institutions	market
rules	plan
enforcement mechanisms	planned economy
organizations	directive plan
public choices	market economy
economic system	indicative plan
self-interest	consumer sovereignty
bounded rationality	planners' preferences
technical–administrative problems	invisible hand
transaction costs	equilibrium
agency–managerial problems	disequilibrum
hierarchy	ownership
association	property rights
decentralized	private ownership
centralized	public ownership
principal	collective ownership
agent	material incentives
information	moral incentives
opportunistic behavior	dictatorship
moral hazard	pure democracy
adverse selection	representative democracy

Notes

1. Alexander Eckstein, "Introduction," in Alexander Eckstein, ed., *Comparison of Economic Systems: Theoretical and Methodological Approaches* (Berkeley: University of California Press, 1971) p. 1; John Michael Montias, *The Structure of Economic Systems* (New Haven: Yale University Press, 1976).
2. Stefan Voigt and Hella Engerer, "Institutions and Transformation—Possible Policy Implications of the New Institutional Economics," in Klaus Zimmerman (ed.), *Frontiers in Economics* (Berlin: Springer-Verlag, 2002), p. 132.
3. Douglass North, *Institutions, Institutional Change and Economic Performance* (Cambridge: Cambridge University Press, 1990), p. 3.

4. Voigt and Engerer, "Institutions and Transformation," p. 133.

5. Montias, *The Structure of Economic Systems*, p. 8.

6. Assar Lindbeck, *The Political Economy of the New Left: An Outsider's View*, 2nd ed. (New York: Harper & Row, 1977), p. 214.

7. Frederic Pryor, *Property and Industrial Organization in Communist and Capitalist Nations* (Bloomington: Indiana University Press, 1973), p. 337. Adapted from T. C. Koopmans and J. M. Montias, "On the Description and Comparison of Economic Systems," in Eckstein, *Comparison of Economic Systems*, pp. 27–28.

8. Herbert A. Simon, *Administrative Behavior*, 2nd ed. (New York: Free Press, 1966), p. xvi.

9. Montias, *The Structure of Economic Systems*, p. 8.

10. This discussion is based on the excellent survey by Avner Ben-Ner, John Michael Montias, and Egon Neuberger, "Basic Issues in Organizations: A Comparative Perspective," *Journal of Comparative Economics* 17 (1993), 207–242. For an early discussion, see Benjamin Ward, "Organization and Comparative Economics: Some Approaches," in Eckstein, *Comparison of Economic Systems*, pp. 103–133.

11. Voigt and Engerer, "Institutions and Transformation," p. 131.

12. A. A. Alchian and H. Demsetz, "Production, Information, Costs and Economic Organizations," *American Economic Review* 62 (December 1972), 777–795. A classic in the study of organizations is Simon, *Administrative Behavior;* for a contemporary survey, see Paul Milgrom and John Roberts, *Economics, Organization and Management* (Englewood Cliffs, N.J.: Prentice-Hall, 1992); see also the classic work of Oliver E. Williamson, *The Economic Institutions of Capitalism: Firms, Markets, Relational Contracting* (New York: Free Press, 1985); Armen A. Alchian and Susan Woodward, "The Firm Is Dead; Long Live the Firm: A Review of Oliver E. Williamson's 'The Economic Institutions of Capitalism,' " *Journal of Economic Literature* 26 (March 1988), 65–79; Alfred D. Chandler, "Organizational Capabilities and the Economic History of the Industrial Enterprise," *Journal of Economic Perspectives* 6 (Summer 1992), 79–100.

13. For a different approach, see Raaj Kumar Sah and Joseph E. Stiglitz, "The Architecture of Economic Systems: Hierarchies and Polyarchies," *American Economic Review* 76, 4 (September 1986), 716–727; see also Roy Radner, "Hierarchy: The Economics of Managing," *Journal of Economic Literature* 30 (September 1992), 1382–1415.

14. There is a large body of literature concerned with issues of centralization and decentralization. For early contributions, see Leonid Hurwicz, "Centralization and Decentralization in Economic Processes," in Eckstein, *Comparison of Economic Systems*, pp. 79–102; Leonid Hurwicz, "Conditions for Economic Efficiency of Centralized and Decentralized Structures," in Gregory Grossman, ed., *Value and Plan* (Berkeley: University of California Press, 1960), pp. 162–183; Thomas Marschak, "Centralization and Decentralization in Economic Organizations," *Econometrica* 27 (1959), 399–430. A summary of different meanings can be found in Pryor, *Property and Industrial Organization*, Ch. 8; for a recent discussion of the issues, see Robert G. Lynch, "Centralization and Decentralization Redefined," *Journal of Comparative Economics* 13 (March 1989), 1–14; Donald Chisholm, *Coordination Without Hierarchy* (Berkeley: University of California Press, 1989).

15. Much attention has been paid to the principal–agent relationship. See, for example, Stephen A. Ross, "The Economic Theory of Agency: The Principal's Problem," *American Economic Review Papers and Proceedings* (May 1973); Glen MacDonald, "New Directions in the Economic Theory of Agency," *Canadian Journal of Economics* 17 (1984), 415–440; George Baker, Michael Jensen, and Kevin Murphy, "Compensation and Incentives: Practice vs. Theory," *Journal of Finance* 43 (1988), 593–616; Bengt Holmstrom and Paul Milgrom, "Multitask Principal–Agent Analyses: Incentive Contracts, Asset Ownership,

and Job Design," *Journal of Law, Economics, & Organization* 7 (1991), Special Issue, 34–52; John Pratt and Richard Zeckhauser, eds., *Principals and Agents: The Structure of Business* (Cambridge, Mass.: Harvard Business School, 1985).

16. It is argued that with the presence of adverse selection and moral hazard, incentive arrangements must be altered. For an early discussion of incentive arrangements in a systems context, see David Conn, ed., "The Theory of Incentives," *Journal of Comparative Economics* 3 (September 1979); for a discussion of incentives in simple cases, see Bernard Caillaud, Roger Guesnerie, Patrick Rey, and Jean Tirole, "Government Intervention in Production and Incentives Theory: A Review of Recent Contributions," *Rand Journal of Economics* 19 (1988), 1–26; Nahum D. Melumad and Stefan Reichelstein, "Value of Communication in Agencies," *Journal of Economic Theory* 47 (1989), 334–368; David E. M. Sappington, "Incentives in Principal–Agent Relationships," *Journal of Economic Perspectives* 5 (Spring 1991); for a discussion of incentive arrangements under adverse selection and moral hazard, see Liang Zou, "Threat-Based Incentive Mechanisms Under Moral Hazard and Adverse Selection," *Journal of Comparative Economics* 16 (March 1992), 47–74.

17. Ronald H. Coase, "The Nature of the Firm," *Economica* 4 (1937), 386–405. Reprinted in George Stigler and Kenneth Boulding, eds., *Readings in Price Theory* (Homewood, Ill: Irwin, 1952).

18. Montias, *The Structure of Economic Systems,* p. 116; for an early survey of the literature, see Erik Furubotn and Svetozar Pejovich, "Property Rights and Economic Theory: A Survey of Recent Literature," *Journal of Economic Literature* 10 (December 1972), 1137–1162; for a discussion in the comparative context, see Pryor, *Property and Industrial Organization;* for a recent discussion, see Alan Ryan, "Property," in John Eatwell. Murray Milgate, and Peter Newman, eds., *The New Palgrave: Dictionary of Economics* (New York: Stockton Press, 1987), pp. 1029–1031; Louis Putterman, "Ownership and the Nature of the Firm," *Journal of Comparative Economics* 17 (1993), 243–263; John P. Bonin, Derek C. Jones, and Louis Putterman, "Theoretical and Empirical Research on Producers' Cooperatives: Will Ever the Twain Meet?" *Journal of Economic Literature* 31 (September 1993), 1290–1320.

19. For a discussion of decision making in the public sector, see V. V. Ramanadham, *Public Enterprise: Studies in Organizational Structure* (London: Frank Cass, 1986); for a discussion of nonprofit organizations, see Avner Ben-Ner and Theresa Van Hoomissen, "Nonprofit Organizations in the Mixed Economy: A Demand and Supply Analysis," *Annals of the Public and Cooperative Economy* 62, 4 (October–December, 1991), 519–550; Susan Rose-Ackerman, ed., *The Economics of Nonprofit Institutions: Studies in Structure and Policy* (New York: Oxford University Press, 1986); Burton A. Weisbrod, *The Nonprofit Economy* (Cambridge, Mass.: Harvard University Press, 1988); Jean-Jacques Laffont and Jean Tirole, "Privatization and Incentives," *Journal of Law, Economics & Public Organization* 7 (1991) Special Issue, 84–105.

20. Pryor, *Property and Industrial Organization,* p. 338.

21. Montias, *The Structure of Economic Systems,* Ch. 13.

22. F. A. Hayek, *The Road to Serfdom* (Chicago: University of Chicago Press, 1944).

23. This section is based largely on Timur Kuran, "Islamic Economics and the Islamic Subeconomy," *Journal of Economic Perspectives* 9, 4 (Fall 1995), 155-174.

24. Zamir Iqbal, "Islamic Financial Systems," *http://www.worldbank.org/fandd/english/0697/articles/0140697.htm*

25. Kuran, "Islamic Economics," p. 161.

26. *Ibid.,* p. 164.

27. Carmelo Mesa-Lago, *Market, Socialist, and Mixed Economies: Comparative Policy and Performance—Chile, Cuba, and Costa Rica* (Baltimore: Johns Hopkins University Press, 2000), Chs. 1–6.
28. *Ibid.,* p. 58.
29. "A Backlash Against the Free Market?" *The Economist,* August 17, 2002, p. 12.
30. See the Latinobarameter indexes of public opinion cited in "Democracy Clings on in a Cold Economic Climate," *The Economist,* August 17, 2002, pp. 29–30.

Recommended Readings

Traditional Sources

A. A. Alchian and H. Demsetz, "Production, Information, Costs and Economic Organizations," *American Economic Review* 62 (December 1972), 777–795.

David Conn, ed., "The Theory of Incentives," *Journal of Comparative Economics* 3 (September 1979).

H. Demsetz, "Toward a Theory of Property Rights," *American Economic Review* 57 (May 1967), 347–359.

Alexander Eckstein, ed., *Comparison of Economic Systems: Theoretical and Methodological Approaches* (Berkeley: University of California Press, 1971).

Erik Furobotn and Svetozar Pejovich, "Property Rights and Economic Theory: A Survey of Recent Literature," *Journal of Economic Literature* 10 (December 1972), 1137–1162.

John Michael Montias, *The Structure of Economic Systems* (New Haven: Yale University Press, 1976).

Egon Neuberger, "Classifying Economic Systems," in Morris Bornstein, ed., *Comparative Economic Systems: Models and Cases,* 4th ed. (Homewood, Ill.: Irwin, 1978).

Frederic Pryor, *Property and Industrial Organization in Communist and Capitalist Nations* (Bloomington: Indiana University Press, 1973).

———, *A Guidebook to the Study of Economic Systems* (Englewood Cliffs, N.J.: Prentice-Hall, 1985).

Herbert A. Simon, *Administrative Behavior,* 2nd ed. (New York: Free Press, 1966).

P. J. D. Wiles, *Economic Institutions Compared* (New York: Halsted, 1977).

———, "What Is Comparative Economics?" *Comparative Economic Studies* 31 (Fall 1989), 1–32.

Oliver E. Williamson, *Markets and Hierarchies* (New York: Free Press, 1975).

Basic, General, Contemporary Sources

Armen Alchian and Susan Woodward, "The Firm Is Dead; Long Live the Firm: A Review of Oliver E. Williamson's 'The Economic Institutions of Capitalism,'" *Journal of Economic Literature* 26 (March 1988), 65–79.

Avner Ben-Ner, John Michael Montias, and Egon Neuberger, "Basic Issues in Organizations: A Comparative Perspective," *Journal of Comparative Economics* 17 (1993), 207–242.

Paul Milgrom and John Roberts, *Economics, Organization and Management* (Englewood Cliffs, N.J.: Prentice-Hall, 1992).

Frederic L. Pryor, "Corporatism as an Economic System: A Review Essay," *Journal of Comparative Economics* 12 (September 1988), 317–344.

Oliver E. Williamson, *The Economic Institutions of Capitalism: Firms, Markets, Relational Contracting* (New York: Free Press, 1985).

———, ed., *Organization Theory: From Chester Barnard to the Present and Beyond.* (Oxford: Oxford University Press, 1990).

Organizations: Historical Aspects

Alfred D. Chandler, "Organizational Capabilities and the Economic History of the Industrial Enterprise," *Journal of Economic Perspectives* 6 (Summer 1992), 79–100.

James S. Coleman, "Constructed Organization: First Principles," *Journal of Law, Economics, & Organization* 7 (1991), Special Issue, 7–23.

R. R. Nelson and S. G. Winter, *An Evolutionary Theory of Economic Change* (Cambridge, Mass.: Harvard University Press, 1982).

Douglass C. North, *Institutions, Institutional Change and Economic Performance* (Cambridge: Cambridge University Press, 1990).

The Structure of Organizations

Sanford Grossman and Oliver Hart, "The Costs and Benefits of Ownership: A Theory of Vertical and Lateral Integration," *Journal of Political Economy* 94 (August 1986), 691–719.

Raaj Kumar Sah and Joseph E. Stiglitz, "The Architecture of Economic Systems: Hierarchies and Polyarchies," *American Economic Review* 76 (September 1986), 716–727.

Paul Milgrom, "Employment Contracts, Influence Activities and Efficient Organizational Design," *Journal of Political Economy* 96 (February 1988), 42–60.

Herbert A. Simon, "Organizations and Markets," *Journal of Economic Perspectives* 5 (Spring 1991), 25–44.

Joseph E. Stiglitz, "Symposium on Organizations and Economics," *Journal of Economic, Perspectives* 5 (Spring 1991), 15–24.

Principal–Agent Relationships

Joseph Farrell, "Information and the Coase Theorem," *Journal of Economic Perspectives* 1 (Fall 1987), 113–129.

Bengt Holmstrom and Paul Milgrom, "Multitask Principal–Agent Analyses: Incentive Contracts, Asset Ownership and Job Design," *Journal of Law, Economics, & Organization* 7 (1991), Special Issue, 34–52.

Glen MacDonald, "New Directions in the Economic Theory of Agency," *Canadian Journal of Economics* 17 (1984), 415–440.

John Pratt and Richard Zeckhauser, eds., *Principals and Agents: The Structure of Business* (Cambridge, Mass.: Harvard Business School, 1985).

Incentive Arrangements

David Conn, "Effort, Efficiency, and Incentives in Economic Organizations," *Journal of Comparative Economics* 6 (September 1982), 223–234.

Jean-Jacques Laffont and Eric Maskin, "The Theory of Incentives: An Overview," in Werner Hildenbrand, ed., *Advances in Economic Theory* (Cambridge: Cambridge University Press, 1982).

Louis Putterman and Gil Skillman, "The Incentive Effects of Monitoring Under Alternate Compensation Schemes," *International Journal of Industrial Organization* 6 (March 1988), 109–120.

Yingyi Qian, "Equity, Efficiency, and Incentives in a Large Economy," *Journal of Comparative Economics* 16 (March 1992), 27–46.

David E. M. Sappington, "Incentives in Principal–Agent Relationships," *Journal of Economic Perspectives* 5 (Spring 1991), 45–66.

Liang Zou, "Threat-Based Incentive Mechanisms Under Moral Hazard and Adverse Selection," *Journal of Comparative Economics* 16 (March 1992), 47–74.

Property Rights

H. Demsetz and K. Lehn, "The Structure of Corporate Ownership: Causes and Consequences," *Journal of Political Economy* 93 (December 1985), 1155–1177.

Louis Putterman, "Ownership and the Nature of the Firm," *Journal of Comparative Economics* 17 (1993), 243–263.

Alan Ryan, "Property," in John Eatwell, Murray Milgate, and Peter Newman, eds., *The New Palgrave: Dictionary of Economics* (New York: Stockton Press, 1987), pp. 1029–1031.

Xiaoki Yang and Ian Wills, "A Model Formalizing the Theory of Property Rights," *Journal of Comparative Economics* 14 (June 1990), 177–198.

The Theory of Cooperatives

John P. Bonin, Derek C. Jones, and Louis Putterman, "Theoretical and Empirical Research on Producers' Cooperatives: Will the Twain Ever Meet?" *Journal of Economic Literature* 31 (September 1993), 1290–1320.

Nonprofit Organizations

Susan Rose-Ackerman, ed., *The Economics of Nonprofit Institutions: Studies in Structure and Policy* (New York: Oxford University Press, 1986).

Walter Powell, ed., *The Nonprofit Sector: A Research Handbook* (New Haven: Yale University Press, 1987).

Burton A. Weisbrod, *The Nonprofit Economy* (Cambridge, Mass.: Harvard University Press, 1988).

The Public Sector

Abram Bergson, "Managerial Risks and Rewards in Public Enterprises," *Journal of Comparative Economics* 2 (September 1978), 211–225.

A. Boardman and A. Vining, "Ownership and Performance in Competitive Environments: A Comparison of the Performance of Private, Mixed, and State-Owned Enterprises," *Journal of Law and Economics* 32 (1989), 1–33.

Estelle James, Egon Neuberger, and Robert Willis, "On Managerial Rewards and Self-Selection: Risk Taking in Public Enterprises," *Journal of Comparative Economics* 3 (December 1979), 395–406.

Jean-Jacques Laffont and Jean Tirole, "Privatization and Incentives," *Journal of Law, Economics, & Organization* 7 (1991), Special Issue, 84–105.

3

Institutions, Systems, and Economic Outcomes

The economic system of a country is determined by its institutions. If the economic system did not affect economic performance, we would have little interest in the system and its institutions as economists. This chapter will show that a country's economic performance depends on the quality of its economic institutions (that is, its economic system), on the environment in which it operates (the quantity and quality of its resources), and on the policies that its leaders select. There is debate on the relative weight of the economic system in explaining economic performance. Contrary to those who argue that conventional environmental and policy factors determine economic performance, Nobel laureate Douglass North writes, 'I wish to assert a much more fundamental role for institutions in society; they are the underlying determinant of the long-run performance of economies.'[1] North's statement suggests that "bad" economic institutions hamper economic performance, whereas "good" institutions promote good economic performance. It also suggests that societies must change their "bad" institutions into "good" institutions if they wish to have good economic performance. Countries that are rich in economic resources can be made poor by the unwise choice of economic institutions.

The Forces Influencing Economic Outcomes

The previous chapter explained that the economic system (ES) is not unidimensional. Rather, it is defined in terms of its many institutions, such as how it manages information, its organizational structure, its provision for property rights, and how it makes public choices. Later in this chapter we shall discuss how these various institutions might be measured, but the definition itself suggests that obtaining actual measures of an economic system is a difficult undertaking.

If we could measure the **economic system (ES)** in a manner that provided ordinal or cardinal rankings, we would still have to measure economic **outcomes (O)** in a meaningful manner. Economic outcomes depend on factors in addition to the economic system—natural resource endowments, the level of economic development, the size of the economy, labor and capital inputs, random events, and so on. These are termed **environmental factors (ENV)**. Economic outcomes also depend on the **policies (POL)** that the policy makers choose to follow.

$$O = f(\text{ES, ENV, POL}) \qquad (3.1)$$

where

> O denotes economic outcomes
> ES denotes the economic system
> ENV denotes environmental factors
> POL denotes policies pursued by the economic system

Equation 3.1 and Figure 3.1 highlight the methodological problems of determining the impact of the economic system (ES) on the observed outcomes (O)—the *ceteris paribus* ("other things being equal") problem. Insofar as outcomes depend on factors in addition to the economic system, we cannot isolate the impact of the system without first controlling for, or holding constant, the influence of the environmental (ENV) factors and the policy variables (POL). To illustrate the problem, let's look at some examples from the real world.

Labor productivity (an "outcome") in the former Soviet Union was relatively low compared with that in Western Europe and the United States.[2] Assuming accurate measurement, is the observed outcome the result of the economic system (planned socialism), environmental factors, policy factors, or some combination of these forces? This question is not easily answered. For example, the level of economic development in the former Soviet Union (as measured by per capita domestic product) was well below levels in the United States and Western Europe, and historical evidence shows that the level of productivity is positively associated with the level of economic development. In this case, is the productivity gap observed in the former Soviet Union a function of the economic system, or are other factors involved?

FIGURE 3.1   Forces Influencing Economic Outcomes

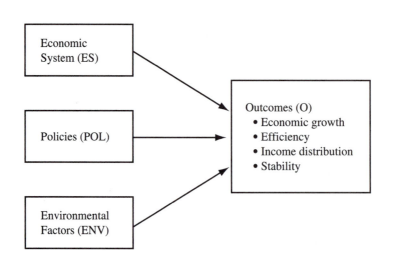

Three countries that have grown rapidly over the past decades are China, Chile, and Singapore. In an effort to determine what factors led to this rapid growth, we would look for changes that would have accelerated growth. In the case of China, we might look at its decision to open up the economy to foreign trade and investment. In Chile, we might look at the privatization of its pension system, which promoted increased capital formation. In the case of Singapore, we might look at its market-oriented programs carried through by a nondemocratic government.

In the 1980s and 1990s, the United States' economy grew more rapidly than Europe's. During this period of time, the United States changed its tax system, passed welfare reform, but also saw the spread of personal computers and the Internet into business and households. Was the higher U.S. growth the result of changes in institutions or the result of the "environmental" factor (the country's reaping the benefits of the computer and the information revolution)?

The sorting out of economic system, environmental effects, and policy effects typically requires statistical or econometric analysis. If we related just one factor to an economic outcome, we might falsely conclude that one had caused the other. Only by examining the effects of all three factors simultaneously can we isolate the effect of the economic system on economic outcomes.

Should we classify changes as *changes in the economic system* or as *changes in policy?* A factor is classified as **policy** if it can be significantly changed without changing the underlying economic system. It is, by contrast, an **attribute** of the economic system if it cannot conceivably be altered without altering the economic system itself. This distinction shows how policy influences and system influences might differ. Consider an economy's openness to international trade. An **open economy** is one in which barriers to trade, such as tariffs and restrictions, are low. A **closed economy** is one in which barriers to trade are high and trade cannot flow freely. How open or closed an economy is acts as a crucial determinant of economic performance. Although the planned socialist economies were largely closed, it is conceivable that they could have adopted policies that would have opened the economy. The open or closed character of an economy is thus a policy that can be changed without changing the economic system itself. China, for example, opened its economy before making substantive changes in its own economic system.

The Evaluation of Outcomes: What Constitutes Success?

When we compare economic outcomes, we wish to determine which economic system or set of institutions performs "best" in achieving its goals. How are we to decide which outcome is "best"? Two problems arise.

First, to evaluate the outcomes, we must select performance criteria. Because people typically do not agree on the appropriate criteria, the selection tends to be subjective. Second, even if agreement can be reached on a list of criteria for evaluating outcomes, how will the criteria be added together? We must somehow add different results together by assigning *weights* to produce a single index of achievement. Clearly, the weights selected will determine the value of the index of achievement, but they are themselves subjective.[3]

An economic system should have as its objective the achievement of a maximal value of the economic outcome (O), subject to the constraints imposed by the economic system (ES), policies (POL), and environmental factors (ENV), which include technology and resource constraints. The objective, then, is to

$$\text{Maximize: O}$$
$$\text{Subject to (ES, ENV, POL)} \qquad \textbf{(3.2)}$$

This formula suggests that evaluating the performance of economic systems would be (theoretically at least) a rather simple matter. After adjusting for differences in environment and policy, we would have only to determine which system achieved the highest economic outcome. If there were agreement on the measurement of outcomes, it would work this way. Instead, the economic outcome (O) is a function of a series of performance indicators:

$$O = \sum_{j=1}^{k} a_j o_j \qquad \textbf{(3.3)}$$

where

o_j = desirable (or undesirable if negative) economic outcomes
a_j = the relative importance of the various outcomes

Consider the following example, in which two economic systems designated A and B are judged according to two criteria. System A receives scores of 1 and 2 on the two criteria. B receives scores of 2 and 1 on the two criteria. Which system has outperformed the other depends on the relative weights applied to the two criteria.

Just as individuals assign different weights (a_j) to different economic goals, so do economic systems assign different weights to those goals.[4] Furthermore, the evaluation of goals changes over time. Societies systematically attach different weights to a rather similar list of economic goals or objectives, as is shown in Figure 3.2.

Equation 3.3 summarizes the crux of the problem. Because different societies assign different subjective weights (a_j) to economic outcomes (o_j), the measurement of economic performance depends not only on o_j but also on a_j, which must remain subjective. For example, one economic system may assign priority to economic growth and allocate resources accordingly. In so doing, it attaches relatively low weights to the other goals. Another economic system may attach a dominant weight to price stability and allocate its resources accordingly. It is likely, in this scenario, that the first system will perform better in terms of the growth objective and that the second system will perform better in terms of price stability. Which system has outperformed the other? The answer depends on one's personal judgment of which goal is more important.

FIGURE 3.2   National Priorities Differ

The Gallup organization carried out a poll of young people aged 19 to 24 in 1977 to determine whether young people in different countries had different views of the world. Young people from eleven countries, both rich and poor, were asked to identify those things in society with which they were dissatisfied. The results are provided below:

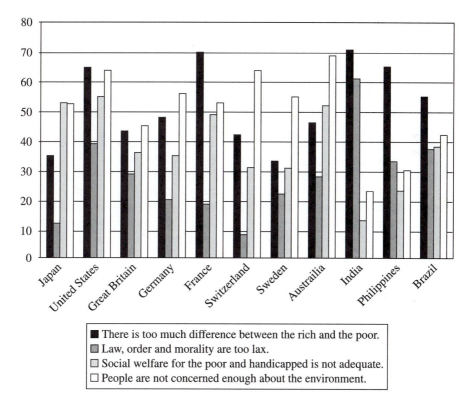

■ There is too much difference between the rich and the poor.
▨ Law, order and morality are too lax.
▤ Social welfare for the poor and handicapped is not adequate.
□ People are not concerned enough about the environment.

Source: George Gallup, *The International Gallup Polls, Public Opinion 1978* (Wilmington, Del.: Scholarly Resources, 1980).

The Determination of System Priorities

How are **national priorities** determined in practice? The involvement of substantial subjective elements does not mean that priorities are not in fact established.

The determination of national priorities differs from economy to economy. In the former Soviet Union, the Communist party played a dominant role in goal formation.[5] This does not mean that other forces had no influence, but their roles were relatively limited. (In socialist societies, where political power was substantially concentrated, the process of modernization itself led to some pluralization of the society and to the formation of influential interest groups.)[6]

In democratic societies, the greater complexity of establishing priorities is reflected in the various arrangements through which individuals can express preferences by voting. The vote may indicate a preference among political candidates with differing positions on national issues, or it may be a "vote" cast in the marketplace indicating what goods and services are desired. However, pressure groups such as trade unions, manufacturers' associations, and professional associations can exert substantial influence. Even though majority voting prevails, legislation that advances minority interests may be passed.[7] Even in a pluralistic democratic society, as power becomes concentrated (whether in the hands of individuals in the form of wealth or in the hands of lobby groups or corporations), there is a tendency for the goal formation process to change.[8] In a democratic society, the change may take place slowly. In a society where power is centralized, change may be more sudden.

If various goals are laudable, why not pursue all of them? Specific goals can often be achieved only by sacrificing other, less important goals. The necessity of choosing to pursue some goals at the expense of others is a consequence of the fundamental scarcity of resources, which prevents every economic system from producing unlimited quantities of goods and services. Instead, choices must be made among goals.

The nature of the tradeoffs is not always clearly defined. Can unemployment be lowered without increasing inflation? Is sustained economic growth compatible with a cleaner environment? Can affluent economies maintain generous welfare and benefits programs without sacrificing economic growth? Can China maintain an open economy *and* the political dictatorship its leaders desire? Tradeoffs matter in at least two ways. First, we cannot assess the performance of economic systems without understanding their tradeoffs among alternatives. Second, when one goal must be sacrificed to achieve another, we should not criticize a system for not achieving a goal that it has, in effect, decided not to pursue.

Performance Criteria

We have selected a number of performance criteria that are generally applied to assess economic outcomes. Our list may omit some criteria (military power, for instance, or environmental quality) that are important. We shall use the following criteria to evaluate economic outcomes:

1. Economic growth
2. Efficiency
3. Income distribution (fairness)
4. Stability (cyclical stability, avoidance of inflation and unemployment)
5. Viability of the economic system

Economic Growth

The most widely used indicator of economic performance is **economic growth**, increases in the volume of real output that an economy generates over time or in output per capita.[9] We are interested in economic output and its growth because material well-being or welfare can be approximated by the volume of goods and services per capita.[10] Changes in output per capita over time normally bring about changes in the welfare of the population in the same direction. Using this interpretation, we can compare levels of well-being in different systems at any time, or over time, to evaluate the rate of economic progress.

Because economic growth is so widely employed as a performance indicator, it is useful to spell out some complications. First, measurement problems arise in assessing economic growth, especially when different economic systems are compared.[11] Second, it is difficult to untangle the causes of differences in economic growth. They may be a consequence of the economic system, but they may also result from environmental and policy factors. The process of economic growth is so complex that it defies easy description; therefore, we can never be sure of the system's impact on growth. For example, the most rapidly growing countries of recent years are located in Asia: China, Singapore, and Taiwan. They began their rapid growth from low levels of income. To what extent was this rapid growth the consequence of changes in the economic system rather than a result of the low "baseline" level of development? When we compare the growth of economic systems over time, when each system begins with a different base, we may expect, *ceteris paribus,* to find differences in growth performance.

Third, the uncertain link between the growth of output and increases in quality of life should be emphasized. Economic growth is enhanced by capital formation, but to expand the capital stock, saving (refraining from current consumption) is required. The savings of the present generation should bear fruit in the form of improvements in the living standard of later generations. The decision to postpone present consumption in favor of future consumption must be confronted, whether the choice is made primarily by consumer or by planner. The outcome of this decision has an impact on growth performance and on current living standards. For example, the Four Tigers of Southeast Asia recorded very high savings rates, and these high rates of capital formation clearly contributed to their rapid growth. In effect, they sacrificed the present for the future.

Some have argued that capitalist systems consistently underrate the merits of future consumption and hence save too little to make adequate provision for the future.[12] Thus we anticipate higher savings rates in socialist systems and, accordingly, a more rapid rate of growth of the capital stock and, *ceteris paribus,* a higher rate of growth of output. The failure of the socialist economies to generate more rapid growth *despite* high rates of savings was one reason for their collapse.

Efficiency

A second measure of system performance is economic efficiency. **Efficiency** is the effectiveness with which a system utilizes its available resources (including knowledge) at a particular time (static efficiency) or through time (dynamic efficiency).[13] Static and dynamic efficiency are interrelated, and both depend on a variety of factors.

The concept of efficiency can be conveniently illustrated by the production possibilities schedule shown in Figure 3.3. The initial production possibilities schedule

FIGURE 3.3   The Hierarchical Command Economy: Principals and Agents

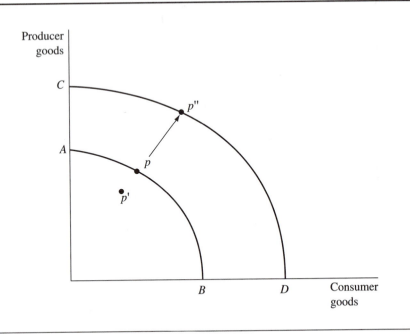

(*AB*) illustrates all feasible combinations of producer and consumer goods that a particular economic system is capable of producing at a particular time by using all available resources at maximal efficiency. The production possibilities schedule shows that, given its existing resources, the system has a menu of production choices open to it. Economic systems must choose where to locate on the schedule. In capitalist societies, the consumer–voter dominates this choice. In planned socialist societies, planners make the decision.

The *shape* of the production possibilities frontier is not accidental. The fact that it is a curve convex from the origin illustrates a basic fact of economic life: As we attempt to produce increasing amounts of, say, consumer goods, we have to give up ever larger amounts of producer goods to obtain identical increases in consumer goods. In more technical terms, there is a diminishing marginal rate of technical substitution between the production of consumer goods and the production of producer goods.

The production possibilities schedule illustrates the concept of efficiency. We have already indicated that *AB* represents the capacity of a particular economy at a particular time. **Static efficiency** requires an economy to be operating on its production possibilities frontier—for example, at point *p*. Output combinations beyond *AB* are impossible at that time; combinations inside *AB* are feasible but inefficient. An economy that has the capacity *AB* but is producing at point *p'* is statically inefficient, because it could move to point *p* and produce *more of both* goods with no increase in available resources.

Dynamic efficiency is the ability of an economic system to enhance its capacity to produce goods and services over time without an increase in capital and labor inputs. Dynamic efficiency is indicated by movement of the frontier outward from *AB* to *CD* from *p* to *p″* (without an underlying increase in resources); the distance of this movement indicates the change in efficiency. Static and dynamic efficiency are subject to measurement problems. The basic approach to measuring static efficiency is to make productivity calculations, as measured by the ratio of output to inputs. Dynamic efficiency is measured by the ratio of the growth of output to the growth of inputs.

Economic growth and dynamic efficiency are not the same. Economies may grow by increasing efficiency (finding better ways of doing things with the same resources) or by expanding the amount of, say, labor but using that labor at a constant rate of effectiveness. The former is termed **intensive growth**, the latter **extensive growth**.

The concepts of intensive and extensive growth are important in understanding the growth experiences of different economic systems. Later chapters will show that the former planned socialist systems of the Soviet Union and Eastern Europe grew more rapidly in their early years and then experienced continuing slowdowns in their later years. The early rapid growth has been widely attributed to a strategy of extensive growth—a growth-oriented policy designed to expand inputs rapidly. As economies reach higher levels of economic development, growth in output is increasingly derived from intensive economic growth. Mature economies no longer experience the increases in population and saving rates necessary for extensive economic growth.

The rightward shift of the production possibilities schedule from AB to *CD* could have three causes. First, it could be due to dynamic efficiency. Dynamic efficiency is usually attributed to technological progress, broadly defined. With dynamic efficiency, output increases without any change in inputs or in the economic system—the phenomenon of intensive growth. Second, output could increase because capital or labor inputs grow—the phenomenon of extensive growth. Third, "negative" institutions that inhibit output (such as trade barriers, corruption, excessive regulation, or insecure property rights) might be improved, allowing output to expand without any increase in inputs or technology.

Income Distribution

How "fairly" an economic system distributes income among households is the third criterion for assessing economic performance. Technically, **income distribution** is measured by the **Lorenz curve** or **Gini coefficient**, as shown in Figure 3.4. Our ability to measure income distributions does not, however, answer the question of what constitutes a "good" distribution. There may be substantial agreement on the definition of "bad" income distributions (for example, where 1 percent of the population receives 95 percent of all income); judgments about intermediate cases are more difficult to make.

What constitutes an equitable distribution of income?[14] Equity involves fairness, though what is considered fair differs from case to case and over time. One criterion of fairness might involve reward according to contribution to the production process. In a capitalist society, personal income is determined by the human and physical capital one owns and by their prices as determined by factor markets. Income differences

FIGURE 3.4   Measuring Income Inequality: The Lorenz Curve

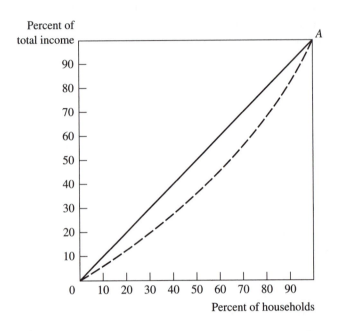

Explanation: Percent of households is measured on the horizontal axis, percent of income on the vertical axis. Perfect equality would be, for example, where 10 percent of households received 10 percent of all income. This would be illustrated by a 45-degree line between the origin (0) and point *A*. Inequality can be illustrated by the dashed line. The further the dashed line away from the 45-degree line, the further from equal the distribution of income. In the diagram, for example, the bottom 20 percent of households receive 10 percent of the income. A comprehensive measure known as the *Gini coefficient* is typically used to measure income inequality. The Gini coefficient is the area between the 45-degree line and the dashed line divided by the entire area under the 45-degree line.

reflect differences in effort (provision of labor services), differences in frugality (provision of capital), inheritance of physical and human capital, luck, and so on. The market distribution of income may be modified by the tax system and by the provision of social services. The extent to which government redistributive action is justified on equity grounds is a matter of continuing controversy in capitalist societies. Under socialism, the factors of production are, with the exception of labor, publicly owned. Capital and land are both socially owned in a socialist society; hence their remuneration belongs to the state, not directly to individuals.

Stability

The fourth criterion is economic stability. By **stability** we mean the absence of significant fluctuations in growth rates, the maintenance of relatively low rates of unemployment, and the avoidance of excessive inflation. Economic stability is a desirable objective for two reasons. The first is that various segments of the population are damaged by instability. Individuals on fixed incomes are hurt by unanticipated inflation; the poorly trained are hurt by unemployment. Second, cyclical instability can lead to losses of potential output, making the economic system operate inside its production possibilities schedule.

Capitalist economies have historically been subject to fluctuations in the level of economic activity—in other words, to business cycles.[15] In planned socialist economies, aggregate economic activity (including investment) was subject to the control of planners. Although cyclical activity did occur in planned socialist economics—through planning errors or transmission through the foreign sector—the socialist society was less likely to suffer cyclical fluctuations.

Stability of economic growth is of practical importance. Potential lost at any particular time is lost forever. A system that, because of cyclical instability, does not reach its potential cannot be expected to achieve its potential rate of growth through time. Thus the matter of cyclical instability, the length and the severity of cycles, and the forms in which they find expression can be indicators of the relative success of economic systems.

Inflation, a second manifestation of instability, may appear in open form as a general rise in the price level, or it may occur in repressed form as lengthening lines for goods and services or as regional and sectoral shortages. In capitalist economies, inflation typically occurs in the first form; in the planned socialist economies (where planners set prices), it historically manifested itself in repressed form. In any event, excessive inflation is viewed as an undesirable phenomenon; it can distort economic calculation (where relative prices are used as sources of information), cause increased use of barter, and alter the income distribution.

Excessive **unemployment** is also undesirable. It implies, along with the personal hardships of those unemployed, less than full utilization of resources. The planned socialist economies did not maintain records on unemployment (which was said to have been "liquidated"). Moreover, the standard definition of unemployment (the unemployed are those seeking employment but unable to find jobs) leaves room for differences in interpretation. There are different types of unemployment, ranging from unemployment associated with the normal changing of jobs to chronic, hard-core unemployment.

These definitions, however, fail to account for the more subtle but important concept of **underemployment**, or the employment of individuals on a full-time basis at work in which they utilize their skills at well under their full potential. Underemployment (which was common in the planned socialist economies) is less visible than unemployment, but it can have a similarly adverse effect on capacity utilization. It typically takes the form of overstaffing, a situation in which ten people are employed for a job that could be done just as well by five.

Viability

The ultimate test of an economic system is its long-term viability. The basic premise of Marxian economics was that over the course of history, "superior" economic systems replace "inferior" ones. In the Marxian scheme, capitalism replaces feudalism, and then socialism replaces capitalism. Inferior systems are beset by internal contradictions that make it impossible for them to survive over the long term. Marx depicted capitalism as unstable, suffering from a number of insurmountable internal contradictions. These internal contradictions, he believed, ensured the eventual demise of capitalism and its replacement by the "superior" system of socialism.

Since the beginning of the Soviet experiment with planned socialism (and its later expansion to one-third of the world's population), discussion had focused on the *relative* economic performance of planned socialism. Most experts felt that planned socialism, though inefficient, would be able to muddle along—to survive at relatively low levels of efficiency and consumer welfare.

Events of the late 1980s highlighted the issue of the long-term viability of planned socialism. The leaders of the former Soviet Union and in Eastern Europe have concluded to transform their planned economic systems into market economies. The rejection of planned socialism casts serious doubt on its ability to deliver an economic performance strong enough to ensure its continued existence.

Among the other basic performance criteria—economic growth, efficiency, income distribution, and stability—the long-term viability of the economic system stands out as the dominant test of performance. If an economic system cannot survive, it has clearly proved itself inferior.

It may be premature to declare the planned socialist system dead. The move away from socialism in the former Soviet Union and in Eastern Europe could be reversed. Socialism continues to have appeal in China, which is combining communist dictatorship with market reform and the opening up of the economy to international trade and investment. It also continues to have a strong emotional appeal because of its promises of equity and stability.

Tradeoffs

The performance criteria we have discussed are not all-inclusive. Other criteria could be added, such as military power, environmental quality, and democratic political institutions. The criteria we have selected are those typically used to measure economic performance.

If all performance criteria were compatible, measuring economic performance would be less complicated. If the achievement of higher growth meant the automatic achievement of the other goals, countries would need only to aim for one goal and expect to achieve the others spontaneously. This is not the way the world works, however. Achieving of one goal often requires sacrificing another.

Consider a society that sets a "fair" distribution of income as its overriding economic goal, where "fairness" requires an equal distribution of income. Dividing output equally among families means that those who have worked harder, who have worked more effectively, or who have taken risks receive the same as those who have not. If unequal effort receives equal reward, this society offers no incentives to encourage hard and effective work, risk taking, and innovation, and in the long run these activities will cease to occur. An equal distribution of income would therefore undermine both efficiency and economic growth.

Consider a society that establishes rapid growth as its overriding goal and seeks to achieve this growth by requiring all teenagers and retired persons to work and by forcing households to save unreasonably large sums for capital formation. Such policies would create economic growth through extensive means (growth through expansion of inputs), but they would probably reduce static efficiency and dynamic efficiency. The capital and labor employed at the margin would not be effective; the loss of household production might make people work less effectively.

Consider a society that wishes to guarantee employment to all those able and willing to work. This guarantee is made in the form of an implicit *job rights* contract, which declares that the state will, as a last resort, provide a job and an income to all.[16] Such a job rights contract would mean that workers have a job no matter how ineffectively and unconscientiously they work. Under such an arrangement, effort would slacken, absenteeism would rise, and employee discipline would fall. These events would depress economic efficiency and cause the society to produce below its production possibilities.

Economic Systems and Performance

Societies do have a choice of economic systems. The countries of the former Soviet Union and Eastern Europe are currently searching for a new economic system. China is experimenting with the combination of political dictatorship, planning, public ownership, and market reform. The nations of the industrialized West are faced with ever-changing choices related to tax systems, industrial policies, and privatization. They must face hard choices between improved growth and efficiency, on the one hand, and, on the other, more equity and stability as provided by their massive social welfare systems. The relatively backward countries of Asia, Africa, and Latin America must decide whether to adopt the free-market policies deployed by the Four Tigers.

The study of comparative economic systems addresses the effect of the system on economic performance. Although the countries of the former Soviet Union and Eastern Europe appear to have rejected this socialist model, it is still important to evaluate its performance, both to complete the historical record and to assess accurately the performance of those countries that continue to use it in modified form, such as China.

It is more difficult to judge the effect of differences in institutional arrangements on performance in countries that use similar economic systems. What is the effect, for example, of worker participation in management on European economic performance? What has been the effect of exceptionally high marginal tax rates in Sweden?

Social experiments, both broad and small, can be costly if erroneously performed. Consider the failed U.S. effort to reform health care in the mid-1990s. America's eventual choice will be enriched by the availability of social experiments that have been conducted in Canada, the United Kingdom, and Germany, which reveal consequences of the choice of various policies. Japan, in its reexamination of its industrial policies, can glean guidance from the experiments with industrial policies in other countries. The poor countries of Asia and Africa can learn from the privatization and free-trade experiments of Hong Kong and South Korea.

Institutions and Economic Performance

The greater the differences are between economic systems, such as the difference between market capitalism and planned socialism, presumably the greater the differences will be in economic performance. Later chapters will discuss the relative performance of the planned socialist economies. It is also possible to compare the economic performance of those economies located in the same geographic region that have chosen different economic systems to identify the effect of the economic system on performance.[17] With the collapse of the socialist economies and the growing interest in economic institutions, we are now able to correlate various measures of institutions with economic performance by using a cross section of countries. A **cross section** of countries is a sample of countries at a particular point in time that differ according to one or more features. For example, a cross section might consist of five countries in the year 2000 that have different economic institutions, such as greater shares of private ownership, and different rates of economic growth. The relationships between institutional differences and economic growth can then be examined by means of statistical tools such as correlation coefficients or scatter diagrams.

Scatter Diagrams: A **scatter diagram** plots two variables taken from the same point in time for different countries to show relationships between the two variables.

FIGURE 3.5(A)   Economic Freedom Index versus Annual Growth Rate: Lower-Middle Income Countries

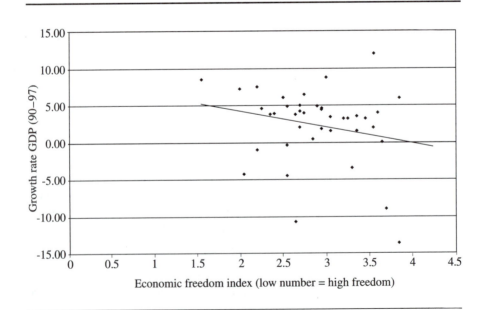

FIGURE 3.5(B)   Corruption versus Growth: Low-Middle Income Countries

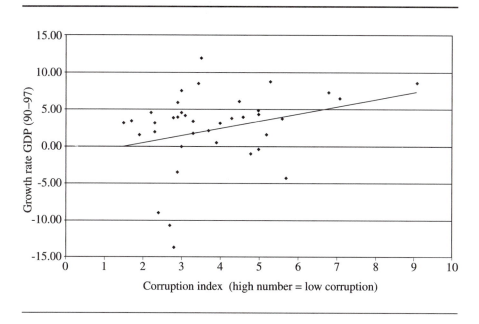

For each country, there is a dot. If the five dots are so arranged that the trend line fitted through them is positively sloped, a positive relationship is suggested. If the dots are so arranged that there is no discernable trend line, there is no relationship between the two variables.

We make extensive use of scatter diagrams in this and subsequent chapters, but they should be handled with care. They only show partial relationships between two variables without taking into account the many other factors that may affect the variable being studied, such as economic growth. A large number of factors affect economic growth. Positive relationships may be the result of some other unseen variables. The lack of relationship may be the result of the omission of another unseen variable from the analysis.

Measures of Institutions and Scatter Diagrams: A number of researchers and organizations compile indexes of economic, social, and political institutions. Among the best known are the Heritage Foundation's Index of Economic Freedom and Transparency International's Corruption Index. Figure 3.5(A) shows a negative relationship between economic growth and a lack of economic freedom. Figure 3.5(B) shows a positive relationship between economic growth and low corruption. These indexes are particularly relevant to the study of comparative economic systems because, as the definition suggests, economic systems (ES) are defined by their institutions (the *I* in equation 2.1). In a world no longer dominated by the great differences between capitalism and socialism, we can still study the effects of different institutions on economic performance to try to identify an "optimal" set of institutions.

Before the collapse of the Soviet Union, a considerable amount of research was devoted to studying the relative performance of Soviet-style planned economies and market economies. These studies, which will be considered in Chapter 13, examined primarily the relative growth rates of output and efficiency in the Soviet Union and Eastern Europe. For the Soviet Union, they show that the Soviet economy grew rapidly in the 1930s and in the 1950s, but growth rates began to decline in the mid-1960s and continued to decline until the end of the Soviet Union. Soviet growth was largely extensive in nature, based primarily on rapid growth of labor and capital inputs.

The growing interest in differing institutional arrangements among capitalist countries has led, in the past two decades, to the compilation of a number of indexes of economic institutions and the study of their correlation with performance indicators such as economic growth. (See Figure 3.5, for example.) A number of researchers and organizations have studied the relationships among institutions and economic performance using measures of democracy, economic openness to trade, property rights, political stability, and economic freedom.

Summary

- Outcomes are influenced by the prevailing economic system (ES) as well as by environmental factors (ENV) and policy factors (POL).
- As different economic systems are evaluated, it is important to develop clear performance criteria and a method of weighting these criteria.
- Five basic economic performance criteria stand out: economic growth, efficiency, income distribution, stability, and viability.
- In real-world economic systems, the formulating of societal objectives is a complex social process that changes through time.
- Economic growth consists of increases in the output of goods and services and/or increases in output per capita.
- Economic development includes societal changes and improvements in the well-being of the population.
- Efficiency is the effectiveness with which a system uses its resources at a given time (static efficiency) or through time (dynamic efficiency). It can be further related to extensive economic growth and intensive economic growth.
- Income distribution is inherently subjective, although it is related to the effectiveness with which participants pursue system objectives.
- The ultimate test of an economic system is it viability.
- When country institutions such as openness, corruption, or economic freedom are correlated with performance indicators such as growth, it is clear that the economic system matters.

Key Terms

economic system (ES)	national priorities	Lorenz curve
outcomes (O)	economic growth	Gini coefficient
environmental factors (ENV)	efficiency	stability
policies (POL)	static efficiency	inflation
policy	dynamic efficiency	unemployment
attribute	intensive growth	underemployment
open economy	extensive growth	cross section
closed economy	income distribution	scatter diagram

Notes

1. Douglass North, *Institutions, Institutional Change, and Economic Performance* (New York: Cambridge University Press, 1990), p. 107.
2. For a discussion of the productivity issue in this case, see the work of Abram Bergson, especially "Comparative Productivity," *American Economic Review* 77 (June 1987), 342–357.
3. See Tjalling C. Koopmans and John Michael Montias, "On the Description and Comparison of Economic Systems," in Alexander Eckstein, ed., *Comparison of Economy Systems: Theoretical and Methodological Approaches* (Berkeley: University of California Press, 1971), pp. 27–78.
4. For the matter of goals or objectives as viewed within the field of comparative economic systems, see John Michael Montias, *The Structure of Economic Systems* (New Haven: Yale University Press, 1976), Ch. 3; G. M. Heal, *The Theory of Economic Planning* (New York: North-Holland, 1973), Ch. 2.
5. For a brief treatment of the role of the Communist party in the formation of national economic objectives in the former Soviet Union, see Paul R. Gregory and Robert C. Stuart *Soviet and Post-Soviet Economic Structure and Performance,* 5th ed. (New York: Harper-Collins, 1994).
6. For a discussion of the various paradigms of political economy, see Barry W. Poulson, *Economic Development: Private and Public Choice* (New York: West, 1994), Part II.
7. The literature on modern public choice has reached some disturbing conclusions about the rationality of majority-rule voting procedures in single and multi-issue settings. See James Buchanan and Gordon Tullock, *The Calculus of Consent* (Ann Arbor: University of Michigan Press, 1962); James M. Buchanan and Robert Tollison, eds., *The Theory of Public Choice II* (Ann Arbor: University of Michigan Press, 1984); for a summary of issues, see Barry W. Poulson, *Economic Development* (New York: West, 1994), Ch. 4.
8. This is a standard element in the socialist critique of capitalism: that under capitalism the impact of the consumer is in fact quite limited, constrained by powerful lobby groups, large corporations, and the like. For a classic treatment, see John Kenneth Galbraith, *The New Industrial State* (Boston: Houghton Mifflin, 1967); Assar Lindbeck, *The New Left: An Outsider's View,* 2nd ed. (New York: Harper & Row, 1977); Samuel Bowles, David M. Gordon, and Thomas E. Weisskopf, *Beyond the Waste Land: A Democratic Alternative to Economic Decline* (New York: Anchor Press/Doubleday, 1983); for a brief summary of these issues, see Poulson, *Economic Development,* Ch. 1.

9. There is much literature on the subject of economic growth. For an introduction, see Malcolm Gillis, Dwight H. Perkins, Michael Roemer, and Donald R. Snodgrass, *Economics of Development,* 3rd ed. (New York: Norton, 1992; Bruce Herrick and Charles P. Kindleberger, *Economic Development* (New York: McGraw-Hill, 1983), Ch. 2.

10. For an example, see Carmelo Mesa-Lago, *Market Socialist and Mixed Economies: Comparative Performance, Chile, Cuba and Costa Rica* (Baltimore: John Hopkins University Press, 2000).

11. The contemporary literature on economic development in fact looks well beyond simple indicators such as per capita output. See, for example, Poulson, *Economic Development,* Ch. 1.

12. The methodological problems of cross-country comparisons have received a great deal of attention in the literature. For early discussions in the U.S.–Soviet context, see Robert W. Campbell, N. Mark Earle, Jr., Herbert S. Levine, and Francis W. Dresch, "Methodological Problems Comparing the U.S. and U.S.S.R. Economies," in United States Congress, Joint Economic Committee, *Soviet Economic Prospects for the Seventies* (Washington, D.C.: U.S. Government Printing Office, 1973), 122–146; for an analysis of growth patterns, see Hollis Chenery and Moshe Syrquin, *Patterns of Development 1950–1970* (London: Oxford University Press, 1975); Moshe Syrquin and Hollis Chenery, "Patterns of Development, 1950–1983," World Bank, Working Papers Series No. 41, 1989; Ross Levine and David Renelt, "A Sensitivity Analysis of Cross-Country Growth Regressions," *American Economic Review* 82, 4 (September 1992), 942–963.

13. This is a rather standard socialist criticism of capitalism. See, for example, the classic work by A. C. Pigou, *Socialism versus Capitalism* (London: Macmillan, 1960), Ch. 8; or the extended discussion in Maurice Dobb, *Welfare Economics and the Economics of Socialism* (Cambridge: Cambridge University Press, 1969); see also Janos Kornai, *The Socialist System* (Princeton, N.J.: Princeton University Press, 1992).

14. A great deal of attention has been paid to the issue of efficiency in connection with the growth analysis of the former planned socialist systems. For a summary of this literature and its application to the Soviet case, see Paul R. Gregory and Robert C. Stuart, *Soviet and Post-Soviet Economic Structure and Performance,* 5th ed. (New York: HarperCollins, 1994), Ch. 10.

15. For an introductory discussion of income distribution, see, for example, Roy Ruffin and Paul Gregory, *Economics* (New York: HarperCollins, 1993); for a development perspective on the distribution of income and wealth, see Poulson, *Economic Development,* Ch. 7.

16. The basic theory of business cycles can be found in any basic work on macroeconomics. See, for example, Andrew W. Abel and Ben S. Berkake, *Macroeconomics* (Reading, Mass.: Addison-Wesley, 1992), Ch. 11. There has been a great deal of interest in the issue of cycles in the formerly planned socialist economic systems. For a summary, see Gregory and Stuart, *Soviet and Post-Soviet Economic Structure and Performance,* Ch. 11.

17. David Granick, *Job Rights in the Soviet Union: Their Consequences* (Cambridge: Cambridge University Press, 1987).

Recommended Readings

Traditional Sources

Kenneth Arrow, *Social Choice and Individual Values,* 2nd ed. (New York: Wiley, 1963).
Trevor Buck, *Comparative Industrial Systems* (New York: St. Martins, 1982).

Edward F. Denison, *Why Growth Rates Differ* (Washington, D.C.: Brookings Institution, 1967).
————, *Accounting for Slower Economic Growth* (Washington, D.C.: Brookings Institution, 1979).
John W. Kendrick, *Understanding Productivity* (Baltimore: Johns Hopkins University Press, 1977).
Etienne S. Kirschen and Lucien Morrisens, "The Objectives and Instruments of Economic Policy," in Morris Bornstein, ed., *Comparative Economic Systems: Models and Cases,* 7th ed. (Homewood, Ill.: Irwin, 1994), 49–66.
Simon Kuznets, *Modern Economic Growth: Rate, Structure and Spread* (New Haven: Yale University Press, 1966).
John Michael Montias, *The Structure of Economic Systems* (New Haven: Yale University Press, 1977).
P. J. D. Wiles, *Distribution of Income East and West* (Amsterdam: North-Holland, 1974).

Economic Growth and Productivity

Robert J. Barro, "Economic Growth in a Cross Section of Countries," *Quarterly Journal of Economics* 106 (May 1991), 407–444.
"Empirical Evidence in Economic Growth Theory," *American Economic Review: Papers and Proceedings* 83, 2 (May 1993), 415–430.
Malcolm Gillis, Dwight H. Perkins, Michael Roemer, and Donald R. Snodgrass, *Economics of Development,* 3rd ed. (New York: Norton, 1992), Chs. 2–3.
Bruce Herrick and Charles P. Kindleberger, *Economic Development,* 4th ed. (New York: McGraw-Hill, 1985).
Ross Levine and David Renelt, "A Sensitivity Analysis of Cross-Country Growth Regression," *American Economic Review* 82, 4 (September 1992), 942–963.
Angus Maddison, "Growth and Slowdown in Advanced Capitalist Economics," *Journal of Economic Literature* 25, 2 (June 1987), 649–698.
E. Wayne Nafziger, *The Economics of Developing Countries,* 2nd ed. (Englewood Cliffs, N.J.: Prentice-Hall, 1990), Ch. 3.
Robert Summers and Alan Heston, "A New Set of International Comparisons of Real Product and Price Levels: Estimates for 130 Countries, 1950–1985," *Review of Income and Wealth* 34 (March 1988), 1–25.

Income Distribution

Anthony B. Atkinson and John Micklewright, *Economic Transformation in Eastern Europe and the Distribution of Income* (Cambridge: Cambridge University Press, 1992).
Malcolm Gillis, Dwight H. Perkins, Michael Roemer, and Donald R. Snodgrass, *Economics of Development,* 3rd ed. (New York: Norton, 1992), Ch. 5.
Margaret E. Grosh and E. Wayne Nafziger, "The Computation of World Income Distribution," *Economic Development and Cultural Change* 34 (January 1986).
Jacques Lecaillon, Felix Paukert, Christian Morrison, and Dimitri Germidis, *Income Distribution and Economic Development: An Analytical Survey* (Geneva: International Labor Office, 1984).
E. Wayne Nafziger, *The Economics of Developing Countries,* 2nd ed. (Englewood Cliffs, N.J.: Prentice-Hall, 1990), Ch. 6.
Barry W. Poulson, *Economic Development* (New York: West, 1994), Ch. 7.

Cyclical Stability

Morris Bornstein, "Unemployment in Capitalist Regulated Market Economies and Socialist Centrally Planned Economies," in Morris Bornstein, ed., *Comparative Economic Systems: Models and Cases,* 7th ed. (Homewood, Ill.: Irwin, 1994), 597–605.

Carlo Frateschi, ed., *Fluctuations and Cycles in Socialist Economies* (Brookfield, Vt.: Avebury Publishers, 1989).

David Granick, *Job Rights in the Soviet Union: Their Consequences* (Cambridge: Cambridge University Press, 1987).

Paul R. Gregory and Robert C. Stuart, *Soviet and Post-Soviet Economic Structure and Performance,* 6th ed. (New York: Addison Wesley Longman, 1997), Ch. 11.

Barry W. Ickes, "Cyclical Fluctuations in Centrally Planned Economies: A Critique of the Literature," *Soviet Studies* 38, 1 (January 1986), 36–52.

4

Changing Institutions

The economic system, the environment in which the system functions, and the economic policies all influence economic outcomes. Many of these influencing forces can, however, be changed. We define **economic reform** as an attempt to modify an existing system, whereas **transition** is the shift from one system to another—for example, the contemporary replacement of plan by market in the countries of the former Soviet Union and Eastern Europe.

Reform of Economic Systems

Although economic reform occurs in both capitalist and socialist economic systems, change occurs differently in different systems. Economic reform in capitalist systems is generally evolutionary in nature, gradual in pace, and, to a significant degree, introduced on a decentralized basis through market-type institutions. In socialist systems, however, change tends to be abrupt and is usually introduced by a central authority—for example, the former Communist parties of Eastern Europe and the Soviet Union. China's move toward modernization also was decided on and introduced by its communist leaders.

Irrespective of how systemic change is classified, modifications that economic systems undergo do change their character. The introduction of command planning and collectivized agriculture in the Soviet Union at the end of the 1920s and the subsequent introduction of such arrangements into Eastern Europe and China after World War II are examples of fundamental and rapid changes in economic systems. In these cases, decision-making arrangements were centralized, the market was replaced by the plan, state ownership supplanted private ownership, and moral incentives became increasingly important. The replacement of command planning by worker-managed socialism in the former Yugoslavia in the 1950s is another case of fundamental change. Finally, in recent times, Eastern Europe and the Soviet Union have shifted from plan to market allocation.

If economic reforms in socialist economic systems are "packages" introduced by a central authority, the reforms of capitalist systems are more difficult to characterize. Today's market economies operate differently from those of 100 years ago. Changes have occurred gradually, without clear milestones. When resources are allocated through markets, changes in allocation procedures are less visible than when a central authority makes sweeping changes by fiat. Some milestones can be identified. Britain's passage of the Corn Laws in the nineteenth century turned the English economy into the world's first open economy. Bismarck's introduction of social security legislation changed Germany's economic system, as did the passage of social security laws in the United States during the Great Depression. Further examples include privatization during the Thatcher years in Great Britain, in the United States the Great Society of Lyndon Johnson in the 1960s, New Zealand's liberalization reforms conducted between 1985 and 1995, Chile's macroeconomic and privatization reforms under Pinochet, Singapore's creation of a forced saving program starting in 1955, and European privatizations of the 1990s. Economic reform attempts to change system characteristics, but the ultimate intent is to change economic outcomes.

Economic Development and Systemic Change

How we view systemic change is influenced by the models used for explaining change. The classical economists in the nineteenth century had a pessimistic view of economic development despite the merits of the invisible hand analyzed by Adam Smith. Economic growth would be limited by diminishing returns. Stagnation was the likely result.

Karl Marx sought to demonstrate the inevitability of the change of one system into another. He formulated the most famous theory of system change. Whether Marx's approach is used as a framework to interpret change or to understand the foundations of socialism, his analysis deserves attention. Other economists, including Joseph Schumpeter, Janos Kornai, and New Institutionalists such as Douglas North and Mancur Olson move beyond the static framework of neoclassical economic theory and seek as well to explain organizational change.

Marx's Theory of Change

Karl Marx (1818–1883) concluded in *Das Kapital* that capitalism is an unstable economic system whose lifespan is inevitably limited.[1] **Marx's theory of capitalism** is based on his materialist conception of history,[2] which teaches that economic forces (called **productive forces**) determine how production relations, markets, and society itself (the **superstructure**) are organized. Weak productive forces (underdeveloped human and capital resources) result in one arrangement for producing goods and services (**production relations**), and strong productive forces lead to different, more advanced production arrangements. A society with underdeveloped economic resources has underdeveloped production relations and superstructure (manifested in barter exchange, serf labor, a rigid social hierarchy, and religious biases against commerce). As the productive forces improve, new economic and social relationships emerge (such as hired rather than serf labor and monetary rather than natural exchange). These new arrangements are not compatible with the old economic, cultural, and social relationships. When they come into contact, tensions and conflicts mount.

Eventually, incompatibilities become so great that a qualitative change (usually the result of violent revolution or war) occurs. New production relations and a new superstructure, compatible with the new productive forces, replace the old order.

These **qualitative changes** are inevitable because societies are destined to evolve from a lower to a higher order. The engine of change is the conflict between old and new, primarily in the form of class antagonisms (the emerging capitalist class versus the landed gentry in feudal societies, the worker versus the capitalist in capitalist societies). The process of evolutionary and inevitable qualitative change through the competition of opposing forces (**thesis versus antithesis**) is the foundation of Marx's theory of **dialectical materialism**, which was based on the teachings of the German philosophers George Wilhelm Hegel and Ludwig Feuerbach.

The upshot of Marx's materialist conception of history was his contention that societies evolve according to an inevitable pattern of social and economic change in which lower systems are replaced by more advanced systems. In this manner, feudalism is bound to replace slavery, capitalism inevitably displaces feudalism, and socialism eventually replaces capitalism.

The victory of capitalism over feudalism represented a qualitative step forward for society. A highly efficient productive machine (capitalism) replaced an inefficient one (feudalism) based on semiservile labor and governed by traditional landed interests. Two landmarks signaled the emergence of capitalism. The first was the initial accumulation of capital by the emerging capitalist class—a process Marx called **primitive capitalist accumulation**. The second indicator was the formation of a "free" labor force at the disposal of capitalist employers. Laborers were separated from control over land, tools, and livestock and were left with only their own labor to sell. At this point the capitalist, who now controlled the means of production, hired this free labor, and capitalist factories were established. In this manner, the basic class conflict of capitalism was created—the conflict between the working class and the capitalist, who "owns" the labor services of the worker.

The feature that distinguishes labor from the other factors of production is that the employer can compel workers to produce a value that exceeds the value that workers need to maintain themselves. However, the employer is not required to pay workers the full value of their production—only enough to allow them to subsist. One worker may have to work 8 hours to produce a value sufficient to meet subsistence needs, yet the employer can force the worker to create a surplus, which will accrue to capitalists, by working 12 hours—4 hours more than are required for subsistence. The exploitation of labor is the source of capitalist profits, which Marx called **surplus value**.

Marx pictured capitalism, in its early stages, as a world of cut-throat competition. The capitalist was driven to maximize profits (surplus value) and to accumulate more capital out of profits. Capitalists, operating in intensely competitive markets, are forced to introduce cost-saving innovations lest their competitors do so first and drive them out of business. One capitalist introduces a new labor-saving technology, attracts competitors' customers through lower prices, and experiences a temporary increase in profits above "normal" levels. The profits are short-lived, however, because competitors respond by introducing the same cost-saving techniques, and new competitors enter the market in response to windfall profits. Excess industry profits are eliminated, and no capitalist ends up better off. But when fixed capital is substituted for labor, the profit rate declines. There is an inherent tendency to substitute capital for labor, even though labor is the sole source of surplus value. Marx predicted that the profit rate would fall, with disastrous consequences for capitalism.

As the profit rate falls, capitalism's internal contradictions and weaknesses become apparent. In an effort to halt the decline in profits, capitalists increase the exploitation of their workers, and alienation and exploitation intensify. The declining profit rate leads to the failure of marginal businesses, and bankrupt capitalists now swell the ranks of the unemployed. Those fortunate enough to be employed are exploited and alienated; the unemployed fare even worse.

A more ominous phenomenon is overproduction. Workers are kept at subsistence wages by high unemployment; capitalists, driven by the desire to accumulate capital, are not willing to increase their spending on luxury goods. Moreover, the ranks of the capitalists are thinning, as monopolies drive out smaller capitalists. Yet all the while, the productive capacity of the economy is growing because of the growing capital-intensity of industry. Aggregate demand falls chronically short of aggregate supply; recessions and then depressions occur, and worldwide crises become commonplace. The declining profit rate leads to declines in investment spending and to further shortfalls in aggregate demand.

Marx described only generally the final stages of the **capitalist breakdown**. Overproduction, underconsumption, disproportions, and the exploitation and alienation of workers combine to create the conditions necessary for the violent overthrow of capitalism.[3] Workers unite against the weakened capitalist class and, through a violent *world* revolution, establish a new socialist order. Marx had little to say about this new order. Implicit in Marx's writings on the final stage of capitalism is that contradictions will be more intense in the most advanced capitalist countries; the socialist revolution would be initiated there.

Schumpeter: The Evolution of Capitalism

Joseph Schumpeter also described the dynamics of capitalist economies.[4] Although Schumpeter was pessimistic about the survival of capitalism and predicted its eventual replacement by socialism, he nevertheless viewed this demise rather differently than Marx.

Schumpeter argued that the capitalist economy could not be understood within the framework of static economic analysis—that is, the pursuit of objectives by existing institutions. Capitalism, he argued, is fundamentally dynamic and can be understood only if change is explained. The important issues, therefore, are not how an organization functions at a point in time but, rather, how that organization comes into being and how it evolves over time as a mechanism generating economic growth.

The driving force of evolution in the capitalist system, according to Schumpeter, is innovation, or the development and implementation of new products, new ideas, and new ways of doing things. Innovation is carried out by an entrepreneurial class, driven by and rewarded through a profit motive. Indeed, the development of new ideas broadly defined was for Schumpeter a process termed **creative destruction**, as the new replaced the old.

According to Schumpeter, the life of a capitalist enterprise was one of struggle. By having a better idea, a superior innovation, or a new product, the enterprise would be able to drive more mature rivals from the field. However, any competitive advantage would be short-lived. Eventually, every business must face creative destruction, even monopolists and giant concerns. Business rivals are constantly in search of better production techniques and better products. Today's dominant firm (the railroad) will become tomorrow's dinosaur as better products (trucking and air freight) are introduced. Today's secure monopoly (such as the Bell system in the 1970s) becomes tomorrow's competitive battlefield (AT&T versus MCI versus Sprint).

Schumpeter viewed the capitalist economy not in terms of the competitive ideal but rather as characterized by concentration. Concentration would eventually lead to the routinization of the entrepreneurial spirit and a lack of social willingness to reward risk takers. The decline in entrepreneurial activity would be a fundamental reason for the eventual decline of capitalism.

Although there are similarities between the Schumpeterian and Marxian interpretations of capitalism (the importance of classes, the cyclical nature of economic activity, the role of profit, and a tendency for profit rates to decline), the Schumpeterian focus is on the innovative power of capitalism and on how to preserve innovation.

The New Institutional Economics

Both Marx and Schumpeter were interested in how institutions change and in how these changes affect economic life. The New Institutional Economics focuses directly on how institutions evolve and on the effect of this evolution on economic performance.[5] The New Institutional Economics has a number of precursors. The early writings of Nobel laureate Friederick Hayek considered the process by which economic institutions change and evolve over time. Hayek argued that economic institutions arise according to a **spontaneous order** in which new organizations, laws, regulations, and customs are tested by daily economic life. Those arrangements that "work" are retained by society; those that do not work fall by the wayside in a Darwinian manner. The corporation arose as a way of raising capital and sharing risk in medieval times. It survived because it served a useful economic function. Worker guilds also arose during the medieval period, to evolve later into craft unions. They served their purpose for a long time, but they will disappear when they outlive their usefulness.

According to Hayek, the institutions of economic life exist in the form of written and unwritten information that is passed from one generation to the next. They are the result of "human action" but not of "human design." They do not have to be codified into law or written into corporate charters or contracts. They evolve in bits and pieces, so no single person or entity knows them in their entirety. Rather, these bits and pieces are known and understood by those who require each bit of specialized knowledge in order to conduct their economic lives. An example is money. All economies use money, but no one designed money. Because money is something that fills a void, it resulted from spontaneous human actions.[6]

Ronald Coase is also a precursor of the New Institutional Economics. Coase, whose ideas we discussed in Chapter 2, explained the rational economic logic according to which organizations are created. Business enterprises arise when the transaction costs of organizing production through markets are too high. Political and social institutions arise in the same fashion. Communities form school districts when the transaction costs of organizing the education of children through individual market contracts are too high. Governments finance the procurement of certain goods when the transaction costs of arranging voluntary contributions are too great.

The basic proposition of the New Institutional Economics, as practiced by Douglass North, Gordon Tullock, Mancur Olson, and many others, is that we can study the evolution of institutions and their effect on economic life by using the logic of economic rationality as reflected in the pursuit of self-interest. Specifically, we can explain many major changes in the course of economic history by examining changes in property rights, transaction costs, and rent-seeking opportunities.[7] For example, the increase in agricultural output and the urbanization of Britain during the Industrial Revolution were enhanced by changes in property rights in the English countryside, as changes in laws and customs reduced the transaction costs of enclosing agricultural land into separate estates. England's making more rapid economic progress than France during the nineteenth century is explained by the creation of stable financial markets as a consequence of parliamentary restraints on arbitrary royal actions. England's long-term decline in the twentieth century is explained by its social and political stability, which allowed rent-seeking *distributional coalitions* to form. The persistence of sharecropping in the American South is explained by imperfect capital markets and excessive information costs. The resistance of French peasants to producing cash crops in the nineteenth century is explained in terms of risk avoidance and the natural insurance provided by the growing of subsistence crops.

As Nobel laureate Douglass North explains, standard microeconomic theory cannot account for the effects of time and institutions on economic performance. Instead, standard theory holds time and institutions constant.[8] The New Institutional Economics argues that changes in institutions can be explained in terms of standard economic logic. They can be explained by changes in property rights, innovations that alter transaction costs, information asymmetries, and opportunities for voluntary behavior.

According to the New Institutional Economics, market institutions—corporations, futures markets, contract law, cartels, commercial banks—were created because they happened to be economically rational given the circumstances of time and place. If economic conditions change—if something happens to lower transaction costs, raise information costs, or change property rights—then our economic institutions will change accordingly.

Whereas Marx viewed institutional change as inevitable and as following a predetermined path, the New Institutional Economics views institutional change as being dictated by economic variables, whose course of change cannot be predicted in advance; nor does this course of change follow an inevitable path. This path depends on the starting point, as measured by an economy's history, culture, resource endowments, and the like—that is, on its *initial conditions.* The path then depends on the course of transaction costs, property rights, and other factors. The course of change is *path-dependent* in that it depends on the initial conditions from which progress begins.

Change in Socialism

Whereas Marx and others believed in the inherent instability of capitalism, a number of critics argued the exact opposite: that socialism is the inherently unstable economic system. Socialism's critics warned against socialist experiments on the grounds that once started, they might be difficult to stop.[9] If a socialist economy was indeed established, it would prove unworkable and would be destined either to collapse or to operate at very low levels of efficiency.

Hayek and Mises

As we noted above, the Austrian economist and Nobel laureate Friederick Hayek argued that capitalism develops its institutions in an efficient manner.[10] If an attempted institutional change does not improve the efficiency of the system, it will disappear. Hayek, together with his colleague Ludwig von Mises, founded a school of economic thought now called Austrian Economics. Both praised the efficiency with which market economies process and utilize information on relative prices. Hayek wrote that the principal problem of economics is "how to secure the best use of resources known to any member of society, for ends whose relative importance only these individuals know."

How is the economy to utilize knowledge about product prices, qualities, and location that is not available to any one person or institution in its entirety? These economists believed that the specialization in information about the price system enables each individual to participate effectively in the economy, acquiring knowledge only about those things that he or she needs to know. Hayek writes of the "marvel" of the price system:

> The marvel is that in a case like that of a scarcity of one raw material, without an order being issued, without more than perhaps a handful of people knowing the cause, tens of thousands of people whose identity could not be ascertained by months of investigation, are made to use the material or its products more sparingly; i.e., they move in the right direction.*

Mises was an early critic of socialism. In his classic article "Economic Calculation in the Socialist Commonwealth," published in 1922, Mises anticipated most of the modern-day problems of the socialist economies, arguing that socialist

---

*Source: Friederick A. Hayek, "The Price System as a Mechanism for Using Knowledge," *American Economic Review* 35, 4 (September 1945), 519–528.

economies would lack market exchange and would hence lack the vital information provided by the price system. Without relative prices, socialist managers would not have enough information to make rational economic decisions. Moreover, lacking property rights, socialist managers would not behave in an economically rational manner but rather would overdemand and waste scarce resources.

According to Hayek and Mises, socialism lacked the informational basis for rational economic calculation, and its institutions were created by "human design" rather than arising according to a spontaneous order.

Experiments with socialism, such as those that took place in Russia after the Bolshevik revolution of 1917, created an economic system of planned socialism that contained a number of internal contradictions. Mises and Hayek felt that a socialist economy would be too complex to plan from the center and would require more information on technology, prices, quantities, and assortments than a central planning board could digest. Moreover, they felt that the task of planning and management could not be effectively decentralized, because in the absence of private property, even the best-intentioned managers of state enterprises could not make economically correct decisions.

For these reasons, Mises and Hayek felt that such socialist experiments as those in the Soviet Union would fail and that the experiment would eventually be abandoned. In this sense, the theories of Mises and Hayek are models of the change of socialism back to capitalism on the grounds of socialism's inferiority as an economic system.

Kornai: The Economics of Shortage

The Hungarian economist Janos Kornai also argued that socialism was inherently unstable because of its natural tendency to generate shortage.[11]

He characterized the planned socialist economy as an **economy of shortage**, where shortage is a systemic, perpetual, and self-reproducing condition. Others had argued earlier that persistent shortages or excess demand in the socialist systems are functions of identifiable, though not necessarily easily corrected, forces. Consumer goods are simply not a high priority and are supplanted by producer goods and military production. Errors in planning, inadequate incentives, and other system characteristics lead to continuing shortages.

From a very different perspective, Kornai argued that the economy of shortages arises from the nature of the enterprise in the planned socialist system. The socialist enterprise operates under fundamentally different rules. The capitalist enterprise is motivated to maximize profits. It makes its input and output decisions on the basis of prices established in markets. As a profit maximizer, the capitalist enterprise has little incentive to overdemand resources. If it employs more resources than technology requires, its profits suffer. The capitalist enterprise operates under a **hard budget constraint**. Faced with input prices and output prices, the capitalist enterprise must cover its costs while earning an acceptable rate of return on invested capital. If it fails to meet its budget constraint, the capitalist firm will fail in the long run. The capitalist firm must live within its means. The hard budget constraint "polices" capitalist enterprise activities and effectively eliminates shortage (in the sense of excess demand for inputs).

The socialist firm operates in a supply-constrained economy. Socialist planners have as their objective the rapid expansion of outputs, and they judge the performance of socialist enterprises on that basis. The manner in which socialist enterprises select inputs to meet their output objectives is of less importance than the output targets themselves. Although socialist enterprises face prices for inputs and outputs, their resource-allocation decisions are aimed at meeting output targets. Relative prices play only a minor role.

The capitalist enterprise that fails to live within its means is punished by bankruptcy. The socialist enterprise that fails to cover costs plus a rate of return on the state's invested capital does not suffer the same consequences. Socialist planners value enterprises for their outputs; socialist enterprises that make losses remain in business by virtue of state subsidies. Accordingly, socialist enterprises face a **soft budget constraint**. Socialist enterprises can live beyond their means, if necessary, over the long run.

The hard budget constraint forces capitalist enterprises to limit their demands for inputs. The soft budget constraint on socialist enterprises fails to reward them for restricting their input demands. Hence the socialist system generates continuous excess demands for inputs. The supply of inputs falls chronically short of the demand for inputs, and persistent shortages or imbalances result.

Economic systems must allocate resources in an orderly fashion. Persistent imbalances and chronic shortages detract from the orderly allocation of resources. With imbalances, those who obtain resources may be those who will not put them to their best and highest use. Kornai's analysis of socialism is related to the complexity and motivation issues raised by Mises and Hayek. Kornai's conclusion is that the socialist motivation system and inattention to relative prices disrupt the orderly allocation of resources under socialism. Accordingly, socialism will not be an efficient economic system.

The New Institutional Economics Critique of Socialism

Public choice economists, in particular Mancur Olson and Peter Murrell, argue that the process of change in socialist economies will be dictated by the extent to which the system's directors (say, a monolithic Communist party spearheaded by a small elite) can prevent rent-seeking distributional coalitions from emerging.[12] A **distributional coalition** is a vested-interest coalition that uses the political process to gain monopoly profits for itself. As long as the socialist system is rigidly controlled by the system's dictator, that dictator will strive to allocate resources to maximize growth. It will be in the dictator's interest, as the beneficiary of economic growth, to create high savings rates, new technologies, and managerial behavior that elicits maximal enterprise capacity. By imposing terror or other coercive policies, the dictator can force agents throughout the economy to work toward the goal of economic growth.

As time passes, however, the power of the dictator may weaken. Dedication to the goal of "overtaking the West" may diminish. Various interest groups (such as a military lobby or a heavy-industry pressure group) emerge, and the primary interests of every such group is promoting its particular branch or enterprise at the expense of others. These coalitions find ways to insulate themselves from the pressure of the dictator, such as concealing information from the center or appropriating resources that could have been used more productively by others. They develop ways to promote their own interests at the expense of the interests of the economy as a whole.

As the power of separate interest groups increases, the center finds it more difficult to impose discipline on the periphery. Power is devolved from the center to lower levels. Interest groups form into coalitions to promote their own interests. Instead of resources being devoted to generating the highest possible growth rates, resources are dissipated among distributional coalitions, which evade central controls and use resources for their own benefit.

The net result of the rising power of interest groups is that growth rates decline and efficiency of resource use drops. The dictator cannot maintain a strong hand forever, but the system works well *only* under a strong hand. As growth rates decline, distributional coalitions become bolder. They begin to engage in outright corruption and theft. No one considers the interest of society as a whole; attention is paid only to the narrow interests of vested-interest groups.[13] Moreover, given that each distributional coalition has vested interests to protect (such as special access to scarce goods and the opportunity to buy at below-equilibrium prices), there is no support for reform, which means that the system will not be able to take corrective action.

Change in Capitalist Economies

Change in capitalist economies is more gradual and less visible than change in socialist economies, which tends to come from above. Long-run changes can occur, however. Some aspects of change can be captured by quantitative statistics, which enable us to see the type and magnitude of change in capitalist economies. These statistics are related to private versus public ownership, friends in competition, and income redistribution.

Property Rights: Private versus Public Ownership

The ownership of property is a distinguishing characteristic of economic systems that can be measured, albeit imperfectly. Significant changes in the shares of public and private ownership of property can alter the nature of a capitalist economic system. Indeed, if the state owned a major share of existing property, we would no longer classify the system as capitalist.

Real-world capitalist systems are mixed, some having higher shares of public ownership than others. **Privatization** occurs when property that had been state-owned is transferred to private owners. State ownership increases when privately owned property becomes publicly owned, or **nationalized**. The shares of public ownership can be increased either by government spending that creates new government-owned capital (such as the U.S. government's Tennessee Valley Authority initiated during the Great Depression) or by direct government buying of existing facilities. By selling

their shares of British Air or Lufthansa, for example, British and German governments increased the share of private ownership.

Public sentiment in favor of public ownership was highest in the United States
during the Great Depression. In the United Kingdom, the elections of Labor governments in the 1940s and 1950s provided political support for nationalization, whereas
the lengthy tenure of a Conservative government from the mid- to late 1970s through
the mid-1990s showed support for privatization. Alternating socialist and conservative
governments in France also reflect rising and falling sentiment for privatization or
nationalization. In Germany, both socialist and conservative governments have consistently favored privatization since the end of World War II. The German government
has sold its shares of major corporations to private owners throughout the postwar era.
It is currently undertaking its largest privatization, the sale of Deutsche Telekom.

In the United States, government shares of structures and land have not changed
noticeably since the early 1930s, nor has the share of output produced by government
enterprises. After a rise in public ownership in the early 1930s, the share of government ownership remained fairly stable, despite a substantial increase in output shares
consumed by government.

Table 4.1 shows the government shares of fixed capital in 1970, 1980, and 1997 in
seven industrialized capitalist countries including Greece. The differences in ownership shares partially result from different accounting procedures, but even so, substantial changes in government ownership shares within each country cannot be observed
from these figures. In some countries, government ownership shares have fallen since
1980 (Canada, Australia, Belgium, and Greece). In others, they have risen (United
Kingdom, Finland, and Sweden). In the majority of countries, government shares of
capital have been stable over the 25-year period. In Germany and Italy, government
ownership shares either were unchanged or changed only slightly.

Figure 4.1 shows that the production of government enterprises as a percent of
GDP varied considerably among industrialized countries but that there was no strong

TABLE 4.1   Share of Government Ownership of Fixed Capital,
Capitalist Countries (percentages of total)

	1970	1980	1997
Australia	17	18	14
Belgium	15	15	13
Canada	20	24	19
Finland	16	16	20
Germany	8	8	8
Greece	2	1	1
Italy	—	15	15
Norway	—	17	18
Sweden	—	13	12
United Kingdom	5	6	7

Source: OECD, *Flows and Stocks of Fixed Capital* (Paris: OECD, various years).

FIGURE 4.1   Public Enterprise Share of GDP (selected industrialized countries)

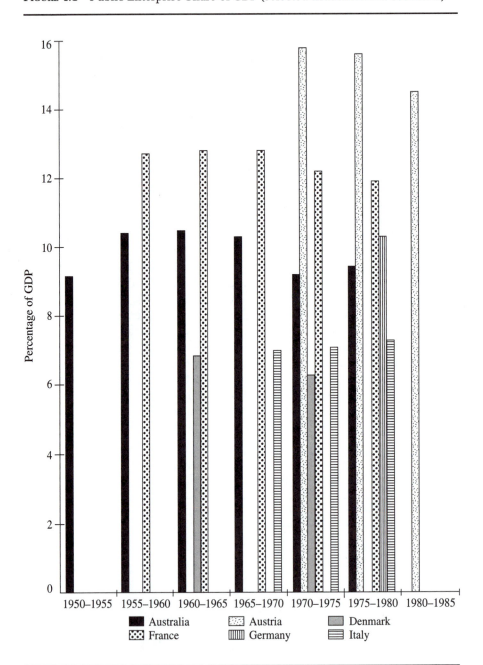

Source: From "The Role of Public Enterprises: An International Statistical Comparison," in Robert Floyd, Clive Gray, and Robert Short, eds., *Public Enterprise in Mixed Economies* (Washington, D.C.: IMF, 1984), pp. 110–196. Reprinted by permission of the International Monetary Fund.

trend prior to the 1980s. Overall there has been little change in private and public ownership shares in capitalist countries, which suggests that these countries have reached a basic consensus on the distribution of public and private ownership. Changes in governments over the years have not notably altered this consensus.

The conservative governments elected in the United States and Western Europe in the 1980s brought a rising tide of privatization. It is difficult to tell whether this trend will continue long enough to change fundamentally their shares of private and public ownership, but in view of the long-term stability of ownership shares, this outcome seems unlikely.

Although government production and shares of capital appear steady, the government's claim on production has increased in most countries. The government does not produce more or own more capital (as a percent of GDP), but its expenditures on goods and services and transfers have generally risen (see Figure 4.2), except for some recent declines in Sweden, the United Kingdom, and the United States.

Trends in Competition

Changes in **competition** alter the nature and operation of a capitalist economy, but they do not result in the system's ceasing to be capitalist. A capitalist economy in which monopoly is prevalent may operate inefficiently and cause consumers to pay high prices, but it is still a capitalist economy.

FIGURE 4.2   Government Consumption as a Percentage of GDP

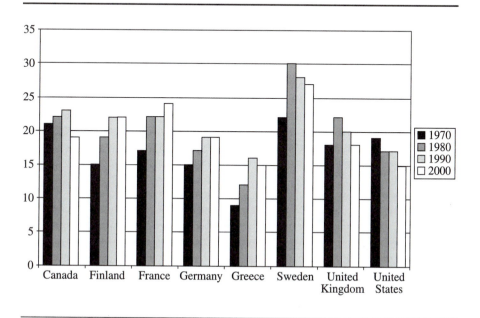

The degree of competitiveness is affected by antitrust laws, regulations, and trade policies. It is difficult to generalize about trends in state policy toward competition. The best-documented trend is the postwar relaxation of international trade barriers. The industrialized capitalist countries created international arrangements for dismantling the restrictive trade barriers that were erected during the Great Depression, and there is little doubt that the degree of international competition expanded rapidly throughout the postwar period. Trade barriers were lowered in both product markets and factor markets (see Figure 4.3). In the early twenty-first century, one can speak of a world capital market in which financial capital flows freely and quickly among Europe, North America, and the industrialized Asian countries.

Deregulation is another visible indicator of state policy toward competition. When a potentially competitive industry is regulated by the state, the degree of competition is reduced. The trend toward deregulation started in the United States in the late 1970s, and it spread from North America to Western Europe and Japan in the 1980s. Deregulation has been most prominent in transportation, communications, and banking, but it remains to be seen whether other capitalist countries will deregulate to the extent of the United States and whether the deregulation experiment will continue into the twenty-first century. The example of U.S. deregulation has clearly been spreading. The European Union has scheduled the deregulation of passenger airline traffic, telecommunications, and financial services as part of Europe's move to a single market.

FIGURE 4.3   Average U.S. Import Duties, 1900–Present

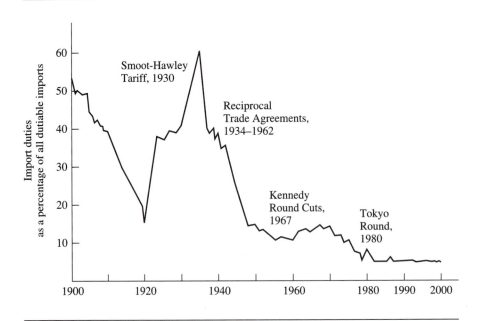

Sources: Historical Statistics of the United States; Statistical Abstract of the United States.

The least visible aspect of state competition policy—and the most difficult to characterize—is antitrust policy. Most industrialized capitalist countries allow more exemptions from antitrust laws than the United States, which exempts primarily farming operations and labor unions; however, antitrust laws that prevent abuse of monopoly power exist in nearly every capitalist country. Unlike the U.S. laws, which declare all formal price-fixing agreements illegal, other industrialized capitalist countries judge price-fixing arrangements on the basis of whether they result in reasonable prices. The European Union now has a cartel office that must approve mergers and acquisitions within the EU.

In the United States, there have been few major changes in antitrust legislation since the 1930s. The changes that have occurred have taken place in the courts. Initially, the courts interpreted the antitrust laws as outlawing anticompetitive behavior, but in the early 1950s, antitrust laws were interpreted as outlawing monopoly power per se, whether this power was abused or not. The 1980s and 1990s have seen a move toward a more liberal interpretation of antitrust laws, stemming from the recognition that businesses must compete in international markets against close substitutes and that antitrust laws should not be used to penalize competitive successes.

Growing international competition and deregulation should increase the degree of competition in capitalist countries. Moreover, rapid technological progress produces a wider variety of competitive products and promotes competition. William Shepherd has attempted to measure the changing degree of competition in the U.S. economy. He concludes that the American economy became more competitive after 1960 as a consequence of growing international competition and deregulation.[14] According to Shepherd, the share of the U.S. economy that was effectively competitive remained fairly stable at 52 to 54 percent between 1939 and 1958 but rose to 77 percent by 1980. Similar studies have not been conducted for the other industrialized capitalist countries, so we do not know whether the American experience is representative. However, because virtually all industrialized capitalist countries have been subject to growing international competition, the impact of this development may be equally strong in other capitalist countries.

An important perspective on deregulation in the American economy is provided by the major changes in airlines, telecommunications, trucking, and other important sectors of the economy during the 1980s.[15] According to a survey of the outcomes of this deregulation, in 1977 fully regulated industries produced 17 percent of gross national product, whereas by 1988 this share had decreased to 6.6 percent.[16] Although the results of this deregulation experience have often been controversial, economic analysis suggests that the benefits have outweighed the costs, resulting in significant net gains for the American public.

Income Redistribution by the State

Capitalism uses material incentives to motivate economic behavior, and a move away from material incentives would signal a fundamental change in the capitalist economic system. If a capitalist state altered the distribution of income earned in factor markets, earnings in factor markets would become less decisive in determining command over resources. For example, if the tax system equalized the distribution of income after taxes, material rewards would cease to guide economic decision making. Changes in tax policy can indeed change the nature of the capitalist economic system.

For a tax system to have a large impact on the reward system, taxes must make up a large share of factor income, and the tax system must redistribute income. Income is redistributed via either a **progressive tax** (which redistributes proportionally away from high-income earners) or a **regressive tax** (which redistributes proportionally away from low-income earners). In a progressive tax system, the tax's share of income rises with income; in a regressive system, that share falls. In order substantially to redistribute income away from high-income earners, the tax system must take up a large share of factor income and must be highly progressive.

Table 4.2 gives information on changes in the tax system's shares of income and in the shares of income taken by several different taxes. The table shows that in all the capitalist countries surveyed, taxes rose as a percentage of GDP. The most modest rise was in the United States—from 27 to 31 percent; the largest rise was in Sweden—from 28 to 59 percent.

The shares of income taxes and taxes on goods provide indirect information on the redistributive role of the tax system. Taxes on income tend to be progressive, whereas taxes on goods are regressive. Assuming no significant changes in income tax rates by income bracket, the tax system would become more progressive as a whole when the share of income taxes rose. The tax system would become more regressive as a whole when the share of taxes on goods rose. Table 4.2 reveals a mixed picture. In six of the countries, the income tax share of total taxes remained stable or fell. In the other two countries, the income tax share rose. In only two countries (Italy's rising share and Sweden's falling share) were the changes substantial. The table also shows a generally declining reliance on taxes on goods. The share of taxes on goods fell substantially in France, Italy, and Japan. Only Canada recorded a small increase in the share of taxes on goods.

Not having readily available information on income tax rates, we can draw only cautious conclusions about Table 4.2. There has been a substantial increase in the share of taxes of factor income in the industrialized capitalist countries, but there has not been a substantial shift in the form of taxation. Although there has been a slight drift away from taxes on goods and toward taxes on income (which should increase progressivity), these changes have been relatively minor, except in Italy. The overall conclusion is that the redistributive role of the tax system has not changed much in capitalist economies, even though the share of taxes has been rising.

What have capitalist governments done with the increasing tax share of GDP? The last columns show the dramatic rises in the shares of social security transfers as a percentage of GDP. The effect of social security transfers on economic rewards depends on how these transfers are distributed. If they are distributed according to contributions, they do not alter the factor distribution of income. If they are distributed in a manner unrelated to contributions (such as in poverty programs), they do alter the distribution of income.

The evidence that has been collected for the United States shows that although the tax system does not materially alter the distribution of income, the distribution of transfers does.[17] The major instrument of state income redistribution in the United

TABLE 4.2 Changes in the Capitalist Tax System

	Taxes as a Percentage of GDP			Share of Total Taxes						Social Security Transfers as Percentage of GDP		
				Income Taxes on Individuals and Corporations			Taxes on Goods					
	1960	1980	2000	1970	1985	2000	1970	1985	2000	1960	1981	2000[a]
Canada	24	32	43	45	43	49	32	33	24	8	10	14
France	32	42	50	18	18	20	38	29	28	14	20	20
Germany	30	38	46	32	33	28	32	27	28	12	17	22
Italy	27	30	46	17	36	35	38	26	26	10	6	19
Japan	20	25	31	41	46	36	22	15	17	4	11	14
Sweden	28	49	59	54	42	41	29	25	22	8	18	16
United Kingdom	28	35	40	40	38	37	29	31	35	7	13	16
United States	27	29	31	48	42	48	19	18	18	5	11	11

[a]Calculated by the authors.

Sources: Statistical Abstract of the United States (international comparisons); OECD, *Historical Statistics* (Paris: OECD, 1990).

States is the distribution of transfer payments to low-income recipients. The growing GDP share of social security transfers suggests that a significant alteration in material rewards may have occurred in capitalist economic systems through the distribution of social security transfers to the less advantaged.

Worker Participation

A fundamental characteristic of capitalism is that the owners of capital (individual proprietors, partners, and corporate shareholders) are rewarded out of profits.[18] Workers are paid wages that do not vary directly with profits. Capitalism can change its character by sharing profits and management control with workers. Such a change would require new incentive arrangements.

Because profits fluctuate more than wage income, the owners of capital are, in effect, making a deal with workers that as long as the business remains solvent, workers will receive their contracted wages. Owners of capital, who bear risk in the form of fluctuating returns on capital, earn a return to reward them for taking that risk. The worker accepts a contractual wage and, in return, is prepared to follow the directions of management.

This relationship between worker and owner of capital can be altered by profit sharing. If rewards to workers depend in part on the profits of the business, the worker becomes a partial capitalist and bears a part of the risk of fluctuating profits. If workers' incomes depend entirely on the profits of the enterprise, then they basically become capitalists.

The advantages of a profit-sharing economy derive from the workers being more materially interested in the profitability of the enterprise. They are more inclined to work in the interests of the enterprise than before, and they are less inclined to shirk work. A profit-sharing economy has another advantage: If workers' pay rises and falls with profits, the economy becomes more flexible. Recessions cause wages to drop, and falling wages stimulate employment.

The notion of profit sharing is not new, but it has gained increasing attention in capitalist economies because of the large-scale use of profit sharing in postwar Japan.[19] In Japan, worker bonuses average about one-quarter of annual earnings, and they are paid out of profits. Japanese workers certainly benefit from higher profits in the form of higher year-end bonuses. In the United States, employees participate in their corporation's profits when the buy their own company's shares for their retirement programs. Often the company will provide shares free of charge to match the employee's purchase. Managerial employees also receive stock options that allow them to benefit from rising share prices.

Government Intervention

Capitalist economic systems rely on the market mechanism to provide information for decision makers. At the same time, there is much debate over the extent to which various failures of the market mechanism might be reduced or eliminated by state intervention.

A significant change in policy has been widespread acceptance of the notion that government is responsible for macroeconomic stability. This change—called the **Keynesian revolution**—took place in the period since World War II, especially in the 1960s and thereafter. Capitalist governments now use fiscal and monetary policies to pursue stabilization. Most capitalist systems have put in place a variety of monetary and fiscal mechanisms designed to implement stabilization policies. Although the role of the state in macroeconomic stabilization remains a subject of discussion and controversy, capitalist countries have generally experienced greater macroeconomic stability in the second half of the twentieth century, despite major energy shocks in the 1970s, than in the first half of the twentieth century or in the nineteenth century. Business cycles have become less severe.

A different sort of change in capitalist systems is represented by the introduction of some sort of planning mechanism—and thus a reduction in reliance on the market mechanism. Great Britain, a country known for the important role government plays in its market economy, has had very limited experience with national economic planning. France, on the other hand, is well known for its application of **indicative planning**, an approach to planning designed to achieve better decision making based on more and better information without being vulnerable to the possibility of authoritarian control in an otherwise democratic system.

There are cases where market capitalist systems have developed some form of planning to supplement and/or modify market outcomes. The Scandinavian countries are cases in point. In the United States, there is no planning in the sense of utilizing a national economic planning mechanism, though one could argue that a great deal of planning does occur through large government branches, powerful corporate entities, and the like. Industrial policy has largely replaced economic planning in capitalist countries. **Industrial policy** is a general strategy of development worked out by government agencies. Industrial policies are designed to promote the health of the capitalist economy—for example, through technological change.[20] Interest in industrial policy peaked with the apparent success of Japan's industrial policy in the period 1950–1970. In Japan, a powerful alliance of government officials, commercial banks, and industrial conglomerates (Sony, Mitsubishi, and so on) decided what products and industries were to be promoted. The South Koreans also used industrial policy in the period 1970 through the 1980s. The prolonged slump of the Japanese economy that began in the 1990s has reduced interest in industrial policy.

Change in Socialist Economies

Although change in the capitalist West may appear to be significant, it has been mild compared to change in the socialist economies of the former Soviet Union, Eastern Europe, and Asia. With the minor exceptions of Cuba and North Korea, planned socialist economies either have been dramatically changed through the process of reform or are being abandoned through the process of transition.

Reform is the process of changing (improving) an existing system. **Transition** is the movement from one economic system (planned socialism) to another (capitalism).

In all cases, reform and transition have been motivated by economic performance. In the cases of the former Soviet Union and Eastern Europe, the decision to begin transition was motivated by declining growth rates, the failure to find ways to grow through **intensive growth** (rather than **extensive growth**), rising consumer dissatisfaction, and the general sense of being left behind by the other world economies.

Many reasons have been advanced to explain the general slackening of their economic performance, but the fact remains that the planned socialist economies found the transformation from extensive to intensive growth very difficult. The basic Stalinist model, though draconian and costly, nevertheless served to bring idle and underused resources into the production process. However, the luxury of idle resources was, for many socialist systems, over by the late 1960s.

We do not know exactly why intensification in socialist systems proved so difficult. Clearly there were consumer pressures in these systems, and clearly they grew more complex over time. Advances in planning methods did not keep pace with the demands on the planning system. The diffusion of technology was inadequate. These systems were not demand-driven, and enterprise rules generally did not stimulate growth in productivity and cost reduction. Efficiency was simply not a hallmark of the Stalinist command economy. Moreover, in contrast to the cyclical nature of productivity problems in market systems, socialist systems seemed to experience long, steady declines in productivity growth through the 1980s.

Interest in socialist reform began in the 1960s and grew in the 1980s and 1990s. By the mid-1980s, performance in most socialist systems had slipped alarmingly. With inadequate incentives, there appeared to be little hope for improved productivity. Moreover, most socialist countries had not been able to compete well enough in export markets to afford significant imports of consumer products. Seen in this perspective, the imperative of reform was evident, although the sudden spread of radical change in the late 1980s caught most observers by surprise.

Backdrop of Reform

The Soviet experiment with planned socialism began in earnest in the late 1920s with the introduction of command planning to industry and of forced collectivization to agriculture. The economic system that Stalin created in the late 1920s and early 1930s proved durable. It was introduced into Eastern Europe by Soviet troops at the end of World War II, and it found its way into China with the victory of communist forces there.

Prior to the early 1960s, reform of the Stalinist economic system was not possible. According to Stalinist dogma, the system was perfect. Any failures encountered were the result of human error or sabotage. Such thinking did not provide fertile ground for reform. The death of Stalin and the ensuing mild liberation allowed discussion of reform to begin. The problems of the planned socialist economy were apparent, and it was natural to consider improving the system.

The Soviet Communist party officially approved such discussion when *Pravda* published the reform proposals of Evsei Liberman in 1962. In this fashion, reform discussion was initiated in the Soviet Union and Eastern Europe. Although official reforms in the Soviet Union were modest, reforms in Eastern Europe were more substantial. Hungary, for example, initiated a long and careful reform process designed to orient its economy more toward the consumer. None of these reforms, either in thought or in content, was designed to replace the planned socialist economy with a market capitalist economy.

China, after experiencing cataclysmic political upheavals in the 1950s and 1960s, embarked on its own reform program in the late 1970s. The Chinese path to reform focused on unleashing private initiative in agriculture and small business and on opening the Chinese economy to world capital and product markets. China's suppression of student revolts in June of 1989 signaled that China was not prepared to combine economic reform with democracy. China's example stands out as a reform that has generated rapid economic growth.

Socialist Reform Models

Reform of planned socialist economic systems focused on changes in some or all of the system components.[21] However, prior to the dramatic changes of the late 1980s and 1990s, most reform in socialist systems was very modest and was characterized as an attempt, by means of very limited changes, to make the existing system work better.

Socialist economic reform has focused on reform models that differ in intensity. We characterize **socialist economic reform** in terms of three basic variants: making planning work better, changes in organizational arrangements, and decentralization of decision making.

Improving the Planning Mechanism   Improving planning is a weak alternative—one that signals unwillingness to make serious changes in the economic system. The arguments in support of this alternative are that problems of economic performance arise largely because planning has not been perfected and that planning can be improved through the application of more sophisticated computer technology. To the extent that enterprise managers make bad decisions because they lack information, ready access to accurate information through an advanced computer network would alleviate the problem. It is assumed that better planning methods, better information channels, and more attention to incentive compatibility could perfect the planning system and improve economic performance. The 1970s were devoted to a number of attempts to improve planning both in the Soviet Union and in Eastern Europe.

Organizational Reform   Changing the organizational arrangements of the existing plan structure represents a second reform alternative. A typical **organizational reform** is the introduction of intermediate organizations into the organizational hierarchy. Ministries, it was argued, are too distant from the enterprises they supervise. Moreover, each ministry supervises enterprises that produce too diverse an array of products. Ministries cannot keep in touch with enterprise behavior and do not truly understand the problems peculiar to the enterprises they oversee. Thus an intermediate agency or association should be inserted between the ministries and groups of enterprises that produce similar products. The intermediate association, it is argued, could understand and manage a particular group of firms more successfully.

Another way to implement organizational reform would be to shift the emphasis from sectoral to regional planning. An economy planned on a sectoral basis may place the interests of the branch above national interests. A shift to regional planning might loosen the grip of an entrenched bureaucracy and encourage a better flow of information among units in the economy. It was this type of reform that Nikita Khrushchev tried, without success, in the Soviet Union of the late 1950s and early 1960s. Most—though not all—past reform attempts in socialist systems have been organizational in nature.

Decentralization   **Decentralization**, the third broad category of socialist economic reform, is a shifting of decision-making authority and responsibility from upper to lower levels. Decentralization is often viewed as "real" reform that can fundamentally change the nature of economic systems and, especially, reduce the role of central planning.

Decentralization implies that decisions about resource allocation was shifted downward in the economic hierarchy. Most important, in a decentralized economy, decisions are not made by planners but are reached at lower levels by means of what were frequently termed **economic levers**—prices, costs, profits, rates of return, and the like. Decentralization of decision making entails both the devolution of decision-making authority and responsibility *and* the use of different decision-making tools in the process. To put it another way, although planning still exists, decentralization implies that local decision makers pay less attention to planners and more attention to market signals.

This type of economic reform was characterized as real reform or significant reform to distinguish it from organizational change. Taken to its limits, it might be called radical reform. Its existence raises new and difficult questions about the development of markets—and thus market signals—in systems previously dominated by planners, by state ownership of property, and by an absence of market signals.

Record of Socialist Reform

China has recorded rapid economic growth since the introduction of its reforms in the late 1970s, but the other attempts to reform the planned socialist economies through organizational change, improvements in planning, and decentralization failed. It is unclear whether China is actually on a path of transition from a planned socialist to a market economy or is engaged in the reform of its current system. Much of Chinese heavy industry remains owned and controlled by the state, China's capital stock is still largely in state hands, and remnants of central planning persist.

The failure of reform in the Soviet Union and Eastern Europe had far-reaching consequences culminating in the decision to abandon the planned socialist system and to move to a market capitalist system. As the dominant force in the former Soviet bloc, the Soviet Union is where the actions that made this move possible originated.

Declining economic performance in the Soviet Union and Eastern Europe, despite repeated reform efforts in the 1970s and early 1980s, convinced the leaders of the Soviet Communist party that radical change was necessary. They appointed a relatively young and vigorous general secretary, Mikhail Gorbachev, to lead this reform effort, which Gorbachev immediately described as radical to distinguish it from the modest reforms of the past. Internationally, Gorbachev relaxed Soviet control over Eastern Europe. As a result, these countries gained their political independence and their freedom to experiment with reform and transition. The collapse of the Soviet Union in December 1991 allowed an additional fifteen former republics of the Soviet Union to select their economic systems freely.

Transition

We shall devote a great deal of attention to transition in later chapters. Once a society has decided in favor of transition, it must decide the speed and sequencing of transition. It may determine that transition should occur on all fronts as quickly as possible. This approach to transition is called *shock therapy*. It may, on the other hand, decide that transition should occur gradually and not on all fronts simultaneously. This approach is called *gradualism*.

The economies of Eastern Europe and the Soviet Union began their transitions in the late 1980s (Eastern Europe) and in late 1991 or early 1992 (the former Soviet Union). Hence we have a growing body of information on transition successes and failures. We have a number of transition successes (Poland, Hungary, the Czech Republic, Slovenia, and the Baltic states). We appear to have even more transition failures. We shall study the characteristics of transition in later chapters.

We can draw a number of general conclusions about the course of transition so far. First, we can say that transition has indeed brought about remarkable changes in every country undergoing transition, be it a transition success or failure. Figure 4.4 shows the degree to which property rights changed from state to nonstate ownership just a few years after transition began in Russia. Transition is for real, and it appears to be including steps that would be very difficult to reverse.

Second, transition is not easy. Transition has been costly both politically and economically. Each country undergoing transition has experienced substantial declines in output, dramatic changes in the distribution of income, and rampant inflation. These costs have created political backlashes that have often returned to power those who favor the old system.

Third, there is no single path to transition. Some countries have tried a gradual approach; others have tried "shock therapy." Although the results are inconclusive, it appears that gradualism does not reduce the costs of transition.

Fourth, the combination of transition and a young democracy has proved to be difficult. Politicians in newly democratic countries must somehow enact transition policies that are costly in terms of lost political support. This difficult combination has created considerable interest in the Chinese reform model, which has combined market-oriented reforms with Communist party dictatorship.

Although the final outcome is still not known, the former Soviet Union and Eastern Europe have taken the first steps of dismantling the power structure on which their planned economic systems were based. The planned socialist economy no longer exists. What has yet to happen is replacement of the old system with a new, stable economic system.

FIGURE 4.4(A)   Nongovernmental Shares of Capital (Russia)

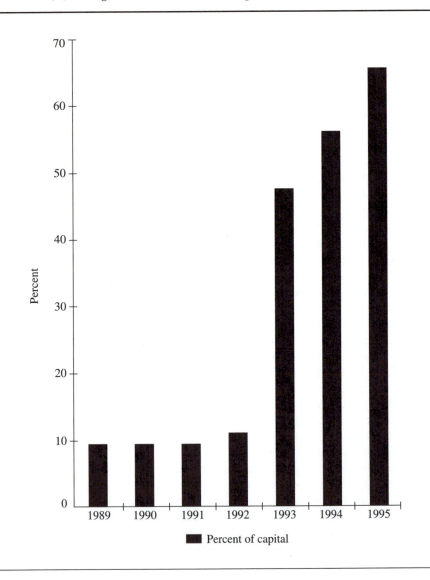

FIGURE 4.4(B)   Distribution of Russian Labor Force (type of enterprise)

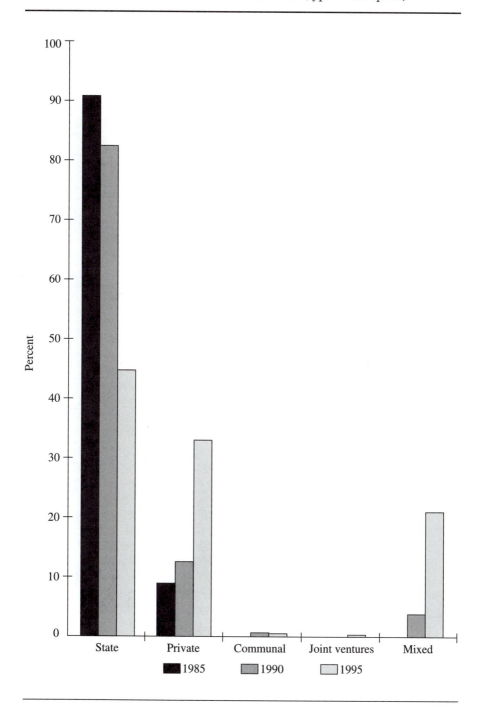

FIGURE 4.4(C)   Privatization of Russian Housing (cumulative totals; percent privatized)

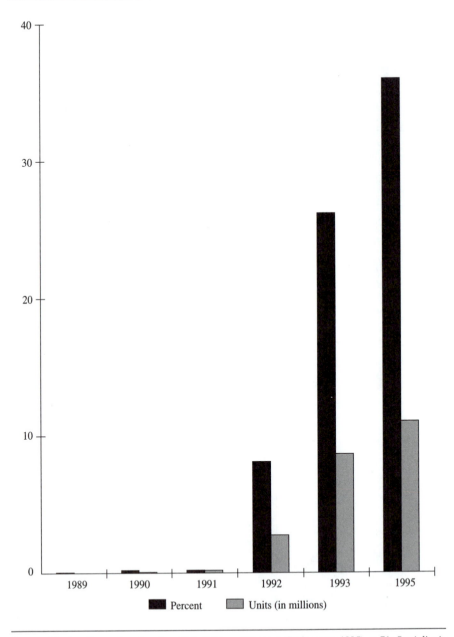

Sources: Natsional'nye scheta Rossii v 1989–1994 gg. (Moscow: Goskomstat, 1995), p. 71; *Sotsial'naia sfera Rossii* (Moscow: Goskomstat, 1995), p. 26.

Summary

- Economic reform usually attempts to improve the functioning of an economic system, although the system itself usually remains unchanged.
- Transition is the replacement of one economic system with another.
- Systemic change is part of the general process of economic development.
- Marx's materialistic/determinist/revolutionary perspective argues that revolutionary system change is an inevitable product of class struggle in an efficient but inequitable system (capitalism).
- Schumpeter articulates the dynamic model of capitalism. Capitalism, in his view, is a constant struggle by firms for long-term survival in the face of creative destruction.
- The New Institutional Economics, inspired by such precursors as Coase (transaction costs) and Hayek (spontaneous order), explain institutional change by examining property rights, transaction costs, and rent seeking.
- Contemporary theories focus on the role of institutions. For example, Austrian Economics argues that the task of planning in the planned socialist economy is too complex to be reasonable and that in the absence of private property, decentralization of decision making would not be an effective means to allocate resources.
- The New Institutional Economics argues that distributional coalitions will retard economic reform.

Key Terms

economic reform
transition
Marx's theory of capitalism
productive forces
superstructure
production relations
qualitative changes
thesis versus antithesis
dialectical materialism
primitive capitalist accumulation
surplus value
capitalist breakdown
creative destruction
spontaneous order
economy of shortage
hard budget constraint
soft budget constraint
distributional coalition

privatization
nationalization
competition
degregulation
progressive tax
regressive tax
Keynesian revolution
indicative planning
industrial policy
reform
transition
intensive growth
extensive griowth
socialist economic reform
organizational reform
decentralization
economic levers

Notes

1. Karl Marx, *Capital* (Chicago: Charles Kerr and Company), Vol. I, 1906; Vols. II and III, 1909. Two works that seek to describe the basics of Marx's economics in the language of conventional economic theory are Oskar Lange, "Marxian Economics and Modern Economic Theory," *Review of Economic Studies*, Vol. II (June 1935); and Murray Wolfson, *A Reappraisal of Marxian Economics* (New York: Columbia University Press, 1966).

2. Our discussion of the economic theories of Marx and Engels is based primarily on the following sources: Paul Sweezy, *The Theory of Capitalist Development* (New York: Monthly Review Press, 1968); Wolfson, *A Reappraisal of Marxian Economics;* Alexander Balinky, *Marx's Economics: Origin and Development* (Lexington, Mass.: Heath, 1970); John Gurley, *Challengers to Capitalism: Marx, Lenin, Mao* (San Francisco: San Francisco Book Company, 1976); William Baumol, Paul Samuelson, and Michio Morishima, "On Marx, the Transformation Problem, and Opacity—A Colloquium," *Journal of Economic Literature* 12 (March 1974), 51–77; *Grundlagen des Marxismus–Leninismus: Lehrbuch,* German translation of the 4th Russian edition (Berlin: Dietz Verlag, 1964); Karl Marx and Friedrich Engels, *The Communist Manifesto,* in Arthur Mendel, ed., *Essential Works of Marxism* (New York: Bantam Books, 1965), pp. 13–44; Paul Samuelson, "Understanding the Marxian Notion of Exploitation: A Summary of the So-called Transformation Problem Between Marxian Values and Competitive Prices," *Journal of Economic Literature* 9 (June 1971), 399–431; Leon Smolinsky, "Karl Marx and Mathematical Economics," *Journal of Political Economy* 81 (September–October 1973), 1189–1204.

3. According to Sweezy, *The Theory of Capitalist Development,* Ch. 11, the Marx–Engels description of the end of capitalism and the coming of socialism was scattered and sketchy. Their failure to deal more thoroughly with the breakdown of capitalism led to the breakdown controversy among socialist writers—Eduard Bernstein, M. Tugan-Baranovsky, Karl Kautsky, Rosa Luxemburg, and others. The central issue of this controversy was whether a violent overthrow of capitalism was obviated by reform of the capitalist system and the capitalist government. For Lenin's view of Kautsky and "revisionism," see V. I. Lenin, *State and Revolution,* in Mendel, *Essential Works of Marxism,* pp. 103–198; and V. I. Lenin, *Izbrannye proizvedeniia, Tom I* (Moscow: Gospolitizdat, 1960), pp. 56–63 ("Marxism and Revisionism").

4. The basic works are Joseph Schumpeter, *Capitalism, Socialism, and Democracy,* 3rd ed. (New York: Harper, 1950); and Joseph Schumpeter, *The Theory of Economic Development* (Cambridge, Mass.: Harvard University Press, 1934).

5. We use the term *New Institutional Economics* to apply to a broad range of schools of economic thought. Our usage includes fields such as the new economic history, public choice economics, and the new political economy.

6. On this, see Friederick von Hayek, *Studies in Philosophy, Politics, and Economics* (New York: Norton, 1969).

7. See, for example, Jon Cohen, in Thomas Rwaski, ed., *Economics and the Historian* (Berkeley: University of California Press, 1996), pp. 60–84; Douglass North and Barry Weingast, "Constitutions and Commitment: The Evolution of Institutions Governing Public Choice in 17th Century England," *Journal of Economic History* 49, 4 (December 1989), pp. 803–832; Mancur Olson, *The Rise and Decline of Nations* (New Haven: Yale University Press, 1982).

8. Douglass North, "Economic Performance Through Time," *American Economic Review* 84, 3 (June 1994), pp. 359–368.

9. F. A. Hayek, *The Road to Serfdom* (Chicago: University of Chicago Press, 1944).

10. F. A. Hayek, ed., *Collectivist Economic Planning,* 6th ed. (London: Routledge & Kegan Paul, 1963); Ludwig von Mises, "Economic Calculation in Socialism," in Morris Bornstein, ed., *Comparative Economic Systems,* rev. ed. (Homewood, Ill.: Irwin, 1969), pp. 61–68.

11. See Janos Kornai, *Economics of Shortage,* Vols. A and B (New York: North-Holland, 1980); "Resource Constrained versus Demand Constrained Systems," *Econometrica* 47 (July 1979), 801–819; *Anti-Equilibrium: On Economic Systems Theory and the Tasks of Research* (Amsterdam: North-Holland, 1971); *Rush versus Harmonic Growth* (Amsterdam: North-Holland, 1972); *Overcentralization in Economic Administration* (London: Oxford University Press, 1959); *Growth, Shortage, and Efficiency: A Macrodynamic Model of the Socialist Economy* (Berkeley: University of California Press, 1983).

12. See Peter Murrell and Mancur Olson, "The Devolution of Centrally Planned Economies," *Journal of Comparative Economics* 15, 2 (June 1991), pp. 239–266. Also see Richard R. Nelson and Sidney G. Winter, *An Evolutionary Theory of Economic Change* (Cambridge, Mass.: Harvard University Press, 1982) for a discussion of the contemporary transition experience from an evolutionary perspective. See, for example, Peter Murrell, "Can Neoclassical Economics Underpin the Reform of Centrally Planned Economies?" *Journal of Economic Perspectives* 5, 4 (Fall 1991), 59–76; Peter Murrell, "Evolution in Economics and in the Economic Reform of the Centrally Planned Economies," in Christopher C. Clague and Gordon Rausser, eds., *Emerging Market Economies in Eastern Europe* (Cambridge: Blackwell, 1992).

13. For descriptions of how these interest groups engage in rent-seeking behavior, see Josef Brada, "The Political Economy of Communist Foreign Trade Institutions and Policies," Michael Mandler and Randi Ryterman, "A Detour on the Road to the Market Coordination, Queues, and the Distribution of Income," and Michael Alexeev, "If Market Clearings Are So Good Then Why Doesn't (Almost) Anybody Want Them?" all in *Journal of Comparative Economics* 15, 2 (June 1991).

14. William G. Shepherd, "Causes of Increased Competition in the U.S. Economy, 1939–1980," *Review of Economics and Statistics* (November 1982), 613–626.

15. Clifford Winston, "Economic Deregulation: Days of Reckoning for Microeconomists," *Journal of Economic Literature* 31, 3 (September 1993), 1263–1289.

16. Robert Crandall and Jerry Elig, *Economic Deregulation and Customer Choice: Lessons for the Electric Industry* (Center for Market Processes, George Mason University, 1996).

17. Edgar K. Browning, "The Trend Toward Equality in the Distribution of Net Income," *Southern Economic Journal* 43 (July 1976), 914.

18. The theoretical foundation of a profit-sharing capitalist economy is provided by Martin L. Weitzman, *The Share Economy* (Cambridge, Mass.: Harvard University Press, 1984); and Martin L. Weitzman, "The Simple Macroeconomics of Profit Sharing," *American Economic Review* 75 (December 1985), 937–953. For an excellent survey of recent developments in the theory of producer cooperatives, see John P. Bonin, Derek C. Jones, and Louis Putterman, "Theoretical and Empirical Studies of Producer Cooperatives: Will the Twain Ever Meet?" *Journal of Economic Literature* 31, 3 (September 1993), 1290–1320.

19. For an analysis of Japanese profit sharing, see Merton J. Peck, "Is Japan Really a Share Economy?" *Journal of Comparative Economics* 10 (December 1986), 427–432.

20. For a discussion of industrial policy in the contemporary American context, see R. D. Norton, "Industrial Policy and American Renewal," *Journal of Economic Literature* 24, 1 (March 1986), 1–40.

21. There is a large body of literature on reform in the former planned socialist economies. For a summary with emphasis on the Soviet case, see Paul R. Gregory and Robert C. Stuart, *Russian and Soviet Economic Structure and Performance,* 6th ed. (Reading, Mass.: Addison Wesley Longman, 1997).

Recommended Readings

Marixst Thought

Paul A. Baran, *The Political Economy of Growth* (New York: Monthly Review Press, 1957).

William Baumol, Paul Samuelson, and Michio Morishima, "On Marx, the Transformation Problem, and Opacity—A Colloquium," *Journal of Economic Literature* 12 (March 1974), 51–77.

John Gurley, *Challengers to Capitalism: Marx, Lenin, Mao* (San Francisco: San Francisco Book Company, 1976).

Oskar Lange, "Marxian Economics and Modern Economic Theory," *Review of Economic Studies* 2 (June 1935).

Karl Marx, *Capital* (Chicago: Charles Kerr and Company), Vol. I, 1906; Vols. II and III, 1909.

Ernest Mandel, *Marxist Economic Theory* (New York: Monthly Review Press, 1970).

Arthur Mendel, ed., *Essential Works of Marxism* (New York: Bantam Books, 1965).

Joan Robinson, *An Essay on Marxian Economics* (New York: Macmillan, 1966).

Paul Samuelson, "Understanding the Marxian Notion of Exploitation: A Summary of the So-called Transformation Problem Between Marxian Values and Competitive Prices," *Journal of Economic Literature* 9 (June 1971), 399–431.

Joseph Schumpeter, *Capitalism, Socialism and Democracy,* 3rd ed. (New York: Harper, 1950).

———, *The Theory of Economic Development* (Cambridge, Mass.: Harvard University Press, 1934).

Leon Smolinsky, "Karl Marx and Mathematical Economics," *Journal of Political Economy* 81 (September–October 1973), 1189–1204.

Paul Sweezy, *The Theory of Capitalist Development* (New York: Monthly Review Press, 1968).

Murray Wolfson, *A Reappraisal of Marxian Economics* (New York: Columbia University Press, 1966).

Socialist Changes

Janos Kornai, *Anti-Equilibrium: On Economic Systems Theory and the Tasks of Research* (Amsterdam: North-Holland, 1971).

———, *Economics of Shortage,* Vols. A and B (New York: North-Holland, 1980).

———, *Growth, Shortage, and Efficiency: A Macrodynamic Model of the Socialist Economy* (Berkeley: University of California Press, 1983).

———, "Resource Constrained versus Demand Constrained Systems," *Econometrica* 47 (July 1979), 801–819.

———, *Rush versus Harmonic Growth* (Amsterdam: North-Holland, 1972).

———, *The Road to a Free Economy* (New York: Norton, 1990).

———. *The Socialist System: The Political Economy of Communism* (Princeton, N.J.: Princeton University Press, 1992).

Richard R. Nelson and Sidney G. Winter, *An Evolutionary Theory of Economic Change* (Cambridge, Mass.: Harvard University Press, 1982).

The Capitalist Economy: Selected Aspects of Change

Richard R. Nelson and Sidney G. Winter, *An Evolutionary Theory of Economic Change* (Cambridge, Mass.: Harvard University Press, 1982).

R. D. Norton, "Industrial Policy and American Renewal," *Journal of Economic Literature* 24, 1 (March 1986), 1–40.

Nitin Nohria and Robert G. Eccles, eds., *Networks and Organizations: Structure, Form, and Action* (Boston: Harvard Business School Press, 1993).

Richard B. Freeman, "Unionism Comes to the Public Sector," *Journal of Economic Literature* 24, 1 (March 1986), pp. 41–86.

William G. Shepherd, "Causes of Increased Competition in the U.S. Economy, 1939–1980," *Review of Economics and Statistics* (November 1982), 613–626.

Grahame Thompson, Jennifer Frances, Rosalind Levacic, and Jeremy Mitchell, eds., *Markets Hierarchies and Networks: The Coordination of Social Life* (London: Sage Publications, 1991).

Michael L. Vasu, Debra W. Stewart, and S. David Garson, *Organizational Behavior and Public Management,* 2nd ed., revised and expanded (New York: Marcel Dekker, 1990).

Leonard W. Weiss and Michael W. Klass, eds., *Regulatory Reform: What Actually Happened* (Boston: Little, Brown, 1986).

Oliver E. Williamson and Sidney G. Winter, eds., *The Nature of the Firm: Origins, Evolution and Development* (Oxford: Oxford University Press, 1991).

Clifford Winston, "Economic Deregulation: Days of Reckoning for Microeconomists," *Journal of Economic Literature* 31, 3 (September 1993), 1263–1289.

The Socialist Economy: Reform and Transition

Robert W. Campbell, *The Socialist Economies in Transition: A Primer on Semi-Reformed Systems* (Bloomington: Indiana University Press, 1991).

Christopher Clague and Gorden Rausser, *The Emergence of Market Economies in Eastern Europe* (Cambridge: Blackwell, 1992).

Sabastian Edwards, "The Sequencing of Economic Reform: Analytical Issues and Lessons from the Latin American Experience," *World Economy* 1 (1990).

Paul R. Gregory and Robert C. Stuart, *Russian and Soviet Economic Structure and Change,* 6th ed. (Reading, Mass: Addison Wesley Longman, 1997), Ch. 12.

Edward P. Lazear, *Economic Transition in Eastern Europe and Russia* (Stanford: Hoover Institution, 1995).

Peter Murrell, "Public Choice and the Transformation of Socialism," *Journal of Comparative Economics* 14 (June 1991), 203–210.

PART **II**

Economic Systems in Theory

5

Theory of Capitalism

This chapter is about the *theory* of capitalism. Subsequent chapters discuss capitalism in practice. This chapter asks: How well should capitalist market economies *in theory* resolve the problem of allocating scarce resources among competing ends? This issue is important for two reasons. The first is that the theories of capitalism and socialism yield hypotheses concerning expected differences in performance, and those hypotheses can be tested against real-world experience. The second is that one may be most interested in what the theoretical models themselves suggest about the performance of economic systems under *ideal conditions*. Because actual economies diverge from the ideal, it could be argued that they cannot be used as a test of the system's "true" performance and that the performance issue must be resolved at the theoretical level.[1]

The "Invisible Hand"

The pioneering analysis of market capitalism is Adam Smith's *The Wealth of Nations,* published in 1776.[2] Speaking against the mercantilist position that free trade could lead to a country's ruin, Adam Smith argued that a highly efficient and harmonious economic system would emerge if competitive markets were left to function freely without government intervention.

Smith's underlying notion was that if individuals were given free rein to pursue their own selfish interests, then the **invisible hand** of competitive markets would cause them to behave in a socially responsible manner. Products desired by consumers would be produced in the appropriate assortments and quantities, and the most efficient means of production would be used. No government or social action would be required, for individuals acting in their own interests could be counted on to do the right thing. In fact, government action would probably interfere with this natural process, so government should be limited to providing essential public services—national defense, a legal system to protect private property, and highways—that private enterprise could not produce on its own. An equilibrium of consumers and producers would be created spontaneously in the competitive marketplace, for if the actions of consumers and producers were not in harmony, the market price would adjust to bring the two groups into equilibrium.

Smith's notion of a natural tendency toward an efficient economic equilibrium was the foundation for the liberal economic thought of the nineteenth century. In the words of one authority, Smith's most important triumph was that "he put into the center of economics the systematic analysis of the behavior of individuals pursuing their self-interest under conditions of competition," and this remains "the foundation of the theory of resource allocation."[3] Most of the later theorizing aimed at a further elaboration of Smith's vision of market capitalism.

Adam Smith's notion of the invisible hand was directed against the philosophy of mercantilism. **Mercantilism** argued that economies must be heavily regulated by the state to prevent a loss of resources to rival nations. Mercantilism was practiced throughout Western Europe but was particularly strong in France, where the state regulated economic activity to such an extent that France's mercantilism has been compared to the Soviet planned economy.[4] The invisible hand argued the exact opposite—that state-regulated economies will perform poorly.

How Markets Work

The theory of capitalism focuses on *markets* in which the interaction of demand and supply determines prices for factors such as labor (factor markets) and products such as consumer goods (product markets). These markets provide a mechanism for harmonizing consumers' desires with producers' ability to satisfy these desires.

Market Equilibrium

Adam Smith's description of markets was left to modern economists to complete. Partial equilibrium assumes that two motivating forces drive market capitalism: the desire of producers to maximize profits and the desire of consumers to maximize their own welfare (utility) subject to the constraint of limited income.[5] Under competitive conditions, producers will be prepared to supply larger quantities at higher prices, combining inputs to minimize costs. Consumers, seeking to maximize their welfare, will purchase less at higher prices. The producer and consumer meet in the marketplace, where their conflicting objectives are brought into equilibrium. If the quantity demanded exceeds the quantity supplied at the prevailing price, the price automatically rises, squeezing out some demand and evoking a larger supply until all those willing to buy and all those willing to sell at the prevailing price can do so. At this point, an equilibrium price is established, the market clears, and there is no tendency to depart from the equilibrium unless it is disrupted by some exogenous change (see Figure 5.1).

This description underscores how market resource allocation works under competitive conditions. All other things being equal, an increase in consumer demand for a particular product disrupts the established equilibrium, and the price starts to rise. As the price rises, producers find it in their interest to supply larger quantities. If larger profits can be obtained at the new price, additional producers enter the market. On the demand side, the rise in the price causes substitution of now less expensive commodities and income effects, thereby reducing the quantity demanded (see Figure 5.2). The increase in demand causes resources to be shifted automatically to the product in greater demand, and the wants of the consuming public are met without intervention from outside forces. Consumers are said to be sovereign because the economy responds to changes in their demand.

FIGURE 5.1   Market Equilibrium in a Competitive Economy

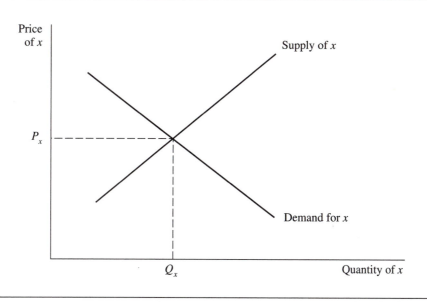

Explanation: In a competitive market economy, the price at which x sells will be P_x. If the price were *below* this level, the quantity demanded would exceed the quantity supplied. The *shortage* of x then would cause the price of x to rise. If the price were *above* P_x, the quantity supplied would exceed the quantity demanded. The surplus of x then would cause the price of x to fall. Only at P_x is the quantity supplied equal to the quantity demanded (Q_x).

Efficiency of Market Allocation

There are two arguments for the **efficiency of market allocation**. One depends on the market being competitive—that is, consisting of a large number of buyers and sellers, none of whom has the power to influence the market price. The other efficiency argument rests on the ability of markets to use information effectively.

The first argument maintains that in perfectly competitive markets, production will take place to the point where the marginal cost of society's resources equals the marginal benefit or utility to consumers. Firms that operate in competitive markets produce the level of output that equates price and marginal cost, and that price is set in the marketplace. When costs and benefits are not equal at the margin, society can gain by producing more or less of the product. For example, if price exceeds marginal cost, the product yields more benefits than costs, and society can gain by producing more. If marginal costs exceed price, too much of the product has been produced, and production should be reduced.

The Austrian economists Friederick Hayek and Ludwig von Mises wrote about the *relative* superiority of market economies over planned socialist economies.[6] Their

FIGURE 5.2   Consumer Sovereignty in a Competitive Economy

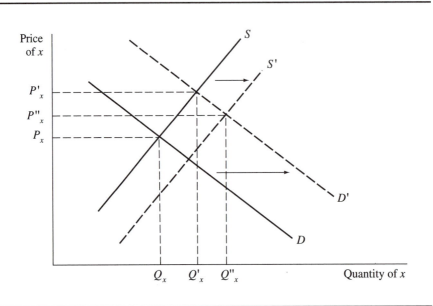

Explanation: We begin with the market for x in equilibrium at price P_x and quantity Q_x. *There is an increase in consumer demand from D to D'.* As a consequence, the price of x rises to P'_x and the equilibrium quantity *rises* to Q'_x. If economic profits are being made at this new price, new firms will enter the market and the supply curve will eventually shift to S'. Now a new long-run equilibrium is established at price P''_x and quantity Q''_x. An increase in consumer demand *automatically* leads to an increase in the quantity produced. The long-run effect on market prices depends on the entry of new firms at the higher price.

arguments rest on the efficient manner in which market economies mobilize and utilize information, in contrast to the inefficient use of information in socialist economies. Hayek wrote that the principal economic problem is not how to allocate given resources but "how to secure the best use of resources known to any member of society, for ends whose relative importance only these individuals know. Or, to put it briefly, it is a problem of the utilization of knowledge not given to anyone in its totality." Economic agents (consumers and producers) specialize in information about prices, products, and location that is relevant to them in their daily lives. Economic agents need not know all prices, products, and locations to behave efficiently in the marketplace. According to Hayek and Mises, the fact that market economies efficiently generate information in the form of market prices, which enable producers and consumers to plan their actions in a rational manner, is the principal advantage of capitalism and will ensure its relative superiority over planned socialism. This is their argument for the theoretical and practical superiority of capitalism. The planned socialist economies would prove too difficult to manage because of the complexity of information and because of incentive problems.

Markets and Institutions

The invisible hand of markets works within a framework of institutions. If these institutions are absent, markets work poorly or do not work at all. Markets work when parties to transactions stick to the terms of the agreement; that is, they enter into contracts which they obey. If contracts are violated, there must be public or private institutions, such as courts or private arbitration commissions, which resolve the dispute. It is also necessary that people respect private property and that illegal violations of private property rights will be punished. These institutions are termed the rule of law. A **rule of law** prevails when participants in society and the economy agree on the legal rules concerning social and economic behavior, they behave according to these rules, and there is a punishment mechanism when the rule of law is violated. Economies must also have established arrangements for monetary and fiscal policy. **Monetary policy** is conducted by a central bank (in most cases), which determines the quantity of money. **Fiscal policy** relates to how the state collects taxes and spends revenue. Economic transactions are carried out in money, which serves as a medium of exchange, unit of account, and standard of deferred payment. If the money supply is not under control, hyperinflation can result, and transactions are carried out in barter rather than money terms. If the state does not have a predictable system for collecting taxes and spending revenues, businesses will not be able to calculate their tax burden and hence make good economic decisions. If the state can confiscate private property via excessive taxes, property rights are not protected. Market economies require financial intermediaries, such as a bank. **Financial intermediaries**, such as banks, accept the deposits of savers and lend them out to borrowers. Savers are usually not those who invest in plant, equipment, and inventories. Savers and investors are brought together by financial intermediaries, who attract the savings of individuals and then make loans to business that require credit. Financial intermediaries cannot operate without a rule of law and without reasonable monetary policy. Savers will not deposit their funds if they cannot trust banks; banks would find it difficult to attract deposits if a hyperinflation were under way.

In a number of countries, the basic rule of law is set out in a constitution. A **constitution** establishes the basic political, economic, and social rules of the game for a society. For example, a constitution might spell out the degree to which private property is protected, the basic rights of citizens, and the cases in which the state can intervene in private economic activity. The United States and modern Germany and Japan are examples of market economies based on formal constitutions. Other countries, such as the United Kingdom and France, have basic rules of the game that evolved over relatively long periods of time and cannot be traced to one single event, such as the ratification of a constitution. Constitutions are not immutable; they can be amended, but the process of amendment is usually difficult and time-consuming.

Captialist economies consist of a wide variety of markets. Some are simple and others complex. **Simple markets** are markets, such as small retail trade in goods and services, that do not require sophisticated institutions. **Complex markets** are markets that deal in nonhomogeneous goods and services that may be bought in one period of time and sold in another period of time or that involve a series of payments over time.[7]

A farmer selling vegetables to final customers at a roadside stand does not require sophisticated legal and business institutions. A bank making a twenty-year mortgage loan to a family and a trader in futures markets for commodities and precious metals need sophisticated business and legal institutions, such as contract enforcement mechanisms, stable monetary policy, and common understanding of ethical business behavior[8] in order to carry out transactions.

State Intervention

The picture of capitalism that we have developed is one of a harmonious and efficient resource-allocation system strongly inclined toward equilibrium in production, especially under competitive conditions. This harmony occurs without the benefit of government intervention and control. Critics of the harmonious model point to the need for **state intervention** to deal with monopoly power, externalities, public goods, and income-distribution problems. They also stress the inherent cyclical instability of capitalism and the problems of making rational public choices.

The appropriate level of state intervention into the affairs of private enterprise is one of the most disputed issues in economics. The neoclassical position, descended directly from Adam Smith, is that in the absence of monopoly power, and in the absence of external effects, the economic role of the state should be strictly limited. The state should supply only those public goods—such as national defense, public roads, a legal system, and foreign policy—that private enterprise on its own would not be able to provide in optimal proportions. The theory of public goods explains why laissez-faire capitalism will underproduce such goods.[9] The question we consider here is in what instances state intervention is necessary to correct deficiencies in market allocation.

Monopoly Power

The nonoptimality of monopoly has been emphasized since, and even before, publication of *The Wealth of Nations*.[10] The crux of the monopoly problem is the monopolist's inclination to hold output below the level that would prevail in a competitive situation. Monopolists underproduce and overcharge relative to competitive producers. Monopoly causes a "deadweight loss," in that the gains of the monopolist are less than the losses to consumers. Figure 5.3 demonstrates that monopolies produce less and charge higher prices than competitive markets.

Monopoly behavior is not explained by extraordinary greed on the part of the monopolist, who is simply attempting to maximize profits. By definition, the monopolist is the sole producer in a particular market. Therefore, to sell a large volume of output, the monopolist must lower the price. Perfectly competitive producers, as price takers, can sell all they desire at the market price. Monopolists fail to expand their output to the point where the marginal cost (which measures the marginal cost of output in terms of society's resources) equals price (which measures the marginal benefit of output to society). Rather, monopolists who wish to maximize profits must restrict their output.

FIGURE 5.3   The Competitive and Monopolistic Models

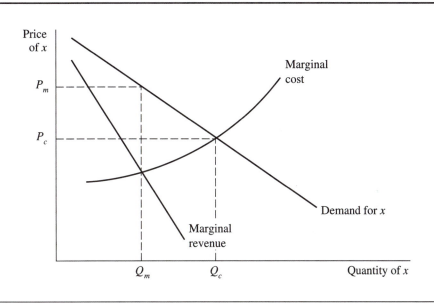

Explanation: This diagram presents the models of price and output determination under conditions of perfect competition and monopoly.

Let us suppose that industry X could be organized either as a monopoly (with a single producer) or as a competitive industry (with a large number of producers). The marginal costs are the same whether the industry is a monopoly or is perfectly competitive. The industry demand schedule and the industry marginal-cost schedule are given in the diagram. The latter is the marginal-cost schedule of the monopolist (in the case of the monopolistic industry) or the sum of the individual marginal-cost schedules of producers (in the case of the competitive industry).

Because the demand schedule is negatively sloped, the monopolist's marginal revenue is less than the product price. To maximize profits, the monopolist produces that output (Q_m) at which marginal cost and marginal revenue are equated and sells this output at the price dictated by the market (P_m). Competitive producers produce output levels at which the product price and marginal costs are equal; therefore, the supply schedule of the competitive industry is the industry marginal-cost schedule. The competitively organized industry produces Q_c, and the product sells for P_c.

The monopoly produces less than the competitive industry and charges a higher price. The monopolist charges a price greater than the marginal costs of production, whereas the competitive industry equates price and marginal cost. Because price and marginal revenue are not equal, an economy made up of monopolies is not efficient.

Economic theory suggests four approaches to the control of monopoly, three of which require state intervention. The first is to use the state's authority to *tax and subsidize* to correct the underutilization of resources by monopolistic producers. The basic idea is to combine subsidization with consumer and producer **taxation** to induce the monopolist to expand output to the competitive level, while at the same time producing a social tax dividend for society. The obvious difficulty is that tax authorities must make quite sophisticated calculations. The use of **subsidies** and taxes to obtain an optimal allocation of resources from a monopolist does not seem too practical, although the theory of how to do so is clear.

The second form of state intervention is **direct regulation** of monopoly. Theoretically, state regulatory authorities could dictate that the regulated monopoly produce the efficient quantity of output at which *P* equals *MC* and force the monopolist to charge a regulated price equal to marginal costs. In this manner, the regulators could dictate directly an efficient allocation of resources. There are two practical difficulties with this approach, however. How are regulators to know market demand and monopoly marginal costs? The monopoly might be tempted to inflate its costs by lax management or other means in order to obtain a higher regulated price. The second difficulty is that marginal-cost pricing would probably force the monopolist to operate at a loss if marginal costs were still declining at the output where *P* equaled *MC*. The existence of regulated losses would require a system of subsidization, which would tend to disrupt the optimal allocation of resources.

The third approach is that recommended by Milton Friedman—to *leave* **natural monopolies** *alone* because regulation is poorly managed and encourages monopolists to be inefficient.[11] The unregulated monopoly, prompted by the desire to maximize profits and keep potential competitors out of the market, would supply a larger quantity at a lower price than that charged by a regulated monopoly. Moreover, even monopolists must face some form of competition in the long run and cannot get by indefinitely with an inefficient use of resources.

The final approach applies to cases where competitive production is also possible. The state, through enforcement of antitrust and anticartel legislation and through the removal of legal obstacles to competition, could transform the industry from monopolistic to competitive.

Modern theory has pondered whether there are natural limitations on monopoly power. Unless freedom of entry were highly restricted, monopolists would avoid charging monopoly prices for fear of attracting competitors in the long run.

External Effects and Collective Action

External effects are brought to bear in situations where the actions of one producer or consumer directly affect the costs or utility of a second producer or consumer.[12] External effects are effects that take place outside of the price system. These external effects may be harmful, in which case they are called an **external diseconomy**, or they may be salutary, in which case they are known as an **external economy**. An example of an external diseconomy of production is the dumping of wastes into a river by one producer, requiring a producer downstream to increase costs by installing water purification equipment.

When external effects are present, the allocation of resources is not optimal, even if the economy is perfectly competitive. Producers of the external effect are not required to take the external impact of their actions into account when making decisions. Rather, they seek to maximize their private profit on the basis of the **private costs** of production, not on the basis of **social costs**. The producer of an external harmful effect therefore produces an output level in excess of the optimum, for the private producer tends to underestimate the true social costs of production (Figure 5.4).

FIGURE 5.4   The Inefficiency of External Costs

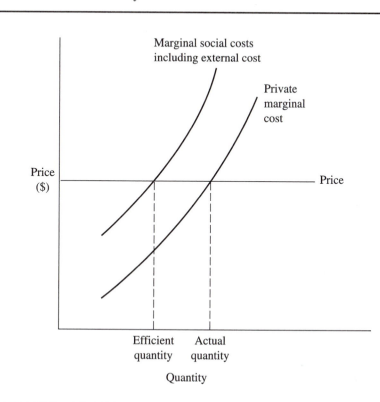

Explanation: When externalities are present, enterprises base their decisions on private marginal costs. This perfectly competitive firm produces where *P* = private marginal cost, not where *P* = full marginal cost. Thus externalities cause competitive firms to produce more than the optimal quantity.

Economic theory suggests remedies to correct for misallocations caused by external effects. One is the internalization of such effects—for example, by merging the enterprises producing external effects and those being affected by them. Consider the example of the waste-dumping factory. If it merged with the downstream factory, the water purification costs would become private costs for the combined enterprise, and waste dumping would be limited as a natural consequence of profit maximization.

In the absence of opportunities for internalization, remedies may require state action, such as taxation and subsidies, to equate private and social costs. If an excise tax equal to the external diseconomy could be levied on the producer, private costs would equal social costs. To maximize private profits, the producer would be forced to limit output to the level at which price and marginal *social* costs are equal—the condition required for an efficient allocation of resources.

When appropriate taxes and subsidies cannot be levied, one alternative is state regulation. Government regulators determine the optimal allocation of resources and administratively decree that producers supply the optimal output. The major drawback is that enforcement and policing costs may be quite high, for it is not clear how one would obtain compliance with regulations. Moreover, there is the enormous problem of calculating private and social marginal costs—the data required for effective regulation.

A third approach to the externality problem is voluntary agreements among the parties involved. This notion was first suggested by Ronald Coase.[13] He contends that under certain conditions, the creator and recipient of the external effect can come to a mutually satisfactory agreement that restores an optimal allocation of resources. Whenever harmful externalities exist, the affected parties have opportunities for gains from trade by striking deals. In the absence of legal obstacles, the amount of shared gains from an agreement must exceed the costs of transacting the agreement. Coase's novel conclusion, therefore, is that if the transaction costs of reaching an agreement are small, private agreements can correct the misallocation of resources caused by external effects. If mutually acceptable bargains are not reached in the presence of small transaction costs, then the divergence between private and social costs is probably inconsequential.

The most important drawback to voluntary agreements is exactly the problem of transaction costs and other impediments to agreement, especially when the number of parties involved is large. When a small number of parties are involved, voluntary agreements are feasible. When the agreement must be ratified by a large number of parties, some of whom have relatively small stakes in the matter, the probability of reaching a mutually acceptable agreement is small.

Problems of Democratic Public Choice

Capitalism is associated with democratic political institutions, although there are exceptions. A partial theory of the positive relationship between free markets and democracy was provided by F. A. Hayek in his 1944 book *The Road to Serfdom,* in which he argued that democracy is possible only in a market economy, but that democracy is fragile. Any effort to introduce state resource allocation, no matter how well intentioned, will necessarily lead to a loss of political freedom and to eventual totalitarianism.[14] The political scientist Seymore Lipset[15] has argued that democracy is strongest and most durable in affluent economies, a proposition that has considerable empirical support. Robert Barro, for example, shows the fragility of democracy in poor countries and its durability in affluent countries.[16]

Public goods—national defense, police protection and a legal system, dams, flood control projects, and the like—will not be supplied in efficient quantities by the private economy for two principal reasons: Nonpayers (called free riders) cannot be prevented from enjoying the benefits of the public good, and one person's use of the good does not generally prevent others from using it. Both of these features make it difficult for the private sector to produce public goods.

Political scientists typically assumed that democracy would ensure "good" public choices. If a government spending project were bad for society, a majority would vote against it, and the measure would be defeated. Such would be the advantage of democracy. Public-choice theorists, such as Nobel laureate James Buchanan, have concluded that certain factors prevent public choices in a democratic (majority-rule) society from being made in an efficient manner.[17]

Efficiency in the case of a public good requires, at a minimum, that the marginal benefits enjoyed by users of the good equal or exceed its marginal costs. Will this necessarily be the case in a society in which public-choice decisions are made by majority-rule voting? Public-choice theory outlines a number of potential problems. First, **majority voting** fails to take into consideration the intensity of preferences among voters. A number of voters may have intense feelings about a specific public-expenditure decision, whereas others may be virtually indifferent. Yet each person's vote counts equally, and changes in preferences typically do not change the voting outcome. This is called the **median voter rule**. Second, there may be a tendency toward vote trading when voters must decide on a number of public-choice issues. A group that favors one public-expenditure program may offer its support for the public-expenditure program of a second group if that group will form a majority coalition. Through such logrolling techniques, public-expenditure programs may be enacted where marginal costs exceed marginal benefits. Moreover, politicians are in the business of getting reelected and are likely to serve special-interest groups that are instrumental in financing election campaigns. The voter, on the other hand, does not have a great incentive to be well informed about public-choice issues. Individual voters are aware that their votes are unlikely to change any outcome, and the costs of gathering information on the large number of technically detailed government programs are high. It is therefore in the rational voter's economic interest to remain "rationally ignorant." Logrolling, vote trading, and rational ignorance cause governments to authorize public programs that are not economically efficient.

Income Distribution

In a capitalist economy, people who own resources that command a high price have higher incomes than those who own resources that command low prices. How equally or unequally should income be distributed? To what extent should the state redistribute income?

The marginal productivity theory of **income distribution** follows from the fact that the private owners of labor, land, and capital are paid the marginal revenue product of their factor. If the factor market is perfectly competitive, the owner receives the actual value of the marginal product of the factor. Thus, argue some economists, the resulting distribution of income is "just," because factor owners receive a reward that is equal to the factor's marginal contribution to society's output. Bestowing rewards according to marginal productivity encourages the owners of the factors of production to raise the productivity of their factors. If the state were to alter this distribution, there would be less incentive to raise the marginal productivity of one's own factors. There would be less investment in human capital and less risk taking, and society's output would accordingly be less.

Critics of this "natural justice" view point out that the marginal productivity of any factor depends on the presence of cooperating factors. An American coal miner may work with millions of dollars of capital equipment, whereas the Indian coal miner works just as hard with only a pick and shovel. The marginal productivity of the American coal miner is therefore many times that of the Indian coal miner. Moreover, marginal productivity is affected by human capital investment, and not everyone has equal access to education.

There are a number of arguments in favor of a redistributive role for the state. First, people are not indifferent to the welfare of others, and their own welfare is diminished by poverty around them. Yet despite altruistic motives, there are strong incentives against charitable contributions. Any one person's contribution can have only a negligible effect on poverty. The insignificance of any one donor creates a substantial free-rider problem, which means that voluntary contributions are unlikely to have a significant impact on the distribution of income. Government income redistribution programs eliminate the free-rider problem. Only the state is in a position to alter the distribution of income.

The philosopher John Rawls has advanced another argument in favor of state intervention.[18] Rawls argues that an unequal distribution of income persists because those who benefit from income inequality are unwilling to accept changes that favor the poor. People are unwilling to agree to redistribution because those who will be rich know fairly early in life their chances of being rich. For this reason, a social consensus can never be formed whereby the rich agree to redistribute income to the poor.

Rawls asks how people would behave if they did not know in advance their lifetime endowment of resources. How would they react if they operated behind a "veil of ignorance"? Rawls maintains that under this condition, people would naturally act to minimize the risks of being poor and would therefore reach a social consensus in favor of a fairly equal distribution of income. If people, operating behind a veil of ignorance, would naturally favor an equal distribution of income, then society should have an equal distribution of income. Insofar as voluntary charitable giving will not effect this result, the state is justified in redistributing income from the rich to the poor.

Macroeconomic Instability

A major challenge to the neoclassical vision of self-regulating capitalism was mounted by John Maynard Keynes in *The General Theory of Employment, Interest, and Money,* published in 1936 against the backdrop of world depression.[19] The depression seemed to deny neoclassical notions of an automatic tendency toward equilibrium over time. Keynes's assertion that activist government action was required to stabilize capitalist economics has come to be called the **Keynesian revolution.**

Keynes   Keynes disputed the mainstay of classical equilibrium theory, Say's Law.[20] According to **Say's Law**, there can be no lasting deficiency of aggregate demand because the act of producing a given value of output creates an equivalent amount of income. If that income were not spent directly on consumer goods, it would be saved. The savings would end up being spent as well, for interest rates would adjust to equate *ex ante* savings and *ex ante* investment. Accordingly, depressions could not be caused by deficiencies in aggregate demand. If we were only patient, eventually prices and wages would adjust to bring about an equilibrium at full employment. If unemployment did exist, it would be because workers were unwilling to accept the lower real wages required for labor market equilibrium. As long as prices and wages are flexible, there will be an automatic adjustment mechanism to restore full employment.

Keynes argued that there is no assurance that equilibrium will occur at full employment or that the automatic adjustment mechanism will work with reasonable speed. Thus—and this is the foundation of the Keynesian revolution—it is the responsibility of government to ensure full employment.

Keynes disputed the conclusions of the neoclassical school in the following manner. First, he argued that wages and prices are not nearly so flexible (especially downward) as the neoclassical economists believed. He pointed out that despite considerable unemployment, money wages were not falling in England in the 1920s and 1930s. Second, he argued that aggregate saving is not significantly affected by the interest rate; rather, it is principally dependent on the level of income. According to Keynes, the investment–savings relationship would be especially troublesome because of the cyclical instability of investment expenditures; only by chance would enough investment be forthcoming to guarantee full employment.

Keynes saw no reason why macroequilibrium should occur at a rate of output sufficient to ensure full employment. Therefore, it is the responsibility of government, by appropriately raising or lowering its spending and taxes (**fiscal policy**) or by controlling investment spending (through **monetary policy**), to ensure that equilibrium occurs near full employment. Because investment spending is quite unstable, government must be prepared to counteract investment fluctuations with compensatory actions.

After World War II, Keynes's advocacy of discretionary monetary and fiscal policy became widely accepted by economists and public officials, who felt justified in abandoning the traditional hands-off policies favored by the neoclassical school. Federal budgets could be openly in deficit in order to stimulate the economy. In the United States, for example, tax cuts and tax increases were imposed for the expressed purpose of manipulating aggregate demand. The practice of demand management became standard procedure in Western Europe, Japan, and Canada. Monetary policy also became an instrument of macroeconomic regulation. At the height of optimism in the mid-1960s, there was talk of being able to "fine-tune" the economy, and the business cycle was declared dead.

Self-Correcting Capitalism: Monetarism and Rational Expectations
Keynes and his contemporary followers questioned the cyclical stability of capitalism. Without government intervention to moderate business cycles, there will be a significant loss of output and employment. Keynesian economics advocates **policy activism**—the discretionary use of monetary and fiscal policy to try to prevent or ameliorate the business cycle. Activist monetary and fiscal policy is required to keep the economy on an even keel.

The **monetarists**, under the intellectual leadership of Milton Friedman, and the rational expectations economists, led by Robert Lucas, argue against the use of activist macroeconomic policy to combat capitalism's cyclical instability.[21] They argue that capitalism is considerably more stable than Keynes thought. In fact, the Great Depression was an aberration caused in large part by blunders in economic policy. The capitalist economy has a built-in self-correcting mechanism that will restore it to full employment or to the natural rate of unemployment. If the economy is operating at an unemployment rate above the natural rate, a slowing down of the inflation rate (or even deflation in extreme cases) will restore the economy to full employment. Lower prices raise aggregate supply, and aggregate employment rises until the natural rate is reached.

The monetarists argue against the use of activist policy. Because fiscal policy is decided primarily by politics rather than economics, monetary policy has been the most flexible tool of activist policy. Monetarists maintain that activist monetary policy is as likely to do harm as good. Lengthy and indeterminate lags separate recognition of a macroeconomic problem, the taking of necessary monetary action, and realization of the effect of that action on the economy. An anti-inflationary policy adopted during a period of rising prices may begin to affect the economy at the very time that an expansionary monetary policy is required. Rather than running the risk of policy mistakes, the monetarists favor a fixed-monetary-growth rule, which would bind monetary authorities to expand the money supply by a fixed rate each year (roughly equal to the real growth of the economy) regardless of the state of the economy.

Advocates of the **rational-expectations theory** also argue against activist policy. They maintain that activist policy will have the desired effect on the economy only if the policy catches people off guard. If taxes are lowered for the purpose of stimulating employment, and people know from experience that lower taxes raise inflation, then people will take actions to defeat the policy. If monetary authorities expand the money supply to raise employment, and workers and employees know that more monetary growth means more inflation, then the higher wages and prices will not raise employment or real output.

Real business cycle theorists argue that the business cycle is caused by random shocks and cannot be controlled by factors other than the self-correcting mechanism. The basic message of the monetarists, the rational-expectations economists, and the real business cycle theorists is that capitalism is much more stable than Keynes thought and that activist policies are likely to harm the economy. They believe it is better to rely on the self-correcting forces of the capitalist economy to restore it to equilibrium than to count on government policy makers to do so.

Growth and State Policy

An economy must grow for living standards to rise. Will a market economy grow appropriately on its own or is state action required to promote and direct growth?

The Austrian economist Joseph Schumpeter argued that market economies are well suited to creating growth.[22] Schumpeter saw growth as a process of **creative destruction**. A particular company or industry will find new ways to produce products or find new products to develop. Such adaptability can become the engine of growth for the entire economy, pulling along laggard branches. The company's success, however, will result in its eventual decline as competitors create substitutes and invent improved technologies.

To prove that economic growth follows the path of creative destruction, Schumpeter pointed out that no company or industry has been able to maintain a dominant position over the long run. The railroads were dominant in the nineteenth century; now they face tough competition from superior technologies, such as truck and air transport. IBM dominated computer production until new technologies enabled smaller, more efficient companies to grab most of IBM's market share.

Although economists such as Schumpeter argue that market economies can grow on their own and can be trusted to select those industries that will grow more rapidly than others, a significant number of economists believe that **industrial policy** can manage growth. Industrial policy uses the state to promote, subsidize, and generally manage the economic growth of a country. The proponents of industrial policy argue that private markets cannot effectively produce growth. Returns from research and development are insufficient to encourage private-sector financing. The state must therefore fund R&D, perhaps in partnership with private industry. The proponents of industrial policy also argue that private industries are not farsighted; they are unable to identify growth industries of the future. Thus government must find, support, and subsidize the growth industries of the future. The real-world model for industrial policy is Japan, which apparently used industrial policy to develop its automobile and electronics industries.

The Performance of Capitalist Economic Systems: Hypotheses

Chapter 3 discussed criteria by which to judge the performance of economic systems: efficiency, stability, income distribution, economic growth, and viability. What hypotheses, if any, follow from the theory of capitalism in each of these areas? First, we must note that it is difficult to formulate hypotheses at this point, because our principal concern is the efficiency of capitalism vis-à-vis other economic systems; these hypotheses would best be stated in relative terms. (See Table 5.1.)

Efficiency

Capitalism should provide a high level of efficiency, especially in the static case. The more competitive the economy, the more efficient the economy. The producer's desire to maximize profits and the consumer's desire to maximize utility lead to a maximal output from available resources under conditions of perfect competition. Imperfect competition and external effects reduce this efficiency. Another point promoting static efficiency is capitalism's apparent ability to process and utilize information more effectively than an economic system in which the market is lacking. Probably the most important point is that profit maximization, under all market arrangements, strongly encourages the efficient (least-cost) combination of resources to produce output.

TABLE 5.1   Hypothesis on the Performance of Capitalist
Economic Systems

Criterion	Performance
Efficiency	Good
Stability	Potentially poor; debate over government role
Income distribution	Unequal in the absence of state action
Economic growth	No clear *a priori* hypothesis; greater efficiency versus potentially lower capital formation

Stability

Stability is the ability of an economic system to grow without undue fluctuations in the rate of growth and without excessive inflation and unemployment. Of course, it is a subjective judgment what *undue* and *excessive* mean in such a context. Keynes argued that capitalist economies are not stable, at least in terms of short-run automatic equilibrating forces. Monetarists and rational-expectations theorists believe that capitalist economies are (or could be) inherently more stable if left to their own devices, so there is considerable disagreement on this point. However, capitalism continues to suffer periodic bouts of inflation, unemployment, and growth fluctuations, which the general public regards as troubling.

Income Distribution

The theory of capitalism cannot make definitive judgments about equity and how resources should be divided among the members of capitalist societies. Only value judgments can provide answers. We lack a consensus about "fairness," and without an agreed-upon definition it is difficult to arrive at hypotheses. Instead, we can only consider empirical measures of income distribution and make statements like the following: Income is distributed more nearly equally in society X than in society Y. It is difficult to proceed further and say that income is distributed "better" ("more fairly") in X or in Y.

The theory of capitalism, however, does suggest the likelihood of significant inequalities in the distribution of income. The factors of production are owned predominantly by private individuals, and the relative value of these factors is determined by the market. Insofar as human and physical capital and natural ability are not likely to be evenly distributed, especially when such things can be passed from one generation to another, private ownership of the factors of production raises the likelihood of an uneven distribution of income and wealth among the members of capitalist societies. Exactly how unevenly income and wealth are distributed will depend on the distribution of human and physical capital and also on the redistributive role of the state.

Economic Growth

One of the supposed advantages of planned socialist economies is their ability to direct resources to specific goals, such as economic growth and military power. To a greater extent than capitalist economies, they can marshal resources for economic growth, if they so desire, by controlling the investment rate and the growth rate of the labor force. Although capitalist governments can and do affect the investment rate, the amount saved is largely a matter of individual choice, and it is likely that individual choice will result in lower savings rates than will a planned socialist economy. Thus if the growth of factor inputs is left to individuals, one would hypothesize a slower rate of growth of factor inputs and hence of economic growth, *ceteris paribus,* under capitalism.

A counterbalancing factor must be considered: the hypothesized efficiency of capitalist economies. Static efficiency means that a maximal output is produced from available resources and (with a given savings rate) a greater volume of savings is available relative to less efficient production methods. Moreover, there is the unresolved matter of the dynamic efficiency of capitalist economic systems. Up to this point, capitalist theory has had relatively little to say about dynamic efficiency. It is conceivable that the greater static and dynamic efficiency of capitalism can compensate for its lesser control over the growth of productive resources.

Viability of the Capitalist System

The viability of capitalism has been demonstrated by both theory and historical experience. Capitalist theory points to its inherent tendencies toward equilibrium. And historical experience shows that capitalism has survived several centuries and that there are no signs of impending collapse.

Summary

- The traditional neoclassical model maintains that capitalist economies have a strong tendency to equilibrium and that they generate and process information efficiently.
- Market capitalism promotes consumer sovereignty, which enables consumers to determine what will be produced.
- In the perfectly competitive market capitalist economy, government would play a very limited role.
- John Maynard Keynes attempted to demonstrate that such an economy could establish a stable macroeconomic equilibrium at less than (or greater than) full employment.
- Keynes believed that it was the responsibility of government, through fiscal and monetary policy, to bring about full employment.

- A major criticism argues that in the real world, perfectly competitive markets are likely to be replaced in part by imperfectly competitive markets, where resources are misallocated.
- The neoclassic model assumes that all costs and benefits, both private and social, can be measured and accounted for in the resource-allocation process.
- Economists argue that certain externalities exist—costs or benefits external to the price system and not accounted for by the decision maker as resources are allocated. As a result, government intervention may be necessary to achieve an optimal allocation of resources.
- The monetarist view of the market economy has mounted a major counterattack against the Keynesian revolution, arguing that government intervention in the economy is not necessarily stabilizing and thus should be minimized.
- Traditional views of market capitalism hold that the markets tend to result in an efficient allocation of resources but that economic activity remains unstable or cyclical.
- It is argued that the distribution of income will be less even in a market capitalist system than in those systems where greater degrees of social ownership or government intervention are present.

Key Terms

invisible hand
mercantilism
efficiency of market allocation
rule of law
monetary policy
fiscal policy
constitution
simple market
complex market
state intervention
monopoly
taxation
subsidies
direct regulation
natural monopoly
external effects

external diseconomies
external economies
social costs
private costs
public goods
majority voting
median voter rule
income distribution
Keynesian revolution
Say's Law
policy activism
monetarists
rational-expectations theory
creative destruction
industrial policy

Notes

1. Examples of how the latter approach has been applied are found in Abram Bergson, *The Economics of Soviet Planning* (New Haven: Yale University Press, 1964); Jaroslav Vanek, *The Participatory Economy* (Ithaca, N.Y.: Cornell University Press, 1971), Chs. 2 and 3; and Benjamin Ward, *The Socialist Economy* (New York: Random House, 1967), Chs. 8 and 9. We also refer the reader to our discussion of the socialist controversy in Chapter 7.

2. Adam Smith, *The Wealth of Nations,* ed. Edwin Cannan (New York: Modern Library, 1937).
3. George Stigler, "The Successes and Failures of Professor Smith," *Journal of Political Economy* 84 (December 1976), 1199–1214.
4. Peter Boettke and G. Anderson, "Soviet Venality: A Rent-Seeking Model of the Communist State," *Public Choice* 93 (1997).
5. It is difficult to single out a few individuals and claim that they are the major contributors to partial-equilibrium analysis, but these three would appear on most lists: Alfred Marshall, *Principles of Economics,* 8th ed. (New York: Macmillan, 1948); J. R. Hicks, *Value and Capital,* 2nd ed. (Oxford, England: Oxford University Press, 1946); and Paul Samuelson, *Foundations of Economic Analysis* (Cambridge, Mass.: Harvard University Press, 1948).
6. Friederick Hayek, "The Price System as a Mechanism for Using Knowledge," *American Economic Review* 35 (September 1945), 519–530; and Ludwig von Mises, *Socialism: An Economic and Sociological Analysis* (New Haven: Yale University Press, 1951).
7. This definition is loosely based on Joseph Stiglitz, "Whither Reform: Ten Years of Transformation," Annual World Bank Conference on Development Economics, Washington, D.C., April 1999.
8. A. Denzau and D. North, "Shared Mental Models: Ideologies and Institutions," *Kyklos* 47 (1004), 3–31.
9. Paul Samuelson, "The Pure Theory of Public Expenditure," *Review of Economics and Statistics* 36 (November 1954), 26–30.
10. For a brief but lucid discussion of monopoly theory, see George Stigler, *The Theory of Price,* rev. ed. (New York: Macmillan, 1952), pp. 204–222.
11. Milton Friedman, "Monopoly and Social Responsibility of Business and Labor," in Edwin Mansfield, ed., *Monopoly Power and Economic Performance,* 3rd ed. (New York: Norton, 1974), pp. 57–68; and George J. Stigler, "The Government of the Economy," in Paul Samuelson, ed., *Readings in Economics,* 7th ed. (New York: McGraw-Hill, 1973), pp. 73–77.
12. The discussion of externalities is based on the following sources: E. J. Mishan, "The Postwar Literature on Externalities: An Interpretive Essay," *Journal of Economic Literature* 9 (March 1971), 1–28; George Daly, "The Coase Theorem: Assumptions, Applications, and Ambiguities," *Economic Inquiry* 12 (June 1974), 203–213; and Eirik Furobotin and Svetozar Pejovich, "Property Rights and Economic Theory: A Survey of Recent Literature," *Journal of Economic Literature* 12 (December 1972), 1137–1162.
13. R. H. Coase, "The Problem of Social Costs," *Journal of Law and Economics* 3 (October 1960), 1–44.
14. F. A. Hayek, *The Road to Serfdom* (Chicago: Chicago University Press, 1944).
15. Seymore Lipset, "Some Social Requisites of Democracy: Economic Development and Political Legitimacy," *American Political Science Review* 53 (1959), 69–105.
16. Robert Barro, *Determinants of Economic Growth* (Cambridge, Mass.: MIT Press, 1997), Ch. 2.
17. James Buchanan and Gordon Tullock, *The Calculus of Consent* (Ann Arbor: University of Michigan Press, 1974); Kenneth Arrow, *Social Choice and Individual Values* (New Haven: Yale University Press, 1976); for a discussion of differing views of the state, see Barry W. Poulson, *Economic Development: Private and Public Choice* (New York: West, 1994).
18. John Rawls, *Theory of Justice* (Oxford, England: Clarendon Press, 1976).
19. John Maynard Keynes, *The General Theory of Employment, Interest, and Money* (New York: Harcourt, 1936). The most important early work to interpret Keynes's general theory for nonspecialists was Alvin Hansen, *A Guide to Keynes* (New York: McGraw-Hill, 1953).

20. There is considerable controversy over what Keynes actually meant to say in *The General Theory,* and some authorities argue that the more popular interpretations of Keynes are incorrect. For discussion of this controversy, see Don Patinkin, *Money, Interest, and Prices,* 2nd ed. (New York: Harper & Row, 1965); Axel Leijonhufvud, *On Keynesian Economics and the Economics of Keynes* (New York: Oxford University Press, 1968); Herschel Grossman, "Was Keynes a 'Keynesian'? A Review Article," *Journal of Economic Literature* 10 (March 1972), 26–30; and Alan Coddington, "Keynesian Economics: The Search for First Principles," *Journal of Economic Literature* 14 (December 1976), 1258–1338. For an historical perspective on the Keynesian revolution, see Alan Sweezy *et al.,* "The Keynesian Revolution and Its Pioneers," *American Economic Review, Papers and Proceedings* 62 (May 1972), 116–141.

21. The discussion of the monetarist school is based on the following sources: Milton Friedman, ed., *Studies in the Quantity Theory of Money* (Chicago: University of Chicago Press, 1956); Milton Friedman and A. J. Schwartz, *A Monetary History of the United States* (Princeton, N.J.: Princeton University Press, 1963); Milton Friedman, *Dollars and Deficits* (Englewood Cliffs, N.J.: Prentice-Hall, 1968); Franco Modigliani, "The Monetarist Controversy, or, Should We Forsake Stabilization Policies?" *American Economic Review* 67 (March 1977), 13; Edmund Phelps, *Microeconomic Foundations of Employment and Inflation Theory* (London: Macmillan, 1974); and Milton Friedman, "Inflation and Unemployment," *Journal of Political Economy* 85 (June 1977), 451–472.

22. For a contemporary view of the Schumpeterian contribution, see F. M. Scherer, "Schumpeter and Plausible Capitalism," *Journal of Economic Literature* 30 (September 1992), 1416–1433. For a discussion of contemporary issues in economic growth, see Paul M. Romer *et al.,* "New Growth Theory," *Journal of Economic Perspectives* 8 (Winter 1994), 3–72.

Recommended Readings

Traditional Sources

F. M. Bator, "The Simple Analytics of Welfare Maximization," *American Economic Review* 47 (March 1957), 22–59.

Abram Bergson, "A Reformulation of Certain Aspects of Welfare Economics," *Quarterly Journal of Economics* 52 (February 1938), 310–334; reprinted in R. V. Clemence, ed., *Readings in Economic Analysis* (Reading, Mass.: Addison-Wesley, 1950), Vol. I, pp. 61–85.

James Buchanan and Robert Tollison, eds., *Theory of Public Choice: Political Applications of Economics* (Ann Arbor: University of Michigan Press, 1972).

James Buchanan and Gordon Tullock, *The Calculus of Consent* (Ann Arbor: University of Michigan Press, 1974).

Edward Chamberlin, *The Theory of Monopolistic Competition,* 6th ed. (Cambridge, Mass.: Harvard University Press, 1948).

R. H. Coase, "The Problem of Social Costs," *Journal of Law and Economics* 3 (October 1960), 1–44.

Alan Coddington, "Keynesian Economics: The Search for First Principles," *Journal of Economic Literature* 14 (December 1976), 1258–1338.

A. S. Eicher and J. A. Kregel, "An Essay on Post-Keynesian Theory: A New Paradigm in Economics," *Journal of Economic Literature* 13 (December 1975), 1293–1314.

Milton Friedman, *Dollars and Deficits* (Englewood Cliffs, N.J.: Prentice-Hall, 1968).

———, ed., *Studies in the Quantity Theory of Money* (Chicago: University of Chicago Press, 1956).

Robert J. Gordon, "What Is the New Keynesian Economics?" *Journal of Economic Literature* 28 (September 1990), 15–71.

J. de V. Graaff, *Theoretical Welfare Economics* (London: Cambridge University Press, 1957).

Herschel Grossman, "Was Keynes a 'Keynesian'? A Review Article," *Journal of Economic Literature* 10 (March 1972), 26–30.

J. R. Hicks, *Value and Capital,* 2nd ed. (Oxford, England: Oxford University Press, 1946).

Axel Leijonhufvud, *On Keynesian Economics and the Economics of Keynes* (New York: Oxford University Press, 1968).

John Maynard Keynes, *The General Theory of Employment, Interest, and Money* (New York: Harcourt, 1936).

E. J. Mishan, "The Postwar Literature on Externalities: An Interpretive Essay," *Journal of Economic Literature* 9 (March 1971), 1–28.

Franco Modigliani, "The Monetarist Controversy, or, Should We Forsake Stabilization Policies?" *American Economic Review* 67 (March 1977), 1–19.

A. C. Pigou, *The Economics of Welfare,* 4th ed. (London: Macmillan, 1946).

John Rawls, *Theory of Justice* (Oxford, England: Clarendon Press, 1976).

Joan Robinson, *The Economics of Imperfect Competition* (London: Macmillan, 1959).

Paul Samuelson, "The Pure Theory of Public Expenditure," *Review of Economics and Statistics* 36 (November 1954), 26–30.

———, *Foundations of Economic Analysis* (Cambridge, Mass.: Harvard University Press, 1948).

Tibor Scitovsky, *Welfare and Competition,* rev. ed. (Homewood, Ill.: Irwin, 1971), Chs. 20 and 21.

Adam Smith, *The Wealth of Nations,* ed. Edwin Cannan (New York: Modern Library, 1937).

The Neoclassical Model

David M. Krebs, *A Course in Microeconomic Theory* (Princeton N.J.: Princeton University Press, 1990).

Eugene Silberberg, *The Structure of Economics: A Mathematical Analysis,* 2nd ed. (New York: McGraw-Hill, 1990).

Hal R. Varian, *Intermediate Microeconomics: A Modern Approach,* 2nd ed. (New York: Norton, 1990).

Macroeconomic Theory

Andrew B. Abel and Ben S. Bernake, *Macroeconomics* (New York: Addison-Wesley, 1992).

William H. Branson, *Macroeconomics: Theory and Policy,* 3rd ed. (New York: HarperCollins, 1989).

Richard T. Froyen, *Macroeconomics: Theories and Policies,* 4th ed. (New York: Macmillan, 1993).

Robert J. Gordon, "What Is the New Keynesian Economics?" *Journal of Economic Literature* 28 (September 1990), 15–71.

———, *Macroeconomics,* 5th ed. (Glenview, Il.: Scott, Foresman, 1990).

Robert E. Hall and John B. Taylor, *Macroeconomics,* 3rd ed. (New York: Norton, 1991).

N. Gregory Markiw, "A Quick Refresher Course in Macroeconomics," *Journal of Economic Literature* 28 (December 1990), 1645–1660.

N. Gregory Mankiw *et al.,* "Keynesian Economics Today" *Journal of Economic Perspectives* 7 (Winter 1993), 3–82.

Paul M. Romer *et al.,* "New Growth Theory," *Journal of Economic Perspectives* 8 (Winter 1994), 3–72.

Market Failure: Imperfect Competition, Income Distribution, and Public Choice

Nicholas Barr, "Economic Theory and the Welfare State: A Survey and Interpretation," *Journal of Economic Literature* 30 (June 1992), 741–803.

Dennis W. Carlton and Jeffrey M. Perloff, *Modern Industrial Organization* (New York: HarperCollins, 1990).

Douglas F. Greer, *Business, Government, and Society,* 2nd ed. (New York: Macmillan, 1987).

F. M. Sherer and David Ross, *Industrial Market Structure and Economic Performance,* 3rd ed. (Boston: Houghton Mifflin, 1990).

R. D. Norton, "Industrial Policy and American Renewal," *Journal of Economic Literature* 24 (March 1986), 1–40.

Barry W. Poulson, *Economic Development: Private and Public Choice* (New York: West, 1994).

Leonard W. Weiss and Michael W. Klass, eds., *Regulatory Reform: What Actually Happened* (Boston: Little, Brown, 1986).

Clifford Winston, "Economic Deregulation: Days of Reckoning for Microeconomists," *Journal of Economic Literature* 31 (September 1993), 1263–1289.

6

Theory of Planned Socialism

Chapter 2 introduced two variants of the socialist economy: centrally planned socialism and market socialism. This chapter discusses the former, and then Chapter 7 looks at market socialism. Before the two major organizational variants of the socialist economy are discussed, it is important to introduce the basic ideas that define the nature of **socialism**.

The Socialist Economy

The definition of a socialist economy in Chapter 2 focused on decision-making arrangements, property rights, and incentive arrangements. These arrangements, along with different policies and a different political system, lead to outcomes different from those under capitalism. Unlike the market capitalist economy, no widely accepted theoretical paradigm of the socialist economy exists.[1] Much of the literature on socialism focuses on its noneconomic aspects and especially on the nature of socialist society. Indeed, many socialists characterize their economic system as one not only based on fundamental social changes with special emphasis on equity but also designed to improve the capitalist system.

Let us consider how socialism resolves the four fundamental tasks of any economic system—what to produce, how to produce, who gets the product, and how to provide for the future.

First, although the output mix could in theory be the same in capitalist and socialist systems, such an outcome is unlikely. Typically, the socialist economic system is directed by a strong central state, which, through state ownership and political power, exercises considerable influence over what will be produced. In most socialist economies, the output mix favors public goods, defense goods, and the socialization of consumption over private consumer goods.

Second, the structure of the socialist economy, through state controls and ownership, can be dictated by forces different from those of the market. Thus the state dictates sectoral expansion and, within sectors, the arrangements for production. Moreover, the technology of production is viewed as simple. The appropriate mix of factor inputs (capital and labor) appears limited and constrained by technology, making it reasonable to assume constant factor proportions over extended periods of time. In such a setting, information problems are not serious, and engineers rather than economists can resolve the issue of factor proportions. Not surprisingly, factor prices are of limited importance in deciding the appropriate input mix.

Third, state ownership of the means of production has fundamental implications for income distribution. For the household, the primary source of income is labor. Private income from capital is absent. Moreover, in a system where the socialization of consumption is an objective, one would expect a more even distribution of income. This expectation—one of the strongest basic tenets of socialism—relies on assumptions about basic human needs, human participation in the economy, and how these basic needs ought to be fulfilled. Specifically, it is assumed that as human needs change, their fulfillment can, in fact, be socialized, and no major differences exist in the ability to benefit from increases in income. All of these assumptions support an egalitarian distribution of income.[2]

Finally, the economy's provision for the future may differ in the socialist case. The capitalist market economy tends to overstate the worth of present consumption at the expense of future consumption. The socialist economy follows policies that expand present savings to offset individual shortsightedness and expand well-being in the future.

Its advocates view socialism as an economic system that can offset the perceived faults of the market capitalist economy. The socialist economy places greater emphasis on economic equality and socialization and, in doing so, uses a variety of state controls and policies to offset the problems of unemployment, inflation, and slow economic growth, which are perceived as inevitable under capitalism.

It is difficult to compare the paradigm of the market with that of the socialist economy because there is no single socialist paradigm other than that of Karl Marx. Marx himself analyzed capitalism, but in doing so, he envisioned socialism (and ultimately communism) as an inevitable outcome of the process of social change.

The Marxist–Leninist View of Socialism

Although Marx did not analyze socialist working arrangements, he did develop a framework for predicting the triumph of socialism over capitalism. For Marx, the historical evolution from primitive societies to communism was inevitable.[3] Capitalism, because of its exploitation of workers and its internal contradictions, would be replaced by socialism. Capitalism would be an engine of economic progress, the results of which would be more evenly shared under socialism.

Socialism itself would be an intermediate step, a system ultimately to be replaced by communism. **Communism**, the highest stage of social and economic development, would be characterized by the absence of markets and money and by abundance, distribution according to need, and the withering away of the state. In the meantime, under socialism, vestiges of capitalism would continue and some familiar institutions would remain. The state would be transformed into a **dictatorship of the proletariat**. Marx emphasized a strong role for the state, a role that was subsequently strengthened by V. I. Lenin.[4] Under socialism, though, the state would be representative of the masses and therefore noncoercive. The state would own the means of production as well as rights to surplus value. Under socialism, each individual would be expected to contribute according to capability, and rewards would be distributed in proportion to that contribution. Subsequently, under communism, the basis of reward would be need. However, need would presumably have a meaning rather different from the one assigned to it under capitalism, where wants are continually expanding.

Many changes and additions have been made to the Marxian model originally developed in the nineteenth century. Lenin wrote extensively on the role of the state under socialism, especially on the tactics of revolution.

Lenin emphasized that inequalities and vestiges of capitalism would still exist under socialism and that, accordingly, coercive actions by the state would be necessary.[5] Indeed, during the "war communisim" period in the former Soviet Union, Lenin promoted a peculiar view of the state in which the task of administering the economy's affairs was viewed as simple, capable of being handled by anyone.[6] There was no need, Lenin argued, for specialists, because the tasks of management were quite routine. These views were subsequently modified, although they form the basis of later Soviet thinking on management.

Marx, Engels, and Lenin wrote about the role of the state and income distribution under socialism. They did not deal with the more fundamental issue of how scarce resources were to be allocated during the socialist phase.

The Socialist Controversy: The Feasibility of Socialism

Resource allocation under socialism has been widely discussed over the past century, and the discussion has been loosely termed the **socialist controversy**. Socialist economic theory must explain how resources are to be allocated under socialism. If the socialist economy is planned, how will planners make rational decisions about the use of scarce resources? Is private ownership necessary for the proper functioning of markets?

Barone: A Theoretical Framework

The first consistent theoretical framework of resource allocation under socialism was developed by the Italian economist Enrico Barone. In 1907, Barone published "The Ministry of Production in the Collectivist State."[7] Here he argued, though in a limited and purely theoretical way, that prices, understood as **relative valuations**, are not bound to the market. A **central planning board** (hereafter designated CPB) could establish prices, or "ratios of equivalence" among commodities.

Barone's model consisted of simultaneous equations relating inputs and outputs to the ratios of equivalence. When solved (Barone admitted that a real-world solution would be impractical), the equations could provide the appropriate relative valuations of resources required to balance demand and supply. A CPB armed with perfect computation techniques would require perfect knowledge of all relevant variables, specifically (1) individual demand schedules, (2) enterprise production functions, and (3) existing stocks of both producer and consumer goods. Barone's principal conclusion was that the CPB's computed resource allocation would be similar to that of competitive capitalism. In fact, he saw no reason for substantial differences.

One could question the practicality of this approach, both at the time Barone was writing and even in the present state of improved computer technology. Nevertheless, it demonstrated that the relative valuations of resources essential for rational resource allocation could be discovered by imputation (solving equations) rather than through the particular institutional arrangements of the market.

The Challenge of Mises and Hayek

The discussion of this matter went little further until the 1920s and 1930s, when three important developments took place. First, Ludwig von Mises and Friederick Hayek mounted a formidable and now famous attack against the case for rational resource allocation under socialism.[8] Second, a number of Soviet authors made significant contributions to the theory of planning, then in its formative stages. Third, the noted Polish economist Oskar Lange set forth his famous model of market socialism, to be discussed in the next chapter.[9]

Hayek and Mises's challenge was directed toward the problem of allocating producer goods in a socialist economic system, a task presumably in the hands of the state (with the allocation of consumer goods left to the market). Mises argued that for a state to direct available resources rationally toward the achievement of given ends, even if resource availabilities and ends were known, a knowledge of relative valuations (prices) would be essential. He maintained that the only way to establish these valuations would be through the market mechanism, which is absent in a socialist system where producer goods are owned and allocated by the state. If prices are the vehicle by which relative scarcities are reflected, why not artificially simulate prices via a system of equations as proposed by Barone? Mises and Hayek argued that it would be difficult if not impossible to separate the allocation function from the workings of the market. Both, he suggested, are tied together through the profit motive and the existence of private property.

Much has been written about the profit motive and private property.[10] Mises argued that individuals are motivated by the urge for material self-betterment, which translates into utility and profit maximization. Second, individuals and enterprises are motivated to produce goods and services as efficiently as possible so as to increase profits. Third, the drive for achievement cannot be socialized; that is, the urge for betterment cannot be translated from the individual to the group. Furthermore, if resources are owned by the state, profits accrue to the state, not to individuals. Thus, Mises argued, the motivation for utilizing available resources in the most efficient way is lost.

The responses to Hayek and Mises's critique have varied. There have been two main interpretations. The first is that they were saying that socialism could not "work" in the sense that resource allocation would be impossible in the absence of a market mechanism. The second and more common interpretation is that socialism cannot work *efficiently*. In fact, the debate over the relative merits of socialism and capitalism has focused on the question of relative efficiency.[11]

The Planned Economy: Formal Organization

Unlike the market economy, where resource allocation takes place on a relatively decentralized basis through supply and demand, allocation here is guided by plans.

Administration of a Planned Socialist Economy

Figure 6.1 is a sketch of the administrative structure of a **planned socialist economy**, directed from above by a Communist party dictatorship. It shows that the rules of the game are set by the top leadership of the Communist party (operating in a Central Committee or even smaller Politburo). Formal decrees are issued by the state administration, at the apex of which is a Council of Ministers, but the top administration of both state and party consists of an interlocking directorate of key political figures

FIGURE 6.1   Administration of a Planned Socialist Economy

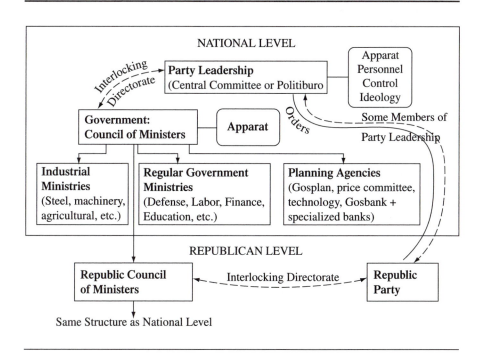

such that distinctions between party and state are blurred at the highest level. In contrast to market economies, decrees and orders are quite specific, instructing some subordinate agency to carry out a designated task. General rules and guidelines are few and far between.

The Council of Ministers, in which the most important ministries and state committees are represented, issues its directives to ministries. "Ministries" are of two types: industrial ministries that supervise productive enterprises and functional ministries that carry out the "normal" state functions, such as education, defense, internal security, justice, and public finance. State committees, such as a state planning commission, perform functions that are specific to a planned economy and usually not found in market economies, such as drawing up national plans. A monopoly state bank assumes all functions of banking, encompassing both central banking and allocations of credit. Its monetary and credit policies are subordinated to the plans prepared by other state committees, and its main job is the distribution of credits according to plan. If the planned economy is a federation of republics or states, the central administrative structure is replicated in the states or republics, the governments of which answer to the Council of Ministers and Communist party. These republican party and state organizations supervise local industries.

The "plan is the law." Given that there are a large number of plans, many conflicting, the administration must engage in considerable negotiating, coercion, and compromising in the absence of overall rules of the game. The party is the "leading institution," which gives it the primary role of negotiator, compromisor, and facilitator. A *nomenklatura* system is used for administrative appointments, promotion, and firings, managed by the party. The *nomenklatura* system operates according to rather clear rules.

Horizontal versus Vertical Transactions

Figure 6.1 shows a vertical, "top-down" planning system. Orders are handed down from the top (the party or the Council of Ministers) to industrial ministries, which hand down orders to enterprises. When all administrative orders are issued by administrative superiors to administrative subordinates, we say that activities are organized in terms of **vertical transactions**. In a vertical planning structure, it is presumed that the subordinates do not deal directly with one another in horizontal transactions. A **horizontal transaction** is one concluded by subordinates at the same level of the administrative structure without the approval of administrative superiors. In a planned socialist economy, presumably, the goal of the dictator (the Communist party or the Council of Ministers) is to ensure that the planned economy runs according to vertical orders and not according to "unplanned" horizontal transactions. If most transactions are horizontal, it is unclear whether the economy is a planned economy.

Early writers on the administrative-command economy, such as Hayek and Mises, paid little attention to the manner in which the dictatorship would organize its bureaucratic staff to manage producers. Mises and Hayek spoke vaguely of a central planning board that would deal directly with enterprises. Students of dictatorship also simplified by assuming "costless coercion"—that the dictator could effectively persuade subordinates to do his bidding.[12] The dictator actively discourages horizontal relations among industrial ministries, regional authorities, or factories, because such alliances weaken control, particularly when they become powerful interest groups. Yet despite the dictator's opposition, informal "horizontal" structures inevitably emerge and weaken the center.

Figure 6.2 shows the source of conflict between vertical and horizontal structures. It depicts the production and allocation of a particular industrial commodity such as pig iron, denoted by X. The demand curve D shows the quantity of X demanded by various potential users at different "prices" of X. The price could be the official price or some more comprehensive price that captures the resources costs of potential users to acquire X. The supply curve S shows the various quantities of X supplied by its producers at different prices.

If this were a market economy (see the figure on the left), the market would determine how much of X would be produced and which potential users would get the available supply. All those willing to pay the market price (P') would get X'. The basic feature of an administrative-command economy (see the figure on the right) is that the dictator decides both how much X is produced and who gets X. The ideal market (on the left) is driven by an invisible hand that does not distinguish among buyers. Anyone who can pay the price will get the good. The dictator, on the other hand, can use his "visible hand" of allocative power to reward and punish for either economic or political ends. In the diagram, the dictator sets the production of X at X^* and its price at P^*. At this price, the producer is supposed to sell the entire output (X^*) to authorized buyers at the official price P^*. In a pure vertical system, the

FIGURE 6.2   Vertical versus Horizontal Structures

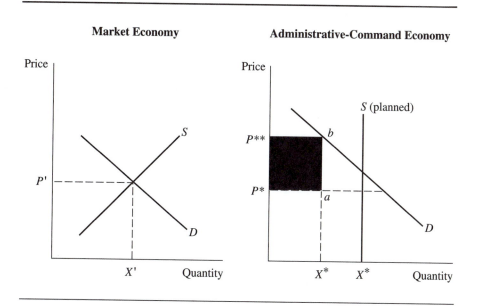

dictator decides who gets X^* among all those willing to pay the official price, P^*. If there is perfect "vertical trust," subordinates will obey orders, and only those designated to receive X will actually get it.

Figure 6.2 illustrates why horizontal structures inevitably compete with vertical structure. The producer of X realizes that it is producing a valuable commodity. In fact, a number of buyers are prepared to pay a "price" well in excess of the official price. Buyers are prepared to buy X^{**} at P^{**}. If the producer of X sells X^{**} to unauthorized buyers at P^{**}, the producer gains a "rent" denoted by the shaded area of the rectangle P^*abP^{**}. Those who are prepared to pay more may also be those who supply the producer of X with another valuable commodity, Y. The producer of Y also realizes that it is producing a valuable commodity for which a large number of buyers are prepared to pay more than the official price. If producers of X and Y follow vertical orders, they receive the official price P^*. They have not violated any orders, and they will receive rewards from the dictator. On the other hand, both have passed up the opportunity to sell above the official price. They could obtain monetary bribes in addition to the official price, maintain good relations with their own best customers, or receive preferential treatment if the buyer happens to be a supplier.

If the reward from the horizontal transaction (the rent) exceeds the reward for vertical loyalty, the producer will engage in "illegal" or "unplanned" horizontal transactions. In extreme cases, horizontal transactions dominate vertical transactions. The dictator loses effective control of transactions and serves instead as a kind of referee, who must organize and control the rents of various competing interest groups.[13] The effective loss of control to interest groups leads to the kind of "red sclerosis" described by Mancur Olson.[14]

Resource Allocation Under Planned Socialism

The socialist controversy raised the key issues of resource allocation under conditions of socialism. On the one hand, it raised the *complexity* issue for planned socialism. Barone showed that the CPB would, in theory, have to gather data and solve simultaneous equations for millions of products. Such a task would be beyond the capabilities of any real-world CPB. On the other hand, the socialist controversy raised the *motivation* issue for both planned and market socialism. If the means of production are owned by society at large, how are managers to be motivated to combine resources efficiently and to take innovative risks?

The discussion that follows pursues these questions for planned socialism. It begins with the origins of the theory of planned socialism in its first real-world experiment, the Soviet Union in the 1930s, and then proceeds to the theory of planning.

Origins: The Soviet Union in the 1920s

The 1920s have been described as "the golden age of Soviet mathematical economics."[15] There was relatively open discussion in the Soviet Union, including discussion about the appropriate path and mechanisms for economic growth under socialism.[16]

The emphasis was on formulating a socialist path of development, guided by Marxist–Leninist ideological principles. Pioneers in mathematical economics, a key area for the subsequent development of the theory of economic planning, were very active. Under these conditions, it is not surprising that prior to the Stalinist crackdown of the late 1920s, Soviet planners and theoreticians pursued the theory of planning under conditions of social ownership. Possibly the most important practical work of this period was the development of **balances of the national economy**, forerunners of the input–output analysis of Wassily Leontief, and of **material balances**, the planning system later used in planned socialist economies. The development of the material balance approach remains a major (though simple) contribution of considerable practical importance.[17]

The material balances formulated by Soviet economists focused on the need to determine aggregate demands and supplies for basic industrial commodities and to bring them in balance without relying on market forces. More specifically, the theoretical underpinning of the material balance approach (input–output analysis) demonstrated that the productive relations of an economic system could be approximated by a system of simultaneous equations along the lines suggested by Barone.

A significant omission in the Soviet discussion of the 1920s was the matter of how enterprises might be guided at the micro level. Some Soviet economists even argued that the whole discussion of relative values (prices) under socialism was irrelevant because the **law of value** would not exist under socialism.

Although there is no necessary inconsistency between Marxian economics and mathematical economics, Stalin thought otherwise. This view ended open discussion in the Soviet Union, a situation that did not change until after Stalin's death in 1953.

Economic Planning: A Paradigm for Planned Socialism

It is not surprising that the Soviet discussions of the 1920s focused on national economic planning. If market resource allocation is to be eliminated, some alternative arrangement must be used in its place.

There has been a tendency to associate national economic planning with socialism in both a political and an economic context. Actually, planning is consistent with a wide variety of organizational and ideological arrangements. Nevertheless, the idea that an economic system could be centrally planned stems in large part from the experience of the former Soviet Union. Even in the countries where most national planning was done—for example, the Soviet Union—the theory of planning was only a set of pragmatic principles; there was no "theory" comparable to the paradigm of the market economy. In this sense, most real-world national planning is a pragmatic exercise.

Planning is a term with differing connotations. Various authors have used different definitions, but there are basic elements in common. Gerald Sirkin writes, "Planning is an attempt, by centralizing the management of the allocation of resources sufficiently, to take into account social costs and social benefits which would be irrelevant to the calculus of the decentralized decision maker."[18] The emphasis here is the appropriate *level* of decision making and the social versus the private element in the decisions taken.

Abdul Qayum defines planning as "a systematic and integrated program covering a definite period of time, approved or sponsored by the state to bring about a rationalization of resources to achieve certain national targets using direct and indirect means with or without state ownership of resources."[19] Here we have a broader and more inclusive definition, which nonetheless includes elements of the previous definition—notably, the implication of centralization in the decision-making process.

Michael Todaro, writing in the context of development planning, defines planning as follows: "Economic planning may be described as the conscious effort of a central organization to influence, direct, and, in some cases even control changes in the principal economic variables (GDP, consumption, investment, savings, and the like) of a certain country or region over the course of time in accordance with a predetermined set of objectives."[20] Todaro further emphasizes that the key concepts are influence, direction, and control, and he defines an economic plan "as a specific set of quantitative targets to be reached in a given period of time."

The concept of plan formulation has been described succinctly by G. M. Heal, who writes that it can be viewed as "solving a constrained maximization problem."[21] Plan formulation involves doing the best one can to achieve objectives, albeit with limitations on available resources.

In contrast to the increasing specificity of these definitions, it is interesting to consider the definition from the Soviet period:

> Socialist planning is based upon strict scientific foundations; it demands the continuous generalization of the practical experience of the construction of Communism as well as the utilization of the accomplishments of science and technology. To operate the economy according to plan means to foresee. Scientific foresight rests on the reconciliation of the objective economic laws of socialism. Plans carry in socialism the character of objectives. The planned direction of the economy requires that priorities be established and the main priorities of the economic plan are the branches of heavy industry, for they determine the development of all industrial branches as well as the economy as a whole.[22]

Although some of the elements of this Soviet definition (for example, the "objective economic laws of socialism") may be difficult to interpret, the definition contains some familiar concepts, such as the ability to foresee and the existence of objectives.

These definitions, though differing in specifics, differ relatively little in substance. They agree that a **national economic plan** is a mechanism to guide the activity of an economy through time toward the achievement of specified goals. The notion of *control* is fundamental to the concept of planning. Planning is more than forecasting. Although forecasting involves projections of future economic activity, planning is substantively different: The planner attempts to *alter* the economy's direction of movement and hence to change economic outcomes. It is convenient to categorize planning as either indicative or directive. In the case of **indicative planning**, targets are set in the hope of affecting economic outcomes by providing information external to the market; typically, individual firms receive no directives from planners. In the case of **directive planning**, however, targets are set by planners with the expectation of directly altering outcomes, because plan targets are legally binding on enterprises.

A popular expression in the Soviet Union was that "the plan is law." Indicative planning will be discussed in more detail in a later chapter.

If the economic activity of a country is to be planned, three basic steps are required. First, a plan has to be constructed that specifies the goals or objectives to be achieved and the means for achieving those goals within a specified time frame. Second, there must be an organizational mechanism for executing the plan and, in particular, a means to guarantee that agents will in fact attempt to achieve plan goals. In short, there must be an incentive system to harmonize the behavior of agents with goal achievement. Finally, there must be a means to evaluate outcomes and, where they differ from targets, to ensure appropriate feedback to adjust the direction of economic activity.

The literature on national economic planning can be conveniently divided into two categories. There is the literature devoted to the planning methods actually utilized in the planned socialist economic systems. This literature describes material balance planning, the Soviet origins of which we have already discussed. And there is the literature on national economic planning models, which usually employ some optimizing procedure. Although the basic principles of planning are common to both, the planned socialist economies have utilized the material balance approach.

Material Balance Planning

The material balance approach to national economic planning has been widely used in the planned socialist economic systems. The central planning board (CPB) specifies a list of goods and services that are to be produced in the plan period. Once the CPB determines the inputs (land, labor, capital, and intermediate products) needed to produce one unit of output (generally on the basis of historical input–output relationships), it can draw up a list of inputs necessary for meeting the specified output objectives. Obviously, the CPB would like to produce as much output as possible, but the availability of inputs limits how much can be produced given available technology.

The CPB must ensure a **balance** between outputs and inputs. For each factor input and intermediate good, the amount needed to produce output (the demand) must be equated with the amount available (the supply). If a balance between the two sides does not exist, administrative steps must be taken to reduce demand and/or expand supply. A balance must exist for each item, and there must also be an aggregate balance of demand and supply.

On the supply side, there are three main sources of inputs: production, stocks on hand, and imports. On the demand side, there are two main elements: **interindustry demand**, where the output of one industry (for example, coal) is used as the input for another industry (for example, steel), and **final demand**, which consists of output that will be invested, consumed by households, or exported. Thus adjustment is possible on both the demand and supply sides, and it is through administrative adjustment that demand and supply are balanced. This adjustment procedure is in basic contrast to market economies, where prices adjust to eliminate imbalances.

For any economy, maintaining an appropriate balance between the supplies and demands for all products would be an enormous task, a point emphasized by Hayek and Mises. In fact, the planned economies that used the material balance approach plan only the most important inputs and outputs, handling others on a more decentralized basis. Although this means that only a portion of total output is under the control of central planners, it is nevertheless sufficient to exert a major degree of influence over the economic outcomes.

Even in this more limited context, Barone's question—how to solve the equations—remains a problem. The problem of balancing supply and demand can be conveniently formalized in the following manner:

$$\text{Sources} \qquad\qquad \text{Uses}$$

$$X_1 + V_1 + M_1 = X_{11} + X_{12} + \cdots + X_{1n} + Y_1$$
$$X_2 + V_2 + M_2 = X_{21} + X_{22} + \cdots + X_{2n} + Y_2$$
$$\vdots$$
$$X_n + V_n + M_n = X_{n1} + X_{n2} + \cdots + X_{nn} + Y_n$$

where n items are included in the balance, and

X_i = planned output of commodity i
V_i = existing stocks of commodity i
M_i = planned imports of commodity i
X_{ij} = interindustry demand, that is, the amount of commodity i required to produce the planned amount of commodity j
Y_i = the final demand for commodity i, that is, for investment, household consumption, or export

Table 6.1 depicts a simplified material balance. Note that for each commodity a balance exists. In the case of steel, there are three sources on the supply side: production of 2,000 tons, no stocks on hand, and imports of 20 tons, for a total supply of 2,020 tons. On the demand side, there are six users of steel: the coal industry using 200 tons, the steel industry using 400 tons, the machinery industry using 1,000 tons, the consumer goods industry using 300 tons, exports of 100 tons, and domestic use of 20 tons, for a total demand of 2,020 tons. In this example, supply and demand are balanced at 2,020 tons.

Computational, administrative, and data-gathering limitations set an upper limit on the number of items that can be handled by material balance planning. Typically, the items that are of major significance to the achievement of state objectives are included in the plan. Items not included in the plan are planned at a lower level in the hierarchy. Plan authorities discovered that the economy can be effectively controlled by manipulating a relatively small number of important inputs.

How does the CPB know how much of each input ($X_{ij}s$) will be necessary to produce a unit of output? The coefficient relating input to output is typically derived from the previous year's planning experience and adjusted somewhat (usually upward) to allow for investment and productivity improvements. Moreover, these coefficients are normally assumed to be constant over varying ranges of output—an assumption that causes problems when an industry is expanding and experiencing increasing (or decreasing) returns to scale. Gathering the information necessary to keep the coefficients up to date is a real problem. Most planned socialist systems rely

TABLE 6.1   Sample Material Balance

	Sources			Intermediate Inputs Required by				Final Uses	
	Output	Stocks	Imports	Coal Industry	Steel Industry	Machinery Industry	Consumer Goods Industry	Exports	Domestic Uses
Coal (tons)	1,000	10	0	100	500	50	50	100	210
Steel (tons)	2,000	0	20	200	400	1,000	300	100	20
Machinery (units)	100	5	5	20	40	10	20	10	10
Consumer goods (units)	400	10	20	0	0	0	100	100	230

Demonstration that a balance exists:

Sources of coal: 1,010 tons   = uses of coal: 1,010 tons
Sources of steel: 2,020 tons   = uses of steel: 2,020 tons
Sources of machinery: 110 units   = uses of machinery: 110 units
Sources of consumer goods: 430 units   = uses of consumer goods: 430 units

Source: Paul R. Gregory and Robert C. Stuart, Soviet Economic Structure and Performance (New York: Harper & Row, 1986), p. 169. Reprinted by permission of HarperCollins Publishers, Inc. Copyright © 1986 by Paul R. Gregory and Robert C. Stuart.

on communications with enterprises, a process that is time-consuming and not necessarily reliable.

Material balance planning must deal with the interrelatedness of economic sectors. Suppose, for example, that a need arises to expand the output of a particular commodity or a previously unknown input shortage is discovered. If more steel is needed, more coal will also be needed for the production of the steel. But to produce more coal, more electricity is needed, and on, and on, and on. These so-called second-round effects reverberate throughout the economic system, making it very difficult to obtain a balance. To what degree can planners take second-round effects into account? In theory, a number of reformulations of the plan would be necessary. In practice, most planners allow for the initial or most serious repercussions, leaving the remainder to be absorbed as shocks by the system.

A plan that achieves a balance of supplies and demands is a **consistent plan**. The balancing of demands with supplies is the essence of material balance planning. But what about optimality? **Optimality** implies selecting the *best* plan of all those consistent plans with which it would be possible to achieve a balance. The best plan is the one that maximizes the planners' objectives. Although it is mathematically possible to elaborate the criteria for selecting an optimal plan from among a number of consistent plans, most planned socialist economies are able to prepare two or three variants at best, and there is no reason for the selected variants to be optimal.

When we examine Soviet planning in practice, we shall have a chance to consider further aspects of material balance planning. At this juncture, let us simply observe that material balance planning was a mechanism that worked, though at a low level of efficiency. Furthermore, it enabled the planners to select key areas on which pressure could be applied to seek rapid expansion, regional economic growth, or whatever. On the other hand, it was cumbersome, and achieving a balance frequently required buffer or low-priority sectors (typically consumer goods) that could absorb planning mistakes.

Raymond Powell examined how economies that operate through material balance planning were able to survive and generate growth.[23] Powell pointed out that material balance planning does not prevent agents and principals in the economy (managers, ministers, and planners) from responding to nonprice scarcity indicators. Because there will inevitably be planning errors (imbalances between output targets and the inputs allocated to produce these targets), managers and planners will be confronted with various indicators of scarcity. Managers will recognize that some materials are harder to acquire than others or that some materials held by the enterprise are scarcer than others. Ministries will receive warnings from their enterprises concerning production shortfalls and material shortages and will have to assess the reliability of this information. On the basis of this **nonprice information**, resources will be reallocated within the firm according to perceived indicators of relative scarcity. Managers may allocate internal resources (personnel and trucks) to seek out and transport scarce materials. Ministries and central planners will reallocate materials to enterprises that, according to the scarcity indicators they receive, have relatively high marginal products. According to Powell, these natural responses to scarcity indicators introduce into material balance planning the rationality that allows it to function and survive.

The Input–Output Model

The **input–output model**[24] offers an alternative approach to administrative material balance planning. In theory, it gives planners an opportunity to determine balances quickly (through high-speed computers) and hence to explore alternative resource allocations.

An input–output table is a graphical presentation of the national accounts of an economy and illustrates the flows among the various sectors. The economy is divided into **sectors**, of which there are two broad types—those that produce output (final output for consumption or intermediate output) and those that use final output (either as an intermediate input to further production or as a final consumption item). Sectors may correspond to industries, the number of which depends on the degree of disaggregation. Naturally, the greater the number of sectors, the more accurately the table reflects real economic interrelationships. At the same time, data and computational problems normally place severe limits on size. A simple input–output table is presented in Figure 6.3.

The sum total of goods and services produced (gross domestic product) is equal to the sum total of factor incomes (gross domestic income) used to produce this output. This concept is illustrated in the input–output table. The sum of all inputs used in, say, agriculture (sum of entries in the second column) is numerically equal to the total output of the agricultural sector (sum of entries in the second row). Each column in the input–output table illustrates both the source and the amount of input that will be used from each source in producing output. The inputs are of two types: **primary inputs** (labor, capital, and land) and **intermediate inputs** (steel, agricultural products). At the same time, each row shows how the output of the particular sector (agriculture in this case) is distributed among the various users (of agricultural products). In this table, there are two types of users: industries that use agricultural products as intermediate inputs for manufacturing, and final consumers who use agriculture products directly without further processing.

The input–output table is a simple yet highly useful picture of resource flows in an economic system. We should emphasize, however, that input–output economics relies on several crucial and limiting assumptions.

1. *Aggregation:* Obviously, the fewer the sectors, the easier it is to manipulate the table. The larger the number of branches, the more realistic the table, but the more difficult it is to compile and manipulate. On the other hand, generalized branches such as "agriculture" and "manufacturing" tell us little about the real working arrangements of an economy.
2. *Time frame:* The simple model presented here is *static* and therefore does not allow for change through time. The amount of labor required to produce a unit of steel is assumed not to change over time.
3. *Returns to scale:* We are assuming constant returns to scale. That is, the input–output ratios are the same, regardless of the *volume* of output being produced.

Our interest focuses largely on Quadrant I, for here are the **technical coefficients** that relate inputs to outputs. Specifically, this quadrant tells us how much of a particular input is required to produce a unit of a particular output. Clearly this technical

FIGURE 6.3   Schematic Input–Output Table

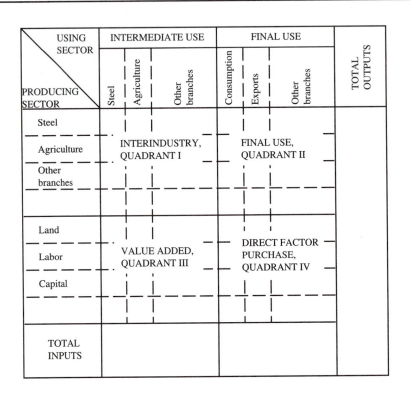

relationship is crucial for specifying what will be produced and what inputs will be available for this production activity. How are these coefficients determined?

If there are i rows and j columns in the input–output matrix, then any cell can be described as a_{ij}, which represents the amount of i that is used to produce a unit of j as a proportion of the total output of j. These technical coefficients are defined in the following manner:

$$a_{ij} = \frac{x_{ij}}{X_j}$$

where

x_{ij} = the amount of input i used in industry j
X_j = the total output of industry j

What is the relationship between the input–output framework and material balance planning? First, knowledge of the matrix of technical coefficients is crucial to the development of a plan, whether that plan is constructed by a simple material balance technique or by more sophisticated methods. For example, if a plan is to be feasible, input availabilities must be sufficient to produce desired outputs. Clearly, knowledge of the technical coefficients can help the planner make such a determination.

Second, if one knows the relationship between inputs and outputs, then with a given feasible objective, one in effect knows the relative worth (value) of different inputs in the production process. Thus a set of **relative prices** can be determined from the input–output model.

Third, the basic input–output model, even with a fair degree of aggregation, provides the planner with important information about the relationship between inputs and outputs.

Suppose the technical coefficients (a_{ij}) are known. How can the planner determine whether a particular objective is possible with available inputs? The input–output model says that for n sectors, the total production of each sector is the sum of intermediate demand and final demand. In notational form, this relationship can be expressed as follows:

$$\sum_{j=1}^{n} x_{ij} + Y_i = X_i \tag{6.1}$$

But we know something about the amount of i needed to produce a unit of j. Specifically, this relationship is

$$x_{ij} = a_{ij}X_j \tag{6.2}$$

Substituting equation 6.2 into equation 6.1, we derive the relationship

$$\sum_{j=1}^{n} a_{ij}X_j + Y_i = X_i \tag{6.3}$$

Rearranging terms yields

$$Y_i = X_i - \sum_{j=1}^{n} a_{ij}X_j \tag{6.4}$$

Equation 6.4 expresses the basic relationship among final demand, interindustry demand, and total production. This basic relationship can be more conveniently expressed in matrix notation as follows:

$$X = AX + Y \tag{6.5}$$

or, by rearranging terms,

$$Y = (I - A)X \tag{6.6}$$

where

I = the identity matrix
X = a vector of planned outputs
A = the matrix of technical coefficients
Y = a vector of final outputs

If the matrix of technical coefficients (A) is known to the planner, then the feasibility of a given vector of plan targets (X) can be readily determined by matrix multiplication. Clearly, even if the focus of the planner should change, knowing any two of the three components of this relationship makes it easier to determine the third component.

How useful is this model in practice? Although aggregation reduces the realism and the practical applicability of the model, it nevertheless remains useful as a method of checking the feasibility of alternative scenarios. The input–output model performs a number of functions: It provides a mathematical formulation of material balances, and it shows how supply–demand balances can be achieved mathematically via computers. Although problems that arise in the real-world collection and manipulation of data limit its applicability, the input–output model supplies the theoretical underpinnings of material balance planning.

Optimization and Economic Planning

Soviet material balance planning was the actual planning method used by the Soviets to allocate resources. As we have noted, Soviet material balance planning was a pragmatic method for planning an economy by administrative means. Its objective was to provide a rough balance between supplies and demands of a relatively limited number of key industrial commodities. Because of its administrative complexity, Soviet material balance planning aimed at achieving a balance; it did not aim at achieving the optimal balance.

The theory of economic planning focuses on the problem of achieving an *optimal* balance. It shows how, in theory, planners can plan for the economy to produce the optimal combinations of outputs, subject to the constraints of limited land, labor, and capital resources. No present-day economy actually allocates resources by using administrative planning techniques that select detailed optimal combinations of outputs. Although the solution to such a planning problem is evident in theory, in practice it is elusive.

The planning problem can be expressed in the following manner:

$$\text{Maximize } U = U(X_1, X_2, \ldots, X_n) \qquad i = 1, \ldots, n \qquad \textbf{(6.7)}$$

Here X_i are products that are produced subject to existing technology:

$$X_i = f(u_1, u_2, \ldots, u_m) \qquad \textbf{(6.8)}$$

where u_j are resources (land, labor, materials, and others) and are subject to

$$u_j \leq b_j \qquad j = 1, \ldots, m \qquad \textbf{(6.9)}$$

where b_j represents resource availabilities, and u_j represents the total amount of resource j used by all producers. Moreover, resources are employed at zero or positive levels:

$$u_j \geq 0 \qquad \textbf{(6.10)}$$

The goal of planning is to achieve the maximal value of equation 6.7, which is termed the **objective function**. The objective function summarizes the planners' economic objectives and provides a precise relationship between the utility derived by society (U) and the output of goods and services (X_i) from which that social utility, or satisfaction, is derived. In turn, the magnitude of goods and services available is a function of resource availabilities (u_j) with given technology. Resources cannot be used beyond their available supplies (b_j), either in the aggregate or for any individual resource.

The critics of the Barone model explained why such optimal planning is virtually impossible in practice. First, an economy produces millions of distinct products and factor inputs. Even with powerful computers, it is not possible to solve the millions of simultaneous equations for the optimal combinations of inputs and outputs. To reduce the computational problem to manageable proportions, planners would have to work with aggregations of distinct commodities (such as tons of steel or square meters of textiles). Real-world economies do not operate with aggregated commodities. Factories require steel goods of specific grades and qualities. To go from a planning solution based on aggregate inputs or outputs to real production and distribution processes is an extremely complicated problem. Second, even if planners could gather the necessary information and make the complicated calculations, it is still not clear how to get enterprises actually to produce the planned commodities by using optimal combinations of inputs. This is the problem of creating an incentive scheme that encourages firms to implement the optimal production and distribution computed by planners. A related problem is the generation and processing of data. The information burden on planners is already excessive even if there is accurate and unbiased reporting by the enterprises. Moreover, planners might find it difficult to elicit accurate information from enterprises, whose success or failure might hinge on these statistical reports.

A final problem with optimal planning is obtaining agreement on the objective function of society. How are planners to know what goods and services are more important than others? Presumably, planners would have some insights on this issue, but the more complex the economy became, the more difficult it might be to determine the relative social valuations of different goods and services. In a complex economy, planners must know whether industrial plastics are more important than stainless steel or ceramics, which might serve similar functions as substitutes.

Coordination: How Much Market? How Much Plan?

In our discussion of planning, two themes emerge. First, there is the matter of how much control the central planning board is to exercise over economic outcomes. Should all decisions be made from above by planners, or should there be some decentralization to lower levels? Second, there is the matter of actually solving the plan to achieve both consistency and optimality. In most planned socialist systems, the practical approaches to these problems involve simplification through limitation of the formal planning procedures to important outputs and inputs, and a downgrading of the optimality criterion. Furthermore, mistakes are typically absorbed by low-priority (buffer) sectors. Also, most real-world systems utilize intermediate arrangements that combine plan and market. For sectors viewed by the planners as crucial to the achievement of state objectives (for example, steel), the CPB plays an important role; for sectors viewed as substantially less important (for example, light industrial goods), the CPB may play a minor role. Most approach planning as only a partial means for the allocation of resources. The "priority principle" (that is, focusing on important sectors such as steel and chemicals) serves to limit the range of inputs and outputs planned at the center. Plan techniques are of the material balance type; they are substantially distant from the more sophisticated and theoretically elegant optimization models that we have described.

Critics of the planned socialist system argue that the complexities of the real world make it impossible for the CPB to handle its tasks, let alone to expect the individual firm to follow its directives. The supporters of planned socialism, on the other hand, have argued that choices in production and consumption are generally much simpler than neoclassical economic theory implies. These sorts of issues remain at the center of the debate over the relative merits of the plan versus the market.

The theory of planning stresses the **formulation of a plan**, consisting of a set of objectives and the means for achieving the objectives. However, plans are of little value unless they are implemented. Implementation calls for incentives that induce economic agents to achieve the goals planners have set. The record of the Soviet Union and other planned socialist economic systems shows that ensuring appropriate motivation is a serious problem. Managers frequently work with plan objectives that are poorly specified, if not contradictory. When managers are asked to **execute plans** with limited information under such conditions, a large element of informal (and often dysfunctional) decision making takes over where plan directives were intended to be dominant.

The Performance of Planned Socialism: Hypotheses

Chapter 5 put forth several hypotheses concerning the expected performance of capitalist economic systems in terms of the performance criteria of income distribution, efficiency, economic growth, and stability. We shall now attempt to do the same for socialist economic systems.

Because we have no paradigm of socialist economic systems, the formulation of hypotheses is especially difficult. Moreover, it is difficult to formulate hypotheses independently of the performance of real-world socialism. We now know a great deal about the efficiency problems of planned socialism in practice. Although it does not constitute a scientific approach to hypotheses formulation, real-world experience is hard to ignore.

Income Distribution

The first hypothesis is obvious. Income should be more evenly distributed under planned socialism than under capitalism. The state (society) owns capital and land, and the returns on these assets go to the state. It is conceivable, but not likely, that the state will distribute this nonlabor income *less* equitably than capitalist societies. Presumably, authorities in planned socialist economies attach considerable importance to the "fair" distribution of income. We therefore expect income to be distributed relatively equally in a planned socialist economy.

Efficiency

The critics of planned socialism believe that planned socialist economies have difficulty in efficiently allocating resources. Planners, they feel, would have great difficulty in processing information, constructing a plan, and motivating participants. Moreover, the planned socialist economy would not automatically generate relative prices that would enable participants to make good use of resources. These theoretical difficulties suggest the hypothesis that planned socialist economies operate at relatively low levels of efficiency. Planning techniques that aim at optimality still have limited real-world applicability, and planned socialist economies have had to use material balance planning procedures that are unlikely to place them on their production possibilities frontiers (see Figure 3.2). In fact, the aim of material balance planning is consistency, not optimality. Thus the hypothesis that the planned socialist economies do not perform well in terms of both dynamic and static efficiency appears to be a fairly safe one.

Economic Growth

In planned socialism, the state is able to exercise greater control over investment and savings rates than under capitalism. This is true because virtually all nonlabor income accrues to the state. One would therefore expect a higher savings rate under both forms of socialism, because the socialist state is likely to adopt rapid growth as a priority objective (the building of socialism).

In the planned socialist economies, rapid growth is promoted both by the high savings rate and by the planners' direction of resources into growth-maximizing pursuits. At first glance, therefore, it would appear that one should hypothesize a higher growth rate for the planned socialist economies. The complicating factor, however, is the hypothesized lower efficiency of the planned socialist economies. Thus we must again refrain from stating a strong hypothesis about the relative growth of planned socialism, an issue that must be investigated empirically.

Stability

We hypothesize that the planned socialist economies will be more stable than their capitalist counterparts. In making this statement, we do not deny that significant concealed instabilities (repressed inflation, underemployment) will be present in the planned socialist economies. We base our hypothesis of greater stability on the following considerations. First, investment spending will be subject to the control of planners and will probably be maintained at a fairly stable rate. Thus fluctuations in investment spending (a major source of instability in capitalist economies) will probably be small. Second, material balance planning will lead to an approximate balance of labor supplies and demands. Third, supplies and demands for consumer goods will be subject to a great deal of state control (planners set industrial wages and determine the output of consumer goods). Moreover, the state will be less subject to popular pressures to pursue inflationary monetary policies. Fourth, firms operating under pressure to meet output targets will provide workers with guaranteed jobs.

Summary

- Socialism emphasizes central planning as a mechanism to organize resource allocation.
- Socialism typically combines a strong state with public ownership and a set of policies designed to change economic outcomes.
- In the socialist system, the primary source of income is labor, socialization of consumption is an objective, and the egalitarian distribution of output is pursued.
- The state exercises substantial control over economic growth and industrial expansion.
- In the view of Marx and Lenin, socialism is the inevitable outcome of social and economic progress.
- At the beginning of the twentieth century, Barone demonstrated the theoretical feasibility of socialist resource allocation but failed to develop a realistic scheme.
- Critics of socialism focus on inefficiencies of resource allocation in a system without markets.
- Hayek and Mises viewed socialism as inefficient because of difficulties in computation and evaluation and a lack of incentives.
- A national economic plan is used to allocate resources within the central planning framework in socialist economies.
- Socialist economies are normally organized in a hierarchial fashion with a central planning board (CPB) that is responsible for directing enterprises in using inputs to produce good and services.
- Socialist systems use a system of balances (material balance planning) even though input–output analysis is the theoretical basis for planning.

Key Terms

socialism

communism

dictatorship of the proletariat

socialist controversy

relative valuations

central planning board

planned socialist economy

vertical transaction

horizontal transaction

balances of the national economy

material balances

law of value

national economic plan

indicative planning

directive planning

balance

interindustry demand

final demand

consistent plan

optimality

nonprice information   technical coefficients
input–output model   relative prices
sectors   objective function
primary inputs   plan formulation
intermediate inputs   plan execution

Notes

1. See A. C. Pigou, *Socialism Versus Capitalism* (New York: St. Martin's, 1960), Ch. 1. For a brief definition, see Benjamin N. Ward, *The Socialist Economy* (New York: Random House, 1967), Ch. 1; for a broader definition, see J. Wilczynski, *The Economics of Socialism* (London: Unwin Hyman, 1970), Ch. 1; for another summary, see Tom Bottomore, *The Socialist Economy: Theory and Practice* (New York: Harvester Wheatsheaf, 1990).

2. If the marginal utility of income is identical and declining for all individuals, then an equal distribution of income would maximize social benefit.

3. In the Marxian schema, capitalism is the engine that was to create the developed and industrialized economy; socialism would be concerned with providing an "equitable" distribution of the productive capacity developed under capitalism. Although socialism was not intended to be the mechanism for economic development, this is precisely the role in which it has been cast.

4. For a survey, see R. N. Carew Hunt, *The Theory and Practice of Communism* (Harmondsworth, England: Penguin Books, 1963), Chs. 6 and 15.

5. Lenin's views on this matter are elaborated in his *State and Revolution,* published in 1917.

6. This view, though largely discredited during the period of war communism in the Soviet Union, has remained influential in present-day Soviet attitudes toward industrial and agricultural management. This attitude is used to support the argument for technical rather than managerial training in large enterprises.

7. The important articles on this debate can be found in F. A. Hayek, ed., *Collectivist Economic Planning,* 6th ed. (London: Routledge and Kegan Paul, 1963).

8. See Ludwig von Mises, "Economic Calculation in Socialism," in Morris Bornstein, ed., *Comparative Economic Systems,* rev. ed. (Homewood, Ill.: Irwin, 1969), pp. 61–68.

9. The best source for the original article by Oskar Lange and related discussion is Benjamin Lippincott, ed., *On the Economic Theory of Socialism* (Minneapolis: University of Minnesota Press, 1938), reprinted by McGraw-Hill in 1964.

10. Pigou, *Socialism Versus Capitalism,* Ch. 1.

11. Abram Bergson, *Essays in Normative Economics* (Cambridge, Mass.: Harvard University Press, 1966), Ch. 9; also see Abram Bergson, "Market Socialism Revisited," *Journal of Political Economy* 75 (October 1967), 663–675; for contemporary views, see Don Lavoie, *Rivalry and Central Planning: The Socialist Calculation Debate Reconsidered* (New York: Cambridge University Press, 1985); Peter Murrell, "Did the Theory of Market Socialism Answer the Challenge of Ludwig von Mises? A Reinterpretation of the Socialist Controversy," *History of Political Economy* 15 (September 1981), 261–276.

12. Ronald Wintrobe, *The Political Economy of Dictatorship.* (Cambridge and New York: Cambridge University Press, 1998).

13. P. Boettke, *Calculation and Coordination* (London and New York: Routledge, 2001).

14. Mancur Olson, "The Devolution of Power in Post-Communist Societies," in Robert Skidelsky, ed., *Russia's Stormy Path to Reform* (London: Social Market Foundation, 1995), pp. 9–42.

15. See Leon Smolinski, "The Origins of Soviet Mathematical Economics," in Franz-Lothar Altmann, ed., *Jahrbuch der Wirtschaft Osteuropas* [Yearbook of East European Economics], Band 2 (Munich: Gunter Olzog Verlag, 1971), pp. 137–154.

16. The most famous Soviet growth model is by P. A. Feldman and is discussed in Evsey Domar, *Essays in the Theory of Economic Growth* (New York: Oxford University Press, 1957), pp. 233–261. The classic work on the Soviet industrialization debate is Alexander Erlich, *The Soviet Industrialization Debate, 1924–1928* (Cambridge, Mass.: Harvard University Press, 1962).

17. R. W. Davies and S. G. Wheatcroft, eds., *Materials for a Balance of the National Economy 1928/29* (Cambridge, England: Cambridge University Press, 1985).

18. Gerald Sirkin, *The Visible Hand: The Fundamentals of Economic Planning* (New York: McGraw-Hill, 1968), p. 45.

19. Abdul Qayum, *Techniques of National Economic Planning* (Bloomington: Indiana University Press, 1975), p. 4.

20. Michael P. Todaro, *Development Planning: Models and Methods* (Nairobi: Oxford University Press, 1971), p. 1.

21. G. M. Heal, *The Theory of Economic Planning* (New York: American Elsevier, 1973), p. 5.

22. *Political Economy: A Textbook,* 4th ed. (Berlin: Deitz, 1964), pp. 496 and 499.

23. Raymond Powell, "Plan Execution and the Workability of Soviet Planning," *Journal of Comparative Economics* 1 (March 1977), 51–76.

24. H. B. Chenery and P. G. Clark, *Interindustry Economics* (New York: Wiley, 1959); R. Dorfman, P. Samuelson, and R. Solow, *Linear Programming and Economic Analysis* (New York: McGraw-Hill, 1958); W. W. Leontief, *Input–Output Economics* (New York: Oxford University Press, 1966); Michael P. Todaro, *Development Planning: Models and Methods* (Nairobi: Oxford University Press, 1971); and Vladimir Treml, "Input–Output Analysis and Soviet Planning," in John Hardt *et al.,* eds., *Mathematics and Computers in Soviet Planning* (New Haven: Yale University Press, 1967); for a discussion in the development context, see E. Wayne Nafziger, *The Economics of Developing Countries,* 2nd ed. (Englewood Cliffs, N.J.: Prentice-Hall, 1990), Ch. 19.

Recommended Readings

Traditional Sources

Abram Bergson, "Socialist Economics," in Howard Ellis, ed., *A Survey of Contemporary Economics* (Philadelphia: Blakiston, 1948).

——, "Market Socialism Revisited," *Journal of Political Economy* 75 (October 1967), 655–673.

R. N. Carew-Hunt, *The Theory and Practice of Communism* (Harmondsworth, England: Penguin, 1963).

G. D. H. Cole, *Socialist Economics* (London: Gollancz, 1950).

Maurice Dobb, *Welfare Economics and the Economics of Socialism* (Cambridge, England: Cambridge University Press, 1969).

F. A. Hayek, ed., *Collectivist Economic Planning,* 6th ed. (London: Routledge and Kegan Paul, 1963).

Michael P. Todaro, *Development Planning: Models and Methods* (Nairobi: Oxford University Press, 1971).

Benjamin N. Ward, *The Socialist Economy* (New York: Random House, 1967).

The Socialist Economy

Pranab K. Bardhan and John E. Roemer, eds., *Market Socialism: The Current Debate* (New York: Oxford University Press, 1993).

Tom Bottomore, *The Socialist Economy: Theory and Practice* (New York: Harvester Wheatsheaf, 1990).

Bernard Crick, *Socialism* (Minneapolis: University of Minnesota Press, 1987).

Don Lavoie, *Rivalry and Central Planning: The Socialist Calculation Debate Reconsidered* (New York: Cambridge University Press, 1985).

Andrew Levine, *Arguing for Socialism: Theoretical Considerations* (London: Routledge and Kegan Paul, 1984).

Peter Murrell, "Did the Theory of Market Socialism Answer the Challenge of Ludwig von Mises? A Reinterpretation of the Socialist Controversy," *History of Political Economy* 15 (September 1984), 261–276.

———, "Incentives and Income Under Market Socialism," *Journal of Comparative Economics* 8 (September 1984), 261–276.

Alec Nove, *The Economics of Feasible Socialism* (Winchester, Mass.: Unwin Hyman, 1983).

S. Pejovich, *Socialism: Institutional, Philosophical, and Economic Issues* (Norwell, Mass.: Kluwer Academic Publishers, 1987).

James A. Yunker, *Socialism Revised and Modernized: The Case for Pragmatic Market Socialism* (New York: Praeger, 1992).

Economic Planning

John Bennett, *The Economic Theory of Central Planning* (Cambridge: Blackwell, 1989).

Morris Bornstein, ed., *Economic Planning, East and West* (Oxford: Ballinger, 1975).

Roger A. Bowles and David K. Whynes, *Macroeconomic Planning* (London: Unwin Hyman, 1979).

Phillip J. Bryson, *Scarcity and Control in Socialism* (Lexington, Mass.: Heath, 1976).

Parkash Chander and Ashok Pavikh, "Theory and Practice of Decentralized Planning Procedures," *Journal of Economic Surveys* 4 (1990), 19–58.

Pawel H. Dembinski, *The Logic of the Planned Economy* (Oxford: Clarendon Press, 1991).

G. M. Heal, *The Theory of Economic Planning* (New York: American Elsevier, 1973).

Zoltan Kenessey, *The Process of Economic Planning* (New York: Columbia University Press, 1978).

Don Lavoie, *National Economic Planning: What Is Left?* (Oxford: Ballinger, 1985).

Abdul Qayum, *Techniques of National Economic Planning* (Bloomington: Indiana University Press, 1975).

Gerald Sirkin, *The Visible Hand: The Fundamentals of Economic Planning* (New York: McGraw-Hill, 1968).

Nicolas Spulber and Ira Horowitz, *Quantitative Economic Policy and Planning* (New York: Norton, 1976).

7

Theory of Market Socialism

Market socialism is, as the term suggests, a hybrid of market and state ownership. It is an economic system that combines social ownership of capital with market allocation. As such, it offers the potential of combining the "fairness" of social-ism with the efficiency associated with market allocation. The state owns the means of production, and returns to capital accrue to society at large. Because resources are allocated primarily by markets, many of the problems of planned socialism—the administrative and computational burdens and the problem of valuing resources—appear to be avoided.

This chapter presents the theory of market socialism. Unlike the perfectly com-petitive model of capitalism, there is no single paradigm of market socialism. Instead, there are alternative visions of market socialism, one characterized by state ownership of the means of production, the other by worker ownership. Both visions rely on mar-kets (or at least artificial markets) to do the job of resource allocation.

Whereas it is possible to study the actual workings of both market capitalism and planned socialism, the world has little experience with market socialism. This lack of real-world practice makes the theory of market socialism even more important. We must rely heavily on theory to understand the properties of this type of economic sys-tem. As this chapter shows, market socialism has both advantages and drawbacks. The major problems appear to be how to motivate participants to use resources effi-ciently and how to make markets work when private individuals do not own capital.

The appeal of market socialism is obvious. The widespread rejection of planned socialism in the late 1980s and 1990s has elevated market socialism to the status of the major alternative to capitalism. The new leaderships of the former Soviet Republic and in Eastern Europe may ultimately find market socialism a more palatable solution than market capitalism insofar as it promises to avoid the more negative features of market capitalism. Put another way, the demise of communism in Eastern Europe does not mean the demise of socialist thought and of democratic variants of social-ism. The latter will continue to have appeal, especially in poor countries striving to achieve improved standards of living.

Market Socialism: Theoretical Foundations

The problems of optimal planning—computational difficulty and motivation—make market socialism appealing. Permitting the market to direct a number of resource-allocation decisions reduces the burden on the **central planning board** (CPB). Also, by allowing individual participants to respond to market incentives, market social-ism may offer greater inducements to combine resources efficiently at the local level.

Advocates of market socialism have had to answer two questions raised by Hayek and Mises (see Chapter 6). If the means of production are owned by society, what assurances are there that capital will be used efficiently? And will the social ownership of capital distort incentives or lead to perverse economic behavior?

The Lange Model

The most famous theoretical model of market socialism is the **trial-and-error model** proposed by the Polish economist Oskar Lange.[1] This model focuses on the use of a general equilibrium framework (emphasized in the writings of Barone, Pareto, and Walras), approaching a "solution" through a number of sequential stages (emphasized by Walras).

A number of economists (most notably H. D. Dickinson and Abba Lerner) con-tributed to the Lange model, and a number of variants of the model exist.[2] Further-more, the **Lange model** of market socialism differs from our definition of market socialism in that Lange envisioned only indirect usage of the market.

What are the essential features of the Lange-type market socialist model? The model posits three levels of decision making (see Figure 7.1). At the lowest level are firms and households; at the intermediate level, industrial authorities; and at the highest level, a CPB. The means of production, with the exception of labor, are state-owned. Consumer goods are allocated by the market.

The CPB would set the prices of producer goods. Producing firms would be informed of these prices and would be instructed to produce in accordance with two rules: Produce the level of output at which price is equal to marginal cost, and min-imize the cost of production at that output. Households could make their own deci-sions about how much labor to supply.

Because the initial prices of producer goods would be arbitrarily set by the CPB, there is no reason to believe that as firms followed the rules (assuming that they did in fact follow the rules), the "right" amount of goods and services would be pro-duced and supplies and demands would be in balance. What would the planners do if there were an imbalance?

If there were an excess supply of a particular good, its price would be lowered by the CPB. If there were excess demand, its price would be raised by the CPB. Thus, in a sequential process, the CPB would adjust prices until they were at the "right" levels—that is, where supply and demand were balanced.

In addition to setting prices, the central planning board would also allocate the social dividend (rents and profits) earned from the use of productive resources owned by the state. This dividend could be distributed in the form of public services or investment, the latter decision being made in conjunction with the intermediate in-dustrial authorities. The state would have a substantial degree of power because it could determine both the magnitude and the direction of investment, though Lange argued that investment funds should be generally allocated to equalize marginal rates

FIGURE 7.1   The Organization of Market Socialism in the Lange Framework

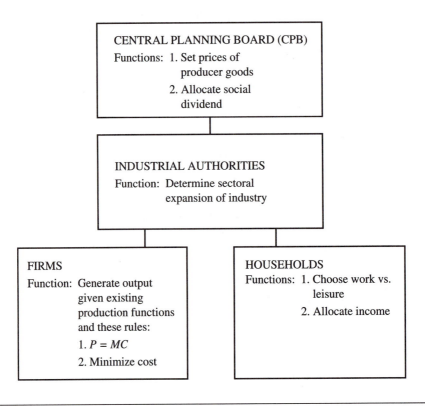

of return in different applications. Considerable central control over the economic system would be maintained by the CPB. At the same time, prices would be used for decision making to relieve the CPB of a substantial administrative task.

Let us examine some of the proposed advantages of the Lange model. Lange envisioned that with the means of production owned by the state, both the *rate* and the *direction* of economic activity would be determined in large part by the state. Thus the returns from and the influence of private ownership would be removed. Accordingly, the distribution of income would be substantially more even than under capitalism. Furthermore, the mix of output would be different, and insofar as the investment ratio would be a major determinant of the rate of economic growth, this rate too would be largely state-determined. Both these features of the Lange model (a more even distribution of income and state control over investment) are presumed advantages.

Lange argued that externalities could be better accounted for because the state could manipulate resource prices. Other economists—for example, Jan Tinbergen and Maurice Dobb—have argued that, in general, decisions made at higher levels rather than lower levels are likely to be "better" in terms of preventing undesirable environmental effects.[3] Lange further presumed that state control over savings and investment would reduce cyclical instability, a mainstay in the socialist critique of capitalism.

Real-world market systems depart from the perfectly competitive model. Simulation of the market, argued Lange, would utilize the positive aspects of the market while eliminating its negative characteristics. In this context, it is ironic that Lange said little about the problems that would arise when difficulties of entry, economies of scale, and changes in technology were present. These forces are crucial in determining the degree of competition in a capitalist economic system. Might not some of these problems arise in the real-world operation of a Lange-type model?

Critics of the Lange Model

The Lange model captured the fancy of many observers over the years, but it has not been without critics. Lange himself recognized that the many tasks assigned to the CPB could lead to a large bureaucracy, long considered a negative feature of socialism. The most outspoken critic on this score has been Nobel laureate Friederick Hayek. Hayek suggested that although the task set for the CPB might be manageable in theory, it would probably be unmanageable in practice.[4]

Abram Bergson and others have pointed to a key problem in the Lange model: that of ensuring appropriate managerial motivation.[5] How would the intermediate authorities, and especially enterprise managers, be motivated to follow Lange's rules of conduct even if they knew marginal costs? The problem of establishing a workable incentive structure has been a major theme in modern socialist economic systems.

Bergson also emphasized the possibility of monopolistic behavior in the Lange framework—if not at the enterprise level, then at the intermediate level. This problem and the matter of relating one level to another are substantially neglected in the original formulation of the Lange model.

Although the Lange model uses features of capitalism, it is also characterized by many elements normally associated with socialism. The scholarly literature, therefore, has tended to focus on whether the Lange model can operate in reality and, if so, how effectively. The Lange model has also sparked great interest because most existing socialist systems use a crude form of trial and error for the setting of prices, at least for consumer goods. Real-world reliance on the trial-and-error methods is important, for mathematical models of planning (and price formulation) have been of limited practical use in spite of their theoretical elegance.[6]

Market Socialism: The Cooperative Variant

A second variant of market socialism is the **cooperative economy** or **labor-managed economy** or, more specifically, the **producer cooperative**.[7] The interest in worker participation stems from both the theory of cooperative economic behavior elaborated in this section and the systems of worker management used in Yugoslavia, Western Europe, and now Eastern Europe.

The cooperative model of market socialism stems from the notion that people should participate in making the decisions that affect their well-being. Jaroslav Vanek, a major early advocate of the **participatory economy**, emphasizes this theme:

> The quest of men to participate in the determination and decision-making of the activities in which they are personally and directly involved is one of the most important sociopolitical phenomena of our times. It is very likely to be the dominant force of social evolution in the last third of the twentieth century.[8]

Vanek uses five characteristics to identify the participatory economy:

1. Firms will be managed in participatory fashion by the people working in them.
2. Income sharing will prevail and is to be equitable—that is, "equal for labor of equal intensity and quality, and governed by a democratically agreed-upon income-distribution schedule assigning to each job its relative claim on total net income."[9]
3. Although the workers may enjoy the fruits of the operation, they do not own, and must therefore pay for the use of, productive resources.
4. The economy must always be a market economy. Economic planning may be used through indirect mechanisms, but "never through a direct order to a firm or group of firms."[10]
5. There is freedom of choice in employment.

In essence, resources are state-owned but are managed by the workers in the enterprises, whose objective is to create a maximal dividend per worker. Cooperative socialism belongs to the more general category of market socialism, because there is state ownership of the means of production but also an exchange of goods and services in the market without intervention by central planners. Producer goods would use market prices, as opposed to prices manipulated by the CPB in the Lange framework. The cooperative form of socialism has been viewed as an important and path-breaking addition to socialist thinking, especially by those who would identify with democratic socialism as a political system.

Theoretical analysis of the cooperative model dates from an article by Benjamin Ward published in 1958 and the subsequent early elaboration of the participatory economy by Vanek and thereafter by many authors.[11] Resources (with the exception of labor) are owned by the state and will be used by each firm, for which a fee will be paid to the state. Prices for both producer goods and consumer goods will be determined by supply and demand in the market. Enterprises will be managed by the workers (who may hire a professional manager responsible to them), who will attempt to maximize the dividend per worker (**net income per worker**) in the enterprise. With this objective, management must decide on input and output combinations.

In addition to levying a charge for the use of capital assets and for land, the state will administer the public sector of the economy and may levy taxes to finance cultural and industrial development. In this environment, how will the cooperative firm behave? Let us examine two cases: first, the short run, where there is a variable supply of labor but capital is fixed; second, the long run, where both labor and capital are variable.

The cooperative model assumes that the enterprise manager wishes to maximize net earnings per worker (Y/L) and that output (Q) is solely a function of the labor input (*L*) in the short run. The output can be sold on the market at a price (*P*) dictated by *market* forces. The firm must pay a fixed tax (*T*) on its capital. In the short-run variant, capital is fixed; so is the tax. Under these conditions, the firm will seek to maximize the following expression:

$$Y/L = \frac{PQ - T}{L} \tag{7.1}$$

where

Y/L = net income per worker
P = price of the product
Q = quantity produced
T = fixed tax levied on capital
L = labor input

Maximum net income per worker in equation 7.1 will be achieved when the amount of labor hired (*L*) is such that the value of the marginal product of the last worker hired is the same as the average net earnings per worker, or, in terms of the notation of equation 7.1, when the following balance is achieved:

$$P \cdot MP_L = \frac{(PQ - T)}{L} \tag{7.2}$$

where

MP_L = marginal product of labor

The logic of this solution is quite simple. If the enterprise can increase average net revenue by hiring another worker—that is, if the marginal product of the last worker hired is greater than average net revenue—then the worker should be hired, and average net revenue can be increased. The addition of workers should continue until the value of the marginal product of the last person hired and the average net revenue are the same. If the manager were to hire, at the margin, a worker the value of whose marginal product was less than the average net revenue per worker, then the net income of the remaining workers would fall.

In the *long run,* the cooperative must select its optimal capital stock (*K*), on which it will pay a rental charge (*r*) per unit of capital used. The firm now seeks to maximize its average net revenue as given by the following expression:

$$Y/L = \frac{PQ - rK}{L} \tag{7.3}$$

where

K = amount of capital
r = charge per unit of capital

The maximal value of this expression (average net revenue per worker) will be achieved in a manner similar to that of the short-run case. As long as the value of the marginal product of capital ($P \cdot MP_K$) is greater than the rental rate (*r*) paid on capital, more capital should be hired and utilized until the return and the cost are equalized ($P \cdot MP_K = r$). This rule applies to the perfectly competitive capitalist firm and the Lange-type firm as well. The same rule as for equation 7.2 would apply for the hiring of labor, except that the charge for variable capital would have to be deducted as follows:

$$P \cdot MP_L = \frac{PQ - rK}{L} \tag{7.4}$$

These two cases, the short run and the long run, are both simple variants of the cooperative model. The short-run case is elaborated diagrammatically in Figure 7.2. Note that the model assumes that both product and factor markets are perfectly competitive and that there is no interference by the state.

The cooperative model works through product and factor markets. Households supply labor services as a consequence of maximizing household utility in the choice of work versus leisure. Labor supply schedules are determined in this way, as are

FIGURE 7.2   The Cooperative Model

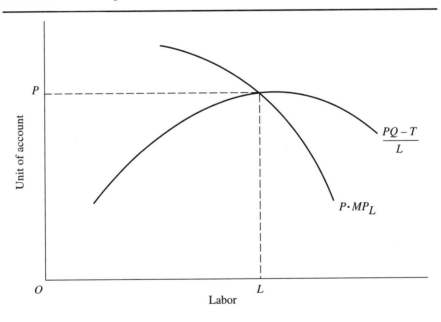

Explanation:

$$\frac{PQ - T}{L} = net \text{ receipts per worker}$$

$$P \cdot MP_L = \text{marginal value product of labor}$$

If the cooperative wishes to maximize the value of net receipts per worker, it should hire labor until the value of the marginal product of the last worker hired is the same as the net receipts per worker. In the diagram, the cooperative would hire *OL* labor, and each worker would receive *OP*.

demand schedules for consumer goods. Firms maximize net revenue per worker and in so doing are prepared to supply goods and services at various prices and, at the same time, to purchase inputs at various prices.

There is a close relationship between the cooperative model and the competitive capitalist and Lange models. In essence, the cooperative model captures the efficiency features of both. In the Lange model, the firm follows two rules, equating price and marginal cost and minimizing average cost of production. In the cooperative model, these two rules are replaced by a single rule (in the short run represented by equation 7.2). In the case of the capitalist market economy, the firm follows the rule of equating marginal cost and marginal revenue, which in the case of perfect competition reduces to the Lange rule; so here too, the cooperative variant simply replaces this rule with equation 7.2.

There is now a considerable body of literature on the cooperative model and its variants. Many pertinent issues have been raised by the model's critics as well as by its admirers.

Criticism of the Cooperative Model

The cooperative model has been analyzed in detail by Benjamin Ward. Ward notes that the two key features of the model are "individual material self-interest as the dominant human motivation" and "the resort to markets as the means of allocating resources."[12] Ward devoted considerable attention to analyzing the response of the cooperative to various changes in capital charges, taxes, input prices, and product prices.[13] For the capitalist and the Lange-type firm, an increase in price induces an increase in output (that is, a positively sloped supply curve). Ward demonstrated that the cooperative supply curve may well be negatively sloped (that is, an increase in price generates a *decrease* in output), especially in the short run.[14] If true, this would certainly be a perverse and undesirable result, especially in an economy where resources are allocated by the market. Such a result might (though it would not necessarily) threaten both the existence and the stability of equilibrium in product markets.

Ward also argued that if two cooperatives producing an identical product use different technologies, there will be a misallocation of labor and capital that would not occur if the two were capitalist firms.[15] In the case of the capitalist firms, both would hire labor until the wage was equal to the value of the marginal product ($W = P \cdot MP_L$), for both would face the same market-determined wage (W) and hence would generate the same value of marginal product. In the case of the cooperative, however, unless the production functions are identical, the average net revenue per worker will differ between the two cooperatives. Although each cooperative equates average net revenue per worker with the marginal product of the last worker hired, overall output could be increased by moving workers to the cooperatives where the value of the marginal product is higher.

Ward also argued that the cooperative might be undesirable if it existed in a noncompetitive environment.[16] Specifically, he contends that the monopolistic cooperative would be less efficient than either its competitive cooperative twin or its monopolistic capitalist twin. The monopolistic cooperative would hire less labor, produce less output, and charge a higher price than either the competitive cooperative or the monopolistic capitalist firm.

Critics of the Lange model raised the issue of how to ensure appropriate managerial motivation. To the extent that the cooperative utilizes hired professional management, the problem of how to motivate and regulate managers will exist. Ward noted that in some cases the cooperative would have the incentive to expand, although in the absence of private property holding, it is not clear who the entrepreneur would be.[17] It is possible that the state would play an important role here because it would control some of the investment funds.

Advantages of the Cooperative Model

Strong support for the cooperative model comes from Jaroslav Vanek, who argues that the participatory economy is an element of social evolution that will be especially important in future years.[18] In addition to prescribing the participatory economy for present-day economies, Vanek argues that it is also the best alternative for developing economies.

Vanek does not agree with Ward's criticisms. He argues that if two cooperative firms have access to identical technology, and if there is free entry and exit, the input–output decisions of the cooperatives will be identical to those of two capitalist firms operating under the same conditions.[19] Moreover, Vanek argues, the result will be much more desirable socially, because in the capitalist case the workers are rewarded according to the value of the marginal products, whereas under the cooperative case, workers are rewarded according to the decision of the collective, which they themselves control.

Vanek also maintains that under certain likely cases, the supply curve of the cooperative firm will not be negatively sloped as Ward suggests. Vanek shows that if the cooperative is a multiproduct firm, or if it faces an external constraint (for example, a limited supply of labor), the firm's supply curve will be positively sloped.

Vanek argues that the imperfectly competitive cooperative firm will be superior to the imperfectly competitive capitalist firm because it will have no incentive to grow extremely large and hence to dominate a particular market. Further, the cooperative will have no incentive to act in a socially wasteful manner—to create artificial demand for a product through advertising. Finally, Vanek maintains that both the demand for investment and the supply of savings will tend to be greater in the cooperative than in the competitive capitalist environment.

Many of the issues surrounding the comparative performance of cooperative and capitalist firms seem highly abstract and theoretical. They are, however, of basic importance to the efficiency of each system. The response of the cooperative firm to market signals determines the extent to which it can meet consumer goals and, in the long run, the extent to which an appropriate industrial structure is established in line with long-term development goals and aspirations.

Many of the supporters of the cooperative model, especially Vanek, argue that beyond these specific performance characteristics, the crucial features of the cooperative would be its "special dimensions." Among the most important is elimination of the capitalist dichotomy between management and labor. It is also argued that there would be greater social justice in the distribution of rewards.[20]

The Participatory Economy in the Twenty-First Century

The pioneering work of Benjamin Ward in the late 1950s and the subsequent elaboration by Jaroslav Vanek in the late 1960s spawned a large and ever-growing body of literature devoted to the broad concepts of labor management and, more specifically, to producer cooperatives as a means of organizing production in an economy. A survey by John Bonin, Derek Jones, and Louis Putterman provides an excellent basis for understanding the current state of the cooperative model.[21]

The body of literature on cooperatives is large but diverse and mainly theoretical; there has been little empirical verification. This is partly because the practical use of cooperatives in real-world economies has been limited, though it has grown in recent years. The lack of empirical work on cooperatives reflects the absence of appropriate data for evaluation purposes; it also reflects the nature of the theoretical models, which tend to be highly abstract, and the great deal of diversity among cooperatives in real-world economies.

In addition, many of the outcomes of the earlier, simple models are evidently not robust under more realistic circumstances. For example, contemporary research demonstrates that the existence of a negatively sloped supply curve depends heavily on the original assumptions of early models and is not generally found in contemporary specifications where "the focus shifts to the membership as the constituent decision-making body or when reasonable labor supply considerations are added."[22] Moreover, limited empirical evidence seems to support the contemporary view.

Contemporary empirical evidence on issues related to worker effort and productivity in producer cooperatives does not provide clear-cut answers. Bonin *et al.,* in their survey of this empirical literature, found that participation variables are important when explaining differences in outcomes. There seems to be a positive relationship between profit sharing and productivity; however, isolating the impact of other types of participation has proved difficult.

Finally, the literature places considerable emphasis on the potential problems of self-financing of producer cooperatives, on the assumption that members will distribute internal funds to themselves rather than expand the capital stock in the absence of appropriate property rights. On the basis of existing empirical evidence, Bonin *et al.* conclude that no econometric evidence supports this proposition.[23]

Despite the relatively few producer cooperatives in contemporary market economies, their existence provides growing evidence that presents them much more favorably than the early and simple models of cooperative behavior. Furthermore, future empirical research will undoubtedly yield at least partial answers to yet-unanswered questions and will shed more light on the evolutionary aspects of cooperatives in market economies.

We must consider that aspects of the participatory economy are encountered in some market economies. Many major U.S. corporations have employee stock options plans (ESOPs) whereby, over time, employees come to own considerable shares of the company. Once the second-largest airline in the United States (United Airlines) was employee-owned before its 2002 bankruptcy. In Germany, worker representatives occupy positions on boards of directors. These "experiments" may provide insight into how a participatory economy will work.

Democratic Socialism?

Proponents of socialism have found it difficult to give up on its feasibility after the collapse of communism in the Soviet Union and Eastern Europe. They specifically cling to socialism's perceived advantages: a more even distribution of income and a greater willingness, as a consequence of state ownership and control, to deal with externalities and monopolies. Lange's market socialism model offers the best prospects for feasible socialism in that it uses markets to allocate resources while retaining the feature of socialism its proponents admire most, state ownership. Specifically, market socialism's contemporary supporters argue that planned socialism failed because it was based on totalitarianism rather than democracy and that it failed to create rules for the efficient operation of state enterprises.

In a detailed argument, James Yunker presents a case for what he terms "pragmatic socialism" based on public ownership and a bureau of public ownership "to enforce upon the executives who manage the publicly owned business corporations a strong profit motivation."[24] This board will also see that the social dividend is disbursed in an egalitarian manner. In addition to dealing with issues such as transition, Yunker devotes substantial attention to such critical areas as investment, growth, and entepreneurship in the socialist economy.

A key issue in any assessment of the feasibility of democratic socialism is whether public ownership and democracy are compatible. In his 1944 book *The Road to Serfdom*, F. A. Hayek wrote that state ownership will eventually lead to political totalitarianism.[25] Ownership by the state will automatically lead to demands for planning and to intrusion into economic decision making by politicians. Hayek maintained that administrative resource allocation necessarily leads to authoritarianism; socialist economies can never be democratically organized. Resources cannot be administratively allocated without the exercise of extreme political power. Administrative orders to subordinates must be backed by the threat of punishment and the use of coercion. Only those with skill in exercising political power will advance in the political apparatus.[26] Such a system requires a talent for unscrupulous and uninhibited moral behavior. As Hayek wrote, "Totalitarianism is a logical consequence of the attempt to centrally plan an economy. Although there may be no original intent to exercise political power over people, the exercise of arbitrary power is the consequence of the desire to plan the economy scientifically."[27] And furthermore, in order to "achieve their end, collectivists must create power—power over men wielded by other men—of a magnitude never before known, and . . . their success will depend on the extent to which they achieve such power."[28]

Even if we grant that socialist economies can be democratically organized, a number of other strictly economic problems must be solved. Andrei Shleifer and Robert Vishny make the case that, for a number of reasons, even a democratically organized market socialist economy will not work.[29] First, with state ownership, state enterprises will be run to achieve political objectives, such as ensuring employment or buying the loyalty of supporters. If the state owners decided to use the most common economic criterion—profit maximization—they would divide the country's enterprises into monopolies because monopolies yield more cumulative profits than competitive firms. Past experience with socialism shows that socialist economies have indeed been organized into monopolies. Second, Shleifer and Vishny argue that public choice decisions will be more inefficient under democratic socialism than market democracy. Like other forms of democracy, democratic socialist governments are prone to exploit the minority for the benefit of the majority or be dominated by interest groups. However, because state ownership is pervasive, these abuses will have more profound effects in socialist economies. Moreover, no matter how hard the democratic socialist economy attempts to avoid it, the management of state-owned firms will become bureaucratized. Criteria like cost economies or technological innovation will be ignored and state enterprises will be run for the convenience of their bureaucratic managers.

Pranab Bardhan and John Roemer counter that the socialist economies that failed were characterized by noncompetitive and nondemocratic politics and by command/administrative allocation of resources and commodities.[30] They maintain that "competitive socialism" could be envisioned through the negation of the latter two characteristics of the failed economies. State-owned firms are not that different from large corporations in market economies, whose managers are separated from their owners. Just as market economies use incentives to ensure that managers work in the interests of the owners, so can socialist economies use similar incentives to motivate state managers. Bardhan and Roemer include an important role for the state, a system using state-owned banks for insider monitoring to solve the traditional problems of enterprise decision making, and the development of political accountability for a state that supervises the banking structure. Shleifer and Vishny counter that even if state banks are used as major shareholders in state enterprises to insure that they are run in a business-like fashion, the state remains the ultimate owner. As such, there is no way to avoid the politicization of the running of the enterprise, and they point to the disappointing performance of state enterprises throughout the world to illustrate this point.

These ongoing discussions send several messages. First, the demise of socialist economic systems in the former Soviet Union and the countries of Eastern Europe did not end discussions about socialism in general and market socialism in particular. Second, much of the discussion now focuses on the nature of the state in a socialist system and on how agency and incentive problems can be resolved. Contemporary organization theory provides useful insights into these problems. Finally, the appeal of a more egalitarian distribution of income remains, yet limited attention is paid to the noneconomic aspects of socialism that many argue are critical to understanding its nature.

The Performance of Market Socialism: Hypotheses

With the exception of the former Yugoslavia, a small country beset by insurmountable political and ethnic problems, we lack real-world experience with market socialism of either the Lange or the worker-managed type. Consequently, we do not have the advantage of long historical experience to test hypotheses concerning the economic performance of market socialism. The following paragraphs represent our best analytical—though somewhat speculative—efforts.

Income Distribution

The easiest hypothesis to formulate concerns the distribution of income under market socialism. Inasmuch as capital continues to belong to society, we would expect income to be distributed more nearly equally under market socialism than under capitalism. Even in the case of worker-managed enterprises, the state must be paid a fee for the use of capital, and the state would presumably divide such income among the population on a fairly equal basis. Some reservations must be expressed, however. As critics have pointed out, prosperous worker-managed firms might protect extraordinarily high earnings by excluding outsiders. This type of behavior could lead to significant inequality in wage income.

Economic Growth

Proponents of market socialism claim that market socialism would yield relatively high rates of growth, primarily because society would plow earnings from capital back into the economy. This conclusion, however, assumes that the socialist state would not be pressured into putting the "social dividend" into current consumption in the form of subsidies and social services. Such pressure would be particularly strong in the case of democratically elected socialist governments. For these reasons, we believe it risky to presume that market socialism will yield higher investment rates—and hence higher rates of growth—than the capitalist model. The outcome is far from certain.

Efficiency

The theory of market socialism does not yield strong propositions concerning economic efficiency. Arguing that market socialism can indeed be more efficient than capitalism, its advocates cite the lack of monopoly, the greater attention to externalities, and individual participation in decision making. Its critics, however, mount equally convincing arguments about the inefficiency of market socialism: motivation problems, perverse supply curves, and the difficulty of finding equilibrium prices. Accordingly, we cannot venture any hypotheses about the relative efficiency of market socialism.

Stability

Advocates of market socialism make the following case for greater economic stability: The state will have greater control over the investment rate, so sharp fluctuations in investment can be avoided. Counterarguments exist, however. If market socialist economies (we are using the Lange model) have trouble adjusting prices to equilibrium, macroeconomic instabilities associated with nonequilibrium prices might be experienced. Moreover, democratically elected officials will be under strong pressure to pursue "popular" economic policies (the political business cycle), while feeling less pressure from market forces to tighten the reins on economic policy. Again, we cannot propose any strong hypotheses concerning the relative stability of market socialism.

Market socialism has sufficient appeal to make it a serious model for discussion. Western Europe has experimented with programs of partial worker management, and major corporations in the United States now have employees as their majority shareholders. Market socialism has appeal for Eastern Europe because it combines the elements of market and socialist economies.

Summary

- The appeal of market socialism is its attempt to combine the efficiency of markets (capitalism) with the more equitable distribution of income (socialism).
- Economic theorists who try to determine whether socialism might be feasible consider both the negative and the positive aspects of socialism in the absence of a paradigm of market socialism.
- The Lange model, named after Polish economist Oskar Lange, combines public ownership and a trial-and-error approach to determining output and equilibrium. Individual enterprises are expected to follow market-type rules, minimizing cost and producing where price equal to marginal cost.
- While households supply labor services, the state distributes the social dividend and decides on sector expansion.
- Critics of the Lange model argue that it is computationally inefficient, lacks in managerial motivation, and is potentially subject to monopoly problems.
- The contemporary cooperative variant of market socialism is theoretically rigorous, but its real-world applications are limited.
- Worker management in enterprise decision making is a key element of the cooperative model.

Key Terms

market socialism	Lange model	producer cooperative
central planning board	cooperative economy	participatory economy
trial-and-error model	labor-managed economy	net income per worker

Notes

1. Benjamin Lippincott, ed., *On the Economic Theory of Socialism* (Minneapolis: University of Minnesota Press, 1938).
2. See, for example, F. M. Taylor, "The Guidance of Production in a Socialist State," *American Economic Review* 19 (March 1929); reprinted in Lippincott, *On the Economic Theory of Socialism,* pp. 39–54; H. D. Dickinson, *Economics of Socialism* (London: Oxford University Press, 1939); and Abba P. Lerner, *The Economics of Control* (New York: Macmillan, 1944).
3. See the discussion in Maurice Dobb, *The Welfare Economics and the Economics of Socialism* (Cambridge: Cambridge University Press, 1969), p. 133 and footnotes thereto.
4. F. A. Hayek, "Socialist Calculation: The Competitive Solution," *Economica* 7 (May 1940), 125–149; reprinted in Bornstein, *Comparative Economic Systems,* pp. 77–97.
5. Abram Bergson, *Essays in Normative Economics* (Cambridge, Mass.: Harvard University Press, 1966), Ch. 9.
6. The sophisticated works of Soviet mathematical economists have been brought to Western readers by Zauberman, Ellman, and others. See Alfred Zauberman, *The Mathematical Revolution in Soviet Economics* (London: Oxford University Press, 1975); Michael Ellman, *Soviet Planning Today* (Cambridge: Cambridge University Press, 1971); Martin Cave, Alastair McAuley, and Judith Thornton, eds., *New Terms in Soviet Economics* (Armonk, N.Y.: Sharpe, 1982).
7. For a recent discussion of the state of the literature on producer cooperatives, see John P. Bonin, Derek C. Jones, and Louis Putterman, "Theoretical and Empirical Studies of Producer Cooperatives: Will the Twain Ever Meet?" *Journal of Economic Literature* 31 (September 1993), 1290–1320.
8. Jaroslav Vanek, *The Participatory Economy* (Ithaca, N.Y.: Cornell University Press, 1971), p. 1.
9. *Ibid.,* p. 9.
10. *Ibid.,* p. 11.
11. For Ward's original contribution, see Benjamin Ward, "The Firm in Illyria: Market Syndicalism," *American Economic Review* 48 (September 1958), 566–589. See also E. Domar, "The Soviet Collective Farm as a Producer Cooperative," *American Economic Review* 56 (September 1966), 734–757; and Walter Y. Oi and Elizabeth M. Clayton, "A Peasant's View of a Soviet Collective Farm," *American Economic Review* 58 (March 1968), 37–59. For a general treatment of Vanek's argument, see Vanek, *The Participatory Economy;* and for a detailed analysis, see Jaroslav Vanek, *The General Theory of Labor-Managed Market Economies* (Ithaca, N.Y.: Cornell University Press, 1970). Since these early contributions, the literature has expanded rapidly. For a survey, see John P. Bonin and Louis Putterman, *Economics of Cooperation and the Labor-Managed Economy* (New York: Harwood Academic Publishers, 1987); see also Bonin, Jones, and Putterman, "Theoretical and Empirical Studies."
12. Benjamin Ward, *The Socialist Economy* (New York: Random House, 1967), p. 183.

13. *Ibid.,* Chs. 8–10.
14. *Ibid.,* pp. 191–192.
15. *Ibid.,* pp. 184 ff.
16. *Ibid.,* pp. 201 ff.
17. *Ibid.,* Ch. 9.
18. For the general treatment, see Vanek, *The Participatory Economy.*
19. See Vanek, *The General Theory.*
20. For background on participatory socialism, see Ellen Turkish Comisso, *Worker's Control Under Plan and Market* (New Haven: Yale University Press, 1979), Chs. 1 and 2; Hans Dieter Seibel and Ukandi G. Damachi, *Self-Management in Yugoslavia and the Third World* (New York: St. Martin's, 1982); Howard M. Wachtel, *Workers' Management and Workers' Wages in Yugoslavia* (Ithaca, N.Y.: Cornell University Press, 1973), Ch. 2.
21. Bonin, Jones, and Putterman, "Theoretical and Empirical Studies."
22. *Ibid.,* 1299.
23. *Ibid.,* 1316.
24. James A. Yunker, *Socialism Revised and Modernized: The Case for Pragmatic Market Socialism* (New York: Praeger, 1992), p. 38.
25. F. A. Hayek, *The Road to Serfdom* (Chicago: University of Chicago Press, 1994).
26. Peter Boettke, *Calculation and Coordination: Essays on Socialism and Transitional Political Economy* (London: Routhage, 2001), pp. 52–56.
27. *Ibid.,* p. 52.
28. Hayek, *Road to Serfdom,* p. 144.
29. Andrei Shleifer and Robert Vishny, "The Politics of Market Socialism," *Journal of Economic Perspectives* 8, 2 (Spring 1994), 165–176.
30. Pranab Bardhan and John E. Roemer, "Market Socialism: A Case for Rejuvenation," *Journal of Economic Perspectives* 6 (Summer 1992), 101–116.

Recommended Readings

Traditional Sources

H. D. Dickinson, *The Economics of Socialism* (London: Oxford University Press, 1938).

Abba P. Lerner, *The Economics of Control* (New York: Macmillan, 1944).

Benjamin Lippincott, ed., *On the Economic Theory of Socialism* (New York: McGraw-Hill, 1964).

Jaroslav Vanek, *The General Theory of Labor-Managed Economies* (Ithaca, N.Y.: Cornell University Press, 1970).

———, *The Labor-Managed Economy* (Ithaca, N.Y.: Cornell University Press, 1971).

———, *The Participatory Economy* (Ithaca, N.Y.: Cornell University Press, 1971).

Benjamin N. Ward, "The Firm in Illyria: Market Syndicalism," *American Economic Review* 48 (September 1958), 566–589.

———, *The Socialist Economy* (New York: Random House, 1967).

The Lange Model

Abram Bergson, "Market Socialism Revisited," *Journal of Political Economy* 75 (October 1967), 663–675.

Benjamin Lippincott, ed., *On the Economic Theory of Socialism* (New York: McGraw-Hill, 1964).

Market Socialism: The Labor-Managed Variant

Katrina V. Berman, "An Empirical Test of the Theory of the Labor-Managed Firm," *Journal of Comparative Economics* 13 (June 1989), 281–300.

John P. Bonin, Derek C. Jones, and Louis Putterman, "Theoretical and Empirical Studies of Producer Cooperatives: Will the Twain Ever Meet?" *Journal of Economic Literature* 31 (September 1993), 1290–1320.

John P. Bonin and Louis Putterman, *Economics of Cooperation and the Labor-Managed Economy* (New York: Harwood Academic Publishers, 1987).

Saul Estrin, "Some Reflections on Self-Management, Social Choice and Reform in Eastern Europe," *Journal of Comparative Economics* 15 (June 1991), 349–361.

Derek C. Jones and Jan Svenjar, eds., *Advances in the Economic Analysis of Participatory and Labor Managed Firms,* Vols. 1–4 (Greenwich: JAI Press, various years).

Kathryn Nantz, "The Labor-Managed Firm Under Imperfect Monitoring: Employment and Work Effort Responses," *Journal of Comparative Economics* 14 (March 1990), 33–50.

Hugh Neary, "The Comparative Statics of the Ward–Domar Labor-Managed Firm: A Profit–Function Approach," *Journal of Comparative Economics* 12 (June 1988), 159–181.

V. Russell and R. Russell, eds., *International Handbook of Participation in Organization* (New York: Oxford University Press, 1989).

Fernando B. Saldanha, "Fixprice Analysis of Labor-Managed Economies," *Journal of Comparative Economics* 13 (June 1989), 227–253.

Feasible Socialism: Contemporary Views

Pranab Bardhan and John E. Roemer, "Market Socialism: A Case for Rejuvenation," *Journal of Economic Perspectives* 6 (Summer 1992), 101–116.

———, eds., *Market Socialism: The Current Debate* (New York: Oxford University Press, 1993).

———, "On the Workability of Market Socialism," *Journal of Economic Perspectives* 8 (Spring 1994), 177–181.

Alec Nove, *The Economics of Feasible Socialism* (Winchester, Mass.: Unwin Hyman, 1983).

S. Pejovich, *Socialism: Institutional, Philosophical and Economic Issues* (Norwell, Mass.: Kluwer Academic Publishers, 1987).

Andrei Schleifer and Robert W. Vishny, "The Politics of Market Socialism," *Journal of Economic Perspectives* 8 (Spring 1994), 165–176.

James A. Yunker, *Socialism Revised and Modernized: The Case for Pragmatic Market Socialism* (New York: Praeger, 1992).

PART **III**

Economic Systems in Practice

8

The Anglo-Saxon Model of Capitalism

Models of Capitalism

The theory of market capitalism (Chapter 5) is the pure theory of capitalism. It showed how an economy could use the invisible hand of markets to allocate resources in an efficient manner, assuming that markets were competitive, that externalities were not overwhelming, and that reasonable macroeconomic stability could be maintained. In practice, capitalist market economies can organize themselves in different ways, while still hewing to this generic definition. In fact, each capitalist country of the globe differs from others in a number of respects.

The next three chapters describe three different models of capitalism, dubbed the Anglo-Saxon model, the European model, and the Asian model. The **Anglo-Saxon model** has its historical origins in Great Britain and is patterned after the classical liberal ideas of Adam Smith and the constitutional precepts of classical liberalism. The Anglo-Saxon model uses common law, which operates with lay judges, broader legal principles, oral arguments, and precedents and is based on the principle that government intervention in the economy should be limited.[1] Although the U.S. economy diverges in a number of respects from this ideal model, it is the best real-world example of the Anglo-Saxon model. The **European model** is patterned after economic principles enunciated in France and Germany in the nineteenth century that place less faith in the invisible hand and call for more state intervention in economic affairs, including more state ownership. Its legal foundation is based on what James Buchanan terms "the constitutional order of socialism." The European model accords the state a higher level of activity in the economy, pays relatively more attention to the common good as opposed to individual property rights, and provides for more regulation of private economic activity. The European model operates on civil (or Roman) law, which uses professional judges, legal codes, and written records. Prime real-world examples of the European model are France, Germany, and Sweden. The **Asian model** is closer in its institutional arrangements to the European model. It focuses on high rates of capital formation and on other devices, often supported by the state, to overcome relative backwardness in as short a time as possible. The Asian model, as a relative latecomer, exists in a variety of forms and involves a considerable amount of experimentation, but its best real-world examples are Japan, South Korea, and Taiwan. The three chapters that follow explain the characteristics of these three models—in particular, how they differ in terms of the functioning of the labor and capital markets.

As we have noted, the grouping of disparate countries under one model is a distortion of reality. Germans consider their economic system as quite different from that of France, and vice versa. The Taiwanese and South Koreans might object to being lumped together with Japan in one model. Nevertheless, the common features are strong enough to warrant our speaking in terms of the three models we have outlined.

Constitutional Foundations of the U.S. Economy

The United States Constitution was ratified in 1787 following a Constitutional Convention and a lengthy public discussion published in what came to be known as the *Federalist Papers,* written by America's founding fathers.[2] The U.S. Constitution was heavily influenced by the classical liberal thinking of the turn of the nineteenth century. James Madison can rightly be called the father of the U.S. Constitution, which bears his indelible imprint and rejects the "stronger state" notions of his rival Alexander Hamilton. Following classical liberalism's belief that a strong state poses a danger to its polity, Madison argued that the Constitution's task was to limit the powers of government. He wrote,

> It may be a reflection on human nature, that such devices should be necessary to control the abuses of government. But what is government itself, but the greatest of all reflections on human nature? If men were angels, no government would be necessary. If angels were to govern men, neither external nor internal controls on government would be necessary. In framing a government which is to be administered by men over men, the great difficulty lies in this: you must first enable the government to control the governed; and in the next place oblige it to control itself. A dependence on the people is, no doubt, the primary control on the government; but experience has taught mankind the necessity of auxiliary precautions.[3]

Madison argued, and the other founders and ratifying states concurred, that the best way to limit the power of government was the separation of powers. The Constitution created three co-equal branches of government—the executive, legislative, and judicial—which could check each other and thus prevent abuse by any one branch of government. Not only would the executive and judicial branches check the legislative branch; the legislative branch itself would be divided into two houses—the Senate and the House of Representatives—that could check each other. In Madison's words, "We see it particularly displayed in all the subordinate distributions of power, where the constant aim is to divide and arrange the several offices in such a manner as that each may be a check on the other—that the private interest of every individual may be a sentinel over the public rights. These inventions of prudence cannot be less requisite in the distribution of the supreme powers of the State."[4]

The founders worried that, with majority rule, a majority might pass laws that discriminated against minorities—in particular against owners of property for the purpose of "more fairly" distributing wealth. In Madison's words,

Measures are too often decided, not according to the rules of justice and the rights of the minor party, but by the superior force of an interested and overbearing majority. However anxiously we may wish that these complaints had no foundation, the evidence of known facts will not permit us to deny that they are in some degree true. The diversity in the faculties of men, from which the rights of property originate, is not less an insuperable obstacle to a uniformity of interests. The protection of these faculties is the first object of government. From the protection of different and unequal faculties of acquiring property, the possession of different degrees and kinds of property immediately results; and from the influence of these on the sentiments and views of the respective proprietors, ensures a division of the society into different interests and parties. The majority, having such coexistent passion or interest, must be rendered, by their number and local situation, unable to concert and carry into effect schemes of oppression.[5]

The founding fathers feared that jealous minorities might pass unfair laws against minorities, such as the owners of businesses and capital. Again in Madison's words,

It is of great importance in a republic not only to guard the society against the oppression of its rulers, but to guard one part of the society against the injustice of the other part. Different interests necessarily exist in different classes of citizens. If a majority be united by a common interest, the rights of the minority will be insecure. There are but two methods of providing against this evil: the one by creating a will in the community independent of the majority—that is, of the society itself; the other, by comprehending in the society so many separate descriptions of citizens as will render an unjust combination of a majority of the whole very improbable, if not impracticable.[6]

Political economist Douglass North concludes that the political structure of the United States "was explicitly oriented to preventing domination by factions. He [Madison] wished to make it unprofitable for groups in society to devote their efforts toward redistributing wealth and income through the political process. The tripartite system of government . . . was designed to make efforts at restructuring property rights to redistribute wealth and income very difficult."[7]

By limiting the power and scope of government, the Constitution embraced the idea of strict restraints on government interventions that would reduce the liberties of private individuals in their economic activities.[8] The Fifth Amendment states, among other things, that no person can "be deprived of life, liberty, or property, without due process of law; nor shall private property be taken for public use, without just compensation."[9] This amendment protected private businesses from government intervention and regulation, with exceptions such as the recognized right of government to take property through the right of eminent domain, the obligation of private persons to pay taxes, and the power of the state to regulate through police power for purposes of public safety and welfare.

We study the American economy as the example *par excellence* of the Anglo-Saxon model. For most American readers, the way the economy is structured is familiar. The American economy is a large and wealthy economy that has enjoyed considerable success. It relies predominantly on markets, with less government intervention than in many other capitalist economies. It is also the most technologically advanced economy, and many experiments, such as deregulation and privatization, originated in the United States. The legal foundation of the U.S. economy is the U.S. Constitution, the original intent of which was to limit the power of the federal government.

The Private Sector versus the Public Sector

The American economy, like other economies, consists of a private sector and a public sector. The economic role of government in the United States is more limited than in most other advanced industrialized economies. Most resource-allocation decisions are made in the private sector, though in areas such as public utilities, government regulation is active.

The **private sector** is the business sector in which private ownership prevails and government regulation or intervention is limited. Milton Friedman has estimated that roughly 25 percent of economic activity was government-operated or government-supervised in 1939, 75 percent conducted in the private sector.[10] Frederic Scherer estimated that in 1965, the government-regulated sector accounted for 11 percent of GNP and that the government-operated sector accounted for another 12 percent, a total close to that for 1939.[11] Clifford Winston estimated that in 1977, 17 percent of the U.S. GNP "was produced by fully regulated industries," whereas in 1988, this share had fallen to 7 percent.[12] The U.S. private sector today amounts to well over 80 percent of the American economy.

The government's claim on labor and capital resources indicates how productive resources are divided between government and business uses. Government (federal, state, and local) employs approximately 16 percent of the American labor force and owns approximately 18 percent of the stock of structures, one-eighth of all land, and one-twentieth of all inventories (see Figure 8.1). Government owned approximately 15 percent of the national wealth and accounted for some 7 percent of total labor, capital, and land inputs in the late 1950s.

At the turn of the century, government accounted for some 4 percent of employment and owned 6 percent of the stock of structures and 13 percent of the stock of land. By 1939, the government's share had increased substantially (to 18 percent of structures and 19 percent of land), whereas its share of the labor force had risen to about 10 percent. Since the late 1930s, government's share of employment has increased substantially, but its share of national wealth has risen only slightly. We have reached a national consensus on the distribution of wealth, which has remained fairly stable for about 50 years. There is now little serious talk of large-scale nationalizations, and most of the major decisions in this area (broadcasting, communication satellites, atomic energy) have come down on the side of private ownership.

FIGURE 8.1   Indicators of Government Participation in Economic Activity and
Wealth in the United States, 1900–2000

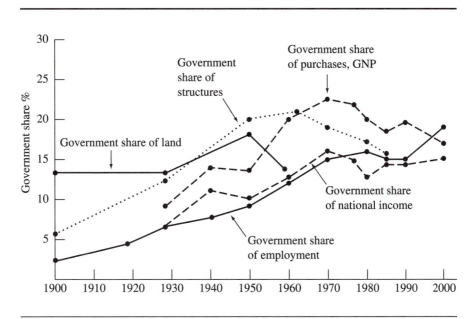

Government produces about 13 percent of national income, of which the over-whelming portion is produced by "general government." Government enterprises account for less than 2 percent of the national income, much less than in other indus-trialized economies. Rather than government enterprises supplanting private enter-prises, it has been the expansion of general government activities that has accounted for rising government output.

The government's share of national income has been rising steadily over the last hundred years (4 percent in 1869 to 8.5 percent in 1919 to 13 percent in 2002). Since the 1930s, the increase in the federal government's share has been more substantial than that of state and local government. Since 1929, business's share of national income has fallen from 91 to 81 percent at the expense of the rise in general gov-ernment and not-for-profit institutions. Government purchases account for about one-fifth of the total. Interestingly, most of the historical increase in the share of gov-ernment purchases has been due to rising state and local government spending and federal defense spending.

It is important to put these U.S. developments in perspective. An examination of other industrialized capitalist countries (Figure 8.2) shows that the scope of the pub-lic sector in the United States is average or even below average if one considers that most countries do not bear a substantial defense burden. If one looks only at non-defense spending, the U.S. government's share of total spending is relatively small by international standards. The rising share of government output and expenditures

FIGURE 8.2   The Size of Government in the United States and Other Countries, 1960, 1970, and 2000

Government Outlays as a Percent of GDP

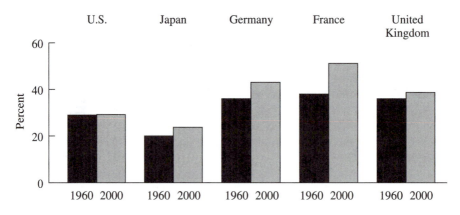

Taxes as a Percent of GDP

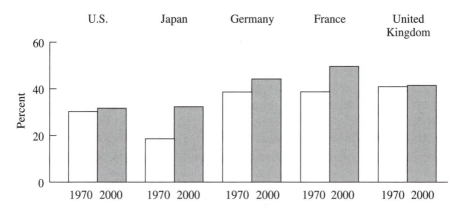

Sources: Handbook of Economic Statistics 1992, CPAS 92–10005, September 1992; *Statistical Abstract of the United States,* 2000.

is also unexceptional; it has characterized the economic growth of capitalism for more than a century. The U.S. tax burden is also relatively modest.

Some people view the rising share of government with alarm; others consider it too small. All one can say for sure is that in the United States, the allocation of resources between the public and private sectors is basically a matter of public choice.

Business Organization

Business enterprises are divided into three categories on the basis of legal organization: sole proprietorships, partnerships, and corporations. The **sole proprietorship** is owned by one individual, who makes all the business decisions and absorbs the profits (or losses) that the business earns. A **partnership** is owned by two or more partners, who make all the business decisions and share in the profits and losses. The major advantages of these forms of business organization are their relative simplicity (the proprietorship is simpler than the partnership) and that, under existing tax law, their profits are taxed only once. They have two major disadvantages: (1) The owners are personally liable for the debts of the business, and (2) the ability to raise capital is limited, dependent as it is on the owners' ability to borrow against personal assets. The third form of business organization, the **corporation**, is owned by its stockholders and has authorization to act as a legal person. A board of directors, elected by the stockholders, appoints management to run the corporation. The advantages of the corporation are (1) that its owners (the stockholders) are not personally liable for the debts of the corporation (limited liability), (2) that its management can be changed if necessary, and (3) that it has more options for raising capital (through the sale of bonds and additional stock). A major disadvantage of the U.S. corporation is that its income is taxed a second time when corporate earnings are distributed to stockholders as dividends. Double taxation gives American corporations an incentive to reinvest earnings rather than pay out dividends.

These three forms of business organization are supplemented in the United States by innovative legal arrangements (such as limited-liability partnerships) designed to circumvent a variety of problems, yet the threefold classification remains valid. Figure 8.3 shows the distribution of U.S. enterprises according to the legal form of business organization. Although sole proprietorships account for most American businesses, they account for only a small percentage of business revenues. Corporations, though few in number (about 20 percent of the total), account for 90 percent of business revenues. The larger size of the corporation is explained by limited liability and the greater ability of the corporation to raise capital. The sole proprietorship is important in agriculture, retail trade, and services; the partnership is important in finance, insurance, real estate, and services; the corporation is the dominant form in other sectors.

Corporate Governance

Although noncorporate forms of business dominate numerically and in terms of employment, the U.S. corporation produces the bulk of output. In other advanced industrial economies, the corporation similarly dominates production. Large corporations in virtually all countries are characterized by a separation of ownership and management. As in most other industrialized countries, the managers of large U.S. corporations own only a small fraction of outstanding shares. The bulk of shares are owned by individuals either directly or through private pension and retirement funds

FIGURE 8.3   Proprietorships, Partnerships, and Corporations, 2000

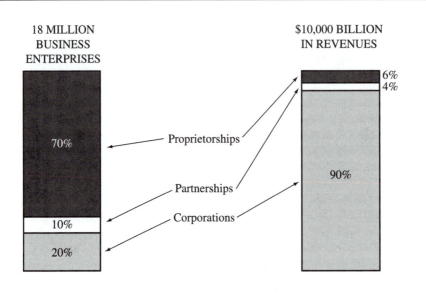

Source: Statistical Abstract of the United States, updated by authors.

in which they have invested. Some 50 percent of Americans own stock—a figure that may be the highest in the world.[13] The separation of ownership and capital, first studied by Adolf Berle and Gardner Means for U.S. corporations,[14] suggests a potential problem of corporate governance. **Corporate governance** raises the question of in whose interests a corporation, in which owners are not managers, will be run. In theory, corporations can be run in the interests of their shareholders, their stakeholders, or the community. **Stakeholders** are those who participate in the operation of the corporation as managers, employees, workers, suppliers, or buyers, but not as owners.

The U.S. corporation tends to be run in the interests of shareholders, where the task of the manager is to maximize **shareholder value**, the value of the corporation in stock markets as measured by its market capitalization. The **market capitalization** of a corporation is the product of the number of shares outstanding and its stock price as determined in the stock market where it is listed, such as the New York Stock Exchange, the American Stock Exchange, or NASDAQ. Insofar as the stock price reflects the anticipated value of future profits, managers committed to maximizing shareholder value will sacrifice stakeholder interests, often including their own, to improve the profit performance of the corporation. If a manufacturing corporation whose goal is creating shareholder value is suffering a slump in profits, management would be expected to downsize the labor force, announce layoffs, or seek lower-cost suppliers. Similarly, an airline would be expected to cease offering service to a low-yielding community, despite the harm to that community.

After Berle and Means first (in 1932) focused attention on the separation of ownership from management, economists began to consider the potential principal–agent problems. If managers are not owners, will they not run the corporation in their own interests or pay too much attention to the interests of employees, rather than making the hard decisions required to maximize profits? Although the issue of how to motivate managers to maximize shareholder value was not resolved for decades, two typically U.S. approaches were apparent by the 1980s: creating a market for corporate control and developing an incentive system for managers that would cause them to maximize shareholder value.

The Market for Corporate Control

One way to ensure that managers maximize shareholder value is the creation of a market for corporate control. A **market for corporate control** is one in which rival management teams have the opportunity to buy control of the corporation from its owners.[15] Prior to the 1980s, there were relatively few changes of management in large corporations, even in cases where the management team did not enable the firm to live up to its profit potential. With a large number of shareholders, the largest owning only a small percentage of shares, it was too difficult for shareholders to organize "hostile" takeovers. Two developments changed this situation. First, as ordinary citizens began investing in private pension funds and in mutual stock funds, these funds began to acquire and control significant shares of large corporations. Today, institutional investors own more than 50 percent of all listed corporate stock and more than 60 percent of the listed stock of the 1,000 largest corporations.[16] For example, the CREF Teacher's Retirement Fund currently has more than $100 billion invested in stocks,[17] virtually enough to be the sole owner of the world's largest corporation, ExxonMobil.

Second, a new breed of **corporate raiders** (individuals such as Carl Icahn, Michael Milliken, and Warren Buffet or investment banks such as Goldman Sachs) emerged with access to substantial funds to engage in hostile takeovers of corporations that they concluded were underperforming. Corporate raiders targeted corporations that were not realizing their potential and, for each such firm, developed a business plan showing that, with new management, the corporation could earn higher profits. The corporate raider would then offer a price above the current stock price to shareholders in an effort to acquire enough shares to replace the current management with a "better" management team.

The U.S. market for corporate control became quite complex and effective in the 1980s and 1990s, using exotic instruments such as the purchase of one company with shares of another. An example is AOL's purchase of Time Warner largely with AOL shares, a transaction that Time Warner later regretted.

Corporate Incentives

Traditionally, U.S. executives received a fixed salary plus a bonus based on the performance of the corporation, such as its profitability in the current year. In the 1980s and 1990s, corporations began introducing more direct incentives to ensure that corporate executives and even middle managers were motivated to maximize shareholder value. The most prominent such instrument was the **stock option**, whereby executives were granted the right to buy a designated number of shares of the company at a specified price (often the stock price on the day the stock options were granted). Stock options, therefore, gave executives the incentive to run the company in such a manner that its stock price would rise and they could "cash in" their stock options at a profit. In theory, the stock price should reflect the long-term, not short-term, profitability of the company. Hence stock options would direct executives to think about the company's long-term performance.

Other incentive devices were to match any employee contributions to their 401K retirement accounts that were invested in the corporation's own stock. Although employees typically have the choice of acquiring the stocks of other corporations for their company retirement accounts, the offer of one "free" share for every share purchased was enticing. The incentive feature of encouraging executives and employees to accumulate shares in their own corporation is that both upper and middle levels of management would then have a personal interest in seeing the value of the stock increase.

A final incentive feature was the golden parachute provision for top executives of corporations. A **golden parachute** is a provision for a limited number of top executives to receive generous severance bonuses if their company is taken over by a new management team. Its purpose is to prevent the existing management from resisting corporate takeovers that, in theory, will install a better management with a better business plan and, in the process, drive up the stock price to the advantage of shareholders.

These and other corporate incentives were all designed to deal with the principal–agent problem in companies in which there is a separation of ownership and management. Preoccupation with shareholder value is a hallmark of the Anglo-Saxon (American) model of capitalism. It has been criticized for a number of reasons: For one thing, it neglects the interests of stakeholders, most specifically employees and managers, who may have worked for the company for decades. Maximization of shareholder value means that corporations will periodically engage in cost cutting and downsizing, which entails the loss of jobs. The interests of other stakeholders, such as the community in which a downsized plant is located, will also be neglected. A second criticism is that maximizing shareholder value can create distortions in stock markets that require accurate information to operate efficiently. Top executives will be tempted (as in the 2001–2002 scandals involving Enron, Arthur Anderson, and WorldCom) to withhold negative information, such as sinking profits, to prevent a decline in the share price. When information is distorted in this fashion, the manner in which corporations are valued in stock exchanges may be faulty, and capital markets themselves will be questioned.

Lawrence Summers, academic economist and former secretary of the treasury, has argued in his academic work that any gains from hostile takeovers are "breaches of trust." Any gains of shareholders are at the expense of wealth losses by stakeholders, such as employees and suppliers, and this will undermine the trust that is necessary for the effective functioning of business.[18]

Capital Markets

The manner in which capital markets function varies with the type of capitalist economic system. The **capital market** is the market in which businesses raise investment finance through the issue of stocks and bonds and bank borrowing. A capital market can be either a primary or a secondary market. In the **primary market**, the business, in this case the corporation, sells (issues) new shares of stocks or bonds to buyers. Such sales of new shares are called **initial public offerings** (IPOs). The secondary market is a "secondhand" market in which shares of stock or bonds that have already been issued are traded by one owner to another. It is in the primary market that investment financing is created.

The American (Anglo-Saxon) capital market is one in which new shares are sold to private investors by **underwriters** who organize the initial sale of shares. It is a "public offering" in the sense that, theoretically, any buyer willing to buy at the offering price can be accommodated. In U.S. stock markets, shares are issued via the various organized stock exchanges, such as the New York Stock Exchange, the American Stock Exchange, the NASAQ Exchange, or numerous smaller exchanges. The listing of shares of stock for sale in the large exchanges must follow the rules of the Securities and Exchange Commission and of the exchange itself. The stock exchanges are private organizations that have established operating rules and have the power to punish underwriters, brokers, or companies that violate their rules.

Full disclosure is the operating principle in the major U.S. stock exchanges. Neither the exchange nor the Securities and Exchange Commission will issue a ruling on the merit of the company. Rather, the task of the Securities and Exchange commission is to ensure that potential buyers of the newly issued stock have full information about the company, such as a list of its officers; the use to which the funds will be put; any outstanding lawsuits; and potential conflicts of interest. The offer to sell new shares will be contained in a published prospectus, which contains obligatory accounting information prepared by a recognized accounting firm according to standard accounting procedures (GAAP). The accounting statement can also include a statement from the accounting firm if there is doubt whether the firm can continue to exist as a "going concern." As long as all relevant information is disclosed and other requirements specific to the exchange are met (such as reaching a minimal capitalization), the underwriter is free to sell the new shares to buyers. Once these new shares are in the hands of owners, they trade in the secondary market.

Unlike the case in Europe (as we shall see in the next chapter), more investment is financed by the issue of stocks and bonds than through bank financing. Table 8.1 shows the financing of U.S. investment in a typical year (1993). This table, which covers all net investment, both corporate and noncorporate, shows that the issue of new stocks and bonds through equity markets accounted for almost 60 percent of all net investment and that retained corporate earnings accounting for another 25 percent, leaving virtually nothing for bank financing, especially considering that much noncorporate investment is financed by other means entirely. In Europe, on the other hand, banks finance two-thirds of business needs.[19]

TABLE 8.1   The Financing of Investment,
U.S. Economy, 1993 (billions of dollars)

Net private domestic investment	474
New security issues, corporations	
Stocks	154
Bonds	114
Total	268
Undistributed corporate profits	121
Other	75

Source: Statistical Abstract of the United States.

The financing of investment through stock markets, which is a characteristic feature of the Anglo-Saxon model, means a separation of those who finance corporations from those who manage corporations. In the European and Asian models, which rely heavily on bank financing, the bank is closely associated with the corporation and would be reluctant to withhold financing from a closely related company. The separation of the financing from management in the Anglo-Saxon model has the advantage that a generally impartial judgment will be made about whether a particular company deserves additional financing. If the corporation cannot make, in its prospectus, a convincing case to potential investors that the investment funds will yield sufficient returns, investors will not buy the stock or bond issue. There is also another way in which the capital market influences who gets capital. If a company is mismanaged or otherwise falls on hard times, its stock price will fall. Buyers of stocks in the secondary model have decided on their own that the corporation's future profits will be small. Now, in order to raise new capital, the corporation must sell new shares at a low price. Earlier, if the stock price was $100, the company could raise $100 million by selling 1 million new shares. If the stock price falls to $25, the company must now sell 4 million shares to raise the same amount of investment finance. Under these circumstances, the corporation will probably decide not to issue new stock and will not obtain more investment financing. Thus the stock market punishes companies that are performing poorly with a low stock price and denies them access to new capital.

Opponents of the Anglo-Saxon model of investment finance argue that stock markets are too volatile and are dominated by emotion. They believe it is better to have knowledgeable bankers deciding who should get investment financing. A disadvantage of bank financing, as we have said, is that the bank tends to get too closely linked to the corporation to make impartial investment decisions.

In Chapter 3, we discussed Joseph Schumpeter's theory of change, called creative destruction. The U.S. capital market promotes dynamic change by its willingness to move capital quickly from one sector to another and from one corporation to another. If one sector develops a new technology and another sector's technology lags, the capital market will automatically direct capital to develop the new technology. If consumer tastes change, new capital will flow to the sector with rising consumer demand. One way to see this dynamic is to compare the changing rankings of the largest U.S. corporation over time. Table 8.2 shows the dramatic changes in ranking over a relatively short, 15 year period. A quite different list of companies occupied the top ranks in 2000 than in 1985. For example, Dow Chemical, which declared bankruptcy as a consequence of a class action litigation, is no longer among the top fifty U.S. companies. Enron and WorldCom, ranked seventh and thirtieth in 2000, no longer exist as viable entities. The U.S. capital market punishes, with great decisiveness and speed, corporations that fail in their business plans.

Competition in the Product Market

Resource-allocation arrangements depend on the degree of **market power** in different product markets. There is no accurate measure of market power, but the most frequently used measure is the **concentration ratio**. The concentration ratio gives the percentage of industry sales accounted for by the largest four, eight, or twenty firms. For example, a four-firm concentration ratio of 80 percent means that the four largest firms account for 80 percent of industry sales. An industry with a very low concentration ratio is generally a "competitive" industry; one with a very high concentration ratio is an "oligopoly" or near-monopoly. The comparison is flawed for various reasons: the difficulties of defining industry boundaries; the availability of competitive substitutes; the fact that some firms operate in regional and local markets, others in national and international markets; and so on.

TABLE 8.2   Ranking of Largest
U.S. Corporations (by sales)

1985	2000
ExxonMobil	ExxonMobil
General Motors	Wal-mart
Ford	General Motors
IBM	Ford
AT&T	General Electric
DuPont	Enron
General Motors	IBM
U.S. Steel	AT&T
United Technologies	Verizon
Boeing	Philip Morris
Procter & Gamble	J. P. Morgan/Chase
Beatrice	Bank of America
Philip Morris	SBC Corporation
Dow Chemical	Boeing

Note: Because of energy mergers, energy companies other than ExxonMobil have been omitted.

Source: Fortune, 1985.

The degree of **competition** in the U.S. economy is hard to measure. Most concentration studies focus on manufacturing, which, although it is the most visible branch of U.S. industry, accounts for less than one-fourth of national income. Many industries that produce raw materials, such as agriculture, forest products, and coal, are organized competitively. Yet government price-support programs in agriculture have affected the behavior of agricultural producers, and the owners of coal mines often band together in associations. Retail stores and most services operate in local markets and in a competitive environment.

Estimates of the overall level of competitiveness (including agriculture, manufacturing, trade, and services) are few and far between. Milton Friedman's estimates for the year 1939 indicate that the private sector was then between 15 percent and 25 percent "monopolistic" and between 75 percent and 85 percent "competitive."[20] A study from the 1980s (Table 8.3) finds that the degree of competition increased for the U.S. economy as a whole since the 1960s.[21]

The surprising feature of U.S. manufacturing is that the degree of concentration appears to have scarcely changed since the turn of the century (see Table 8.4). According to G. Warren Nutter's famous study, in 1900 roughly one-third of manufacturing net output came from industries wherein the four largest firms accounted for half or more of industry output. In 1963 and 1982, the figure was still one-third. Morris Adelman reports similar findings for the period 1947–1958, when the average concentration ratio of the four largest firms in each industry rose only from 35 percent

TABLE 8.3   Trends in Competition in the U.S. Economy, 1939–1980

Sector of the Economy	Share of Each Sector That Was Effectively Competitive (percent)		
	1939	1958	1980
Agriculture, forestry, and fisheries	91.6	85.0	86.4
Mining	87.1	92.2	95.8
Construction	27.9	55.9	80.2
Manufacturing	51.5	55.9	69.0
Transportation and public utilities	8.7	26.1	39.1
Wholesale and retail trade	57.8	60.5	93.4
Finance, insurance, and real estate	61.5	63.8	94.1
Services	53.9	54.3	77.9
Total	52.4	56.4	76.7

Note: In this table, an effectively competitive industry is one in which the four-firm concentration ratio was below 40 percent, entry barriers were low, market shares were unstable, and prices were flexible. The extent of oligopoly in the economy is the measure of the combined shares of dominant-firm and tight-oligopoly industries.

Source: William G. Shepherd, "Causes of Increased Competition in the U.S. Economy, 1939–1980," *Review of Economics and Statistics,* November 1982, 613–626. Used by permission of Elsevier Science Publishers, Amsterdam.

to 37 percent. Between 1931 and 1960, the share of the 117 largest manufacturing firms in total manufacturing assets remained stable at 45 percent.[22]

Economic theory suggests that concentrated industries with a great deal of market power will enjoy larger profit rates. Joe S. Bain and H. Michael Mann have shown that profit rates in the 1930s and 1950s tended to rise with concentration and with barriers to entry, although this effect was more pronounced in the 1950s.[23] Later studies found that at concentration ratios above 70 percent, concentration was strongly related to profit rates. Barriers to entry appear to have an even stronger positive effect on profit rates. At lower rates of concentration, the relationship among profits, concentration, and entry barriers appears weak or even nonexistent.[24]

Another gauge of the degree of competition in the U.S. economy is how much output would increase if monopoly were eliminated. Researchers—notably Arnold Harberger and David Schwartzman—have calculated such "monopoly welfare losses."[25] They conclude that if monopoly were to disappear, national income would increase by less than 1 percent. These calculations do not deny that the distribution of income between the monopolist and the consumer is distorted by monopoly. Rather, what is calculated is the "dead-weight loss" of monopoly—that is, the net loss of output due to monopoly.

Critics of monopoly such as Gordon Tullock and Anne Krueger have pointed out that monopoly rent seeking raises society's losses above dead-weight losses.[26] Examples of monopoly rent seeking include bribing public officials to gain monopoly franchises and lobbying to gain protection from foreign imports. Because substantial profit gains accrue to the monopolist, people are prepared to expend substantial

TABLE 8.4   Trends in Concentration in American Manufacturing:
Two Measures

Year	Percentage of Output by Firms with Four-Firm Concentration Ratio of 50 percent or Above (1)	Percentage of Output of 100 Largest Firms (2)
1895–1904	33	n.a.
1947	24	23
1954	30	30
1958	30	32
1972	29	33
1977	28	33
1982	24	33

Sources: G. Warren Nutter, *The Extent of Enterprise Monopoly in the United States, 1899–1939* (Chicago: University of Chicago Press, 1951); pp. 35–48, 112–140; F. M. Scherer, *Industrial Market Structure and Economic Performance* (Boston: Houghton Mifflin, 1980), pp. 68–69; *Concentration Ratios in Manufacturing, 1977 Census of Manufacturing,* MC77-SR-9; *1982 Census of Manufacturers,* MC82-S-7.

resources to turn a competitive industry into a monopoly. Harvey Leibenstein emphasized the "organizational slack" or "X-inefficiency" of monopoly. Because monopolists are faced with less competition, they are under less pressure to minimize costs of production. The competitive firm that fails to minimize costs may be forced out of business, but the monopoly can relax. If one takes monopoly rent seeking and X-inefficiency into account, society's losses from monopoly may be considerable.

Harold Demsetz argues in a different vein that the higher profits of large enterprises result from their superior cost performance.[27] If prices are set competitively so that each firm acts like a price taker, then economic profits accrue to those firms that have lower costs of production. The higher profit rates found in highly concentrated industries are the result of the superior efficiency of large firms.

Regulation

The Constitution's due process clause was designed to protect private property from government regulation. If a federal, state, or local government is able to dictate to owners how they may or may not use their property, their property rights are abridged. The due process clause of the Constitution creates a dilemma: What should the state do to protect the general welfare from the misuse of property by private owners? Clearly the Constitution did not intend for government to refrain from all action affecting property rights. The state's right to tax owners of property is clear, and the Constitution allowed the **right of eminent domain**—the right of the state to take property under certain conditions in the public interest (such as buying land for the construction of railways or making way for an interstate highway). However, from the period of the Constitution's adoption to the 1930s, the right of the federal government to regulate private businesses was strictly limited.

Under Chief Justice John Marshall, the U.S. Supreme Court consistently ruled that the Constitution's contract clause protected the right of contracts from state laws. Marshall himself was a delegate to the Virginia ratifying convention and was the justice most knowledgeable about the original definition of the contract clause.[28] Marshall himself viewed courts as "tribunals which are established for the security of property and to decide human rights." Following Marshall, the Supreme Court consistently ruled that state laws that diminished the right of contract, such as state laws that prohibited the buying of insurance from out-of-state companies or established minimum wage laws, were unconstitutional.

Constitutional protection of private property and of the sanctity of private contracts was gradually weakened starting in 1877 when the state court of Illinois ruled, in *Munn* v. *Illinois,* that businesses "affected with the public interest" were subject to regulation and control by the state of Illinois.[29] A decade later, the Interstate Commerce Commission was set up to regulate the railroads; the Pure Food and Drug Administration was created in 1906, followed by the Federal Trade Commission in 1914. Constitutional protection of private property rights was further weakened during the Great Depression and Roosevelt's New Deal, when it was successfully argued that businesses that affected the public interest could be regulated. A decision written by the Supreme Court in 1934 declared that the economic emergency justified a state law affecting private mortgage debt obligations.[30] Such decisions, rendered largely during the Great Depression, opened the door for increased government regulation of private business. Of the almost thirty major federal departments and agencies, more than half have significant regulatory functions, such as the Environmental Protection Agency, Labor, OSHA, Commerce, Health and Human Services, and Transportation.

The federal government can make decisions affecting business either through the legislative process, in which a bill is passed by Congress and signed by the president, or by executive order and regulation. Regulatory authority creates the danger of passing legislative authority to the executive branch. For example, in the final quarter of 2001, the Clinton administration published over 26,000 pages of regulations in the *Federal Register.*[31] Table 8.5 provides a list of laws extending government regulation of business that were passed between 1962 and 1978 alone.

Regulation has been exercised by a wide variety of local, state, and federal agencies.[32] Other kinds of regulation—control by the courts or by the terms of franchises, charters, and city ordinances—have proved ineffective, and the public has turned instead to administrative regulation, either by an official of executive government or by semi-independent commissions operating under general legislative authority.[33]

Government regulation can be classified as *social regulation* or *economic regulation.*[34] Social regulation is regulation of health, safety, and environment. Examples include consumer product safety rules, environmental protection, and automobile safety and gasoline mileage requirements. Economic regulation is government involvement in markets, such as setting prices, restricting corporate decision making, and controlling competition. Examples of economic regulation include government regulation of utility rates and market structures and the setting of local taxi rates.

Both economic regulation and social regulation impose costs and create benefits. One of the costs of regulation is the costs of compliance—the associated paper work, creating facilities for the handicapped, and so on. The *Federal Register,* which publishes all federal regulations, has reached 100,000 pages per year. Estimates of the compliance costs of regulation are provided in Table 8.6.

U.S. businesses are regulated by government in the interest of protecting the public good. The Air Pollution Control Act of 1962, the Cigarette Labeling and Advertising Act of 1965, the Consumer Product Safety Act of 1972, and the Toxic Substance Control Act of 1976 were all intended to promote the public good. Government regulations impose costs on businesses, and presumably when Congress debates regulatory measures or when regulatory agencies pass new regulations, they should consider both the costs and the benefits. On September 30, 1993, President Bill Clinton issued Executive Order 12866, "Regulatory Planning and Review," requiring federal agencies to ensure that regulations achieve the desired results with a minimal societal burden. Under the executive order, each agency was directed to choose the approach that maximizes net benefits, unless the statute requires another regulatory approach; to assess the costs and benefits of regulatory alternatives, including the alternative of no regulation; and to tailor regulations to impose the least possible burden on society.

A study of regulatory costs that was prepared for Congress in 1995 (Figure 8.4) shows the costs of regulation broken down by type of regulation from 1977 to 1995.

TABLE 8.5   Extension of Government Regulation of Business, 1962–1978

Year of Enactment	Name of Law	Purpose and Function
1962	Food and Drug Amendments	Requires pretesting of drugs for safety and effectiveness and labeling of drugs by generic names
1962	Air Pollution Control Act	Provides first modern ecology statute
1963	Equal Pay Act	Eliminates wage differentials based on sex
1964	Civil Rights Act	Creates Equal Employment Opportunity Commission (EEOC) to investigate charges of job discrimination
1965	Water Quality Act	Extends environmental concern to water
1965	Cigarette Labeling and Advertising Act	Requires labels on hazards of smoking
1966	Fair Packaging and Labeling Act	Requires producers to state what a package contains, how much it contains, and who made the product
1966	Child Protection Act	Bans sale of hazardous toys and articles
1966	Traffic Safety Act	Provides for a coordinated national safety program, including safety standards for motor vehicles
1966	Coal Mine Safety Amendments	Tightens controls on working conditions
1967	Flammable Fabrics Act	Broadens federal authority to set safety standards for inflammable fabrics, including clothing and household products
1967	Age Discrimination in Employment Act	Prohibits job discrimination against individuals aged 40 to 65
1968	Consumer Credit Protection Act (Truth-in-Lending)	Requires full disclosure of terms and conditions of finance charges in credit transactions
1968	Interstate Land Sales Full Disclosure Act	Provides safeguards against unscrupulous practices in interstate land sales
1969	National Environmental Policy Act	Requires environmental impact statements for federal agencies and projects
1970	Amendments to Federal Deposit Insurance Act	Prohibits issuance of unsolicited credit cards. Limits customer's liability in case of loss or theft to $50. Regulates credit bureaus and provides consumers access to files

TABLE 8.5   Extension of Government Regulation of Business, 1962–1978 (cont.)

Year of Enactment	Name of Law	Purpose and Function
1970	Securities Investor Protection Act	Provides greater protection for customers of brokers and dealers and members of national securities exchanges. Establishes a Securities Investor Protection Corporation, financed by fees on brokerage houses
1970	Poison Prevention Packaging Act	Authorizes standards for child-resistant packaging of hazardous substances
1970	Clean Air Act Amendments	Provides for setting air quality standards
1970	Occupational Safety and Health Act	Establishes safety and health standards that must be met by employers
1972	Consumer Product Safety Act	Establishes a commission to set safety standards for consumer products and bans products that sent undue risk of injury
1972	Federal Water Pollution Control Act	Declares an end to the discharge of pollutants into navigable waters by 1985 as a national goal
1972	Noise Pollution and Control Act	Regulates noise limits of products and transportation vehicles
1972	Equal Employment Opportunity Act	Gives EEOC the right to sue employers
1973	Vocational Rehabilitation Act	Requires federal contractors to take affirmative action on hiring the handicapped
1973	Highway Speed Limit Reduction	Limits vehicles to speeds of 55 miles an hour
1973	Safe Drinking Water Act	Requires EPA to set national drinking water regulations
1974	Campaign Finance Amendments	Restricts amounts of political contributions
1974	Employee Retirement Income Security Act	Sets new federal standards for employee pension program
1974	Hazardous Materials Transportation Act	Requires standards for the transportation of hazardous materials
1974	Magnuson–Moss Warranty Improvement Act	Establishes federal standards for written consumer product warranties

(*continued*)

TABLE 8.5   Extension of Government Regulation of Business, 1962–1978 (cont.)

Year of Enactment	Name of Law	Purpose and Function
1975	Energy Policy and Conservation Act	Authorizes greater controls over domestic energy supplies and demands
1976	Hart–Scott–Rodino Antitrust Amendments	Provides for class action suits by state attorneys general; requires large companies to notify the Department of Justice of planned mergers and acquisitions
1976	Toxic Substances Control Act	Requires advance testing and restrictions on use of chemical substances
1977	Department of Energy Organization Act	Establishes a permanent department to regulate energy on a continuing basis
1977	Surface Mining Control and Reclamation Act	Regulates strip mining and the reclamation of abandoned mines
1977	Fair Labor Standards Amendments	Increases the minimum wage in three steps
1977	Export Administration Act	Imposes restrictions on complying with the Arab boycott
1977	Business Payments Abroad Act	Provides for up to $1 million penalties for bribing foreign officials
1977	Saccharin Study and Labeling Act	Requires warning labels on products containing saccharin
1978	Fair Debt Collection Practices Act	Provides for the first nationwide control of collection agencies
1978	Age Discrimination in Employment Act Amendments	Raises the permissible mandatory retirement age from 65 to 70 for most employees

Source: Murray Medenbaum, *Business Government and the Public,* 2nd ed. (Englewood Cliffs, N.J.: Prentice-Hall, 1981), pp. 8–10.

It concludes that regulation cost business almost $700 billion in 1995, which constituted almost 10 percent of GDP. If we apply these percentages to 2002, regulation costs the U.S. economy more than $1 trillion per year, or to put it differerently, about 9 cents of every dollar of output produced by the economy. In 1992, the cost of regulation was in excess of $5,000 per employee for small firms and was around $3,000 for large companies. In manufacturing, where the regulatory burden is higher, the cost per employee ranged from $9,000 for small companies to $5,000 for large companies. Translating these figures to 2002 suggests that small businesses in manufacturing pay

TABLE 8.6   Costs of Regulation in the United States

	Cost (billions)	Percent GDP	Cost per Capita
1976	$63	3.5	$289
1979	$103	4.0	$458
1990	$400	7.0	$1606
1992	$600	8.0	$1961
2002	$1,100	10.0	$3900

Source: Federal Reserve Bank of Dallas, *America's Economic Regulation Burden,* Fall 1996, p. 2. Figure updated to 2002 by authors.

a regulatory cost of $12,000 for each employee and that large manufacturing firms pay about $7,000 per employee. An independent estimate prepared by the Federal Reserve Bank of Dallas in 1996 came to similar conclusions about the costs of regulation. As updated by the authors, this estimate suggests that regulation cost each man, woman, and child on average almost $4,000 in 2002. For a family of four, the cost of regulation would therefore be some $16,000. The truth of these estimates of the high costs of regulation is borne home by the fact that all fifty titles to the U.S. Code of Federal Regulations plus the previous twelve months of the complete *Federal Register* must be packed into a series of CD-ROM disks that businesses can buy on the Internet for $399 per year, including quarterly updates.[35]

Students of economics know that the current $1 trillion regulatory burden, like any other tax, can be shifted forward to final consumers, depending on conditions of supply and demand. Although it is unclear how the burden is distributed between business and households, the best guess is that households pay most of this burden in higher prices.

Proponents of regulation point to its significant beneficial effects. Over the past thirty years, the United States has made substantial progress in cleaning up air, water, and land, reducing automobile emissions, reducing lead pollution, and improving safety and design in airbags and infant safety seats. Regulation, however, cannot be evaluated only in terms of its benefits. A regulation is economically and socially beneficial only if it yields benefits in excess of its costs. In fact, all regulations are now required to be subject to a cost/benefit test. According to the 1995 report to Congress cited above, however, "Unfortunately, although the benefits of regulations are important, no reliable estimates of total benefits exist." The government's own report concludes that the benefits of reducing air pollution exceed its costs, whereas the benefits of reducing water pollution fall short of its costs by as much as $20 billion per year. And "for other environmental areas, we lack comparable data. The general trend appears to be the adoption of regulations whose benefits do not exceed their costs. The 1990 Clean Air Act Amendments very likely will impose additional compliance costs of $30 billion annually while generating far smaller additional benefits. This trend is driven in part by the fact that many of the low-cost options for lessening risks already have been adopted."

FIGURE 8.4   Annualized Regulatory Costs in Billions of 1995 Dollars

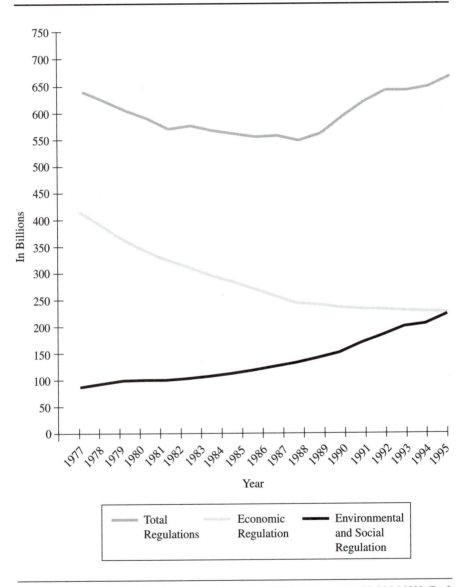

Source: Thomas D. Hopkins, "Profiles of Regulatory Costs," SBA Contract SBAHQ-95-M-0298 (Draft Final Report, 1995), Table A.

These calculations capture only the direct costs of federal regulations. There are also significant indirect costs of regulation, called unfunded mandates. An **unfunded mandate** is a regulation, such as asbestos removal requirements or handicap-access regulations, that the private business must pay for out of its own pocket without government assistance. The calculations cited above also do not include the cost of state and local regulation of business, which comes in the form of prohibitions, licenses, and other regulatory acts.

Another complication in evaluating the costs of regulation is the absence of counterfactual information. **Counterfactual information** indicates what would have happened in the absence of a particular event. It is presumed that improvements in automobile safety, gasoline mileage, and seat belt technology, as well as safer foods and drugs and the like, are due to government regulation and would not have occurred in its absence. This assumption ignores the fact the private businesses might have been motivated by profit maximization to produce the same results without regulation. Automobile manufacturers, for example, might find it in their narrow interest to produce a more fuel-efficient or a safer car because such a car would be easier to market and would command a higher price.

Given the high costs of regulation, federal government agencies have shown a willingness to entertain new regulatory ideas in the area of environmental protection. The most significant change has been the greater use of "economic" regulation of the environment. In particular, regulatory agencies understand that different companies are able to reduce pollution at different resource costs. They have therefore allowed trading in "rights to pollute." In a particular industry, for example, the environmental regulatory agency establishes emission limits and issues the number of "licenses to pollute" that will keep emissions within the prescribed limits. The companies receiving these licenses, however, are free to sell them to the highest bidder. Companies that can reduce their emissions at low cost will be willing to sell their pollution rights to high bidders who cannot reduce their emissions efficiently. In fact, markets located in Chicago and New York now conduct active trading in pollution emission rights. Notably, the prices of emission rights have been falling steadily, driven down by the incentive to create new pollution abatement technologies.

Deregulation

In the 1960s and 1970s, the high costs and perceived inefficiencies of regulation prompted a movement toward **deregulation**—the reduced incidence of government regulation of business and the return of decision making to the private businesses themselves. Deregulation was promoted by anecdotes of enormous regulatory inefficiencies: trucks being required by federal regulations to return empty from long hauls, airlines being forced to serve communities with few customers, slower railroad freight being required to charge the same prices as more flexible trucking, and so forth. The proponents of deregulation argued that if decisions were returned to the businesses themselves, customers would benefit from lower prices and better service.

The deregulation of the American economy began in the late 1970s. The Airline Deregulation Act, signed in October of 1978, allowed the airlines rather than the Civil Aeronautics Board (which went out of existence in 1984) to set fares and choose routes, according to the availability of landing slots at airports.[36] In 1980, the Motor Carrier Act curbed the role of the Interstate Commerce Commission in interstate trucking. Also in 1980, the Staggers Rail Act led to major changes in railroad transport, and the Depository Institution Deregulation and the Monetary Control acts significantly changed the way the banking sector sets charges, enters markets, and the like. The AT&T Settlement of 1982 and the Cable Television Deregulation Act of 1984 brought major and well-known changes in the telecommunications and cable television industries, respectively.

Much of this deregulation was motivated by the message of microeconomic theory—namely, that the development of competitive markets could provide benefits that would outweigh associated costs. At the same time, the opponents of deregulation warned of deteriorating service, pricing wars, and general instability in deregulated industries.

U.S. experience has shown that deregulation leads to lower prices for most—but not all—consumers. Consumers in small markets characterized by high costs are no longer protected and now have to pay prices closer to costs. Deregulation has increased the diversity of services offered and has given consumers more freedom of choice. Firms that had been protected by regulation have lowered their costs substantially, and these lower costs are being passed on to their customers. Deregulation has also had its losers. Firms that could not meet competitive pressures have gone out of business or have been acquired by more successful firms. Employees have seen their earnings fall as firms have sought ways to lower their costs.

In the airline industry, the problems of high fuel prices, terrorism, and high debt resulted in the concentration of the industry in the hands of a few giant airlines. In banking, a number of problems (such as corruption and the inflation of the 1970s and 1980s) led to massive failures both in the savings and loan industry and in commercial banking. These negative experiences have caused some to question the wisdom of deregulation. There is, however, widespread agreement that consumers have been the prime beneficiaries of deregulation. Consumers now have a broad choice of long-distance carriers, airline fares, and financial services, offered at competitive prices.

Support for deregulation continued into the early 2000s. The most controversial area of expansion of deregulation is the electricity market. Previously, electricity was supplied by regulated electrical utilities that were granted monopolies over geographic markets, subject to rate regulation by state regulatory agencies.[37] A number of experiments were tried that created a private unregulated market in electricity. With the development of transmission technology and a national grid system of high-voltage cables, electricity could be transmitted at low cost from one geographic region to another, thereby creating the opportunity for a competitive market in electricity. Under deregulation, local utilities would serve as common carriers obligated to transmit electricity purchased from various supplies to the national power grid. Marketers of electricity can enter into contracts with businesses and ultimately consumers whereby they supply the end user with electricity purchased from the cheapest source. Under this system, the forces of competition, not regulatory agencies, will determine the price of electricity.

The year 2001 found electricity deregulation under intense scrutiny. California passed deregulation legislation that froze the retail price of electricity, while allowing the wholesale price to be set in the deregulated electricity market. Moreover, California passed rules that required that wholesale electricity be purchased in short-term markets, forbidding purchases in long-term forward markets. As energy prices (and electricity prices) rose unexpectedly in world markets, California electricity retailers found that their retail prices did not cover their wholesale prices, and to avoid massive bankruptcies, the state of California had to cover the price differential through the state budget, which was thrown into a severe deficit as a consequence. The later, unrelated failure of Enron Corporation, one of the electricity marketers to California, introduced further confusion into the picture of electricity deregulation.

Deregulation has indeed had the consequences predicted by economists. In general, prices have fallen; industries are making their own decisions about prices and services, and the result, such as in the airlines industry and electricity market, has been increased volatility and business uncertainty—a characteristic of capitalism. A large number of airlines have declared bankruptcy; the state of California has a huge budget deficit; the banking and securities industry has concentrated as large national banks and brokerage firms have taken dominant positions in their industries. As a consequence of deregulation, to quote one of its major proponents,

> Federal regulation, for better or worse, has changed dramatically since 1977. Most of the older forms of economic regulation, some dating from the nineteenth century, have now been substantially reduced or eliminated—including most of the industry-specific regulation of agriculture, communications, energy, finance, and transportation. In most cases, the reduction has led to lower real prices, increased services, and broad popular support. The only significant current threat to continued deregulation is a consequence of the Enron collapse—the threat of increasing regulation of accounting, corporate governance, and securities.[38]

The Labor Market

The Anglo-Saxon (U.S.) labor market differs substantially from its European and Asian counterparts. As we have noted, the U.S. corporation is managed to maximize shareholder value, not stakeholder value. The major stakeholders in a corporation are its managers, employees, and workers. Their interests, such as staying on the job during economic downturns, are regarded as less important than those of the shareholders. Hence, in principle, there should be less job security in the American labor market than in the European labor market, where stakeholder rights are greater.

The functioning of a nation's labor market depends on a number of factors. One is the legal framework: What are the rules and regulations that employers must follow? Second, the labor market's functioning depends on the degree to which workers are organized into labor or trade unions. A **labor** or **trade union** is an organization of employees and workers of a company, occupation, or branch that comes together for the purpose of affecting conditions of work and pay. Third, an economy's labor market is determined by history and custom. Particular companies or branches of the economy may have hiring and firing practices that have evolved over a long period of time and that continue to affect the way that market functions today.

Labor is allocated largely through labor markets in the United States.[39] In competitive labor markets, employers demand larger quantities of labor at low wages.

The supply of labor is a positive function of the wage rate offered, and a wage rate equating the supply and the demand for labor is established automatically in the marketplace.

Unions

Less then 13 percent of the U.S. labor force belongs to labor unions. In the 1930s, union members accounted for 6 to 7 percent of the labor force. Union membership rose in the 1940s and peaked at 25 percent in the mid-1950s. Since then the percentage has declined—despite the notable increase in union membership among public employees—largely because of the rapid growth of white-collar employment. Government employees now count for the majority of unionized workers. The American trade union movement is more decentralized than its counterparts in Europe. More authority rests with local unions, and the movement has failed to produce its own political party. The American union movement consists of loose federations of local unions banded into national unions.

Most American unions are associated with the AFL-CIO (American Federation of Labor–Congress of Industrial Organizations). The AFL-CIO accounts for almost 80 percent of all union members.

American workers were slower to organize than their European counterparts, because unfavorable legislation existed until the early 1930s: The Sherman Antitrust Act of 1890 was initially applied against "monopolistic" labor unions, court orders prohibited union activity, and "yellow dog" contracts required employees to agree not to join a union. The Norris–LaGuardia Act of 1932 and the Wagner Act of 1935 laid the legislative foundation for the growth of unionism.

Most studies show that unions raise wages in unionized industries. Unions control wages through their power to strike and to control the supply of (and in some cases, through work rules, the demand for) labor. Unions raised wages in the unionized sector some 25 percent during the mid-1930s, 5 percent during the late 1940s, and some 10 to 15 percent during the 1950s. More recent studies show that union wages are 15 to 18 percent higher than they would have been in the absence of unions. For the entire economy, the impact of unionization is probably small. Union wages are emulated in the nonunionized sector, and higher union wages reduce employment in the unionized branches and hence place downward pressure on wages in nonunionized branches.

What has been the effect of unions on productivity? Economists have traditionally believed that unions have a negative effect on productivity through disruptive strikes, featherbedding practices, and distortion of union–nonunion wages. Some economists have questioned this view. Albert Hirschman, Richard Freeman, and James Medoff maintain that unions actually raise productivity by giving union members a collective voice. Without union representation, the only way workers can raise their voice against bad employers is to exit—that is, to leave the enterprise. With unions, workers can gain effective representation and can work from within to improve conditions. Unions can have a positive effect on productivity in three ways: Unions reduce worker turnover and thus limit hiring and training costs. In the union setting, senior workers are more likely to provide informal training and assistance. And the union provides for an improved information flow between workers and managers.

The most notable differences between the American and European labor movements are that U.S. trade unions, although they are closely associated with the Democratic party, do not have their own political party. American union members split their votes between the Republican and Democratic parties, although the clear majority vote for Democrats. More important, U.S. labor unions generally do not bargain at a national level, as do the German unions, where the metal workers and public-sector employees set wage patterns for the entire labor force. Also, there is less cohesion among U.S. labor unions, so it would be difficult to organize a general strike that would paralyze the entire economy.

Although U.S. labor unions use collective bargaining and the threat of strike to set their wages and conditions of work, collective-bargaining agreements are primarily about conditions of pay, although there are cases where the employer will guarantee a specified level of employment. If business turns down in the course of the contract, the employer is free to lay workers off. The pattern of layoffs is governed by union rules, such as the workers with least seniority being laid off first and the most senior workers being hired back first. But generally speaking, U.S. labor union members are accustomed to periodic layoffs, thereby creating a flexible labor market. A **flexible labor market** is one in which wage rates and employment can be varied within the short run. In unionized sectors that operate on the basis of multiyear collective-bargaining contracts, there is usually more flexibility in employment than in wages.

Government Intervention in the Labor Market

Government (usually local or state government) affects wages through licensing and other procedures that regulate the supply of labor in particular occupations. It also affects the supply of labor in the long run through its policies toward public education and job training. Moreover, antidiscrimination legislation, hiring quotas, and the like affect employment practices.

The most notable difference between the U.S. and European labor markets is the much more limited degree of government regulation in American labor markets. Although U.S. employers feel that they are subject to extensive regulation, such regulation is relatively minor compared to the major European labor markets in Germany, France, and Italy, as will be explained in the next chapter. U.S. employers are regulated by several acts.

The **Fair Labor Standards Act of 1938** establishes standards for minimum wages, overtime pay, record keeping, and child labor. The act covers enterprises with $500,000 or more in annual dollar sales—less if they are engaged in interstate commerce. It also covers domestic service workers who earn at least $1,300. It exempts executive, administrative, and professional employees (including teachers and academic administrative personnel in elementary and secondary schools), outside sales employees, and certain skilled computer employees, as well as a long list of other specialized workers.

The act requires employers of covered employees to pay a minimum wage of not less than $5.15 an hour, exempting student learners and those with specified disabilities. Employers must keep records on wages, hours, and other information as set forth in the Department of Labor's regulations. It is a violation of the act to fire or in any other manner discriminate against an employee for filing a complaint or for participating in a legal proceeding under the act. The act also prohibits the shipment, in interstate commerce, of goods that were produced in violation of the minimum wage, overtime pay, child labor, or special minimum wage provisions. Willful violators may be prosecuted criminally and fined up to $10,000. A second conviction may result in imprisonment.[40]

The **Occupational Safety and Health Act of 1970 (OSH Act)** covers all employers and their employees,[41] either directly by the Federal Occupational Safety and Health Administration (OSHA) or by an OSHA-approved state job safety and health plan. The act does not cover self-employed persons, farms that employ their own family members, or employees of state and local governments. OSHA sets health and safety standards and conducts inspections to ensure safe and healthful workplaces. OSHA standards may require that employers adopt certain practices, means, methods, or processes reasonably necessary and appropriate to protect workers on the job. Employees must comply with all OSHA rules and regulations. The general duty clause states that each employer "shall furnish . . . a place of employment which is free from recognized hazards that are causing or are likely to cause death or serious physical harm." Each employer must advise the nearest OSHA office of any accident that results in one or more fatalities or the hospitalization of three or more employees. OSHA handles employee complaints and grants employees the right to complain to OSHA about safety and health conditions and to have their identities kept confidential. Each year the Office of the Federal Register publishes all current regulations and standards in the U.S. Code of Federal Regulations. Every establishment covered by the act is subject to programmed or unprogrammed inspections by OSHA compliance safety and health officers. Establishments with high injury rates receive programmed inspections, and unprogrammed inspections are used in response to fatalities, catastrophes, and complaints. An employer who willfully violates the act may be assessed, for each violation, a civil penalty of not more than $70,000 but not less than $5,000. A willful violation that has resulted in the death of an employee is punishable by a court-imposed fine or by imprisonment for up to six months, or both, and by fines of up to $250,000 for an individual or $500,000 for a corporation.

Although these regulations may appear onerous at times to U.S. employers, they do not dictate hiring and firing procedures. Some U.S. labor markets, such as the civil service, academic labor markets, and the postal service operate according to stringent rules on hiring, tenure, and firing practices, but in most cases procedures for hiring and firing are set by the enterprises themselves, including probation periods, pay scales, promotion practices, and seniority privileges. Some procedures are worked out between the employer and the labor union; an example is airline contracts, which set hours of work, vacation time, and furlough procedures.

In fact, unionized industries appear to have worked out a system of sophisticated **implicit contracts**, which are unwritten rules about hiring and layoff practices.[42] These implicit contracts are usually agreements that less-senior union members will be laid off first during business downturns, that the wages of those that stay on the payroll will not be reduced, and that laid-off workers will be recalled to their old jobs in accordance with seniority.

Welfare

U.S. government public assistance has been limited to public education, some low-cost health care for the poor, and social security insurance for retirement, disability, and unemployment. Such services are typically supplied on a mixed private-enterprise–public-service basis with the user paying a portion of the cost.

The mix of private and public support has shifted toward public provision, reflecting a changing public attitude toward government responsibility. Over the last half-century, this change has been most dramatic in the areas of health expenditures, social welfare expenditures, and social insurance (Table 8.7), which earlier had been regarded as private or charitable obligations. Prior to the 1930s, nearly all retirement, health, and unemployment insurance was purchased on a voluntary private basis; in 1929 only 10 percent of personal health expenditures were funded by governmental agencies. Public elementary and secondary education has dominated the American education system for quite a while, but the government share of support for higher education has increased substantially over the last 50 years. During that time, public universities have supplanted private universities as the dominant institutions in higher education.

TABLE 8.7   Expenditures on Public Assistance in the United States, 1890–2000

Year	Public Social Welfare Expenditures as a Percent of GDP[a]	Social Insurance Expenditures as a Percent of GDP	Government Health Care Expenditures as a Percent of GDP
2000	19.0	8.0	6.7
1994	21.0	8.4	5.9
1990	19.1	9.3	5.0
1987	18.4	10.8	4.2
1985	18.4	10.1	4.2
1980	18.6	8.0	3.6
1970	14.8	5.7	2.5
1955	8.6	2.6	0.9
1929	3.9	0.2	0.4
1920	—	—	—
1900	—	—	—
1890	2.4	—	0.1

[a]Social welfare expenditures include social insurance and public aid, education, veterans' programs, child nutrition, and rehabilitation programs.

Sources: U.S. Department of Commerce, *Historical Statistics of the United States: Colonial Times to 1970; Statistical Abstract of the United States* (selected years).

Two general rules have governed public assistance. The first is that, if feasible, goods should be provided on an "in-kind" basis (for example, subsidized school lunches and food stamps) rather than as income payments. This rule suggests an unwillingness to rely on freedom of choice and a feeling that the poor are not to be trusted to allocate their incomes wisely. The second general rule is that families should not have the power to shop around for education or public health, despite arguments that making such choice possible would force suppliers to be more efficient and responsive to the consumer.

In the 1990s, discussion of the U.S. public assistance programs turned to their potential effects on economic efficiency and to their unanticipated consequences. It was argued that public assistance programs based on calculated "need" encouraged families on welfare to reduce their incomes. In particular, "needs-based" programs actually created incentives for fathers to desert their families in order to reduce the income of the family on welfare. Government unemployment insurance programs, designed to mitigate the costs of unemployment, may serve to encourage longer spells of unemployment. Government health insurance programs, by increasing the demand for medical care, may cause medical costs to rise more rapidly, thereby making them less affordable to the uninsured.

In the mid-1990s, Congress passed and President Clinton signed a major change in the aid to families with dependent children (AFDC) program with the passage of the Personal Responsibility, Work Opportunity and Medicaid Restructuring Act of 1996. Its major provision was to limit recipients (mothers on welfare) to two years of eligibility to receive public assistance. Programs were put in place to train welfare-dependent mothers and place them in jobs so that they could become self-supporting. Prior to the passage of this bill, the number of individuals receiving aid to families with dependent children had more than tripled since 1965. More than two-thirds of these recipients were children, 89 percent of whom were living in homes in which no father was present. While the number of children receiving AFDC benefits increased threefold, the total number of children declined by 5.5 percent. The rate of no-marital teen pregnancy rose 23 percent from 54 pregnancies per 1,000 unmarried teenagers in 1976 to 66.7 such pregnancies in 1991, and young women 17 and under who gave birth outside of marriage were more likely to go on public assistance and to spend more years on welfare once enrolled. Only 9 percent of married-couple families with children less than 18 years of age had income below the national poverty level, but 46 percent of female-headed households with children less than 18 were below the national poverty level. Between 1985 and 1990, the public cost of births to teenage mothers under the AFDC program, the food stamp program, and the Medicaid program was $129 billion.

Under the 1996 bill, states were required to submit programs designed to provide assistance to needy families with (or expecting) children and to provide parents with job preparation and support services to enable them to leave the program and become self-sufficient. Welfare recipients were required to engage in work once the state deemed the recipient prepared for work or after twenty-four consecutive months of assistance. The states were also to establish goals and take action to reduce out-of-wedlock pregnancies, with special emphasis on teenage pregnancies.[43]

Limiting welfare assistance and promoting self-reliance through the acquisition of job skills is consistent with the precepts of the Anglo-Saxon model. Although critics of the Personal Responsibility, Work Opportunity and Medicaid Restructuring Act of 1996 declared it too harsh, it brought about a drastic reduction in the number of young mothers on welfare and a dramatic increase in their employment.

Income Distribution

The distribution of income is measured by the Lorenz curve (defined in Chapter 3), which compares family income by rank (say, the lowest fifth to the highest fifth of all families) with percentage share of income either before or after taxes. Some studies "tailor" the Lorenz curve by adjusting for age differences, for differences in family size, and for the distribution of government services.[44]

As measured by the Lorenz curve before taxes and any other adjustments, the U.S. distribution of income seems to have changed little since 1950. In 1950, the lowest fifth and the highest fifth of families accounted for 5 and 45 percent of all income, respectively. By 1995, those figures were 4 and 46 percent. The change since 1929 has been more substantial: The share of the highest fifth of U.S. families declined from 54 to 47 percent between 1929 and 1995.[45] It has been argued that if one adjusts these figures for differences in age and family size, then the trend toward greater equality becomes even more evident.[46]

The traditional view is that government has not played a significant role in redistributing income from upper-income to lower-income groups. Although the federal tax system is progressive (upper-income families pay a higher percentage of their income in taxes than do lower-income families), state and local taxes are regressive (upper-income families pay a lower percentage of income). On balance, therefore, the total tax system is roughly proportional (each income group pays the same percentage of its income in taxes), and the after-tax distribution of income is little different from the before-tax distribution. Remember, though, that all such calculations are inexact because of the difficulty of determining what proportion of business and property taxes are passed on to the consumer in the form of higher prices. Joseph Pechman and Benjamin Okner have found that if one assumes such taxes are almost entirely passed on to the consumer, then the tax system is proportional. If one assumes they are borne by the producer, however, Pechman and Okner found that the tax system becomes progressive, but only at the very top and very bottom of the income distribution.[47]

According to some, the state plays a greater redistributive role than is commonly thought.[48] The basis for such claims is that lower-income groups receive larger shares of government in-kind benefits (food stamps, welfare, public education) than their shares of money income. If one includes the value of these benefits in income and then subtracts income and payroll taxes, the distribution of disposable income is much more nearly equal than the unadjusted figures suggest. Figure 8.5 shows calculations from a study by Edgar Browning to illustrate this position. The redistributive role of government in the United States is probably much less significant than in other industrialized capitalist countries. Thus, relatively speaking, the government plays a modest role in the redistribution of income in the United States.

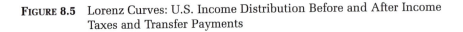

FIGURE 8.5   Lorenz Curves: U.S. Income Distribution Before and After Income
Taxes and Transfer Payments

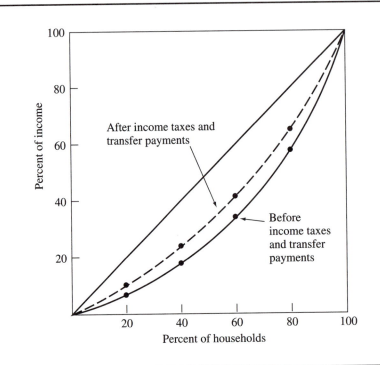

Source: Data from 1972 based on Edgar K. Browning, "The Trend Toward Equality in the Distribution of
Net Income," *Southern Economic Journal* 43 (July 1976), 914.

Providing for Income and Security

The "pure" Anglo-Saxon (American) model espouses the principle of self-reliance.
The state is not responsible for the income and security of its citizens; rather, this responsibility lies with the families, local community, and private charities. Individuals,
not the state, are responsible for providing for retirement. The life cycle of earnings
is predictable; therefore, during their prime earning years, rational individuals should
accumulate savings to be used during retirement. Obviously, there must be deviations
from this pure model in the real world. No country can ignore the income and security of its citizens in need because of special circumstances such as disability, death
of a spouse, and so on.

The major break with the nonintevention philosophy occurred in the summer of
1934, when President Franklin D. Roosevelt announced his intention to create a program for social security. The Social Security Act was signed into law on August 14,
1935, creating a social insurance program to pay retired workers aged 65 or older a
continuing income after retirement. The original act provided only retirement benefits,

and only to the worker. The 1939 amendments added payments to the spouse and minor children of a retired worker (so-called dependents benefits) and survivors benefits paid to the family in the event of the premature death of the worker. This change transformed social security from a retirement program for individuals into a family-based economic security program. In 1972, the law was changed to provide automatic annual cost-of-living adjustments (COLAs).

The Social Security Amendments of 1954 launched a disability insurance program that provided the public with additional coverage against economic insecurity. In 1956, the Social Security Act was amended to provide benefits to disabled workers aged 50 to 65 and to disabled adult children. The most significant change involved the passage of Medicare, which extended health coverage to social security beneficiaries aged 65 or older (and eventually to those receiving disability benefits as well). Nearly 20 million beneficiaries enrolled in Medicare in the first three years of the program. In 1977, a reorganization created the Health Care Financing Administration (HCFA), which assumed administrative responsibility for Medicare.

Since its inception, social security has been a pay-as-you-go system. The social security taxes paid into the system by workers and employees were placed in the general fund and were used to pay social security benefits as well as other general government outlays. As the ratio of active to retired workers fell, the social security program faced an impending financing crisis in the 1980s. In 1940, there were 42 workers per retiree. Today the ratio is 3 to 1; by 2050 it will be 2 to 1. President Ronald Reagan appointed a blue-ribbon panel, known as the Greenspan Commission, to study the financing issues and make recommendations for legislative changes. The final bill, signed into law in 1983, made numerous changes in the social security and Medicare programs, including the taxation of social security benefits and the raising of retirement ages. On April 7, 2000, President Clinton signed the Senior Citizens' Freedom to Work Act of 2000, which spared approximately 900,000 people who were collecting benefits but were still working from having their benefits reduced because of their earnings.

Social security has become a mainstay of U.S. life. One in six Americans receives a social security benefit, and about 98 percent of all workers are in jobs covered by social security. Almost 45 million people receive social security benefits, and nearly 1 in 3 beneficiaries is not a retiree.[49] In 2001, social security paid retirement and survivors benefits to 38.8 million people and disability benefits to 6.7 million. Meanwhile, 153.4 million workers contributed to the program. The average social security benefit in 2000 was $767 per month, or $9,204 per year. Among retirees, 64 percent depend on social security for half or more of their income, 29 percent rely on social security for 90 percent or more of their retirement income, and 18 percent rely on the program for all their retirement income.[50] Hence, about half of American retirees depend almost exclusively on social security for their retirement income.

The social security system is funded by a payroll tax on employees, a tax burden that is split evenly between employee and employer. The 2002 contribution rate, also known as the FICA tax, for employees was 7.65 percent, with the employer matching the employee's contribution. Self-employed persons pay 15.3 percent. The maximum tax withheld in 2002 was $5,263, although high-income earners must pay more than this because Medicare contributions are not subject to any maximum income limit. Social security contributions constitute the second-largest source of federal revenue and are equal to over 70 percent of federal income tax receipts. For about one-third of U.S. families, the social security tax is the only tax they pay on income.

Despite proposals to privatize social security by allowing current workers to invest in their own earmarked accounts, social security is still organized on a pay-as-you-go basis. Payments to beneficiaries are paid out of social security tax receipts (which are currently in excess of payments) and out of general tax revenues if needed. With the declining number of active workers per retiree, social security payments will, in the future, have to be made out of general tax revenues. The social security system has been calculated to have an unfunded liability of several trillion dollars. An **unfunded liability** is the shortfall in funds currently available to meet the future obligations of a retirement program, such as social security.

Although it has not proved politically possible to privatize social security, steps have been taken to encourage workers and employees avail themselves of opportunities to accumulate retirement funds to supplement social security. Such vehicles include 401K pension plans and IRA accounts, which permit employees to invest pretax income in retirement accounts that cannot be tapped (without penalty) until retirement. These private retirement funds have grown to enormous proportions. Employees contributed to 401K and IRA accounts at an average rate of $100 billion per year in the 1990s, and the value of assets in such accounts averaged around $1 trillion.[51]

Whether the retirement system is a public pay-as-you-go system or a private system based on purchases of stocks and bonds in private capital markets has an effect on savings and economic growth. In a pay-as-you-go system, retirement contributions are used to pay current retirees and to cover general expenditures, if necessary. There is no increase in private investment as a consequence. If the funds are invested in private accounts in the form of corporate stocks and bonds, these funds are used to finance investment and to grow the capital stock. With the growth of the capital stock, the economy will expand, as will the standard of living.

The Anglo-Saxon (U.S.) model deals with employment insecurity and poverty via programs administered by the federal and state governments in association with the social security administration. Protection against poverty is provided primarily by the Aid to Families with Dependent Children (AFDC) program, which provides income payments to families that do not meet minimum income standards. Employment security and antipoverty programs were established during the Great Depression but were increased substantially with Lyndon Johnson's Great Society programs, passed in 1964.

Privatization

In recent years, interest has been growing in **privatization**, the shift of economic activity from the public sector to the private sector.[52] In part, this new interest stems from the vast privatization efforts taking place in the former Soviet Union and Eastern Europe economies and in Western Europe. In this sense, privatization represents one way to reduce the role of government in a market economy. But the contemporary

American economy focuses more on efficiency, or the notion that goods and services can be provided more efficiently (that is, at lower cost) in the private sector than in the public sector. As noted above, there is limited public enterprise in the United States. Hence any substantial privatization would have to be of services typically supplied by government.

Thus, whereas privatization in other countries consists primarily of changes in equity arrangements from public to private, privatization in the United States is more likely to consist of government contracting for the private production of traditionally public-sector goods and services, such as trash collection, homes for the elderly, local transportation services, schools, and even prisons.

Privatization is a matter of considerable controversy in the contemporary American economy. Accordingly, it is easy to find strongly held views on both sides of the subject. Those who favor privatization in the provision of municipal services, for example, argue that beyond immediate cost reduction, quality will improve as a result of competitive markets and that in the long term, the role of government in the economy will be reduced. Those who oppose privatization argue that, in fact, only limited empirical evidence indicates actual cost reductions. Moreover, because measuring its impact is difficult, the role of government might not be reduced, competitive provision of services might not prevail, and quality might, in fact, be threatened. Inevitably, privatization threatens government employees, who are likely to oppose the trend.

A case in point has been the battle over vouchers in public education. If government gave parents vouchers that could be used to pay for education in the school of the parents' choice, this would result in a de facto privatization of U.S. public education. Vouchers have therefore been strongly opposed by teacher unions.

What is the status of privatization in the United States in early 2000s? First, although past trends have been toward contracting, there are publicly owned facilities, such as airports, roads, water systems, and sports centers, to which the privatization discussion has been applied. Second, although considerable variation exists from one city or region to another, there is a substantial amount of private initiative in the provision of local services. Finally, opinion expressed in the scholarly literature remains divided. However, as more case studies are examined, empirical evidence will doubtless help in understanding privatization, in determining whether it is a realistic alternative for cost savings, and in sorting out the preconditions that are necessary to achieve such savings.

Macroeconomic Planning

Planning for macroeconomic stability in the United States is limited to using the indirect tools of monetary and fiscal policy. No national economic plan is drafted by government. In this, the United States differs significantly from other industrialized capitalist countries, most of which have some form of national economic planning or industrial policy. Congressional proposals to introduce a mild form of economic planning have generated considerable controversy.[53]

Prior to the Great Depression, the prevailing notion in government circles was that monetary and fiscal policies should be neutral. "Neutral" meant interfering as little as possible with private economic activity. After the Great Depression and the acceptance of Keynesian economics, this view changed; by the 1960s, both major political parties came to accept the view that discretionary monetary and fiscal policies should be used to counter cyclical unemployment and inflation. Although some American monetarists and rational-expectations theorists have spoken out in favor of a return to the traditional neutralist view, monetary and fiscal planners continue to engage in countercyclical policy.

The Federal Reserve System (the Fed) is in charge of formulating monetary policy. Established in 1913, the Federal Reserve System consists of twelve Federal Reserve district banks coordinated by the Board of Governors in Washington, D.C. In the United States the "central bank" is more decentralized along regional lines than is common for central banks, but it nonetheless performs the functions of a central bank—regulating the money supply through open-market operations, managing the discount rate, setting reserve requirements, and so on.

Authority over fiscal policy is diffused among the various executive and legislative bodies in charge of government spending and taxation, and the balance of authority has tended to shift over time. It is therefore difficult to describe briefly how important fiscal decisions are made. The president can propose budgets, but only Congress can approve them. The Treasury Department can propose changes in the tax structure, but it is the Congress that amends and approves such executive suggestions.

The conduct of monetary policy is more divorced from the business of day-to-day politics than is that of fiscal policy. Members of the Board of Governors of the Fed are appointed for fourteen-year terms, and although they are ultimately responsible to Congress, a tradition of independence for the Fed has evolved. Recurring proposals call for greater congressional control of the Fed, and there is evidence that the Fed does seek to pursue a monetary policy consistent with that of the current administration. The conduct of fiscal policy is very much a matter of politics, so it has proved difficult to conduct countercyclical fiscal policy. This is especially true during periods of inflation, when politically unpopular budget cuts and tax increases are shunned.

On the whole, the distinctive feature of economic planning in the United States is its virtual absence. Price and wage controls have been applied during periods of inflation, in the form of either voluntary guidelines or mandatory wage and price limitations. The most dramatic examples were the price freezes of 1971–1973, which showed the American public the disastrous consequences of wage and price controls. The negative effects of interfering in the price system were again apparent when efforts were made to control gasoline prices during the energy crises of the 1970s.

Final Comments

The Anglo-Saxon model was developed in England in the eighteenth century. Under it, England became the world's largest and most affluent nation, despite its island status. The tradition of the Anglo-Saxon model was passed on to the United States, which expanded that tradition in its Constitution. The United States appears to follow the Anglo-Saxon model most closely in its capital and labor markets. The rise in regulation of business since the 1930s has made the U.S. economy a highly regulated economy with a regulatory burden of at least $4,000 per capita, despite a significant deregulation of traditionally regulated industries beginning in the late 1970s.

The economic successes of the United States after 1982 have encouraged other countries to adopt some features of the Anglo-Saxon model, such as deregulation and privatization. The "liberalization" of capital and labor markets has proved more difficult in other countries, such as those in Europe, where liberalization efforts encounter significant barriers. Some countries, such as Ireland in the 1990s and, to a lesser extent, the Netherlands, have deliberately adopted some features of the Anglo-Saxon model. In both cases, the move to the Anglo-Saxon model has improved their economic performance.

Summary

- The Anglo-Saxon model of American capitalism is patterned after the classical liberal ideas of Adam Smith, such as the notion of the invisible hand.
- By contrast, the European model places less faith in the invisible hand and calls for more state intervention.
- The Asian model, which is similar to the European model in terms of institutional arrangements, is focused on capital formation.
- The U.S Constitution specifies three branches of government—executive, legislative, and judicial—each of which represents a substantial check over the other branches.
- The original intent of the U.S. Constitution was to limit the power and scope of the federal government.
- The private sector (business sector) accounts for approximately 75 percent of economic activity, the government sector for roughly 25 percent.
- There are three primary forms of business organizations: sole proprietorships, partnerships, and corporations.
- Corporate governance is concerned with the issue of for whose interest a corporation is operated.
- U.S. corporations are run for the benefit of shareholders, or owners, as measured by increases in market capitalization.
- The market for corporate control is a market wherein rival management teams have the opportunity to buy control of the corporation from its owners.
- The capital market is the market for long-term financial assets such as stocks and bonds.
- Regulation of private business evolved for the purpose of protecting the public interest, as evidenced by almost 30 different regulatory bodies.
- In 2002, the cost of business regulation was approximately $1 trillion, or about 9 percent of GDP.
- Deregulation, on balance, has reduced real prices and increased services.

Key Terms

Anglo-Saxon model
European model
Asian model
private sector
public sector
sole proprietorship
partnership
corporation
corporate governance
stakeholders
shareholder value
market capitalization
market for corporate control
corporate raiders
stock option
golden parachute
capital market
primary market

initial public offering
underwriters
market power
concentration ratio
competition
right of eminent domain
regulation
unfunded mandate
counterfactual information
deregulation
labor or trade union
flexible labor market
Fair Labor Standards Act of 1938
Occupational Safety and Health Act
    of 1970 (OSH Act)
implicit contracts
unfunded liability
privatization

Notes

1. Edward Glaeser and Andrei Shleifer, "Legal Origins," NBER Working Paper 8272, *http:// www.nber.org/papers/w8272*
2. *http://federalistpapers.com*
3. James Madison, *Federalist 51,* "The Structure of the Government Must Furnish the Proper Checks and Balances Between Different Departments," *http://federalistpapers.com*
4. *Ibid.*
5. James Madison, *Federalist 10,* "The Same Subject Continued (The Union as a Safeguard Against Domestic Faction and Insurrection)."
6. Madison, *Federalist 51.*
7. Douglass North, "Structure and Performance: The Task of Economic History," *Journal of Economic Literature* 41 (September 1978), 968.
8. Harry Scheiber, "Original Intent, History, and Doctrine: The Constitution and Economic Liberty," *American Economic Review* 78, 2 (May 1988), 140.
9. *http://www.law.emory.edu/FEDERAL/usconst/amend.html*
10. Milton Friedman, "Monopoly and Social Responsibility of Business and Labor," in Edwin Mansfield, ed., *Monopoly Power and Economic Performance,* 3rd ed. (New York: Norton, 1974), pp. 57–68.
11. Frederic Scherer, *Industrial Structure and Economic Performance,* 2nd ed. (Boston: Houghton Mifflin, 1980), p. 519.
12. Clifford Winston, "Economic Deregulation: Days of Reckoning for Microeconomists," *Journal of Economic Literature* 31, 3 (September 1993), 1263–1289.
13. Christopher Caldwell, "Europe's Social Market Economy," *Policy Review* 109 (October– November 2002), 38.

14. Adolf Berle and Garder Means, *The Modern Corporation and Private Property* (New York: Macmillan, 1932).

15. Henry Manne, "Mergers and the Market for Corporate Control," *Journal of Political Economy* 73 (1965), 110–120; Philippe Aghion, Oliver Hart, and J. Moore, "The Economics of Bankruptcy Reform," *Journal of Law, Economics and Organizations* 8 (1992), 523–546.

16. "Corporate Governance: Enhancing the Return on Capital Through Increased Corporate Responsibility," *www.corpgov.net*

17. *Participant: Quarterly News and Performance from TIAA-CREF* (August 2002), p. 24.

18. See, for example, Andrei Shleifer and Lawrence Summers, "Hostile Takeovers as Breaches of Trust," FMG Discussion Papers, June 1987, *http://netec.mcc.ac.uk/BibEc/data/Papers/fmgfmgdpsdp0008.html*

19. Caldwell, "Europe's 'Social Market,' " p. 38.

20. Friedman, "Monopoly and Social Responsibility of Business and Labor," pp. 57–68.

21. William G. Shepherd, "Causes of Increased Competition in the U.S. Economy, 1939–1980," *Review of Economics and Statistics,* November 1982, 613–626.

22. See Scherer, *Industrial Market Structure,* pp. 68–70; James V. Koch, *Industrial Organization and Prices,* 2nd ed. (Englewood Cliffs, N.J.: Prentice-Hall, 1980), p. 181; and Morris Adelman, "Changes in Industrial Concentration," in Mansfield, *Monopoly Power and Economic Performance,* pp. 83–88.

23. Joe S. Bain, *Barriers to New Competition,* pp. 192–200; H. Michael Mann, "Seller Concentration, Barriers to Entry, and Rates of Return in Thirty Industries," *Review of Economics and Statistics* 58 (August 1966), 296–307.

24. Leonard W. Weiss, "Quantitative Studies of Industrial Organization," in Michael D. Intrilligator, ed., *Frontiers of Quantitative Economics* (Amsterdam: North-Holland, 1971); Leonard Weiss, "Concentration–Profits Relationship and Antitrust," in Goldschmidt *et al.,* eds., *Industrial Concentration: The New Learning* (Boston: Little, Brown, 1974), pp. 184–233.

25. The Harberger results can be found in Arnold Harberger, "Monopoly and Resource Allocation," *American Economic Review* 44 (May 1954), 77–87.

26. Anne Krueger, "The Political Economy of the Rent-Seeking Society," *American Economic Review* 64 (June 1974), 291–303; Gordon Tullock, "The Welfare Cost of Tariffs, Monopolies, and Theft," *Western Economic Journal* 5 (June 1967), 224–232; Harvey Leibenstein, "Allocative Efficiency vs. X-Inefficiency," *American Economic Review* 56 (June 1966), 392–415.

27. Harold Demsetz, "Industry Structure, Market Rivalry, and Public Policy," *Journal of Law and Economics* 16 (April 1973), 1–10.

28. Bernard Siegan, *Economic Liberties and the Constitution* (Chicago: University of Chicago Press, 1980), pp. 65, 99, 111–113.

29. North, "On Economic History," p. 969.

30. Scheiber, "Original Intent," p. 142.

31. Susan Dudley, "Reversing Midnight Regulations," *Regulation* 9 (Spring 2001).

32. The following discussion of regulation is based on these sources: Wilcox, *Public Policies Toward Business,* Part III; Scherer, *Industrial Structure and Economic Performance,* Ch. 18; Paul MacAvoy, "The Rationale for Regulation of Field Prices of Natural Gas," in MacAvoy, *The Crisis of the Regulatory Commissions,* pp. 152–168; Robert E. Litan and William D. Nordhaus, *Reforming Federal Regulation* (New Haven: Yale University Press, 1983); and Lawrence J. White, *Reforming Regulation* (Englewood Cliffs, N.J.: Prentice-Hall, 1981).

33. The first of these commissions was established in New England before the Civil War, with authority over the railroads, and in the Midwest in the 1870s. Commissions for the regulation of public utilities were set up only in the early twentieth century (1907); in some instances, public utility supervision was entrusted to the already established railroad

commissions. Federal regulation was initiated in 1887 with the Interstate Commerce Commission, the first major federal regulatory commission.

State commissions in almost all states have jurisdiction over railroads, motor carriers, water, electricity, gas, and telephones, and such bodies in about half the states have the authority to regulate urban transit, taxicabs, and gas pipelines. Commissioners are either elected or appointed by the governor of the state. The staffs of the commissions are generally small and are generally poorly funded compared to the legal staffs of the industries they regulate.

There are five federal commissions. The Interstate Commerce Commission (established in 1887) regulates railroads, interstate oil pipelines, and interstate motor and water carriers. The Federal Power Commission (established in 1920) has jurisdiction over power projects and the interstate transmission of electricity and natural gas. The Federal Communications Commission (established in 1933) regulates interstate telephone and telegraph and broadcasting. The Securities and Exchange Commission (established in 1934) regulates securities markets. The Civil Aeronautics Board (established in 1938) supervised domestic and international aviation before it was closed in 1984. These federal commissions are staffed by commissioners appointed by the U.S. president for terms of five to seven years, and their staffs range from 1,000 to 2,000 employees. In general, the professional staffs on the federal commissions are better paid and better qualified than their state counterparts, but their salaries are not competitive with those paid by the regulated industries.

34. Federal Reserve Bank of Dallas, *America's Economic Regulation Burden,* Fall 1996, pp. 1–6.
35. *http://cfr.law.cornell.edu/cfr/#TITLES*
36. This discussion is based on Roy J. Ruffin and Paul R. Gregory, *Principles of Microeconomics,* 3rd ed. (Glenview, Ill.: Scott, Foresman, 1988), Ch. 14; Elizabeth E. Bailey, "Price and Productivity Change Following Deregulation: The U.S. Experience," *Economic Journal* 96 (March 1986), 1–17. See also C. Winston, "Conceptual Developments in the Economics of Transportation," *Journal of Economic Literature* 23 (1985), 57–94; T. Keeler, *Railroads, Freight, and Public Policy* (Washington, D.C.: Brookings Institution, 1983); A. F. Friedlander and R. H. Spady, *Freight Transport Regulation* (Cambridge, Mass.: MIT Press, 1981); Clifford Winston, "Economic Deregulation: Days of Reckoning for Microeconomists," *Journal of Economic Literature* 31, 3 (September 1993), 1263–1289.
37. Robert Bradley, Jr., "The Origins of Political Electricity: Market Failure or Political Opportunism?" *Energy Law Journal* 17, 59 (1996), 59–102.
38. William A. Niskanen, "Regulatory Change over the past Quarter-Century," *Regulation* 25, 2.
39. Our discussion of the U.S. labor market and the figures cited are from the following sources: William Bowen and Orley Ashenfelter, eds., *Labor and the National Economy,* rev. ed. (New York: Norton, 1975); H. Gregg Lewis, *Unions and Relative Wages in the United States* (Chicago: University of Chicago Press, 1963); Stanley Masters, *Black–White Income Differentials* (New York: Academic, 1975); Cynthia Lloyd, ed., *Sex, Discrimination and the Division of Labor* (New York: Columbia University Press, 1975); Michael Boskin, "Unions and Relative Real Wages," *American Economic Review* 62 (June 1972), 466–472; George Johnson, "Economic Analysis of Trade Unionism," *American Economic Review, Papers and Proceedings* 65 (May 1975), 23–28; Albert Rees, *The Economics of Trade Unions* (Chicago: University of Chicago Press, 1963); C. J. Paisley, "Labor Union Effects on Wage Gains: A Survey of Recent Literature," *Journal of Economic Literature* 18 (March 1980), 1–31; Richard Freeman and James Medoff, "The Two Faces of Unionism," *Public Interest* 57 (Fall 1979), 73–80; Ronald G. Ehrenberg and Robert S. Smith, *Modern Labor Economics,* 3rd ed. (Glenview, Ill.: Scott, Foresman, 1988); "Rising Wage Inequality in the United

States: Causes and Consequences," *American Economic Review: Papers and Proceedings* 84, 2 (May 1994), 10–33; "Lessons from Empirical Labor Economics: 1972–1992," *American Economic Review: Papers and Proceedings* 83, 2 (May 1993), 104–121.

40. *http://www.dol.gov/asp/programs/handbook/minwage.htm*
41. *http://www.dol.gov/asp/programs/handbook/osha.htm*
42. Sherwin Rosen, "Implicit Contracts," *Journal of Economics Literature* 23, 3 (September 1985), 1144–1175.
43. *http://libertynet.org/~edcivic/welfbill.html*
44. See, for example, Morton Paglin, "The Measurement and Trend of Inequality: A Basic Revision," *American Economic Review* 65 (September 1975), 598–609; and Edgar Browning, "The Trend Toward Equality in the Distribution of Income," *Southern Economic Journal* 43 (July 1976), 912–923.
45. These figures are from Department of Commerce, *Historical Statistics of the United States,* series G; and *Statistical Abstract of the United States.*
46. Paglin, "The Measurement and Trend of Inequality," pp. 598–609.
47. Joseph Pechman and Benjamin Okner, *Who Bears the Tax Burden?* (Washington, D.C.: Brookings Institution, 1974).
48. Browning, "The Trend Toward Equality," pp. 912–923. Also see Edgar Browning and William R. Johnson, *The Distribution of the Tax Burden* (Washington, D.C.: American Enterprise Institute, 1979).
49. *http://www.ssa/gov*
50. *http://www.mysocialsecurity.org/quickfacts/*
51. *Statistical Abstract of the United States 2000,* p. 388.
52. For background, see Janet Rotherberg Pack, "Privatization of Public Sector Services in Theory and Practice," *Journal of Policy Analysis and Management* 6 (1987), 523–540; John B. Donahue, *The Privatization Decision* (New York: Basic Books, 1989); a useful summary of the American experience can be found in Richard L. Worsnop, "Privatization," *Congressional Quarterly Researcher,* November 13, 1992, 979–999.
53. Richard Musgrave, "National Economic Planning: The U.S. Case," *American Economic Review, Papers and Proceedings* 67 (February 1977), 50–54; see also R. D. Norton, "Industrial Policy and American Renewal," *Journal of Economic Literature* 24, 1 (March 1986), 1–40.

Recommended Readings

Traditional Sources

F. M. Bator, "The Simple Analytics of Welfare Maximization," *American Economic Review* 47 (March 1957), 22–59.

——, "The Anatomy of Market Failure," *Quarterly Journal of Economics* 72 (August 1958), 351–379.

H. G. Lewis, *Unionism and Relative Wages in the United States* (Chicago: University of Chicago Press, 1963).

Paul MacAvoy, ed., *The Crisis of Regulatory Commissions* (New York: Norton, 1970).

Product Markets

William J. Baumol, John C. Panzar, and Robert D. Willig, *Contestable Markets and the Theory of Industry Structure* (New York: Harcourt, 1982).

Oliver Williamson, *The Economic Institutions of Capitalism* (New York: Free Press, 1985).

Factor Markets

Ronald Ehrenberg and Robert Smith, *Modern Labor Economics,* 3rd ed. (Glenview, Ill.: Scott Foresman, 1988).

Richard B. Freeman, "Unionism Comes to the Public Sector," *Journal of Economic Literature* 24, 1 (March 1986), 41–86.

"Lessons from Empirical Labor Economics: 1972–1992," *American Economic Review: Papers and Proceedings* 83, 2 (May 1993), 104–121.

James B. Rebitzer, "Radical Political Economy and the Economics of Labor Markets," *Journal of Economic Literature* 31, 3 (September 1993), 1394–1434.

Government and the Economy

Andrew B. Abel and Ben S. Bernanke, *Macroeconomics* (New York: Addison-Wesley, 1992).

Douglas H. Blair and Robert A. Pollack, "Rational Collective Choice," *Scientific American* 249, 2 (August 1983), 88–95.

John B. Donahue, *The Privatization Decision* (New York: Basic Books, 1989).

Federal Reserve Bank of Dallas, *America's Economic Regulation Burden,* Fall 1996.

Frank Levy and Richard J. Murname, "U.S. Earning Levels and Earnings Inequality: A Review of Recent Trends and Proposed Explanations" *Journal of Economic Literature* 30, 3 (September 1992), 1333–1381.

N. Gregory Mankiw, "Symposium on Keynesian Economics Today," *Journal of Economic Literature* 7, 1 (Winter 1993), 3–82.

Robert Moffitt, "Incentive Effects of the U.S. Welfare System: A Review," *Journal of Economic Literature* 30, 1 (March 1992), 1–61.

Joseph Pechman, *Who Paid the Taxes, 1966–85?* (Washington, D.C.: Brookings Institution, 1985).

Janet Rotherberg Pack, "Privatization of Public Sector Services in Theory and Practice," *Journal of Policy Analysis and Management* 6 (1987), 523–540.

Harvey S. Rosen, *Public Finance,* 3rd ed. (Homewood, Ill.: Irwin, 1992).

F. M. Scherer and David Ross, *Industrial Market Structure and Economic Performance,* 3rd ed. (Boston: Houghton Mifflin, 1990).

Eugene Singer, *Antitrust Economics* (Englewood Cliffs, N.J.: Prentice-Hall, 1968).

James Schmitz, "The Role Played by Public Enterprises: How Much Does It Differ Across Countries?" Federal Reserve Bank of Minneapolis, *Quarterly Review,* Spring 1996, 2–15.

Don E. Waldman, ed., *The Economics of Antitrust* (Boston: Little, Brown, 1986).

Leonard Weiss and Michael Klass, eds., *Regulatory Reform: What Actually Happened* (Boston: Little, Brown, 1986).

Clifford Winston, "Economic Deregulation: Days of Reckoning for Microeconomists," *Journal of Economic Literature* 31, 3 (September 1993), 1263–1289.

Richard L. Worsnop, "Privatization," *Congressional Quarterly Researcher* (November 13, 1992), 979–999.

9

The European Model

The previous chapter introduced three models of capitalism: Anglo-Saxon (American) capitalism, European capitalism, and the Asian model of capitalism. This chapter explores the European model. The countries that follow the European model are the affluent countries of Western Europe that participated in the original Industrial Revolution and were already highly industrialized by the second half of the nineteenth century. Although there are more than twenty such countries, we focus on the most populous: Germany, France, and Italy. The United Kingdom will be discussed briefly as exhibiting characteristics of both the Anglo-Saxon model (it is the historical source of this model) and the European model.

Although the nations of continental Western Europe vary in history, ethnicity, customs, and traditions, they are lumped together in one economic system for two reasons: The model's main characteristics do apply generally to these countries, and Europe itself has become one "common market" of almost 400 million people. The countries of the European Union combine to create a common market roughly equivalent in size to the United States.

Starting more than 50 years ago with the "one Europe" concept of the French politician Jean Monnet, Europe has gradually developed into a single market that functions much like the fifty states of the United States. The **European Union (EU)** was established via a series of treaties. The Treaty of Paris, signed in 1951, established the European Coal and Steel Community. The Treaty of Rome, signed in 1957, established the **European Economic Community,** generally referred to as the European Common Market. It decreed that Europe was to become one common market by eliminating import duties and quotas. The momentous **Maastricht Treaty,** signed in February of 1992, concluded that Europe should have a common currency and one central bank and should move toward a political union. The Treaty of Amsterdam, signed on October 2, 1997, abolished border patrols and passport requirements between member states, calling for the removal of immigration barriers among EU member countries by 2004. The Nice Summit of December 2000 spelled out procedures for expansion of membership rights to other countries and for voting rights. The Barcelona Summit of 2002 took the first step toward liberalizing gas and electricity sectors. On January 1, 1999, the European Central Bank was established, and a common currency, the euro, was adopted for all bank transactions, although member countries temporarily continued to use their own national currencies. Member countries withdrew their national currencies from circulation on January 1, 2002, and the euro became the sole currency for the EU. Three countries—England, Sweden and Denmark—opted out of the common currency. England will hold a referendum at some point to determine whether to adopt the euro in place of its pound sterling.[1]

In the course of creating the European Union (EU), the European countries had to agree on a multinational form of government, consisting of, among other agencies, a European Council of Ministers, located in Strassbourg, a European Parliament, located in Brussels, and a single central bank, the European Central Bank, located in Frankfurt. They also had to agree on a common set of rules and procedures to ensure that all countries operated on a level playing field (prohibiting, for example, preferential treatment for national industries) and establishing common fiscal policies and the free movement of resources. The most spectacular agreement was to allow free migration among the EU member countries despite substantial income differentials, particularly when poorer countries such as Greece and Portugal were admitted. Figure 9.1 shows the structure of the European Union.

The creation of a single European central bank means that monetary policy is no longer made by the individual countries; rather, interest rates are set for all EU members by one bank. In fact, the **European Central Bank** shares many features with the Federal Reserve Bank of the United States. Its board consists of representatives from the national banks of the various EU members, just as the Federal Reserve Board comprises representatives from the district banks. The European Union also requires a common fiscal policy based on the rule that no member country can run a budget deficit greater than 2 percent of its GDP. A larger deficit triggers substantial penalties.

The EU is a monumental experiment. Many of its provisions remain to be finalized. Precedents are being set. Voting rules must be established; provisions for its enlargement must be approved; and the rights and powers of the elected legislative branch, the European Parliament, must be weighed against those of the European Commission and the European Council of Ministers, which are staffed by technocrats. The Council of Ministers is pledged to consider the common interest of the EU, whereas, the members of the European Parliament are supposed to represent the interests of their respective nations. Thus the EU must resolve a principal–agent problem between the Council of Ministers and Parliament. The danger of relying entirely on technocrats is that they use rigid bureaucratic rules and are not answerable to voters.

The EU currently consists of fifteen countries (see Table 9.1), twelve of which are members of the euro zone (as we have noted England, Sweden, and Denmark chose not to adopt the euro). The EU's population is 376 million, which exceeds that of the United States (at 277 million) by almost 100 million persons. At roughly $8 trillion, however, the GDP of the EU is less than the $10 trillion GDP of the United States. Hence the per capita GDP of the EU is some 60 percent of that of the United States. The formation of the EU has therefore created a market that is roughly equal in size to that of the United States, and it has created a currency, the euro, that could ultimately challenge the world dominance of the dollar.

Ideological and Philosophical Foundations

The ideological and intellectual origins of the Anglo-Saxon model can be traced directly to the classical liberalism of the late eighteenth century. Its economic framework was provided by Adam Smith, who argued that individuals should have the economic liberty to pursue profits and self-interest. Government interference, he

FIGURE 9.1 Structure of the European Union

Commission—Made up of twenty commissioners, two each from France, Germany, Italy, Spain and the United Kingdom, and one each from Luxembourg, Belgium, Greece, the Netherlands, Portugal, Austria, Sweden, Denmark, Finland, and Ireland. Appointed by their national governments for five-year terms, the commissioners owe loyalty to the EU, not to their national interests.

The Commission proposes legislation, is responsible for administration, and ensures that provisions of the treaties and the decisions of the institutions are properly implemented. It has investigative powers and can take legal action against entities that violate EU rules. It manages the budget and represents the EU in international trade negotiations.

Council of Ministers—Made up of fifteen ministers, one from each member state. The Council tries to strike a balance between national and EU interests. It enacts EU laws and can accept or reject legal suggestions made by the Commission. Unlike the Commission, the ministers can defend their national interests.

Council of Ministers Presidency—Rotates among member states every six months.

Parliament—Made up of 626 members elected to five-year terms by the 370 million citizens of the EU. The Parliament's president is elected for a term of two and a half years. Parliament cannot enact laws but can veto legislation in certain policy areas, amend or reject the EU budget, dismiss the entire Commission through a two-thirds vote, and supervise the EU's new employment policy.

Court of Justice—Made up of fifteen judges, one from each member state, appointed for renewable terms of six years. It ensures that the treaties are interpreted and applied correctly by other EU institutions and by the member states. The court has final decision-making powers. Its judgments are binding on EU institutions, member countries, national courts, companies, and private citizens, and they supersede those of national courts.

Court of Auditors—Made up of 15 members appointed by the Council for renewable six-year terms. The Court has extensive powers to examine the legality and regularity of receipts and expenditures and the sound financial management of the EU budget.

Member States—The fifteen countries that are part of the European Union.

Source: European Union.

maintained, will have only negative effects. Individuals, in pursuing their own self-interest, will be lead by an "invisible hand" to further the general social interest. The political origins of the Anglo-Saxon model date to classical liberal political thinkers, largely in the United States, such as Thomas Jefferson and James Madison, who argued that that government is best that governs least. Government is a force that must be restrained by a clear rule of law that protects individuals from government.

TABLE 9.1   Gross Domestic Product in the European Union and the Eurozone

Country	Population (millions)	2000 GDP ($ billions)	Share of EU GDP	Share of Eurozone GDP	Per Capita GDP
Austria	8	189.6	2.42%	3.15%	
Belgium	10	227.8	2.91	3.78	
Denmark	5	161.2	2.06		
Finland	5	119.7	1.53	1.99	
France	58	1,294.1	16.51	21.47	
Germany	81	1,680.4	23.99	31.19	
Greece	11	112.2	1.43	1.86	
Ireland	4	94.2	1.20	1.56	
Italy	59	1063.1	13.56	17.64	
Luxembourg	4	18.6	0.24	0.31	
Netherlands	16	367.4	4.69	6.09	
Portugal	11	103.7	1.32	1.72	
Spain	40	557.0	7.11	9.24	
Sweden	9	229.2	2.92		
United Kingdom	59	1421.1	18.13		
			100.00%	100.00%	
EU Total	376	7,839.3			20,848
Eurozone Total	303	6,027.9			19,891
United States	277	9,926.6			35,834

Source: OECD Statistics GDP, *http://cecd.org/std/gdp.htm*; *Statistical Abstract of the United States.*

The economic and political ideology of the European model has quite different origins and arrives at the conclusion that the state is a necessary force to promote the general welfare. Individual economic freedoms, property rights, and private contracts may have to be abridged by a powerful state in the name of the public interest. This conclusion follows from mercantilism, a philosophy that was particularly strong in France and England in the seventeenth and eighteenth centuries. In fact, Adam Smith's *The Wealth of Nations* was conceived as an attack on mercantilist conclusions.

According to the tenets of **Mercantilism** a strong state is necessary to regulate and control the domestic and international operations of a national economy in order to promote the political and economic strength of the country vis-à-vis its neighbors. Unlike classical liberalism, which had the founding father of modern economics (Adam Smith) as its leader, mercantilism had no intellectual founder. Mercantilism was not a "scholar's doctrine but a folk doctrine," and "no scholar of even third rank made a contribution to it."[2] As a folk doctrine, it had no organized opposition, although various interest groups sought to use it to achieve their ends. Mercantilism grew out of practice, in England and France, between the sixteenth and eighteenth centuries, reaching its peak in France under Colbert in the 1660s. During that time, mercantilism was "a common approach to the European problem,"[3] which encompassed not only France and England but also Germany and Scandinavia. As a "system of state making," it extended regulation over business and commerce, took control of guilds, and took formal charge of international trade by issuing charters to select companies. Under mercantilism, the state collected its revenues by selling licenses, charters, and other monopoly rights to special-interest groups. The basic political conclusion of mercantilism was that only a strong state could keep the economy from ruin. If individuals were given economic freedom, the country would quickly lose its wealth and power to rivals.

Karl Marx also influenced the European model indirectly through his warnings about the inherent instability of capitalism.[4] Western Europe, composed of prosperous nations ruled by Marx's hated bourgeoisie, feared that if an economy were left to its own devices, Marx's prediction of collapse would come true, and the proletariat would overthrow the ruling class. Indeed Marx's predictions appeared to be coming true when something resembling a socialist revolution (the Paris Commune) struck France in 1871. Chancellor Otto von Bismarck introduced social welfare legislation in Germany between 1883 and 1888, despite violent political opposition, as a direct attempt to stave off Marx's socialist revolution. The Great Depression strengthened belief in the accuracy of Marx's predictions and paved the way for New Deal legislation in the United States.

In Germany, there developed a more prominent strain of economic thought known as the German historical school. Its most influential proponent was Gustav Schmoller, who founded the influential *Verein fuer Sozialpolitik* in 1872. After the German political unification in 1871, the opinions of German economists moved with public opinion, as academic economists became adherents to nationalist, anti-democratic, and expansionist doctrines dominant in the German ruling class—an intellectual phenomenon with few parallels in economic history.[5] Schmoller argued that there are no universal principles of economics. Instead, we can understand the workings of the economy only by long observation of facts, rather than by trying to identify general principles via theoretical abstraction. All economic interactions depend on their historical context. Schmoller's antitheoretical approach dominated the teaching of economics in Germany, and a whole generation of teachers, government officials, and politicians were trained without understanding basic economic principles, such as the relation between money and inflation. "The economic education of the Prussian bureaucracy lay for many years in the hands of Schmoller and his students. Its negative consequence was seen in the inflation crisis of the early 1920s. The bureaucracy did not have the faintest idea of the simplest economic concepts. There was practically no one in the Finance Ministry who understood something about inflation."[6] The political message of the German historical school was that a strong state is necessary to correct social injustices and to regulate the economy.

After World War II, a new school of economic thought developed in Germany and had a substantial impact on implementation of the European model of the social market economy. Its intellectual heritage can be traced to the Freiburg school of neo-liberalism, headed by Walker Euchen and Alfred Muller-Armack.[7] The Freiburg school believed that the state should ensure the workability of the competitive market system but that the market should allocate resources. The state should be prepared to intervene, however, to achieve necessary social goals. Intervention should be compatible with the underlying market order; thus policies that disrupt the working of the market, such as direct orders and price freezes, should be avoided.

The political background of the social market economy can be traced to the immediate postwar years of Allied occupation. The initial Allied policy was to continue the wartime controls. Until 1947 its objective was to enforce payment of reparations and to destroy the German military potential. When the emphasis turned to recovery, direct controls were dismantled, and the running of the country's economy was gradually returned to German hands. Ludwig Erhard, the minister of economics during the Adenauer years, was a proponent of the Freiburg school. He strongly favored decontrol, deregulation, and the turning of economic decisions over to the impersonal hands of the market.[8] The choice of market versus plan was heatedly debated, the social democrats favoring strong state planning. Memories of the chaos of the inflationary 1920s and the depression of the 1930s convinced many German politicians of the dangers of a market economy. The Currency Reform and Price Reform of June 1948 and the passage in May 1949 of the Basic Law of the Federal Republic (the German constitution) established the sanctity of private property, the foundation of economic policy in the postwar era.

The economic goals of the Federal Republic were written into law. These goals are price stability, a stable currency, full employment, balance-of-payments equilibrium, and stable economic growth. Three social goals closely associated with the social market economy were later also identified: social equity, social security, and social progress. These social goals provided much of the basis for later state intervention in economic affairs in the Federal Republic.[9]

These disparate forces came together to create a philosophy of social democracy, which reflected the view that the state is a necessary force for good and must intervene actively in economic affairs. Rather than concentrating on the rights of the individual, social democracy focused on the obligation of the state to intervene when necessary.

Legal Foundations: Civil Law

Whereas the Anglo-Saxon model is based on **common law** (custom, usage, and court decisions), the European model uses civil (or Roman) law, a code-based legal system operated by professional judges interpreting a detailed set of written rules and regulations. The **civil law** system grew out of the European tradition of monarchies and feudal lords. In countries like France and Germany, where feudal princes were as powerful as the sovereign, laws and rules could be abused at the local level, creating great uncertainty in their application. In such a case, written laws with clear rules seemed to work better than unwritten laws based on tradition and precedent.[10] If laws could be abused by local potentates, there could be no rule of law. Hence written laws, approved by the sovereign and enforced by professional judges, were the only alternative. Civil law gave less weight to individual rights, such as the right of property and the right of private contract, and more to the rights of the state.

Table 9.2 lists several countries that follow the common-law tradition and civil-law tradition. Note that the EU and Eurozone countries, with the exceptions of the United Kingdom and Ireland, use civil law. More countries follow civil than common law, and those that use common law tend to be former English colonies or English offshoots, such as the United States. In today's world, there are more civil-law than common-law countries.

Features of the European Model

We discussed the Anglo-Saxon model in terms of the functioning of its product market, capital market, and labor market and in terms of how provision was made for income and job security. We used the United States as the sole example of the Anglo-Saxon model. In contrast, we can choose among fifteen EU member countries to illustrate the European model. EU member countries, while recognizing that they have much in common, might regard their internal differences as just as prominent as those between EU members and the United States. The European common market, with its level playing field, is the strongest proof that a common model is operating. We shall use different European countries to illustrate selected aspects of the

TABLE 9.2   Civil-Law and Common-Law Countries

Use Civil Law	Use Common Law
Argentina	Australia
Austria	Canada
Belgium	Hong Kong
Denmark	Ireland
Finland	Israel
France	New Zealand
Germany	Singapore
Greece	United Kingdom
Italy	United States
Japan	
South Korea	
Mexico	
Netherlands	
Norway	
Portugal	
Spain	
Sweden	
Switzerland	

Source: Laura Benny, "Do Shareholders Value Insider Trading Laws? International Evidence," Discussion Paper No. 345, 12/2001, Harvard John M. Olin Discussion Papers Series, *http://www.law. harvard.edu/programs/olin_center*

European model. We use primarily Germany (and to a degree France) to describe the European labor market; we use Sweden to illustrate an extreme case of the state's provision of income security. We again use Germany to describe European corporate governance procedures, but we describe the European capital market in general terms without reference to a specific European country. We use France's earlier experiences with indicative planning, or *planification,* to describe a more extreme historical example of European industrial policy in contrast to the virtual absence of planning/industrial policy in the Anglo-Saxon model. And we examine deregulation and privatization in European terms rather than in terms of a specific country.

Corporate Governance

The previous chapter discussed different models of **corporate governance** in terms of the friction between **stakeholders**, such as workers, suppliers, buyers, and owners, and **shareholders**. In the Anglo-Saxon model, the primary aim of corporate management is to maximize shareholder value, even if that means sacrificing the interests of stakeholders. In the European model, managerial capitalism replaces shareholder capitalism.

Managerial capitalism   **Managerial capitalism** is a system of corporate governance that places the interests of stakeholders above those of shareholders. Whereas shareholder capitalism requires managers to focus on profitability, managerial capitalism focuses on other objectives, such as providing a stable work environment for managers and employees or maintaining stable relationships with banks, suppliers, and major customers, who may also be shareholders. Managerial capitalist corporations are presumed to have some advantages. For example, they receive more loyalty from their employees, who have a long-term stake in the company. Stakeholder companies can therefore invest more in employee training and education, knowing that trained employees will not leave to join other firms.[11] Managerial capitalism provides more stable employment. Downturns in business will be absorbed by lower profits, not by layoffs. Stakeholder companies create a more nearly equal distribution of income within the company, because payments are not tied to profits. Stakeholder corporations may take a longer view of technological improvements than shareholder corporations, which may be more interested in short-term profits.[12]

Shareholdings   Whereas shareholder corporations in the United States tend to be broadly owned by a large number of investors, stakeholder corporations in Europe tend to be held by a smaller number of investors, many of whom hold significant stakes. For example, the largest German bank, Deutsche Bank, and Germany's largest insurance company, Allianz, hold 5 percent and larger shares in most major German corporations. DeGussa, a large German metals and chemicals concern, has had Dresdner Bank, Henkel, Veba, and its successor Eon as major shareholders. A minority of shares are held by the public, often in the 25 to 33 percent range. With a few large shareholders, smaller shareholders have little chance to influence policy, and the rights of minority shareholders may not be of prime concern to the management.

People will be reluctant to buy shares of companies if their interests are not protected. In shareholder corporations, the board of directors has a fiduciary responsibility to protect the interests of all shareholders, not just the interests of majority shareholders. Given the strong protection of property rights under common law, minority shareholders can sue the management or the board of directors for violation of their rights. For example, the management may issue additional shares to majority shareholders, to management, or to related parties, thereby diluting (reducing the ownership interests of) the minority shareholder. If management can be proved to have abrogated its fiduciary responsibility to minority shareholders, the action could be reversed and the minority shareholders compensated.

With broad public ownership, disgruntled shareholders can punish corporations for poor performance by selling their shares and pushing down the share price. A low share price makes raising capital more expensive.

Insider Trading   Insiders (managers, board members, and the like) have more information about the corporation's performance than do public shareholders. Insiders, for example, might know that the corporation's profits will collapse in the coming quarter. They can profit from this information by selling their shares while the price is still high. Outsiders, lacking this information, cannot sell their shares in time and will incur losses. In Anglo-Saxon countries, stock exchanges and securities commissions have more strict laws against **insider trading** than do those in European countries. In the United States, for example, managers and directors are subject to "blackout periods" prior to the public disclosure of information—periods during which they cannot sell or buy shares. Also, insider stock transactions must be reported to the Securities and Exchange Commission for publication. Insider trading does occur, but if it is discovered, it is punishable by civil and even criminal penalties. In the European model, there are fewer restrictions on insider trading.

Table 9.3 ranks countries by their ownership structure based on samples of corporations from various countries that use either civil or common law. The "Control Owner" column shows the percentage of firms that are owned by a single controlling interest. The "Widely Held" column shows the percentage of corporations that have broad stock ownership. The "Severity of ITL" column ranks countries according to the severity of their insider-trading laws, where 5 (for example, the United States) denotes the strictest laws and 1 (for example, Mexico) denotes the most lax laws. The table shows that there is more "control ownership" in Europe but relatively little in the United States and the United Kingdom. There is little broad ownership of stock in Europe and much broad ownership in the United States and the United Kingdom. Insider-trading laws are stricter in countries that have common law. Empirical studies show that companies that have strict insider-trading rules have stock market valuations suggesting that investors discount corporations in which there is uninhibited insider trading.[13]

In Germany, for example, there was no insider-trading law until January 1995, when the Security Trading Law was adopted. Prior to that time, all efforts to pass meaningful prohibitions on insider trading were rebuffed through lobbyists' efforts. The 1995 law stated that a well-functioning securities market requires the faith and

TABLE **9.3**   Ownership, Insider-Trading Laws, and Legal System

	Control Owner	Widely Held	Severity of ITL
Common Law			
Australia	0.19	0.44	4
Canada	0.35	0.31	5
Hong Kong	0.91	0.05	3
Ireland	0.21	0.26	4
Israel	0.95	0.05	3
New Zealand	0.71	0.05	4
Singapore	0.65	0.13	4
United Kingdom	0.02	0.69	3
United States	0.04	0.74	5
Civil Law			
Austria	0.91	0.05	2
Belgium	0.95	0.00	3
Denmark	0.80	0.00	3
Finland	0.64	0.09	3
France	0.36	0.29	4
Germany	0.57	0.13	3
Greece	1.00	0.00	2
Italy	0.86	0.05	3
Japan	0.29	0.36	2
South Korea	0.36	0.29	5
Mexico	1.00	0.00	1
Netherlands	0.50	0.23	3
Norway	0.76	0.05	1
Portugal	0.90	0.00	4
Spain	0.71	0.05	4
Sweden	0.77	0.10	3
Switzerland	0.42	0.36	3
Common Law Avg.	0.301	0.439	4
Civil Law Avg.	0.674	0.133	2.93

Note: ITL stands for Insider-Trading Law; 5 is most strict.

Source: Laura Benny, "Do Shareholders Value Insider Trading Laws? International Evidence," Discussion Paper No. 345, 12/2001, Harvard John M. Ohlin Discussion Papers Series, *http://www.law.harvard.edu/programs/olin_center*

confidence of investors, which cannot be established if insider information is protected. In practice, the German insider-trading law has been applied rarely, and offenders have been punished with monetary penalties only.[14] Note that Germany ranks in the middle of European countries in terms of severity of insider-trading laws. Thus European insider-trading laws are relatively toothless compared to those of the United States.

Transparency   In order for shareholders to be informed about their ownership interests, shareholder corporations must supply the public with regular, accurate, and transparent information concerning the company's profits and balance sheet. The **transparency** requirement is less vital in a stakeholder company that is run primarily for the benefit of insiders. Accordingly, stakeholder corporations use less uniform accounting standards and reveal less about company operations. These accounting differences are felt when a European corporation wishes to be listed on an American stock exchange, such as the New York Stock Exchange. To be listed according to U.S. standards, the European company must reveal more information about itself than is customary in its home country. Table 9.4 compares French accounting standards with International Accounting Standards (IAS). Note that French accounting standards do not require the disclosure of transactions with related parties or diluted earnings per share (which result from the issue of additional shares by management) or the disclosure of changes in equity (the value of the corporation). Such disclosures are considered essential in U.S. stock exchanges, and the collapse of Enron Corporation in 2002 was associated with the nondisclosure of transactions with related parties and of changes in equity.

TABLE 9.4   French Accounting Standards

French requirements are based on the Commercial Code, company law and decrees, and rules established by the Committee of Accounting Regulation (including the General Accounting Plan) and interpretations of the Urgent Issues Committee that apply to consolidated financial statements.

French accounting may differ from that required by International Accounting Standards (IAS) because of the absence of specific French rules on recognition and measurement in the following areas:

- Impairment of assets
- Impairment tests for goodwill and intangibles with depreciable lives in excess of twenty years
- Accounting for employee benefit obligations, because it is not mandatory to recognize a liability for postemployment benefits
- The discounting of provisions
- The calculation of basic and diluted earnings per share

There are no specific rules requiring disclosures of:

- A primary statement of changes in equity
- Transactions with related parties (except for limited requirements)
- Discontinuing operations
- Segment liabilities
- The FIFO or current cost of inventory when LIFO is used
- The fair values of investment properties

Source: http://www.ifad.net/content/ie/ie_f_gaap_frameset.htm

Hostile Takeovers and the Market for Corporate Control   A shareholder corporation has shares that are publicly traded, and large blocs may be owned by institutional investors who are prepared to sell the stock if its performance falters. In European corporations, large owners tend to be stakeholders as well and are less inclined to sell the stock if profits decline. Our discussion of corporate governance in the Anglo-Saxon model focused on corporate takeovers, including **hostile takeovers**, as a disciplining device for management. If the current management team is not maximizing shareholder value, the **market for corporate control** will install a new and (it is hoped) more profit-oriented management team. That management team may reduce the work force, change suppliers, or work with different banks, thus instituting a wholesale change in stakeholders. A stakeholder society, in contrast, would wish to erect barriers to the development of any market for corporate control. With cross-ownership of corporations—a supplier may own shares in the company, as does the company's largest bank—there will be a limited market for corporate control. When management changes do occur through mergers and acquisitions, they tend to be friendly takeovers approved by the current management team.

Although it is difficult to obtain comparable statistics, mergers and acquisitions in the United States economy numbered between 4,000 and 5,000 in the 1990s. A **merger** or **acquisition** occurs when one corporation buys another either by purchase or through the exchange of stock, corporate debt, or borrowed money. There were more than 400 acquisitions of foreign companies by U.S. companies each year in this period. The number of mergers considered by the European Merger Control of the EU (presumably, only large mergers were reported) was less than 400 in the late 1990s and early 2000s.[15] Of these several hundred mergers, few if any were hostile takeovers.

Codetermination   The European model is also characterized by codetermination (*Mitbestimmung* in German). **Codetermination** places worker representatives on the boards of directors of corporations. Codetermination is widely used in France, Germany, and Italy, but we shall focus on Germany and Scandinavia. The objective of this policy is "industrial democracy," or forcing management to consider workers' interests when making policy. Initially applied only to selected industries, codetermination has applied to nearly all industry since German law was revised in 1976.[16] Firms with 2,000 or more employees fall under the codetermination legislation. A separate codetermination law applies to the coal, iron, and steel industries.

According to the 1976 law, shareholders and workers should have equal numbers of representatives on the board of directors. For example, if the board consists of twelve members, six represent the shareholders and six the employees. Of the latter, two must be representatives of the labor union, and at least one must be a "leading employee" (such as a foreman). The codetermination law requires the election of a chairman (*Vorsitzender*) of the board of directors. In the absence of a majority, the chairman is elected by the representatives of the shareholders. In this way, the codetermination law seeks to avoid stalemates by giving the chairman the deciding vote. Although labor and stockholders appear to have parity on the board of directors, the shareholders actually have the advantage because of the way the chairman is selected and because "leading employees" often side with the stockholders. The 1976 regulations are still being tested in the German courts. Because codetermination rules call for a nearly equal voice for labor, they call into question the protection of private property guaranteed in the German constitution. Another objection to codetermination is that it puts labor representatives on both sides of the collective-bargaining table and thus gives labor an unfair advantage. In steel industry negotiations, however, labor representatives on the management boards sided with management against the steel workers' demand for a 35-hour workweek. It is not obvious, therefore, how labor representatives will behave when they in effect join management.

The Enterprise Constitution Law (*Betriebsverfassungsgesetz,* or BVG) of 1972 also gives labor a voice in shop-floor decisions. The BVG requires the election of an enterprise council in enterprises that employ five or more workers; "leading employees" are not eligible. The enterprise council has codetermination responsibilities for wages, length of the working day, firings, and layoffs. The influence of the enterprise council is strongest in personnel areas; termination requires the approval of the enterprise council.

The BVG law of 1972 substantially constrains management in the area of personnel decisions. On the positive side, worker participation may boost worker loyalty and enthusiasm and reduce turnover; on the negative side, worker participation may prevent management from making necessary personnel changes.

Codetermination is one of the most distinctive features of the European model because it formally gives nonowners of companies (employees) the same rights as owners to make decisions about how that property will be used. It was hoped that giving stakeholders a prominent voice would enable the economy to operate on the basis of consensus. Codetermination principles have been enshrined in EU legislation under its work council provisions (discussed below).

Capital Markets

In the Anglo-Saxon model, corporations raise funds primarily by issuing stocks and bonds in private capital or equity markets. A prospectus is prepared, the stock or bond issue is registered with the exchanges and with securities regulators, and an initial public offering (IPO) takes place in which, theoretically at least, any and all buyers who are prepared to pay the initial offering price can be accommodated. In the European model, the initial capital of the company is usually supplied by a bank. Instead of private venture capitalists evaluating projects and providing the initial financing, a bank's technical department makes the determination on start-up capital. The funding bank then becomes the company's "house bank" and may eventually arrange to issue shares so as to pay back part of the bank's loans. The house bank continues to occupy a seat on the board of directors and, through its retained ownership shares, holds significant interests in the company. These significant interests owned by the house bank and other stakeholder companies prevent hostile takeovers of the company.[17]

Historically, European banks have exercised broader functions than U.S. commercial banks, which until recently were prevented from engaging in stock brokerage, insurance, and investment-banking activities. European banks are **universal banks**, which can perform not only traditional banking but also risk-sharing, stock sales, and merchant-banking functions. The mammoth German universal banks (Deutsche Bank, Bayerische Hypo-und Vereinsbank, and Dresdner Bank) are the sixth-, twenty-first-, and twenty-third-largest concerns in Germany.[18]

Figure 9.2 reveals the clear distinction between the financing of enterprises in the United States and in Europe. At somewhat less than 20 trillion dollars, the stock market capitalization of U.S. companies is almost double U.S. GDP; Europe's stock market capitalization (at about 6 trillion dollars) is less than its GDP. Whereas these figures also reflect the stock market's higher evaluation of U.S. companies than of European companies, they show the greater reliance of U.S. corporations on the sale of new stock shares. On the other hand, bank assets (primarily loans to businesses, mortgages, and consumer credit) are almost twice GDP in Germany but are just equal to GDP in the United States. Whereas bank loans to businesses in Europe equal over 40 percent of Europe's GDP, they constitute only 7 percent of GDP in the United States. Figure 9.2 demonstrates rather conclusively that U.S. corporations are financed primarily through equity markets, while European businesses are financed by banks.

FIGURE 9.2   Financing of Business in the European Union and the United States, 2000

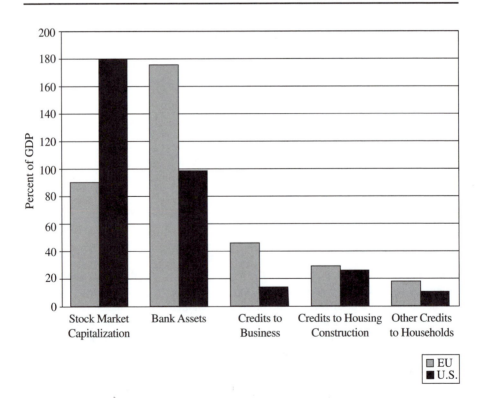

Source: European Central Bank, Monthly Reports, 2001.

In Europe, banks provide venture capital to start-up companies. In the United States, start-up capital is provided by private venture capitalists. Start-up capital is a key ingredient of economic growth, and the volume of venture capital in the United States rose from 7 billion dollars in 1994 to 45 billion dollars in 1999. In Europe, venture capital also rose rapidly but at a slower pace, from 5 billion euros to 20 billion euros in the same period.[19] Venture capital investment rose by a factor of seven in the United States over the five-year period and by a factor of four in Europe.

Bank financing is presumed to offer some advantages. Banks examine business risks carefully because if they back poorly run companies, their loans will not be repaid. Banks also diversify their risks; therefore, a downturn on one sector will not snowball into downturns elsewhere. Banks monitor any business to which they have lent money to prevent gross mismanagement. Insofar as the stocks of the universal banks themselves are traded in major stock exchanges, they are ultimately subject to the discipline of the stock market. If these banks make bad loans, their share prices will fall. The venture capital statistics suggest that the U.S. "market-based" system does a better job of raising venture capital; this may be explained by banks' bureaucratic decision making, which is not well suited to new ventures and new ideas. The corporate governance of European companies also explains the more limited use of stock markets to raise capital. With the lesser protection of property rights by civil law, and the lesser interest in minority shareholder rights, smaller investors may be wise not to purchase stock in European companies.[20]

The previous chapter underscored the dynamism of American capitalism by showing that the ranking of the top twenty industrial concerns changes over relatively short periods of time. Table 9.5 shows that the reverse is true for Germany. The largest German corporations in 1992 were also the largest corporations at the end of the 1990s. The 1998 ranking contains the familiar list of well-known German industrial giants, some of which have been in the top ranks for half a century or longer (Hoechst, Siemens, Daimler, BASF). The two newcomers to the 1998 list were created by a merger with a British company (VIAG) and by the emergence of a trading company (Metro), whose revenues may be overstated.

The failure of new giant concerns to emerge in Germany to replace aging giants appears to be attributable to Germany's capital market and its corporate governance. This system does not promote venture capital well, and cross-holdings of stock do not allow capital to be reallocated from declining to rising industries. Rather, when a new type of industry develops, such as personal computers or VCR recorders, old established German companies must change their profile to produce these new goods (for example, Siemens producing PCs and BASF producing VCR tapes), rather than new companies emerging. Thus Schumpeter's "creative destruction" plays a less prominent role in Europe than in the United States.

The Labor Market

The European labor market is much more highly regulated than that of the United States. Regulation of labor conditions began in the second half of the nineteenth century with the introduction of work councils on the shop floors of German businesses. Germany's social market economy, based on a social consensus between management

Table 9.5   The Largest German Companies, 1992 and 1998

1998	1992
Deutsche Telekom	Deutsche Post
Daimler	Daimler
Volkswagen	Siemens
Siemens	Deutsche Telekom
Deutsche Post	Volkswagen
RWE	RWE
Deutsche Bank	VEBA
Bayer	Bosch
VEBA	Bayer
BASF	RAG/Ruhrkohle
Bosch	Thyssen
Mannesmann	Hoechst
RAG/Ruhrkohle	BASF
Thyssen	Mannesmann
Metro	Deutsche Bank
BMW	BMW
Lufthansa	Krupp
Opel	Opel
VIAG	Dresdner Bank
Bayerische Hypo-und Vereinsbank	Mannesmann
DresdnerBank	Lufthansa

Source: Monopolkommission, Wettbewerbspolitik in *Netstruckturen,* 1998/1999, 1992/1993.

and workers, allowed for regulation of conditions of work through the process of co-determination. Countries such as Germany, France, Italy, and Spain have among the most highly regulated labor markets in the world (see Figure 9.3).

Labor-Market Regulation   EU policy requires a level playing field in labor markets. The Treaty of Amsterdam of 1997 called for the creation of a coordinated strategy for employment and for promoting a skilled, trained, and adaptable work force and labor markets. To implement this objective, the EU has put in place, beginning with legislation passed in 1976, elaborate directives in the area of social policy, regulating such issues as equal pay, minimum annual paid holidays, hours of work, portability of pensions, health and safety standards, maternity and paternity leave, and gender equality. Figure 9.4 offers excerpts from the 1975 and 1993 EU labor-market regulations. These EU-wide regulations spell out the minimum standards for work time, paid vacations, and work conditions. Member countries can offer even more generous provisions, such as the 35-hour workweek in France, the two years maternity leave available in Germany, and the provision to Swedish parents of 480 days off for each child at 80 percent of pay.[21] In Germany, unemployed workers qualify for unemployment insurance for 32 months and are not required to take open jobs that necessitate their moving or that offer lower wages than they had earned previously.[22]

FIGURE 9.3   OECD Indexes of Labor-Market Intervention

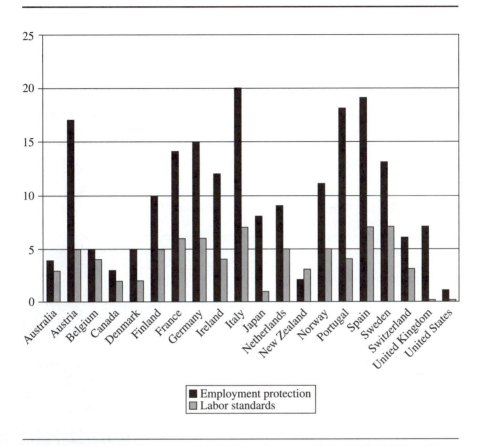

Source: Statistics compiled in Stephen Nickell, "Unemployment and Labor Market Rigidities: Europe versus North America," *Journal of Economic Perspectives* 11, 3 (Summer 1997), 61.

In the highly regulated labor markets of Europe, employers cannot easily fire or lay off workers. Significant layoffs have to be approved by works councils, and layoffs must follow rigid and time-consuming procedures.

According to German law, for example, thirty days before any termination, firms must inform the State Employment Office of the grounds for the termination, the criterion used, and the time period in which the termination will occur. Those to be terminated must be identified by age, gender, and other characteristics. The employer must simultaneously inform the work council and must supply to the Employment Office the work council's position with respect to the planned layoffs. The works council has the right to inform the Employment Office independently of its opinions. Workers have the right to appeal in a complicated and time-consuming process. The Employment Office must approve the termination. If the termination does not take place within ninety days, the application process must start from the beginning.[23]

FIGURE 9.4   EU Labor Regulations, 1975 and 1993 (excerpts)

RECOMMENDATION OF 22 July 1975 on the principle of the 40-hour week and the principle of four weeks' annual paid holiday

1. The principle of the *40-hour week* whereby the length of the normal working week (i.e. the period to which provisions for overtime do not apply), as laid down by national legislation, collective agreements or by any other means, must not exceed 40 hours, shall be applied throughout the Community in all sectors by 31 December 1978 at the latest and as far as possible before that date.

2. The application of the principle set out in point 1 *may not entail a reduction in earnings;*

3. The principle of *four weeks annual paid holiday* whereby the minimum standard for annual paid holiday for all persons who have satisfied all the requirements entitling them to full holiday rights must, depending on the Member States' choice, be either four weeks or correspond to the exemption of a number of working days equal to four times that agreed per week, shall be applied throughout the Community in all sectors by 31 December 1978 at the latest and as far as possible before that date.

Council Directive 93/104/EC of *23 November 1993* concerning certain aspects of the organization of working time:

Article 1

1. This Directive lays down minimum *safety and health requirements* for the organization of working time.

2. This Directive applies to:
    (a) *minimum periods of daily rest, weekly rest and annual leave, to breaks and maximum weekly working time;* and
    (b) certain aspects of *night work, shift work and patterns of work.*

3. This Directive shall apply to all sectors of activity, both public and private, within the meaning of Article 2 of Directive 89/391/EEC, without prejudice to Article 17 of this Directive, with the exception of air, rail, road, sea, inland waterway and lake transport, sea fishing, other work at sea and the activities of doctors in training.

Article 3

Daily rest
Member States shall take the measures necessary to ensure that every worker is entitled to a minimum daily rest period of 11 consecutive hours per 24-hour period.

Article 4

Breaks
Member States shall take the measures necessary to ensure that, where the working day is longer than six hours, every worker is entitled to a rest break, the details of which, including duration and the terms on which it is granted, shall be laid down in collective agreements or agreements between the two sides of industry or, failing that, by national legislation.

FIGURE 9.4   EU Labor Regulations, 1975 and 1993 (excerpts) (cont.)

Article 6

Maximum weekly working time
Member States shall take the measures necessary to ensure that, in keeping with
the need to protect the safety and health of workers:

1. The period of weekly working time is limited by means of laws, regulations or
   administrative provisions or by collective agreements or agreements between
   the two sides of industry;

2. The average working time for each seven-day period, including overtime, does
   not exceed 48 hours.

Article 7

Annual leave

1. Member States shall take the measures necessary to ensure that every worker
   is entitled to paid annual leave of at least four weeks in accordance with the
   conditions for entitlement to, and granting of, such leave laid down by national
   legislation and/or practice.

Pattern of work

Member States shall take the measures necessary to ensure that an employer who
intends to organize work according to a certain pattern takes account of the general
principle of adapting work to the worker, with a view, in particular, to alleviating
monotonous work and work at a predetermined work-rate, depending on the type
of activity, and of safety and health requirements, especially as regards breaks
during working time.

Sources: http://europa.eu.int/smartapi/cgi/sga_doc?smartapi!celexapi!prod!CELEXnumdoc&lg=EN&
numdoc=31975H0457&model=guichett; http://europa.eu.int/smartapi/cgi/sga_doc?smartapi!celexapi!
prod!CELEXnumdoc&lg=EN&numdoc=31993L0104&model=guichett

As a consequence of such regulations, hours worked per employed person have
dropped dramatically in Europe. In 1980, U.S. workers worked over 1,800 hours per
year on average, whereas workers in France, Germany, and Italy worked between
1,700 and under 1,800 hours each. In 2001, U.S. workers still average about 1,800
hours per year, but Italian workers have fallen to 1,600, French workers to slightly
over 1,500, and German workers to well under 1,500 hours per year. German workers
averaged about 80 percent of the hours of U.S. workers per year.[24]

Works Councils   The European Works Council Directive, adopted in September
1994, enacted "consult and inform" requirements obligating employers to consult
with employees about decisions that could directly or indirectly affect their jobs and
to keep them informed about the financial health of the business. These directives

were enacted into national laws by September 1996, applying to all companies with at least 1,000 employees within the EU, and with at least 150 employees in each of at least two member states. By September 22, 1999, when the first phase of the law became subject to a EU Commission review, more than 2,000 companies had negotiated **works council** agreements.[25] When Renault of France closed its two-year-old Belgian plant employing more than 3,000 workers, Renault's European Works Council sued Renault for failure to fulfill its information and consultation obligations under the directive. In both France and Belgium the courts decided against Renault, requiring it to pay heavy fines and provide for a costly layoff plan. The Belgium plant closure became a European Works Council issue because Renault wanted to transfer its production to low-cost Portugal, a move that social policy advocates refer to as "social dumping."[26] Unions are currently seeking sanctions that would punish a company for taking actions similar to those of Renault and are asking that the threshold of employees for the establishment of a works council be reduced from 1,000 to 500. Given the fact that many European and U.S. companies operate in a large number of countries, works council advocates propose to apply the works council provision on a worldwide scale.

Costs of Labor-Market Regulations   EU member countries must implement EU's labor regulations, including those, such as the United Kingdom and Ireland, that have less regulated labor markets. The U.K. government estimates place the compliance costs alone at over $10 billion per year. Since the EU's "Working Time Directives" were implemented in 1999, the number of British workers taking complaints to employment tribunals rose from under 50,000 to more than 100,00 per year.[27] Obviously, the cost of the labor market is not simply the compliance cost. The paid vacations, maternity leaves, and liberal unemployment benefits must be paid by someone. In Germany, unemployment benefits cost 2.2 percent of GDP per year, or roughly $40 billion per year.

Table 9.6 shows the costs of maintaining the highly regulated EU labor market, as measured by its income tax and social security contribution costs. EU member countries such as Germany, France, and Austria have income and social security taxes that account for almost half of labor costs. The highest rates are in Belgium, where taxes account for 57 percent of labor costs. In the United States, the same taxes account for about 30 percent of labor costs. The highly regulated European labor market has therefore created the paradox of a relatively wealthy group of nations, whose per capita income is 60 percent that the United States, with labor costs equal to U.S. labor costs. Not only do European workers cost as much as or more than U.S. workers, but they work only 80 percent of the hours of American workers. Hence, unless European workers are at least 20 percent more productive, they will be more expensive than U.S. workers. Thus, the highly regulated European labor market has made its own labor uncompetitive with other parts of the world. The natural reaction of employers, is to transfer jobs aboard, perhaps first to the lower-wage countries of the EU ("social dumping") and then to lower-wage countries in Eastern Europe or Asia.

The monetary costs of labor do not include the costs of labor inflexibility to the employer. If labor were a variable cost, the employer could more readily deal with

TABLE 9.6   Income Tax and Social Security Contributions as a Percent of Labor Costs, 1998

Country	Labor Costs[a] (dollars)	Percent of Labor Costs			
		Total	Income Tax	Social Security Contributions	
				Employee	Employer
United States	31,300	31	17	7	7
Belgium	40,995	57	22	10	26
Germany	35,863	52	17	17	17
Italy	32,351	47	14	7	26
Netherlands	32,271	44	6	23	14
Denmark	32,214	44	34	10	1
Canada	32,211	32	20	5	6
Norway	31,638	37	19	7	11
Austria	29,823	46	8	14	24
Sweden	29,768	51	21	5	25
Australia	29,590	25	24	2	—
Finland	29,334	49	22	6	21
United Kingdom	29,277	32	15	8	9
France	28,198	48	10	9	28
Japan	27,664	20	6	7	7
Ireland	24,667	33	18	5	11
Spain	24,454	39	11	5	24
Korea, South	22,962	15	1	4	9
Greece	17,880	36	2	12	22
Portugal	13,903	34	6	9	19

(Data are for a single individual at the income level of the average production worker.)

[a]Adjusted for purchasing power parities. Labor costs include gross wages plus employers' compulsory social security contributions.

Source: Taxing Wages, 1998–1999 (Paris: Organization for Economic Cooperation and Development, 2000).

its high cost. During bad times, the employer could cut back on employment through layoffs. In the case of the EU, this option is not available. The employer is saddled with high-priced labor that cannot be shed during economic downturns.

Different EU member countries deal with the problem of high-priced and inflexible labor differently. France, which has the most rigid labor laws on the books, adds flexibility by hiring temporary and part-time workers. In England, 7 percent of workers work on temporary contracts, and a quarter work part-time. Germany, on the other hand, has rigid labor laws that are more likely to be strictly enforced. In fact, proposals to loosen up German labor laws are met with stiff political opposition, even during periods of high unemployment and labor-market stress.

One consequence of the high cost and rigidity of Europe's labor market has been persistently high unemployment, even during periods of economic expansion. While the U.S. unemployment rate has settled in the 5–7 percent range, European unemployment rates have settled, with few exceptions, in the 8–11 percent range. Nevertheless, the political opposition to change in Europe's labor laws is overwhelming and is spearheaded by Europe's unions. In Italy, Spain, and France, even relatively modest proposals to relax rigid labor laws are met with warning strikes and even general strikes. These three countries lead Europe in days lost to strikes for the period 1994–1999, Spain having lost 250 days per year per 1,000 workers, Italy 100 days, and France 90 days.[28] In the United States, the comparable figure is about 10 days. In Germany, where there is a close alliance between the currently ruling SPD party and the labor unions, the government has been warned that any amendments to labor laws will be met by major strike actions.

Public Enterprise: Nationalization, Privatization, and Deregulation

The Anglo-Saxon model calls for a limited role of government and for protection of private property. Hence public enterprise should play only a minor part. Indeed, publicly owned enterprises account for between 1 and 2 percent of U.S. GDP. The European model welcomes a larger economic role for the state. Therefore, we would expect a greater share of public ownership. Figure 9.5 confirms that as of 1980, there was more extensive public ownership in Europe, including Great Britain, than in the United States.

In the postwar period, Europe has had a relatively even balance between social democratic (trade union) and conservative political parties. The major French political figures of the postwar period were Charles de Gaulle (conservative) and François Mitterrand (socialist). The dominant German political figures were Konrad Adenauer, Ludwig Erhardt, and Helmut Kohl (conservatives) and Willy Brandt and Helmut Schmidt (social democrats). In the United Kingdom, there were a succession of relatively weak Labor prime ministers and one strong Conservative prime minister, Margaret Thatcher. This pattern continued through the 1990s and the early 2000s, the political pendulum swinging back and forth between social democratic governments and conservative governments. In 2001 and 2002, the pendulum appeared to be swinging back to the conservatives, with the election of conservative governments in Spain and Italy. In the early years of the new century, differences between political parties have become less striking as both parties seek to position themselves in the middle. Cases in point were Tony Blair in England and Gerhard Schroeder in Germany, who offered voters a "middle way."

In the early postwar years, the choice of government affected the extent of public enterprise. Social democratic and trade union governments favored **nationalization**, and conservative governments opposed it. Hence, nationalizations were followed by privatizations of major industries in metallurgy, transportation, and banking as political regimes changed. As Figure 9.5 indicates, France, at the start of the lengthy

FIGURE 9.5   Extent of State Ownership of Industry, 1980

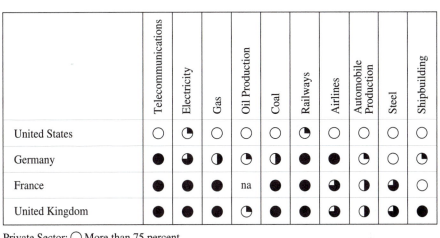

	Telecommunications	Electricity	Gas	Oil Production	Coal	Railways	Airlines	Automobile Production	Steel	Shipbuilding
United States	○	◑	○	○	○	◑	○	○	○	○
Germany	●	◕	◐	◑	◑	●	●	◑	○	◑
France	●	●	●	na	●	●	◕	◐	◕	○
United Kingdom	●	●	●	◑	●	●	◕	◐	◕	●

Private Sector: ○ More than 75 percent

Public Sector: ● More than 75 percent; ◕ 75 percent; ◐ 50 percent; ◑ 25 percent;
na = not available

Source: J. Vickers and V. Wright, *The Politics of Privatisation in Western Europe* (London: Frank Cass, 1989), p. 11.

Mitterrand tenure in the early 1980s, had extensive state ownership in industry, transportation, and banking.

The initial Mitterrand years witnessed a substantial increase in the role of government. Beginning in late 1981 and early 1982, a policy of nationalization was announced, especially in the large industrial trusts where state involvement was already substantial. Substantial nationalization took place in the banking sector as well. The public sector share rose from zero to 71 percent in iron ore, from 1 to 79 percent in iron and steel, from 16 to 66 percent in other metals, from 16 to 52 percent in basic chemicals, and from zero to 75 percent in synthetic fibers.[29] These figures suggest a clear trend toward greater government ownership. After the return of the Gaullists to power in the mid-1980s, there was a reversal in the trend toward nationalization and growth of the public sector, but state ownership remained substantial.

Public enterprise was highly visible in the British economy throughout the postwar era, but its overall contribution was not a large share of GDP.[30] Although the share of public corporations in capital formation grew, the contribution of public enterprises to output remained moderate. In 1950, public enterprise accounted for just over 8 percent of GDP; the equivalent figure for 1967 was just over 7 percent.[31]

It is difficult to quantify the effects of British public enterprise on overall economic performance. What counts is not only the relative size of the public sector but also how well or poorly it was operated. Many public enterprises (such as coal and steel) were nationalized not because of ideology but to prevent bankruptcy. Others were large, visible companies, such as British Airways, that were run by coalitions of unions and management. Others, like British Gas, were operated according to political rather than economic rules.

The role of public enterprise in postwar Germany has also been substantial. Not only did state enterprises dominate transportation and communication and the construction of apartment dwellings, but there was significant state participation in mining and metallurgy.[32] In some cases, government participation was indirect (as in the case of the Krupp industries); in others it was carried out through holding companies. Prior to the 1980s, the German experience with nationalization was the reverse of the British experience. In Germany, the emphasis was on denationalization (*Privatisierung*). The Federal Treasury Ministry was established in 1957 to deal with public enterprises. It was set up to lay the foundations for denationalization. The management of public enterprises has typically been decentralized to the enterprise itself. Two methods of denationalization were used: (1) the sale of public enterprises to private persons or private groups and (2) **social denationalization**, achieved by selling a new type of equity, the so-called popular share, to low-income citizens on a preferential basis. The main early denationalizations were those carried out at Volkswagen and Veba. Union-owned and -organized enterprises represent a mix of public and private enterprise. The union-owned *Gruppe Neue Heimat* was once the largest European apartment construction firm, the *Bank für Gemeinwirtschaft* was the fourth-largest German interregional bank, and the *Coop-Unternehmen* was the second-largest retail distributor in the 1970s.

When Germany was reunited in 1989, the German government inherited an East German economy comprising only state enterprises and state farms. The sale of these public enterprises was handled by a special privatization bureau, which faced the massive task of privatizing thousands of enterprises, most of which were unprofitable.

In the 1990s and early 2000s, discussion of nationalization was replaced by discussion of **privatization**—the conversion of enterprises owned by the state into enterprises at least partially owned by private owners. Wide-scale privatization was begun in England under Thatcher, who argued that private ownership would convert the massive, bureaucratic, and unprofitable public enterprise of Britain into profitable, well-managed companies.

British Telecom was Britain's first privatization in a series of large companies—such as British Airport Authority, British Gas, British Airways, Rolls-Royce, and various electricity and water authorities. They were subsequently joined by British Steel, British Coal, and Northern Ireland Electricity. To be added eventually were British Rail, the U.K. nuclear power industry, and even the London Underground. Privatization proceeds from sales of public enterprises were between 8 and 15 percent of the deficit in the period 1994–1997. The British government has sought, through a so-called Private Finance Initiative (PFI) program, to increase private-sector participation in the provision of both capital assets and services in areas that had previously been restricted to the public sector.[33]

Traditionally, little empirical evidence has been available for assessing the impact of privatization. However, a study of a large number of newly privatized firms (including the British case) revealed significant benefits, including performance improvements (sales, profitability, and the like) and sustained employment.[34] For example, British Airways, one of the more poorly performing international air carriers, became more innovative and profitable after its privatization, although it remains subject to the ups and downs of international aviation.

In France the first period of privatization, from 1986 to 1988, yielded 70 billion French francs to the budget. From 1988 to 1990, official policy aimed at maintaining the status quo ("neither privatization nor nationalization"). Partial privatizations began again in 1991. A law of July 19, 1993 earmarked twenty-one crucial companies in banking and industry for privatization. By 1995, total privatization sales had yielded 185 billion French francs (roughly $37 billion). The sales of this period included the large companies Rhône-Poulenc, Banque Nationale de Paris, Elf-Acquitaine, and Union des Assurances de Paris, but the effort encountered market resistance when it proved difficult to find major investors for Usinor-Sacilor. The total yield of 185 billion French francs was also rather modest when compared to the total budget expenditures for 1995 of 1,592 billion French francs and to a deficit for that same year of 322 billion French francs (some 4.5 percent of GDP).[35]

Privatization in Germany included the sale of substantial shares in Lufthansa and the conversion of Deutsche Post and Deutsche Telekom into publicly traded companies with significant government ownership shares.

Privatization does not automatically mean that the privatized company will behave as an ordinary private corporation. Nicolas Spulber summarizes the situation as follows:

> The role of the government after privatization is also not as simple and transparent as one might assume. Of course, *in principle* privatization aims to free enterprises from government's ownership and control in order to increase their efficiency. Indeed, in some cases, the government does remove itself up to a point from the operation of the privatized firms. But more often than not, the government decides to *continue to play* a role—for instance, that of a critical shareholder—while in other cases, it vests new and extensive controlling powers over the privatized enterprises in the hands of regulatory authorities. Furthermore, shares are not always placed competitively through the financial markets.[36]

As part of underlying arrangements, a substantial number of shares are kept by the state or are placed in the hands of certain groups of investors. As we already know, the government may reserve "golden shares" for itself or may select a "hard core" (*noyaux durs*) of investors to whom it allocates a proportion of the capital, with restrictions placed on its disposal over a number of years. Again, privatization, just like its opposite, nationalization, allows the state bureaucracies and the party in power to transfer wealth and award patronage to their supporters. It also allows for political rather than economic decision making. An example was the politically motivated firing of the chairman of Deutsche Telekom in the summer of 2002 to clear the decks for Schroeder's reelection campaign. In all the Western countries considered, and in particular under both Thatcher's and Chirac's privatizations, reliable political friends were placed at the head of privatized public enterprises. On the other hand, change-resistant employees of public enterprises may also be encouraged to acquire stock in these companies as they are privatized. Methods include offering free shares to the employees or giving the latter priority in the allocation of shares sold to the public. This much-advertised way of promoting "popular capitalism" does not, however, necessarily lead to "shareholder democracy," because people are attracted to this kind of transaction mostly in order to make a quick profit. In any case, ill-informed and largely uninterested small shareholders have few effective powers. In sum, privatization does not necessarily herald a more market-oriented economy, but only a *differently structured* economy.

Privatization and **deregulation** are interrelated. The deregulation process that began in the United States in the late 1970s and early 1980s was at least partially credited with the rejuvenation of the U.S. economy after 1982. Thatcher's deregulation of the British economy in the 1980s also appeared to strengthen the British economy. In light of these successes, deregulation became an official policy of the European Union. Given the EU's policy of creating a common market based on a level playing field, deregulation appeared as a necessary component of industrial strategy. The regulated markets were largely in transportation, in utilities, and in banking, which had been characterized by state ownership in the 1980s. National regulatory agencies would probably give preference to state-owned companies of their own nation.

At the EU summit in Barcelona in March of 2002, the European Commission advocated the opening of the European gas and electricity market to competition by 2005, in the EU's drive to make Europe the world's most competitive and dynamic economy. The French opposed this because of the intense resistance of the powerful lobby of French public-sector workers. At Barcelona, France agreed to consider the opening of gas and electricity markets to foreign competition after a two-year preparatory period but insisted on limiting the deregulation to business customers. The European Commission proposed complete liberalization by 2005, with liberalization of factories, offices, and shops by 2003 and 2004. The matter of national regulatory agencies remains unresolved, even though Scandinavia, Britain, Austria, and Germany have largely liberalized their own gas and electricity markets. Germany, for example, has liberalized its market but has preserved its national regulatory agency, which has been accused of restraining sales of foreign companies.[37] There has been more progress in deregulating passenger air travel in Europe. As of 2000, virtually any carrier is free to compete in any EU market. However, the national airlines have been reluctant to set up competitive operations in other countries, although British Air has established a competitor airline in Germany, called Deutsche BA. The real competition has come not from national carriers but, rather, from low-cost private carriers such as RyanAir, which are offering lower fares from smaller airports.

French Indicative Planning

The privatization and deregulation movement that swept Europe after 1980 meant a decision to place more resource-allocation authority in the hands of private owners and private markets. Such thinking represents a major about-face from the early postwar period, when there was greater confidence in the state's ability to regulate economic activity through some kind of planning. Although planning apparatuses were in place in Germany and Great Britain in the aftermath of World War II, they were dismantled, and neither Britain nor Germany made any serious attempts to "plan" their postwar economies beyond traditional monetary and fiscal policies. The major experiment with planning took place in France between 1945 and 1980. Even with the accession of a socialist government in 1980, there was limited interest in planning after the mid-1970s. The French experiment with **indicative planning**—an attempt to create non-binding plans that provide guidance to private and public companies—was a quite different effort from the compulsory planning that took place in the Soviet Union.

The French have tended to view their economy in a rather long-term perspective, emphasizing the importance of balanced economic growth.[38] The mixed enterprise in which the state and the private sector combine their entrepreneurship and managerial skills also has a long history in France. The pattern of interchanging executives between the public and the private sector has created a tight-knit network of officials.[39] The recruitment of top executives for the public sector from the upper echelons of management creates a peculiarly French managerial style.[40] The basic case for indicative planning rested on the need for information to guide the economy in the face of uncertainty.[41] It was argued that decision making can be improved if a planning agency disseminates information to decision makers. Such indicative planning is nonauthoritarian; no directive targets are issued, and economic agents are encouraged to pursue plan objectives via indirect incentives. French planning began immediately after World War II, as England and Germany were dismantling wartime controls. The first French plan, begun in 1946 and subsequently extended to 1952, was a transitional plan closely associated with Jean Monnet,[42] who headed the General Planning Commissariat. As time passed, French indicative planning moved away from direct controls to reliance on the more indirect mechanisms that became the hallmark of French planning.[43] French planning sought to forge a social consensus among business, trade unions, and regions. The main planning organ was the relatively small General Planning Commissariat. Some thirty "vertical" and "horizontal" **modernization commissions** were responsible for sectoral projections. Consultation, a major feature of the French system, was achieved through the work of the Economic and Social Council.

The plan itself constituted alternative projected-growth paths, including major state priorities, formulated by the Planning Commissariat. In essence, the plan consisted of broad sectoral growth targets related to input, output, investment, and productivity. The mechanisms for plan implementation, both direct and indirect, were another distinctive feature of French planning.[44] The state had two major instruments for influencing economic outcomes: the *budget* and *public ownership*. Plan control over investment in large public enterprises was considerable, but such control was limited in the case of local government investments.[45] Almost one-third of investments in structures were undertaken by government—more than double the proportion of public investment in the United Kingdom.[46] Given the significant public ownership of French industry, the share of investment undertaken by state-owned industry was also substantial. With public ownership in key sectors such as banking, coal, gas and electricity, transportation, and auto and aircraft production, the state could influence economic activity through its control of credit, electricity, and tax incentives. The French plan was designed to create a predictable and harmonious business environment.[47]

Evidence suggests that French firms in fact paid attention to the plans, especially firms important enough to know that the plan might influence their operation.

Monnet argued that a plan is likely to be carried out if those who will be implementing it have a voice in its creation.[48] Indeed, the modernization commissions brought labor, the state, and business together to forge a consensus. The relationship between business and the state in France fostered an interchange of ideas and understanding where there would otherwise be antagonism.

Events of the 1970s resulted in a loss of interest in planning. France was ruled by a conservative government from 1974 to 1981. The election of a socialist president in 1981 presented an opportunity for renewed planning activity.[49] By the 1980s, issues of European integration superseded interest in planning. Although French plans continued, their impact was minimal.

Most observers argue that French planning was of limited importance, especially after 1970.[50] Only limited amounts of information were used to generate the plan, and plan objectives were too simplistic. Plan information was of little value to industrial firms, even state-owned firms. French firms did consider the plan important, especially in providing useful information and creating a dynamic business environment.[51] In a study of plan fulfillment, Vera Lutz, a critic of French planning, argues that, on balance, the achievement record of French planning was dismal.[52] In fact, French planning was not planning at all. It was little more than "collective forecasting." Lutz's examination of the plan target and achievement data suggests that fulfillment varied widely from one target to another and, overall, probably did not improve over time. Other researchers found that "the national planning process did have some influence on the *general* measures and macroeconomic programs used by the state to shape the economic environment in which companies and industries worked."[53] The plan influenced economic outcomes through its *indirect* use of state influence, such as credit and tax credits. Saul Estrin and Peter Holmes argue that in spite of its theoretical basis, planning in France "lost practically all practical relevance after 1965."[54] Thus Estrin and Holmes emphasize the growing lack of interest in planning, poor planning, and inadequate mechanisms to implement plans. The fact that scholars must debate whether French planning had any influence at all suggests that French indicative planning was not effective in allocating resources. Martin Cave points out that indicative planning ceased to play an important role, even after Mitterrand's socialist governments tried to revive it in the early 1980s.[55] The Mitterrand government preferred traditional macroeconomic tools and did not place confidence in the plan.

Economic institutions are judged by their durability. Institutions that work persist. Those that fail are abandoned. The disappearance of indicative planning is probably the best indicator of its limited workability and utility to a society.

The Limits of Income Security: Sweden

Societies wish for prosperity, growth of that prosperity, good jobs, and economic security. Market economies are subject to all kinds of shocks. You could be employed in an industry where demand is declining or in an industry that is being outmoded by a new technology. As a consequence of these shocks, you could lose your job and suffer a loss of income. People yearn for economic security in a market economy, yet the market economy even when it functions well, generates insecurities for certain segments of the population.

All countries make some kind of provision for economic security. It may be provided through private charities, or it may be provided by the state, with greater or lesser generosity. In the European model, economic security is provided by the state, with greater generosity than in the Anglo-Saxon model with its emphasis on individual reliance. Given the old rule of economics that "there is no such thing as a free lunch," economic security must be provided by redistributing resources from the "secure" to the "insecure." It is generally assumed that private transfers through charity will be inadequate, so the government is the institution that arranges this transfer. Arthur Okun used the analogy of a leaky bucket to characterize such a transfer.[56] As income is being transferred from one person to another, some of the income leaks from the leaky bucket, leaving less income for all. The reason for the leak is that those losing income in the transfer have less of an incentive to earn income, and the size of the income pie shrinks accordingly.

Sweden conducted the most ambitious experiment in transferring income and benefits from one group to another in the 1960s and 1970s.[57] At the start of this experiment, Sweden, as a consequence of its extremely rapid growth over the previous half-century, was the world's fourth most affluent nation. By the time Sweden backed away from its "Swedish model," it was the world's sixteenth most affluent country. The only other country that has undergone such a dramatic loss of position is the United Kingdom, which after World War II fell from second place to eleventh place. Prior to its experimentation in the 1960s and 1970s, Sweden did not stand out relative to its European neighbors in terms of government activity, taxation, or economic policy.

The "Swedish model" aimed at providing economic security, including full employment, and egalitarianism, which included both reducing income differences and eliminating poverty. The institutions created to carry out the Swedish model were a large public sector funded by high tax rates; strong stabilization policies, including active labor-market intervention and centralized wage bargaining; highly centralized decision making by a small group of individuals; and concentrated holdings of assets by a few financial institutions. These institutions were put in place at different times. Wage bargaining was already centralized by the 1950s, but the decision to squeeze out wage differentials was the result of the "solidarity wage policy" of the late 1960s. Tight regulation of the labor market was not introduced until the 1970s. Tax rates were raised gradually, culminating in the 1971 tax reform that left workers with a marginal take-home pay rate of less than 30 percent and executives with a marginal take-home pay rate of some 10–15 percent. These rates show the worker's available consumable income from an extra dollar of earnings after taxes. Hence, if workers earned an extra 1,000 kroner, they could keep 300 at the 30 percent rate. If executives earned an additional 1,000 kroner, they could keep between 100 and 150![58]

Like the German "social market economy," the Swedish model was consensus-oriented, dating back to an agreement made between the Swedish trade unions and

Swedish employers in 1938. This agreement was designed to settle disputes peacefully. Union ambitions to gain power reached their peak in the 1970s, when they proposed the creation of a tax-financed wage earners fund to buy Swedish corporate stock and basically make labor the owners of the Swedish private economy. The unions also succeeded in putting in place provisions that would hold down profits and hold down wages in high-productivity firms relative to those in lower-productivity firms.

Sweden's famed cradle-to-grave welfare system matured in the 1960s and 1970s and was based on the notion of **universal coverage**—that is, anyone could qualify for benefits irrespective of work situation or other criteria. Under this system, people without work or not working for reasons such as maternity or sick leave would automatically have 90 percent of their income replaced by state programs. Retirees would automatically have 65 percent of their previous income replaced. Parents received a year of income for each child if they stayed home to care for the infant. Obviously, such benefits were costly, and total public-sector expenditures starting in the late 1970s were in the range of 60–70 percent of GDP, compared to 45–50 percent for the other European countries.[59]

Perhaps the most remarkable feature of the Swedish model was the shift from private-sector employment to living from the state budget. In 1960, 40 percent of individuals were "market-financed" (living from jobs provided by the private sector). In 1995, almost two times as many individuals lived from tax-financed activities (working for a state company or state administration, sick leaves, maternity leaves, pensions, early retirement, etc.). According to the 1995 figures, 2.2 million Swedes lived from market-financed activities and 4.1 million lived from tax-financed activities.[60]

As a consequence of these programs, the Swedish distribution of income became markedly more even. The Swedish Gini coefficient changed from a fairly normal .28 in the mid-1960s to an exceedingly low .20 in the early 1980s. (The higher the Gini coefficient, the more unequal the distribution of income.) This narrowing of income equalities was entirely due to government income redistribution. The distribution of factor income (before taxes and benefits) had a Gini of .33 whereas the distribution of disposable income (after taxes and benefits) was .20.[61] Unions, in wage bargaining, went from the slogan of "equal pay for equal work" to "equal pay for all work."[62] Under the policy of restricting profits, and as a general consequence of the Swedish model with its state distribution of capital, profit rates fell from between 6 and 10 percent in the 1950s to 2–5 percent in the 1970s and 1980s. With such low profit rates, there was little incentive to invest.[63]

Swedish growth of per capita income began to lag relative to that of the rest of Europe starting in the 1970s. Whereas Europe's GDP per capita in the late 1990s was nearly double that of 1970, Swedish GDP per capita was only 40 percent higher, and Swedish real wages did not rise at all during this entire period.[64]

The Swedish welfare system provides an extreme microcosm of welfare programs in other parts of Europe. In Germany, France, Italy, and other EU countries, transfers for pensions, unemployment, maternity leaves, and other benefits are paid out of general revenues on a pay-as-you-go basis. Although individuals are free to save on their own for retirement or health emergencies, the generosity of the pay-as-you-go system is such that there is relatively little incentive to save. In the United States, where people invest in tax-deferred 401K and IRA accounts, massive private savings accumulate to be invested in the private sector. In Europe, with the exceptions of the Netherlands and Switzerland, private pension funds are largely lacking. Instead, Europeans save largely to buy a home. They plan to retire on a generous state pension. Just as the United States is considering the politically explosive issue of the partial conversion of its pay-as-you-go social security system into a private-pension-fund approach, Europe must eventually consider whether it can continue to pay for its generous welfare-state programs. In most of Europe, the problem is more acute than in the United States: Europe's population is aging because birth rates are lower than the rate of replacement. As Europe ages and shrinks in population, there will be fewer contributors to the pay-as-you-go system, and there is limited opportunity to raise taxes on labor above the current rates of near 50 percent.

Summary

- After early postwar efforts, the major European nations began the European integration process with the Maastricht Treaty of 1992. There followed a series of treaties and agreements that created the European Union. The integration process culminated with the establishment of a common European currency, the euro, in 1999. The European Union must still adopt a constitution and resolve its governance procedures and principles.
- The theoretical and philosophical foundations of the European model include mercantilism and the teachings of the German economist Gustav Schmoller. After World War II, the European model was influenced by the ideas of the social market economy. The European model has its legal foundations in civil law, as opposed to common law.
- The European model is characterized by greater interest in stakeholder than in shareholder value. European firms tend to be closely held rather than widely publicly traded, and there is a less active market for corporate control (fewer hostile takeovers). Companies are financed primarily through banks as opposed to stock markets.
- The European model uses codetermination in enterprises, which gives employees a greater say in management, such as seats on corporate boards.
- The European labor market is characterized by rigidities caused by numerous rules and regulations that reduce labor mobility and lower hours of work, and thereby raise the costs of labor to employers.
- The European model is characterized by a greater amount of public enterprise, although in recent years, European countries have begun to initiate privatization and deregulation.
- Within Europe, France has experimented with indicative planning, and Sweden has tested the limits of the welfare state.

Key Terms

European Union (EU)

European Economic Community

Maastricht Treaty

European Central Bank

mercantilism

common law

civil law

corporate governance

stakeholders

shareholders

managerial capitalism

insider trading

transparency

hostile takeovers

market for corporate control

merger

acquisition

codetermination

universal banks

works councils

nationalization

social denationalization

privatization

deregulation

indicative planning

modernization commissions

universal coverage

Notes

1. For a concise description of the European Union, see Jay Levin, *A Guide to the Euro* (Boston: Houghton Mifflin, 2002).
2. Jacob Viner, "The Economist in History," *American Economic Review,* 1963, 3.
3. Herbert Heaton, "Heckscher on Mercantilism," *Journal of Political Economy* 45 (June 1937), 371.
4. James Buchanan, "Notes on the Liberal Constitution," *Cato Journal,* 14, 1.
5. Viner, "The Economist in History," p. 20.
6. Quoted in Erich Schneider, *Einfuehrung in die Wirtschaftstheorie, IV Teil* (Tuebingen: Mohr, 1965), p. 326.
7. H. Jorg Thieme, *Soziale Markiwirtschaft: Konzeption und wirtschaftspolitische Gestalt-Martwirtschaft: Verschahte Zukunft* (Stuttgart: Seewald, 1973), pp. 40–45.
8. L. Erhard and A. Muller-Armack, *Soziale Markwirtschaft* (Frankfurt am Main: Ullstein, 1972).
9. See Gutman *et al., Wirtschaftsverfassung,* Ch. 8.
10. Edward Glaeser and Andrei Shleifer, " Legal Origins," NBER Working Paper 8272, May 2001.
11. Christopher Caldwell, "Europe's Social Market," *Policy Review* 109 (October–November 2001), 32.
12. Michel Albert, *Capitalism vs. Capitalism: How America's Obsession with Individual Achievement and Short-Term Profit Has Led to the Brink of Collapse* (New York: Four Walls Eight Windows, 1993).
13. Laura Benny, "Do Shareholders Value Insider Trading Laws? International Evidence," Discussion Paper No. 345, 12/2001, Harvard John M. Olin Discussion Papers Series, *http://www.law.harvard.edu/programs/olin_center*
14. *http://www.arnaud.de/Insidertrading.htm*
15. *http://europa.eu.int/comm/competition/mergers/cases/stats.html; Statistical Abstract of the United States,* Mergers and Acquisitions Summary.

16. Martin Schnitzer and James Nordyke, *Comparative Economic Systems,* 2nd ed. (Cincinnati, Ohio: Southwestern, 1977), p. 328.

17. Ronald Dore, William Lazonik, and William O' Sullivan, "Varieties of Capitalism in the Twentieth Century," *Oxford Review of Economic* Policy 15, 4 (Winter 1999).

18. *Monopolkommission, Wettbewerbspolitik in Netzstruktur,* 1998/1999.

19. Mechthild Schrooten, *"Finanzmaerkte und Gesamtwitschaftliche Dynamik: USA und Europa,"* in Lars Roller and Christian Wey, eds., *Die Soziale Marktwirtschaft in der Neuen Weltwirtschaft, Jahrbuch 2001* (Berlin: WZB, 2001), p. 393.

20. *Ibid.,* pp. 400–401.

21. "Short Work Hours Undercut Europe in Economic Drive," *Wall Street Journal,* August 8, 2002.

22. "Germany to Tackle Its Labor Taboos," *Wall Street Journal,* August 8, 2002.

23. *http://jurcom5.juris.de/bundesrecht/kschg/BJNR004990951BJNG000300311.html*

24. "Short Work Hours Undercut Europe in Economic Drive," *Wall Street Journal,* August 8, 2002.

25. *http://carbon.cudenver.edu/public/inst_intl_bus/gef/issues/98july/labor.html*

26. *http://carbon.cudenver.edu/public/inst_intl_bus/gef/issues/98july/labor.html*

27. *Wall Street Journal Europe,* "Focus on Labor," June 21–23, 2002.

28. "Caution Could Bog Down Broader Labor Reforms," *Wall Street Journal Europe,* June 21–23, 2002.

29. Bela Balassa, *The First Year of Socialist Government in France* (Washington, D.C.: American Enterprise Institute, 1982), pp. 2–5.

30. A great deal has been written about the nationalized industries in Great Britain. For a brief survey, see Richard Pryke, "Public Enterprise in Great Britain," in Morris Bornstein, ed., *Comparative Economic Systems: Models and Cases,* 3rd ed. (Homewood, Ill.: Irwin, 1974), pp. 77–92. For in-depth treatment, see R. Kelf-Cohen, *Twenty Years of Nationalisation* (London: Macmillan, 1969); R. Kelf-Cohen, *British Nationalisation, 1945–1973* (New York: St. Martin's, 1973); and Leonard Tivey, ed., *The Nationalized Industries Since 1960: A Book of Readings* (Toronto: University of Toronto Press, 1973). For a discussion of issues in the 1970s, see T. G. Weyman-Jones, "The Nationalised Industries: Changing Attitudes and Changing Roles," in W. P. J. Maunder, ed., *The British Economy in the 1970s* (London: Heineman Educational Books, 1980), Ch. 8.

31. Steel (denationalized in 1954 and nationalized again in 1965) is not included. See Pryke, "Public Enterprise in Great Britain," p. 82.

32. J. H. Kaiser, "Public Enterprise in Germany," in W. G. Friedman and J. F. Garner, *Government Enterprise: A Comparative Study* (New York: Columbia University Press, 1970).

33. Nicolas Spulber, *Redefining the State: Privatization and Welfare Reform in the East and West* (Cambridge, Cambridge University Press, 1997).

34. William L. Megginson, Robert C. Nash, and Mathias van Randenburgh, "The Financial and Operating Performance of Newly Privatized Firms: An International Empirical Analysis," *Journal of Finance* 44 (June 1994), 403–452.

35. Measures of government involvement are from Gould, "The Development of Government Expenditures in Western Industrialized Countries: A Comparative Analysis," pp. 42–43.

36. Nicholas Spulber, *Redefining the State: Privatization and Welfare Reform in Industrial and Transitional Economies* (Cambridge: Cambridge University Press, 1997), p. 59.

37 "French Giving In?" *International Herald Tribune,* March 16–17, 2002.

38. Schonfield, *Modern Capitalism,* pp. 156–157.

39. The importance of technical planning experts in different planning efforts has been emphasized: a major role in the French case, a minimal role in the British case. For a comparison, see *ibid.,* pp. 155–156.

40. The differing national styles of executive development have been examined in David Granick, *The European Executive* (New York: Doubleday, 1962). For a later comparative analysis, see David Granick, *Managerial Comparisons of Four Developed Countries: France, Britain, United States and Russia* (Cambridge, Mass.: MIT Press, 1972).

41. For a survey of views on planning in the United States, see Zoltan Kenessey, *The Process of Economic Planning* (New York: Columbia University Press, 1977). For a comparative viewpoint, see Morris Bornstein, ed., *Economic Planning, East and West* (Cambridge, Mass.: Ballinger, 1975). On the relevance of the French planning experience, see Stephen S. Cohen, *Recent Developments in French Planning: Some Lessons for the United States* (Washington, D.C.: U.S. Government Printing Office, 1977). For an excellent survey of views, see Saul Estrin and Peter Holmes, *French Planning in Theory and Practice* (Boston: Allen and Unwin, 1983), Chs. 1–2.

42. See Schonfield, *Modern Capitalism,* Ch. 7.

43. Vera Lutz, *Central Planning for the Market Economy: An Analysis of the French Theory and Experience* (London: Longmans Green, 1969), Ch. 6.

44. Any discussion of the French planning system invariably devotes a great deal of attention to the mystique of the planning system, the ability of the state and the planners to get things done in the absence of coercive power, flexibility and strength, democracy, and direction. For a generally balanced treatment of these features of French planning, see Schonfield, *Modern Capitalism,* Ch. 7; for a critical view, see Lutz, *Central Planning for the Market Economy;* for a brief but useful discussion of pro and con views and references to the literature, see J. R. Hough, *The French Economy* (New York: Holmes & Meier, 1982), Ch. 5; for a more recent view, see Bernard Cazes, "Indicative Planning in France," *Journal of Comparative Economics* 14, 4 (December 1990), 607–620.

45. See Hans Schollhammer, "National Economic Planning and Business Decision Making: The French Experience," in Morris Bornstein, ed., *Comparative Economic Systems: Models and Cases,* 3rd ed. (Homewood, Ill.: Irwin, 1974), pp. 52–76.

46. For a useful discussion of the relationship among the state, the sources of investment funds, and the plan, see J.-J. Carre, P. Dubois, and E. Malinvaud, *French Economic Growth* (Stanford, Calif.: Stanford University Press, 1975), Ch. 10.

47. Changing the nature of the business environment and the extent to which planning (as opposed to simple forecasting) is useful have been controversial. For a discussion of information flows and the French planning system, see *ibid.,* Ch. 14; for a discussion of the theoretical question of reducing uncertainty through planning, see J. E. Meade, *The Theory of Indicative Planning* (Manchester, England: Manchester University Press, 1970); see also Estrin and Holmes, *French Planning in Theory and Practice,* Chs. 1–2; see also Joseph Brada and Saul Estrin, eds., "Advances in Indicative Planning," *Journal of Comparative Economics* 14, 4 (December 1990), 523–812.

48. Lutz, *Central Planning for the Market Economy.*

49. For a discussion of changes in the French planning system, see Martin Cave, "Decentralized Planning in Britain: Comment," *Economics of Planning* 19, 3 (1985), 141–144; Martin Cave, "French Planning Reforms, 1981–1984," *ACES Bulletin* 26, 2–3 (1984), 29–38; Saul Estrin, "Decentralized Economic Planning: Some Issues," *Economics of Planning* 19, 3 (1985), 150–156.

50. Such a case is made in Estrin and Holmes, *French Planning in Theory and Practice.*

51. See Schollhammer, "National Economic Planning and Business Decision Making," p. 52–76.

52. Lutz, *Central Planning for the Market Economy.*
53. John H. McArthur and Bruce R. Scott, *Industrial Planning in France* (Boston: Graduate School of Business Administration, Harvard University, 1969), pp. 26–27.
54. Estrin and Holmes, "Preface," *French Planning in Theory and Practice,* p. vii.
55. Martin Cave, "French Planning Reforms."
56. Arthur Okun, *Equality and Efficiency: The Big Tradeoff* (Washington, D.C.: Brookings Institution, 1975).
57. Our discussion of Sweden is based primarily on Assar Lindbeck, "The Swedish Experiment," *Journal of Economic Literature,* 35, 3 (September 1997), 1273–1319.
58. *Ibid.,* p. 1298.
59. *Ibid.,* pp. 1278–1279.
60. *Ibid.,* p. 1279.
61. *Ibid.,* p. 1281.
62. *Ibid.,* p. 1282.
63. *Ibid.,* p. 1291.
64. *Ibid.,* pp. 1284, 1308.

Recommended Readings

General Sources

Clive Archer and Fiona Butler, *The European Union: Structure and Process,* 2nd ed. (New York: St. Martin's, 1996).
Charles R. Bean, "Economic and Monetary Union in Europe," *Journal of Economic Perspectives* 6, 4 (Fall 1992), 31–52.
Robert Leonardi, *Convergence, Cohesion and Integration in the European Union* (New York: St. Martin's, 1994).
Stephen Nickell, "Unemployment and Labor Market Rigidities: Europe versus North America," *Journal of Economic Perspectives,* 11, 3 (Summer 1997), 55–74.
Horst Siebert, "Labor Market Rigidities," *Journal of Economic Perspectives,* 11, 3 (Summer 1997), 37–54.
Stelios Stavridis, Elias Mossialos, Roger Morgan, and Howard Machin, *New Challenges to European Union* (Brookfield, Vt.: Ashgate, 1997).
Bart van Art and Nicholas Crafts, eds., *Quantitative Aspects of Post-War European Economic Growth* (New York: Cambridge University Press, 1996).
William Wallace, *Regional Integration: The West European Experience* (Washington, D.C.: Brookings Institution, 1994).

France

Bela Balassa, *The First Year of Socialist Government in France* (Washington, D.C.: American Enterprise Institute, 1982).
Joseph Brada and Saul Estrin, eds., "Advances in Indicative Planning," *Journal of Comparative Economics* 14 (December 1990), 523–812.
J.-J. Carre, P. Dubois, and E. Malinvaud, *French Economic Growth* (Stanford, Calif.: Stanford University Press, 1975).
Bernard Cazes, "Indicative Planning in France," *Journal of Comparative Economics* 14 (December 1990), 607–619.

Juny Chater and Brian Jenkins, *France: From the Cold War to the New World Order* (New York: St. Martin's Press, 1996).

Stephen S. Cohen, *Modern Capitalist Planning: The French Model* (Berkeley: University of California Press, 1977).

————, *Recent Developments in French Planning: Some Lessons for the United States* (Washington, D.C.: U.S. Government Printing Office, 1977).

Stephen S. Cohen and Peter A. Gourevitch, eds., *France in a Troubled World Economy* (Boston: Butterworth, 1982).

Saul Estrin and Peter Holmes, *French Planning in Theory and Practice* (Boston: Allen and Unwin, 1983).

John and Anne Marie Hackett, *Economic Planning in France* (Cambridge, Mass.: Harvard University Press, 1963).

Stanley Hottman and William Andrews, eds., *The Fifth Republic at Twenty* (New York: State University of New York Press, 1980).

J. R. Hough, *The French Economy* (New York: Holmes & Meier, 1982).

Richard F. Kuisel, *Capitalism and the State in Modern France* (New York: Cambridge University Press, 1981).

Vera Lutz, *Central Planning for the Market Economy: An Analysis of the French Theory and Experience* (London: Longmans Green, 1969).

John H. McArthur and Bruce R. Scott, *Industrial Planning in France* (Boston: Graduate School of Business Administration, Harvard University, 1969).

John Sheahan, *An Introduction to the French Economy* (Columbus, Ohio: Merrill, 1969).

W. Allen Spivey, *Economic Policies in France 1976–1981* (Ann Arbor: University of Michigan Graduate School of Business Administration, 1983).

Great Britain

David S. Bell, ed., *The Conservative Government, 1979–84: An Interim Report* (London: Croom Helm, 1985).

Frank Blackaby, ed., *De-industrialisation* (London: Heinemann Educational Books, 1979).

M. J. Buckle and J. L. Thompson, *The United Kingdom Financial System,* 2nd ed. (New York: St. Martin's, 1995).

Richard E. Caves and Associates, *Britain's Economic Prospects* (Washington, D.C.: Brookings Institution, 1968).

Richard E. Caves and Lawrence B. Krause, eds., *Britain's Economic Performance* (Washington, D.C.: Brookings Institution, 1980).

Carlo M. Cipolla, ed., *The Economic Decline of Empires* (London: Methuen, 1970).

B. E. Coates and E. M. Rawstron, *Regional Variations in Britain* (London: Batsford, 1971).

T. A. J. Cockerill and R. Brown, eds., *Prospects for the British Economy* (Brookfield, Vt.: Ashgate, 1997).

Charles Feinstein, ed., *The Managed Economy* (Oxford: Oxford University Press, 1983).

Andrew Gamble, *Britain in Decline* (New York: St. Martin's, 1995).

John and Anne Marie Hackett, *The British Economy: Problems and Prospects* (London: Allen and Unwin, 1967).

Paul Hare, *Planning the British Economy* (London: Macmillan, 1985).

Werner Z. Hirsch, *Recent Experience with National Economic Planning in Great Britain* (Washington, D.C.: U.S. Government Printing Office, 1977).

Ken Holden, Kent Matthews, and John Thompson, *The U.K. Economy Today* (New York: St. Martin's, 1995).

R. Kelf-Cohen, *British Nationalization, 1945–1973* (New York: St. Martin's, 1973).

W. P. J. Maunder, ed., *The British Economy in the 1970s* (London: Heinemann Educational Books, 1980).

F. V. Meyer, D. C. Corner, and J. E. S. Parker, *Problems of a Mature Economy* (London: Macmillan, 1970).

National Institute of Economic and Social Research, *The United Kingdom Economy* (London: Heinemann Educational Books, 1976).

Sidney Pollard, *The Wasting of the British Economy* (New York: St. Martin's, 1982).

Grahame Thompson, *The Conservatives' Economic Policy* (London: Croom Helm, 1986).

Alan Walters, *Britain's Economic Renaissance* (New York: Oxford University Press, 1986).

Germany

George A. Akerlof, Andrew K. Rose, and Janet L. Yellen, "East Germany in from the Cold: The Economic Aftermath of Currency Union," paper presented at the Conference of the Brookings Panel on Economic Activity, Washington, D.C., April 4, 1991.

Gary R. Beling, "Selling Off the Family Silver? The Privatization of State Enterprises: The East German Case," unpublished paper, Princeton University, May 17, 1991.

Eduardo Borensztein and Manmohan S. Kumar, "Proposals for Privatization in Eastern Europe," IMF Working Paper, Washington, D.C., April 1991.

Doris Cornelsen, "GDR: Current Issues," in NATO, *The Central and East European Economies in the 1990s: Perspectives and Constraints* (Brussels: NATO, 1990).

Irwin Collier, "The Estimation of Gross Domestic Product and Its Growth Rate for the German Democratic Republic," World Bank Staff Working Papers #773, Washington, D.C., 1985.

Paul Gregory and Gert Leptin, "Similar Societies Under Differing Economic Systems: The Case of the Two Germanys," *Soviet Studies* 29, 4 (October 1977), 519–544.

Lutz Hoffmann, "Integrating the East German States Into the German Economy: Opportunities, Burdens, and Options," paper presented at the American Institute for Contemporary German Studies, Johns Hopkins University, Washington, D.C., November 13, 1990.

Barry W. Ickes, "What to Do Before the Capital Markets Arrive: The Transition Problem in Reforming Socialist Economies," paper presented at the Conference on the East European Transformation, Princeton University, May 3, 1991.

Henning Klodt, "Government Support for Restructuring the East German Economy," paper presented at the American Institute for Contemporary German Studies, Johns Hopkins University, Washington, D.C., November 14, 1990.

Jack K. Knott, *Managing the German Economy* (Lexington, Mass.: Heath, 1981).

Oliver Letwin, *Privatizing the World* (London: Cassell, 1988).

Leslie Lipschitz and Donough McDonald, *German Unification: Economic Issues,* IMF Occasional Paper #75, Washington, D.C., December 1990.

Philip L. Paarlberg, "Sectoral Adjustments in Eastern Germany Due to Market Forces," *Review of International Economics* 2 (June 1994), 112–122.

Martin Myant, Frank Fleischer, Kurt Hornschild, Křižena Vintrová, Karel Zeman, and Zdeněk Sovček, *Successful Transformations?* (Brookfield, Vt.: Edward Elgar, 1997).

Claus Schnabel, "Structural Adjustment and Privatization of the East German Economy," paper presented at the American Institute of Contemporary German Studies, Johns Hopkins University, Washington, D.C., December 1990.

Martin Schnitzer, *East and West Germany: A Comparative Economic Analysis* (New York: Praeger, 1990).

————, *Income Distribution: A Comparative Study of the United States, Sweden, West Germany, East Germany, the United Kingdom, and Japan* (New York: Praeger, 1974).

Wolfgang Stolper, *The Structure of the East German Economy* (Cambridge, Mass.: Harvard University Press, 1960).

Helmut Wagner, "Reconstruction of the Financial System in East Germany," *Journal of Banking and Finance* 17 (1993), 1001–1029.

Norbert Walter, "Beyond German Unification," *International Economy* (October–November 1990).

Sweden

Barry P. Bosworth and Alice M. Rivlin, eds., *The Swedish Economy* (Washington, D.C.: Brookings Institution, 1987).

Timothy A. Canova, "The Swedish Model Betrayed," *Challenge* 37 (May–June, 1994), 36–40.

Richard Freeman, Birgitta Swedenborg, and Robert Topel (eds.), *Reforming the Welfare State: The Swedish Model in Transition* (Chicago: University of Chicago Press, 1997).

Peter Lawrence and Tony Spybey, *Management and Society in Sweden* (London: Routledge and Kegan Paul, 1986).

Assar Lindbeck, "The Swedish Experiment," *Journal of Economic Literature* 35, 3 (September 1997), 1273–1319.

Assar Lindbeck *et al., Turning Sweden Around* (Cambridge, Mass.: MIT Press, 1994).

Erik Lundberg, "The Rise and Fall of the Swedish Model," *Journal of Economic Literature* 23 (March 1985), 1–36.

Michael Maccoby, ed., *Sweden at the Edge* (Philadelphia: University of Pennsylvania Press, 1991).

Per-Martin Meyerson, *The Welfare State in Crisis—The Case of Sweden* (Stockholm: Federation of Swedish Industries, 1982).

Henry Milner, *Sweden: Social Democracy in Action* (New York: Oxford University Press, 1989).

Bengt Ryden and Villy Bergstrom, eds., *Sweden: Choices for Economic and Social Policy in the 1980s* (London: Allen and Unwin, 1982).

The Swedish Economy Autumn 1993 (Stockholm: National Institute of Economic Research, 1993).

10

The Asian Model

The Asian model applies to those countries located in South and East Asia, far removed from the industrialized core of Europe and North America. A Eurasian country with some similarities in its pattern of economic development was the Soviet Union—the pioneer of *the socialist planned-economy model of development.* This model is discussed in Chapter 11. Japan is the notable pioneer of the **Asian model**, followed, in the second half of the twentieth century, by the Four Tigers of Southeast Asia: Taiwan, South Korea, Singapore, and Hong Kong. Another country with Asian development features is China, a country that has experienced rapid growth in the last three decades. China began its development as a planned socialist economy and now appears to be developing as a *market-socialist economy.* China will be discussed in Chapter 12.

The Asian model applies to Asian countries that began their development from a low initial level of per capita income in a largely rural economy. Their main task was not the more efficient utilization of resources, as in Europe, but the creation of capital and the drawing of labor out of agriculture, where workers were underemployed or redundant, into industry. In order for this transfer to take place, capital formation in industry was necessary, and this requires savings, from the predominant rural sector or from such sources as foreign capital.

Given the greater gap in per capita incomes, the Asian model argues that a strong state hand is needed to raise the formation of capital, to allocate that capital, and to draw labor from agriculture to industry

This high-investment model covers a wide gamut of choices. At one extreme is the *Stalinist model,* which uses extreme state power to force high rates of capital formation and rapid transfer of resources from agriculture to industry. At the other extreme, we have the models of Japan and Southeast Asia, using state industrial policy to direct investment resources to defined targets. Japan was the pioneer, with its heavy emphasis on land taxes and other devices to shift savings from industry to agriculture and its heavy-handed reliance on industrial policy supported by a close alliance between the state and big business.

Asia includes the world's two largest countries, China and India, which together account for some 40 percent of the world's population. Clearly, what happens in these two countries will determine the shape of the twenty-first century. India, a perennial laggard in economic growth, has shown dramatic signs of life over the past decade. If both India and China continue their economic progress, the face of the twenty-first century will be much brighter.

This chapter treats Asia as a single model even though there are substantial differences among countries. Those economies that come closest to the Anglo-Saxon model, Hong Kong and Singapore, are city-states, quite different in many respects from the populous, middle-income countries of South Korea and Taiwan. The poorer, developing-market countries of Thailand, the Philippines, and Malaysia differ as much from these middle-income countries as they do from the gigantic and very poor India. We devote the most attention to Japan as the pioneer of the Asian model and its longest practitioner. The fact that Japan has scarcely grown for a decade is scrutinized carefully to determine whether those following it on the path to the Asian model will experience a similar slowdown. The unifying features of the Asian model that override these differences are the high rates of savings and investment and the distinctive organization of capital markets and corporate governance.

Ideological and Theoretical Foundations

The ideological, legal, and theoretical lineages of the Anglo-Saxon and European models were described in the two previous chapters. The foundations of both models could be traced to economic and constitutional philosophies. The roots of the Asian model are quite different. The Asian model originated in Japan, which, until the late 1860s, was isolated from Western thought. The Asian model spread to the Korean peninsula with its annexation by Japan in 1910. Japan, planning to make Korea a permanent Japanese territory, introduced its style of business, finance, and industrial organization there and assumed ownership of most Korean businesses. When Korea was freed from Japanese occupation in 1945, it was left with a strong imprint of the Japanese system.[1] The Japanese model spread throughout Southeast Asia in the 1960s and 1970s as Japan, by then the world's second-largest economy and by far the dominant Asian economy, exerted influence through its apparent "economic miracle" and its investments in the region.

Modern Japanese history began with two major events. The first was the forced opening of Japan by Admiral Matthew Perry on his second voyage to Japan with eight military ships in February of 1854. In the sixteenth century, Japan's rulers had discontinued relations with the West because of its corruptive influences. The imposition of "unequal treaties" on Japan by the more powerful American military came as a profound shock to a nation that believed in its cultural superiority to all things foreign. The humiliation of the forced opening taught Japan that it must modernize to protect itself from foreign enemies—an insight institutionalized in an 1868 imperial memo stating that Japan must stop looking at the world "as a frog from the bottom of a well" and be willing to learn from foreigners and adopt their best points.[2] In the decades that followed, Japanese were sent to the West to learn from universities, industrialists, philosophers, and statesmen. The second major event was the Meiji Restoration in 1868, which replaced the military regime with a new government of progressive officials determined to embark on modernization.[3] The Meiji leaders had no blueprint, other than the general acceptance of an "emperor system" that nominally gave the emperor absolute power to be exercised by appointed officials rather than feudal lords. By 1900, Japan's top officials were largely appointed through competitive exams.

Initially, the Meiji rulers lacked a strong centralized government, because land, the basic source of revenue, was disbursed among feudal lords. Gradually, however, the central government extended control over feudal land in return for fixed payments. Eventually, the central government engineered a massive buyout of feudal lands, and this enabled the state to impose a land tax, which served as its main source of revenue. Deprived of land, talented samurai entered government or business positions. The central government, patterning itself after Western-style governments, became increasingly efficient. The period's most famous document issued in the emperor's name, the Charter Oath of 1868, stated that all matters would be decided ultimately by the emperor—but on the basis of broad consultation, taking into account the interests of all Japanese.[4] Japan's constitution was prepared after numerous study expeditions to the West. Although there were calls for a democratically elected legislature, the Constitution of 1889 assigned most power to the emperor and his advisors rather than to such an elected body.

Japan, China, Korea, and other East Asian countries were strongly influenced by Confucianism, the religion of the educated classes in ancient Japan and China. Confucianism emphasized the qualities of loyalty, nationalism, social solidarity, collectivism, benevolence, faith, and bravery. The Koreans and Chinese placed emphasis on the last three, whereas the Japanese emphasized loyalty and bravery—a "loyalty centered Confucianism."[5] In Japan, this emphasis led to an amalgamation of civil religion, work ethic, and business ideology. The relationship between religion and law was formalized in imperial edits, such as the 1872 "Great Teaching" that included injunctions to respect the gods, revere the emperor, love one's country, and obey the rules of moral behavior. The Great Teaching constituted a code of civic duty for all Japanese. It institutionalized the emperor as a figurehead who was to preside over Japan's transformation and give legitimacy to those who developed his policies.

Confucianism teaches the notion of a virtuous government, and in China, Japan, and Korea, a positive role of government was taken for granted. Throughout Asia, government is expected to play a significant and positive role in the economy. Thus the public was prepared to accept government administrative guidance in Japan and government instructions in Korea in their early years of industrialization.[6] Moreover, there is greater acceptance of powerful leadership, such as the authoritarian presidencies of Park Chung Hee in postwar Korea and Chaing Kai-Shek and Chaing Ching-Koo in Taiwan (marshal rule was not relaxed until 1988), the symbolic authority of the monarchy in Thailand, the strong rule of Lee Kuan Lew in Singapore, and the intrusive role of the state sultans of Malaysia.

If Japan's political governance was influenced by foreign ideas at all, it was by German notions of the late nineteenth century—the idea of the "right of the state," which gave the state priority over individuals. Thus the ideas of Japan's rulers were far removed from the teachings of Adam Smith and of classical liberal thinking. It is no surprise, then, that Japan's economy was organized on the principle of a strong state to which the individual was subordinated.

Relative Backwardness

The economic historian Alexander Gerschenkron formulated his **theory of relative backwardness** to explain how a poor country, such as Japan at the end of the nineteenth century, could rather quickly overcome its relative economic backwardness.[7] An economically backward country that is grossly underutilizing its potential, if it becomes aware of the dangers of backwardness, can take steps to accelerate its economic growth. In Japan's case, the necessary shock was delivered when Admiral Perry's forced opening of Japan demonstrated that it could not compete militarily with the West. This experience forced Japan to confront the gap between its actual and its potential economic achievements and to find innovative ways of overcoming its backwardness. Lacking bureaucrats, Japan created a professional bureaucracy in short order by adopting Western methods and sending young people abroad. Lacking domestic industrial technology, Japan borrowed technology from other countries. Lacking an entrepreneurial class, it turned to the young samurais who had lost their land. The state substituted industrial policy for market decision making. To economize on entrepreneurial resources, Japan fostered large integrated concerns and syndicates. In short, it made up for missing preconditions with innovative substitutions. Many of these substitutions were passed on to Korea, which was left, after Japan's brutal occupation, with Japan's educational system; modernized industry, agriculture, and mining; a centralized administrative structure; and the beginnings of the integrated concerns that dominated the Korean economy in the postwar years.[8]

Gerschenkron's empirical prediction was that relatively backward countries would grow more rapidly than the industrialized countries once they decided upon a policy of industrialization. Indeed, Japan began its modern era in the late 1880s with a GDP per capita of around $1,000. In the first year of the new millennium, Japan's per capita GDP, despite a decade of slow growth, was $25,600—almost 10 percent above the EU average.[9] Japan's dramatic rise in relative living standards was achieved via higher rates of economic growth. Whereas the major industrial countries grew between 2 and 3 percent per year over the long run, Japan's growth (see Figure 10.1) tended to be well above that of countries and accelerated from the prewar period through the 1970s. And whereas capital grew at the same rate as output in the industrialized countries, there were significant periods in which capital growth exceeded output growth in Japan (see Figure 10.1).

Japan's "economic miracle" dates to the period 1953 to 1971, when growth averaged 14 percent and capital grew at 9 percent. Since then growth rates have declined, reaching less than 2 percent for the decade 1990–2000.

Clearly, Japan's growth was fostered by high rates of investment and national savings. Throughout the postwar period, Japan continued to have exceptionally high national savings rates and investment rates. Figure 10.2 shows that the Japanese economy was able to maintain high investment rates through significant domestic savings. Excess savings were then exported, as national savings exceeded gross domestic investment, especially in 1965–1973 and 1983–1989. One would expect countries with high savings rates to invest more abroad as they mature and domestic rates of return

FIGURE 10.1   Real GDP and Aggregate Gross Capital Stock in Japan
             (average annual growth rates)

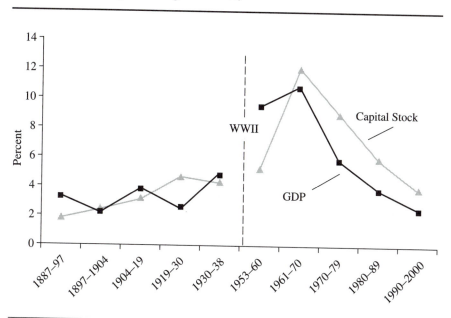

Sources: K. Ohkawa and M. Shinohara, eds., *Patterns of Japanese Economic Development: A Quantitative Appraisal* (New Haven: Yale University Press, 1979); Denison and W. Chung, eds., *How Japan's Economy Grew So Fast* (Washington D.C.: Brookings Institution, 1976); Penn World Table 5.6, Global Development Finance & World Development Indicators, OECD.

decline. Japanese savings flooded into Southeast Asia, spurring economic development. With this capital went Japanese business methods.

The economic explanations for Japan's rapid economic growth were a technology gap, a high rate of capital formation, and the availability of labor. After being a closed economy for centuries, Japan had a technology gap and thus could absorb Western technology through imports of capital, a high propensity to save, and the state's promotion of capital formation.[10] The excess of agricultural labor facilitated the shift from agriculture to the modern sector at a rate dictated by the needs of the advanced sector, and wage increases lagged behind advances in productivity.[11]

Japanese growth was export-driven. While modern industry was growing, exports were primarily traditional industries such as textiles. As modern technology was assimilated, exports shifted toward the high-technology products that Japan, owing to its productive but relatively inexpensive labor, could produce with comparative advantage. Industrial development at home was enhanced by the state's policy of starting import-competing industries.

Noneconomic factors contributed to growth as well. First, the state gave direction to economic growth. Government offices (*genkyoku*) supervised individual industries,

FIGURE 10.2   National Savings and Gross Investment Rates in Japan, 1887–2000

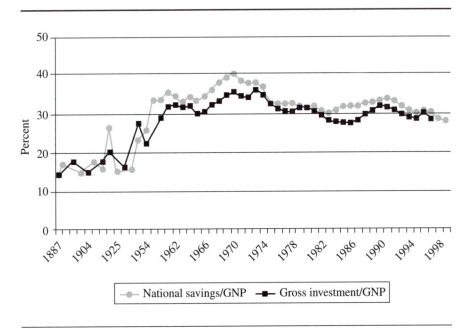

Sources: K. Ohkawa and M. Shinohara, eds., *Patterns of Japanese Economic Development: A Quantitative Appraisal* (New Haven: Yale University Press, 1979); Global Development Finance & World Development Indicators; IMF's International Financial Statistics.

and ministries supervised sectors of the economy. The government was directly involved in the encouragement of industrial projects through low-interest loans from the Japan Development Bank.[12] Second, labor had a growth-conducive attitude: the "permanent employment" system and the submissive attitude of labor toward the industrial establishment.[13] Prior to World War II, the government suppressed trade unions. Since their recognition in the postwar period, trade unions have had a voice in wages, supplemental benefits, and working conditions. They remain enterprise unions, enrolling long-term employees. Their primary strength is in the largest industrial enterprises.[14]

The rest of Asia had to wait until the postwar period for its Gerschenkronian burst of economic growth. Perhaps these countries had to await Britain's decision to dismantle its colonial empire after World War II. The **Four Tigers**—Hong Kong, Singapore, South Korea, and Taiwan—are so named because of their exceptionally rapid growth, which started in the early 1970s (see Figure 10.3) and continued until it was interrupted by the Asian crisis of 1997 (to be discussed below). Note that the rapid growth of the Four Tigers proved contagious, spreading to other parts of Asia, such as Indonesia, Thailand, the Philippines, and Malaysia. In the 1980s, the growth laggard, India, began to grow as well and was one of the world's most rapidly growing economies in the 1990s.

FIGURE 10.3   Growth of the Four Tigers and Other Asian Countries, 1970 to Present

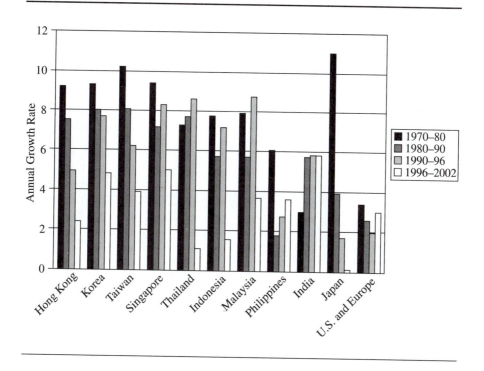

Figure 10-4 shows that two Asian countries, Hong Kong (which is now a part of China) and Singapore, have reached the level of affluence of Western industrialized countries and Japan. South Korea and Taiwan have become "middle-income" countries. The other rapidly growing Asian countries remain poor.

The Four Tigers achieved rapid growth with little if any increases in inequality, as will be shown later. They are therefore systems generating both efficiency and equity. They generated exceptionally high rates of savings, most of which was invested at home, but significant amounts were also invested in nearby developing Asian economies. They also invested in health and education. The burden of taxes was generally light.

Their growth was driven by export-led industrialization. Exports have been largely manufactures, but in recent years a somewhat more diversified export pattern has emerged (for example, financial services in the case of Singapore).[15]

Each of the Four Tigers has a different political system. South Korea and Singapore have been more repressive than Hong Kong, which has not suppressed labor unions. Singapore has been strongly opposed to trade unionism. In South Korea, an active and noisy form of trade unionism has developed.

State policy has been consistent in its support of *export promotion* over *import substitution*. **Export promotion** consists of state policies to promote exports. Such

FIGURE 10.4   GDP per Capita, 2000

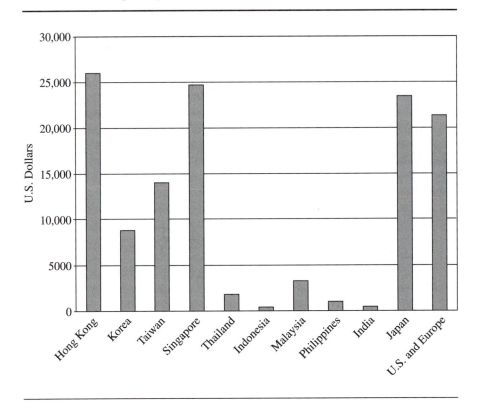

policies range from subsidies of export industries to free-trade practices for the economy as a whole. **Import substitution** consists of policies that protect domestic industries from foreign competition via tariffs or other barriers.

The World Bank classified Hong Kong, Singapore, and South Korea as the world's most outward-oriented economies among the developing countries during the periods 1963–1973 and 1973–1985 and India as among the most inward-oriented during that same period.[16] More general statistical studies confirm that the relationship between export orientation and economic growth is positive.[17]

A number of factors explain the rapid growth of the Four Tigers:

1. The rapid demographic transitions from high fertility and high mortality to low fertility and low mortality caused substantial increases in savings rates. With declining fertility, the ratio of dependents to adult workers fell, freeing discretionary income for savings.[18]

2. Governments in the region promoted a stable investment climate by adopting stable macroeconomic policies and providing stability, reasonably secure property rights, and tranquil industrial relations. Some governments created development banks that took a longer-run view of investment and monitored industrial borrowers.

3. The governments promoted universal education and investment in human capital, such as in public health. The high levels of human capital at the start of growth contributed substantially to the rapid economic growth.[19]
4. Openness to international trade was one of the most important factors in the region's rapid growth. Outward-oriented policies varied from the use of incentives to undervalued exchange rates, the avoidance of import restrictions, and trade liberalization policies.[20] Competing in world markets forced domestic producers to become more efficient and to learn new technologies. Exports generated foreign exchange that could be used to import raw materials and capital goods.
5. Some East Asian governments promoted foreign direct investment to supplement domestic savings and attract new technologies. Policies toward foreign direct investment varied widely; Japan and Korea were hostile, whereas Hong Kong and Singapore promoted foreign investment. Foreign direct investment has been significant in parts of East Asia, but only in Singapore was direct foreign investment more than 10 percent of capital formation.

The most controversial issue is the extent to which the Asian miracle was made possible by market-oriented policies versus state-interventionist policies. These matters will be discussed later in this chapter.

The Asian growth figures raise a number of questions: First, what caused growth to be so rapid starting in Japan around the turn of the twentieth century? Second, why did Japanese growth decline over the past decade? Is this a temporary or a permanent setback, and will other Asian countries eventually experience declining growth as well? Third, what caused the acceleration of growth in other parts of Asia, extending even to India? Did these countries simply follow the Japanese path, or did they create their own models? The ultimate issue is the viability and performance of the Asian model. We have less information on this issue, because we have only one long-run experience combined with the short-run experiences of a relatively small number of countries.

The Lewis Two-Sector Model

The Nobel laureate economist W. Arthur Lewis pioneered the **two-sector model** that was later refined by J. Fei and G. Ranis. This model can be used to explain the rapid growth of Japan and the Four Tigers.[21] Lewis's two-sector model assumed a traditional agricultural sector in which, because of population pressures, labor is redundant, the marginal worker produces no additional output, and agricultural output is allocated among the farm population by tradition rather than by commercial decision making. Alongside the traditional agricultural sector there exists a relatively small modern industrial sector in which decisions are made commercially. The task of development, therefore, is to transfer labor from agriculture, where it is redundant, to industry, where its marginal product is positive.

Figure 10.5 contrasts the traditional agricultural sector with the modern industrial sector. Panel A shows agriculture with an employment level of N_a and a production level of Q_a. From the shape of agriculture's production function, it is clear that

FIGURE 10.5   The Two-Sector Model

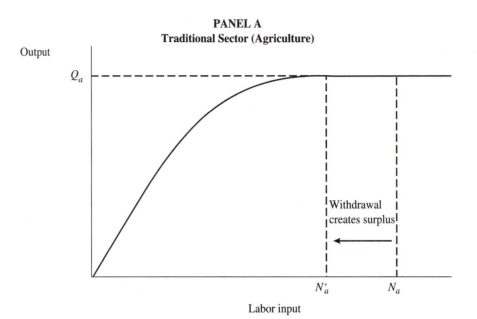

PANEL A
Traditional Sector (Agriculture)

Output

Q_a

Withdrawal
creates surplus

N_a' N_a

Labor input

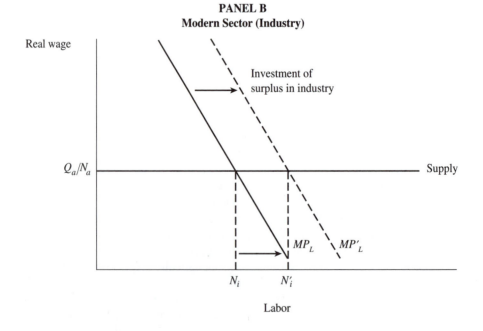

PANEL B
Modern Sector (Industry)

Real wage

Investment of
surplus in industry

Q_a/N_a Supply

MP_L MP_L'

N_i N_i'

Labor

agricultural output would not decline if employment in agriculture could be reduced. The average wage in agriculture is Q_a/N_a. Agricultural workers simply decide to divide the available output evenly among themselves according to tradition and custom.

Panel B shows labor supply and demand in industry. The demand for labor depends on the marginal product of labor MP_L (remember that in industry, decisions are made on the basis of standard marginal analysis). Initial industry employment is N_i; the marginal product of labor in industry is positive. If additional employment could be created in industry, more industrial output could be produced.

The development task of this poor, agricultural economy is therefore to transfer labor from agriculture to industry—which will occur only if the demand for industrial labor can be increased. In order for demand for industrial labor to increase, there has to be an increase in industrial investment. Additional industrial investment raises the marginal product of labor and increases the demand for labor. The supply of labor to industry will be horizontal at Q_a/N_a (the traditional agricultural wage), because there will be a ready supply of labor to industry as long as the traditional agricultural wage is not bid up. This bidding up will not occur until agricultural surplus labor is transferred out of agriculture.

Consider what would happen if, by some mechanism, the supply of labor to agriculture could be reduced to N'_a. Because agricultural labor is redundant, the same amount of agricultural output (Q_a) continues to be produced. Workers who remain in agriculture will continue to receive the same wage as before, so a "surplus" is created that equals agricultural output (Q_a) minus the wages (in the form of agricultural goods) received by those workers who remain in agriculture. As long as the agricultural population continues to receive the same wage as before, the transfer of labor out of agriculture generates a surplus, which is free to flow from agriculture to industry as industrial investment.

The investment of the agricultural surplus in industry raises the marginal product of labor in industry (from MP_L to MP'_L), which raises the demand for industrial labor, which increases industrial output and employment. The net result is that the economy has not lost any agricultural output but has increased its production of industrial output. Thus, as long as a mechanism can be found to harness the agricultural surplus for industrial investment, labor can continue to be transferred out of agriculture, industrial investment can continue to grow, and economic development can proceed.

The theoretical model is clear. What is unclear is the mechanism that will cause the agricultural surplus to be transferred from agriculture to industry and will keep the agricultural wage at its initial level even though labor is leaving agriculture.

A number of mechanisms have been suggested. One is to use the market to transfer the surplus. The farm population could be offered the opportunity to deposit savings into financial intermediaries, which would then lend these funds to industry. Agricultural entrepreneurs could supply capital to industrial firms in return for ownership shares. Another mechanism is for the state to impose taxes on the agricultural population to force them to save. The state would then accumulate budget surpluses that could be used as a fund to invest in industry. Finally, the state could "nationalize" agriculture, through collectivization or some other means, to force the transfer of savings from agriculture to industry.[22]

Japan illustrates the workings of the Lewis model (Figure 10.6)—namely, how the labor surplus was drawn rapidly out of agriculture into industry and how the capital stock grew rapidly as well. Presumably, the movement of redundant labor from low-productivity agriculture to high-productivity industry created the surplus from which the capital stock was built.

High rates of investment in both physical and human capital characterized Japanese economic growth. Japan invested heavily in the education and health of its population, creating a society that was 100 percent literate (as is the case in Western Europe). Japan's high rate of investment in health is shown by a people/doctor ratio comparable to that of Western Europe. Japan's commitment to investment in physical capital is shown by its high rates of national savings and its high rates of domestic

FIGURE 10.6   Japan as an Illustration of the Lewis Model, 1888–1930

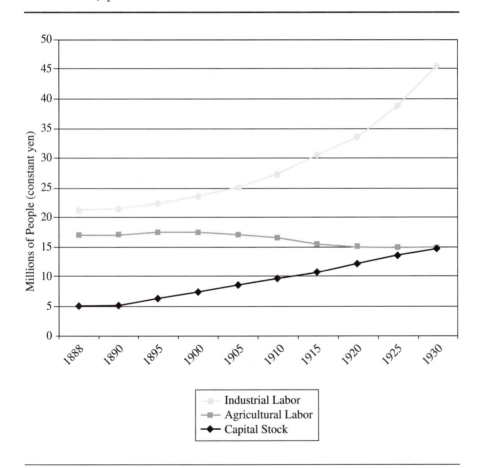

Source: John Fei and Gustav Ranis, *Development of the Labor Surplus Economy* (Homewood, Ill.: Irwin, 1964), pp. 126–129.

investment. The high rate of national savings appears to be a constant of Japanese life. It enabled Japan, particularly in the 1970s and 1980s, to invest its savings surpluses in other countries, like the Four Tigers of Southeast Asia. Net foreign investment occurs when a country's national savings rate exceeds its domestic investment rate. Table 10.1 shows Japan's national savings rate (in the mid-1990s) to equal 34 percent, exceeding its domestic investment rate of 33 percent by 1 percent, which constitutes Japan's net foreign investment. Table 10.1 also shows that high rates of investment in human and physical capital are common to the Asian model. The Four Tigers all have exceptionally high national savings rates, in excess of their already high domestic investment rates, indicating that they, like Japan, are making net investments in other countries, primarily other Asian countries. They also have high rates of literacy, and they make substantial investments in health, as is indicated by their people/doctor ratios.

Table 10.1 reveals yet another common feature: a relatively low tax burden. Whereas Europe's average tax burden was 40 percent of GDP, the Asian countries range from a high of 29 percent for Japan to a low of 14 percent for Hong Kong.

Characteristics of the Asian Model

In the previous two chapters we examined the institutional features of the Anglo-Saxon and European models in terms of capital markets, corporate governance, labor markets, privatization, regulation versus deregulation, and provision of income security. We also examined the role of planning or industrial policy, which was largely lacking in the Anglo-Saxon model but present in the European model, particularly in the case of French indicative planning. The same type of analysis can be performed on those countries that adhere to the Asian model.

TABLE 10.1   Asian versus European Models, Late 1980s

	Europe	Japan	Hong Kong	Singapore	Korea	Taiwan
Per capita GDP, 93 $	17,089	20,523	16,601	13,021	6,548	7,249
GDI/GDP	20%	33%	27%	35%	35%	18%
Gross saving	20%	34%	35%	43%	37%	31%
Literacy	100	100	88	91	96	92
People/doctor	611	609	933	753	1078	9811
Taxes/GDP	40%	29%	14%	21%	19%	n.a.[a]

[a]Not available.

Sources: Roy Ruffin, "The Role of Foreign Investment in the Economic Growth of the Asian and Pacific Region," *Asian Development Review* 11, 1 (1993), 3–5; Cormac O'Grada and Kevin O'Rourke, "Irish Economic Growth, 1945–88," in Nicholas Crafts and Gianni Toniolo, eds., *Economic Growth in Europe Since 1945* (Cambridge: Cambridge University Press), 1996, p. 405; *The World Factbook 1988,* country statistics.

Corporate Governance

The Asian model of corporate governance, which was developed in Japan in the early postwar period, is based on the following principles: extensive reciprocal (cross) shareholdings by one company of other companies; contracting based on trust rather than on impersonal, arms-length transactions; and selective intervention and coordination by key shareholders.[23] This corporate strategy was executed by conglomerates of horizontally or vertically integrated companies owned by a single owner or a small group of owners, working closely with government and with banks.[24]

Before World War II, Japanese industry was dominated by giant holding companies called *zaibatsu,* which represented a complex maze of interlocking directorships, banking relationships, and family ties.[25] By the end of the war, this concentration of ownership had reached the point where fewer than 4,000 zaibatsu-connected families owned almost 50 percent of all the outstanding shares. The American occupation forces sought to eliminate zaibatsu dominance by outlawing holding companies, breaking up monopolies, and making mutual shareholdings among zaibatsu firms illegal. In the postwar era, shareholding in Japanese industry and banking became more evenly distributed. New industrial groupings called *kieretsu* replaced the old zaibatsu organizations. Kieretsu can be either vertical or horizontal: either a large firm in charge of smaller firms ("children") or a horizontal association of interest groups. These new groups are less powerful than the old zaibatsu, and it is possible for a firm within a grouping to place its own interests above those of the group.

The Asian model differs from the Anglo-Saxon and European models most distinctly in its patterns of ownership and corporate governance. A strong Confucian family ideology is reflected in East Asian corporate institutions, where the company is the "head of the family" and the workers the "children." Instead of management and ownership being separate, the owners tend to be powerful families who also serve as the management team. Moreover, these families or groups of related individuals own not one company but groups of companies in a complex pattern of cross-ownership. In Europe, cross-ownership by banks, suppliers, and customers is common. It is common in Asia as well, but instead of institutions owning parts of other institutions, it is one family that owns a number of companies in a kind of overlapping directorate.

Table 10.2 shows that ownership concentrated in the hands of single individuals or families is characteristic of most Asian countries except Japan. Notably, individual and family ownership is also characteristic of Latin America, which shares this feature with the Asian model.[26] Individual or family ownership applies to both large and small companies, whereas in the United States and Europe, family ownership is common only in small businesses. In the Philippines and Indonesia, one-sixth of all market capitalization can be traced to a single family (the Ayalas in the Philippines and the Suhartos in Indonesia). Even in Hong Kong, the territory that most resembles the Anglo-Saxon model (such as the use of common law), more than 50 percent of listed companies have a single shareholder or a family that holds the majority of shares. These major families have cross-holdings in other companies. Unlike in Europe, where banks hold significant shares, banks hold insignificant shares and are not part of the corporate governance team. In the mammoth Korean conglomerates, or

TABLE 10.2   Ownership Concentration of the
Ten Largest Firms

Asia		Latin America	
India	38%	Argentina	50%
Indonesia	53	Brazil	31
Korea	23	Chile	41
Malaysia	46	Colombia	63
Philippines	56	Mexico	64
Thailand	44		

Source: Rafael LaPorta *et al.,* "Corporate Ownership Around
the World," NBER Working Paper Series, No. 6625, June 1998.

chaebols (such as Daiwo, Hyundai, and Samsung), the largest single shareholder
owns a relatively small share, such as 10 percent. However, closely affiliated firms
own enough of the company—say, an additional 30 percent—to give the largest
single shareholder effective control of the conglomerate. Although ownership does
not equate directly with control, in most cases the owners either directly manage the
company or are represented by a senior executive who manages the company in the
interest of the family.

Table 10.3 shows the patterns of ownership in various East Asian countries. It
shows that, except in Japan, publicly traded companies are owned primarily by family or individual owners. In Singapore, Malaysia, and Thailand, there is significant
state ownership as well. Only in Japan are there widely held corporations. Unlike the
Anglo-Saxon model, where institutional investors own substantial shares of stock,

TABLE 10.3   Control of Publicly Traded Companies in East Asia (weighted by
market capitalization)

Country	Number of Corporations	Widely Held	Family	State	Widely Held Financial	Widely Held Corporation
Hong Kong	330	7.0	71.5	4.8	5.9	10.8
Indonesia	178	6.6	67.3	15.2	2.5	8.4
Japan	1240	85.5	4.1	7.3	1.5	1.6
Korea	345	51.1	24.6	19.9	0.2	4.3
Malaysia	238	16.2	42.6	34.8	1.1	5.3
Philippines	120	28.5	46.4	3.2	8.4	13.7
Singapore	221	7.6	44.8	40.1	2.7	4.8
Taiwan	141	28.0	45.5	3.3	5.4	17.8
Thailand	167	8.2	51.9	24.1	6.3	9.5

Source: Stijn Claessens, Simon Djankov, and Larry Lang, "Who Controls East Asian Corporations?"
World Bank, December 1998.

institutional investors (except for some foreign institutional investors) are not prominent in Asia, and they rarely participate in management.

Both the Anglo-Saxon and the European models rely on a "rule of law" when they enter into contracts, although the rule of law may be less crucial in the European model, where cross-holdings and bank ownership are prevalent. In Asian countries, which, with the exceptions of Hong Kong and India, use civil law, the "rule of law" appears to be less important in regulating the dealings among companies.

Two generic types of contracting regimes can be identified: **Relational contracting** is based not on a formal rule of law but on personal relationships and trust. **Market-based contracting** is an impersonal form of contracting based on formal contracts backed by a rule of law. Market-based contracting is the primary form of contracting used in, say, the United States, whereas relational contracting is the primary form of contracting used in Asia. Relational contracting is used in countries that have a relatively weak rule of law; a prominent example is modern-day Russia. Asian firms usually deal with other firms on the basis of personal agreements, informal enforcement mechanisms, customs, or existing trust relationships and rely less on formal contracts and their enforcement by the courts. The courts themselves may be inefficient or even corrupt. For example, influenced by bribes to judges, a court-appointed supervisor declared a perfectly solvent Canadian company operating in Indonesia bankrupt. Such cases prompted the World Bank's chief representative to Indonesia to declare, "The pattern of outcomes from the courts is very hard to understand except in terms of corruption and probably incompetence."[27]

With their family-based ownership system, Asian companies appear to have resolved the key principal–agent problem between owners and manager: The owners are the managers. Principal–agent conflicts do arise, however, between the principal owner and minority shareholders and among the various companies owned by the same family. In cases where relational contracting is used and there is extensive cross-ownership, the rights of minority shareholders tend to be abused. In Thailand and Korea, shareholder meetings make decisions without a quorum of shareholders. The rights of minority shareholders can be diluted by decisions of the major shareholder to issue new shares to insiders. In Japan, the Asian country with the broadest public ownership of corporations, minority shareholders, even foreign shareholders with significant minority interests, are unable to influence management decisions.

Disputes involving the Japanese company Tokyo Style provide a microcosm of the problems of minority shareholders. In the spring of 2002, a Japanese sort of corporate raider organized minority shareholders (about 30 percent of shares were held by foreign owners) to force Tokyo Style to pay out some of its huge cash holdings to shareholders as dividends or, at least, to buy back its own shares to raise the stock price. Minority shareholders attempted to place this proposal on the agenda of a shareholder meeting in May of 2002, an action practically unheard of in Japan. The minority-shareholder proposals were rebuffed by the long-time president of Tokyo Style (he had worked for the company since the age of 18), who marshaled the support of cross-shareholders like Fuji Bank. Fuji Bank was quoted as saying that it would risk ruining its relationships with other customers if it failed to side with management.[28]

Cross-shareholding creates a further risk of expropriation of minority shareholders. The family owner of a number of companies can divert assets from one company to another. In Korea, for example, it is common for companies owned by one family to make uneconomical loans to other family-controlled firms. Shareholders of the lending firm are basically expropriated of their assets via such transfers. Such diversions of assets cannot take place without the collusion of employees and managers, whose careers are controlled by the family owner.

Given the web of cross-ownership in Asian countries, hostile takeovers are practically impossible. Owners can count on related parties to repel any such attempts. Cross-holdings make bankruptcy a less effective instrument for weeding out poorly managed companies. If the insolvent company is part of a family-owned conglomerate, other companies will be called on to bail out the faltering company with loans or asset transfers.

The most fundamental risk is not to minority shareholders but to the company itself. By relying on relational rather than on market-based contracting, the company fails to use price signals in its decision making. For example, in an Anglo-Saxon company, transactions would occur "at arm's-length" and would be subjected to rate-of-return calculations by third parties such as investment bankers. Poor investments would be ruled out, as would irrational asset transfers among companies.[29] When relational contracting is used, such "market" controls are largely absent. Business errors, large and small, are the result. Figure 10.7 summarizes the features of corporate governance in Asia.

Publicly traded Asian countries are not required to be as transparent as companies that operate in the Anglo-Saxon legal and accounting environment. Public investors will be reluctant to become shareholders of companies that do not supply adequate accounting information. Figure 10.8 contrasts the disclosure requirements of publicly traded Japanese companies with the disclosures required by the International Accounting System (IAS). The list of deviations is long, and the most significant omission is any requirement to reveal transactions with related parties. Furthermore, Japanese companies can value their assets at their acquisition costs, which mean that losses due to declining asset values are not disclosed to shareholders. In Japanese firms there are few outside directors. Virtually all directors are involved in management; therefore, accounting statements cannot be vetted by outside, impartial directors.[30]

The Capital Market

The corporate governance of Asian companies has a profound effect on the functioning of its capital markets. Given the widespread use of relational contracting, the lack of protection of minority shareholders, and the limited amount of accounting disclosure, there are only limited purchases of stock by minority buyers. Capital must come from the owners; it will not come from a large number of small investors as it does in Anglo-Saxon equity markets. Those with funds to invest, either parties in the country itself or foreigners, would therefore invest in bank deposits or in government debt. Foreign investment would be through the purchase not of shares but

FIGURE 10.7   Corporate Governance in East Asia and Other Emerging Economies

Variables	Description/Effect	Korea	Indonesia	Malaysia	Philippines	Thailand	Mexico	India
Right to call emergency shareholder meeting	Facilitates shareholders' control	Yes	Yes	Yes	Yes	Yes	Yes	Yes
Right to make proposals at shareholder meeting	Facilitates shareholders' control; increased opportunity to prevent biased decisions by insiders	Yes	Yes	Yes		Yes	NA	NA
Mandatory shareholder approval of interested transactions	Protects against abuse and squandering of company assets by insiders	Yes	Yes	Yes	Yes	Yes	NA	NA
Preemptive rights on new stock issues	Protects against dilution of minority shareholders; prevents insiders from altering ownership structure	Yes	Yes		Yes	Yes	NA	NA
Proxy voting	Facilitates shareholders' control	Yes	No	Yes	Yes	Yes	No	Yes
Penalties for insider trading	Protects against use of undisclosed information at the expense of current and potential shareholders	Yes	Yes	Yes	Yes	Yes		
Provisions on takeover legislation	Protects against violation of minority shareholders' rights	Yes		Yes	Yes	Yes		
Mandatory disclosure of nonfinancial information	Both financial and nonfinancial information data are important in assessment of a company's prospects.	Yes	Yes	Yes		Yes		
Mandatory disclosure of connected interests	Protects against abuse by insiders	Yes			Yes	Yes		
Mandatory shareholder approval of major transactions	Protects against abuse by insiders. Protection can be enhanced through supramajority voting.	Yes	Yes	Yes	Yes	Yes	Yes	
One share–one vote	A basic right. Some shareholders may waive their voting rights for other benefits such as higher dividends.	Yes	No	Yes	No	No	Yes	No
Allows proxy by mail	Facilitates shareholders' control	Yes	No	No	No	No	No	No

Note: Blank denotes no regulation.

Source: Stijn Claessens, Simon Djankov, and Larry Lang, East Asian Corporations: Growth, Financing and Risks over the Last Decade (World Bank, 1998).

of short-term debt. (Share owners know that they have little legal protection, so they invest in the least-risky funds—namely, short-term debt.) This practice creates considerable volatility in Asian capital markets because short-term capital, unlike equity capital, can flee a country on a moment's notice if there are signs of weakness of the economy. If there are no restrictions on currency outflows, domestic savers prefer to invest in safe-haven countries, such as the United States, where their holdings are protected by a strong rule of law.

The overall result is that Asian countries finance themselves by borrowing, not by selling new shares of stock. This means that Asian companies are highly **leveraged**; that is, they have heavy debt burdens, which must be serviced by regular interest and principal payments. The danger of high leverage is that if revenues fall as a consequence of declining demand, the company will not be able to pay its interest obligations and may become insolvent. In Korea, the weak financial structure of the corporate sector made it vulnerable to mass bankruptcies. Korea's debt-to-equity ratio (the ratio of debt to the underlying value of the company) for the 30 largest chaebols in 1995 was almost 350; these firms had borrowed an average of more than three times the company's net worth. Not all Asian countries have such high debt-to-equity ratios. In the same period, Taiwan's was only one-sixth of Korea's.[31]

We have already seen that households in Asian countries have exceedingly high rates of savings. Thus, there should be a ready supply of capital for Asian businesses from domestic savings. Given the reluctance of households to invest in stocks as minority shareholders, their savings flow primarily into banks, if not abroad. For example, for many years, most Japanese household savings automatically flowed into the state postal bank. In the European model, banks act as the primary financial intermediaries; therefore, the Asian flow of household savings into banks is similar to the European practice. To a greater degree than in Europe, Asian banks base their lending on political and industrial-planning criteria. For many years, Japan's powerful planning ministry (MITI, recently renamed METI) directed banks to lend to industries and companies singled out for development. In Korea, banks were basically owned by the state until their privatization in 1982. Despite financial liberalization and deregulation, strong intervention continued as the government appointed CEOs of banks, and Korean banks continued to function like state-owned institutions. In the Philippines, banks are owned by families, and there are weak laws to prevent them from serving as a "cash vault" of business groups.[32] In Taiwan, banks were tightly controlled by the government until the early 1990s. After 1992, the banking industry was deregulated, and the government placed regulations on lending to affiliated groups.

Irrespective of their ownership, most Asian banks are not subject to strong supervision. In Japan, a large number of banks were technically insolvent in the early 2000s as a consequence of bad loans, many backed by real estate the value of which had collapsed. Japan's banking regulatory agency, the Financial Services Agency, continues to support generous deposit insurance that prevents insolvent banks from being restructured and placed on a solid financial footing. Throughout Asia, banks and other financial institutions are poorly regulated, and large financial institutions count on being bailed out by the government if they are threatened by insolvency. The promise of bailouts encourages bad and risky lending, thereby exacerbating the problems of the banking system. In Japan, the moral-hazard problem can be traced

FIGURE 10.8   Japanese Accounting Standards

Japanese requirements are based on the Commercial Code, the standards of the Business Accounting Deliberation Council, and statements of the Japanese Institute of Certified Public Accountants. Because March year-ends are the most common in Japan, this analysis is prepared on the basis of Japanese standards in force for accounting periods ending on March 31, 2002.

Japanese accounting may differ from that required by IAS because of the absence of specific Japanese rules on recognition and measurement in the following areas:

• The classification of business combinations as acquisitions or unitings of interest	IAS 22.8
• The setting up of provisions in the context of business combinations accounted for as acquisitions	IAS 22.31
• Impairment of assets	IAS 36
• The discounting of provisions	IAS 37.45
• The recognition of lease incentives	SIC 15
• Accounting for employee benefits other than severance indemnities	IAS 19

There are no specific rules requiring disclosures of:

• A primary statement of changes in equity	IAS 1.7
• The FIFO or current cost of inventories valued on the LIFO basis	IAS 2.36
• The fair values of investment properties	IAS 40.69
• Discontinuing operations	IAS 35
• Segment reporting of liabilities	IAS 14.56

There are inconsistencies between Japanese and IAS rules that could lead to differences for many enterprises in certain areas. Under Japanese rules:

• It is acceptable that overseas subsidiaries apply different accounting policies if they are appropriate under the requirements of the country of those subsidiaries.	IAS 27.21
• Under a temporary regulation, land can be revalued, but the revaluation does not need to be kept up to date.	IAS 16.29
• Preoperating costs can be capitalized.	IAS 38.57
• Leases, except those that transfer ownership to the lessee, can be treated as operating leases.	IAS 17.12/28
• Inventories can generally be valued at cost rather than at the lower of cost and net realizable value.	IAS 2.6
• Inventory cost can include overheads in addition to costs related to production.	IAS 2.6
• The completed contract method can be used for the recognition of revenues on construction contracts.	IAS 11.22
• Some trading liabilities are measured at fair value, but the category is not clearly defined.	IAS 39.93
• Provisions can be made on the basis of decisions by directors before an obligation arises.	IAS 37.14

FIGURE 10.8 Japanese Accounting Standards (cont.)

• Proposed dividends can be accrued in consolidated financial statements.	IAS 10.11
• The discount rate for employee benefit obligations can be adjusted to take account of fluctuations within the previous five years.	IAS 19.78
• Any past service cost of employee benefits is spread over the average service lives of active employees, even if the cost is vested.	IAS 19.96
• The portion of a convertible debenture that is in substance equity is not normally accounted for as such.	IAS 32.23
• Extraordinary items are defined more widely.	IAS 8.6/12
• Segment reporting does not use the primary/secondary basis.	IAS 14.26
In certain enterprises, these other issues could lead to differences from IAS:	
• It is possible, though unusual, for dissimilar subsidiaries to be excluded from consolidation if the consolidation of such subsidiaries would mislead stakeholders.	IAS 27.14
• There are no requirements concerning the translation of the financial statements of hyperinflationary subsidiaries.	IAS 21.36

Source: Adapted from *http://www.ifad.net/content/ie/ie_f_gaap_frameset.htm*

to the government's practice of insuring virtually all accounts. Depositors see no risk in depositing their funds in poorly run banks, which are thus not punished for bad lending practices by bankruptcy.[33]

A nation's capital market must be judged not only by how much investment finance it raises but also by how it distributes these funds among competing claimants. Figure 10.9 provides devastating evidence on rates of return on capital investments in manufacturing industries in Japan and the United States.[34] For the entire period of 1986 to 1999, the rate of return to U.S. capital investment was markedly higher than in Japan and the difference was widening. In 1999, the manufacturing rate of return was 30 percent in the United States and 1.4 percent in Japan. Like Japan, Korea experienced declining rates of profitability starting in the late 1980s, making it vulnerable to crises. The decline in Korea's profits can be attributed to increased competition from China and rising wage rates.[35]

Labor Markets

The advantage of the Anglo-Saxon "hire and fire" labor market is that it is flexible and moves labor resources from one activity to another quickly. The European model basically rejects the Anglo-Saxon model as inconsistent with fairness to workers and

FIGURE 10.9   Return on Equity (ROE) in Manufacturing, Japan and
the United States

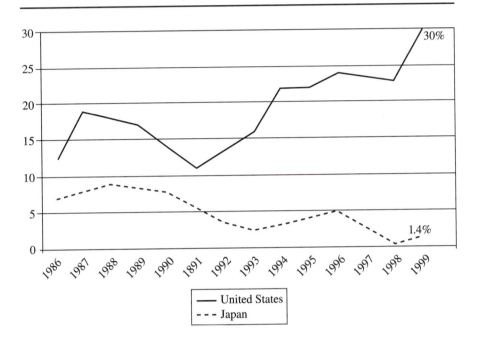

Source: Nikkei (October 8, 2000). Japan: 1,345 Corp.; U.S.: S&P 400; cited in Schulz, "The Reform of (Corporate) Governance in Japan," p. 531.

replaces it with a highly regulated model that makes firing difficult. There are economic theories that argue that a more inflexible labor market may actually be efficient. Workers who have implicit contracts that promise them long tenure are more loyal to the firm and are willing to get training specific to the firm. Workers who are paid a "fair" wage exert more effort on behalf of the firm, and the fair wage may be above the current market wage.

The Asian labor market has some features of both the Anglo-Saxon and the European labor markets, with the added twist of paternalism toward workers that may be traced back to Confucian philosophy. Unlike in Europe, and with the clear exception of South Korea, labor unions have been relatively weak. In Japan, labor unions tend to be enterprise unions (such as the Sony union) and do not represent economy-wide branches or crafts. In fact, a number of authoritarian governments banned labor unions in the early postwar period, and unions were banned in Japan prior to World War II. In most Asian countries, workers are poorly protected from "hire and fire" provisions, but they may receive the protection afforded by paternalistic attitudes toward the work force—workers are regarded as part of an extended family.

The stereotype of the postwar Japanese labor market is one in which there is an "implicit" lifetime labor contract between those working for a large company and the company itself. Thus a college graduate hired by Sony or Mitsubishi could expect lifetime employment at the company as a "salaryman." Lifetime employment contracts have been regarded both as a plus for the system (increased loyalty, better-trained workers) and as a minus (companies are unable to shed workers during economic downturns). Indeed, tenure at Japanese firms is longer than in U.S. firms. In the United States, the average male employee spends 7.5 years in one company, whereas the average Japanese male employee spends 12.9 years. The longest Japanese tenures are in large companies. The average tenure in manufacturing is 13.1 years; in electricity, gas, and water, it is 17.3 years.[36]

Established employees of large companies are, in effect, guaranteed lifetime employment. They are taught to think of the company as their family, and they believe that if they work hard for the company, the company will take care of them. John M. Montias singled out this characteristic of the Japanese enterprise for study and found that this "permanent employment" constraint on Japanese management is likely to alter resource-allocation patterns.[37]

Indeed, the Japanese economy has been characterized as a **share economy**, based on a framework suggested by Martin Weitzman.[38] The evidence for this characterization—the bonus system in Japan—is not strong, though differences in the allocation system make Japanese labor markets of great interest to the comparative analyst.[39]

The concepts of industrial paternalism and lifetime employment have received a great deal of attention, in large part because the system seems so different from those in other capitalist countries. In the Japanese case, the difference between appearance and substance is considerable.[40] In fact, a number of forces at work in the Japanese economy limit the impact of guaranteed employment. First, not all members of the Japanese labor force are covered by guaranteed employment. Roughly 30 percent of the industrial labor force is covered by some form of guaranteed employment.[41] Second, Japanese firms have ways to create flexibility in employment. For example, a temporary labor force can be utilized, and the bonus payment system serves as an inducement for employees to work hard. Third, Japanese firms rely on subcontracting for industrial parts, thus lessening the need to hire the labor force necessary to produce these parts on a sustained basis. Finally, guaranteed employment does not mean that inefficient firms are in some way maintained. On the contrary, both the pressures of the market and the role played by government agencies encourage the productive sectors and discourage the unproductive sectors. All these factors substantially mitigate what would otherwise appear to be a starkly different system of labor–management relations.

The importance of lifetime contracts in Japan is called somewhat into question by the following facts: Small firms lay off employees readily. Large firms retire employees early. If lifetime contracts were in effect, the large company could formalize that practice rather than leaving it implicit. Prior to World War II, Japanese companies, large and small, did not hesitate to fire or lay off employees. If lifetime employment had deep-rooted cultural causes, they would have been in effect in this earlier period as well. Thus it may not be that large companies want lifetime contracts but, rather, that the legal system forces such contracts on them. According to current Japanese labor law, employees can not be fired unless the company is prepared to argue that it will otherwise fail. Small firms are willing to make such assertions, but large firms are not.[42]

The greater flexibility of the Japanese labor market than its stereotype is suggested by its lower unemployment rates even during periods of economic downturn. In the rigid European labor market, unemployment rates are high during normal periods but worsen during economic downturns. Those outside the European job-tenure system simply cannot find work. In Japan, there is apparently enough flexibility, through part-time work and contracting to smaller firms, for the labor market to respond to economic downturns.

The affluent Singapore's labor laws are a microcosm of Asia's limited regulation of labor markets. Singapore's "liberal" Employment Act simply limits the workweek to forty-four hours and specifies one and one-half times regular pay for overtime. New employees are allowed one week of annual leave and one additional day for each year of service, up to a maximum of fourteen days per year. Employees can be dismissed on one day's notice if they have been employed for less than twenty-six weeks and on four weeks' notice if they have been employed for five years or more.[43]

Income Distribution

As we have seen, East Asia recorded remarkable economic growth from 1965 to the present. One of the often-overlooked aspects of this growth is that the East Asian economies have combined high growth with relatively low and declining inequality of income.

Figure 10.10 is a scatter diagram for forty economies, showing the relationship between economic growth and income inequality as measured by the ratio of the income share of the richest 20 percent to that of the poorest 20 percent of the population. As the figure shows, there are seven high-growth–low-income-equality countries, and all seven are in East Asia. The East Asian economies began their era of rapid growth with relatively even distributions of income, and most of them have ended with a more nearly equal distribution than when they started.[44] As the author of a substantial survey of the East Asian growth experience comments, "East Asian economies have relatively equal income distributions, and growth in the region is especially noteworthy in that it has not been at the expense of equity."[45]

How was it that East Asia was able to combine growth and equity? One factor has been that the governments of the region adopted policies to ensure that all groups benefited from economic growth. These programs included universal education and public-housing programs, land reform, and control of fertilizer and agricultural prices to raise rural incomes. History also contributed to the more nearly equal distribution of income: Japan's defeat in World War II, the destruction during the Korean War, and the defeat of the Chinese nationalist forces made possible rural land reform and eliminated the property assets of the elite.[46]

East Asia's relatively equitable distributions of income may contribute to their more rapid growth. Less inequality usually means greater political stability. It also

FIGURE 10.10   Income Inequality and Growth of GDP, 1965–1989

GDP growth per capita (percent)

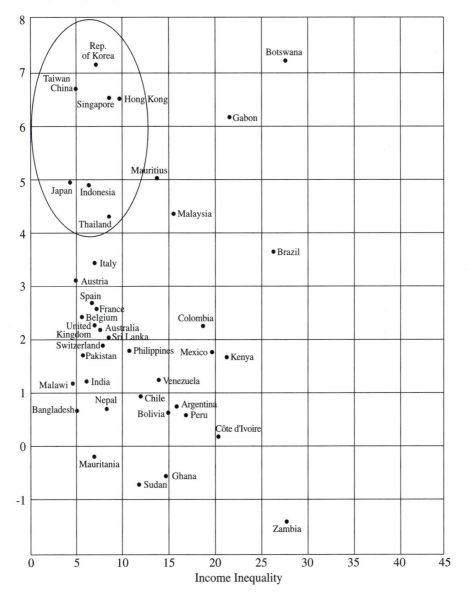

Income Inequality

Note: Income inequality is measured by the ratio of the income share of the richest 20 percent to the income share of the poorest 20 percent of the population.

Source: World Bank data.

means a more equitable distribution of education. A high degree of income inequality may promote labor unrest and political conflict, both of which inflict greater risks on the economy and raise the cost of capital.[47] The most likely cause of low income inequality is the more even distribution of human capital (education and health) in Asia.

Industrial Policy

Japan was the pioneer of the Asian brand of industrial policy. The government has played an important role in the Japanese economy since the early years of industrialization.[48] The Japanese ministerial structure has a substantial impact on the economy, not only through direct participation in key aspects of economic life, but also through its indirect influence. The Ministry of Finance, along with the Bank of Japan, is responsible for the traditional functions of monetary control. In the outside world, however, it is the **Ministry of International Trade and Industry** (MITI, recently renamed METI) that receives the most attention.[49] The close relationships among manufacturing, banks, and government has meant that banks have allocated capital on the basis of an implicit industrial policy. Prior to 1998, this meant that Japanese enterprises were virtually guaranteed cheap capital through the banking system.

MITI is responsible for international trade, domestic production, and domestic industrial structure. MITI is the purveyor of an "industrial policy" geared to promoting rapid economic growth.[50] MITI is responsible for guiding and influencing economic decisions by promoting key sectors of the economy and endeavoring to phase out low-productivity sectors. MITI uses public funds for research and development and provides assistance for organizational change, such as mergers.

Traditional measures of government involvement do not capture the essence of the Japanese system. In the absence of a major formal role for government and planning, the government is nevertheless able to influence both short- and long-term decision making. Rather than formal and powerful involvement in a few traditional and noticeable areas, the government exerts its influence through a myriad of arrangements that guide economic growth. Enthusiasts of an industrial policy cite the Japanese experience.

During the 1970s, early admiration for the Japanese economic system grew. In a time of general economic turmoil, the Japanese were perceived to have found the keys to sustained economic growth. The 1970s, however, were not a tranquil decade for the Japanese economy. In the early 1970s, Japan sustained two major shocks. The first was the end of a long-fixed exchange rate between the American dollar and the Japanese yen and the move toward a flexible exchange rate.[51] The second event was the energy crisis of 1973. The average annual rate of growth of real GDP declined from above 10 percent in the late 1960s to generally lower rates in the mid-1970s. The average annual rate of inflation reached almost 25 percent in 1974. Other performance indicators showed similar trends. Output per labor-hour in manufacturing declined, and manufacturing unit costs increased dramatically. The late 1970s brought on a second, less severe energy crisis and (possibly more important) a sharply increasing positive balance on the current account. Once again, the problem of balancing Japanese–American trade became a major issue.

Japan's dramatic decline in economic performance in the 1990s has dimmed the luster of the Japanese model. The reliance on large industrial conglomerates has been seen to inhibit competition and to retard the growth of smaller and more innovative businesses. The intimate relationship between banks and large industrial concerns has caused banks (often prompted by government) to make large, unprofitable loans. The cozy relationship between government and business has created a vast system of corruption, where more than half of Japan's business enterprises have admitted to breaking the law in order to conduct their routine business operations. The close link between government and business has spawned campaign-funding abuses more severe than those encountered in the United States. The lifetime employment offered by Japan's large industrial concerns has prevented them from downsizing to become more efficient in the world marketplace.

Japan's famous industrial policy—the attempt on the part of the state bureaucracy to pick upcoming industrial winners—has also been questioned. An example is the Japanese government's ill-fated decision to promote high-definition television. Japan still lags well behind the United States in technological innovation, a gap that many attribute to the Japanese economic system.

It now appears that Japan's decline in the 1990s is not cyclical but structured. We do not know whether Japan can recover its status as one of the world's fastest-growing economies. In the early 2000s, prospects did not appear bright. Japan's political system was in paralysis, unable to implement meaningful reforms. Growth remained anemic. Japan's banks were left with large portfolios of questionable loans, and respected financial enterprises were forced to close their doors.

Japan's experience with industrial policy is the most prominent, but the Four Tigers also pursued industrial policies in their own way. The industrial policies of the Four Tigers had one consistent theme—the promotion of exports. In this regard, South Korea is fairly typical.[52] Korean industrial policy aimed at promoting exports and fostering infant industries that had the potential to export. This policy was executed through a virtual free-trade regime for export activity (capital and intermediate goods could be imported without tariffs) and the allocation of credits through government control of banks. The government set quarterly export targets and gave large-scale establishments temporary monopolies and preferential access to credits, rewarding them according to the proportion of output that they succeeded in exporting.

Promotion of exports is an extremely important aspect of Asian industrial policy. Asian firms that tied their fate to the export market and to competition according to world market prices had to learn how to compete and how to introduce the technology that would allow them to do so. Countries that used industrial policy to protect their domestic industries, in effect, cut themselves off from these competitive signals and languished.

Provision of Income Security

One of the prime features of the European model was its generous provision of income security for practically everyone. Sweden served as the extreme example of the European welfare state, but other Western European countries did not lag far behind in terms of benefits. Providing for the public welfare is focused principally on the health and pensions of the aged, although the provision of health care by the state has become an increasingly important factor in Europe and in the United States. The demand for old-age security depends in part on the age structure of the population. Figure 10.11 shows that all the Asian countries except Japan have a young population. Less than 5 percent of their populations are 65 and older. In Japan, Europe, and the United States, the proportion of older people is much greater.

Partially as a consequence of the different age structure of the population, the Asian countries have a much smaller welfare state. And despite having an age structure that is quite similar to that of Europe, Japan has social security contributions that (as a percent of wage income) are about half of Europe's. As late as 1979, South Korea devoted only 1 percent of its GDP to social security expenditures.[53] Judging from Japan's and South Korea's social security contribution rates, we suspect that the rates in other Asian countries are even lower.

Japan did not have a public pension system until 1961, after three-quarters of a century of industrialization. It also did not have public health insurance until 1961, and the system in effect discriminates sharply between employees and those out of the labor force or self-employed. From a European perspective, "Japanese welfare services remain underdeveloped. . . . Japanese social protection services are

FIGURE 10.11   The Welfare State: The Asian Model in Perspective

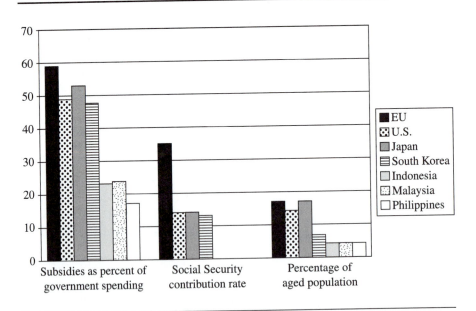

Sources: World Bank, "Role of Government in the Economy," in *World Development Report; Statistical Abstract of the United States,* International Statistics.

still limited compared to other developed countries. But their potential volume is already similar to continental European countries."[54]

The affluent Singapore is an exception to the rule of limited social security protection, but it has relied on a private-market solution.[55] All Singapore employees are required to contribute to a Central Provident Fund for retirement. The contributed funds are invested in Singapore government securities or approved listed stocks. Employees may use these funds to purchase property and also to pay educational expenses. In effect, the contributed funds belong to the contributor and are intended to be used for retirement and for major investments. A Medisave account is part of the Provident Fund. Each contributor has a medical fund to be used as a standby for exceptional medical expenses. At age 55, the contributor can withdraw his or her fund after setting aside a minimum amount in a retirement account. Thus Singapore has a "privatized" social security system, the cost of which is a 25 percent contribution by the employee and a 15 percent contribution by the employer.

The lesser role of the welfare state in the Asian model can also be attributed to cultural factors and tradition. Confucianism and other Asian religions emphasize the role of the family and the obligation of younger generations to take care of family elders in their retirement years. These cultural norms have been gradually breaking down as Asian countries industrialize and urbanize, but they remain strong.

Because of the relative lack of public pension protection, private households must provide for their own old age, either by relying on their children for assistance or by saving for their own retirement. The high rates of savings that characterize the Asian model are often ascribed to the absence of such a pay-as-you-go retirement system as prevails in Europe and the United States. Japan, which has the most developed welfare-state system in Asia, spends 5.8 percent of GDP on health of state and private funds, while spending a total of 7.4 percent of GDP on health. This means that private households themselves spend almost 2 percent of GDP on health care. In the EU, more than 10 percent of GDP is spent on health, between 7 and 8 percent being paid by the state. The United States spends 13 percent of its GDP on health care, but about half of that is paid by private households (see Figure 10.11).

Summary

- The Asian model was developed in Japan and China in isolation from Western influence. It is based on history and religion, largely Confucianism, which teaches a positive role for virtuous government. Asian economic development is described by the relative-backwardness model of Alexander Gerschenkron.
- The Asian model is characterized by rapid growth fostered by high rates of capital formation. Japan experienced rapid and accelerating growth through the 1970s, and the Four Asian Tigers began to grow rapidly in the 1960s and 1970s.
- The Lewis two-sector model has been used to explain the rapid growth of Asia.
- The Asian model is characterized by corporations closely held by wealthy families or small groups of individuals, by relational rather than market-based contracting, and by the relatively small role of widely held, publicly traded corporations.

- Asian corporations tend to obtain their financing from banks that are closely related to the enterprises themselves. Asian banks tend to be loosely regulated.
- The Asian labor market combines the limited regulation of the Anglo-Saxon model with paternalistic practices that protect employment during downturns. Paternalism appears to characterize large firms more than small firms, which have considerable flexibility in hiring and firing.
- The Asian model has combined high growth with a relatively even distribution of income.
- Many Asian economies have used heavy-handed industrial policy combined with consistent promotion of export.
- The Asian model has largely rejected the European model of state provision of income and healthy security. The Asian countries' public spending on health is relatively low.

Key Terms

Asian model
theory of relative backwardness
Four Tigers
import substitution
two-sector model
relational contracting

market-based contracting
leverage
share economy
Ministry of International Trade and
    Industry

Notes

1. Lee-Jay Cho and Yoon Hyung Kim, "Political and Economic Antecedents," in Lee-Jay Cho and Yoon Hyung Kim, eds., *Economic Development in the Republic of Korea: A Policy Perspective* (Honolulu: East–West Center, 1991), pp. 3–9.
2. *Ibid.,* p. 55.
3. This historical section is largely based on W. G. Beasley, *The Rise of Modern Japan* (New York: St. Martin's, 1995), Chs. 1–6.
4. *Ibid.,* p. 56.
5. Lee-Kay Cho, "Culture, Institutions, and Economic Development in East Asia," in Lee-Jay Cho and Yoon-Hyung Kim, *Korea's Political Economy* (Boulder, Colo.: Westview, 1991), pp. 5–19.
6. *Ibid.,* p. 15.
7. Alexander Gerschenkron, *Economic Backwardness in Historical Perspective* (Cambridge, Mass.: Harvard University Press, 1965).
8. Cho and Kim, "Political and Economic Antecedents," pp. 6–7.
9. Angus Maddison, *The World Economy: A Millennial Perspective* (Paris: OECD, 2001); and *www.OECD.org*
10. For a survey of Japanese economic growth, see Kazushi Ohkawa and Henry Rosovsky, *Japanese Economic Growth* (Stanford, Calif.: Stanford University Press, 1973), Ch. 2.
11. Various aspects of the Japanese labor market are discussed in G. C. Allen, *The Japanese Economy* (London: Weidenfeld and Nicolson, 1981), Ch. 9; Taira, *Economic Development.*

12. For a useful survey of organizational features of the Japanese economic system, see Kanji Haitani, *The Japanese Economic System* (Lexington, Mass.: Heath, 1976).

13. Ohkawa and Rosovsky, *Japanese Economic Growth*, Ch. 5.

14. In addition to Taira, *Economic Development*, see Robert E. Cole, *Japanese Blue-Collar: The Changing Tradition* (Berkeley: University of California Press, 1971); for a summary, see Robert E. Cole, "Industrial Relations in Japan," in Morris Bornstein, ed., *Comparative Economic Systems, Models and Cases*, 3rd ed. (Homewood, Ill.: Irwin, 1974), pp. 93–116.

15. Eddy Lee, ed., *Export-Led Industrialization and Development* (Geneva: ILO, 1981); Robert A. Scalapino, Seizaburo Sato, and Jusuf Wanandi, eds., *Asian Economic Development—Present and Future* (Berkeley: University of California Press, 1985).

16. World Bank, *World Development Report 1987* (Oxford: Oxford University Press, 1987).

17. Sebastian Edwards, "Openness, Trade Liberalization and Growth in Developing Countries," *Journal of Economic Literature* 31 (September 1993), 1387.

18. Geoffrey Carliner, "Comment on Anne Krueger, 'East Asian Experience and Endogenous Growth Theory,'" in Taakatoshi Ito and Anne Krueger, eds., *Growth Theories in Light of the East Asian Experience* (Chicago: University of Chicago Press, 1995), pp. 30–33; and Joseph Stiglitz and Marilow Uy, "Financial Markets, Public Policy, and the East Asian Miracle," *World Bank Research Observer* 1, 2 (August 1996), 249–276.

19. Ronald Lee, Andrew Mason, and Timothy Miller, "Saving, Wealth, and the Demographic Transition in East Asia," Conference on Population and the East Asian Miracle, Program on Population, East-West Center, Honolulu, Hawaii, January 7–10, 1997; Jeffrey Williamson and Mathew Higgins. "The Accumulation and Demography Connection in East Asia," Andrew Mason, ed., *Population and the East Asian Miracle* (East-West Center Working Papers, Population Series, No. 88-24, August 1997).

20. Robert Barro and Xavier Sala-l-Martin, *Economic Growth* (New York: McGraw-Hill, 1995).

21. W. Arthur Lewis, "Economic Development with Unlimited Supplies Labor," *Manchester School* 22 (May 1954), 139–191; John Fei and Gustav Ranis, *Development of the Labor Surplus Economy* (Homewood, Ill.: Irwin, 1964).

22. As is well known, collectivization was the transfer mechanism used in the Soviet Union in the 1930s and in China in the 1950s.

23. Carl Kester, *Japanese Takeovers: The Global Contest for Corporate Control* (Boston, 1991).

24. Martin Schulz, "The Reform of (Corporate) Governance in Japan," in *Japan: How to Overcome the Difficult Decade*, Vierteljahrshefte zur Witschaftsforschung, Heft 4, no. 70, 2001.

25. Kozo Yamamura, "Entrepreneurship, Ownership and Management in Japan," in M. M. Postan *et al., Cambridge Economic History of Europe*, Vol. 7, Part 2 (Cambridge: Cambridge University Press, 1978), pp. 215–264. See also Eleanor M. Hadley, *Antitrust in Japan* (Princeton, N.J.: Princeton University Press, 1970); Richard E. Caves and Masu Uekusa, *Industrial Organizations in Japan* (Washington, D.C.: Brookings Institution, 1976); and Kanji Haitani, *The Japanese Economic System* (Lexington, Mass.: Heath, 1976).

26. Much of this section is based on Il Chong Nam, Yeongjae Kang, and Joon-Kyong Kim, "Comparative Corporate Governance Trends in Asia," Korea Development Institute, December 1999.

27. "World Banker Assails Indonesia's Corruption," *New York Times*, August 28, 2002.

28. "Proxy Fight to Redress Tokyo Style," *Wall Street Journal*, May 13, 2002.

29. Schulz, *The Reform of (Corporate) Governance*, p. 528.

30. *Ibid.*, p. 537.

31. Joon-Kyung Kim and Chung H. Lee, "Insolvency in the Corporate Sector and Financial Crisis in Korea," *Journal of the Asian Pacific Economy* 7, 2 (2002).

32. Nam, Kang, and Kim, "Comparative Corporate Governance Trends in Asia."

33. "Rough Start for Regulator in Japan," *New York Times,* World Business, August 23, 2002.

34. Schulz, *The Reform of (Corporate) Governance,* p. 531.

35. Kim and Lee, "Insolvency in the Corporate Sector."

36. These figures are cites in Y. Miwa and J. M. Ramsauer, "The Myth of the Main Bank, Japan, and Comparative Corporate Governance," Harvard Law School, Discussion Paper 333, September 2001.

37. John M. Montias, *The Structure of Economic Systems* (New Haven: Yale University Press, 1976), Part 5.

38. Martin Weitzman, *The Share Economy* (Cambridge, Mass.: Harvard University Press, 1984).

39. Merton J. Peck, "Is Japan Really a Share Economy?" *Journal of Comparative Economics* 10 (1986), 427–432.

40. For a discussion, see Gregory B. Christainsen and Jan S. Hagendorn, "Japanese Productivity: Adapting to Changing Comparative Advantage in the Face of Lifetime Employment Commitments," *Quarterly Review of Business and Economics* 23 (Summer 1983), 23–39. For a discussion of the labor–management issue in a growth context, see Harry Oshima, "Reinterpreting Japan's Postwar Growth," *Economic Development and Cultural Change* 31 (October 1982), 1–43.

41. Christainsen and Hagendorn, "Japanese Productivity," p. 30.

42. *Ibid.*

43. Geoffrey Murray and Audrey Perera, *Singapore: The Global City State* (New York: St. Martin's, 1996), pp. 231–233.

44. World Bank, *The East Asian Miracle: Economic Growth and Public Policy* (Oxford: Oxford University Press, 1993), Fig. 1.3, p. 31; Fig. 3, p. 4.

45. John Bauer, "Economic Growth and Policy in East Asia," Conference on Population and the Asian Economic Miracle, Program on Population, East-West Center, Honolulu, Hawaii, January 7–10, 1997.

46. D. H. Perkins, "There Are at Least Three Models of East Asian Development," *World Development* 4 (April 1994), 655–662.

47. For a discussion of income distribution and growth, see Vito Tanzi and Ke-young Chu, eds., *Income Distribution and High-Quality Growth* (Cambridge Mass.: MIT Press, 1998).

48. Assessing the role of government in the importance of the "public" sector in the Japanese economy is difficult for definitional reasons. For a discussion, see Chalmers Johnson, *Japan's Public Policy Companies* (Washington, D.C.: American Enterprise Institute, 1978).

49. Much has been written about MITI. For basics, see Haitani, *The Japanese Economic System.* For more detail, see Chalmers Johnson, *MITI and the Japanese Miracle* (Stanford, Calif.: Stanford University Press, 1982); and Christainsen and Hagendorn, "Japanese Productivity."

50. For a more restrained view of the role of MITI in the 1970s, see Kozo Yamamura, "Success That Soured: Administrative Guidance and Cartels in Japan," in Kozo Yamamura, ed., *Policy and Trade Issues of the Japanese Economy* (Seattle: University of Washington Press, 1982), pp. 77–112. On the role of the state in supporting key sectors, see also Gary R. Saxonhouse, "What Is All This About 'Industrial Targeting' in Japan?" *World Economy* 6 (September 1983), 253–273.

51. The movement from fixed to flexible exchange rates was, of course, much more an issue than U.S.-Japanese trade. See Patrick and Rosovsky, *Asia's New Giant,* Ch. 6. See also Takafusa Nakamura, *The Postwar Japanese Economy* (Tokyo: University of Tokyo Press, 1981), Part 3; for specific references to the impact of oil shortages, see Yoichi Shinkai,

"Oil Crises and Stagflation in Japan," in Yamamura, *Policy and Trade Issues of the Japanese Economy,* pp. 173–193.

52. Larry Westphal, "Industrial Policy in an Export-Propelled Economy: Lesson from the South Korean Experience," *Journal of Economic Perspectives* 4 (Summer 1990), pp. 41–60.

53. Chung Kee Park, "The Health Insurance Scheme," in Cho and Kim, "Political and Economic Antecedents," p. 332.

54. Tetsuo Fukawa, "Japanese Welfare State Reforms in the 1990s and Beyond: How Japan Is Similar to and Different from Germany," in *Japan: How to Overcome the Difficult Decade,* p. 572.

55. Murray and Perera, *Singapore,* Ch. 11.

Recommended Readings

Japan

J. G. Abegglen, *The Japanese Factory* (Glencoe, Ill.: Free Press, 1958).

G. C. Allen, *The Japanese Economy* (London: Weidenfeld and Nicolson, 1981).

W. G. Beasley, *The Rise of Modern Japan* 2nd ed. (New York: St. Martin's, 1995).

Thomas F. Cargill, Michael M. Hurchison, and Takatoshi Ito, *The Political Economy of Japanese Monetary Policy* (Cambridge, Mass.: MIT Press, 1997).

Edward F. Denison and William K. Chung, *How Japan's Economy Grew So Fast: The Sources of Postwar Expansion* (Washington, D.C.: Brookings Institution, 1976).

Ronald Dore, *Flexible Rigidities* (London: Athlone Press, 1986).

Kanji Haitani, *The Japanese Economic System* (Lexington, Mass.: Heath, 1976).

Christopher Hause, *The Origins of Japanese Trade Supremacy: Development and Technology in Asia from 1540 to the Pacific War* (Chicago: University of Chicago Press, 1996).

Ronald I. McKinnon and Kenichi Ohno, *Dollar and Yen: Resolving Economic Conflict Between the United States and Japan* (Cambridge, Mass.: MIT Press, 1997).

Toru Iwami, *Japan in the International Financial System* (New York: St. Martin's, 1996).

Japanese Economic Research Center, *Economic Growth: The Japanese Experience Since the Meiji Era,* Vols. I and II (Tokyo: Japanese Economic Research Center, 1973).

Chalmers Johnson, *Japan's Public Policy Companies* (Washington, D.C.: American Enterprise Institute, 1978).

————, *MITI and the Japanese Miracle* (Stanford, Calif.: Stanford University Press, 1982).

Lawrence Klein and Kazushi Ohkawa, eds., *Economic Growth: The Japanese Experience Since the Meiji Era* (Homewood, Ill.: Irwin, 1968).

Edward J. Lincoln, *Japan: Facing Economic Maturity* (Washington, D.C.: Brookings Institution, 1988).

William Lockwood, ed., *The State and Economic Enterprise in Japan* (Princeton, N.J.: Princeton University Press, 1965).

Angus Maddison, *Economic Growth in Japan and the USSR* (London: Allen and Unwin, 1969).

Ryoshim Minami, Kwan S. Kim, Fumio Makino and Joung-Hae Seo, *Acquisition, Adaptation and the Development of Technologies* (New York: St. Martin's, 1994).

Ryoshin Minami, *The Economic Development of Japan* (London: Macmillan, 1986).

Carl Mosk, *Competition and Cooperation in Japanese Labor Markets* (New York: St. Martin's, 1994).

Takafusa Nakamura, *The Postwar Japanese Economy* (Tokyo: University of Tokyo Press, 1981).

Meiko Nishimizu and Charles R. Hulten, "The Sources of Japanese Economic Growth, 1955–71," *Review of Economics and Statistics* 60 (August 1978), 351–361.

Kazushi Ohkawa and Henry Rosovsky, *Japanese Economic Growth* (Stanford, Calif.: Stanford University Press, 1973).

Kazushi Ohkawa and Hirohisa Kohama, *Lectures on Developing Economies: Japan's Experience and Its Relevance* (Tokyo: University of Tokyo Press, 1989).

Hugh Patrick and Henry Rosovsky, eds., *Asia's New Giant: How the Japanese Economy Works* (Washington, D.C.: Brookings Institution, 1976).

M. M. Postan *et al.*, eds., *Cambridge Economic History of Europe,* Vol. VII, Part 2 (Cambridge: Cambridge University Press, 1978), Chs. 3–5 on Japan.

Ozawa Terutomo, *Multinationalism Japanese Style* (Princeton, N.J.: Princeton University Press, 1979).

Kazuo Sato, *The Transformation of the Japanese Economy* (Armonk, N.Y.: Sharpe, 1996).

———, *The Japanese Economy and Business* (Armonk, N.Y.: Sharpe, 1996).

Ryuzo Sato, "U.S.–Japan Relations Under the Clinton and Hosokawa Administrations," *Japan and the World Economy* 6, 1 (1994), 89–103.

Yoshio Suzuki, *Money, Finance, and Macroeconomic Performance in Japan* (New Haven: Yale University Press, 1986).

Yosho Tsurumi, *The Japanese Are Coming: A Multinational Interaction of Firms and Politics* (Cambridge, Mass.: Ballinger, 1976).

Kozo Yamamura, ed., *Policy and Trade Issues of the Japanese Economy* (Seattle: University of Washington Press, 1982).

M. Y. Yoshino, *Japan's Multinational Enterprises* (Cambridge, Mass.: Harvard University Press, 1976).

South Korea, Singapore, Taiwan, Hong Kong

Edward K. Y. Chen, *Hyper-Growth in Asian Economies* (London and Basingstoke, England: Macmillan, 1979).

Shirley W. Y. Kao, Gustav Ranis, and John C. H. Fei, *The Taiwan Success Story: Rapid Growth with Improved Distribution in the Republic of China, 1952–1979* (Boulder, Colo.: Westview, 1981).

Paul Krugman, "The Myth of Asia's Miracle," *Foreign Affairs* 73 (November–December 1994), 62–78.

Paul Kuzner, "Indicative Planning in Korea," *Journal of Comparative Economics* 14 (December 1990), 657–676.

Eddy Lee, ed., *Export-Led Industrialization and Development* (Geneva: ILO, 1981).

Roy A. Matthews, *Canada and the Little Dragons* (Montreal: Institute for Research on Public Policy, 1983).

Miron Mushkat, *The Economic Future of Hong Kong* (Boulder, Colo., and London, England: Hong Kong University Press, 1990).

George Rosen, *Economic Development in Asia* (Brookfield, Vt.: Ashgate, 1996).

J. L. Saking, "Indicative Planning in Korea: Discussion," *Journal of Comparative Economics,* 14, 1 (December, 1990), 677–680.

Robert A. Scalapino, Seizaburo Sato, and Jusuf Wanandi, eds., *Asian Economic Development—Present and Future* (Berkeley: University of California Press, 1985).

Miyohei Shinohara and Fu-chen Lo, *Global Adjustment and the Future of the Asian-Pacific Economy* (Tokyo and Kuala Lumpur: Institute of Developing Economies and Asian and Pacific Development Centre, 1989).

A. H. Somjee and Geeta Somjee, *Development Success in Asia Pacific* (New York: St. Martin's, 1995).

Julian Weiss, *The Asian Century* (New York: Facts on File, 1989).

Jon Woronoff, *Asia's "Miracle" Economies* (Armonk, N.Y.: Sharpe, 1986).

World Bank, *The East Asian Miracle: Economic Growth and Public Policy* (Washington, D.C.: World Bank, 1993).

India

A. N. Agrawal, *Indian Economy,* 2nd ed. (New Delhi: Vikas, 1976).

Jagdish Bhagwati and Sukhamoy Chakravaty, "Contributions to Indian Economic Analysis: A Survey," *American Economic Review* 59 (September 1969), 4–29.

Kaushik Basu, *Agarian Questions* (New Delhi: Oxford University Press, 1998).

William A. Byrd, "Planning in India: Lessons from Four Decades of Development Experience," *Journal of Comparative Economics* 14 (December 1990), 713–736.

Pramit Chaudhuri, ed., *Aspects of Indian Economic Development* (London: Allen and Unwin, 1971).

Francine R. Frankel, *India's Green Revolution* (Princeton, N.J.: Princeton University Press, 1971).

————, *India's Political Economy, 1947–1977* (Princeton, N.J.: Princeton University Press, 1978).

Ira N. Gang, "Small Firm 'Presence' in Indian Manufacturing" *World Development* 20 (1992), 1377–89.

Raj Krishna and G. S. Raychaudhuri, "Trends in Rural Savings and Capital Formation in India, 1950–1951 to 1973–1974," *Economic Development and Cultural Change* 30 (January 1982), 271–298.

William A. Long and K. K. Seo, *Management in Japan and India* (New York: Praeger, 1977).

Angus Maddison, *Class Structure and Economic Growth: India and Pakistan Since the Moghuls* (New York: Norton, 1971).

Wilfred Malenbaum, "Modern Economic Growth in India and China: The Comparison Revisited, 1950–1980," *Economic Development and Cultural Change* 31 (October 1982), 45–84.

Dilip Mookhergee, *Indian Industry: Policies and Performance* (New Delhi: Oxford University Press, 1997).

Rakesh Mohan and Vandana Aggarwal, "Commands and Controls: Planning for Indian Industrial Development, 1951–1990," *Journal of Comparative Economics* 14 (December 1990), 681–712.

Arvind Panagariya, "Indicative Planning in India: Discussion," *Journal of Comparative Economics* 14 (December 1990), 736–742.

Prabhat Patnaik, *Macroeconomics* (New Delhi: Oxford University Press, 1997), pp. 12–36.

C. H. Shah and C. N. Vakil, eds., *Agricultural Development of India: Policy and Problems* (New Delhi: Orient Longman, 1979).

Subramanian Swamy, "Economic Growth in China and India, 1952–1970: A Comparative Appraisal," *Economic Development and Cultural Change,* 21 (July 1973), 1–84.

11

The Soviet Command Economy

Although the organization of the Soviet economy varied during the years following the 1917 **Bolshevik revolution**, state ownership, national economic planning, and the collectivization of agriculture remained constants of the system after they were introduced in the late 1920s. The **administrative-command economy** was the mechanism for resource allocation in the former Soviet Union for more than sixty years. The Soviet experience therefore remains the prime attempt to create a socialist society and to forge rapid economic development with minimal use of markets. Although economic reform received a great deal of attention in the Soviet Union from mid-1950 on, reform did little to change the fundamentals of the system. From 1928 through 1985, when Mikhail Gorbachev introduced Perestroika, there is a long period in which to examine the Soviet economic system.

The demise of the administrative-common system in the former Soviet Union and in Eastern Europe necessarily focuses attention on performance. A later chapter examines these systems' performance to explore the reasons for their demise and their legacy for transition in the 1990s.

History

The Soviet experience was marked by radical changes. Just as the Gorbachev era that began in 1985 represented a sharp break with the Soviet past, the Bolshevik revolution of 1917 was a sharp break with the preceding **czarist era**.[1] Indeed, Soviet experimentation between 1917 and 1928 provides insights into the roots of the administrative-command system.

The era of the czars came to a close and the era of the Soviets began with the Bolshevik revolution of 1917. Although the Soviet plan era dates from 1929, analysis must begin with the *level* and *rate* of economic development at the end of the czarist era. Russian economic development as of 1917 was at a relatively low level, judged by indicators such as per capita GDP. However, there had been considerable increase in rate of growth, especially industrial growth, during the last three decades of czarist rule, and the Soviets could therefore build on an existing base of transportation, industrial capacity, minerals, and (notably) foreign capital.

At the end of the 1920s, Joseph Stalin, the Soviet leader who had succeeded V. I. Lenin, made three momentous decisions. First, a comprehensive system of central planning based on compulsory state and party directives was established. An abrupt end to the prevailing system of market relations in industry ensued, and there was a marked shift in industrial production away from consumer goods and toward producer goods. Second, agriculture was collectivized. A vast network of **collective farms (kolkhozy)** was created, in which more than 90 percent of Soviet peasant households were living by the mid-1930s.[2] Third, a totalitarian system of political governance was put in place that enshrined the Communist party and its leaders or leader in the "leading role." The Communist party assumed dictatorship, its economic commands being communicated throughout the system by the "general line" of the party.[3] These three major decisions, though sudden at the time, did not arise out of a vacuum.

Two economic "experiments" were conducted in the decade following the revolution of 1917: **war communism** (1917–1921) and the **New Economic Policy (NEP,** 1921–1928).[4] Both responded to the needs to consolidate power and to marshal economic resources in a time of crisis.[5] War communism, implemented by Lenin during the Russian Civil War, saw the introduction of substantial state ownership through massive nationalization, an attempt to eliminate market relationships in industry and trade, and the forced requisitioning of agricultural products from the peasants. These moves suggest that Lenin was attempting to bypass socialism and move directly to a communist system. Whatever the intent, the economic consequences were a disaster. By the end of the civil war, the economy was in ruin.[6]

To instill economic recovery, Lenin introduced the New Economic Policy (NEP) in 1921. NEP signaled a partial return to private ownership (although the so-called commanding heights of industry remained nationalized), reintroduction of the market for resource allocation, and implementation of a tax on agriculture to replace requisitions. By 1927, the Soviet economy had recovered from the losses of civil war and war communism and was at, and in some cases above, the prewar level.[7] In effect, NEP was a form of market socialism, with its combination of state ownership of industry and market allocation.

The period from 1917 to 1928 provided some lessons that permeated Soviet thinking. First, if the market were to be eliminated, some mechanism for coordination had to take its place. During war communism, Lenin nationalized industries and eliminated the market, but he did not replace the market with a plan or some other substitute mechanism. Second, partly as a result of inept state policies, the peasants came to be viewed as having a dangerous influence on the pace of industrialization.[8] After all, the economy was largely agricultural, so resources would have to come primarily from the rural sector. Third, the attempt to introduce payment in kind and to downgrade the importance of money during war communism made it obvious that **material incentives** were crucial to motivate labor.

In addition to the experience of war communism and NEP, the 1920s witnessed remarkably open discussions within the upper reaches of the party over the proper course of industrialization and planning.[9] The debate on industrialization focused on modes of industrialization and, in particular, on differing roles for the agricultural and industrial sectors. All participants agreed that industrialization was essential and that the peasants would play a key role. The end result, however, was not readily foreseen by the debate's participants.

The economic system that Stalin put in place in the early 1930s was radically different from any prior system. Although the economic system evolved through time, and a variety of reform attempts were made beginning in the late 1950s, the system Mikhail Gorbachev inherited in 1985 looked surprisingly similar to that of earlier years.

The Setting

By almost any measure, the Soviet Union was a very large country. It occupied 8.6 million square miles, an area more than twice that of the United States. In terms of population, the Soviet Union entered the 1990s with approximately 290 million persons, some 15 percent more than the U.S. population. The majority of the Soviet population (roughly 65 percent) lived in urban areas, and approximately 80 percent of the labor force was in industry and related nonagricultural occupations. Urbanization characterized the Soviet experience, along with the traditional shift of the labor force away from rural/agricultural pursuits.

Equally significant, the Soviet Union was a very diverse nation consisting of fifteen union republics. The largest of these, the Russian Republic, accounted for just over 50 percent of the Soviet population. The remainder of the population comprised the Latvians, Lithuanians, and Estonians; the Ukrainians; the peoples of Central Asia, including Uzbekistan, Kirgizstan, Tadzhikistan, and Turkmenistan; and those of the Caucasus, including Georgia, Azerbaidzhan, and Armenia. These and other peoples of the Soviet Union infused it with vast ethnic, cultural, and historical diversity. Ethnic and regional differences remained significant in the post-Soviet era, as the newly independent former Soviet republics created their own transition paths.

Sharp differences also existed in the Soviet Union's natural environment. The climate ranged from the hot, dry areas of Central Asia to the cold expanses of Siberia and the cool, wet plains of the west. Needless to say, significant regional differences in climate dictated major variations in resource usage, especially in agriculture.

Finally, the Soviet Union had an extraordinarily rich resource base. In addition to being a major producer of fish and forest products, the Soviet Union was amply endowed with minerals and was the world's largest producer of petroleum, coal, and iron ore. Indeed, there are very few minerals for which the Soviet Union had inadequate domestic reserves.

The Soviet Economy: A Framework

Economic systems are characterized by five basic attributes: decision-making *levels,* *market* and *plan* mechanisms of information, property rights, incentive systems, and system of political governance.

As we examine the Soviet command economy and its organizational arrangements, we must ask two questions: How did this system differ from the ideal of planned socialism? How should the actual command system be categorized on our five criteria?

In terms of decision-making arrangements, the Soviet economy was organized in a vertical hierarchical fashion of the sort described in Chapter 2. The Soviet state, operating through government ministries, and the **Communist party**, operating through its top ranks, shared authority and responsibility. There were several decision-making layers, including the state and party structure at the top, the ministries and regional authorities and sometimes trust organizations in the middle, and the basic production units (enterprises and farms) at the lower level.

The Soviet system was a highly centralized economic system. The presumed dominant mechanism for generating and using information was the national economic plan. The state and party organizations made key decisions on production, distribution, and accumulation that were spelled out in the long- and short-term plans. Although administrative allocation was dominant, there were instances in which market forces and influences affected that process—for example, in the allocation of labor and in the second, or underground, economy. The Soviet state, as the primary property owner, controlled virtually all aspects of property utilization. Although collective farms, for example, were exceptions to full state ownership, such distinctions were not particularly important. State ownership of property meant that there were no capital or land markets and no formal system of rewards for these inputs. Rather, income generated from their use accrued directly to the state, and Wage income was the method of payment to workers. Beyond material incentives, however, the Communist party placed considerable emphasis on moral incentives, a distinguishing characteristic of socialist systems.

We can examine the Soviet administrative-command system as it was supposed to have worked in theory or as it worked in practice. As with most economic systems, the way an economy works in practice diverges from how theory says it should work. Just as the U.S. economy has some "command" elements, so did the Soviet economy have significant "unplanned" elements and informal rules and practices that in theory are supposed not to exist. Let us begin with how the Soviet system was supposed to work.

The Decision-Making Hierarchy

From the beginning of the plan era in 1929, there was considerable continuity in working arrangements. Under these arrangements (Figure 11.1), the Soviet Union was nominally governed by an elected government, but the operative organ was the Council of Ministers at the federal (all-Union) and republican levels. A parallel structure, the Communist Party of the Soviet Union (CPSU), was the principal organ of decision making, control, and supervision. It operated through a complex centralized structure beginning at the national level, with its Politburo of top leaders and Central Committee of national and regional leaders, and terminating with individual party cells in each industrial enterprise, farm, and organization.[10] Regional and local party organizations controlled and monitored the allocation of resources at lower levels.

All capital, with only limited exceptions, was owned by the state; firms and other organizations operated under the control of the state and party apparatus.[11] Agriculture was organized into state farms, collective farms, and private plots, the latter governed by strict regulations.

FIGURE 11.1   The Organization of the Soviet Economy: The Command Model

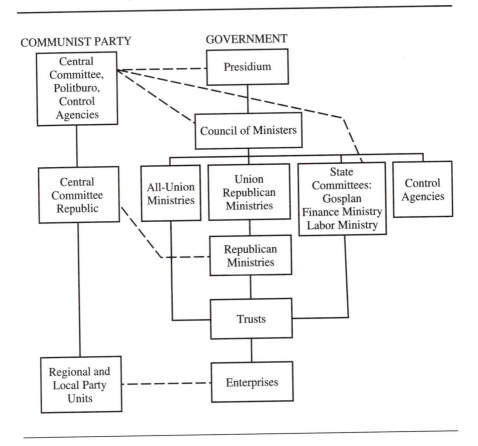

The operational decisions were made through **Gosplan**, the state planning agency. The Communist party developed the general directives on resource allocation. Gosplan then converted those directives into operative plans, with the aid of ministeries and, to a degree, the individual enterprises. It was the responsibility of the individual enterprises to carry out the plan directives. Information flowed from top to bottom and vice versa. Transactions among enterprises were coordinated by a plan, and money and markets were to play only a limited role.

Planning in Theory

The industrial activity of enterprises and the agricultural activities of farms were organized by the **ministry**. Ministries were hierarchically organized by type of production: steel, agriculture, and machinery. The ministerial structure was shifted to organization on a *regional* basis in 1957, under the reform leadership of Nikita Khrushchev, to break down the tendency of ministries to become self-sufficient and to ignore interactions with other ministries. The reform did not work and was abandoned when Khrushchev fell from power in 1964. Ministries differed in importance, depending on their function. The most important branches of industry were governed by all-Union ministries. Investment decisions concerning, for example, steel production facilities were made at the center. Union republican ministries dispersed a measure of decision-making authority to the level of the fifteen republics. The ministries were the organizational superiors of the industrial and agricultural enterprises. Organizational reforms experimented with combining enterprises into trusts to serve as an intermediary between the enterprise and the ministry.

Mises and Hayek argued that a single planning organization cannot plan all economic activity from the center. Indeed, Gosplan simplified the planning task by planning only a limited number of products and by planning the work of ministries, not the work of enterprises. The ministries produced the real operational plans of the economy, while Gosplan concentrated on more general directives. Gosplan prepared short-term (1-year and quarterly), longer-term (5- or 7-year), and even 20-year "perspective" plans. The annual and quarterly plans, which directed economic activity, were of central interest. The essence of the plan was the **material balance system**, the theoretical basis of which we examined in Chapter 6.[12] The plan was formulated in the following manner. General directives were provided by the CPSU and converted into control figures by Gosplan. The control figures, or tentative production targets, were transmitted through the ministries down to the level of individual enterprises, with comment and informational input being sought from each level in the hierarchy. The control figures then moved back up through the hierarchy and at the Gosplan level were "balanced"; that is, for major items in the plan, supply and demand had to balance. Once balance was achieved, the plan was disaggregated and the targets were once again disseminated down through the ministries to the individual enterprises. The final result, the **techpromfinplans** (technical–industrial–financial plans), were legally binding and contained detailed directives for enterprise operations during the forthcoming year.

The formulation of this plan was time-consuming and complex, and clearly could not approach the theoretical ideals outlined in Chapter 6. Intense bargaining, haggling, interplay among the various units, and delays were integral parts of planning. Frequently the new plan was late in arriving, so the enterprise would continue to operate under the old plan. This planning system worked in large part because it had built-in simplifications. The planning process did not start from scratch each year. The plan for year t was, in effect, little more than a revision and update of the plan for year $t - 1$. This practice, **planning from the achieved level**, simplified the planning process, but it created rigidities. Gosplan planned only major commodities such as steel and machinery, which were called **funded commodities** or **limited commodities**. Their number varied over time from a few hundred to a few thousand. Other commodities were planned at progressively lower levels, depending on their importance. This simplified the planning process but left much to be done at the lower levels, in the various republics and ministries.

In constructing balances for major materials, planners faced a dilemma. On the one hand, they wanted the **balance** to be achieved at the highest possible level; on the other hand, they knew that the more **taut** the plan—that is, the closer the targets were to maximum capacity—the more likely it was that errors and supply imbalances would occur.[13] Planners had to compile a plan that was demanding yet at the same time in balance. Planners did not employ sophisticated planning techniques to "balance" supplies and demands. In fact, ad hoc tallies of sources and material requirements were compiled, and past experience was the principal guide. Accordingly, planners were usually satisfied if they were able to come up with a **consistent plan**; they did not have the luxury of seeking out the **optimal plan** from among all possible consistent plans.

Planning in Reality

Our picture of Soviet planning is one of "scientific planning"—a planning procedure that, despite its faults and ad hoc nature, attempted to produce the best economic results possible for the country. It also assumes that these plans were the actual instruments by which resources were allocated. Presumably, the operational plans issued binding instructions to ministries, which converted them into binding instructions for enterprises. The reality of Soviet planning was far different.

Eugene Zaleski, in his study of Soviet planning from 1933 to 1952, found that the deviations of actual performance from planned performance were so great that he doubted that this was a planned economy at all. Rather, he suggested that resources were actually allocated by **resource managers** in the party and state apparatus after the plan had been completed. The plan is simply a vision of the future, designed to show the population that better times are ahead. No manager, however, is prepared to limit the demand for resources, and the plan declares that production will be abundant. Hence the material balance will be grossly *unbalanced* by excess demands. As enterprises and ministries clamor for resources, state and party officials decide who gets what. They, not the plan, allocate resources. No less an authority than Stalin himself confirmed that resources were allocated by resource managers and not by the plan:[14]

> For us, for Bolsheviks, the five year plan is not something that is a law that is forever given. For us the five year plan, like any plan, is only a plan approved *as a first approximation* which must be made more precise, to change and improve on the basis of experience, on the basis of executing the plan. No five year plan can consider all the possibilities, which are hidden in the foundation of our movement and which are uncovered only in the process of work, in the process of carrying out the plan in factories, plants, and collective farms, in the regions, and so forth. Only bureaucrats can think that planning work ends with the creation of the plan. The creation of the plan is only the beginning. The real direction of the plan develops only after the putting together of the plan.[15]

Recent studies of actual Soviet planning based on the recently opened Soviet state and party archives show planning to be a chaotic process that produced virtually no "final" plans.[16] All plans were preliminary and subject to change at any time by virtually any resource manager in the state or party. Although the enterprise plan was supposed to contain numerous plan targets, the operational plans that were available when resources were actually allocated gave only output and assortment targets. The other targets, such as labor, costs, productivity, new technologies, and new products, were reconstructed retrospectively at the end of the planning period. Ministries and enterprises, when ordered by resource managers to amend the plan, could not appeal to earlier agreements because they were all preliminary.

Enterprises and ministries therefore developed a number of devices to protect themselves from arbitrary resources managers: They either failed to provide planners with information or provided them with false information; they prepared two plans, one for internal use, the other for external consumption; and, most important, they created networks of informal resource allocation with others at the same level in the hierarchy.[17] The archives reveal a high-level "unplanned" exchange system among ministries—a system in which disputes were largely adjudicated informally rather than through appeal to the center. Even products that were subject to the strictest level of planning and control, such as vehicles, were subject to informal allocation.[18]

The Soviet system of resource allocation was therefore incredibly complex and multifaceted. Some products were "planned"; others were "resource-managed"; still others were allocated by the participants themselves via horizontal unplanned exchanges. In effect, these unplanned exchanges can be regarded as a form of "quasi-market"—a market in which two planned state enterprises or even ministries agree on exchanges of products that are unsanctioned and perhaps illegal. Clearly, central authorities were aware of these quasi-markets. They had any number of high-level control commissions that investigated wrongdoing by party members.[19] That they chose to tolerate unplanned exchanges suggests that these were probably essential to keeping production moving.

It is not possible to characterize precisely the balance between the formal and the informal forces that determined resource allocation in the Soviet Union. We know that compared to market economies, the balance was strongly in favor of centralized administrative allocation, but the role of informal forces was also recognized.[20]

The Soviet Manager:
The Principal–Agent Problem

Soviet enterprises had a plan, specified in annual terms but broken down into quarterly and monthly periods. The plan was supposed to be a comprehensive document covering all facets of the firm's operations. The plan specified both inputs and outputs in physical and financial terms; it specified the sources and the distribution of funds. However, it would be erroneous to think that the Soviet manager was fully regimented. In fact, quite a lot of managerial freedom existed.

Soviet managers were required to fulfill the plan. The plan was the "law of the land."[21] Yet it was unclear what it meant to "fulfill" a plan that consisted of a large number of indicators, such as outputs, the mix of output, the introduction of new products, a profit target, a cost reduction target, and a wage bill.

The manager therefore had a success indicator problem. Managers were offered rewards and advancement for achieving planned objectives, but those objectives were multifaceted.[22] **Gross value of output** was the most important target. The manager's performance was judged on the basis of fulfillment of production, but planners could not specify output objectives unequivocally. If managers were told to maximize the gross value of output, they would ignore items that made a small contribution, relative to their use of scarce resources, to gross value and would overproduce items that made a large contribution. The *mix* or assortment of goods within the plan would be ignored, if ignoring it was necessary to meet the gross output target. Such behavior, though potentially disruptive, was rewarding to the manager and the enterprise. The bonus system typically paid little or nothing until the output plan was 100 percent fulfilled. Then rewards were paid for production over this level, resulting in an average managerial bonus of 25 or 35 percent of base salary.[23] Top managers received bonuses in excess of 50 percent. Managerial behavior was clearly affected by the reward system.[24] Soviet managers earned substantial monetary bonuses for meeting targets. There were other rewards, such as housing, vacations, automobiles, and promotions. On the negative side, managers who did not perform were dismissed or even imprisoned or executed—sanctions that were widely used in the early days of Soviet planning.[25] Managerial perks and job tenure also depended on fulfillment of the gross output target. Generally taut targets and uncertain supply (especially for "limited" goods) were combined with substantial rewards for fulfillment of planned output targets. The result was informal and dysfunctional managerial behavior—a problem not anticipated by the socialist theorists, who assumed that managers would obey all rules handed down by superior authorities.

The combination of different objectives and different access to information created a classic **principal–agent conflict** between enterprise managers and their superiors. The manager was required by law to fulfill the plan, primarily to produce the output targets and the assortment, and would suffer presumably dire consequences in the event of failure. But only the manager knew the true productive capacity of the enterprise and its true needs for materials. The manager's superiors in the ministry or in Gosplan could only guess at capacity or material requirements. This **information asymmetry** enabled the manager to engage in **opportunistic behavior** relative to principals in the hierarchy who wanted maximum production with the minimum expenditure of society's resources. The manager's opportunism extended into the following areas:

First, managers, during the plan formulation stage, attempted to secure "easy" targets—that is, targets that were a low vis-à-vis the actual capacity of the enterprise. An easy target meant low outputs and ample inputs and investment.

Second, managers emphasized what was important in terms of their rewards and neglected other areas. Thus cost-saving targets, along with assortment targets, could be sacrificed for the sake of meeting the gross output targets. Neglect of assortment explained the shortage of spare parts, whose manufacture disrupted production lines and did not contribute sufficiently to rewards.

Third, managers could seek "safety" in various other practices. They could stockpile materials that were in short supply; they could avoid innovation; and they could establish informal or "family" connections to ensure a supply of crucial inputs.

Managers were able to focus on production at the expense of other targets—most notably, the efficiency with which output was produced—because they understood that their production was so valuable to their principals that they would not be allowed to fail. In effect, Soviet enterprises operated on the basis of a **soft budget constraint**. The soft budget constraint meant that enterprises that failed to cover their costs could count on automatic subsidies from their ministry, which redistributed profits from profitable to unprofitable enterprises, or from the state budget. With a soft budget constraint, enterprises were free to overuse resources and to avoid cost-saving innovations. It also meant that profitability was not an important indicator of managerial success. Therefore, later efforts to introduce profits as a criterion for success were doomed to failure as long as the soft budget constraint was retained.

Many features of the informal Soviet managerial milieu were disruptive and shifted the results of production away from those envisaged by the planners. Others were necessary to correct for errors made by planning authorities and for breakdowns in the supply system. Plan execution, therefore, was subject to a substantial measure of flexibility not envisaged in the theoretical models: People simply did not do what they were told.

Monitoring of Agents

It would appear that the principals of enterprise managers in the ministries, in Gosplan, and in the party and state would want to weed out all dysfunctional actions of opportunistic agents. The organization chart given in Figure 11.1 shows that both the party and the state had their own control commissions to ferret out and punish illegal managerial behavior. The party control commission, for example, had the right to punish any and all party members (except those in the top leadership). Insofar as all responsible positions were filled with party members through **nomenklatura appointments** (operated by the party personnel commission), the party control commission could oversee the actions of virtually all managers. Party and state control commissions, however, faced a dilemma: Virtually all Soviet managers were forced by circumstances to break the "plan-law." Any serious investigation would therefore prove that any manager had violated rules and laws, and the managers were personally responsible for plan fulfillment. Thus any and every investigation could theoretically result in the removal of the manager. Yet the supply of managers who knew how to produce output was limited. Control commissions could punish only a few token violators at best. These token punishments, which could often be transferred to lower-level scapegoats in the enterprise,[26] were not an effective deterrent to opportunistic behavior. The inability to deter opportunistic behavior was therefore a paradox of the Soviet system: One of history's most totalitarian regimes was unable to control effectively its most important agents, its managers.

The CPSU itself served as a control institution. All organizations contained party cells, and enterprise managers were nearly always party members, aware of party priorities. Despite these pervasive controls, there was a bias in favor of reporting successful results. If local enterprises performed well, the careers of local party officials were advanced. Another monitoring device was the state bank (Gosbank).[27] Most Soviet enterprises were budget-financed, which meant that funds both to and from enterprises flowed through the state bank into and out of the state budget. The state budget was the major source of enterprise investment funds or, for an enterprise that lost money, of subsidy funds. Profits, too, were channeled through the state bank, and profit taxes were the major source of Soviet budgetary revenue. Each enterprise was required to hold all accounts with the state bank, where all transactions were recorded. Not only were the firm's labor requirements specified in the plan, but the fund that was used to pay for the labor was held and monitored by the state bank.

Ruble control is based on the accounting principle that all physical transactions must have parallel financial transactions. If an enterprise is ordered to produce 10 tons of steel and sell it to a buyer at 20 rubles per ton, when the physical sale is made, the seller will receive 200 rubles in its bank account, and the buyer's account will be debited 200 rubles. Planners therefore can follow the financial flows to see what is happening to physical flows. In theory, this ruble control should work well. All enterprises must maintain their bank accounts in the state bank, which can serve as a huge financial monitoring center. In practice, however, ruble control was not that easy. Plan targets were usually stated in aggregated terms, such as tons of steel or meters of textiles. Financial flows, on the other hand, were for microeconomic transactions conducted at lower levels of aggregation. Moreover, just as enterprises could receive "unofficial" supplies by trading with other enterprises, they could evade ruble control by granting each other unofficial credits or by paying cash.

Prices and Money

The founders of the administrative-command economy hoped money and prices would play only a small role in the economy. They hoped that goods and services could be directly distributed to consumers by a rationing system and that money could perhaps disappear. Ruble control suggests that money and prices play at most a passive role. To translate physical tasks into monetary values, prices would be needed as accounting units to add physical quantities, such as products and labor together. In market economies, prices and money play a key role. Relative prices tell participants in the economy what is cheap and what is expensive and guide resource-allocation decisions. Money clearly affects the price level, and it may affect the level of real output and employment. If, indeed, resources are allocated by an administrative plan, prices should not be expected to play an allocative role. Hence they would not be the mechanism by which supplies and demands are equated, nor would they be indicators of relative scarcity.

Soviet prices were primarily set by administrative authorities.[28] In the case of collective farm markets, and in services provided by moonlighting workers, prices were formed by supply and demand. Industrial prices were set to equal the average cost of the industrial branch plus a small profit markup. **Branch average cost** excluded rental and interest charges, and this practice resulted in enterprises making both planned profits and planned losses within the same branch. Pricing authorities sought, through periodic price "reforms," to raise prices enough to make the average branch enterprise profitable. When price reform was introduced, the average enterprise broke even, but others made profits or losses. The administrative difficulty of frequent price reforms dictated that prices lag behind cost, and there were times when the majority of enterprises in particular branches made planned losses. During the last quarter-century of the Soviet system, major price reforms were infrequent. Wholesale prices established in 1955 remained generally in effect until 1966. The 1966–1967 price reform remained in effect until the general price reform of 1982. Prices had limited use, because they were unrelated to relative scarcities.

Wholesale prices played primarily an accounting role, for supplies and demands were administratively planned and were not dependent on prices. However, when a product left the wholesale level to be sold at the retail level, the matter was not so simple. Figure 11.2 illustrates retail price formation.

The supply of consumer goods was determined largely by the planners, although producers, if they had a choice in output mix, might choose products with higher relative prices. Thus we draw the supply curve (*S*) with a steep upward slope. The consumer demand curve (*D*) is a function of relative prices, incomes, and tastes and could not be controlled by the planners. Planners sought to achieve a balance of

FIGURE 11.2   Soviet Turnover Tax

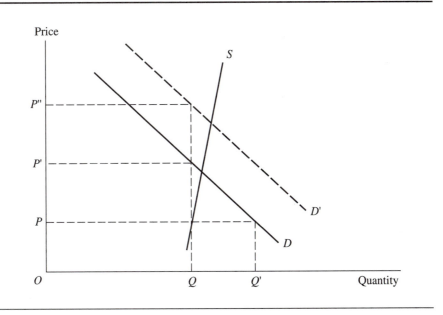

supply and demand by setting the retail price at or near a market-clearing level, such as P', by adding a **turnover tax**. If the retail price were set at the wholesale price (P in Figure 11.2), there would be an excess demand of $Q'Q$, for OQ would be produced and OQ' demanded. Some form of rationing would be required in this case, such as administrative rationing or rationing through long lines. The turnover tax was used to balance supply and demand. The difference between the retail and wholesale prices is the turnover tax. If the authorities chose to ration via equilibrium pricing, the retail price would be set at OP' and a near-equilibrium would prevail. Raising the retail price *did not* raise the quantity supplied above OQ, because the enterprise continued to receive the wholesale price OP for the product.

Unlike Western sales taxes, the turnover tax, in this case PP', differed widely from one product to another, and it was included in the price rather than being added on at the time of sale. Its share of retail prices declined over time, as planners increased supplies of consumer products and raised the wholesale prices of farm products.

Although prices approached equilibrium at the retail level, the result was different from a market economy. What in the Soviet case was a tax would in the capitalist system be something resembling a profit, signaling existing producers to expand supply and new producers to enter the market. There was no such signal in the Soviet case, because the producer was unaware of and largely uninterested in retail prices. The link between consumer demand and the producer was broken. Say demand increases from D to D'. As the producer continues to receive the wholesale price OP, the quantity produced remains at OQ. But at the old retail price OP', there is now an excess of quantity demanded over quantity supplied. The state reacts by raising the turnover tax by $P'P''$.

In the Soviet case, the mix of consumer goods was determined by **planners' preferences**, not by **consumer demand** (although planners may well have considered consumer signals when establishing plan targets). Thus prices played only a very limited allocative role and were used primarily for measurement, control, and manipulation of the distribution of income. In our diagram, the level of production is set administratively, not by the price.

Price policy emphasized the desirability of pricing some goods and services relatively "low" and others relatively "high." This policy reflected a very different socialist attitude toward the "equitable" distribution of income and toward necessities and luxuries. Books, housing, medical care, and transportation were priced very low, and automobiles and vodka were priced very high. Price policy affected the distribution of real incomes in accordance with state objectives.

Input Prices

The prices of inputs—land, labor, and capital—reflected a peculiar combination of Marxian orthodoxy, pragmatism, and necessity. There was, for the most part, no rental price for agricultural land. Land was allocated to collective and state farms administratively. Planners determined land utilization within the framework of the plan, taking into account technical and local conditions. The absence of land charges made farm accounting a questionable exercise, prompting an endless debate over the role of land rent under socialism. Despite some interest in land valuation, there was never a formal system of land valuation. However, planners attempted to extract a rent from the Soviet countryside by using regionally differentiated procurement prices and differential charges for state machine services.

The allocation of labor in the Soviet Union was a very different case, for there was a price for labor in the form of a wage rate.[29] Wage differentials were the primary mechanism to allocate labor. The demand for labor was primarily plan-determined. Once output targets were established, labor requirements were determined by applying technical coefficients of labor required per unit of output under existing technology. On the supply side, households were substantially free to make occupational choices. The state set wage differentials—for example, by occupation and by region—in an attempt to induce appropriate supplies to meet planned demands.

Wage-setting was straightforward. For an industrial branch, a base rate determined the relative wage level for that branch. A branch schedule of skill grades established the pattern of wage differentials within the branch. Thus the level and differential could be adjusted by manipulating either the base or the schedule. Trade unions and workers played virtually no role in setting wages; wages were set by administrative authorities. Unlike other areas, planners were willing to use these differentials to manipulate labor supply. There was a substantial degree of market influence on the structure of Soviet wages.[30]

In addition to wage differentials, nonmarket devices were used to manipulate labor supply. Higher- and technical-education institutions expanded in direct relation to the desired composition of the labor force, as directed by state control. Nonmonetary rewards, adulation in the press, social benefits, and other moral incentives were also used to control the supply of labor. **Organized recruitment** was used in early years but declined after World War II, except for the seasonal needs of agricultural production.[31]

Soviet labor policies, including the forced-labor campaigns of the 1930s, ensured a high rate of labor force participation to promote rapid economic development. The participation rate (the civilian labor force as a proportion of the able-bodied population) generally exceeded 90 percent. Structural problems grew more serious as the system matured and became a major test of the ability of central planning to allocate labor. The rapid rate of urbanization left shortages in some areas, surpluses in others. Labor imbalances especially characterized the regional distribution of labor. Soviet authorities were consistently unable to meet the labor needs of Siberia and the Far North. In addition, the restrictive role of Soviet trade unions and the policy of "full employment" resulted in overemployment—artificially high levels of staffing at the enterprise level. It was quite difficult to lay off workers even if they were redundant. Although there was experimentation with programs to encourage the firing of unproductive workers, the problems of **guaranteed-employment policies** were not solved and remained a grave difficulty for the transition.

Financial Planning and Money

Value categories, such as prices, costs, and profits, always existed, but they were supposed to play only a limited role in allocating resources. In a centralized economy where few decisions are made at local levels, households made decisions about working and what they would buy. How could planners ensure that there would be a **macroeconomic balance** of consumer goods? The balancing of aggregate consumer demand and supply can be illustrated in the following formulas:

$$D = WL - R \tag{9.1}$$

$$S = P_1 Q_1 \tag{9.2}$$

where

> D = aggregate demand
> S = aggregate supply
> W = the average annual wage
> L = the number of worker-years of labor used in the economy
> R = the amount of income not spent on consumer goods
>   (equal to the sum of direct taxes and savings)
> Q_1 = the real quantity of consumer goods produced
> P_1 = the price level of consumer goods

The conceptual problem is quite simple. As the Soviet economy grew rapidly in the early plan years, it paid labor increasingly high wages to motivate higher participation and greater effort, but the state wanted that labor to produce producer goods, not consumer goods (Q_1). Thus the state permitted wages (W) to rise rapidly in order to encourage labor inputs (L) to rise. In so doing, planners were hoping that labor force decisions would be based on nominal and not real wages—in other words, that Soviet workers would be subject to money illusion. In the absence of sharp increases in Q_1, however, alternative steps were required to achieve a balance between S and D—notably to let P_1 rise along with R (the latter through forced bond purchases). However, prices were not allowed to rise fast enough to absorb the full increase in demand; an imbalance between aggregate supply and demand was allowed to develop. This phenomenon, known as **repressed inflation**, was used widely throughout the entire Soviet era.[32]

After World War II, the quantity of consumer goods increased, although simultaneous increases in purchasing power made it difficult to determine to what degree excess demand was reduced. Indeed, as noted earlier, Janos Kornai developed a general model of the socialist economy suggesting why shortages persist, even when expansion of consumer goods is taking place.

The consumer-goods-balance formula shows the importance of money. Virtually all consumer purchasing power originated from wage earnings, which were paid by enterprises in cash. Enterprises typically preferred more labor rather than less. The more labor they had, the easier it would be to meet production targets, even if some of this labor might be redundant. They were persistently pressing on planning officials' requests for more labor and on banking officials' requests for more cash to pay labor. Although the enterprise had a soft budget constraint for the purchase of materials, it appeared to have a hard budget constraint on cash to pay labor.[33] In fact, the highest political authorities in the land had to approve the emission of new currency, and ministers of finance could be fired if the money supply expanded too rapidly.[34]

The consumer-goods-balance equation shows why enterprise cash for wages was a hard budget constraint. Basically, the demand for consumer goods roughly equaled the amount of cash paid as wages throughout the economy. If financial authorities had treated wages like materials and allowed enterprises virtually unlimited access to cash, the inflationary consequences would have been substantial. As it was, the problem of too much purchasing power plagued the Soviet economy in its final years.

At the end of the Soviet era, the focus of discussion was on repressed inflation.[35] In a system where excess demand is unlikely to result in price increases, **disequilibrium analysis** can be used as an effective tool of analysis. Savings were regarded as evidence of repressed inflation, assuming that people save because there is nothing to buy at prevailing prices. Soviet authorities feared a savings overhang—forced savings that could destabilize consumer markets.

Capital Allocation

Capital is not a value-creating input in the Marxian scheme[36] and hence should not generate an interest charge. Nevertheless, capital has an implicit value because less is available than is demanded, and some means must be devised for its allocation. Furthermore, if a "price" of capital is allowed, presumably all capital is owned by the state, and the "income" from capital accrues to the state, not to individuals.

Soviet investment was largely controlled by planning authorities and the ministries. In drawing up the output plan, planners used technical coefficients to determine and authorize the investment necessary to produce the planned increases in output. Some funds were available from internal enterprise sources, but even those funds remained under control of the state banking system. The aggregate supply of investment funds was largely under the control of planners. It is not surprising, therefore, that the ratio of saving to GDP was higher than under industrialized capitalism. The high investment rate illustrates a basic feature of planners' preferences. In a capitalist economy, saving is largely determined by individuals and businesses as they choose between consumption in the present and greater consumption in the future. In the Soviet context, the state controlled savings (primarily by the state and by enterprises). In a capitalist economy, savings arise as undistributed profits in enterprises and as income that is not consumed in households. Both *types* of savings existed in the Soviet case, but because wages and prices were set by the state, the state itself could determine savings rates. The control of savings and investment was a powerful mechanism to promote more rapid capital accumulation than would be tolerated in an economy directed by consumer sovereignty.

Starting in the late 1960s, Soviet enterprises paid an interest charge for the use of capital. This charge was typically low and was designed to cover the administrative costs of making the capital funds available to the enterprise. The introduction of interest charges was less significant than it might appear. Interest charges were simply added as a cost of production, but, as noted above, production costs did not determine the use of outputs or inputs.

At the micro level, authorities devised rules for choosing among investment projects. Suppose there was a directive to raise the capacity to generate the volume of electric power. Will the new capacity be hydroelectric, nuclear, coal-fueled, or what? How can one compare the capital-intensive variant that has low operating costs with the variant that requires less capital initially but has high annual operating costs? Although quasi-market techniques for making this sort of decision were rejected by Stalin in the 1930s in favor of planners' wisdom, those methods surfaced again in the late 1950s and were used widely until the end of the Soviet Union.

Planners accepted the principle that the selection among competing projects should be based on cost-minimizing procedures. A general formula, called the **coefficient of relative effectiveness**, was used to compare projects:

$$C_i + E_n K_i = \text{minimum}$$

where

C_i = current expenditures of the ith investment project
K_i = the capital cost of the ith investment project
E_n = the normative coefficient

This formula was used to weigh the tradeoff between higher capital outlays (K_i) and lower operating costs (C_i). The principle was that the project variant should be selected that yields the minimal full cost, where an imputed capital charge is included in cost. The capital cost was calculated by applying a "normative coefficient" (E_n) to the projected capital outlay.

To illustrate, assume that a choice must be made between two projects, the first having an annual operating cost (C) of 10 million rubles and a capital cost (K) of 30 million rubles, the second having a C of 7 million rubles and a K of 50 million rubles. Applying a normative coefficient of 10 percent yields a full cost of 13 million rubles for the first project and 12 million rubles for the second. The second project should be chosen, because it is the minimal-cost variant. However, suppose a normative coefficient of 20 percent is applied. In this case, the full cost of the first variant is 16 and that of the second variant is 17. In this case—and all that has changed is the normative coefficient—the first variant should be chosen.

It is a distinctive feature of this formula that the higher the normative coefficient, the higher the imputed capital cost, and the *less* likely it is that capital-intensive variants will be selected. Between 1958 and 1969, a system of differentiated normative coefficients gave priority to heavy industry by applying low E_n's to heavy-industrial branches and high E_n's to light industry. In 1969, a new **Standard Methodology** replaced the earlier differentiated system with a standard normative coefficient of 12 percent,[37] supposedly to be applied equally to all branches.

The principle that capital should be allocated on the basis of rate-of-return calculations should not obscure the fact that the basic allocation of capital still proceeded through an administrative investment plan, which itself was a derivative of the output plan. The rate-of-return calculations were used only to select among projects that followed planners' preferences in the first place. Thus they were used to decide what type of plant should be used to generate electricity, not whether the investment should be in the generation of electricity or in steel production. In fact, the standardized coefficient introduced in 1969 was watered down thereafter by numerous exceptions for particular branches of heavy industry and for various regions.

Market Forces

The Soviet economy, at least until the era of *Perestroika*, was a planned economy in which market forces were of only moderate and secondary importance. Markets were an exception to the plan.

In some areas of the Soviet economy—for example, labor allocation—planners used markets to influence outcomes. Wage differentials were used to influence the distribution of labor by region, by season, and by profession; retail prices were used to allocate consumer goods. The fact that wages and retail prices were set by planners does not rule out market forces. In such instances, planners were actually using the market as a tool.

Unlike labor and retail prices, the **second economy** fell outside the range of state control. The second economy has been analyzed extensively by Gregory Grossman, Dimitri Simes, Vladimir Treml, Michael V. Alexeev, Aron Katsenelinboigen, and others.[38] It consisted of a number of market activities of varying importance and degrees of legality, all facilitating "unplanned" exchange among consumers and producers. According to Grossman, second-economy activities must meet at least one of the following two criteria: (1) the activity is engaged in for private gain; (2) the person engaging in the activity knowingly contravenes existing law.

Examples of second-economy activities abound. Indeed, since the demise of the Soviet Union, a good deal more has been learned about the second economy. A physician would treat private patients for higher fees. A salesperson would set aside quality merchandise for customers who offered large tips. The manager of a textile firm would reserve goods for sale in unofficial supply channels. A collective farmer would divert collective farm land and supplies to his private plot. Black marketeers in port cities would deal in contraband merchandise. Owners of private cars transported second-economy merchandise. In some cases, official and second-economy transactions were intertwined. Managers would divert some production into second-economy transactions to raise cash to purchase, unofficially, supplies needed to meet the plan. The official activities of an enterprise would serve as a front for a prospering second-economy undertaking.

Second-economy activities were concentrated in collective farms and in transportation. Apparently, the supervision of collective farms was more lax; they therefore served as better fronts for the second economy. Transportation enterprises were critical to the second economy, for its merchandise had somehow to be moved. The increase in private ownership of automobiles apparently enhanced the operation of the second economy.

It is difficult to estimate accurately the magnitude of second-economy activity. In a survey of Soviet émigrés conducted by Gur Ofer and Aron Vinokur, earnings derived during the early 1970s from activity other than that at the main place of employment were found to account for approximately 10 percent of earnings.[39] A study of Soviet alcohol production and consumption, conducted by Vladimir Treml in the mid-1980s, found that between 20 and 25 percent of transactions were illegal. Although the second economy was important in the overall command economy, there were substantial variations from one sector to another. It was not surprising for secondary activities to arise in a setting of increasing incomes and devotion of limited resources to the service sector.

The second economy had its advantages and disadvantages as far as the planners were concerned. It helped to preserve incentives, because higher wages and bonus payments could be spent in the second economy. Moreover, the second economy reduced inflationary pressures on the official economy. On the negative side, the second economy diverted effort from planned tasks and loosened planners' control. Soviet authorities long tolerated the second economy. Reforms of the late 1980s moved to legalize a number of second-economy activities that did not involve the use of hired labor.

Yet another area of market influence was the private sector of Soviet agriculture. Under certain restrictions, the farm family could use a plot of land, hold animals, and raise crops. The resulting products were sold in the kolkhoz market—a practice tolerated by the authorities—at prices established by supply and demand. Such sales accounted for a substantial portion of the farm family's income. It was not by accident that the private plots produced farm products that were poorly suited to planning, such as fruits, vegetables, and dairy products—all of which required much personal care and motivation.

Agriculture

In advanced market economies, agriculture plays a more modest role than it did in the Soviet economy. In the mid-1980s, agriculture accounted for 20 to 25 percent of Soviet GDP and absorbed a great deal of the Soviet labor force. For this reason alone, we should study agriculture. However, there is a second reason for looking more closely at Soviet agriculture: It had unique organizational arrangements, and the results achieved were modest in spite of continuing attention from Soviet policy makers.

During war communism and the New Economic Policy, various forms of organization existed, but private peasant agriculture dominated.[40] The rural sector was seen as crucial to any Soviet development effort, because industrialization would depend on agricultural deliveries. Whether or not the perception of agriculture in the 1920s as the key to industrialization was correct, it was the rationale for Stalin's decision to collectivize in 1929.[41]

Two major institutions dominated Soviet agriculture after 1928. The collective farms (kolkhozy) were operated like cooperatives; the **state farms (sovkhozy)**, in which the farmers were paid like industrial workers, in effect were "factories in the fields." The sovkhoz was a state enterprise with state-appointed management.[42] The kolkhoz was, in theory, a cooperative with elected management. Sovkhoz workers were state employees and received fixed wages like other state employees. Kolkhoz peasants initially received a dividend instead of a wage payment. Because this unique payment system was the cornerstone of Stalin's attempt to extract a surplus from the countryside, dwelling on it for a moment is worthwhile.

Before 1966, payment for peasants in the kolkhoz was established in the following fashion. For a particular task assigned to a peasant, a certain number of labor days would be recorded in the peasant's work book. The **labor day** was not necessarily a measure of time or effort but, rather, an often arbitrary measure of work input. At the end of the year, the *value* of one labor day would be determined by the following formula:

Value of one labor day = farm income after required deliveries and
other expenses ÷ total number of labor days
for entire kolkhoz

Once the value of a labor day was determined, each individual was paid a "dividend" by multiplying the number of labor days accumulated by the value of one labor day.

The labor-day system of payment was highly arbitrary. The work demanded for one labor day could and did vary regionally, seasonally, and from farm to farm. Furthermore, contrary to the principles of any good incentive system, peasants had little idea in advance what they would earn per labor day. The labor-day system was finally abandoned in 1966 and replaced with a guaranteed wage.[43]

In both the kolkhoz and the sovkhoz, families were entitled to small plots of land (typically about half an acre) for their private use.[44] The produce from this land, important in the case of truck garden and dairy products, could be consumed on the farm, sold to the state, or sold in collective-farm markets. To give some idea of the importance of the private sector, in the 1960s, the private sector accounted for roughly 60 percent of total potato output, 70 percent of total vegetable output, and 30 percent of total milk output. Throughout the postwar period, the private sector accounted for approximately 40 percent of family income on collective farms. Peasants were also entitled to hold some animals, although the permitted number of each type varied over time. For example, roughly 40 percent of all cows were owned privately in the 1960s.

Changes in Agriculture

Organizational arrangements in agriculture changed substantially after the 1930s, although the kolkhoz, the sovkhoz, and the private sector remained at least in name through 1991.[45]

First, after the 1940s, mergers and consolidations sharply reduced the number and importance of kolkhozy; at the same time, the number of sovkhozy increased, and their average size became greater. In 1940 there were 237,000 kolkhozy, with an average sown area of 1235 acres. By the mid-1980s, the number of kolkhozy had been reduced to just over 26,000, and each kolkhoz had an average sown area of just over 8600 acres. As for sovkhozy, in 1940 there were 4200, averaging just over 6900 acres of sown area on each farm. By the mid-1980s, the number of sovkhozy had increased to almost 22,700, with an average sown area of almost 12,000 acres per farm.[46] In 1940 roughly 78 percent of all sown area was accounted for by kolkhozy; this was reduced to 44 percent by the mid-1980s.

Second, **Machine Tractor Stations** were abolished in 1958, and their equipment was sold to the farms, a move that gave farm managers enhanced control over farm equipment.

Third, rural incomes increased sharply after the 1950s, generally more rapidly than industrial incomes. In addition, a pension system introduced in the 1960s substantially improved the welfare of rural workers and peasants and reduced the rural–urban income differential.[47] However, expanded production costs at the farm level, along with unwillingness to raise retail food prices significantly, resulted in a very large subsidy to the agricultural sector.[48]

Fourth, after a period of extensive campaigns by Nikita Khrushchev in the 1950s (the Virgin Land Campaign, the corn program, and so on) designed to expand inputs, the emphasis in the 1960s and 1970s shifted to improvement of productivity through increases in agricultural investment.

Soviet agricultural policy was a focal point of controversy from the beginning, and it remained so in those East European nations where the Soviet model was imposed after World War II. During the postwar era, there was probably no sector in the Soviet economy to which so much attention was devoted with so few results. Agriculture remains a major challenge for the leaders of the post-Soviet era.

International Trade

Foreign trade played a substantive but less important role in the Soviet development experience than in that of other industrialized economies.[49] The policies and the systemic arrangements of foreign trade in the command model differed widely from those in market economies. Throughout the Soviet period, foreign trade was planned and executed by the foreign-trade monopoly. Decision making—what will be traded, with whom, and on what terms—was centralized in three major institutions: the Ministry of Foreign Trade (MFT), the *Vneshtorgbank* or **Bank for Foreign Trade (BFT)**, and the various **foreign-trade organizations (FTOs)**. The formal organization of Soviet foreign trade is represented in Figure 11.3. The **Ministry of Foreign Trade**, like other Soviet ministries, was a centralized body concerned with issues of foreign-trade planning—the development of import/export plans, material supply plans, and balance-of-payments plans—all of which were an integral part of the Soviet material balance planning system.

Individual Soviet enterprises did not deal with the external world until the reforms of Gorbachev in 1987. Rather, for both imports and exports, enterprises dealt with the FTOs in domestic currency at domestic prices, and the FTOs dealt with the external world via financial arrangements handled by the Ministry of Foreign Trade and the BFT. The domestic users or producers of goods entering the foreign market were isolated from foreign markets by this foreign-trade monopoly. Soviet foreign trade operated according to the rule "Export what is available to be exported to pay

FIGURE 11.3   The Organization of Soviet Foreign Trade: The Command Model

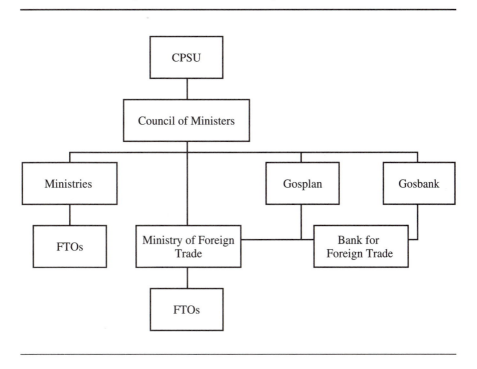

for necessary imports, and limit the overall volume of trade to control the influence of market forces on the Soviet economy."

Most Soviet trade, even with other socialist countries, was bilateral—that is, directly negotiated for each trade deal with each trading partner. Bilateral trade meant that Soviet exports and imports were handled largely on a barter basis. The difficulties of operating according to offsetting barter deals hampered Soviet trade volume through the years. In part, bilateral trading arrangements arose from and contributed to the nonconvertibility of the Soviet ruble, which was not used as a medium of exchange in world markets.

Soviet trading arrangements were not conducive to an expanding and competitive position in world markets, but Western economists generally argued that the Soviet Union followed a policy of deliberate **trade aversion**.[50] Dating from the late 1920s and early 1930s, Soviet trade ratios (that is, the ratio of imports and exports to GDP) generally declined. For many years the Soviet trade ratio remained low by world standards. This pattern partially resulted from the Soviet Union's adverse position in world markets at that time, or it may have been in part a deliberate policy response. In any event, for the trade that was conducted, a very successful effort was made to redirect Soviet imports away from consumer goods and toward producer goods, an outcome that contributed to the development effort.

The latter years of the Soviet era witnessed some changes in Soviet foreign trade. First, Soviet trade ratios increased, signaling a growing participation in the world economy. The extent of this rise was difficult to estimate because of the peculiarities of Soviet foreign-trade accounting,[51] but Soviet participation in foreign trade in the 1980s was well above the rates of the 1950s and 1960s. Second, the 1960s and 1970s saw organizational changes aimed at making enterprises more responsive to world markets and streamlining the FTOs. Third, there were changes in Soviet attitudes toward foreign trade, with renewed interest in neoclassical trade theory and in the development and application of criteria on which to base trade decisions. Fourth, the Soviet Union, though fundamentally conservative throughout the command era, displayed increasing interest in participating in world trade arrangements and organizations. Thus Soviet attitudes toward the external world changed even before the Gorbachev era.

Despite changes in attitudes toward international markets near the end of the Soviet period, the Soviet economy remained isolated from world product and capital markets. Whereas other countries became increasingly a part of globalized markets, the Soviet economy remained isolated.

Summary

- State ownership, national economic planning, and the collectivization of agriculture characterized the Bolshevik revolution.
- The administrative-command economy was the resource-allocation model used in the former Soviet Union for over sixty years.
- The Soviet system was a relatively centralized economic system. The broad objectives of the Communist party were implemented through Gosplan (the state planning agency), the ministries, and individual firms and agricultural units.
- The essence of Soviet planning was the material balance system, in which balances were developed to equate the demand and supply of key industrial commodities, labor inputs, and the like. This system emphasized consistency, not optimality, and there was only minimal reliance on money and prices for the allocation of resources.
- Soviet enterprises were responsible for fulfilling plan targets, and managers were motivated within an incentive framework.
- Prices were cost-based, and the demand side had little or no influence. Capital was allocated primarily by administrative decree.
- Market-type influence existed in the allocation of labor. Market mechanisms played an important role in the private sector of Soviet agriculture.
- Collective farms, state farms, and the private sector traditionally dominated Soviet agriculture. In later years, agro-industrial integration became an important mechanism for combining farm activity with industrial processing.
- Soviet foreign trade was a state monopoly. Soviet domestic enterprises were largely isolated from world markets through the intermediary function of the foreign-trade organizations and the nonconvertible ruble.

Key Terms

Bolshevik revolution
administrative-command economy
czarist era
collective farms (kolkhozy)
war communism
New Economic Policy (NEP)
material incentives
Communist party
Gosplan
ministry
material balance system
techpromfinplan
planning from the achieved level
funded commodities
limited commodities
balanced plan
taut plan
consistent plan
optimal plan
resource manager
gross value of output
principal–agent conflict
information asymmetry
opportunistic behavior

soft budget constraint
nomenklatura appointments
ruble control
branch average cost
turnover tax
planners' preferences
consumer demand
organized recruitment
guaranteed-employment policy
macroeconomic balance
repressed inflation
disequilibrium analysis
coefficient of relative effectiveness
Standard Methodology
Perestroika
second economy
state farms (sovkhozy)
labor day
Machine Tractor Stations
Bank for Foreign Trade (BFT)
foreign-trade organizations (FTOs)
Ministry of Foreign Trade
trade aversion

Notes

1. For a general treatment of the Soviet economy and references to the specialized literature, see Paul R. Gregory and Robert C. Stuart, *Soviet and Post-Soviet Economic Structure and Performance,* 6th ed. (Reading, Mass.: Addison Wesley Longman, 1997); Alec Nove, *The Soviet Economic System,* 3rd ed. (New York: Unwin Hyman, 1986); and Michael Ellman, *Socialist Planning* (New York: Cambridge University Press, 1989). For useful background papers, see U.S. Congress, Joint Economic Committee, *Soviet Economy in the 1980s: Problems and Prospects,* Parts 1 and 2 (Washington, D.C.: U.S. Government Printing Office, 1982). For a briefer treatment of the Soviet economy, see Franklyn D. Holzman, *The Soviet Economy: Past, Present, and Future* (New York: Foreign Policy Association, 1982); and James R. Millar, *The ABC's of Soviet Socialism* (Urbana: University of Illinois Press, 1981).

2. For a discussion of these years, see M. Lewin, *Russian Peasants and Soviet Power* (London: Allen and Unwin, 1968); for a brief survey, see Gregory and Stuart, *Soviet and Post-Soviet Economic Structure and Performance,* Ch. 5.

3. Paul Gregory, *Command: The Political Economy of Stalin's Command System* (New York: Cambridge University Press, 2003), Ch. 1.

4. A considerable amount has been written about the Soviet economy during these early years. See, for example, Alec Nove, *An Economic History of the U.S.S.R.,* rev. ed. (London: Penguin Books, 1982); Eugene Zaleski, *Planning for Economic Growth in the Soviet Union, 1928–1932* (Chapel Hill: University of North Carolina Press, 1971); Maurice Dobb, *Soviet Economic Development Since 1917,* 5th ed. (London: Routledge and Kegan Paul, 1960); E. H. Carr and R. W. Davies, *Foundations of a Planned Economy, 1926–1929,* Vol. I, Part 2 (New York: Macmillan, 1969); Roger Munting, *The Economic Development of the USSR* (London: Croom Helm, 1982); R. W. Davies, *The Socialist Offensive, the Collectivization of Soviet Agriculture 1929–30* (London: Macmillan, 1980); and Thomas F. Remington, "Varga and the Foundation of Soviet Planning," *Soviet Studies* 34 (October 1982), 585–600.

5. There is considerable debate about the *level* of economic development in the Soviet Union in 1917 and hence about the readiness of that country, in the Marxian schema, for the introduction of socialism. For a discussion of this issue, see Gregory and Stuart, *Soviet and Post-Soviet Economic Structure and Performance,* Ch. 2; for more detail, see Paul R. Gregory, "Economic Growth and Structural Change in Tsarist Russia: A Case of Modern Economic Growth?" *Soviet Studies* 23 (January 1972), 418–434; Paul R. Gregory, *Russian National Income 1885–1913* (New York: Cambridge University Press, 1983); and R. W. Davies, ed., *From Tsarism to the New Economic Policy* (Basingstoke, England: Macmillan, 1990).

6. By 1920 the index of industrial production (1913 = 100) had fallen to 20, the index of agricultural production to 64, and the index of transportation to 22. See Gregory and Stuart, *Soviet and Post-Soviet Economic Structure and Performance,* p. 58.

7. By 1928 the index of industrial production (1923 = 100) had risen to 102, the index of agricultural production to 118, and the index of transportation to 106. *Ibid.,* p. 56.

8. For a discussion of the policy issues of this period, see Jerzy F. Karcz, "From Stalin to Brezhnev: Soviet Agricultural Policy in Historical Perspective," in James R. Millar, ed., *The Soviet Rural Community* (Urbana: University of Illinois Press, 1971), pp. 36–70; and Davies, *The Socialist Offensive.*

9. The classic work is Alexander Erlich, *The Soviet Industrialization Debate, 1924–1928* (Cambridge, Mass.: Harvard University Press, 1960). For a translation of original contributions to the debate, see Nicolas Spulber, *Foundations of Soviet Strategy for Economic Growth* (Bloomington: Indiana University Press, 1964).

10. There was, however, only a single candidate for each position, although Gorbachev later proposed changes. For a comprehensive discussion of the Soviet government and party structure, see Jerry F. Hough and Merle Fainsod, *How the Soviet Union Is Governed* (Cambridge, Mass.: Harvard University Press, 1979); and T. H. Rigby, *Political Elites in the USSR* (Brookfield, Vt.: Edward Elgar, 1990).

11. For a study of the Communist party of the Soviet Union, see Leonard Shapiro, *The Communist Party of the Soviet Union* (New York: Random House, 1971); and Hough and Fainsod, *How the Soviet Union Is Governed.* For a statistical survey of party membership, see T. H. Rigby, *Communist Party Membership in the U.S.S.R., 1917–1967* (Princeton, N.J.: Princeton University Press, 1968). For further evidence, see T. H. Rigby, "Soviet Communist Party Membership Under Brezhnev," *Soviet Studies* 28 (July 1976), 317–337; and Jan Adams, *Citizen Inspectors in the Soviet Union: The People's Control Committee* (New York: Praeger, 1977).

12. The material balance technique has been analyzed in some detail. The classic article is J. M. Montias, "Planning with Material Balances in Soviet-Type Economies," *American Economic Review* 49 (December 1959), 963–985; for a summary, see Gregory and Stuart, *Soviet and Post-Soviet Economic Structure and Performance,* p. 163 ff. For a theoretical

discussion, see Raymond P. Powell, "Plan Execution and the Workability of Soviet Planning," *Journal of Comparative Economics* 1 (March 1979), 51–76.

13. This important point represents a sharp difference between the functioning of a planned economy and that of a market economy. In the market economy, the producing enterprise normally has supply contracts for required inputs. However, the firm can, with limitations, enter the market either to secure better contractual arrangements or to find a replacement if existing arrangements are interrupted for some reason. In the planned economy, the producing enterprise relies on an inter-enterprise delivery specified in the annual plan. If this delivery is interrupted for any reason, the producing enterprise has no market to which it may turn. In such cases production is typically interrupted. Unless formal or informal stop-gap measures can be taken, the imbalances tend to accumulate throughout the economy.

14. Eugene Zaleski, *Stalinist Planning for Economic Growth, 1933–1952* (Chapel Hill: University of North Carolina Press, 1980).

15. I. V. Stalin, *Voprosy Leninizma,* 10th ed. (Moscow, 1937), p. 413.

16. Paul Gregory, *The Political Economy,* Ch. 8.

17. Eugenia Belova and Paul Gregory, "Dictators, Loyal and Opportunistic Agents: The Soviet Archives on Creating the Soviet Economic System," *Public Choice* 113 (2002), 265–286.

18. Valery Lazarev and Paul Gregory, "The Wheels of a Command Economy," *Economic History Review* 55, 2 (July 2002), 324–328.

19. Eugenia Belova, "Economic Crime and Punishment," in Paul Gregory (ed.), *Behind the Façade of Stalin's Command Economy* (Stanford, Calif.: Hoover Institution Press, 2001).

20. The role of the Soviet second economy was the focus of a major research effort undertaken by Gregory Grossman and Vladimir Treml. The Grossman–Treml project involved interviews with Soviet émigrés concerning their personal experiences in the second economy. Gur Ofer and Aaron Vinokur have conducted studies of second-economy earnings among Soviet émigrés to Israel, and the Soviet Interview Project has studied second-economy earnings among Soviet emigrants to the United States. For initial results from these surveys, see J. R. Millar, ed., *Politics, Work, and Daily Life in the USSR* (New York: Cambridge University Press, 1987).

21. *Ibid.*

22. There is a substantial body of literature on the problems of Soviet enterprise management. See Joseph Berliner, *Factory and Manager in the USSR* (Cambridge, Mass.: Harvard University Press, 1957); David Granick, *The Red Executive* (New York: Doubleday, 1960); David Granick, *Managerial Comparisons of Four Developed Countries: France, Britain, United States and Russia* (Cambridge, Mass.: MIT Press, 1972); William J. Conyngham, *The Modernization of Soviet Industrial Management* (New York: Cambridge University Press, 1982); and Jan Adams, "The Present Soviet Incentive System," *Soviet Studies* 32 (July 1980), 360.

23. Gregory and Stuart, *Soviet and Post-Soviet Economic Structure and Performance,* pp. 215–216.

24. Incentives—how to make enterprises do what the center wants—have been the subject of a considerable amount of research. See David Conn, special ed., *The Theory of Incentives,* published as vol. 3, no. 3, *Journal of Comparative Economics* (September 1979); and J. Michael Martin, "Economic Reform and Maximizing Behavior of the Soviet Firm," in Judith Thornton, ed., *Economic Analysis of the Soviet-Type System* (New York: Cambridge University Press, 1976).

25. In contemporary times, the rate of turnover of Soviet industrial managers declined.

26. Paul Gregory, *Restructuring the Soviet Economic Bureaucracy* (New York: Cambridge University Press, 1990), pp. 35, 73, 129.

27. Unfortunately, relatively little research has been done on the structure and functions of the Soviet state bank. For a survey, see Paul Gekker, "The Banking System of the USSR," *Journal of the Institute of Bankers* 84 (June 1963), 189–197; and Christine Netishen Wollan, "The Financial Policy of the Soviet State Bank, 1932–1970" (Ph.D. dissertation, University of Illinois, Urbana, 1972).

28. For a basic survey of Soviet price policy and citation of the important literature, see Gregory and Stuart, *Soviet and Post-Soviet Economic Structure and Performance,* Ch. 8; Morris Bornstein, "Soviet Price Policy in the 1970s," in U.S. Congress, Joint Economic Committee, *Soviet Economy in a New Perspective* (Washington, D.C.: Government Printing Office, 1976), pp. 17–66; Morris Bornstein, "The Administration of the Soviet Price System," *Soviet Studies* 30 (October 1978), 466–490; and Morris Bornstein, "Soviet Price Policies," *Soviet Economy* 3, 2 (1987), 96–134.

29. For a discussion of Soviet wage-setting procedures, see Leonard J. Kirsch, *Soviet Wages: Changes in Structure and Administration Since 1956* (Cambridge, Mass.: MIT Press, 1972); B. Arnot, *Controlling Soviet Labour* (London: Macmillan, 1988); D. Granick, *Job Rights in the Soviet Union: Their Consequences* (New York: Cambridge University Press, 1987); and Silvana Malle, *Employment Planning in the Soviet Union* (Basingstoke, England: Macmillan, 1990).

30. See Abram Bergson, *The Economics of Soviet Planning* (New Haven: Yale University Press, 1964), Ch. 6.

31. The provision of appropriate manpower to the Soviet economy was a matter of both interest and complexity because it involved analysis of Soviet demographic trends. For a summary of statistical trends, see Murray Feshbach and Stephen Rapawy, "Soviet Population and Manpower Trends and Policies," in Joint Economic Committee, *Soviet Economy in a New Perspective,* 113–154. For the specific case of agriculture, see Karl-Eugen Wadekin, "Manpower in Soviet Agriculture—Some Post-Khrushchev Developments and Problems," *Soviet Studies* 20 (January 1969), 281–305. More recent evidence is presented in Murray Feshbach, "Population and Labor Force," in Abram Bergson and Herbert S. Levine, eds., *The Soviet Economy: Towards the Year 2000* (Winchester, Mass.: Allen and Unwin, 1983), pp. 79–111; Jan Adams, ed., *Employment Policies in the Soviet Union and Eastern Europe,* 2nd ed. (New York: St. Martin's, 1987); and P. R. Gregory and I. L. Collier, "Unemployment in the Soviet Union: Evidence from the Soviet Interview Project," *American Economic Review* 78 (September 1988), 613–632.

32. Since the mid-1970s, there has been a debate over the extent of repressed inflation in the former Soviet Union. See D. H. Howard, "The Disequilibrium Model in a Controlled Economy: An Empirical Test of the Barro-Grossman Model," *American Economic Review* 66 (December 1976), 871–879; Richard Portes, "The Control of Inflation: Lessons from East European Experience," *Economics* 44 (May 1977), 109–130; Richard Portes and David Winter, "A Planners' Supply Function for Consumption Goods in Centrally Planned Economies," *Journal of Comparative Economics* 1 (December 1977), 351–365; and Richard Portes and David Winter, "The Demand for Money and for Consumption Goods in Centrally Planned Economies," *Review of Economics and Statistics* 60 (February 1978), 8–18.

33. David Granick, *Job Rights in the Soviet Union: Their Consequences* (Cambridge: Cambridge University Press, 1987).

34. Gregory, *The Political Economy,* Ch. 9.

35. Joyce Pickersgill and Gur Ofer conducted early empirical studies of Soviet saving behavior and concluded that Soviet citizens appear to save for the same reasons Westerners do. On this, see Gur Ofer and Joyce Pickersgill, "Soviet Household Saving: A Cross-Section Study of Soviet Emigrant Families," *Quarterly Journal of Economics* 95 (August 1980),

121–144; and Joyce Pickersgill, "Soviet Household Saving Behavior," *Review of Economics and Statistics* 58 (May 1976), 139–147. Other scholars see increases in excess demand as the cause of increases in saving. On this, see D. W. Bronson and Barbara S. Severin, "Recent Trends in Consumption and Disposable Money Income in the USSR," U.S. Congress, Joint Economic Committee, *New Directions in the Soviet Economy,* Part II-B (Washington, D.C.: Government Printing Office, 1966); and Igor Birman, *Secret Income and the Soviet State Budget* (Boston: Kluwer, 1981).

36. For a brief summary of the socialist attitude toward an interest charge for capital, see A. C. Pigou, *Socialism versus Capitalism* (London: Macmillan, 1937), Ch. 8. For a discussion of Soviet investment planning, see Gregory and Stuart, *Soviet and Post-Soviet Economic Structure and Performance,* Ch. 7. For details, see David A. Dyker, *The Process of Investment in the Soviet Union* (Cambridge: Cambridge University Press, 1983).

37. For a discussion of the rules, see Alan Abouchar, "The New Soviet Standard Methodology for Investment Allocation," *Soviet Studies* 24 (January 1973), 402–410; P. Gregory, B. Fielitz, and T. Curtis, "The New Soviet Investment Rules: A Guide to Rational Investment Planning?" *Southern Economic Journal* 41 (January 1974), 500–504; Frank A. Durgin, "The Soviet 1969 Standard Methodology for Investment Allocation versus 'Universally Correct' Methods," *ACES Bulletin* 19 (Summer 1977), 29–53; Frank A. Durgin, Jr., "The Third Soviet Standard Methodology for Determining the Effectiveness of Capital Investment (SM-80, Provisional)," *ACES Bulletin* 24 (Fall 1982), 45–61; and Janice Giffen, "The Allocation of Investment in the Soviet Union: Criteria for the Efficiency of Investment," *Soviet Studies* 33 (October 1981), 593–609. For a useful summary, see David Dyker, *The Process of Investment in the Soviet Union* (New York: Cambridge University Press, 1981).

38. Gregory Grossman, "The 'Second Economy' of the USSR," *Problems of Communism* 26 (September–October 1977), 25–40; Aron Katsenelinboigen, "Coloured Markets in the Soviet Union," *Soviet Studies* 29 (January 1977), 62–85; Dimitri Simes, "The Soviet Parallel Market," *Survey* 21 (Summer 1975), 42–52; and *Studies on the Soviet Second Economy* (Durham, N.C.: Berkeley–Duke Occasional Papers on the Second Economy in the USSR, December 1987).

39. Vladimir Treml, "Alcohol in the USSR: A Fiscal Dilemma," *Soviet Studies* 41 (October 1973), 161–177; Dennis O'Hearn, "The Consumer Second Economy: Size and Effects," *Soviet Studies* 32 (April 1980), 221; and Vladimir G. Treml, *Purchase of Food from Private Sources in Soviet Urban Areas* (Durham, N.C.: Berkeley–Duke Occasional Papers on the Second Economy in the USSR, September 1985).

40. For a discussion of the various forms of agricultural organization, see D. J. Male, *Russian Peasant Organization Before Collectivization* (Cambridge: Cambridge University Press, 1971); and Robert G. Wesson, *Soviet Communes* (New Brunswick, N.J.: Rutgers University Press, 1963).

41. For a survey of thinking on this issue, see Karcz, "From Stalin to Brezhnev."

42. Because the sovkhoz was a relatively straightforward state enterprise operating under the same general principles as the industrial enterprise, relatively little attention had been paid to its structure and operation. It is important to note, however, that whereas the sovkhoz was state-owned property, the kolkhoz was an ideologically inferior form of property holding known as kolkhoz-cooperative property. Many of the changes in the kolkhoz could be explained by the implementation of state policy designed to "improve" the kolkhoz and raise it to the same level as the sovkhoz.

43. For a detailed discussion of the kolkhoz and the labor-day mechanism, see Robert C. Stuart, *The Collective Farm in Soviet Agriculture* (Lexington, Mass.: Heath, 1972); and

R. W. Davies, *The Industrialization of Russia,* Vols. 1 and 2 (Cambridge, Mass.: Harvard University Press, 1980). Research has supported the view that during the introduction of the collectives there was no increase in the net surplus generated by agriculture. For a discussion of this question, see James R. Millar, "Soviet Rapid Development and the Agricultural Surplus Hypothesis," *Soviet Studies* 22 (July 1970), 77–93; and M. J. Ellman, "Did the Russian Agricultural Surplus Provide the Resources for the Increase in Investment in the USSR During the First Five-Year Plan?" *Economic Journal* 85 (December 1975), 844–863. For a summary, see Gregory and Stuart, *Soviet and Post-Soviet Economic Structure and Performance,* Ch. 5. For a critical view, see David Morrison, "A Critical Examination of A. A. Barsov's Empirical Work on the Value of Balance Exchanges Between the Town and the Country," *Soviet Studies* 34 (October 1985), 570–584.

44. For an in-depth discussion of the private sector in Soviet agriculture, see Karl-Eugen Wadekin, *The Private Sector in Soviet Agriculture* (Berkeley: University of California Press, 1973); and A. Lane, "U.S.S.R.: Private Agriculture on Center Stage," in U.S. Congress, Joint Economic Committee, *Soviet Economy in the 1980s: Problems and Prospects,* Part 2 (Washington, D.C.: U.S. Government Printing Office, 1982), pp. 23–40.

45. For a survey of postwar developments in Soviet agriculture and references to the specialized literature, see Gregory and Stuart, *Soviet and Post-Soviet Economic Structure and Performance,* Ch. 6.

46. Robert C. Stuart, "The Changing Role of the Collective Farm in Soviet Agriculture," *Canadian Slavonic Papers* 26 (Summer 1974), 145–159.

47. Rural income levels are discussed in David W. Bronson and Constance B. Krueger, "The Revolution in Soviet Farm Household Income, 1953–1967," in Millar, *The Soviet Rural Economy,* pp. 214–257; and in more general terms in Gertrude E. Schroeder and Barbara S. Severin, "Soviet Consumption and Income Policies in Perspective," in Joint Economic Committee, *Soviet Economy in a New Perspective,* pp. 620–660.

48. For a discussion of subsidies, see W. G. Treml, "Subsidies in Soviet Agriculture: Record and Prospects," in U.S. Congress, Joint Economic Committee, *Soviet Economy in the 1980s: Problems and Prospects* (Washington, D.C.: U.S. Government Printing Office, 1982), pp. 171–186.

49. For a survey of Soviet foreign trade and references to the literature, see Gregory and Stuart, *Soviet and Post-Soviet Economic Structure and Performance,* Ch. 9.

50. For a different view, see Steven Rosefielde, "Comparative Advantage and the Evolving Pattern of Soviet International Commodity Specialization, 1950–1973," in Steven Rosefielde, ed., *Economic Welfare and the Economics of Soviet Socialism* (New York: Cambridge University Press, 1981), pp. 185–220.

51. See Vladimir Treml and Barry Kostinsky, *Domestic Value of Soviet Foreign Trade: Exports and Imports in the 1972 Input-Output Table,* Foreign Economic Report No. 20, U.S. Department of Commerce, October 1982.

Recommended Readings

General Works

Robert W. Campbell, *The Soviet-Type Economies: Performance and Evolution,* 3rd ed. (Boston: Houghton Mifflin, 1981).

R. W. Davies, ed., *The Soviet Union* (Winchester, Mass.: Unwin Hyman, 1989).

David A. Dyker, *The Future of the Soviet Planning System* (Armonk, N.Y.: M. E. Sharpe, 1985).

Paul R. Gregory and Robert C. Stuart, *Soviet and Post-Soviet Economic Structure and Performance,* 5th ed. (New York: HarperCollins, 1994).

Franklyn D. Holzman, *The Soviet Economy: Past, Present, and Future* (New York: Foreign Policy Association, 1982).

Tania Konn, ed., *Soviet Studies Guide* (London: Bowker–Saur, 1992).

James R. Millar, *The ABC's of Soviet Socialism* (Urbana: University of Illinois Press, 1981).

Alec Nove, *The Soviet Economic System,* 2nd ed. (London: Unwin Hyman, 1981).

United States Congress, Joint Economic Committee, *Gorbachev's Economic Plans,* Vols. I and II (Washington, D.C.: U.S. Government Printing Office, 1987).

Soviet Economic History

E. H. Carr and R. W. Davies, *Foundations of a Planned Economy, 1926–1929,* Vol. 1, Parts 1 and 2 (New York: Macmillan, 1969).

R. W. Davies, *The Industrialization of Soviet Russia,* Vols. I and II (Cambridge, Mass.: Harvard University Press, 1980).

R. W. Davies, Mark Harrison, and S. G. Wheatcroft, eds., *The Economic Transformation of the Soviet Union 1913–1945* (Cambridge: Cambridge University Press, 1994).

Maurice Dobb, *Soviet Economic Development Since 1917,* 5th ed. (London: Routledge and Kegan Paul, 1960).

Alexander Erlich, *The Soviet Industrialization Debate, 1924–1928* (Cambridge, Mass.: Harvard University Press, 1969).

Paul R. Gregory, *Russian National Income, 1885–1913* (New York: Cambridge University Press, 1983).

Gregory Guroff and Fred V. Carstensen, *Entrepreneurship in Imperial Russia and the Soviet Union* (Princeton, N.J.: Princeton University Press, 1983).

Moshe Lewin, *Political Undercurrents in Soviet Economic Debates: From Bukharin to the Modern Reformers* (Princeton, N.J.: Princeton University Press, 1974).

Roger Munting, *The Economic Development of the USSR* (London: Croom Helm, 1982).

Alec Nove, *An Economic History of the U.S.S.R.,* rev. ed. (London: Penguin Books, 1982).

Nicolas Spulber, *Soviet Strategy for Economic Growth* (Bloomington: Indiana University Press, 1964).

The Communist Party and the Manager

Donald D. Barry and Carol Barner-Barry, *Contemporary Soviet Politics: An Introduction,* 2nd ed. (Englewood Cliffs, N.J.: Prentice-Hall, 1982).

William J. Conyngham, *The Modernization of Soviet Industrial Management* (New York: Cambridge University Press, 1982).

Andrew Freiis, *The Soviet Industrial Enterprise* (New York: St. Martin's Press, 1974).

David Granick, *Managerial Comparisons of Four Developed Countries: France, Britain, United States, and Russia* (Cambridge, Mass.: MIT Press, 1972).

Leslie Holmes, *The Policy Process in Communist States* (Beverly Hills: Sage Publications, 1981).

Jerry F. Hough and Merle Fainsod, *How the Soviet Union Is Governed* (Cambridge, Mass.: Harvard University Press, 1979).

David Lane, *Politics and Society in the USSR,* 2nd ed. (London: Martin Robertson, 1978).

Nathan Leites, *Soviet Style in Management* (New York: Crane Russak, 1985).

Leonard Shapiro, *The Government and Politics of the Soviet Union,* 6th ed. (Essex, England: Hutchinson Publishing Group, 1978).

Selected Aspects of the Soviet Economy

R. Amann and J. M. Cooper, eds., *Industrial Innovation in the Soviet Union* (New Haven: Yale University Press, 1982).

Joseph S. Berliner, *The Innovation Decision in Soviet Industry* (Cambridge: MIT Press, 1976).

Morris Bornstein, ed., *The Soviet Economy: Continuity and Change* (Boulder, Colo.: Westview, 1981).

Robert W. Campbell, *Soviet Energy Technologies* (Bloomington: Indiana University Press, 1980).

David A. Dyker, *The Process of Investment in the Soviet Union* (Cambridge: Cambridge University Press, 1983).

Franklyn D. Holzman, *International Trade Under Communism* (New York: Basic Books, 1976).

Alastair McAuley, *Women's Work and Wages in the Soviet Union* (London: Unwin Hyman, 1981).

Mervyn Matthews, *Education in the Soviet Union* (London: Allen and Unwin, 1982).

————, *Poverty in the Soviet Union* (New York: Cambridge University Press, 1987).

James R. Millar, *Politics, Work, and Daily Life in the USSR* (New York: Cambridge University Press, 1987).

Henry W. Morton and Robert C. Stuart, eds., *The Contemporary Soviet City* (Armonk, N.Y.: M. E. Sharpe, 1984).

Robert C. Stuart, ed., *The Soviet Rural Economy* (Totowa, N.J.: Roman and Allenheld, 1983).

Murray Yanowitch, *Social and Economic Inequality in the Soviet Union* (London: Martin Robertson, 1977).

Eugene Zaleski, *Planning Reforms in the Soviet Union, 1962–1966* (Chapel Hill: University of North Carolina Press, 1967).

Planning

Alan Abouchar, ed., *The Socialist Price Mechanism* (Durham, N.C.: Duke University Press, 1977).

Edward Ames, *Soviet Economic Processes* (Homewood, Ill.: Irwin, 1965).

Abram Bergson and Herbert S. Levine, eds., *The Soviet Economy: Towards the Year 2000* (London: Allen and Unwin, 1983).

Martin Cave, Alastair McAuley, and Judith Thornton, eds., *New Trends in Soviet Economics* (Armonk, N.Y.: M. E. Sharpe, 1982).

Michael Ellman, *Soviet Planning Today: Proposals for an Optimally Functioning Economic System* (Cambridge: Cambridge University Press, 1971).

David Granick, *Job Rights in the Soviet Union: Their Consequences* (New York: Cambridge University Press, 1987).

Kenneth R. Gray, ed., *Soviet Agriculture* (Ames: Iowa State University Press, 1990).

Donald W. Green and Christopher I. Higgins, *SOVMOD I: A Macroeconometric Model of the Soviet Economy* (New York: Academic, 1977).

Paul R. Gregory, *The Soviet Economic Bureaucracy* (Cambridge: Cambridge University Press, 1990).

John Hardt *et al., Mathematics and Computers in Soviet Planning* (New Haven: Yale University Press, 1977).

Peter Murrell, *The Nature of Socialist Economies: Lessons from Eastern European Foreign Trade* (Princeton, N.J.: Princeton University Press, 1990).

Steven Rosefielde, ed., *Economic Welfare and the Economics of Soviet Socialism* (New York: Cambridge University Press, 1981).

Robert C. Stuart, ed., *The Soviet Rural Economy* (Totowa, N.J.: Roman and Allenheld, 1983).

Judith Thornton, ed., *Economic Analysis of the Soviet-Type System* (New York: Cambridge University Press, 1976).

Alfred Zauberman, *Mathematical Theory in Soviet Planning* (Oxford: Oxford University Press, 1976).

12

China: Market Socialism?

We discussed the theory of market socialism in Chapter 7. Unlike the other theoretical models of economic systems—market capitalism and planned socialism, both of which can be illustrated with real-world examples—market socialism lacks a clear-cut real-world manifestation. Recall that **market socialism** combines market resource allocation with state ownership. In different market-socialist models, state ownership need not be pervasive; there may be private ownership of smaller businesses, but the state should own the most significant "means of production" of society. This ownership may be practiced in the form of state ownership or ownership by workers. The market allocates consumer goods and labor, but market simulation techniques such as trial-and-error pricing may be used for producer goods. Management of state enterprises may be carried out by state managers answerable to the state, or it may be executed by managers appointed by worker-owners. There is no single form of market socialism; it is sufficiently flexible to encompass a range of institutional arrangements. Its most basic feature, however, is its combination of state ownership with market allocation.

If we search for real-world models of market socialism, we can cite the Yugoslav economy before the disintegration of what was once Yugoslavia. The Yugoslavs abandoned the Soviet planned economy in the aftermath of World War II as Yugoslavia, under the leadership of J. Tito, avoided being swallowed up in the Soviet bloc. Having rejected the Soviet model, the Yugoslavs settled on worker ownership and management, a relatively open economy, and extensive use of market allocation tempered by strong state interventionist policies. Interest in the Yugoslav form of market socialism disappeared with the collapse of Yugoslavia as a nation-state.

The transition economies of Eastern Europe and the former Soviet Union (to be discussed in later chapters) could perhaps also serve as examples of market socialism except for the fact that most of them are aiming for an end result that is not market socialism. As they go through their transitions, their economies are characterized by extensive state ownership combined with the increasing importance of market allocation. However, their ultimate goal appears to be the creation of a capitalist market economy rather than a market-socialist economy. The market-socialist features of the transition economies, however, will be noted in our discussion of them.

China began its current economic reform in the late 1970s. Prior to the adoption of these reforms, the Chinese economy strongly resembled the Soviet administrative-command economy (almost complete state ownership, collectivized agriculture, an industry managed by directive plans, priorities set by the Communist party) but with necessary amendments to account for China's rural nature. The reforms begun by Deng Xiaoping introduced dramatic change. Deng permitted a form of private ownership in agriculture, trade, and small-scale industry; opened the economy to world product and capital markets; and allowed the formation of various financial markets and institutions, such as stock markets, commercial banks, and credit markets. Throughout the first two decades of reforms, China retained two features of the administrative-command model: state ownership of heavy industry and other "commanding heights" activities and the continued political dictatorship of the Chinese Communist party. The continued dominance of the Communist party was signaled by the crackdown on dissidents in June of 1989 in Tianenmin Square in Beijing. Since that landmark event, there has been no serious challenge to the party's monopoly of political power.

This chapter examines the Chinese experience as the country moved from the administrative-command model to a model that resembles market socialism. The Chinese story is not complete without accounts of the various political upheavals that, although they occurred for political and ideological reasons, had major negative effects on economic performance. An unusual feature of Chinese development has been exogenous political catastrophes, such as the Great Leap Forward and the Cultural Revolution, both of which set back economic progress, often for a decade or more.

We are attracted to China for two reasons. First, with its 1.2 billion citizens, China is the world's most populous country. It has the world's largest standing army, and it has shared borders with no fewer than 14 countries. Given its size and geographic location, China is bound to play a major role in the twenty-first century. Second, we are drawn to China as a part of the "East Asian economic miracle." Like several of its East Asian neighbors, China has grown at rapid rates for more than two decades. If this rapid growth continues, China could become a relatively affluent economy of immense political and economic power. There is, therefore, major interest in the contemporary Chinese economy, emerging as it has from the Soviet model, but with the introduction of markets and sustained state control.

Revolution and Upheaval

The Setting

China's 1.2 billion inhabitants make it the world's most populous country. China has a land area of just over 3.6 million square miles, about the size of Canada, making it one of the most densely populated countries of the globe. But if the Chinese population continued to increase at the average annual rate of the past two decades, a new Canada, in terms of population, would arise in China roughly every 15 months!

China is a relatively resource-rich country. Although coal is a major source of energy, only recently has China undertaken to utilize its oil riches. Sharp variations in climate and fertility, along with large areas of rough terrain, mean that large amounts of capital are needed to exploit its mineral and land resources.

China is the oldest existing civilization in the world, a source of great pride to the Chinese people. Although there are numerous ethnic minorities in China (primarily in the western part of the country), the dominant group is the *han* nationality.

The Chinese language comprises many varying dialects; the Mandarin dialect is dominant. The rich heritage of the Chinese people is an important if unmeasurable influence on their attitudes toward and participation in the modernization process.

China remains today a poor country despite rapid growth. Substantial economic progress has been made since the early 1950s, but China in 2002 had a per capita income of about $4,000. China's per capita income, though above that of its immediate neighbors India and Pakistan ($2,000 and $1,600, respectively), ranks well below that of Taiwan at around $15,000.

Another unique feature of China is the notion of a greater China. The political definition of "Greater China" is mainland China plus Taiwan, Hong Kong, and Macao, the last Portuguese colony. Hong Kong is now under the rule of mainland China. The prospering Taiwan is vigorously seeking to maintain its independence in the face of mainland Chinese efforts at reunification. In addition to Greater China's geographic boundaries, "Greater China" also includes the diaspora of more than 50 million ethnic Chinese located mainly in Southeast Asia; their wealth is said to equal that of China's own population of 1.2 billion. "Greater China" accounts for economic and labor resources that make it a fourth pillar in the world economy, along with the United States, Europe, and Japan.[1]

The Early Years and the Soviet Model

We cannot understand the Chinese economic system without an excursion into its pre-reform history. China was much more backward in 1949, when it adopted the Soviet economic model, than Russia was in 1917. Chinese leaders faced several key problems in adapting the Soviet model. How could the Chinese economy, in the absence of the advantages enjoyed by Russian leaders in 1917 (a basic industrial capacity, a transportation network, and so on), institute a planned socialist economic system in a large and very poor peasant economy? In developing such a planned socialist economy, modifications of the Soviet model had to be made to account for the very large Chinese population, its relative poverty, and its primarily rural character.

China at the time of the 1949 revolution was a classic poor country with low per capita income, significant population pressure on arable land and other resources, and an absence of institutions appropriate for economic development. China, with a land mass about half that of the Soviet Union, and with a population roughly three and one-half times that of the Soviet Union, began in 1949 to implement the Soviet model. The result was economic growth and development interrupted when ideological and political factors gained supremacy over economic factors. Many of the policies and institutions developed in China were similar to those used in the Soviet Union. There were, however, important differences, especially the impact of ideology.

The Chinese People's Republic was proclaimed by Mao Zedong in 1949. Between 1949 and 1952, two goals were pursued. First, land was redistributed to individual households in preparation for collectivization. Collectivization was pursued without undue haste. Second, nationalization and consolidation of industry took place in preparation for national economic planning. Financial reform, educational reform, and other changes were undertaken to prepare for the beginning of the first five-year plan in 1953. In this respect, China's first steps were much like those of the Soviet Union in the 1920s, as it prepared for its five-year-plan era.[2]

China's approach to agriculture differed from the Soviet's in the early 1930s. Inasmuch as Soviet collectivization brought with it serious negative consequences, the Chinese leadership wished to avoid Soviet mistakes. On the surface, both countries utilized initial land reform and similar experimental forms of organization to eliminate class differences, distributed machinery and equipment through centralized facilities, and applied pressure to hold down rural food consumption. China, however, avoided substantial destruction of cattle, facilities, and equipment when it collectivized agriculture in the 1950s.[3] The Chinese countryside was better prepared in terms of ideological and organizational factors, though certainly not in terms of machinery and equipment.

The early 1950s also saw the nationalization of industry and the development of a system of national economic planning. There was a gradual transition from private to socialist industry—certainly more gradual than in the Soviet Union after 1928. The shift was intended to be slow, though toward the latter part of the first five-year plan it became rapid. The pattern of change was from private ownership to what the Chinese called elementary state capitalism, then to advanced state capitalism, and finally to socialist industry. By 1955, 68 percent of the gross value of output was produced by state industry and only 16 percent by joint state–private enterprises. Eventually, even handicraft production was brought under state control in moves reminiscent of the excessive nationalization of Soviet war communism dating from 1918 to 1920. The socialist transformation of both agriculture and industry accelerated in 1955–1956 as ideology and political considerations dominated economic considerations.

Chinese planning, put in place in the early 1950s, was initially similar to the Soviet model.[4] The basic unit of production activity was the enterprise. As in the Soviet Union, a dual party–state administrative structure drew up and implemented (and often interrupted) five-year plans for both agriculture and industry. Chinese plans were formulated by a State Planning Commission, which, like Gosplan in the Soviet Union, operated through an industrial ministry system communicating with regional and enterprise officials. Once it was approved by the State Council, that plan became law for enterprises. Chinese planning produced problems similar to those in the Soviet case: imbalance and shortages, poor quality, late plans, and deviation of results from targets. Chinese thinking on reform began to surface in the mid-1950s, but it was overshadowed by the political and ideological upheavals of the late 1950s.

The first ten years of the Chinese industrialization show the influence of the Soviet model. "In general, it can be said that during 1953–1957, the Chinese followed the broad outlines of the Stalinist strategy of selective growth under conditions of austerity with three important qualifications."[5] First, less pressure was placed on agriculture, in recognition of the large, poor, rural population. Chinese leaders apparently learned from the Soviet experience with rapid collectivization, for the extreme costs of the Soviet case were avoided.

Second, unlike the Soviet case, where state resources were directed through state farms and Machine Tractor Stations, agriculture was largely self-financed in the early years a consequence of the much lower economic development of China in 1949 than of the Soviet Union in 1928.[6]

Third, the Chinese relied heavily on the state enterprise as a revenue source for state investment funds. Revenue from state enterprises accounted for roughly 35 percent of total budgetary revenue in 1953 and for 46 percent by 1957. In comparison, the most important source of budgetary revenue in the early years of Soviet industrialization was the turnover tax. The decision not to rely on taxes forced from the peasants reflected the realities of a subsistence agriculture.

During the 1950s, the Chinese generally followed the Soviet "industry first" strategy. Between 1953 and 1957, heavy industry in China absorbed an average of 85 percent of industrial investment. Only 8 percent of state investment was devoted to agriculture, whereas aggregate investment accounted for 20 to 25 percent of the national product.[7] These investment figures suggest a relatively high rate of accumulation for a poor country, with emphasis on industry in general and heavy industry in particular.

China's economic growth during the 1950s was generally strong, though uneven. There was an impressive doubling of GNP per capita, a ninefold increase in industrial production, and a modest increase in agricultural production. The first five-year plan witnessed substantial growth; thereafter, China's growth was largely determined by cataclysmic political and ideological upheavals.

The First Upheaval: The Great Leap Forward

Chinese economic development through the 1970s was characterized by intermittent political upheavals that tended to erase economic progress. Massive ideological disruptions appealed to the aging group of communist revolutionaries led by Mao, who worried about the decline of revolutionary fervor and the bureaucratization of Chinese economic and political life. Chinese upheavals originated from the highest levels of the ruling elite; they were introduced to achieve goals and objectives desired by that leadership.

After the liberal **Hundred Flowers Campaign** (1956–1957), during which there was open discussion and criticism of the system, the **Great Leap Forward** was launched (1958–1960) by Mao.[8] The Great Leap was a massive resurgence of ideology, which replaced rationality. Campaigns were instigated with revolutionary fervor to emphasize a new role for the peasantry, especially through small-scale industry in the countryside and the introduction of communes. Development of water resources was also stressed. A brutal campaign against the educated elite was mounted.

The disruptions of the Great Leap were substantial. There was an economically irrational attempt to move heavy industry from the city to the countryside, contrary to all economic principles of mass production and economies of scale. Agriculture was reorganized into massive communes encompassing thousands of households. The exacting of farm products from the countryside was so stringent that massive starvation occurred in provinces that were exporting grain "surpluses." The true toll of the great Leap Forward was initially concealed by Chinese authorities, but by all official statistics, the Great Leap caused a stagnation of Chinese economic growth.

Although the Great Leap was abandoned by 1960, the commune system, introduced in 1958, remained.[9] The **Rural Peoples Communes** were initially set up as very large units combining a number of collectives (advanced cooperatives) to produce agricultural and handicraft products and to serve as local units of government. The original communes (roughly 26,000 in number and averaging about 4,600 households each) faced obvious difficulties. They were too large to coordinate, and individual incentives were lacking. The striking feature of Chinese economic performance in the 1950s was the impact of ideological disruptions. GDP grew at an annual rate of 6 percent from 1952 to 1956.[10] The 1958 level of GDP, however, was not regained until 1963. Thus the Great Leap Forward caused an enormous setback in Chinese growth.

The Great Leap Forward was abandoned in the late 1950s at a time when relations between China and the Soviet Union were deteriorating rapidly. The ideological and economic break between the two countries was almost complete by 1960. Although the role of outside aid was minimal, the Soviet contribution was important in the early years, especially in the area of technical assistance. The break would prove to be a sobering experience for Chinese leaders and planners.

1960–1978: Development and Disruption

Like the 1950s, the 1960s were divided into two very different periods: moderation in the early 1960s and upheaval in the late 1960s. The early 1960s was a period of relative calm in which Chinese leaders looked toward balance in economic development, modernization of agriculture, and recovery from the aftermath of the Great Leap. In industry, the 1960s was a period of reform—a movement away from the overwhelming importance of gross output (the major success indicator of the 1950s) toward quality in production and the elimination of major deficiencies in the planning system.

Both central control and local initiative changed during this period. The center tried to put pressure on enterprises to improve quality, to be concerned with efficiency, and to enhance the role of technical expertise in the decision-making process. Many decisions, especially minor ones, were shifted to the local level. Local industrial establishments were set up to serve local (especially rural) needs. Although the emphasis on enterprise efficiency and profitability came under sharp attack in the 1960s, these modifications for the most part withstood later upheavals.

During the early 1960s, new emphasis was placed on the need for mechanization and reorganization of the agriculture. Because communes were too large, the intermediate (brigade) and lower-level (team) units assumed new importance. Emphasis on nonmaterial rewards, a hallmark of the earlier commune system, was changed in favor of material incentives and the reintroduction of private plots. Although the number of communes was reduced during the 1960s, their role in the social, cultural, and political affairs of the countryside remained intact through the 1970s.

In addition to organizational changes and policy shifts, the 1960s witnessed a widespread educational campaign. There was an effort to re-educate the population in the ways of Mao. This campaign laid the foundations for the **Cultural Revolution**.

If the early 1960s was a period of rationality—reform and change along a well-defined continuum—the opposite could be said of the Cultural Revolution of 1966–1969. The Cultural Revolution, which is difficult for the Western observer to comprehend, was an upheaval of ideas, an abandonment of much that had preceded it. Emanating from a Communist party struggle, the Cultural Revolution was not a debate over economic ideas. In fact, its disastrous disruption of economic activity became apparent only later.

The Cultural Revolution had a dramatic effect on China's educated classes, including its elite. Scholars and officials were ignominiously shipped to hard industrial labor or labor in the countryside by radical bands of youths motivated by Mao's revolutionary ideas. China's entire educational establishment ceased to function in the backlash against education and Western teaching. Like the Great Leap, the Cultural Revolution had a devastating effect on economic performance. Disruption was so great that meaningful estimates of GDP during the Cultural Revolution are not available. GDP failed to increase between 1965 and 1970—a loss of output equal to or more severe than that of the Great Leap.[11]

The early 1970s was a period of recovery from the events of the Cultural Revolution.[12] The return to normalcy was interrupted, however, by events of the early and mid-1970s. Zhou Enlai, an advocate of a moderate path of industrialization, died in early 1976. The following September, Mao Zedong, the father of the revolution and an advocate of continuing the revolutionary mentality, died. Shortly thereafter, in October of 1976, the **Gang of Four**, representing the revolutionary left and espousing a continuation of the Stalinist mode of industrialization, were arrested amid great ideological fervor.[13] These events paved the way for what would be fundamental changes in the Chinese economic system under the leadership of Deng Xiaoping.

China's Modernization Reform: The Deng Era

Both China and the Soviet Union sought to make the administrative-command system work—the Soviet Union from 1928 to 1985, China from 1950 to 1978. Both, disillusioned by the weaknesses of the administrative-command system, turned to reformers to modify their systems. The Soviet Union turned to a young and vigorous general secretary of the Communist party, Mikhail Gorbachev, who opted to alter the Soviet political, social, and economic system, with the result that the Soviet Union and its centralized party dictatorship ceased to exist. China turned to Deng Xiaoping, an elderly veteran of the Chinese civil war and a victim of the worst of China's upheavals, the Cultural Revolution, to reform the Chinese system.[14]

The path chosen by Deng roughly a decade before Gorbachev yielded quite different results: Deng opted to avoid the political and social liberalization—democratization and openness—that Gorbachev later introduced into the Soviet system. He chose instead to preserve the dictatorship of the Chinese Communist party and not to tolerate dissent, but rather to unleash the productive and entrepreneurial talents of the Chinese people while retaining significant control and ownership of the "commanding heights" of the Chinese economy. This decision can be likened to V. I. Lenin's decision in 1921 to return the Soviet economy to a mixed economic system that encouraged private initiative and openness to the outside world, while the state retained control of the "commanding heights." During the Gorbachev era, agrarian reform was of limited importance. In China, agrarian reform was the catalyst of change.

Although the Deng reforms, which began to be introduced in 1978, were intended to be gradual (a process Deng described as "fording the river by feeling for the stones"), in reality the reforms moved quickly, particularly in the countryside. Specifically, the Deng reforms made two major changes in the vast Chinese countryside: Chinese farmers were allowed to work for themselves rather than for the collective farm, and townships were permitted to create "township enterprises" or "township and village enterprises" (TVEs). These reforms spread across the countryside so rapidly because the party and state chose not to stop them, and because they resulted from the unleashing of existing entrepreneurial forces.

Agricultural Reforms   Prior to 1978, the commune was the unit of organization in agriculture.[15] Agricultural production was in the hands of the **production team**, which comprised a number of households within a village. Production teams would combine to form a brigade, brigades to form a commune. Above the commune, the county was the state unit responsible for directing agricultural activity. It implemented the national economic plan administered by the Ministry of Agriculture and Forestry.[16]

The commune had a reward system not unlike that used in the collective farms of the former Soviet Union prior to 1966. Individuals would accumulate points for daily work done. The value of the points hinged on communal income, which was not known until the end of the period.

The **contract responsibility system** was introduced in the late 1970s.[17] The release of local agricultural markets and contracting by the state with households for the sale of major crops effectively brought collectivization to an end. The system for distributing output changed, as did the ability of households to purchase inputs. Although restrictions remained on the availability of land for household farming, by the early 1980s, the commune and production-team arrangements had virtually disappeared.[18] The impact of these changes on agricultural performance was immediate and dramatic, as is shown by Figure 12.1. By 1983, the collective form of social responsibility had given way to something approximating individual farming. Families were allotted former collective land for a period of fifteen years in exchange for agreeing to meet certain tax and delivery obligations.[19]

The Soviet experience revealed that private agriculture could not exist if the sole purchaser was the state. Prior to 1979, the state set obligatory delivery quotas at state-set delivery prices. In earlier years, the delivery prices were set low, but starting in 1979, the state began raising prices to provide greater production incentives. As state payments to farmers increased, the state budget found itself in a squeeze because it did not want to raise prices to consumers. The state ended up paying subsidies as it paid more to farmers than it was realizing at the retail level. The government therefore had a fiscal incentive to withdraw from the business of purchasing grain and to turn this matter over to private markets. A bumper harvest in 1984 provided the opportunity to move to a market system of farm-product purchases.[20]

FIGURE 12.1   The Growth of Agriculture in the Early Years of Chinese Reform

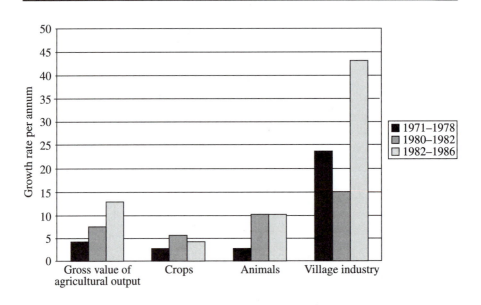

Source: State Statistical Bureau, cited in Dwight Perkins, "Reforming China's Economic System," *Journal of Economic Literature* 36, 2 (June 1988), 612.

Figure 12.1 shows the almost immediate improvement in agricultural production brought about by agrarian reforms. Agricultural production growth rose from under 4 percent immediately prior to the reforms, to 7 percent immediately after the introduction of reforms, and then to 14 percent throughout the rest of the 1980s. Notably, the improvement in agricultural output came more from animal husbandry and village production than from staple crops such as wheat.

Small-Scale Industry and Entrepreneurship   In the late 1970s, at the outset of China's reforms, a debate raged between those communist leaders who wished to keep a state-controlled system and those who favored market-oriented industry. At that time, the consensus was that China should have both a state industry and a non-state industry, the relative proportions of which remained to be resolved. In October of 1984, the Chinese government released its official reform of the urban sector, initially calling for the increased role of economic levers such as prices and profits. By the middle of the 1980s, surveys showed that managers had turned their attention away from Soviet-style gross-value indicators to profits, quality, and marketing. Under the Soviet-style system, profits were not important because they were shuffled from profitable to unprofitable enterprises to enforce soft-budget constraints. As the tax system was reformed to allow profitable enterprises to retain profits, enterprise managers began focusing on profits. The Chinese introduced a bankruptcy law, and the first bankruptcy occurred in 1987. Thereafter, bankruptcies of large enterprises, though possible, were rare. In fact, the story of the large state-owned enterprise sector continued to be the propping up of insolvent companies with loans, subsidies, and other forms of assistance. With the increased attention to profits and the freedom to reinvest these profits, investment shifted from budget-financed projects (more than half the total in the 1950s and 1960s) to investment financed from the companies' own resources. By the mid-1980s, almost 40 percent of state enterprise investment originated outside the state budget, and only 28 percent of total investment came from the state budget.[21] Companies that wanted to grow should earn profits.

The State Enterprise Sector[22]   China began its reforms in the late 1970s with virtually complete state ownership of industry, transportation, and commerce. Reforms began with changes in ownership relationships in agriculture and in small-scale trade, manufacturing, and service establishments, but the problem of dealing with large state-owned companies remained. The Chinese leaders were educated from their youth years to believe in the superiority of state ownership. Making the final move from state to private ownership of the "commanding heights" has been the most difficult step to take. State ownership is the hallmark of market socialism. If China were indeed to privatize its **state-owned enterprises (SOEs)**, it would cease to be classified as a market-socialist economy. Chapter 7 described the debate between the advocates and opponents of market socialism. Its proponents argued that state-owned enterprises could adopt corporate governance procedures to make them work efficiently in the interests of the owner (the state), just as privately owned capitalist corporations could adopt measures to make hired managers operate the company in the interests of private shareholders. China serves as a testing ground for this very debate.

The first two decades of SOE reform applied an incremental approach to reduce the scope of planning, increase managerial authority, and rely more on market forces. The late 1990s saw a more clearly enunciated SOE policy under the slogan "retain large SOEs and release small ones." Smaller state-owned companies (non–commanding heights enterprises) could go to private owners, but the state should continue to own the largest. Instead of privatization occurring, the form of state ownership itself was to be transformed from direct state supervision and management to state "shareholding" operated by "independent" managers backed by a state asset-management commission, outside directors, and supervisory committees. SOEs were to be **corporatized**; this means the state remains the owner of the majority of shares but management is independent. The aim was to ensure that the corporatized SOEs would operate like corporations in industrialized market economies. To do so, however, the state would have to let an independent management make its own decisions concerning executive compensation, hiring and firing, and investment.

Acceptance of the de-politicization of SOEs has proved difficult for Chinese officials. Their control of large companies has been a source of political power and patronage, and their ideological biases, shaped under communist rule, naturally favor state ownership over private ownership. Hence the transition from state ownership to something more closely representing private ownership has been slow and gradual, with many reversals.

The continued preference of officials for public ownership can be seen in a number of ways: Bank credit, where banks tend to be controlled by political authorities, is extended preferentially to SOEs despite their poor financial condition, whereas the private sector has limited access to credit. State ownership of the majority of shares of corporatized companies discourages share purchases by minority shareholders, who rightly fear the enterprise will be run for political rather than economic gain. Unable to sell shares, corporatized companies are left with bank lending or the state budget as the only sources of finance. The state's majority ownership means that there can be no hostile takeovers by a rival management group. In short, Chinese officialdom remains hostile to the development of a healthy private financial and industrial sector. Laws and the tax system favor state-owned enterprises over private corporations, and few tax incentives are offered for forming private companies.[23]

Under the Soviet-style system, insolvent SOEs could count on state bailouts, through either redistributions of profits or state credits. Although state credits are supposed to be based on commercial principles, there is still official pressure on banks to make loans that are unlikely to be repaid. Insolvent SOEs are kept afloat by cash infusions and rollovers of nonperforming debt. Because it is politically difficult to allow the bankruptcy of a large local enterprise, political pressure on bank authorities remains intense, and China's banking system has accumulated substantial inventories of bad bank loans that constitute a problem for the entire economy.

Throughout the reform process, China has allowed the private sector to grow, but in core areas, such as the state banking and other "commanding heights" industries, the state wishes to maintain control. The government response to economic problems is not to eliminate the poorly performing firms, as would happen in Western-style markets, but rather to try new types of reforms that will save all firms. The Chinese notion that ways can be found for markets to salvage all enterprises has put off the resolution of bad debt and commercialization of bank lending. China has not allowed the market to winnow out the low performers and replace them with the high performers. Someone must pay the cost of maintaining failing enterprises. To a great extent, that cost has been shifted to private enterprise and taxpayers.[24]

The investment decisions of privatized companies in China should be based on rate-of-return considerations. Given the large volume of foreign investment, Chinese companies affiliated with Western partners would also make investment decisions based on commercial principles. In the state-owned sector, investment decision making still suffers from political intervention. Because the approval process takes into account the impact of investment on regional economic development, the majority of large investment projects are decided by the clout of their high-level political supporters, not by market research or rate-of-return analysis. One expert on China draws the following conclusions about investment choice in China: "Despite the impact of two decades of reform, the fundamental nature of investment processes in China has not changed substantially from the pre-reform circumstances."[25]

Thus the Chinese economy, in the early years of the twenty-first century, appears to be a dual economy consisting of (1) small and medium-scale establishments that operate on the basis of commercial principles and are not particularly favored by state policy and (2) large-scale corporatized SOEs that remain subject to political tutelage and support. There is little evidence that the restructuring of SOEs has improved performance so far. Factor productivity for corporatized "shareholding entities" declined between 1993 and 1996. The decline was so precipitous in output per unit of fixed assets that the productivity of corporatized SOEs fell below that of state enterprises.[26]

It remains to be seen whether the state will eventually be removed from management decisions and whether economics will replace politics in the decision making of large enterprises. If the problem of large enterprises cannot be resolved, they will either pull down the rest of the economy or gradually whither away, to the point where they no longer constitute a national problem.

Although most of industry and transportation remained under state control and ownership, the Deng reforms permitted villages and townships to form their own enterprises, concentrating initially on services and light industry. They accounted for one-third of Chinese manufacturing by the mid-1980s. Chinese township enterprises were largely free of state planning and bureaucratic controls and could form joint ventures with foreign partners, who supplied capital and export-marketing expertise.

Before 1978, Stalinist priorities and restrictions against services prevailed; however, between 1978 and 1981, the share of total investment devoted to heavy industry fell from 54.7 percent to 40.3 percent, a sharp drop in a very short time.[27] Indeed, the average annual rate of growth of services was 6.1 percent between 1970 and 1980 and 11.2 percent between 1980 and 1991.[28] The labor force in the service sector doubled from 48.7 million in 1978 to 99.5 million in 1988.

The Opening of the Chinese Economy   The common denominator of the Asian model is its openness to world trade and investment. Even though the companies of Hong Kong, Taiwan, South Korea, and Singapore are subject to industrial policy and to state credit allocation, participation in the world market plays a vital disciplinary role. Companies that do not produce high-quality products efficiently and with modern technology simply cannot sell in world markets. Companies that do not offer reasonable protection to investors cannot attract equity capital in world capital markets. Even state bureaucrats, who wish to control all aspects of the economy, realize that they cannot affect conditions in the world market but must simply accept the world market as a given. The opening of China's economy, therefore, was probably the most significant step in the Chinese reform process. It is noteworthy that China's reform leaders deliberately decided to emulate the openness of Southeast Asia after studying the success of countries there. Figure 12.2 shows the magnitude of China's participation in world trade. China's ratio of imports plus exports to GDP exceeds 200 percent, a figure rivaled only by the city-state Singapore. China's trade proportions are particularly high given its size. Large countries such as the United States and India tend to have lower trade proportions.

The opening of China's economy began in 1977 and 1978, and China's exports increased from 7.6 billion dollars in 1977 to $22 billion in 1981—a near tripling in just a few years. China returned to membership in the World Bank and the International Monetary Fund and began to borrow from these institutions. It passed joint-venture

FIGURE 12.2   China's Trade Proportion (exports plus imports as a percent of GDP) versus Other Countries, 2000

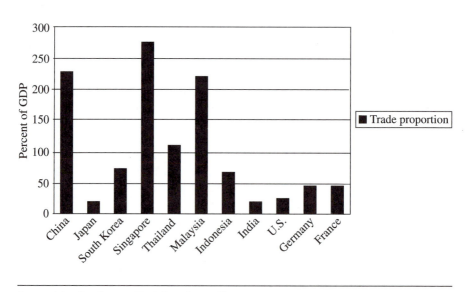

Source: Asian Development Bank, *http://www.adb.org*

laws to encourage foreign companies to set up shop in China with Chinese partners. Remarkably, China became the world's top recipient of foreign direct investment among the developing economies. **Foreign direct investment (FDI)** is investment by foreign investors in the form of acquiring substantial shares in domestic companies or entering into partnerships with domestic companies through joint ventures. FDI contrasts with **portfolio investment**, whereby foreign investors simply purchase shares or debt of domestic companies. Table 12.1 shows China's astonishing success in attracting FDI, which reached a peak of 40 percent of world FDI in the mid-1990s. China began its reform era with less than $2 billion of FDI annually and entered the twenty-first century with over $40 billion annual FDI. China was able to finance some 40 percent of its gross capital formation in the decade of the 1990s with FDI; the remaining 60 percent was financed through domestic savings.[29]

Figure 12.3 shows that most FDI to China came from Asia, the largest donor being Hong Kong (perhaps playing the role of intermediary for overseas Chinese in various countries). Less than one-quarter of FDI in the mid-1990s came from countries outside of Asia, although this proportion has increased since then.

Some 400 of the 500 world's largest companies have invested in over 2,000 projects in China. They include the world's leading computer, electronics, telecommunications equipment, pharmaceutical, and petrochemical companies. Transnational corporations such as Microsoft, Motorola, GM, GE, Samsung, Intel, Nokia, and Siemens, to name just a few, have established R&D ventures in China. Microsoft, for

TABLE 12.1   China's Share in FDI Inflow in the World and as a Share of
Developing Countries, 1982–2000

	Year			
	1982–1987 (annual average)	1990	1994	2000
China (billion $US)	1.4	3.5	33.8	41
All Countries (billion $US)	67.2	159.1	225.7	1271
China's Share in World FDI	2	2.2	15	3.2
All Developing Countries (billion $US)	14.7	34.7	84.4	240
China's Share in Developing Countries FDI	9.5	10.1	40	17.1

Sources: Data for 1982–1987 annual averages are cited from the United Nations, *World Investment Report 1994,* Annex table 1. Data for 1990, 1994, and 2000 are from the United Nations, *World Investment Report 2001.* The 1982–1987 averages are cited from Chen Chunlai, *Foreign Direct Investment in China,* Chinese Economy Research Unit (Adelaide, Australia: University of Adelaide, April 1996).

example, has invested $80 million in a Chinese research institute and intends to make additional investments to create a Microsoft Asian Technology Center. The effect of FDI can be seen in China's increasing ability to export high-technology products. In 2000, China exported 37 billion worth of high-technology products, 81 percent of which were produced by foreign affiliates in China.[30]

When transnational companies make foreign direct investments in China, they must usually partner with a Chinese joint-venture partner or affiliate. Hence they must deal, through their local partner, with all the peculiarities and problems of Chinese corporate governance that we have discussed. The assets that foreigners acquire through their direct investments must be managed within China according to Chinese business practices and are subject to the interventions and frequent irrationalities of the Chinese economic system.

China's major advances in trade and investment were solidified with China's accession to the World Trade Organization (WTO) in an agreement signed at its Fourth Ministerial Conference in Doha on November 10, 2001.[31] China's accession to the WTO obligates it to comply with WTO rules and regulations concerning international copyright laws, trademarks, visas, business licenses, and protection of domestic industries. China, for example, has already taken advantage of its membership to file a complaint against the United States for its protection of its domestic steel industry.[32] China's admission to the WTO serves as an important symbol of China's formal acceptance into the world trading community. (Russia remains the only large nation that has not become a member of the WTO.) Complying with WTO rules will represent a serious test for China's economic practices. The WTO does not allow governments to subsidize their domestic industries to protect them from foreign competition. Under WTO rules, foreign banks must be allowed to do business in China and to compete against Chinese banks. Some argue that the most important long-run effect of the

FIGURE 12.3   Distribution of FDI in China by Source Country, 1996

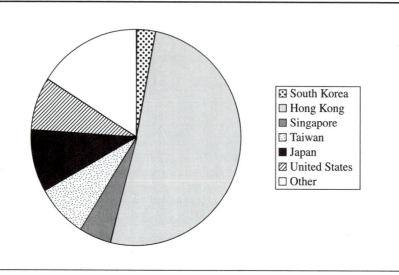

WTO on China will be to force it to make the final reforms of corporate ownership and governance that it has so far been unwilling to make.

In focusing on the outside world, Chinese reformers knew that they had to take advantage of the presence of capital and technology in nearby Hong Kong, Taiwan, and East Asia. However, such capital would not be forthcoming unless the Chinese could offer reasonable safety for foreign investment. Given that Chinese legal protection of property rights was weak and that Chinese courts could not be counted on to enforce the property rights of foreigners, Chinese reformers set up various "free enterprise or trade zones," most located initially in close proximity to Hong Kong, that were exempted from the more restrictive Chinese taxation and regulatory arrangements. Moreover, China liberalized its joint-venture laws to encourage the creation of export-oriented joint ventures in these zones.

The result of this activity was a massive influx of Western capital after 1978 (see Figure 12.3). Starting initially with modest amounts, direct foreign investment in China exceeded a cumulated total of $40 billion by 1996.[33] As Figure 12.3 shows, almost 60 percent of this direct investment initially came from "Greater China" sources—Hong Kong, Macao, and Taiwan.

Although the increase in direct foreign investment was substantial, it remains relatively small on a per capita basis, given China's massive population. In 1994, for example, China attracted $26 of foreign investment per capita, well above India's $1 per capita but well below Mexico's, Chile's, Hungary's, Poland's, and Malaysia's.[34] A major payoff from this foreign investment has been the installation of technology and the creation of marketing savvy that has permitted China to increase its exports. In 1985 Chinese companies with foreign investors exported goods worth less than $1 billion per annum and accounted for about 1 percent of Chinese exports. By 1995 they accounted for almost $50 billion in exports and for 32 percent of Chinese total exports.

Chinese Economic Growth

China's story after 1978 is one of exceedingly rapid economic growth. Figure 12.4 contrasts Chinese and U.S. growth from 1970 to the present. The Chinese series, beginning in 1970, captures the declining growth of China before the reform and the exceedingly rapid growth after its start at the end of the 1970s. In fact, it was this stagnation in the 1970s that provided the impetus for the economic reform itself.[35] Since then, China's economic growth has been among the most rapid in the world, rivaled only by that of the Four Tigers of Southeast Asia and, more recently, of India.

The growth-rate figures are the official figures of the Chinese State Statistics Committee. They have been criticized as being overstated and, in recent years, politicized.[36] Anecdotal evidence, eye witness accounts, and the dramatic changes that are obvious even to casual visitors all confirm, however, that China's growth over more than two decades has been remarkable and that China has been transformed into a different country through its considerable economic progress. The extent of Chinese growth is confirmed by anthropomorphic data: Chinese youths have become much taller, with more healthy body weights, since the reform began.[37] In the concluding chapter, we shall consider whether this progress is likely to continue.

FIGURE 12.4   Real GDP Growth for China and United States, 1970–2000 (in percent)

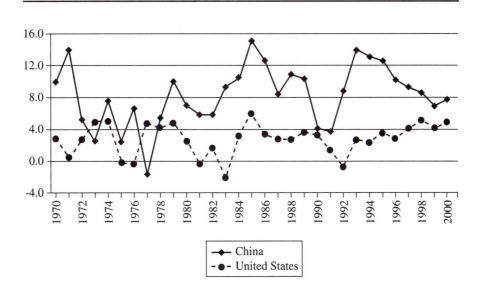

Source: World Development Indicators database.

The Chinese Economic System

We have focused so far on the history of Chinese reform and its remarkable success in terms of economic growth, expansion of exports, and the attraction of direct foreign investment. China's success is remarkable because it lacks many of the usual ingredients required for economic success. Although ownership in agriculture and small-scale service and industrial establishments appears to be in private hands, the ownership of large establishments remains either in the hands of the state or subject to political intervention. There is no standardized "rule of law" in the form of either civil law or common law. Instead, the supreme law emanates from the authority of the Communist party and of top government officials, whose word or influence outweighs any formal law or regulation. What has made China "work" in the absence of clear property rights is, in effect, the guarantee of the party that reform will continue and that China's economy will remain open. These guarantees are far from perfect. A future Communist party leadership could decide to embark on an entirely different course.

We have singled China out for examination in a separate chapter because it exhibits the two main features of market socialism: state ownership and market allocation. There is no doubt that market allocation prevails in China, despite substantial state intervention with respect to large companies. The openness of China's economy means that it must compete in unforgiving world markets that do not tolerate poor economic decision making for long.

Corporate Governance and Property Rights

The matter of "state ownership" is more complicated. As we noted in Chapter 2, ownership entails formal ownership, control rights, and the right to receive the income and other benefits that the property generates. China's formal property rights are remarkably weak. Even in agriculture and small-scale enterprises, formal private ownership is disguised by long-term "leases" or by "township" or "corporative" ownership. There exist few formal-ownership registers, which establish clear-cut documentation of property ownership. These property rights instead are guaranteed by an implicit contract with state and party authorities, who tacitly agree to the exercise of these property rights.

China's "property rights limbo" is nowhere more evident than in the corporatized SOEs. The state is the formal owner of the corporatized shares, but the management is supposed to operate the company according to market criteria, independently of the owners. One expert on China, however, concludes that "Shareholding enterprises, despite receiving a great deal of attention, have not been able to deliver markedly better results than the Soviet-style SOEs they are replacing. This goes to show that the property rights structure for shareholding firms is still not stable, that property rights relations remain relatively confused, that the reform process still encounters large fluctuations."[38] Although management is theoretically guided and supervised by shareholders, the monitoring capacity of corporate shareholders is not yet established. Some enterprise managers have complete authority; others are directed by state and political leaders. Corporate directors are ill-informed about the enterprises on whose boards they serve. Corporate directorates are often simply renamed government offices. The State Asset Management Bureau, which was established in the 1980s to consolidate supervision and monitoring of state property into a single agency, failed to perform its intended function, in part because of tensions with other government departments. It was abolished as a national-level agency in the late 1990s, and its functions were distributed between the Ministry of Finance and the industrial supervision arm of the Chinese Communist party.

In the earlier period, "the plan was the law." Although it was often difficult to determine what constituted plan fulfillment, it was clear that "laws" were set in the form of plan targets and directives and that the failure of an enterprise or a collective farm to fulfill its plan was a violation of the law of the land. With the move toward a complex open-market economy with numerous forms of ownership (joint ventures, SOEs, corporatized state enterprises, and township enterprises), various businesses have to deal with one another through markets and through administrative agreements. Just as for corporations in other countries, some transactions are made through markets and others are based on administrative orders from the management or from state officials. In either case, there must be a means of ensuring that the transaction is carried out in accordance with agreements made by the contracting parties. If a transnational corporation decides to invest $2 billion in a joint venture with a Chinese company, it must be certain that all parties will meet their contractual obligations. In the Anglo-Saxon and European models, a "rule of law" helps provide this assurance, but rule-of-law enforcement requires clearly defined property rights and an accepted enforcement mechanism, such as courts. If a contract is violated, the injured party may receive, from the offender, damages based on the monetary loss of value to property. This threat (plus other factors, such as harm to reputation and image) induces parties to honor contracts in other countries. In the Chinese case, the transnational corporation would not expect the Chinese courts to protect its property rights; rather, it would expect specific government or party officials—be they local, regional, or national—to act as guarantors of contracts. Hence Chinese contracts are primarily regulated by *relational contracting,* rather than by a rule of law. Given the enormous volume of foreign direct investment in China, Chinese relational contracting appears, to date, to have provided sufficient protection to allow the influx of billions of dollars of investment every year.

The ultimate guarantor of property rights is the Chinese Communist party. Power in China is exercised through the largest coercive apparatus in the world. At the top of this apparatus are 25 to 35 people who make the major policy decisions for the country—the Politburo of the Chinese Communist party. Its standing committee consists of seven individuals who oversee the main functional areas of power, such as public security, the education system, propaganda, and the economy. The branch of the party that influences Chinese daily life the most is concerned with personnel and organization. Every employee of a state enterprise is assigned to a work unit, which controls the employee's housing and oversees the employee's work record. Job moves are approved by personnel committees. In attracting foreign investment, it is, in effect, declaring to the outside world that it will continue its reform course and will be a pillar of stability. The guarantee of the Community party, however, is valuable only so long as that body makes "rational" decisions and remains a stable institution dedicated to economic development. Maintaining the Communist party as a force for stability is more difficult than it appears. First, the party consists of many layers with many interests. The national party has one set of goals; regional party officials must look after the interests of their regions; municipal party leaders are interested in the success of their city. Regional, municipal, and local party leaders represent narrow vested interests that pursue narrow goals. For example, the national interest may require the closing of a large, inefficient plant, but the city party leadership must lobby against its closing to prevent the loss of local employment. Second, in order to be credible, the Chinese Communist party must arrange for the orderly transition of power. If a transnational company is contemplating a billion-dollar investment that will pay off only over decades, it must be confident of an enlightened leadership over this period of time. If aging leaders refuse to retire (perhaps they fear retribution for earlier decisions), a new generation of leaders with new ideas cannot advance. How the Chinese Communist party itself adapts to change and handles the myriad of principal–agent problems within its hierarchy will determine how long it can serve as an anchor for the relational contracts on which the Chinese economy is based.

Capital Markets

The Chinese capital market resembles those of Europe and other parts of Asia inasmuch as most companies obtain their funding through banks, not through stock markets. China, however, is an exceptional case in which FDI investment sometimes accounts for 40 percent of Chinese industrial investment (such as in the 1990s). China has been the world's largest recipient of FDI among the developing countries. FDI has been attracted by China's exceptional growth, its presumed political stability, and its low labor costs. Figure 12.5 shows that China had a 37 percent gross domestic investment rate and a 31 percent gross domestic savings rate in 2000, indicating that a remarkable 16 percent of China's gross domestic investment (equipment, structures, and inventories) was funded by direct foreign investment. Figure 12.5 also confirms China's affinity to the Asian model. Like the other Asian countries, China has an exceptionally high rate of savings. One out of every four dollars of GDP is saved by households or businesses. In the United States, the corresponding figure is one out of every seven dollars. These figures underline the fact that capital formation explains part of China's exceptional growth.

The financial market (equity markets and banks) intermediates between businesses and households with funds to invest and businesses that wish to borrow for investment purposes. An "efficient" system of financial intermediation allocates savings to the investment projects that offer the highest rates of return. If projects that yield 30 percent per annum are passed up in favor of projects that yield 3 percent, financial intermediaries are not doing their work effectively and capital is being misallocated. FDI is allocated among countries and among projects in a cut-throat process of international competition for funds. If transnational companies

FIGURE 12.5   Gross Domestic Savings and Gross Domestic Investment,
China and Other Countries, 2000

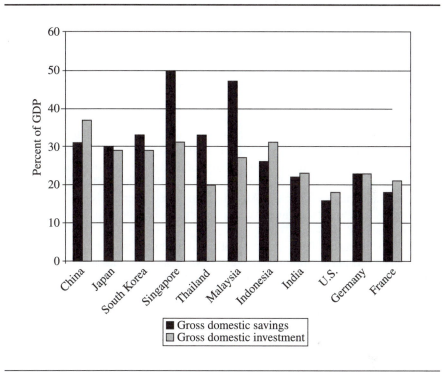

choose to invest in China, they have concluded that China offers the highest rates of return. We must therefore assume that FDI is allocated efficiently to its highest and best uses in China. The same cannot be said of bank loans.

Commercial banks are the major source of financing for Chinese companies.[39] The average Chinese company does not attract FDI and cannot sell new shares of stock because of the corporate governance problems discussed above. Since China reopened its capital market in 1992, funds raised through the sale of new stocks and bonds has accounted only for between 2 percent and 14 percent of total financing. In 2001, 110 billion yuan ($13 billion) was raised in the capital market, whereas banks extended 1,300 billion yuan ($157 billion) of new loans. Thus equity market finance was only 8 percent of the total. The stock market capitalization of China is only 18 percent of GDP, excluding the state-owned stock that cannot be traded in the market, compared with a much higher world average. China falls well below the 30 to 50 percent capitalization of middle-income countries. As a consequence of relying on bank loans, Chinese companies operate with high debt burdens. In the early 1990s, company debt exceeded assets by 25 percent. With such high "leverage," downturns in revenues mean that companies cannot repay their bank loans.

Since initiating its reforms, China has had to rebuild its commercial banking sector. Under the old Soviet-style banking system, there was no distinction between the central bank and commercial banks. A monopoly banking system allocated credit according to credit plans tied to the economic plan. Throughout the early reform period, banks remained the property of the state, and they disbursed loans according to the directives of government and party officials, giving preferential treatment to state enterprises. Private-sector companies had to finance their own activities through their retained earnings and were starved of banking services. The regime has been particularly hostile toward banks not owned by the state, which are taxed heavily and in a discriminatory fashion. Interest rates are regulated on both the loan and deposit sides. Thus the fate of private banks is largely in the hands of banking officials.[40] The Big Four commercial banks—Bank of China, Industrial and Commercial Bank of China, Agricultural Bank of China, and China Construction Bank—control about two-thirds of the banking system. Each of these giant banks employs hundreds of thousands of people at thousands of branches. Although top management has tried to institute reforms, it is hard to get such massive bureaucratic organizations to change their way of doing business.

As a consequence of state direction of credits, China's commercial banks have a high ratio of **non-performing loans (NPLs)**. NPLs are loans that are not being serviced with interest and principal payments and will probably not be repaid. The NPL ratio for the state-owned banks and municipal banks averages 25 percent; for joint stock banks, the NPL ratio is 13 percent—a much improved figure, but unacceptably high by any international banking standard. These ratios suggest that, at best, $13 of every $100 of loans will eventually be repaid. China's banks therefore face a major bad-loan problem that would challenge the management of any bank, but China's banks are run by relatively inexperienced staffs and have their own corporate culture dominated by political intervention.

Banks with such high proportions of NPLs typically write them off and take the losses. If the losses are not too high, the bank can survive. In China's case, Chinese banks have not had to write off bad loans because the Central Bank and the Ministry of Finance have served as lenders of last resort. In order to improve the operations of commercial banking, the government began a series of major reforms in 1997. Independent asset-management companies were established to dispose of the massive volume of NPLs held by the stated-owned commercial banks. In order to provide China's ailing banks with adequate capital to handle the almost $150 billion of bad loans, a total of $30 billion was injected into the state-owned commercial banks by the government.[41] To provide a sense of proportion, China's GDP is around $1.3 trillion; therefore, bad loans equal about 10 percent of GDP. China's official budget deficit in 2000 was around 1 percent of GDP, or about $13 billion. The government's injection of credit was therefore greater than the entire government deficit.[42]

China's accession to the World Trade Organization (WTO) poses additional challenges for China's commercial banks. Under WTO provisions, domestic banks must compete with foreign banks. Under promises that Beijing made when China joined the WTO, by the end of 2006, foreign banks will have the same rights as domestic banks. Chinese banking officials worry that transnational banks such as Citibank, based in

New York, or HSBC, based in London, will come to dominate the Chinese banking market. China is therefore currently inviting foreign investors to take minority stakes in smaller banks so that the small bank can learn Western banking skills from them. Although foreign banks usually do not like joint ventures, they may be willing to make compromises as the price of entry into China. HSBC has already purchased an 8 percent stake in Bank of Shanghai, which has begun to compete in selling "new banking products," such as credit cards, mutual funds, and insurance, to Bank of Shanghai's 6 million customers.[43]

Labor Markets

Under China's old Soviet-style system, employees of SOEs had a virtual guaranty of lifetime employment. Large SOEs were often the major employer in the city or region, providing for the social, health, educational, and cultural needs not only of employees but also of the community. Labor unions were state-sponsored, and their job was to ensure that workers fulfilled the plan, not to lobby for better wages and working conditions. Under the old system, there was no concern about unemployment. The plan would ensure that every able-bodied person had a job. Enterprises operated under soft budget constraints. With little interest in profits, enterprises kept too many employees on the payroll. Even redundant employees could be useful at times to fulfill a difficult plan.

This type of labor market was clearly not suited to new market conditions. As private enterprises gained ascendancy in agriculture and small-scale establishments, they limited their hiring to employees who could add to profits. Competition in world markets dictated that the product be produced efficiently and at high quality; there was no room for redundant workers in export industries. Thus the last haven for redundant workers was the SOE, which still received subsidies and credits to keep it in business. In this new environment, a rebirth of a strong, independent labor movement was not to be expected. Labor unions were regarded by the party leadership as potential political competitors. Lacking formal work rules, such as procedures for hiring and firing, maximum work hours, and overtime pay, the new Chinese labor market was among the most unregulated in the world. The major constraint on the political leadership was that layoffs and unemployment should not lead to massive labor unrest.

Given initial overemployment, one measure of reform is employment trends. Despite official fears of urban unrest, employment in the entire state sector dropped from the 1994–1995 peak of 112 million to 85.7 million at year-end 1999, with further cuts in store. Some 20 million workers were furloughed, eventually to be cut off entirely from state-owned enterprises.[44] It may be that such cuts have been facilitated by the growth of the economy at large and by the expansion of private employment opportunities. Nevertheless, there are communities where the SOE remains a key source of employment. Managers of state enterprises still lack the power to reward key personnel. They are still subject to political supervision, despite their new status as shareholder companies. For example, Beijing's municipal government issues guidelines for wage payments to workers, technicians, and managers in enterprises operating under state, collective, and "other" ownership.

It remains unclear whether China's unregulated labor market will continue as is. The WTO is considering adding labor standards and environmental regulations to its repertoire of potential reforms. The WTO's foray into social issues would be at odds with China's interest in maintaining a cheap and flexible labor force, thus creating another source of conflict with WTO rules.

Economic Security and Inequality

The Chinese Constitution of 1982 (Articles 44 and 45) provides that retirees shall enjoy the benefits of social security and that the state shall establish a system of social insurance, social assistance, and medical care. Under current provisions, state enterprises are supposed to pay a social security tax equal to 20 percent of their payroll, plus another 8 percent for health and unemployment insurance. The state finances only the administration of the system; it makes no other contribution. As in Europe and the United States, the Chinese state social security system is a pay-as-you-go system, and social security taxes go into the general revenue fund. This system went into effect only in 1991, so the coverage of those in the system before that date remains unclear. Moreover, because of the financial condition of state-owned enterprises, only about 70 percent of the social security taxes are actually collected. China is also experimenting with privatized social security accounts. The state system covers primarily employees in urban state enterprises and excludes those out of the labor force and those living in the countryside. Hence the state system covers less than 20 percent of the population. The privatized social security accounts are meant to cover the remainder. The state system currently replaces only 20 percent of pre-retirement income.[45] Although retirement ages of state employees remain the same, there is now the question of how pensions will be funded, particularly if large state-owned enterprises are allowed to fail. Those falling outside the state system, who work for private companies or for themselves, must see to their own retirement.

The weakness of the official social security system explains, in large part, the high rate of household savings in China, which is an astronomical 40 percent of household income.[46] Cultural factors explain the rest—self-reliance and family support are strong values. Figure 12.6 makes it clear that the Chinese government does not have the resources to support a massive European-style social security system. Its GDP share of taxes is less than 15 percent, a figure that is in line with other poor Asian countries.

China began its reform era with a relatively even distribution of income. All property was owned by the state; able-bodied persons worked either in collective or state farms or in state enterprises earning wages set by the state. Entrepreneurial incomes were illegal. Workers, with a guarantee of lifetime employment and an obligatory retirement age of 60 (men) and 55 (women), would receive a state pension upon retirement. China's market reforms have changed the distribution of income dramatically. Figure 12.7 shows that China's income distribution is now similar to that of other relatively poor Asian countries and is on a par with the United States. The dramatic rise in inequality is exactly what would be expected from the move to private enterprise, the increase in entrepreneurship, and the stagnation of the large SOEs.

FIGURE 12.6   China's Tax Burden Compared with Other Countries, 2000

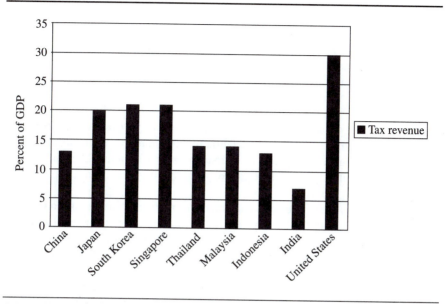

Source: Asian Development Bank.

FIGURE 12.7   Chinese Inequality of Income Distribution as Measured by
the Gini Coefficient

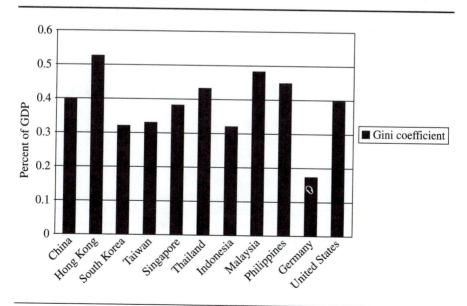

Source: Asian Development Bank, Poverty Database, *http://www.abd.org*

Summary

- China, the world's most populous country, has had exceptionally rapid growth for more than two decades, as it has moved toward a model of market socialism that combines market forces with strong state and party control.
- In the early years of communist rule in China, the Soviet model was applied with substantial regional diversity but abundant natural resources. Between 1949 and the contemporary reform era, the beginnings of Chinese socialism unfolded under Mao Zedong.
- During the first decade of socialism in China, the basic Soviet model was implemented, characterized by the socialization of agriculture, by nationalization, and by the development of a system of national economic planning. A major feature of this era was the dominance of ideology, exhibited by the Great Leap Forward campaign of the mid- to late 1950s.
- The latter half of the 1960s was characterized by the dominance of the Cultural Revolution. Although the ideological changes made during this period had major impacts on the Chinese economy, the basic organizational arrangements of the economic system seemed to undergo relatively little change.
- The reforms begun by Deng Xiaoping opened the Chinese economy to world trade and FDI and created new forms of ownership, while maintaining the political monopoly of the Communist Party. These reforms created rapid economic growth.

Key Terms

market socialism

Hundred Flowers Campaign

Great Leap Forward

Rural Peoples Communes

Cultural Revolution

Gang of Four

production team

contract responsibility system

state-owned enterprises (SOEs)

corporatized

foreign direct investment (FDI)

portfolio investment

non-performing loans (NPLs)

Notes

1. "Survey China," *The Economist,* March 8, 1997, p. 5.
2. For a useful long-term comparison of basic economic and developmental indicators, see Arthur G. Ashbrook, Jr., "China: Economic Modernization and Long-Term Performance," in U.S. Congress, Joint Economic Committee, *China Under the Four Modernizations,* Part 2, Section 5 (Washington, D.C.: U.S. Government Printing Office, 1982), pp. 151–368.
3. There was some unrest and disruption in China, but markedly less than that which occurred in the Soviet Union. For a comparison, see Jan S. Prybyla, *The Political Economy of Communist China* (Scranton, Pa.: International Textbook, 1970), Ch. 5.
4. For a useful outline of the basic features of the Chinese administrative structure and changes through time, see Thomas G. Rawski, "China's Industrial System," in U.S. Congress, Joint Economic Committee, *China: A Reassessment of the Economy* (Washington, D.C.:

U.S. Government Printing Office, 1975), pp. 175–198. For a later comparison of the Chinese experience and the Soviet experience, see Robert F. Dernberger, "The Chinese Search for the Path of Self-Sustained Growth in the 1980s: An Assessment," in Joint Economic Committee, *China Under the Four Modernizations,* Part 1, pp. 19–76.

5. Prybyla, *The Political Economy of Communist China,* pp. 144–145.

6. For example, in terms of agricultural performance, we might make the following crude comparison. In China in 1949, grain production was 0.20 metric tons per capita; in the Soviet Union in 1928–1929, grain production was 0.47 metric tons per capita. Chinese data are from Ashbrook, "China: Economic Modernization and Long-Term Performance," p. 104; Paul R. Gregory and Robert C. Stuart, *Soviet Economic Structure and Performance,* 3rd ed. (New York: Harper & Row, 1986), p. 244; and TsSU (Central Statistical Administration), *Naselenie SSSR 1973* (Moscow: Statistika, 1975), p. 7.

7. These data are from Prybyla, *The Political Economy of Communist China,* pp. 135 ff.

8. For a discussion of this period, see Roderick MacFarquhar, *The Hundred Flowers Campaign and the Chinese Intellectuals* (New York: Praeger, 1960).

9. For a discussion of the early commune, see Kenneth R. Walker, "Organization of Agricultural Production," in Alexander Eckstein, Walter Galenson, and Ta-Chung Liu, eds., *Economic Trends in Communist China* (Chicago: Aldine, 1968), pp. 440–452. For a study of the private sector, see Kenneth R. Walker, *Planning in Chinese Agriculture: Socialization and the Private Sector, 1956–1962* (Chicago: Aldine, 1965). For an update on organizational changes into the 1970s, see Frederick W. Crook, "The Commune System in the People's Republic of China, 1963–74," in Joint Economic Committee, *China: A Reassessment of the Economy,* pp. 366–410; a useful recent source is Frederic M. Surls and Francis C. Tuan, "China's Agriculture in the Eighties," in Joint Economic Committee, *China Under the Four Modernizations,* Part 1, pp. 419–448.

10. Subramanian Swamy, "Economic Growth in China and India 1952–1970: A Comparative Appraisal," *Economic Development and Cultural Change,* 21 (July 1973), 62.

11. *Ibid.*

12. An excellent survey of these years can be found in Dernberger, "The Chinese Search for the Path of Self-Sustained Growth," pp. 19–76.

13. For a discussion of the revolutionary left in the economic context, see Robert F. Dernberger and David Fasenfest, "China's Post-Mao Economic Future," in U.S. Congress, Joint Economic Committee, *Chinese Economy Post-Mao* (Washington, D.C.: U.S. Government Printing Office, 1978), pp. 3–47.

14. There is a great deal of literature pertaining to the Chinese economy. For a useful survey of events in the 1990s, see Dwight Perkins, "Completing China's Move to the Market," *Journal of Economic Perspectives* 8 (Spring 1994), 23–46; Gary H. Jefferson and Thomas G. Rawski, "Enterprise Reform in Chinese Industry," *Journal of Economic Perspectives* 8 (Spring 1994), 47–70; Shahid Yusuf, "China's Macroeconomic Performance and Management During Transition," *Journal of Economic Perspectives* 8 (Spring 1994), 71–92; "China's Economic Reforms: Structural and Welfare Aspects," *American Economic Review Papers and Proceedings* 84 (May 1994), 266–284; and *China: Statistical Yearbook 1993* (Bejing: State Statistical Bureau of the People's Republic of China, 1993).

15. Frederick W. Crook, "The Commune System in the People's Republic of China, 1963–1974," in Joint Economic Committee, *China: A Reassessment of the Economy,* pp. 411–437.

16. For a discussion of pre-reform arrangements, see Henry J. Groen and James A. Kilpatrick, "China's Agricultural Production," in Joint Economic Committee, *Chinese Economy Post-Mao,* Vol. 1, pp. 607–652.

17. For a discussion of changes in the rural economy, see Kuan-I Chen, "China's Changing Agricultural System," *Current History* 82 (September 1983), 259–263, 277–278; Kuan-I Chen,

"China's Food Policy and Population," *Current History* 82 (September 1983), 257–260, 274–276; Yak-Yeow Kueh, "China's New Agricultural-Policy Program: Major Economic Consequences, 1979–1983," *Journal of Comparative Economics* 8 (December 1984), 353–375; Nicholas R. Lardy, *Agriculture in China's Modern Economic Development* (Cambridge: Cambridge University Press, 1983); Dwight Perkins and Shahid Yusuf, *Rural Development in China* (Baltimore: Johns Hopkins University Press, 1984); Kenneth R. Walker, "Chinese Agriculture During the Period of Readjustment, 1978–83," *China Quarterly* 100 (December 1984), 783–812; Kenneth R. Walker, *Food Grain Procurement and Consumption in China* (Cambridge: Cambridge University Press, 1984); Peter Nolan and Dong Fureng, eds., *Market Forces in China* (London: Zed Books, 1990); and Anthony Y. C. Koo, "The Contract Responsibility System: Transition from a Planned to a Market Economy," *Economic Development and Cultural Change* 38 (July 1990), 797–820.

18. Perkins, "Completing China's Move to the Market," p. 26.
19. Dwight Perkins, "Reforming China's Economic System," *Journal of Economic Literature* 36, 2 (June 1988), 609.
20. *Ibid.,* pp. 809–810.
21. *Ibid.,* pp. 615–616.
22. This section is largely based on Thomas G. Rawski, "Is China's State Enterprise Problem Still Important?" prepared for a Workshop on "China's SOE Reform and Privatization," University of Tokyo, June 25, 2000.
23. Report by John Langlois, Summer Conference of American Enterprises Institute, May 3, 2001, entitled "Challenges Facing China's Reform," *http://www.aei.org*
24. Report by Edward Steinfield, Summer Conference of American Enterprises Institute, May 3, 2001, entitled "Challenges Facing China's Reform," *http://www.aie.org*
25. Rawski, "Is China's State Enterprise System Still Important?"
26. Gary H. Jefferson, Thomas G. Rawski, Wand Li, and Zheng Yuxin, "Ownership, Productivity Change, and Financial Performance in Chinese Industry," *Journal of Comparative Economics,* 28, 4 (2000), 786–813.
27. Chu-yuan Cheng, "China's Industrialization and Economic Development," *Current History* 82 (September 1983), 266.
28. World Bank, *World Development Report 1993* (New York: Oxford University Press, 1993), Table 2.
29. United Nations, *World Investment Report 2001,* p. 27, Figure 1.
30. *World Investment Report 2001,* p. 26.
31. *http:www.chinalegalchange.com*
32. "China Seeks Tariff Talks," *International Herald Tribune,* March 16–17, 2002.
33. *The Economist,* 1997, p. 10.
34. *Ibid.*
35. Nicolas Lardy, *Agriculture in China's Modern Economic Development* (Cambridge: Cambridge University Press, 1983), pp. 88, 159.
36. Thomas Rawski, "What's Happening to China's GDP Statistics?" *China Economic Review,* 12, 4 (December 2001).
37. Stephen Morgan, "Richer and Taller: Stature and Living Standards in China, 1979–1995," *China Journal* 44 (July 2000), 1–40.
38. Quoted in Rawski, "What's Happening to China's GDP Statistics?"
39. This section is largely based on Jiang Jianquing, "China: Government Initiatives Vital to Growth of Commercial Banking Sector," *Asian Banker,* April 1, 2002, *http://www. theasianbanker. com*

40. Remarks by Yasheng Huang, Summer Conference of American Enterprises Institute, entitled "Challenges Facing China's Reform," May 3, 2001, *http://www.aei.org*

41. We are using an exchange rate of approximately of 0.11 yuan to the dollar.

42. These figures are from Asian Development Bank, *Country Strategy and Program Update, 2002–2004,* Table 26.

43. *Beltonhttp://www.businessweek.com/bwdaily/dnflash/aug2002/nf20020829_4026.htm*

44. Remarks by Yasheng Huang, Summer Conference of American Enterprises Institute.

45. Yang Yansui, "The Analysis of the Structure of the Social Security System in China," CCER-NBER Annual Meeting, Analysis and Structure of the Social Security System in China, March 2002, *http://www.ccer.edu.cn/en/*

46. Calculated from World Bank, *World Development Indicators 1999,* p. 220.

Recommended Readings

General Works

Richard Baum, ed., *China's Four Modernizations: The New Technological Revolution* (Boulder, Colo.: Westview Press, 1980).

Chu-yuan Cheng, *China's Economic Development: Growth and Structural Change* (Boulder, Colo.: Westview Press, 1982).

Gregory Chow, *The Chinese Economy* (New York: Harper & Row, 1984).

Robert F. Dernberger, ed., *China's Development Experience in Comparative Perspective* (Cambridge, Mass.: Harvard University Press, 1980).

Audrey Donnithorne, *China's Economic System* (New York: Praeger, 1967).

Alexander Eckstein, *China's Economic Development: The Interplay of Scarcity and Ideology* (Ann Arbor: University of Michigan Press, 1975).

————, *China's Economic Revolution* (New York: Cambridge University Press, 1977).

————, *Communist China's Economic Growth and Foreign Trade* (New York: McGraw-Hill, 1969).

Alexander Eckstein, Walter Galenson, and Ta-Chung Liu, eds., *Economic Trends in Communist China* (Chicago: Aldine, 1968).

Christopher Howe, *China's Economy: A Basic Guide* (New York: Basic Books, 1978).

Gary H. Jefferson and Wenyi Yu, "The Impact of Reform on Socialist Enterprises in Transition: Structure, Conduct, and Performance in Chinese Industry," *Journal of Comparative Economics* 15 (January 1991), 45–54.

Zhiling Lin and Thomas Robinson, eds., *The Chinese and Their Future: Beijing, Taipei, and Hong Kong* (Washington, D.C.: American Enterprise Institute, 1994).

Thomas P. Lyons, *Economic Integration and Planning in Maoist China* (New York: Columbia University Press, 1987).

Nicholas Lardy, *Economic Growth and Distribution in China* (New York: Cambridge University Press, 1979).

Jun Ma, *Intergovernmental Relations and Economic Management in China* (New York: St. Martin's, 1997).

Jan S. Prybyla, *The Chinese Economy: Problems and Policies,* 2nd ed. (Columbia: University of South Carolina Press, 1981).

————, *The Political Economy of Communist China* (Scranton, Pa.: International Textbook, 1970).

Carl Riskin, *China's Political Economy* (New York: Oxford University Press, 1987).

Kai Yuen Tsui, "China's Regional Inequality, 1952–1985," *Journal of Comparative Economics* 15 (March 1991), 1–21.

U.S. Congress, Joint Economic Committee, *China: A Reassessment of the Economy* (Washington, D.C.: U.S. Government Printing Office, 1975).

———, *China Under the Four Modernizations* (Washington, D.C.: U.S. Government Printing Office, 1982).

———, *Chinese Economy Post-Mao* (Washington, D.C.: U.S. Government Printing Office, 1978).

———, *An Economic Profile of Mainland China,* Vols. 1 and 2 (Washington, D.C.: U.S. Government Printing Office, 1967).

———, *China's Economic Dilemmas in the 1990s: The Problems of Reforms, Modernization, and Interdependence,* Vols. 1 and 2 (Washington, D.C.: U.S. Government Printing Office, 1991).

The Rural Economy

William A. Byrd and Lin Qingsong, eds., *China's Rural Industry* (New York: Oxford University Press, 1991).

Kang Chao, *Man and Land in Chinese History: An Economic Analysis* (Stanford, Calif.: Stanford University Press, 1987).

Kuan-I Chen, "China's Food Policy and Population," *Current History* 86 (September 1987), 257–260, 274–276.

Christopher Findlay, Andrew Watson, and Harry X. Wu, eds., *Rural Enterprises in China* (New York: St. Martin's, 1994).

Yak-Yeow Kueh, "China's New Agricultural-Policy Program: Major Economic Consequences, 1979–1983," *Journal of Comparative Economics* 8 (December 1984), 353–375.

Justin Yitu Lin, "Rural Reforms and Agricultural Growth in China," *American Economic Review* 82 (March 1992), 34–51.

Nicholas R. Lardy, *Agriculture in China's Modern Economic Development* (Cambridge: Cambridge University Press, 1983).

Victor Nee and Frank W. Young, "Peasant Entrepreneurs in China's 'Second Economy': An Institutional Analysis," *Economic Development and Cultural Change* 37 (January 1991), 293–310.

Dwight H. Perkins, *Agricultural Development in China, 1368–1968* (Chicago: University of Chicago Press, 1969).

———, ed., *Rural Small-Scale Industry in the People's Republic of China* (Berkeley: University of California Press, 1977).

Shugiei Wao, *Agricultural Reform and Grain Production in China* (New York: St. Martin's Press, 1994).

Economic Reform

Willam A. Byrd, ed., *Chinese Industrial Firms Under Reform* (Oxford: Oxford University Press, 1992).

Richard Conroy, *Technological Change in China* (Paris: OECD, 1992).

Kang Chen, Gary H. Jefferson, and Inderjit Singh, "Lessons from China's Economic Reform," *Journal of Comparative Economics* 16 (1992), 201–225.

Directorate of Intelligence, *The Chinese Economy in 1991 and 1992: Pressure to Revisit Reform Mounts* (Washington, D.C.: Central Intelligence Agency, 1992).

————, *China's Economy in 1992 and 1993: Grappling with the Risks of Rapid Economic Growth* (Washington, D.C.: Central Intelligence Agency, 1993).

————, *China's Economy in 1994 and 1995: Overheating Pressures Recede, Tough Choices Remain* (Washington, D.C.: Central Intelligence Agency, 1995).

————, *China's Economy in 1995–97* (Washington, D.C.: Central Intelligence Agency, 1997).

Qimiao Fan and Peter Nolan, *China's Economic Reforms* (New York: St. Martin's, 1994).

Joseph Fewsmith, *Dilemmas of Reform in China* (Armonk, N.Y.: M.E. Sharpe, 1994).

David Granick, *Chinese State Enterprises: A Regional Property Rights Analysis* (Chicago: University of Chicago Press, 1990).

Keith Griffin and Zhao Renwei, eds., *The Distribution of Income in China* (New York: St. Martin's, 1993).

————, *China's Economy in 1983 and 1984: The Search for a Soft Landing* (Washington D.C.: Central Intelligence Agency, 1994).

Gary H. Jefferson and Thomas G. Rawski, "Enterprise Reform in Chinese Industry," *Journal of Economic Perspectives* 8 (Spring 1994), 47–70.

Gary H. Jefferson, Thomas G. Rawski, and Yuxin Zheng, "Growth, Efficiency, and Convergence in China's State and Collective Industry," *Economic Development and Cultural Change* 40 (1992a), 239–266.

Hsueh Jien-tsung, Sung Yun-wing, and Yu Jingyuan, *Studies on Economic Reform and Development in the People's Republic of China* (New York: St. Martin's, 1993).

Deborah A. Kaple, *Dream of a Red Factory* (New York: Oxford University Press, 1994).

Anthony Y. C. Koo, "The Contract Responsibility System: Transition from a Planned to a Market Economy," *Economic Development and Cultural Change* 38 (July 1990), 797–820.

Deepak Lal, "The Failure of the Three Envelopes: The Analytics and Political Economy of the Reform of Chinese State-Owned Enterprises" *European Economic Review* 34 (September 1990), 1213–1231.

Nicholas R. Lardy, *China in the World Economy* (Washington, D.C.: Institute for International Economics, 1984).

Justin Yitu Lin, Fang Cai, and Zhou Li, *The China Miracle* (Hong Kong: Chinese University Press, 1996).

Ike Mathur and Chen Jui-Sheng, *Strategies for Joint Ventures in the People's Republic of China* (New York: Praeger, 1987).

Barry Naughton, *Growing Out of the Plan: Chinese Economic Reform, 1978–1993* (New York: Cambridge University Press, 1993).

Ole Odgaard, *Private Enterprises in Rural China* (Brookfield, Vt.: Ashgate, 1992).

Dwight H. Perkins, "Completing China's Move to a Market Economy," *Journal of Economic Perspectives* 8 (Spring 1994), 23–46.

Elizabeth J. Perry and Christine Wong, *The Political Economy of Reform in Post-Mao China* (Cambridge, Mass.: Harvard University Press, 1987).

Jan S. Prybyla, "Mainland China's Economic System: A Study in Contradictions," *Issues & Studies* 30, 8 (August 1994), 1–30.

Susan L. Shirk, *The Political Logic of Economic Reform in China* (Berkeley: University of California Press, 1993).

Clement Tisdell, *Economic Development in the Context of China* (New York: St. Martin's, 1993).

George Totten and Zhou Shulian, eds., *China's Economic Reform* (Boulder, Colo.: Westview, 1992).

Lim Wei and Arnold Chao, eds., *China's Economic Reforms* (Philadelphia: University of Pennsylvania Press, 1983).

Gordon White, "The Politics of Economic Reform in Chinese Industry: The Introduction of the Labour Contract System," *China Quarterly* 11 (September 1987), 365–389.

Christine P. Wong, "The Economics of Shortages and Problems of Reform in Chinese Industry," *Journal of Comparative Economics* 10 (December 1986), 363–387.

Susumi Yabuki, *China's New Political Economy: The Giant Awakes* (Boulder, Colo.: Westview, 1995).

Shahid Yusuf, "China's Macroeconomic Performance and Management During Transition," *Journal of Economic Perspectives* 8 (Spring 1994), 71–92.

13

The Command Economies: Performance and Decline

There is probably no issue in the field of comparative economic systems of greater relevance than the issue of comparative performance. After all, in the early chapters of this book, we emphasized that systems and policies differ and that performance differences can be related to these differences. If we are to assess the relative merits of different arrangements, then we need to be able to associate these arrangements with performance. Moreover, the collapse of the command economies ushered in the transition era to which we turn in the remaining chapters of this book.

In this chapter, we focus on two important performance issues. First, returning to the classification of economic systems that we developed in the early chapters of this book, can we compare performance across real-world variants of these systems in order to make some basic judgments about comparative performance as it relates to the economic system? Second, in light of the demise of a number of the planned socialist economic systems, can we relate problems with economic performance to systemic arrangements in these cases? To put it differently, what factors led to the demise of the administrative-command systems?

The reader might well ask why are we interested in the performance of systems that have collapsed. There are several reasons. From both a theoretical and a practical standpoint, the reasons for the decline of the planned economies are important. These major system variants, some of which still exist, experienced major economic problems. Moreover, as these systems collapsed, many of the economic problems that they experienced remained (and in some cases still remain) in the transition era. Moreover, many contemporary systems are in fact mixed systems, in which components from a wide variety of systems are employed. Their experience is therefore fundamental to our knowledge about contemporary economic systems—and especially about the nature of change in modern economic systems.

Problems of Evaluation

In Part I of this book, we emphasized that system objectives differ from one case to another. Socialist systems have typically pursued different objectives than capitalist systems. The pursuit and achievement of each objective represent a cost in terms of resources used, so difficult choices must be made in any system. Unfortunately, unless different systems pursue the same goals and in fact assign the same weight to each, it is difficult to evaluate the overall performance of the differing economic systems.

There is no way in which we can identify single or dominant **system objectives**, so in the end, we find ourselves making subjective judgments about which goals are "best" as we make comparisons of performance.

Evaluating economic performance is not easy even if we isolate a single dominant objective—for example, economic growth. Suppose we wish to compare the growth experience of socialist and capitalist economic systems. Assuming that we can agree on basic system definitions, how will we decide what systems to evaluate, and over what time frame will the evaluation be performed? How will we control nonsystem characteristics such as the level of economic development? Some criterion for selection must be used. For example, should we choose **representative economic systems**, and if we do so, how will we approach the selection process? If we consider a sampling approach, the relatively small number of planned socialist systems in that particular population poses serious problems.

For performance comparisons to be valid, the *ceteris paribus* assumption must hold. The economies compared should be alike *in all respects* except their economic systems. In Chapter 3, the *ceteris paribus* problem was described as follows: Outcomes (O) are a function of a variety of environmental factors (ENV; for example, natural and human resource endowments and level of development), economic policy (POL), and the economic system (ES).

$$O = f(\text{ENV, POL, ES}) \tag{13.1}$$

Because ENV and POL differ by country, one cannot make a statement about the impact of ES on outcomes without clearly understanding the role of the ENV and POL factors.

Labor productivity in the Soviet Union was always low relative to that in the United States and industrialized Western Europe.[1] The question, however, is whether this was a consequence of the *system* or a product of the other factors (ENV, POL). The level of economic development of the Soviet Union always lagged behind that of the United States and Western Europe, and productivity is positively associated with economic development. Can the Soviet productivity gap be accounted for entirely by these other factors, or was the economic system itself to blame? *Long-term* economic growth in the Soviet Union outpaced that in the United States and Western Europe through the 1970s.[2] Was this a consequence of the economic system or of other factors?

Two related approaches can be used to deal with this problem. The first is to compare economies that are alike in all respects other than economic system. In terms of equation 13.1, this means making performance comparisons only in instances where ENV and POL are equal so that any differences in performance can be attributed to the system. Perhaps the best example (though an imperfect one) is the comparison of previously unified countries that belonged to different economic blocs (East and West Germany or North and South Korea, for example), but such examples are rare.[3] The basic drawback is that real-world cases where all factors other than the economic system are constant do not exist.

The econometric approach to the *ceteris paribus* problem requires estimation of the impact of the ENV and POL factors on O. Once their impact is known, these factors can be held constant, revealing the impact of the economic system on performance.

This approach requires the investigation of *groups* of capitalist and socialist economies that differ in ENV and POL characteristics, so that their impact can be isolated and held constant.[4]

Because economic systems are multidimensional, their attributes are difficult to measure, and we cannot formulate an *objective* and *quantitative* measure of ES that differentiates among economies in terms of the degree of capitalism or of planned or market socialism. We cannot determine whether the Soviet economy was "more planned socialist" than the East German economy was or whether the U.S. economy is "more capitalist" than the British economy. Therefore, we must bunch real-world economies into political–economic groupings without being able to hold constant the effect of variations in ES *within* a particular group.

Real-world economies are grouped into two categories: capitalism and planned socialism. This requires combining economies that differ in important respects. In the comparisons that follow, intermediate- and low-income countries such as Greece, Spain, Turkey, and India are included in the "capitalist" group, despite their substantial differences from industrialized capitalist countries. There was much greater homogeneity within the planned socialist group prior to the reforms of the late 1980s. Yet even they had differences (ownership and control arrangements in agriculture), so the planned socialist economies were by no means uniform.[5]

How well the representatives of economic systems have actually performed is the appropriate standard for evaluating the performance of economic systems. What counts is not how an economic system might conceivably perform under ideal circumstances, but how well it performs in the real world.

The Performance of Systems

Recognizing the difficulties inherent in evaluating economic systems, we use the most important performance indicators—economic growth, economic efficiency, the "fairness" of the distribution of income, and economic stability—to determine how well selected representatives of capitalism and socialism have performed. The available empirical evidence is updated with any new evidence that exists.

The Choice of Countries

The selection of representatives of capitalism and socialism is constrained by the availability of data. Data limitations dictate that we emphasize comparisons of the former Soviet Union and East European nations with the industrialized and near-industrialized capitalist nations.[6] The data for the smaller Asian communist countries (North Korea, Vietnam, Cambodia, and Mongolia) are too meager to support meaningful comparisons.[7]

How about the performance of China during the command era vis-à-vis its non-communist Asian counterparts? China may be representative of planned socialism in a large and backward economy. Chinese economic performance has been significantly affected by political upheavals. There is the further difficulty of finding appropriate counterparts against which to gauge China's economic performance. Should China be measured against Japan (an immediate Asian neighbor), against India[8] (another Asian neighbor, almost equally populous), or against the large and small noncommunist Asian nations combined? If the yardstick is Japan, then Chinese performance will not be impressive; if Bangladesh, it will be. Moreover, in the era since the late 1970s, major reforms in China (examined in Chapter 12) have significantly altered the nature of the Chinese economic system.

Data: Concepts and Reliability

Economic aggregates, such as GDP, industrial production, and per capita consumption, were not compiled uniformly by the statistical agencies in Eastern and Western countries.[9] The planned socialist nations used the concept of *net material product* and excluded from final output "nonproductive" services—those that did not directly support material production. The aggregate figures used in this chapter are recalculations that make the planned socialist figures conform as closely as possible to Western national accounting practices.[10] Western recalculations of Soviet and East European national accounts made adjustments for omitted costs and for omitted product categories (such as services). They all used the **adjusted factor cost concept** pioneered by Abram Bergson.[11] Western economists were not in a position to recalculate the output of planned socialist economies on the basis of utility values. If planners dictated the production of goods and services that did not raise welfare (such as excessively heavy reinforced concrete, inferior shoes, and the collected works of Leonid Brezhnev), we have no choice but to value those goods and services at the cost of supplying them. A market economy might reject these goods and services (by setting zero prices), but a planned socialist economy dictated by planners' preferences would continue to order their production.

The *Glasnost* movement that swept through the Soviet Union and Eastern Europe in the second half of the 1980s raised serious questions about statistical reliability.[12] For example, Romanian statistical authorities subsequently revealed that their statistics contained wild exaggerations of economic performance. Independent estimates by Soviet economists and journalists claim that official Soviet statistics overstated growth by a factor of more than 2.[13] These issues, as we will see later, have made it very difficult to develop meaningful comparisons of the command and transition eras.

The demise of the Soviet Union and the other planned socialist economies of Eastern Europe has made the matter of accessing accurate and meaningful statistical information complex. Although the situation may appear dramatically better, that is not necessarily the case. First, because the former planned socialist systems generally began the conversion to Western accounting practices at or just prior to the end of the plan era, new series for earlier years (for example, relating to the components of national income) were not necessarily generated. Second, the new empirical evidence that has become available is highly variable. Finally, the availability of new data does not necessarily mean that new analysis has been done in the 1990s.

An Economic Profile: Structural Characteristics of East and West

Table 13.1 provides an economic profile of the planned socialist countries and selected capitalist countries. This profile shows what factors should be held constant in performance comparisons, and it offers insights into the socialist model of industrialization.[14] We focus on the mid-1980s as a period of relative "normalcy" in Eastern Europe prior to the dramatic changes of the late 1980s.

In terms of per capita income, the Soviet Union and Eastern Europe were well behind the advanced capitalist countries in the mid-1980s. The per capita incomes in the more advanced planned socialist economies (Czechoslovakia, East Germany, and the Soviet Union) were well below those in Japan and the United Kingdom and between those in Italy and Spain. Poland, Romania, and Hungary and the less advanced Bulgaria were well below Italy and Spain but close to Greece. The planned socialist countries as a group were less advanced than the industrialized Western countries with which they were most often compared.

Despite relatively low per capita income, the share of industry and construction in GDP in the socialist countries was roughly equal to that of the capitalist countries in the mid-1980s. In fact, the socialist industry share averaged 43 percent; the average of capitalist countries (United States to Italy) was 36 percent. One would have to conclude that if per capita income were held constant, the planned socialist industry share would be high relative to capitalism. The socialist shares of agriculture and services were even more different from their Western counterparts. Agriculture's share of both GDP and labor force emerged as quite high in the planned socialist countries once per capita income was held constant, but the share of the service sector was well below that of capitalist countries at similar levels of development. The data on investment rates do not yield a clear trend. The socialist countries tended to have investment rates in the high ranges of 24 to 38 percent, but one can find similarly high investment rates among the capitalist countries. The East German investment rate, on the other hand, was relatively low.

Other differences, not recorded in Table 13.1, can also be noted. If one breaks down the industry sector into heavy and light industry, the planned socialist shares of heavy industry were well *above* those of a capitalist country at a similar level of development. The shares of the urban population of the socialist countries were well *below* those of a capitalist country at a similar stage of economic development.

All of these features constitute the distinguishing characteristics of the socialist industrialization model and are important components of the initial conditions as we examine the transition to market arrangements during the 1990s. What was the logic behind the socialist model? It aimed at "building socialism" as quickly as possible. In order to do so, industrialization had to be accorded priority. Activities that did not contribute to material production, such as services, would be limited, and within industry, priority had to be granted to heavy industry, which laid the foundation for socialism. Urbanization should be retarded to limit the flow of scarce investment resources into social overhead capital, a form of capital that does not lead immediately

TABLE 13.1   An Economic Profile of Socialist and Capitalist Countries in the 1980s

	(1) Per Capita GNP, 1985 (U.S. $)	(2) Population 1985 (millions)	(3a) Share of Industry and Construction in GDP (1982)	(3b) Agriculture	(3c) Services	(4) Proportion of Labor in Agriculture (1985)	(5) Gross Investment as a Percentage of GDP (1982)
A. Planned Socialism							
East Germany	10,440	16.7	51	13	36	10	24
Czechoslovakia	8,750	15.5	49	15	36	13	25
Hungary	7,560	10.6	38	26	36	18	29
Soviet Union	7,400	278.9	42	19	39	19	30
Poland	6,470	37.2	37	27	36	29	27
Bulgaria	6,420	9.0	46	23	31	20	28
Romania	5,450	22.7	46	26	28	29	38
China	340	1,042.4	45	35	20	68	28
B. Capitalism							
Norway	16,719	4.2	41	5	54	9	26
United States	16,710	238.6	34	3	63	3	19

	(1) Per Capita GNP, 1985 (U.S.$)	(2) Population 1985 (millions)	(3a) Share of Industry and Construction in GDP (1982)	(3b) Agriculture	(3c) Services	(4) Proportion of Labor in Agriculture (1985)	(5) Gross Investment as a Percentage of GDP (1982)
Canada	16,538	25.4	32	4	64	5	25
Denmark	14,603	5.1	22	5	73	7	16
West Germany	14,432	61.0	53	3	44	6	23
France	13,755	55.0	41	4	55	9	21
Japan	13,312	120.7	40	5	55	10	31
Belgium	13,219	9.9	42	4	54	3	18
Netherlands	12,741	14.5	33	4	63	5	18
Austria	12,343	7.6	39	4	57	9	26
United Kingdom	12,042	56.4	33	2	65	3	17
Italy	10,928	57.1	41	6	53	13	21
Spain	9,008	39.1	34	6	60	18	20
Greece	6,854	10.0	31	17	52	31	25
Turkey	2,135	45.1	31	22	47	60	25
India	250	767.7	26	36	38	70	25

Sources: U.S. Department of Commerce, *Statistical Abstract of the United States, 1981* (Washington, D.C.: U.S. Government Printing Office, 1981), pp. 876–879; National Foreign Assessment Center, *Handbook of Economic Statistics 1986* (Washington, D.C.: Central Intelligence Agency, 1986); World Bank, *World Tables,* 3rd ed. (Baltimore: Johns Hopkins University Press, 1984); OECD, *Historical Statistics, 1960–1985* (Paris: OECD, 1987); Thad Alton, "East European GNPs," Joint Economic Committee, *East European Economics: Slow Growth in the 1980s,* Vol. 1 (Washington, D.C.: U.S. Government Printing Office, 1985), pp. 81–132. The East European investment rates are calculated by subtracting the rates of defense spending and the GDP from Alton's residual expenditure category (p. 95).

to expanded industrial capacity. Extra resources were devoted to agriculture to promote self-sufficiency, even if this worked against comparative advantage. Resources
were channeled away from consumption into investment in order to achieve a high
investment rate.

The socialist industrialization model is important for several reasons. First, it has
been of great interest in Third World countries, such as India, where socialist economic policies and economic planning were borrowed from the past Soviet experience. Second, examining the socialist growth record will reveal that these countries
were not indifferent to what was being produced. Thus, although growth was emphasized in these systems, that emphasis was directed toward particular sectors, such as
heavy industry, while other sectors, such as services, were neglected. It is important
to note that when we examine efficiency measures, inputs are related to all output, not
just to the output of priority sectors.

Economic Growth

Table 13.2 and Figure 13.1 supply data on GDP growth rates for the postwar period
in socialist and capitalist countries. One should be cautious about attaching importance to small differences in growth rates, for there is measurement error in such
calculations. Moreover, the measured growth rate of economies experiencing substantial structural changes can be ambiguous—the problem of index number relativity.[15] Growth rates must be regarded as approximate and often ambiguous
measures of the expansion of real goods and services. This is especially true of
East–West comparisons, where substantial adjustments must be made to render the
past GDP data comparable.

In Table 13.2, we have assembled growth rates of real GDP and of real GDP per
capita for the entire postwar period. In panel A we supply growth rates for the Soviet
Union, Eastern Europe, and China. We also supply growth rates for a number of capitalist countries at various stages of economic development (panel B). We include
comparative growth data for China and India, two poor and populous Asian giants,
one a planned socialist economy, the other a basically capitalist economy.

Are there systemic differences in growth rates? Was economic growth more rapid
in the planned socialist economies? Table 13.2 examines postwar economic growth
from the heady growth of the 1950s and 1960s to the generally slower growth of the
mid-1970s and 1980s. It illustrates the dangers of using a pair of countries (such as
the United States and the Soviet Union) to judge the growth performance of capitalism and socialism. One can find capitalist countries (such as Japan) that have grown
much more rapidly than most socialist countries, and one can find socialist countries
(such as Bulgaria and China) that have grown more rapidly than most capitalist countries. Moreover, some countries grew rapidly in one period (Bulgaria in the 1950s and
1960s) and then grew slowly in another period (Bulgaria in the period 1975 to 1980).

It is difficult to reach firm conclusions about the growth performance of capitalism and socialism on the basis of these data. If one simply takes unweighted averages

of the eight planned socialist and the sixteen capitalist countries, the socialist group grew slightly more rapidly in the 1950s (5.7 percent per year versus 5.0 percent for the capitalist group). The capitalist group grew more rapidly in the 1960s (5.5 percent versus 4.4 percent in the first half and 5.5 percent versus 4.3 percent in the second half). The capitalist group experienced severe growth recessions in the mid-1970s, whereas the socialist group enjoyed a noticeable growth advantage for the first half of the 1970s (4.8 percent versus 3.9 percent). The growth of the capitalist group continued to lag during the second half of the 1970s (at 3.4 percent), but the slowdown of growth was even more severe in the socialist group (growth fell to below 3 percent). For the period 1980 to 1985, the average socialist growth rate exceeded the average capitalist rate. The marked slowdown of socialist growth in the second half of the 1980s (coupled with the recovery of capitalist growth rates) gives the clear advantage to the capitalist group. Trends in per capita GDP, given in parentheses in Table 13.2, mirror these GDP growth trends.

Because only eight planned socialist countries are covered, growth of any one has a strong effect on the averages of the group. As Table 13.2 shows, China's growth up to the mid-1970s was not so different from that of the other socialist countries. From 1975 onward, however, China's rapid growth stood in marked contrast to the slowing growth rates of the other socialist countries. If China is excluded from the socialist group, their average growth rate sinks well below that of the capitalist group from 1975 on. For example, for the period 1980 to 1985, the average socialist growth rate without China was a meager 1.2 percent per annum, compared to the capitalist rate of 1.9 percent per annum. In fact, if one omits the soaring Chinese growth rates of the mid-1970s and 1980s, the decline in socialist growth rates is very pronounced: from above 4 percent per annum, to 2 percent in the late 1970s, to 1 percent in the 1980s. From 1985 to 1990, the collapse of socialist growth is so pronounced that Western growth outstrips socialist growth by a large factor, whether China is included or not. We will return to this point later in the chapter because it bears upon issues related to the collapse of the command economies and subsequent transition.

One contrast between capitalism and planned socialism that holds over the entire postwar period is the lesser variability of growth rates among socialist countries. From 1950 to 1960, for example, the gap between the lowest and highest socialist growth rates was the difference between 4.6 percent and 7.9 percent; for the capitalist group, the difference was that between 3.0 percent and 7.9 percent The capitalist averages conceal more variation than the socialist averages. This pattern was altered somewhat by the marked contrast in growth rates between China and the other socialist countries after 1975, but it persisted within the Soviet and East European group. The planned socialist economies avoided the extreme differences among capitalist countries.

Direct comparisons of planned socialist and capitalist average growth rates did not reveal significant growth differences. However, if one makes a rule-of-thumb adjustment for differences in per capita income by including only the capitalist countries that fall within the approximate per capita income range of the socialist sample—say $3,000 to $6,000—some striking findings emerge. The rationale for this adjustment is that growth rates in the postwar period have tended to vary inversely with the level of development. Countries with low per capita income have

TABLE 13.2   Average Annual Growth of GDP and GDP per Capita in Socialist and Capitalist Countries, 1950–1990 (percentage; per capita figures in parentheses)

	1950–1960	1960–1965	1965–1970	1970–1975	1975–1980	1980–1985	1985–1990
A. Planned Socialist Countries							
Czechoslovakia	4.8 (3.9)	2.3 (1.6)	3.4 (3.2)	3.4 (2.7)	2.2 (1.5)	1.5 (1.2)	1.2 (1.2)
East Germany	5.7 (6.7)	2.7 (3.0)	3.0 (3.1)	3.4 (3.8)	2.3 (2.5)	1.8 (1.9)	1.6 (1.6)
Soviet Union	5.7 (3.9)	5.0 (3.5)	5.2 (4.2)	3.7 (2.7)	2.7 (1.8)	2.0 (1.1)	1.8 (1.1)
Poland	4.6 (2.75)	4.4 (3.2)	4.1 (3.4)	6.4 (5.4)	.7 (0)	.7 (-.1)	.2 (.2)
Hungary	4.6 (4.0)	4.2 (3.9)	3.0 (2.7)	3.4 (2.9)	2.0 (1.9)	1.7 (1.7)	.7 (.7)
Romania	5.8 (4.55)	6.0 (5.3)	4.9 (3.7)	6.7 (5.8)	3.9 (3.0)	1.0 (.8)	.6 (.6)
Bulgaria	6.7 (5.9)	6.7 (5.7)	5.1 (4.2)	4.6 (4.2)	.9 (.9)	1.2 (1.0)	.4 (.4)
China	7.9 (5.6)	4.0 (2.5)	7.1 (4.0)	7.0 (4.5)	6.2 (4.6)	9.3 (8.0)	8.6 (7.2)
Unweighted average	5.7 (4.7)	4.4 (3.6)	4.3 (3.6)	4.8 (4.0)	2.6 (2.0)	2.4 (2.0)	1.9 (1.5)
Without China	5.4 (4.5)	4.5 (3.7)	4.1 (3.5)	4.5 (3.9)	2.1 (1.7)	1.4 (1.1)	.9 (.8)
B. Capitalist Countries							
United States	3.3 (1.5)	4.6 (3.2)	3.1 (2.1)	2.3 (1.6)	3.7 (2.6)	2.4 (1.4)	3.1 (2.1)
Canada	4.6 (1.3)	5.7 (3.8)	4.8 (3.0)	5.0 (3.6)	2.9 (1.9)	2.2 (.9)	3.3 (2.3)

	1950–1960	1960–1965	1965–1970	1970–1975	1975–1980	1980–1985	1985–1990
West Germany	7.9 (6.3)	5.0 (3.5)	4.4 (3.9)	2.1 (1.7)	3.6 (3.7)	1.1 (1.4)	2.8 (2.4)
Denmark	3.6 (2.9)	5.1 (4.3)	4.5 (3.7)	2.8 (2.4)	2.7 (2.4)	2.3 (2.3)	2.4 (2.4)
Norway	3.6 (2.5)	4.8 (4.3)	4.8 (3.9)	4.6 (4.0)	4.6 (4.2)	3.0 (2.8)	3.3 (3.3)
Belgium	3.0 (2.5)	5.2 (4.5)	4.8 (4.4)	3.9 (3.5)	2.5 (2.3)	.4 (.4)	2.7 (2.7)
France	4.4 (3.8)	5.8 (4.5)	5.4 (4.5)	4.0 (3.2)	3.2 (2.9)	1.2 (.7)	2.7 (2.2)
Netherlands	5.0 (3.3)	4.8 (3.5)	5.5 (4.4)	3.2 (2.0)	2.6 (1.9)	.5 (.1)	2.1 (1.6)
Japan	7.9 (6.6)	10.0 (9.0)	12.2 (11.2)	5.0 (3.8)	5.1 (4.2)	3.9 (3.2)	3.8 (3.4)
Austria	5.6 (5.4)	4.3 (3.7)	5.1 (4.6)	3.9 (3.5)	4.0 (4.0)	2.8 (2.8)	2.2 (2.2)
United Kingdom	3.3 (2.3)	3.1 (2.4)	2.5 (2.2)	2.0 (1.4)	1.6 (1.6)	1.7 (1.3)	3.1 (2.9)
Italy	5.6 (4.8)	5.2 (4.3)	6.2 (5.4)	2.4 (1.5)	3.9 (3.4)	.8 (.5)	2.9 (2.7)
Spain	6.2 (5.3)	8.5 (7.5)	6.2 (5.2)	5.5 (4.6)	2.3 (1.3)	1.4 (.8)	4.1 (3.7)
Greece	6.0 (5.0)	7.7 (7.2)	7.2 (6.6)	5.0 (4.5)	4.4 (3.2)	1.0 (.4)	1.8 (1.8)
Turkey	6.4 (3.4)	4.8 (2.8)	6.6 (3.7)	7.5 (5.0)	3.1 (.6)	4.9 (2.7)	5.1 (2.7)
India	3.8 (1.9)	4.0 (1.7)	5.0 (2.6)	3.0 (1.0)	3.4 (1.6)	4.1 (1.9)	6.0 (3.9)
Unweighted average	5.0 (3.7)	5.5 (4.4)	5.5 (4.5)	3.9 (2.95)	3.4 (2.6)	2.0 (1.5)	3.2 (2.7)

Sources: Thad Alton, "Economic Structure and Growth in Eastern Europe," in U.S. Congress, Joint Economic Committee, *Economic Developments in Countries of Eastern Europe* (Washington, D.C.: U.S. Government Printing Office, 1970), p. 49; Thad Alton, "Comparative Structure and Growth of Economic Activity in Eastern Europe," in U.S. Congress, Joint Economic Committee, *East European Economies Post Helsinki* (Washington, D.C.: U.S. Government Printing Office, 1977), p. 237; Thad Alton, "Production and Resource Allocation in Eastern Europe: Performance, Problems, and Prospects," in U.S. Congress, Joint Economic Committee, *East European Economic Assessment*, Part 2 (Washington, D.C.: U.S. Government Printing Office, 1981), p. 381; U.S. Congress, Joint Economic Committee, *USSR Measures of Economic Growth and Development, 1950–1980* (Washington, D.C.: U.S. Government Printing Office, 1982), pp. 15–21; *Statistical Abstract of the United States, 1981*, pp. 878–879; Wilfred Malenbaum, "Modern Economic Growth in India and China: The Comparison Revisited, 1950–1980," *Economic Development and Cultural Change* 31 (October 1982), 53; *Handbook of Economic Statistics 1990*; Thad Alton et al., Occasional Papers Nos. 75–79 of the Research Project on National Income in East Central Europe, New York, 1983, pp. 7–12, 25; Rush Greenslade, "The Real Gross National Product of the USSR, 1950–75," in U.S. Congress, Joint Economic Committee, *Soviet Economy in a New Perspective* (Washington, D.C.: U.S. Government Printing Office, 1975), p. 271; World Bank, *World Tables*, 3rd ed. (Baltimore: Johns Hopkins University Press, 1983); OECD, *National Accounts, 1960–1985* (Paris: OECD, 1987); "Eastern Europe: Long Road to Economic Well-Being," Tables C-1 to C-21.

FIGURE 13.1   Average GDP Growth Rate, Planned Socialist and Capitalist
Countries, 1950–1990 (unweighted annual average growth rates)

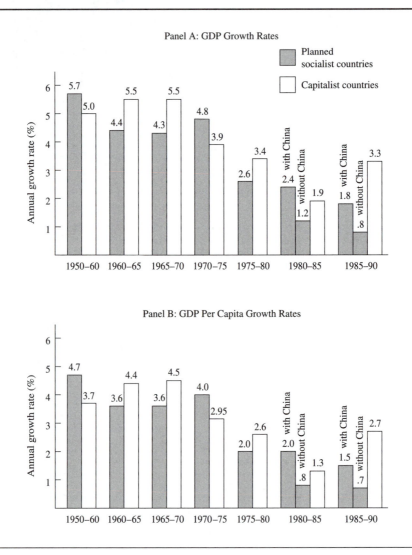

Source: Table 13.2.

grown more rapidly as a group. Only four capitalist countries fall within this income
range (Spain, Greece, Italy, and Venezuela), but comparing their average growth
rates with those of the former Soviet Union and Eastern Europe is nevertheless informative. For the entire postwar period, the unweighted average annual growth rate
of these four capitalist economies was almost 6 percent (4.25 percent on a per capita
basis). Even when China is included, the planned socialist average was around 4.5
percent per annum (3.8 percent on a per capita basis). Among countries at a similar

stage of development, the planned socialist economies experienced slower growth than their capitalist counterparts.[16]

Frederic Pryor examined the comparative growth rates of capitalist and socialist economies for the period 1950 to 1979, using econometric methods to hold factors other than the economic system constant. Pryor found that although the socialist-system effect was negative, the system coefficient was not statistically significant either for the growth of GDP or for the growth of GDP per capita.[17]

The pattern of decline of planned socialist growth rates goes a long way toward explaining the desire to convert from planned socialism to market resource allocation. Both East and West experienced relatively high rates of growth from 1950 through 1970. In the West, growth was well above long-term historical performance during this period. The growth rates of the planned socialist economies began their descent in the mid-1970s; lower growth rates were recorded in each successive half-decade. In the Soviet Union and Eastern Europe, economic growth had all but ceased by the latter half of the 1980s.

On the other hand, the West (after slow growth in the early 1980s) continued to grow at approximately its long-term historical rates. For the West, the first two decades after the war were periods of peak economic performance, after which it returned to its long-run historical pattern. The West, with two hundred years of recorded growth history, had demonstrated its ability to grow over the long run. The East, on the other hand, with a limited history of economic growth, feared that the planned socialist system had lost its ability to generate economic growth.

The Chinese and Indian comparisons shed light on the growth performance of capitalism and planned socialism in large and very poor countries. Although the Chinese data are fairly rough, most authorities agree that China has outperformed India in GDP growth and per capita GDP growth. It is likely that India and China entered the postwar era with similar levels of per capita income. China's current advantage in per capita income is the consequence of its more rapid growth.

The importance of China as a development model for poor, populous countries requires that we look further at Chinese economic growth in an Asian context. Table 13.3 gives the annual growth rates of seven Asian countries for the periods 1960–1991 and 1990–1997. It shows that Chinese economic growth has indeed been rapid even compared with that of other rapidly growing Asian economies, such as Japan, South Korea, and Taiwan. Chinese economic performance looks even better when compared with that of poor, populous Asian countries. Chinese growth has been more than double that of India and Pakistan and has accelerated significantly following the market-oriented reforms of recent years.[18]

There is no evidence that the planned socialist countries as a group outgrew their capitalist counterparts. One would have to conclude that the growth rates of capitalism and planned socialism were quite similar until the collapse of growth in the East after 1985.

The conclusion that economic growth was not more rapid in the planned socialist economies is a strong one in view of the priority of growth in these countries and the low weight attached to economic growth by many of the capitalist countries. If one makes a crude *ceteris paribus* adjustment for differences in per capita income, capitalist growth even emerges as more rapid.

TABLE 13.3 Annual GDP Growth Rates of Selected Asian
Economies, 1960–1991 and 1990–1997

China	6.9	11.6
Taiwan	7.6	n.a.
South Korea	7.9	7.2
Japan	5.7	1.5
Philippines	4.2	3.3
India	4.1	6.0
Pakistan	4.0	4.2

Sources: National Foreign Assessment Center, *Handbook of International Economic Statistics 1992* (Washington, D.C.: Central Intelligence Agency, 1992), Table 8 and Table 13.2.; World Bank, *World Development Indicators 1999* (Washington, D.C.: World Bank, 1999), Table 4.1

The Sources of Economic Growth

Socialist growth rates were in many ways comparable to those in capitalist systems, although differences in priorities, levels of economic development, and other such influences affect this conclusion. Toward the end of the planned socialist era in the Soviet Union and Eastern Europe, growth rates declined seriously. In the Soviet Union, the rate of growth of output became negative by 1990 as the collapse drew near.

Why did rates of **economic growth** ultimately decline sharply in the planned socialist economic systems? Were declining rates of economic growth a symptom of more basic economic difficulties in these systems? To answer these questions, it is necessary to look closely at the sources of economic growth and especially at issues of efficiency.

Chapter 3 distinguished between extensive growth and intensive growth. Extensive growth is the growth of output from the expansion of inputs, land, labor, and capital. Intensive growth is the growth derived from increasing output per unit of factor input—that is, from the better use of available inputs.

The sources of economic growth are important for two reasons. First, historical experience shows that as economies grow and develop, the sources of growth tend to change. During the early stages of development, the task is to bring idle resources into production, a model where output expansion is achieved largely from using more inputs. As economic development proceeds, the tendency is to generate growth from the better use of inputs (and from improvements in input quality). The distinction between intensive and extensive growth is important, for input expansion comes from sacrificing leisure time, increasing work time, and reducing current consumption with the hope of greater improvements in the future. Intensive growth, however, is derived largely from increased efficiency—for example, through improved managerial systems and technological change.

It is relevant to ask which economic system has done a better job of generating economic growth, where *better* is defined in terms of the relative weights of **intensive growth** and **extensive growth**. Two such comparisons are relevant here. The first, **static efficiency**, takes a snapshot of planned socialist and capitalist countries at a particular point in time to determine how much output they are generating from a given amount of factor inputs. The second, **dynamic efficiency**, probes the question of efficiency performance over time—that is, the extent to which output expands more rapidly than inputs, the difference being the growth rate of factor productivity.[19]

Dynamic Efficiency

Table 13.4 supplies information on the dynamic efficiency of the planned socialist and the industrialized capitalist countries. Specifically, it provides the annual growth rates of aggregate employment $(\hat{L})$ and reproducible capital $(\hat{K})$, which we then compare with the growth rate of aggregate output $(\hat{Q})$. By subtracting the growth rates of employment and capital, respectively, from the growth rate of output, we obtain the growth rates of **labor productivity** $(\hat{Q} - \hat{L})$ and **capital productivity** $(\hat{Q} - \hat{K})$, respectively.

Because the productivity of labor or capital is affected by substitutions between the two factors, it is desirable to have a comprehensive measure of the growth rate of combined labor and capital productivity. One must first calculate the growth rates of labor and capital combined $(\hat{L} + \hat{K})$, or total factor input. This is typically done by taking a weighted average of the growth rates of labor and capital, where the weights represent each factor's share of national income. Thus **total factor productivity** is defined as $\hat{Q} - (\hat{L} + \hat{K})$. Here

$$\hat{K} + \hat{L} = \hat{K} W_K + \hat{L} W_L$$

where

$$W_K = \text{capital's share of income}$$
$$W_L = \text{labor's share of income}$$

We use rates of growth of labor and capital combined $(\hat{L} + \hat{K})$, calculated in this manner. Inasmuch as a return to capital was typically not included in prices in the planned socialist countries, "synthetic" factor shares must be used to calculate their $\hat{L} + \hat{K}$ growth rates.[20] Once the growth rate of combined factor inputs is calculated, it is subtracted from the growth rate of output to obtain the growth rate of factor productivity $[\hat{Q} - (\hat{L} + \hat{K})]$. All of these figures are given in Table 13.4.

The approximate nature of these productivity calculations is worth emphasizing. Factors of production, especially labor, can expand in both quantitative and qualitative terms, yet our measure captures only their quantitative advance.[21] If comparable data were available, we could calculate a more comprehensive measure of labor's growth by adjusting for the growth in education, training, and composition of the labor force. Because we use employment rather than actual hours, we are not even capturing the quantitative growth of labor accurately. Moreover, the capitalist data do not adjust for unemployment (which rose over this period). We use the official capital-stock estimates of the planned socialist economies, except for the Soviet Union. We have no way of knowing whether they are comparable to Western data or of assessing their reliability.[22]

What conclusions are to be drawn from Table 13.4? The first is that through the mid-1980s, the growth rates of capital and labor inputs were similar for capitalism and socialism. The planned socialist and capitalist averages suggest roughly equivalent rates of growth of employment, and although the socialist growth rate of capital was probably slightly lower during the 1950s and higher thereafter, for the entire period capital grew at an average rate of roughly 5 percent in each economic system. The stereotype, fostered by the rapid growth of both labor and capital in the Soviet Union, that the planned socialist system generates a more rapid rate of growth of inputs is not supported. The rates of growth of labor and capital combined round to 2 percent per annum for both capitalism and planned socialism.

Unlike GDP growth, the variability of factor-input growth by country appears to have been as great under planned socialism as under capitalism. Some planned socialist countries (East Germany, for example) experienced low growth of both labor and capital, whereas others (the Soviet Union and Poland, for example) experienced rapid input growth. One finds similar variability among the capitalist countries, with some (notably Japan) experiencing quite rapid growth of both labor and capital inputs.

Both the socialist and the capitalist countries experienced a slowdown in productivity growth after the 1960s: The planned socialist growth rate of output declined after 1960 by about 40 percent; yet inputs, both labor and capital, grew more rapidly after 1960 (about one-quarter faster). Thus both labor and capital productivity and total factor productivity declined dramatically after 1960 in the planned socialist economies—labor productivity from an average of 4.8 percent to 2.5 percent, total factor productivity from 3.5 percent to 0.9 percent. Efforts to stabilize the growth of output by raising the growth of inputs did not succeed; rather than becoming more intensive, the growth of the planned socialist economies became more extensive after 1960. This is a serious criticism of the command role.

The greater extensivity of socialist growth after 1960 is apparent when we compare the growth rates of total factor productivity with the growth rates of output. Taking those five socialist countries for which capital data are available, the average GDP growth rate was 5.2 percent per annum between 1950 and 1960, whereas the growth of efficiency (factor productivity) was 3.5 percent. Thus 67 percent (3.5/5.2) of economic growth was accounted for by increasing output per unit of input. The corresponding figures for the 1960 to 1983 period are 0.9 percent and 3.0 percent. Thus from 1960 to 1983, only 30 percent of growth was accounted for by increasing inputs. The declining growth of productivity was felt by both labor and capital, but the decline in capital productivity from a positive rate to a negative rate of 2.1 percent per annum was especially prominent.

The capitalist group also experienced a slowdown in productivity growth after 1960. Average labor productivity growth fell from 3.9 percent to 2.8 percent; capital productivity growth fell from zero to 1.0 percent; and total factor productivity growth fell from 3.0 percent to 1.8 percent. In the 1950s, some 65 percent (3.0/4.8) of growth in the capitalist group was explained by the growth of efficiency; for the period 1960–1985, 49 percent (1.8/3.7) of growth was explained by efficiency gains.

Table 13.4 shows the planned socialist economies in a favorable light because it does not include the productivity collapse of the second half of the 1980s. During this period, all the planned socialist economies experienced negative productivity growth except the USSR, which experienced zero productivity growth. The special features

TABLE 13.4 Annual Growth of Inputs and Output per Unit of Inputs in Socialist and Capitalist Countries

		(1) Employment ($\hat{L}$)	(2) Fixed Capital ($\hat{K}$)	(3) Labor and Capital ($\hat{L}+\hat{K}$)	(4) Output ($\hat{Q}$)	(5) Labor Productivity ($\hat{Q}-\hat{L}$)	(6) Capital Productivity ($\hat{Q}-\hat{K}$)	(7) Total Factor Productivity $\hat{Q}-(\hat{L}+\hat{K})$
		A. Planned Socialist Countries						
Czechoslovakia	1950–60	0.7	3.5	1.4	4.8	4.1	1.3	3.4
	1960–83	1.0	4.7	2.1	2.6	1.6	-2.1	0.5
East Germany	1950–60	0.0	2.0	0.5	6.1	6.1	4.1	5.6
	1960–83	0.3	4.0	1.4	2.8	2.5	-1.2	1.4
Soviet Union	1950–60	1.2	9.4	3.4	5.8	4.6	-3.6	2.4
	1960–85	1.3	7.3	2.8	3.6	2.3	-3.7	0.8
Poland	1950–60	1.0	2.6	1.4	4.6	3.6	2.0	3.2
	1960–83	1.5	4.7	2.5	3.3	1.8	-1.4	0.8
Hungary	1950–60	1.0	3.6	1.7	4.6	3.6	1.0	2.9
	1960–83	0.3	5.0	1.7	2.9	2.6	-2.1	1.2
Romania	1950–60	1.1	—[a]	—	5.9	4.8	—	—
	1960–85	0.4	—[a]	—	4.6	4.1	—	—
Bulgaria	1950–60	0.2	—[a]	—	6.7	6.5	—	—
	1960–85	0.5	—[a]	1.7	3.7	3.2	—	1.0
Unweighted average	1950–60	0.8	4.2	1.7	5.5[b] (5.2)[c]	4.8	1.0	3.5
	1960–83(85)	0.8	5.1	2.1	3.3[b] (3.0)[c]	2.5	-2.1	0.9

(continued)

TABLE 13.4   Annual Growth of Inputs and Output per Unit of Inputs in Socialist and Capitalist Countries (cont.)

		(1) Employ-ment $(\hat{L})$	(2) Fixed Capital $(\hat{K})$	(3) Labor and Capital $(\hat{L} + \hat{K})$	(4) Output $(\hat{Q})$	(5) Labor Productivity $(\hat{Q} - \hat{L})$	(6) Capital Productivity $(\hat{Q} - \hat{K})$	(7) Total Factor Productivity $\hat{Q} - (\hat{L} + \hat{K})$
		B. Capitalist Countries						
United States	1950–60	1.4	3.6	1.8	3.1	1.7	−0.5	1.3
	1960–85	2.0	3.3	2.4	3.1	1.1	−0.2	0.7
Canada	1960–85	2.7	4.7	3.3	4.2	1.5	−0.5	0.9
Belgium	1950–62	0.6	2.3	1.0	3.2	2.6	0.6	2.2
Denmark	1950–62	0.9	5.1	1.8	3.5	2.6	−1.6	1.7
	1950–60^d	0.1	4.2	1.0	4.9	4.8	0.7	3.9
	1960–85	0.7	4.8	1.8	3.9	3.1	−0.9	2.1
West Germany	1950–60^d	2.0	6.4	3.1	7.3	5.3	0.9	4.2
	1960–85	0.0	4.8	1.2	3.1	3.1	−1.7	1.9
Italy	1950–62	0.6	3.5	1.3	6.0	5.4	2.5	4.7
Finland	1960–85	0.7	4.6	1.9	3.9	3.2	−0.5	2.0
Sweden	1962–83	0.6	3.5	1.5	2.8	2.2	−0.7	1.3
Netherlands	1950–62	1.1	4.7	1.9	4.7	3.6	0.0	2.8
Norway	1950–60^d	0.2	4.2	1.2	3.5	3.3	−0.7	2.3
	1960–85	0.5	3.6	1.4	4.2	3.7	0.6	2.8
United Kingdom	1950–60^d	0.7	3.4	1.2	2.3	1.6	−1.1	1.1
	1960–85	0.5	3.2	1.1	2.3	1.8	0.9	1.2

		(1) Employment ($\hat{L}$)	(2) Fixed Capital ($\hat{K}$)	(3) Labor and Capital ($\hat{L} + \hat{K}$)	(4) Output ($\hat{Q}$)	(5) Labor Productivity ($\hat{Q} - \hat{L}$)	(6) Capital Productivity ($\hat{Q} - \hat{K}$)	(7) Total Factor Productivity $\hat{Q} - (\hat{L} + \hat{K})$
Japan	1953–70	1.7	9.8	3.8	10.0	8.3	0.2	6.2
	1970–85	0.9	8.2	2.3	4.4	3.5	–3.8	2.1
Greece	1960–85	0.4	5.8	2.0	5.1	4.7	–0.7	3.1
Unweighted average[e]	1950–60	0.9	4.7	1.8	4.8	3.9	0.1	3.0
Unweighted average	1960–85	0.9	4.7	1.9	3.7	2.8	–1.0	1.8

Note: All figures are annual growth rates.
$\hat{L}$ = growth rate of employment
$\hat{K}$ = growth rate of reproducible capital
$\hat{Q}$ = growth rate of output
$(\hat{L} + \hat{K})$ = growth rate of labor and capital combined

[a] The official Romanian and Bulgarian capital-stock series are not cited because they are in current, not constant, prices.
[b] Average of all seven countries.
[c] Average of first five countries.
[d] 1950–1962.
[e] Includes Japan, 1953–1970.

Sources: **Panel A:** *Employment:* Andrew Elias, "Magnitude and Distribution of the Labor Force in Eastern Europe," in U.S. Congress, Joint Economic Committee, *Economic Developments in Countries of Eastern Europe* (Washington, D.C.: U.S. Government Printing Office, 1970), pp. 208–214; Thad Alton, "Comparative Structure and Growth of Economic Activity in Eastern Europe," in U.S. Congress, Joint Economic Committee, *East European Economies Post Helsinki* (Washington, D.C.: U.S. Government Printing Office, 1977), p. 218; *Handbook of Economic Statistics 1980*, p. 47. *Capital Stock:* Official CMEA estimates of productive funds (*osnovnye fondy*) from *Statisticheski ezhegodnik stran-chlenov Soveta Ekonomicheskoi Vzaimopomoschi 1974* (Moscow: Statistika), p. 27; Alton, "Production and Resource Allocation in Eastern Europe," p. 372; *Handbook of Economic Statistics 1980*, p. 58; and Alton, "Comparative Structure and Growth," p. 223. *Output:* Paul R. Gregory and Robert C. Stuart, *Comparative Economic Systems* 6th ed. (Boston: Houghton Mifflin, 1999), Table 9.2, pages 220–1. **Panel B:** *Growth Rates of Employment, Reproducible Capital, and Output:* Edward Denison, *Why Growth Rates Differ* (Washington, D.C.: Brookings Institution, 1967), pp. 42, 190, and Ch. 21; Edward Denison, *Accounting for United States Economic Growth, 1929–1969* (Washington, D.C.: Brookings Institution, 1974), pp. 32, 58; Edward Denison and William Chung, *How Japan's Economy Grew So Fast* (Washington, D.C.: Brookings Institution, 1976), pp. 19, 31; OECD, Department of Economics and Statistics, *Flows and Stocks of Fixed Capital, 1960–1985* (OECD: Paris, 1987); *Handbook of Economic Statistics 1986; World Table*, 3rd ed.

of the Soviet case, notably extensive growth and a low elasticity-substitution of capital for labor, are discussed by Easterly and Fischer.[23]

What are the overall conclusions concerning the growth of efficiency under capitalism and planned socialism? As in the case of economic growth, there appears to be no evidence to suggest a more rapid rate of growth of productivity under planned socialism (see Figure 13.2). It appears that the productivity performance of planned socialism deteriorated seriously since 1960, at least, and that socialist growth became

FIGURE 13.2   Productivity Growth in Socialist and Capitalist Countries, 1960–1985

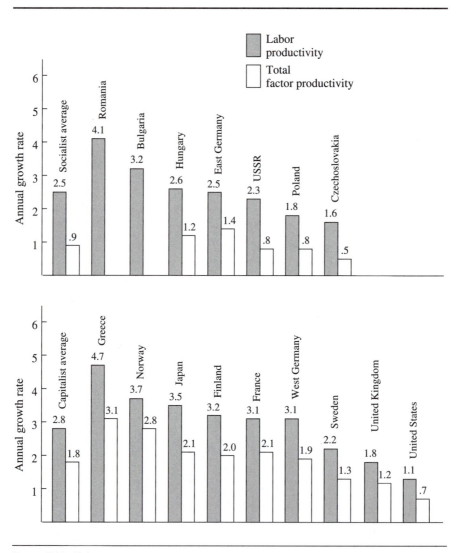

Source: Table 13.4.

much more extensive in character. We must emphasize that these conclusions are based on approximate data and do not reflect the qualitative growth of inputs. We believe, however, that they would hold up even if more exhaustive data were available.

Consumption Costs of Growth

One cost of economic growth is the sacrifice in current consumption required to add to the nation's stock of capital. Although growth rates in the East and West have been similar, it is not true that this growth was achieved with a similar allocation of resources between consumption and investment. Information on resource-allocation policies is summarized in Table 13.5.[24] Although the capitalist and socialist data cover slightly different time periods, they tell an interesting story. Again the GDP growth rates are quite similar, but personal consumption fared relatively better than investment under capitalism. In fact, whereas personal consumption grew on the average at a more rapid rate in the capitalist sample (4.7 percent versus 3.6 percent), gross investment grew faster under planned socialism (6.4 percent versus 5.6 percent).

Of even greater interest, when one takes the ratio of the growth rates of consumption and investment as a measure of resource allocation, a distinct pattern emerges. Although there seems to be a positive relationship between this ratio and per capita income, the socialist consumption–investment ratios appear to be well below those of capitalist countries at a similar stage of development. The achievement of similar rates of growth in East and West has required a greater sacrifice of current consumption under planned socialism. In fact, the resource-allocation pattern of the socialist countries was remarkably uniform and was closest to the pattern of the less-industrialized capitalist countries (such as Turkey and Spain).

Given the higher investment rates under planned socialism in the 1950s and 1960s, it follows that socialist per capita consumption was lower for a given level of per capita national income *ceteris paribus*. This is the other side of the coin—namely, the cost of maintaining economic growth through expansion of capital inputs.[25] The absolute level of per capita consumption depends on the economic potential of the country, and to argue that one country has outperformed the other simply because its standard of living is higher begs the question. The major issue is what standard of living is being supplied, given the economic resources at the nation's disposal. Such a comparison shows that the socialist living standards are low relative to per capita income. This reflects the decision of growth-oriented socialist planners to devote a relatively larger share of GDP to investment than under capitalism. However, the telling point is that this decision did not lead to a notably higher rate of growth for the planned socialist nations. The planners' consumption policies did not pay off in terms of more rapid growth.

These findings have negative implications concerning the viability of the planned socialist systems. We have not yet considered the reasons for the productivity problem, but the negative impact on the incentive of the socialist consumer to purchase must have been harmful to these economies. First, the systems, especially that of the former Soviet Union, emphasized a basic socialist postulate—sacrifice now through expanded savings and reduced consumption (such as that which took place in the

TABLE 13.5   Annual Rates of Growth of Personal Consumption, Investment, and GDP in Planned Socialist and Capitalist Countries

Country	(1) Personal Consumption	(2) Gross Investment	(3) GDP	(4) Consumption Growth as a Percentage of Investment Growth, (1) ÷ (2)
A. Planned Socialist Countries				
Czechoslovakia (1950–1967)	2.2	5.2	3.2	0.42
East Germany (1960–1975)	3.7	6.1	4.9	0.61
Hungary (1950–1967)	3.4	5.2	4.0	0.65
Poland (1950–1967)	4.2	7.9	5.1	0.53
Soviet Union (1950–1980)	4.3	7.7	4.7	0.56
Unweighted average	3.6	6.4	4.4	0.56
B. Capitalist Countries, 1950–1977				
United States	3.4	3.1	3.6	1.10
Canada	4.7	4.6	4.8	1.02
West Germany	4.7	5.0	4.8	0.94
Denmark	3.5	4.9	3.8	0.71
Norway	3.9	4.6	4.2	0.85
Belgium	3.7	4.6	4.0	0.81
France	5.0	6.1	5.0	0.82
Netherlands	4.6	4.2	4.5	1.09
Japan	7.8	11.0	8.4	0.71
Austria	5.4	5.1	4.9	1.06
United Kingdom	2.2	4.4	2.5	0.50
Italy	4.6	5.0	4.8	0.92
Greece	6.0	7.1	6.4	0.85
Spain	5.2	6.7	5.6	0.77
Turkey	6.1	8.2	6.3	0.74
Unweighted average	4.7	5.6	4.9	0.84

Sources: Thad Alton, "Economic Structure and Growth in Eastern Europe," in U.S. Congress, Joint Economic Committee, *Economic Developments in Countries of Eastern Europe* (Washington, D.C.: U.S. Government Printing Office, 1970), pp. 52–53; *Deutsches Institut fur Wirtschaftsforschung Wochenbericht* 44 (June 1977), 199; Rush Greenslade, "The Real Gross National Product of the USSR, 1950–75," in U.S. Congress, Joint Economic Committee, *Soviet Economy in a New Perspective* (Washington, D.C.: U.S. Government Printing Office, 1975), p. 275; World Bank, *World Tables 1980* (Baltimore: Johns Hopkins University Press, 1980), country tables; U.S. Congress, Joint Economic Committee, *USSR: Measures of Economic Growth and Development, 1950–80* (Washington, D.C.: U.S. Government Printing Office, 1982), pp. 65–67.

1930s) to enjoy significant gains in consumption in the future. But in general those gains did not materialize. When they did, the pace of improvement was slow, a fact that Soviet consumers could recognize as they watched other countries outperform their own system. Although these patterns are not easily quantifiable, the effort contributed by the Soviet worker must have suffered, especially in the 1970s and 1980s.

Static Efficiency

Static efficiency is a difficult concept to measure. To do so correctly requires first a notion of an economy's productive potential, as defined by its total resources, and then a determination of how closely the economy comes to meeting that potential. This problem is explained in Figure 13.3. To show that the Soviet Union, for example, obtained half as much output as the United States from a given amount of conventional

FIGURE 13.3   Why It Is Difficult to Evaluate Static Efficiency: Different Country Production Possibilities

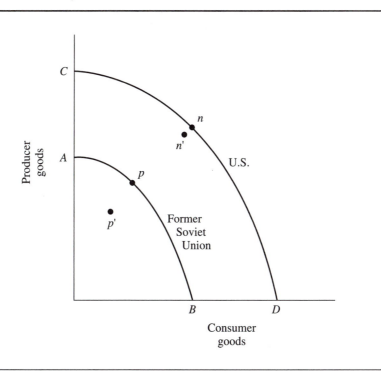

Explanation: CD represents the production possibilities frontier (PPF) of, say, the United States. *AB* is the PPF of, say, the former Soviet Union. The U.S. PPF is to the northeast of the Soviet PPF because of greater resources and better technology. The relevant measure of static efficiency is how closely each economy comes to operating on its PPF. If, for example, the United States operates very close to *n* at *n'* and the Soviet Union operates at *p'*, which is very far from *p*, then the United States is more efficient. In real-world measurement, all we observe is *p'* and *n'*. We have no way of knowing what *p* and *n* are.

labor and capital inputs would not unambiguously prove the greater static efficiency of the American economy. The measurement of conventional inputs may fail to capture the full range of resources (in both qualitative and quantitative terms) at the disposal of each economy.

One way to illustrate the problem of measuring static efficiency is to note the strong positive relationship between the level of economic development and output per unit of input. Any evaluation of the static efficiency of capitalism and planned socialism must distinguish between "normal" differences caused by unequal economic development and differences due to the economic system. What is missing is information on what the economy should be able to produce from its resources at maximum efficiency.

Abram Bergson has made a careful study of comparative productivity under capitalism and socialism that sheds light on the issue of relative productivity performance.[26] Bergson's data for 1975 are reproduced in Table 13.6. They give per capita outputs and labor (adjusted for quality differences), capital, and land inputs of various capitalist and socialist countries (where the socialist group includes Yugoslavia) as a percentage of the U.S. per capita figures. Table 13.6 shows, for example, that Italy had a per capita output 61 percent of that of the United States, a per capita employment 75 percent of that of the United States, and a per capita capital stock 62 percent of that of the United States. The Soviet Union had a per capita output 60 percent of that of the United States, a per capita employment 104 percent of that of the United States, and a per capita capital stock 73 percent of that of the United States.

TABLE 13.6   Per Capita Output, Employment, Capital, and Land, 1975
(United States = 100)

Country	Output per Capita	Employment per Capita Adjusted for Labor Quality	Reproducible Capital per Capita	Farm Land per Capita
United States	100.0	100.0	100.0	100.0
West Germany	90.0	84.0	107.3	14.8
France	92.2	88.3	83.0	40.1
Italy	61.3	75.2	61.6	24.9
United Kingdom	67.2	89.6	77.2	14.5
Japan	82.8	129.0	95.2	5.4
Spain	64.6	95.4	47.7	67.0
Soviet Union	60.0	104.1	73.2	103.5
Hungary	61.1	115.6	70.9	59.8
Poland	54.8	122.7	51.6	50.4
Yugoslavia	41.5	98.8	35.9	45.6

Source: Abram Bergson, "Comparative Productivity: The USSR, Eastern Europe, and the West," *American Economic Review* 77 (June 1987), 347. Used by permission.

The issue is whether the socialist countries systematically obtained less output from their available inputs than the capitalist countries. The data for Italy and the Soviet Union show that Italy obtained more output from its available inputs. Italy and the Soviet Union had the same per capita output when compared with the United States, yet the Soviet Union used more labor and capital per capita to produce that output.

Bergson demonstrates that there was a systematic tendency for the output per worker (labor productivity) in socialist economies to fall short of output per worker in capitalist countries, when inputs are held constant. According to Bergson's calculations, output per worker in the socialist group fell 25 percent to 34 percent short of output per worker in the capitalist group *ceteris paribus.*

Bergson's findings are important, though this sample is small. It will be a long time before a similar experiment on a larger number of countries can be performed. Meanwhile, we believe it is appropriate to conclude that socialist economies have relatively lower productivity, *ceteris paribus,* than industrialized capitalist countries.[27]

As previously shown, it is difficult to assess the comparative static efficiency of socialist and capitalist economic systems because it is not possible to determine how closely to their production possibilities frontier real-world economies operate. However, beginning with the work of Judith Thornton in 1971, a number of predictive studies inclusive of the early 1990s have attempted to examine **allocative efficiency** by estimating various production functions and by focusing on the allocation of inputs among industries in socialist economies.[28] These studies generally found that there was allocative inefficiency in that reallocation could raise the value added; that was increasingly so through the 1970s. Similar studies conducted in the 1980s resulted in similar conclusions, although the estimated magnitudes of inefficiency were generally not very large. These types of studies generally supported the existence of allocative inefficiency, but their results have sparked controversy, especially because of a variety of basic measurement problems that remain unresolved.

A number of studies of **enterprise (technical) efficiency** have looked at enterprises in socialist and capitalist systems and, in some cases, have made comparisons. Although generalizing across a wide variety of studies that differ in scope and approach is difficult, most studies have not shown unusually low levels of efficiency in enterprises of planned socialist economic systems. But, like measures of allocative efficiency, these measures of technical efficiency are difficult to interpret because of basic underlying measurement problems.

In sum, these studies have led to a general presumption that efficiency was lower in the planned socialist systems than in market capitalist systems. The issue remains controversial, however, and undoubtedly will spur further analyses in the future.

Income Distribution

Another measure of the performance of economic systems is the distribution of income among the members of society. What constitutes a good **income distribution** must be a subjective matter, but most would agree that a distribution in which the top 5 percent of the population receives 95 percent of all income is "unfair" and that a completely even distribution is "unfair." Marx himself rejected the notion of an equal distribution of income during the transition from socialism to communism, arguing instead for a distribution that reflected the individual's contribution to the well-being of society.[29]

Another reason why most people reject a perfectly equal distribution of income is that rewards must be offered for differential effort and for scarce resources; otherwise, incentives will diminish and the economy will not produce its potential output. The issue, therefore, is to construct a distribution of income that both is "fair" and provides necessary incentives. Both socialism and capitalism must address this issue.

What differences would one expect in the distribution of income under capitalism and socialism? In capitalist societies, the two major sources of income inequality are the unequal distribution of property ownership (land and capital resources) and the unequal distribution of human capital. Both forms of capital yield income—the first in the form of property income from rent, interest, dividends, and capital gains, the second from wages and salaries.

Under both planned and market socialism, property other than consumer durables and housing is owned by the state, and the return from this state-owned property is at the state's disposal. Under capitalism, the bulk of property is owned privately, and property income accrues to private individuals.

The distribution of human capital depends on the manner in which schooling and on-the-job training are provided. Free or subsidized public schooling is available in both types of societies, although there is a greater tendency for the state to pay for higher education in socialist societies. Nevertheless, the differences between the two systems would not be expected to be great.

The major distinction is the absence of private ownership of income-earning property under socialism. Unless offset by higher earnings differentials, the distribution of property plus labor income should be more nearly equal under socialism. The distribution of income after taxes depends on the extent to which the state uses redistributive taxes and transfers to equalize income distribution.

As to earnings differentials, planned socialist societies recognized that labor cannot be allocated administratively and must be allowed relative freedom of choice of occupation. Therefore, the distribution of wage and salary income under socialism should follow roughly the same principles as under capitalism.

Arguments can be made, however, that the distribution of labor incomes varies according to the economic system.[30] Some maintain that labor income is more nearly equally distributed under socialism because of the more nearly equal distribution of education and training and because the government can control the power of labor groups. Moreover, socialist governments have a greater doctrinal commitment to equality.

Frederic Pryor made an extensive econometric study of the distribution of labor income among workers for the late 1950s and early 1960s.[31] He found that the distribution of labor income was *more nearly equal* under socialism, once per capita income and the size of the country were held constant. He also found that labor incomes were less nearly equal in the Soviet Union than in the other socialist countries; therefore, studies that generalize from the Soviet experience are likely to give a false impression.

Subsequent data on the distribution of earnings for full-time wage and salary earners confirm most of Pryor's findings for the 1950s and early 1960s.[32] Earnings were more nearly equally distributed in Eastern Europe, Yugoslavia, and the Soviet Union than in the United States in the 1970s. For the USSR, this was a relatively new phenomenon, for as late as 1957, Soviet earnings were less nearly equal than those in the United States.[33]

We now turn from the distribution of **labor income** to the distribution of **total income**. Table 13.7 gives data on the distribution of per capita income, after income taxes, in a limited number of planned socialist and capitalist countries for which data are available.[34] The socialist data generally excluded top income-earning families (party leaders, government officials, artists, and authors), including instead only families of workers and employees. Many second-economy activities considered legal in capitalist societies (the provision of private repair and medical services, for example) were not recorded. Also, a relatively larger volume of resources (even excluding free educational and medical benefits) was provided in socialist societies on an extra-market basis—shopping privileges, official cars, vacations—and such resources were not included in reported income.

Table 13.7 shows that income was distributed more unequally in the capitalist countries in which the state played a relatively minor redistributive role either through progressive taxation or through the distribution of social services (the United States, Italy, and Canada). Yet even where the state played a major redistributive role (the United Kingdom and Sweden), the distribution of income appeared to be slightly more unequal than in the planned socialist countries (Hungary, Czechoslovakia, and Bulgaria). The Soviet Union in 1966 appears to have had a less egalitarian distribution of income than its East European counterparts. The USSR distribution was scarcely distinguishable from the British and Swedish distributions (it may even have been more unequal). Table 13.8 reveals that Soviet income distribution was more nearly equal than that in Australia, Canada, and the United States but not much different from that in Norway and the United Kingdom.

The **Gini coefficient** is a convenient summary measure of income inequality. The higher the Gini coefficient, the more unequal the distribution of income. A Gini coefficient of zero denotes perfect equality; a Gini coefficient of 1 denotes perfect inequality. Gini coefficients for Great Britain and Sweden for the early 1970s are both around 0.25. The Czech, Hungarian, and Polish Gini coefficients for the same period are 0.21, 0.24, and 0.24, respectively—that is, very close to the British and Swedish coefficients. The Canadian and U.S. Gini coefficients, on the other hand, are 0.34 and 0.35, respectively, well above the socialist coefficients.[35]

Figure 13.4 provides Lorenz curves for Hungary, Sweden, West Germany, Spain, Mexico, and Yugoslavia. The reader will recall from Chapter 3 that the further the Lorenz curve departs from the line of perfect equality, the more unequal the distribution. These curves, which refer to the early 1970s, confirm the basic pattern shown in Table 13.7: Hungary was about the same as Sweden but was much more egalitarian than West Germany and Spain (two capitalist countries without considerable state income redistribution); Yugoslavia did not differ significantly from West Germany and Spain. However, there apparently was a narrowing of differentials in Yugoslavia between the early 1960s and the early 1970s.

The Mexican Lorenz curve is included to make a general point about the Yugoslav (and Hungarian, Polish, Soviet, and Czech) distribution. As the Mexican curve

TABLE 13.7   Distribution of Per Capita Income Among Families After Income Taxes in Planned Socialist and Capitalist Countries

	U.K. 1969	U.S. 1968	Italy 1969	Canada 1971	Sweden 1971	Hungary 1964	Czecho-slovakia 1965	Bulgaria 1963–1965	USSR 1966
Per capita income of individual in 95th percentile ÷ that of individual in 5th percentile	5.0	12.7	11.2	12.0	5.5	4.0	4.3	3.8	5.7
Per capita income of individual in 90th percentile ÷ that of individual in 10th percentile	3.4	6.7	5.9	6.0	3.5	3.0	3.1	2.7	3.5
Per capita income of individual in 75th percentile ÷ that of individual in 25th percentile	1.9	2.6	2.5	2.4	1.9	1.8	1.8	1.7	2.0

Source: P. J. D. Wiles, *Economic Institutions Compared* (New York: Halsted Press, 1977), p. 443. By permission of Basil Blackwell, Oxford.

TABLE 13.8 An International Comparison of Income Shares of Selected Percentile Groups, Distributions of Households by Per Capita Household Income, and GDP Per Capita

Distribution, Country and Year	Percentage Income Share of			
	Lowest 10%	Lowest 20%	Highest 20%	Highest 10%
Nonfarm households (pretax)				
USSR, 1967	4.4	10.4	33.8	19.9
Urban households (post-tax)				
USSR, 1972–1974	3.4	8.7	38.5	24.1
All households (pretax)				
Australia, 1966–1967	3.5	8.3	41.0	25.6
Norway, 1970	3.5	8.2	39.0	23.5
U.K., 1973	3.5	8.3	39.9	23.9
France, 1970	2.0	5.8	47.2	31.8
Canada, 1969	2.2	6.2	43.6	27.8
U.S., 1972	1.8	5.5	44.4	28.6
All households (post-tax)				
Sweden, 1972	3.5	9.3	35.2	20.5

Source: Abram Bergson, "Income Inequality Under Soviet Socialism," *Journal of Economic Literature* 22 (September 1984). Used by permission.

shows, inequality tends to be negatively related to level of development.[36] If one could adjust for lower per capita income, the socialist distributions would appear even more nearly equal than they do in direct comparisons.

In general, we conclude that the differences in distribution of income between the planned socialist economies and the capitalist welfare states have been relatively minor. This is a surprising conclusion. One would have expected the absence of private ownership of property to make more of a difference. Nevertheless, differences are apparent when one contrasts the socialist distributions with those of the capitalist nations in which the state does not play a major redistributive role. In this instance, the expected contrast emerges, although we must re-emphasize the difficulty of interpreting the socialist distributions because of the omitted income categories. As we examine the former command economies in the transition era, we will note significant increases in income inequality.

Economic Stability

A final indicator of economic performance is economic stability. By economic stability we mean the absence of excessive movements in prices, unemployment, and output. Stability also implies the absence of persistent (as opposed to cyclical) high unemployment rates or inflation rates.

FIGURE 13.4   Lorenz Curves of the Distribution of Per Capita Income in Hungary,
             Sweden, West Germany, Spain, Yugoslavia, and Mexico[a,b]

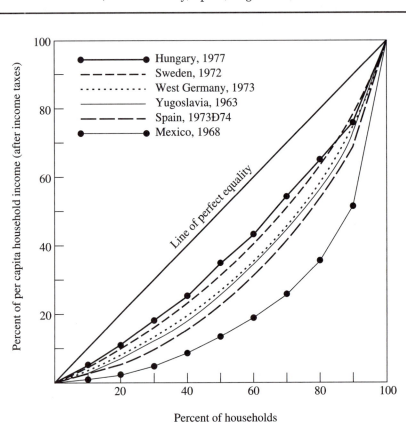

[a] For an explanation of the Lorenz curve, see Chapter 3.
[b] Mexican data are prior to income taxes, but we doubt that their inclusion would move the Mexican Lorenz curve dramatically.

Sources: Malcolm Sawyer, *Income Distribution in OECD Countries* (Paris: OECD, 1976), p. 17; Jan Adams and Miloslav Nosal, "Earnings Differentials and Household-Income Differentials in Hungary—Policies and Practice," *Journal of Comparative Economics* 6 (June 1982), 197; and Wouter van Ginneken, "Generating Internationally Comparable Income Distribution Data," *Review of Income and Wealth* 28 (December 1982), 374.

The postwar era witnessed several recessions in the major capitalist countries, the most severe occurring in the mid-1970s and at the start of the 1980s. Socialist countries experienced "growth recessions"—that is, periods when the growth rate declined but remained positive—but they largely avoided recessions before 1980. In the 1980s, however, the majority of the planned socialist countries experienced periods of negative growth.

The literature recognizes that cyclical fluctuations are present in planned socialist economies, but it was believed that socialist fluctuations were less pronounced.

However, Frederic Pryor found that socialist fluctuations in GDP, industrial output, and investment are not statistically distinguishable from capitalist fluctuations. Moreover, socialist fluctuations in agricultural output were more pronounced than those in capitalist agriculture.[37]

The planned socialist economies claimed that socialist planning "liquidated" unemployment. No society can eliminate unemployment entirely, for at any given time some people are in the process of changing jobs. It does appear that the planned socialist economies reduced the rate of unemployment to small proportions relative to capitalist economies.[38] This was a consequence of deliberate full-employment planning and the resulting **underemployment**. Enterprises were either unwilling or unable to release underemployed workers, which created such a problem that experiments were attempted to encourage the laying off of redundant workers. Generally, however, enterprises were given hiring quotas for new graduates, and the planning system served to provide employment for able-bodied individuals, whether in a necessary or an underemployed position.[39]

Moreover, the planned system avoided unemployment problems by not allowing enterprises to fail. Enterprises have typically been rewarded on the basis of output rather than sales, and the existence of the enterprise has been guaranteed regardless of its performance.

If one examines price inflation under capitalism and planned socialism, a striking contrast emerges from the official statistics (see Table 13.9). Between 1960 and 1980, for example, the capitalist countries experienced considerable inflation, which accelerated after 1970. According to official socialist indexes, on the other hand, consumer prices rose at a very modest pace over this period. The planned socialist economies' claims of virtual price stability for the 1960s and 1970s evoke skepticism about the official consumer price series.[40] First, the official price series ignored substantial price increases for "new" or "higher-quality" products. Often an enterprise could obtain a higher price by claiming superficial or nonexistent quality improvements in its products. Second, the official series failed to capture the price increases of goods sold in legal and illegal free markets. Third, the official indexes did not include the costs of standing in line or of the bribes required to obtain goods. When these circumstances prevail, demand exceeds supply at the established official price, and **repressed inflation** results. Supplies offered at established state prices were rationed out via standing in line, special shopping privileges, or ration coupons.

There is evidence that the official price series understated actual inflation in the socialist countries. Recalculated price indexes (shown in parentheses in Table 13.9) suggest that prices rose more rapidly than official sources claim for the period 1960 to 1980. The relatively stable state retail prices concealed an unknown degree of repressed inflation, which has had a serious destabilizing effect in some planned socialist economies, such as Poland. For political and other reasons, authorities were unwilling to raise official consumer prices to market-clearing levels. Price stability was achieved only at the cost of serious shortages, redirection of purchasing power into collective farm markets and black markets, and growing discontent.

The second column of Table 13.9 gives inflation rates for 1980 to 1989, a period that saw the partial liberalization of state price controls in the East. In the two countries that have converted most to market prices (Poland and Hungary), inflation well

TABLE 13.9   Indexes of Consumer Prices in 1980 and 1989
            (recalculated socialist indexes in parentheses)

	1980 (1960 = 100)		1989 (1980 = 100)	
	A. Socialist Countries			
	Official	Recalculated	Official	Recalculated
Soviet Union	100	(140)	109	(—)
Bulgaria	130	(207)	113	(126)
Czechoslovakia	126	(173)	116	(115)
East Germany	98	(127)	110	(114)
Hungary	169	(210)	215	(220)
Poland	185	(254)	6515	(—)
Romania	120	(—)	130	(141)
Yugoslavia	1449		246560	
	B. Capitalist Countries			
United States	280		150	
Canada	287		170	
Belgium	261		150	
France	382		178	
Italy	546		236	
Japan	420		119	
Netherlands	295		124	
United Kingdom	547		172	
West Germany	213		126	

Sources: Statistical Abstract of the United States, 1981, p. 881; Economic Report of the President, 1981, p. 355; Martin Kohn, "Consumer Price Developments in Eastern Europe," in U.S. Congress, Joint Economic Committee, Eastern European Economic Assessment, Part 2 (Washington, D.C.: U.S. Government Printing Office, 1981), p. 3330; Thad Alton et al., Official Alternative Consumer Price Indexes in Eastern Europe, 1960–1980, OP-68, Research Project on National Income in East Central Europe (New York, 1981); Directorate of Intelligence, CIA, Soviet Gross National Product in Current Prices, 1960–80, SOV 83-10037 (March 1983), pp. 6, 22; Handbook of Economic Statistics 1990, p. 45; "Eastern Europe: Long Road Ahead to Economic Well-Being," 1990, Tables C-2 to C-21; and Narodnoe Khoziaistvo SSSR 1988, p. 125.

outpaced that in the West. Even in the Soviet Union, Bulgaria, and Romania, where prices remained state-controlled during this period (and where the official statistics probably understated inflation), inflation was about the same as in such low-inflation Western countries as Japan, Germany, and the Netherlands.

The rapid increase of prices in Poland and Hungary shows the extent of repressed inflation on the eve of liberalization. The freeing of prices led to very high rates of inflation. In Poland, the result was a 65-fold increase in prices in 1989 as price controls were removed, after which prices stabilized. The apparent price stability of earlier periods (as reflected in the official statistics) has concealed churning inflationary forces. In fact, the pent-up inflationary forces present a serious obstacle to economic reform. The conversion to a market economy requires releasing inflationary pressures. In Eastern Europe, both the governments and the public have a strong fear of inflation—of its effect on output and on the distribution of income. This fear of inflation reduces public support for market reform.

Yugoslavia experienced a more rapid rate of inflation than any capitalist country in our sample. After 1980, Yugoslavia experienced hyperinflation. Moreover, the Yugoslav unemployment rate was higher than that in the planned socialist countries.[41] Thus Yugoslavia does not appear to have matched the planned socialist record of stability but was more like a capitalist developing country in this regard. In fact, Yugoslavia's rates approximated those of Portugal and Turkey. After the end of the command era, formerly fixed prices were generally released. The immediate result was a spike of inflation varying significantly from country to country, but providing interesting information on the extent of command-era repressed inflation.

Performance Comparisons and Decline

At the beginning of this chapter we posed two questions: First, to what extent and in what ways did the performance of the former planned socialist economic systems differ from the performance of market capitalist systems? Second, to what extent and in what ways can the demise of many of these systems be attributed to economic factors?

Economic Decline in the Planned Socialist Systems

Although empirical evidence suggests that some aspects of socialist performance were good in earlier years, noticeable declines in the growth rate of output and productivity were observed in the 1970s and 1980s. That declining performance attracted considerable attention as well as many explanations.

A popular approach to understanding the growth slowdown in the planned socialist economies focused on analysis of input and output growth (production function analysis).[42] Such analyses seemed to suggest that the growth of total factor productivity, while generally (though not always) positive, declined rather steadily during the 1970s and 1980s. Moreover, studies examining labor and capital productivity usually demonstrated a positive and declining labor productivity and an increasingly negative capital productivity. The simple conclusion was that overall diminishing returns and/or declining marginal product of capital occurred in a setting where capital was substituted for labor. This evidence was used to conclude that planned socialist systems, rather than becoming more intensive, were in fact, achieving increasingly less growth from a given input expansion.

Examination of these concepts required the use of production function analysis to relate inputs to outputs in a formal econometric model. Lack of technological progress has been a problem, but for some periods, diminishing returns to capital has also been an explanatory factor.

Beyond the statistical analysis of economic growth in the planned socialist economic systems, a variety of other theories have attempted to provide reasons for the observed slowdown. Many of these theories focus on problems with information and/or incentives.

The microeconomics of the planned socialist systems revealed various sources of inefficiency. In the absence of the pressures of competition and for cost minimization, socialist industrial and agricultural production units demonstrated little interest in efficiency, functioning in an environment of persistent excess demand, along with shortages and bottlenecks in the material supply system. Moreover, lack of innovative activity became understandable in a system where few if any rewards were reaped for either product or process innovation.[43]

Besides the microeconomic problems, a number of observations have been made about more general macroeconomic issues. For example, the evolutionary approach to change may have conferred a growth advantage for the early years of such systems, but it became a disadvantage in later years.[44] Thus it has been argued that the devolution of the planned economies occurred because micro-units, responding to central directives, could be directed and controlled in the early years. But as time passed, those units learned how to collude, restricting and manipulating information flows, which limited the effectiveness of the central planners and their control over the economy. This argument is interesting in light of the sustained existence of an important underground economy in some of the transition economies—for example, Russia.

In addition, the growing complexity of the planned socialist systems could have contributed to the lagging performance.[45] There is, in fact, empirical evidence to suggest that as an economy grows, more units produce more products with increasingly varied inputs. As a result, the basic coordination function becomes increasingly difficult, especially when efforts have been made to avoid the decentralizing of decision making to local levels where the necessary information is available.

A major problem in the planned socialist systems was the nature of incentives. Incentive arrangements may possibly provide the broadest indictment of the planned socialist systems. Although it is difficult to demonstrate empirically, some have argued that the lack of perceived improvements in standards of living, and especially shortages of quality consumer goods, caused the labor force to become increasingly unwilling to make the effort required to stimulate growth and efficiency.

Finally, a variety of issues are related to the general development patterns of socialist economic systems. In a variety of dimensions, especially structural ones, socialist development patterns were different from those observed in market capitalist systems. Sectoral expansion paths differed; for instance, the socialist system emphasized heavy industry at the expense of consumer and service sectors. Although attempts (such as the expansion of social consumption) were made to offset the slow growth in private consumption, the bias against market patterns undoubtedly influenced the forces affecting economic growth. Although structural issues were discussed in a growth context during the era of the planned socialist economic systems, we will see in this book's discussion of transition that structural issues continued to influence the rate and pattern of adjustment in the 1990s—what we broadly term the issue of initial conditions.

Although there is no general and decisive explanation for the decline of the planned socialist economic systems, their so-called strengths at lower levels of economic development might have become weaknesses in subsequent years. These systems were largely incapable of institutional adaptation. To put it another way, traditional economic reform failed, and even last-minute efforts, such as the Soviet Union's attempts at perestroika, were too little and too late. Moreover, in places like Hungary, where change may have been more successful, it served mainly to make the ultimate transition to markets easier as political support for the socialist regime collapsed.

Summary

- Although performance comparisons are important for understanding different economic systems, meaningful comparisons and overall conclusions are difficult to make without using some subjective criteria—for example, whether economic growth is more or less important than, say, full employment. It is possible, however, to compare economic performance by using a series of separate indicators to see how well different systems measure up.
- Cases of rapid economic growth in socialist systems do exist, but despite the importance given to economic growth in socialist systems, these systems have generally not surpassed their capitalist counterparts. Indeed, if one were to control for other factors, such as the level of economic development, rates of economic growth were highest in capitalist systems, even though there has been a capitalist slowdown in contemporary times. Socialist growth rates slowed markedly in the final years of the Soviet and East European experiences.
- Structural differences between socialist and capitalist economic systems are important. If one attempts to control for per capita income, a comparison of the two systems reveals that industry shares were high under socialism, service-sector shares low, and urbanization underemphasized, all of which outcomes are characteristic of the socialist industrialization model. All are important initial conditions that have an impact during transition.
- To understand differences in economic growth, it is necessary to examine the sources of growth, especially the increased use of inputs (extensive growth) vis-à-vis the better use of inputs (intensive growth). The differing systems were broadly similar in growth of inputs during the postwar years, though after 1980, factor inputs probably grew more rapidly under planned socialism, despite the declining rate of output growth in this era.
- During the early postwar era, productivity growth was broadly similar in both systems. For example, during the 1950s, improved efficiency accounted for more than 60 percent of the growth in planned socialist systems, a figure close to the capitalist achievement during that same period. In the era after 1960, however, planned socialist economic growth became more extensive, a troubling sign because almost 80 percent of socialist growth was accounted for by the expansion of inputs.
- The phenomenon of a more extensive growth pattern in the socialist systems was evident in both the levels and the differential growth rates of consumption and

investment; this indicates greater consumer sacrifices in the socialist systems, precisely the opposite of what socialist theory would suggest for advanced levels of economic development. Other inputs remaining constant, the planned socialist countries generally achieved less output per unit of labor input than their capitalist counterparts.

- Income distribution was always difficult to measure in the socialist systems because of the lack of meaningful data. However, past studies have generally argued that income is distributed more nearly equally in those systems in which the state plays a major redistributive role. Thus the differences between the planned socialist systems and the capitalist welfare states are surprisingly small.
- Conventional measures of stability suggest, for the most part, that the socialist systems were more stable than the capitalist systems. But common measures, such as inflation and unemployment, are difficult to interpret across systems because of the serious underemployment and repressed inflation in the socialist setting.
- The apparent decline in rates of economic growth in the planned socialist systems has been analyzed largely by using production function analysis. Although the evidence is mixed, the focus is on diminishing returns and/or declining productivity of capital due to substitution of capital for labor with lack of technological change.
- In addition to an analysis of slowdowns in growth, a number of more general explanations have been given for the slowing economy. They include the growing complexity and the devolution of the system and its general inability to adjust to changes over time.

Key Terms

system objectives
representative economic systems
adjusted factor cost concept
economic growth
intensive growth
extensive growth
static efficiency
dynamic efficiency
labor productivity
capital productivity

total factor productivity
allocative efficiency
enterprise (technical) efficiency
income distribution
total income
labor income
Gini coefficient
underemployment
repressed inflation

Notes

1. Abram Bergson, *Planning and Productivity Under Soviet Socialism* (New York: Columbia University Press, 1968).
2. Paul R. Gregory and Robert C. Stuart, *Soviet Economic Structure and Performance,* 7th ed. (Reading, Mass.: Addison Wesley Longman, 2001), Chs. 10–11.
3. See Joseph Chung, "The Economies of North and South Korea" (Annual Meeting of the American Economic Association, Atlantic City, N.J., September 1976); and Paul Gregory

and Gert Leptin, "Similar Societies Under Differing Economic Systems: The Case of the Two Germanys," *Soviet Studies* 24 (October 1977), 519–542. Also see the papers on the panel "Different Strategies, Similar Countries: The Consequences of Growth and Equity" (Annual Meeting of the American Economic Association, New York, December 1982).

4. Gur Ofer, "Industrial Structure, Urbanization, and the Growth Strategy of Socialist Countries," *Quarterly Journal of Economics* 90 (May 1976), 219–243; Gur Ofer, *The Service Sector in Soviet Economic Development* (Cambridge, Mass.: Harvard University Press, 1973); Paul Gregory, *Socialist and Nonsocialist Industrialization Patterns* (New York: Praeger, 1970); Frederic L. Pryor, *Public Expenditures in Communist and Capitalist Nations* (Bloomington: Indiana University Press, 1973); and Frederic L. Pryor, *Property and Industrial Organization in Communist and Capitalist Nations* (Bloomington: Indiana University Press, 1973). For a discussion of the pure methodology of econometric performance evaluation, see Edward Hewett, "Alternative Econometric Approaches for Studying the Link Between Economic Systems and Economic Outcomes," *Journal of Comparative Economics* 4 (September 1980), 274–294. For a discussion of the methodology of growth comparisons, see Gur Ofer, "Soviet Economic Growth, 1928–1985," *Journal of Economic Literature* 25 (December 1987), 1767–1833.

5. For example, Gregor Lazarcik found that the centrally planned economies with more decentralized agriculture (such as Hungary and Poland) have performed better in terms of output and efficiency than those with centralized agriculture. On this, see Gregor Lazarcik, "Comparative Growth, Structure, and Levels of Agricultural Output, Inputs, and Productivity in Eastern Europe, 1965–79," in U.S. Congress, Joint Economic Committee, *East European Economic Assessment,* Part 2 (Washington, D.C.: U.S. Government Printing Office, 1981), pp. 587–634.

6. The major sources of data on the Soviet Union, Eastern Europe, and China are reports to the U.S. Congress prepared by the Joint Economic Committee. See, for example, *East European Economies: Slow Growth in the 1980s,* Vols. 1–3 (Washington, D.C.: U.S. Government Printing Office, 1986) and *Gorbachev's Economic Plans,* Vols. 1–2 (Washington, D.C.: U.S. Government Printing Office, 1987). Another useful statistical compendium is the Directorate of Intelligence, Central Intelligence Agency, *Handbook of Economic Statistics.* The most useful official East European source is the CMEA handbook: *Statisticheski ezhegodnik stran chlenov Sovet Ekonomicheskikh Vzaimopomoshichi,* various annual editions. For data on the Chinese economy, see U.S. Congress, Joint Economic Committee, *China: A Reassessment of the Economy* (Washington, D.C.: U.S. Government Printing Office, 1975); and Alexander Eckstein, ed., *Quantitative Measures of China's Economic Output* (Ann Arbor: University of Michigan Press, 1980).

7. Statistical comparisons of industrialized capitalism and planned socialism include Maurice Ernst, "Postwar Economic Growth in Eastern Europe," in U.S. Congress, Joint Economic Committee, *Economic Developments in Countries of Eastern Europe* (Washington, D.C.: U.S. Government Printing Office, 1970), pp. 41–67; and Thad Alton, "East European GNPs," in Joint Economic Committee, *East European Economies: Slow Growth in the 1980s,* Vol. 1, pp. 81–132. Also see Andrew Stollar and G. R. Thompson, "Sectoral Employment Shares: A Comparative Systems Context," *Journal of Comparative Economics* 11 (March 1987), 62–80; and Thad Alton, "Production and Resource Allocation in Eastern Europe: Performance, Problems, and Prospects," in Joint Economic Committee, *East European Economic Assessment,* Part 2, pp. 348–408.

8. See, for example, Subramanian Swamy, "Economic Growth in China and India, 1952–1970: A Comparative Appraisal," *Economic Development and Cultural Change* 21 (July 1973), 1–84; and Wilfred Malenbaum, "Modern Economic Growth in India and China: The Comparison Revisited," *Economic Development and Cultural Change* 31 (October 1982), 45–84.

9. For a discussion of CMEA statistical practices, see Thad Alton, "Economic Structure and Growth in Eastern Europe," in Joint Economic Committee, *Economic Developments in Countries of Eastern Europe,* pp. 43–45; and Alton, "Production and Resource Allocation in Eastern Europe," pp. 384–408. See also Paul Marer *et al., Historically Planned Economies: A Guide to the Data* (Washington, D.C.: World Bank, 1992).

10. The pioneering work on reconstructing planned socialist national income accounts was for the Soviet Union and was carried out by Abram Bergson and his associates. For an account of these early efforts, see Abram Bergson, Introduction, *Real National Income of Soviet Russia Since 1928* (Cambridge, Mass.: Harvard University Press, 1961).

11. Bergson, *Real National Income of Soviet Russia Since 1928,* Chs. 2 and 3.

12. On this, see Directorate of Intelligence, Central Intelligence Agency, *Measuring Soviet GNP: Problems and Solutions: A Conference Report,* SOV 90–10038, September 1990; "Eastern Europe: Long Road Ahead to Economic Well-Being," paper by the Central Intelligence Agency presented to the Subcommittee on Technology and National Security of the Joint Economic Committee, May 1990; and Directorate of Intelligence, Central Intelligence Agency, *Revisiting Soviet Economic Performance Under Glasnost: Implications for CIA Estimates,* SOV 88–10068, September 1988.

13. Directorate of Intelligence, *Measuring Soviet GNP: Problems and Solutions,* p. 187.

14. For discussions of the socialist industrialization model, see Gregory, *Socialist and Nonsocialist Industrialization Patterns;* Ofer, "Industrial Structure, Urbanization, and the Growth of Socialist Countries" and *The Service Sector in Soviet Economic Development;* and Gregory and Stuart, *Soviet Economic Structure and Performance,* Ch. 12.

15. For a discussion of index number relativity, see Bergson, *Real National Income of Soviet Russia Since 1928,* Ch. 3.

16. This result was noted first by Abram Bergson in "Development Under Two Systems: Comparative Productivity Growth Since 1950," *World Politics* 20 (July 1971), 579–617.

17. Frederic Pryor, *A Guidebook to the Comparative Study of Economic Systems* (Englewood Cliffs, N.J.: Prentice-Hall, 1985), p. 78.

18. See, for example, Swamy, "Economic Growth in China and India," pp. 81–83; and Malenbaum, "Modern Economic Growth in India and China," pp. 45–84.

19. For a discussion of the measurement of static and dynamic efficiency, see Bergson, *Planning and Productivity Under Soviet Socialism.*

20. Edward Denison and William Chung, *How Japan's Economy Grew So Fast* (Washington, D.C.: Brookings Institution, 1976), p. 30.

21. The classic treatment of the measurement of factor productivity is Edward Denison, *Why Growth Rates Differ* (Washington, D.C.: Brookings Institution, 1967).

22. Apparently the Romanian and Bulgarian capital-stock figures are in current prices. On this, see Alton, "Comparative Structure and Growth of Economic Activity in Eastern Europe," p. 223.

23. Wililam Easterly and Stanley Fischer, "The Soviet Economic Decline," *World Bank Economic Review* 9, 3 (September 1995), 341–371.

24. A considerable amount of research has gone into the subject of the relative growth of investment and consumption in Eastern Europe. Unfortunately, studies that cover the 1970s have not succeeded in calculating directly the real growth of investment. For a discussion of this point, see Alton, "Production and Resource Allocation in Eastern Europe," pp. 314–367. Also see Alton, "East European GNPs," pp. 94–98.

25. See the following studies of per capita consumption in the USSR and Eastern and Western Europe: Terence Byrne, "Levels of Consumption in Eastern Europe," in Joint Economic Committee, *Economic Developments in Countries of Eastern Europe,* pp. 297–315; and U.S. Congress, Joint Economic Committee, *Consumption in the USSR: An International Comparison* (Washington, D.C.: U.S. Government Printing Office, 1981).

26. Abram Bergson, "Comparative Productivity: The USSR, Eastern Europe, and the West," *American Economic Review* 77 (June 1987), 342–357. For Bergson's earlier work on this subject, see his discussion of relative Soviet output per unit in Abram Bergson, *The Economics of Soviet Planning* (New Haven: Yale University Press, 1964), Ch. 14. Also see Bergson, *Production and the Social System: The USSR and the West* (Cambridge, Mass.: Harvard University Press, 1978).

27. This view is shared by Pryor, *Property and Industrial Organization in Communist and Capitalist Nations,* p. 80.

28. Padma Desai and Ricardo Martin, "Efficiency Loss from Resource Misallocation in Soviet Industry," *Quarterly Journal of Economics* 98 (August 1983), 441–456. Also see Judith Thornton, "Differential Capital Charges and Resource Allocation in Soviet Industry," *Journal of Political Economy* 79 (May/June 1971), 545–561. A useful summary of major studies can be found in Peter Murrell, "Can Neoclassical Economics Underpin the Reform of Centrally Planned Economies?" *Journal of Economic Perspectives* 5 (Fall 1991), 59–76.

29. For comprehensive discussions of income distribution under capitalism and socialism, see P. J. D. Wiles, *Economic Institutions Compared* (New York: Halsted Press, 1977), Ch. 16; Martin Schnitzer, *Income Distribution: A Comparative Study of the United States, Sweden, West Germany, East Germany, the United Kingdom, and Japan* (New York: Praeger, 1974); Abram Bergson, "Income Inequality Under Soviet Socialism," *Journal of Economic Literature* 22 (September 1984); C. Morrison, "Income Distribution in East European and Western Countries," *Journal of Comparative Economics* 8 (1984), 121–138; and Anthony B. Atkinson and John Micklewright, *Economic Transformation in Eastern Europe and the Distribution of Income* (Cambridge: Cambridge University Press, 1992).

30. See Pryor, *Property and Industrial Organization in Communist and Capitalist Nations,* pp. 74–75.

31. *Ibid.,* pp. 74–89.

32. John R. Moroney, ed., *Income Inequality: Trends and International Compromise* (Lexington, Mass.: Heath, 1978), p. 5.

33. Janet Chapman, "Earnings Distribution in the USSR, 1968–1976," *Soviet Studies* 35 (July 1983), 410–413.

34. See also a specialized study for the Soviet Union by Alastair McAuley, "The Distribution of Earnings and Income in the Soviet Union," *Soviet Studies* 29 (April 1977), 214–237.

35. Harold Lydall, "Some Problems in Making International Comparisons of Income Inequality," in Moroney, *Income Inequality,* pp. 31–33. For a recent analysis of the available evidence, see Atkinson and Micklewright, *Economic Transformation in Eastern Europe and the Distribution of Income.*

36. Simon Kuznets, *Modern Economic Growth* (New Haven: Yale University Press, 1966).

37. For studies of socialist business and trade cycles, see C. W. Lawson, "An Empirical Analysis of the Structure and Stability of Communist Foreign Trade, 1960–68," *Soviet Studies* 26 (April 1974), 224–238; G. J. Staller, "Patterns and Stability in Foreign Trade, OECD and COMECON," *American Economic Review* (September 1967); Josef Goldman, "Fluctuations and Trends in the Rate of Economic Growth in Some Socialist Countries," *Economics of Planning* 4, 2 (1964), 89–98; Oldrich Kyn, Wolfram Schrette, and Jiri Slama, "Growth Cycles in Centrally Planned Economies: An Empirical Test," Osteuropa Institute, Munich, Working Papers No. 7, August 1975; and Gerard Roland, "Investment Growth Fluctuations in the Soviet Union: An Econometric Analysis," *Journal of Comparative Economics* 11 (June 1987), 192–206. Pryor's results are in Pryor, *A Guidebook,* pp. 114–118.

38. P. J. D. Wiles, "A Note on Soviet Unemployment in U.S. Definitions," *Soviet Studies* 23 (April 1972), 619–628; and David Granick, *Job Rights in the Soviet Union: Their Consequences* (Cambridge: Cambridge University Press, 1987).

39. Morris Bornstein, "Unemployment in Capitalist Regulated Market Economies and Social-ist Centrally Planned Economies," *American Economic Review, Papers and Proceedings* 68 (May 1978), pp. 38–43; and Paul Gregory and Irwin Collier, Jr., "Unemployment in the Soviet Union: Evidence from the Soviet Interview Project," *American Economic Review* 78 (September 1988), 613–632.

40. Authoritative discussions of official socialist price indexes and repressed inflation are found in Richard Portes, "The Control of Inflation: Lessons from East European Experience," *Economica* 44 (May 1977), 109–129. For some empirical estimates, see Richard Portes and David Winter, "The Demand for Money and Consumption Goods in Centrally Planned Economies," *Review of Economics and Statistics* 60 (February 1978), 8–18; and Martin J. Kohn, "Consumer Price Developments in Eastern Europe," in Joint Economic Committee, *East European Economic Assessment,* Part 2, pp. 328–347.

41. World Bank, *World Tables 1976* (Baltimore: Johns Hopkins University Press, 1976).

42. For a summary of views, see "The Soviet Growth Slowdown: Three Views," *American Economic Review: Papers and Proceedings* 76 (May 1986), 170–185.

43. See, for example, Joseph S. Berliner, *The Innovation Decision in Soviet Industry* (Cambridge, Mass.: MIT Press, 1976).

44. Peter Murrell and Mancur Olson, "The Devolution of Centrally Planned Economies," *Journal of Comparative Economics* 15 (June 1991), 239–265.

45. Abhijii V. Banerjee and Michael Spagat, "Productivity Paralysis and the Complexity Problem: Why Do Centrally Planned Economies Become Prematurely Gray?" *Journal of Comparative Economics* 15 (December 1991), 646–660.

Recommended Readings

General References

Trevor Buck, *Comparative Industrial Systems* (New York: St. Martin's, 1982).

Michael Cox, ed., *Rethinking the Soviet Collapse* (London and New York: Pinter, 1998).

William Easterly and Stanley Fischer, "The Soviet Economic Decline," *World Bank Economic Review* 9, 3 (September 1995), 341–71.

Michael Ellman and Vladimir Kontorovich, eds., *The Destruction of the Soviet Economic System* (Armonk, N.Y.: M. E. Sharpe, 1998).

Tania Konn, ed., *Soviet Studies Guide* (London: Bowker-Saur, 1992).

Irving B. Kravis, "Comparative Studies of National Incomes and Prices," *Journal of Economic Literature* 22 (March 1984).

Irving B. Kravis, Allen Heston, and Robert Summers, "Real GDP Per Capita for More Than One Hundred Countries," *Economic Journal* 88 (June 1978).

Irving B. Kravis, *World Product and Income: International Comparisons of Real Gross Product* (Baltimore: Johns Hopkins University Press for the World Bank, 1982).

Frederic L. Pryor, *Property and Industrial Organization in Communist and Capitalist Nations* (Bloomington: Indiana University Press, 1973).

———, *A Guidebook to the Comparative Study of Economic Systems* (Englewood Cliffs, N.J.: Prentice-Hall, 1985).

Economic Growth

Thad P. Alton *et al., Economic Growth in Eastern Europe 1970 and 1975–1985,* Research Project on National Income in East Central Europe (New York: L. W. International Financial Research, Inc. (occasional paper no. 90).

Abram Bergson, *Soviet Post-War Economic Development* (Stockholm: Almquist & Wicksell, 1974).

———, "The Soviet Economic Slowdown," *Challenge* 21 (January–February 1978), 22–27.

Norman E. Cameron, "Economic Growth in the USSR, Hungary, and East and West Germany," *Journal of Comparative Economics* 5 (March 1981), 24–42.

Stanley Cohn, "The Soviet Path to Economic Growth: A Comparative Analysis," *Review of Income and Wealth,* March 1976, 49–59.

Edward Denison, *Why Growth Rates Differ: Postwar Experience in Nine Western Countries* (Washington, D.C.: Brookings Institution, 1967).

Padma Desai, *The Soviet Economy: Efficiency, Technical Change and Growth Retardation* (Oxford: Blackwell, 1986).

———, "Soviet Growth Retardation," *American Economic Review Papers and Proceedings* 76 (May 1986), 175–179.

Stanislaw Gomulka, "Soviet Growth Slowdown: Duality, Maturity and Innovation," *American Economic Review Papers and Proceedings* 76 (May 1986), 170–174.

Vladimir Kontorovich, "Soviet Growth Slowdown: Econometric vs. Direct Evidence," *American Economic Review Papers and Proceedings* 76 (May 1986), 181–185.

Sima Lieberman, *The Growth of European Mixed Economies* (New York: Halstead Press, 1977).

Angus Maddison, *Economic Growth in Japan and USSR* (New York: Norton, 1969).

———, "Growth and Slowdown in Advanced Capitalist Economies," *Journal of Economic Literature* 25 (June 1987), 649–698.

Paul Marer *et al., Historically Planned Economies: A Guide to the Data* (Washington, D.C.: World Bank, 1992).

Wilfred Malenbaum, "Modern Economic Growth in India and China: The Comparison Revisited," *Economic Development and Cultural Change* 31 (October 1982), 45–84.

Productivity

Abram Bergson, "Comparative Productivity: The USSR, Eastern Europe, and the West," *American Economic Review* 77 (June 1987), 342–357.

———, *Planning and Productivity Under Soviet Socialism* (New York: Columbia University Press, 1967).

———, *Productivity and the Social System: The USSR and the West* (Cambridge, Mass.: Harvard University Press, 1978).

———, "Productivity Under Two Systems: The USSR versus the West," in Jan Tinbergen *et al.,* eds., *Optimum Social Welfare and Productivity: A Comparative View* (New York: New York University Press, 1972).

Padma Desai, "Total Factor Productivity in Postwar Soviet Industry and Its Branches," *Journal of Comparative Economics* 9 (March 1985), 1–23.

Padma Desai and Ricardo Martin, "Efficiency Loss from Resource Misallocation in Soviet Industry," *Quarterly Journal of Economics* 98 (August 1983), 441–456.

Herbert S. Levine, "Possible Causes of the Deterioration of Soviet Productivity Growth in the Period 1976–80," in U.S. Congress, Joint Economic Committee, *Soviet Economy in the 1980s: Problems and Prospects,* Part 1 (Washington, D.C.: U.S Government Printing Office, 1982), 153–168.

Peter Murrell and Mancur Olson, "The Devolution of Centrally Planned Economies," *Journal of Comparative Economics* 15 (June 1991), 239–265.

Gertrude Schroeder, "The Slowdown in Soviet Industry, 1976–1982" *Soviet Economy* 1 (January–March 1985), 42–74.

Subramanian Swamy, "The Economic Growth in China and India, 1952–1970: A Comparative Appraisal," *Economic Development and Cultural Change* 21 (July 1973), 1–84.

U.S. Congress, Joint Economic Committee, *USSR: Measures of Economic Growth and Development, 1950–1980* (Washington, D.C.: U.S. Government Printing Office, 1982).

———, *East European Economies: Slow Growth in the 1980s,* Vols. 1–3 (Washington, D.C.: U.S. Government Printing Office, 1985).

Martin Weitzman, "Soviet Postwar Economic Growth and Capital–Labor Substitution," *American Economic Review* 60 (December 1970), 676–692.

Technology

R. Amann and J. Cooper, eds., *Industrial Innovation in the Soviet Union* (New Haven: Yale University Press, 1982).

Abram Bergson, "Technological Progress," in Abram Bergson and Herbert S. Levine, eds., *The Soviet Economy Towards the Year 2000* (London: Allen and Unwin, 1983).

Joseph S. Berliner, *The Innovation Decision in Soviet Industry* (Cambridge, Mass.: MIT Press, 1976).

Income Inequality

Michael V. Alexeev and Clifford G. Gaddy, "Trends in Wage and Income Distribution Under Gorbachev: Analysis of New Soviet Data," (Durham, N.C.: Berkeley–Duke Occasional Papers on the Second Economy in the USSR, No. 25, 1991).

Anthony B. Atkinson and John Micklewright, *Economic Transformation in Eastern Europe and the Distribution of Income* (Cambridge: Cambridge University Press, 1992).

Abram Bergson, "Income Inequality Under Soviet Socialism," *Journal of Economic Literature* 22 (September 1984).

Janet Chapman, "Are Earnings More Equal Under Socialism? The Soviet Case, with Some United States Comparisons," in J. R. Moroney, ed., *Income Inequality: Trends and International Comparisons* (Lexington, Mass.: Heath, 1979).

———, "Earnings Distribution in the USSR, 1968–1976," *Soviet Studies* 35 (1983), 410–413.

———, "Income Distribution and Social Justice in the Soviet Union," *Comparative Economic Studies* 31 (1989), 14–45.

John Moroney, *Income Inequality: Trends and International Comparisons* (Lexington, Mass.: Heath, 1978).

Martin Schnitzer, *Income Distribution: A Comparative Study of the United States, Sweden, West Germany, East Germany, the United Kingdom, and Japan* (New York: Praeger, 1974).

P. J. D. Wiles, *The Distribution of Income, East and West* (Amsterdam: North-Holland, 1974).

Welfare Issues

Anthony B. Atkinson and John Micklewright, *Economic Transformation in Eastern Europe and the Distribution of Income* (Cambridge: Cambridge University Press, 1993).

Abram Bergson, "The USSR Before the Fall: How Poor and Why?" *Journal of Economic Perspectives* 5 (Fall 1991), 29–44.

M. Matthews, *Privilege in the Soviet Union* (London: Allen and Unwin, 1978).

Alastair McAuley, *Economic Welfare in the Soviet Union* (Madison: University of Wisconsin Press, 1979).

———, "The Welfare State in the USSR," in T. Wilson and D. Wilson, eds., *The State and Social Welfare* (London: Longmans, 1991).

G. Ofer and A. Vinokur, *The Soviet Household Under the Old Regime* (Cambridge: Cambridge University Press, 1992).

A. Vinokur and G. Ofer, "Inequality of Earnings, Household Income, and Wealth in the Soviet Union in the 1970s," in James R. Millar, ed., *Politics, Work, and Daily Life in the USSR* (Cambridge: Cambridge University Press, 1987).

Murray Yanowitch, *Social and Economic Inequality in the Soviet Union* (White Plains, N.Y.: M. E. Sharpe, 1977).

Appendix 13A:
The Index Number Problem in International Comparisons

In this chapter we cited a large number of statistics comparing the level of GDP, output per worker, and so on, among capitalist and socialist countries.[1] For purposes of simplicity, we glossed over the fact that the price system that underlies these valuations can have a substantial impact on the outcome. For example, for us to compare levels of GDP meaningfully, the GDPs of all countries being compared must be valued in some common currency (dollars, rubles, marks, pounds, or whatever). These issues bear scrutiny because they are basic to international comparisons.

Let us take the case of comparing the levels of GDP of the Soviet Union and the United States in 1980. To simplify the illustration, let us say that both countries produce only two goods, wheat and lathes. In the USSR, wheat is expensive relative to lathes; in the United States, wheat is cheap relative to lathes (as judged by Soviet prices). Production and domestic prices of these two commodities in each country are given in Table 13A.1.

From this information, we can make two types of calculations: We can calculate the GDPs of both countries using U.S. prices, or we can calculate the GDPs of both countries using Soviet prices.

In U.S. prices, we get

$$\text{Soviet GDP} = (\$2 \times 10) + (\$2 \times 20) \quad \text{or} \quad \$\ 60$$
$$\text{U.S. GDP} = (\$2 \times 30) + (\$2 \times 40) \quad \text{or} \quad \$140$$

Result: In U.S. prices, Soviet GDP is 60/140 = 43 percent of U.S. GDP.

In Soviet prices, we get

$$\text{Soviet GDP} = (5R \times 10) + (1R \times 20) \quad \text{or} \quad 70R$$
$$\text{U.S. GDP} = (5R \times 30) + (1R \times 40) \quad \text{or} \quad 190R$$

Result: In Soviet prices, Soviet GDP is only 70/190 = 37 percent of U.S. GDP.

The comparison is more favorable when the prices of the other country are used than when the country's own prices are used. Why is this typically the case? It is an empirical fact that the relative prices of any country tend to be inversely related to the relative quantities produced by that country. Products that can be produced relatively cheaply (because of abundant domestic resources) tend to be produced in abundance, and products that can be produced relatively expensively tend to be limited in production. Insofar as relative prices differ among countries (as a result of differences

TABLE 13A.1

	Output		Price	
	Wheat	Lathes	Wheat	Lathes
Soviet Union, 1980	10	20	5R	1R
United States, 1980	30	40	$2	$2

in human capital and natural resources), we find that each country emphasizes the production of relatively cheap commodities. Therefore, when the GDP of one country is valued using the different relative prices of another country, its total output appears relatively large.

To take a real-world example of this index number phenomenon, we can cite studies of Soviet per capita consumption as a percentage of U.S. consumption. In 1976, Soviet and U.S. consumption per capita were 1,116R and 4,039R, respectively, when valued in rubles. In other words, the Soviet Union stood at 28 percent of the U.S. level. Valued in dollars, Soviet and U.S. per capita consumption were $2,395 and $5,598, respectively; that is, Soviet consumption per capita was 43 percent of the U.S. level. Which figure (28 percent or 43 percent) is the correct one? There is no "true" value in such comparisons. One comparison is as real as the other, for each system of relative prices yields a different answer.

It should be noted that for the comparisons in this chapter, we consistently use dollar valuations. Dollar valuations make Soviet and East European values look more favorable than they would have if, say, ruble prices had been used.

Note

1. U.S. Congress, Joint Economic Committee, *Consumption in the USSR: An International Comparison* (Washington, D.C.: U.S. Government Printing Office, 1981), p. 6.

References

Trevor Buck, *Comparative Industrial Systems* (New York: St. Martin's, 1981), Ch. 5.

Irving B. Kravis *et al., A System of International Comparisons of Gross National Product and Purchasing Power* (Baltimore: Johns Hopkins University Press, 1975).

Richard Moorsteen, "On Measuring Productive Potential and Relative Efficiency," *Quarterly Journal of Economics* 75 (August 1981), 451–467.

PART IV

Systemic Change in a Global Perspective: Transition

14

An Introduction
to Transition

Concepts and Context

In Chapter 4 we examined the concepts of economic reform and transition from the broad perspective of socioeconomic change. In this chapter, we resume our examination of transition to explore the dramatic events of the post-command era of the 1990s. Transition is the replacement of one **economic system** by another.[1] The precise identification of real-world examples of transition is not always an easy task. Although there are wide variations from country to country, transition has typically entailed replacement of a **command economy** with a **market economy**.

In spite of conceptual difficulties in applying our definition of *transition* to real-world settings, most observers identify the transition economies as the fifteen separate countries that emerged from the Soviet Union, along with the countries of Central and Eastern Europe (including countries emerging from former Yugoslavia). In fact, as we will see, transitional change has been broader in scope. Although the terms used to identify and characterize change vary from one case to another, **economic reform** generally refers to the modification of an existing system, and **transition** refers to the replacement of one economic system by a new and different economic system. In this sense, countries like China and Vietnam are of immense interest as **emerging market economies** but usually are not formally classified as transition economies. In both cases the government structure remains substantially unchanged, these countries being governed by a single communist political party, whereas in the transition economies identified above, political change and democratization have been a pivotal part of the transition experience. However, important components of transition—for example, privatization—have been major policy imperatives in both China and Vietnam, and indeed in many other countries. Thus, as we examine important components of transition, it is often useful to examine a broad set of country experiences.

Transition was not a concept that emerged gradually during the 1970s and 1980s. Indeed, as we observed in Chapter 13, the performance of the command economies of the Soviet Union and Eastern Europe showed significant decline during this period. Moreover, the collapse of these political and economic systems was rapid, following the lead of the Soviet Union at the end of the era of Perestroika in the late 1980s. Because the collapse of the command systems was rapid, in nearly all cases there were no clear theoretical or practical system models from which the course of transition could be charted. Moreover, as we emphasize throughout this book, the starting conditions of transition in the various transition economies were very different, a fact that would influence the success of transition in complex ways.

Differences in Background and Initial Conditions

Systemic change was not well understood at the end of the 1980s. Moreover, the impact of past command arrangements was quite different in the various transition economies. In the Soviet Union, itself a very large country composed of fifteen different republics, the command system was introduced in 1928, whereas in Eastern Europe the command type of economic system dated from the end of World War II. Indeed, Yugoslavia was classified not as a command economy but rather as an example of market socialism under the arrangements of worker management. In the Soviet Union, the command economy functioned for roughly sixty years; in Eastern Europe, it functioned for roughly forty years. The extent and impact of change from within (economic reform) during the command era also differed widely in these economies. During the 1980s, for example, there was significant economic reform in Hungary and Poland and minimal reform in the Soviet Union.[2] Thus, as we will see, the starting positions of the transition era were very different across the various transition economies.[3] It is the need to understand these different starting positions that prompted our earlier discussions of the command systems.

The sudden collapse that occurred in the late 1980s also occurred in a variety of very different settings. Table 14.1 notes important basic differences among twenty-six transition economies.[4] For example, the Soviet Union was an immense entity (in geographic area, output, and population) consisting of fifteen very different republics, most of which had functioned within the command environment for a long time.[5] Policy imperatives and applications in, say, Moldova were not an outcome of Moldavian decision making but rather were, for many years, a product of decision making in Moscow. Although we should not overstate the extent and influence of centralized power in the Soviet Union, Moldova was effectively a region of a large centralized economy, not a country pursuing economic activity in its own right. Thus the size and nature of the decision-making unit (country) changed fundamentally during the transition era. Understandably, the collapse of the command order presented serious problems in the Soviet Union—problems very different from those in a single political and geographic entity such as Hungary. As the republics became countries, how would the infrastructure be divided, and how would formerly national issues (such as the debt of the USSR) be handled?

By any indicator chosen in Table 14.1, the countries that emerged from the former Soviet Union are fundamentally very different from each other. Figure 14.1 shows the important differences in size and location.

Regional issues were important in the Soviet Union, and they remain important—though fundamentally different—among the nations carved from the Soviet Union. For example, after roughly ten years of transition, the per capita income of Estonia was $10,000 (measured in U.S. dollars), whereas the per capita income of Tajikistan was $1,140 (measured in U.S. dollars). Even if measurement problems make these estimates of per capita income only broadly reflective of actual differences, the differences are very important.[6]

Eastern European countries were generally much smaller than the major transition economies emerging from the Soviet Union (Russia, Kazakhstan, and Ukraine); were

TABLE 14.1   Transition: Countries and Country Indicators

Country	Land Area (square kilometers)	Population (millions), July 2001 Estimate	Per capita GDP (U.S.$), Mid-2001 Estimate (ppp)[a]	Per Capita GDP, 1999 (1989 = 100)
Albania	27,398	3.5	3,000	95
Armenia	28,400	3.3	3,000	42
Azerbaijan	86,100	7.8	3,000	47
Belarus	207,000	10.4	7,500	80
Bosnia/ Herzegovina	51,129	3.9	1,700	n.a.
Bulgaria	110,550	7.7	6,200	67
Croatia	56,414	4.3	5,800	78
Czech Republic	77,276	10.3	12,900	95
Estonia	43,211	1.4	10,000	77
FYR Macedonia	24,856	2.0	4,400	74
Georgia	69,700	5.0	4,600	34
Hungary	92,340	10.1	11,200	99
Kazakhstan	2,669,300	10.7	5,000	63
Kyrgyzstan	191,300	4.8	2,700	63
Latvia	64,589	2.4	7,200	60
Lithuania	65,200	3.6	7,300	62
Moldova	33,371	4.4	2,500	31
Poland	304,465	38.6	8,500	122
Romania	230,340	22.4	5,900	76
Russia	16,995,800	145.5	7,700	57
Slovakia	48,800	5.4	10,200	100
Slovenia	20,253	1.9	12,000	109
Tajikistan	142,700	6.6	1,140	44
Turkmenistan	488,100	4.6	4,300	64
Ukraine	603,700	48.8	3,850	36
Uzbekistan	425,400	25.2	2,400	94

[a]Purchasing power parity estimate.

Source: Central Intelligence Agency, *The World Factbook 2001* (Washington, D.C.: CIA, 2001); European Bank for Reconstruction and Development, *Transition Report 2000* (London: EBRD, 2000).

homogeneous in many dimensions, having undergone a much shorter command experience; and were located in geographic proximity to Western Europe (see Figure 14.2). Most of the transition economies remained as identifiable entities before and during transition, although there were important and interesting exceptions. Czechoslovakia split into the Czech Republic and Slovakia (1993), and the German Democratic Republic (GDR) became unified with the Federal Republic of Germany (FRG) to form a single country and economy.[7] Isolating the elements of transition in the German case is especially difficult, because the entire process has taken place under a single political

FIGURE 14.1   The Independent Republics of the Former Soviet Union

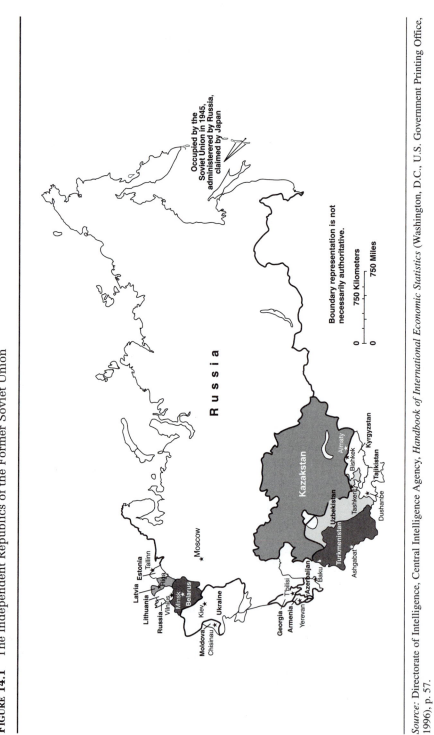

Source: Directorate of Intelligence, Central Intelligence Agency, *Handbook of International Economic Statistics* (Washington, D.C., U.S. Government Printing Office, 1996), p. 57.

FIGURE 14.2   Europe

Source: Central Intelligence Agency, Washington, D.C., 1995.

entity in a unique cultural, historical, and geographic setting. Yugoslavia's experience has been complicated by internal conflict.[8] However, the republics of the former Yugoslavia became independent entities. In Table 14.1, we include four newly independent nations: Bosnia-Herzegovina, Croatia, FYR Macedonia, and Slovenia.

Subsequent events and the analysis of transition outcomes have demonstrated that the differences noted above matter in a variety of ways. It is important to understand that even though we characterize transition broadly as the replacement of the command economy with a market economy, in fact the command experience itself differed from one country to another. In the case of Yugoslavia, for example, not only have the transition economies emerged from a single country, but the Yugoslav economy was not generally classified as a command economy. Although Yugoslavia was governed by a single Communist party, the economy was often characterized as market socialism using a system of worker management.[9] (The theoretical basis of market socialism was examined in detail in Chapter 7.) The contemporary division of the former Yugoslavia is shown in Figure 14.3.

Country size and location are significant in many ways. Some countries, especially the smaller East European countries, were relatively open economies even during the command era, whereas others experienced only very limited trading engagement with the external world.[10] This differing trade experience not only had an impact on resource allocation during the command era but also left some of the new countries with any trading experience to exploit as they entered a global environment during transition. Arguably, the republics of the Soviet Union were "closed" to a much greater degree than Hungary and Poland. This fact affects far more than the simple mechanics of exporting and importing, influencing areas such as specialization patterns and the potential impact (or lack of impact) of foreign technology. Geography also matters in another important respect: the proximity of the countries of Eastern and Central Europe to the European Economic Community.

In the transition economies, the **resource bases** differ greatly, a fact which influenced industrial structure and trade patterns during the command era. These differences have largely persisted during the transition era in critical areas such as energy supplies. All of these resource differences were important in the command era, and most remain influential, though in varying degrees, in the transition era. Again, there are important differences among the former republics of the Soviet Union and vis-à-vis the East European transition economies.

Effects of the Rapidity of Transition

The fact that the transition era emerged quickly presented a variety of special difficulties that have been far more important than was imagined during the early years of transition. First, transition has always been much more than an economic phenomenon. It is also fundamentally a political and a social phenomenon with far-reaching implications for populations long isolated from Western democratic ideas and institutions. The extent and impact of this isolation varied a great deal from country to country. Clearly, Albania and Belarus were far more isolated over a longer period of time than Hungary and Poland.

FIGURE 14.3   The Former Yugoslavia

Source: Central Intelligence Agency, Washington, D.C., 1996.

Second, social policies—or, more narrowly, economic incentives—were fundamentally different in the command economies. Great reliance was placed on the socialization of incentives, and this became an important issue as social policies began to change dramatically during transition. The new incentive structure would be a major determinant of population support for the new political regime and its transition policies. One could argue that in the command economies, the attempted socialization of incentives failed. However, citizens became accustomed to full employment, access to education, and the provision of old-age pensions on reasonable terms, even if consumer goods were not always available in retail stores. Changes in the safety net during the transition of the 1990s have been of major importance in all the transition economies during an era when the social contract has been fundamentally redefined.

Third, it is perhaps ironic that many countries, suddenly faced with the need for institutional change, would look to the discipline of economics for guidance. Neoclassical economics has never, until recently, embraced institutional change as a fundamental component of its paradigm. This is why models of systemic change were simply not available to policy makers in the emerging market economies.[11] The dominant model of socioeconomic change in the East—namely the **Marxist–Leninist framework**—was generally not accepted in the West and subsequently was largely abandoned in the East. However, we must not overlook the impact of European, Asian, and other cultural and historical forces on the outcomes of transition. To put it differently, the former command economies are pursuing the development of market capitalism, although the forms of capitalism may differ considerably from those we are familiar with in the industrialized world. Transition economies may well be identified as mixed economic systems to a greater degree than the traditional industrialized (market) economies. In the transition context, it is important to identify a mixed system as mixed in at least two important dimensions: (1) There may well be a tendency to combine systemic elements from the old order—specifically, instruments of state control and/or intervention—with traditional market mechanisms. (2) It is likely that there will be important policy differences (for example, greater concern for the safety net in transition economies) to soften the outcomes more typical of market economies.

The decade of the 1990s has been dominated by interest in and observation of these emerging systems, the different paths they have chosen, and the varied outcomes they have achieved. The lessons learned from these transition economies have been important for the other emerging market economies. However, judging the success of the transition economies themselves and assessing the relevance of their experiences to other countries is a complex undertaking. Even after a decade of transition experience, there are some countries (such as Ukraine and Belarus) where the impact of transition has been minimal. And there are other countries (such as Hungary and the Czech Republic) where some would argue that models of transition no longer apply to these small, open, market economies.

Thus far we have emphasized basic historical and natural features of the transition economies. As transition began in the late 1980s and early 1990s, attention quickly turned to the collapse of the command systems, the gradual emergence of new arrangements, and perhaps most important, changes in output. We turn our attention to these issues.

Differences in Output Performance

The index of output for transition economies given in Table 14.1 and the graphical presentation in Figure 14.4 demonstrate the existence of major differences in output performance during the transition era of the 1990s. Thus in 1999, the per capita output of Moldova (as an example) was 31 percent of its level in 1989. Collapse on this

Figure 14.4   GDP: Percentage Change (year to year in constant prices)
Selected Transition Economies, 1990–2002[a]

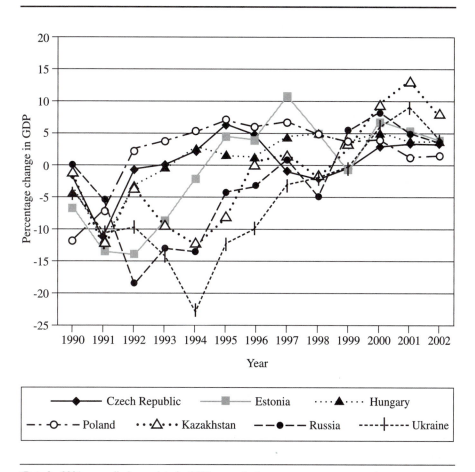

Legend:
———◆——— Czech Republic   ———■——— Estonia   ····▲···· Hungary
— · —○— · — Poland   ··△·· Kazakhstan   ——●—— Russia   ----+---- Ukraine

[a]Data for 2001 are preliminary; data for 2002 are projections.

Source: Data are from EBRD, *Transition Report Update* (London: EBRD, May 2002), Annex 1.1.

scale has been experienced in many transition economies. There are, of course, exceptions, such as Poland and Slovenia, and in countries such as Estonia and Romania the collapse has been less severe. Moreover, this evidence on the output patterns of transition economies presents us with one of the most frequently discussed stylized pictures of transition: the "J curve," or the pattern of severe collapse and subsequent recovery observed in virtually all transition economies. In Figure 14.4 we present a summary picture of the growth of output in a selection of transition economies. What accounts for this striking pattern and for the important differences in output growth from one country to another?

In broad perspective, one of the most characteristic aspects of transition is the initial collapse of output and its slow recovery. Obviously, any judgment about transition tends to focus on output—specifically, the magnitude of the collapse and its pattern and duration. Even with this seemingly simple indicator, there are disagreements about measurement and interpretation, and yet striking differences emerge. Although the general pattern of decline and subsequent recovery is clearly evident, there are substantial differences among the countries examined in this chart, differences that reflect what we observe in Table 14.1.

The collapse of the Polish economy was by any measure modest and the recovery rapid. By contrast, the collapse of the Russian economy was deep and the recovery very slow; after the collapse in 1989, positive economic growth appeared for the first time in the late 1990s! Thus both the nature and the pattern of economic growth are major indicators for judging transition, though in many cases there are serious problems of data availability, accuracy, and interpretation.[12] For example, in the important case of Russia, the presence of a large virtual (shadow) economy, especially in the late 1990s, makes traditional measurement approaches inadequate.[13] As we will observe in subsequent discussion, the issue of a shadow economy, especially important in Russia, significantly complicates traditional approaches to measurement.[14]

Output is of course a function of many underlying forces, so naturally these forces are of interest. Privatization is a first step, but restructuring is essential and is a major indicator of systemic change. Trade is important, but the contribution of trade to economic growth and to the enhanced well-being of the population is also of fundamental importance. Therefore, both the nature of economic growth and the forces that contribute to this growth are crucial to a successful transition. Characterizing systemic change and the components of systemic change is a major challenge as we seek to understand the transition experience.

Much as economists favor examination of institutional, policy, and other underpinnings of the growth experience, we cannot assess transition without considering the populace's quality of life. As we noted earlier in this book, the socialist era may have had a leveling effect on living standards, imposing a more even income distribution than tends to occur under alternative systemic and policy arrangements. But the era of markets has been very different: Some economies have prospered, some have held their own, and some have found their standard of living significantly lowered. Increasing inequality was to be expected. At the same time, human adjustment to these new conditions is a major story of the transition experience. The human side of transition is especially important in the European setting, where there is less tolerance for inequality than in the United States.

Should we emphasize the starting points, or **initial conditions**, that prevailed at the beginning of transition some ten years ago? Or is the major emphasis to be placed on other factors, such as the natural environment, the extent of political modernization, and the emerging policy framework? Although these questions will interest scholars and policy makers long into the twenty-first century, a decade of practical experience can certainly provide us with important perspectives. Transition is one of the most important events of the twentieth century, and it will clearly remain so during the early years of the twenty-first.

Transition in a Global Setting

We have noted that the emergence of transition in the late 1980s was a relatively sudden event. Its impact, however, is far more than local (domestic) in character—a fact which dominates the contemporary discussion of transition economies. There are a variety of reasons for this global emphasis.

First, when transition began, it did so in economies that had been, for a variety of reasons, largely isolated from the globalization process. Although we have noted that this isolation was of greater consequence for some countries (such as the Soviet Union) than for others (such as Poland and Hungary), the structural impact of years of isolation from both the negative and the positive effects of world market forces left many countries with archaic resource-allocation arrangements and resulting **structural distortions** in resource allocation. The normal market influences of specialization and trade, for example, were sharply modified in countries such as the Soviet Union. Furthermore, the Soviet Union was almost totally isolated from the impact of world financial markets and world financial forces. Some of the distortions that grew out of the isolation of the command economies were quite basic (distorted commodity trade patterns), and some were more complex (the lack of impact of foreign technology). The emergence of markets and market forces in the transition economies brought necessary—but sudden and sometimes brutal—changes as noncompetitive industries collapsed while new, formerly nonexistent industries emerged. Another important example is the command economies' well-known bias in favor of industry and heavy industry, which results in sectoral allocation patterns very different from what one might expect under market arrangements. Of course, structural changes have occurred in many countries (consider the production of steel in the United States after World War II), but in market economies, these changes occurred relatively slowly. Large segments of the command economies were isolated from world competitive forces, and inefficient domestic economic activity was sustained by large state subsidies funded by the extraction of surplus value from the population. These arrangements changed suddenly during transition. The associated social disruption (for example, significant unemployment in declining sectors) has been important.

Second, the transition economies have had to adapt to an external (global) environment that itself has been undergoing rapid change. Perhaps the most dramatic example of such change is the development of the **European Union**. The emergence of the EU has been controversial in the West, but even more so in the East, where EU rules of entry prescribe the implementing of difficult but critical policy, structural, and other changes.

Third, the global setting has prompted some to ask about the end of transition. For example, one could argue that the Czech economy is a small open economy at a medium level of economic development pursuing stable and sustained economic growth. Why not simply characterize the Czech economy in this way rather than thinking about it in terms of the framework of transition? Our choice in this matter will dictate what tools are appropriate for analyzing the Czech economy. If we abandon the characterization of the Czech economy as a transition economy, then we imply that we understand the objectives of transition and that these objectives have been achieved.

Moreover, we imply that the impact of the command era has been erased or, at a minimum, has no impact on contemporary economic events. In other words, the Czech economy would be characterized as returning to its long-term "normal" growth path having eliminated the structural distorting of the command era. These important and controversial issues will be discussed further in subsequent chapters of this book.[15]

Assessing Transition: Contemporary Perspectives

More generally, how might we characterize the end of transition? There are a variety of indicators, none of which is completely satisfactory and most of which are difficult to measure precisely. It is, however, critical that we be able to characterize both the successes and the failures of the transition experience. The output data presented in Table 14.1 and Figure 14.4 gives us only a modest start in our assessment of transition outcomes. But, we need to focus on varying frames of reference that can be used to characterize transition and to assess outcomes.

During the early years of the transition era, there has been a tendency to look at organizational indicators of transition (for example, the importance of private ownership) and to argue that when this indicator reaches a level comparable to that in other economies at similar levels of economic development, this element of transition has been completed. In the case of our example (private ownership), that level would be reached when private property had replaced state property, and markets had been put in place. One could make a similar argument for policy measures—for example, using the development of monetary and fiscal institutions and associated macroeconomic policies to gauge the extent to which institutions and policies of the command era have in fact been replaced by market-based institutions and policies. It is for this reason that liberalization has been a major theme of the literature on transition. **Liberalization** is the reduction of state controls and the introduction of markets. As we will see, there have been a variety of attempts to develop indexes measuring the degree to which markets and market policies have emerged in the transition economies. In a sense, such a perspective looks at transition in terms of organizational arrangements (inputs) rather than outputs.

One could argue that from a longer-term perspective, transition is really over when the economy in question has returned to a long-term market trajectory of economic growth. Such an outcome might be measured in terms of such long-term structural characteristics as sectoral output shares, trade shares, and aggregate growth patterns. This was, after all, a popular framework in which to view the command economies as suffering from distortion in their earlier outcomes. Indeed, we often characterized the command economies as being distorted, a concept that implied nonmarket outcomes (an example is the well-known industry bias in these economies). From this point of view, the changing institutional arrangements and policies are secondary characteristics that we examine to determine the outcome of the allocation process and to observe when such outcomes revert to "normal," or noncommand, patterns. The empirical literature on transition has yet to fully characterize transition from this perspective. Moreover, this type of assessment brings the field of transition economics very close to the field of development economics. Indeed, for some transition economies that had only limited success in the 1990s, one could argue that the tools of economic development may be more relevant than the tools of transition. That is, the tools of transition are inappropriate for those economies that have not experienced any measurable amount of economic growth and development.

Finally, much of the transition literature focuses on quite traditional indicators of success. We have already emphasized the importance of output patterns in the transition economies. Equally important are indicators such as employment, medical care, pension benefits, and elimination of poverty.

A Systems Perspective

Those who observe transition economies in the context of comparative economic systems tend to take a long-term view of the transition process. From a systems perspective, it can be argued that differences in outcomes are to be expected when institutional arrangements and policy imperatives differ even moderately. It might also be argued, especially in cases such as Russia, that the long-term impact of socialist policies in the command setting is very difficult to erase. The analyst of differing economic systems would maintain, therefore, that even when we do not impose the traditional simplistic characterization of systems inherent in the "isms" framework, economic systems remain very different. Indeed, we have already noted that the concept of a mixed system may receive much more attention in the transition economies than has been typical in market economies. The economic systems of Great Britain and the United States are very different, as are the economic outcomes in these countries. These differences will remain important as the discipline of economics becomes better able to provide useful theoretical and analytical tools with which to understand them. The disappearance of simplistic categories of economic systems is a positive though complex outgrowth of the transition era. However, system differences persist, as do other fundamental differences such as natural setting and resource endowment. Thus in the end, and with only limited exceptions, most transition economies are in fact mixed systems and differ significantly from one another. They will, however, be analyzed not in terms of simple categorizations (the "isms"), but rather in terms of their architecture and internal working arrangements using agency theory, information economics, and so on.

We have already noted that the impact of the global era is important in yet another dimension: Transition has not taken place in isolation from more general changes occurring in various nontransition countries, such as the emergence of the European Union. Consider, for example, the role of the state and public sector in the economy. This issue can be approached in ideological terms, but it can also be cast within the framework of public-choice theory in market-capitalist economies. In the past, these two approaches have been quite distinct.

Whereas explicit policies of **privatization** have been pursued in transition economies to replace command instruments with market mechanisms of resource allocation, Western market economies have placed major emphasis on privatization with the immediate objective of increasing economic efficiency. Thus replacing public enterprise with private enterprise has been a major policy imperative in both East and West, but in very different settings and with somewhat different objectives and results. Indeed, as we will observe, the decline of the state sector in economies East and West, developed and developing, is a contemporary phenomenon of great importance, with implications far beyond the singular case of privatization in the transition setting. The contribution that examining this process will make to our knowledge of differing economic systems promises to be immense.

Finally, the social impact of transition is a complex issue of great importance to our assessment of transition outcomes. Although social policies differed considerably from one command economy to another, on balance all pursued a social contract very different from that pursued under contemporary capitalism.[16] It is understandable that the former command economies saw the need for efficiency, but it is also necessary to emphasize the long-run importance of equity issues. The latter will be critical to defining the successes or failures of the transition economies.

The Framework of Transition: Theory and Evidence

In the remaining chapters of this book, we examine the transition era of the 1990s. Our approach relies heavily on the experiences of individual countries for the light they shed on similarities and differences between various transition scenarios and on the components of the transition process. Framing the experience of transition is not a straightforward task. Much of the literature generated during the early years of transition is cast in terms of two broad approaches: the big push and the evolutionary approach. We will discuss both approaches in greater detail in subsequent chapters, although most analysts now treat these early transition models as simplistic and prefer to address basic issues of speed, sequencing, and complementarities when formalizing the transition experience. The modeling of transition approaches is not ideal, but there is much agreement on the typical components of the transition experience. It is these components that form the framework of the remainder of this book.

Traditionally, the literature on transition has been usefully characterized in four major dimensions. First, there is a large literature on *the process of privatization and the development of factor and product markets.* During the early years of transition, this literature focused on the mechanisms for privatization and typically assessed the immediate results by examining the sectoral shares of output and employment derived from private economic activity. During the latter years of the 1990s and into a new century, the literature has focused mainly on **restructuring**, or changing the nature of corporate governance to achieve efficiency objectives.

The second major component of the transition literature has been the *development of the macroeconomy,* both institutions and policies. Immediately after the collapse, the focus was on stabilization, but the more recent focus has been on "normalization" of the macroeconomy, specifically the budgetary process and the banking system, including the development of financial markets for the purpose of financial intermediation. These issues are especially important during transition because financial institutions had limited influence on resource allocation in the command economies. The challenge here is to develop new institutions and a new stock of human capital to guide them.

Third, although integration of the command economies into the global economy is fundamentally intertwined with development of the macroeconomy, it is useful to examine foreign trade as a major and identifiable policy issue for transition economies. Beyond the development of new market-oriented institutional arrangements for both physical and financial flows, a major issue has been the introduction of a convertible currency and the implementation of an exchange rate regime capable of sustaining a reasonable foreign and domestic balance.

Fourth, the literature on transition economies has placed a great deal of emphasis on safety-net issues, both in and of themselves and as part of a more general assessment of the successes and failures of transition. Interest in safety-net issues derives in part from our appreciation of the major social impact of transition, an issue we have emphasized in this chapter. But we must also remember that, because in the former command economies the safety net was largely socialized in the hands of the state, maintaining that safety net is challenging as the functions of the state diminish in the transition era.

When we turn our attention to the components of transition, it is the theory underlying these components that provides a framework for analysis. For example, there is a considerable body of theoretical reasoning on privatization. This theorizing provides a framework for assessing the process of privatization and its results in the transition economies. Likewise, there is a large body of theory that can be used to understand and assess the process of globalization—specifically, the development of new institutional arrangements and exchange rate regimes in the transition economies.

The unifying theme for the systemic change that the transition economies are experiencing is liberalization, the replacement of command mechanisms with market mechanisms and market policies. Liberalization is hard to measure, but indexes are available to measure the extent of institutional and policy change and to relate these changes to performance outcomes.

In the end, assessing the evidence on transition is difficult. Some twenty-six countries have been engaged in the transition process, and we have had a full decade to observe transition and collect empirical evidence on it. How will the successes and the failures of transition be judged? Once again, there are a variety of indicators; the choice depends on the interests of the observer.

Summary

- Transition is the replacement of the command economic system with a market or mixed economic system.
- There are many transition economies, most having originated from the collapse of the former Soviet Union, the collapse of economic systems in Eastern Europe, or the collapse of the market-socialist experience of the former Yugoslavia.

- Beyond those countries that we generally and typically classify as transition economies, important aspects of transition (for example, privatization) have been fundamental components of change in other emerging market economies, such as Vietnam and China.
- As the command economies collapsed quickly in the late 1980s, models of system change were not readily available. This led to considerable experimentation and controversy, much of the latter arising from Western advice on how markets should emerge in the new transition economies.
- The transition economies, with their varying backgrounds and very different initial conditions, have pursued the introduction of markets to varying degrees, through varying approaches, and with very different results. Nearly all transition economies, however, experienced an initial decline in output and then a subsequent recovery, although the patterns of change in output varied from case to case throughout the transition era of the 1990s.
- Transition emerged in countries that had been largely isolated from the global economic community during the command era. This fact has been of great importance as the transition economies have developed and implemented new institutions and policies to facilitate their participation in the growing global economy.
- From a systems perspective, analysis of the transition era has moved us away from the era of "isms" toward an era in which organizational (institutional) arrangements and policy variants are the central components of new economic systems that are emerging in settings where very different command arrangements recently dominated. The economic analysis of these emerging arrangements is based on contemporary microeconomic theory—for example, agency theory and information economics.
- We have emphasized the fact that our discussion will focus on the beginnings of transition—that is, the setting inherited from the command era, measurement issues, and assessing transition alternatives. Finally, we examine the content of transition by isolating its main components: privatization, restructuring and liberalization, development of the macroeconomy, introduction of new trade regimes, and, finally, the building of a new safety net.

Key Terms

economic system	Marxist–Leninist framework
command economy	initial conditions
market economy	structural distortions
economic reform	European Union
transition	liberalization
emerging market economies	privatization
resource base	restructuring

Notes

1. The economic system is defined as the organizational arrangements (the organizational hierarchy and the rules governing behavior within the hierarchy) used for the allocation of resources in a given (country) setting.

2. We observed in Part I that although much attention was paid to economic reform in the Soviet Union, there was seemingly little impact on the economic system, the policies followed, or the performance results achieved. In a case such as Hungary, however, the long-term pursuit of the system of New Economic Management (NEM) may in fact have been more important, especially for subsequent privatization and enterprise restructuring.

3. Differences in starting positions matter in two respects. First, it can be argued that command economies with more serious economic reform (for example, Hungary) were in fact different economies as they entered the transition era. Second, the collapse of the command economies occurred at different points in calendar time. Thus, as we examine performance issues during the transition era, it will be useful to distinguish between transition in **calendar time** and in **transition time**. Using calendar time, we select a useful and broadly accurate date (for example, 1989) to examine patterns of change. Using transition time, we examine the transition process dated from the actual date on which the transition process began. The latter differs from country to country. For example, we might date the beginning of transition in Russia from December 1991 when the Soviet Flag was removed from the Kremlin in Moscow.

4. Throughout our discussion of the transition economies, the reader will note that we use various groupings of the transition economies to illustrate various points. Data on all of the transition economies are readily available in the major sources that we identify, limiting the need for a more expansive and inclusive treatment here.

5. During the Soviet command era (after 1928), three republics (Latvia, Lithuania, and Estonia) were added to the Soviet political entity.

6. Throughout this book we rely heavily on various estimates of per capita output (GDP) as a measure of the level and rate of change of economic activity in transition economies. It is important to emphasize that whatever methods are used to generate these data (for example, conversion to U.S. dollars using exchange rates or purchasing power parity approaches), there are significant measurement problems. In addition, there is wide variation in the extent of the shadow economy in transition and nontransition economies. This issue is discussed in Friedrich Schneider and Dominik H. Enste, "Shadow Economies: Size, Causes, and Consequences," *Journal of Economic Literature* 38, 1 (March 2000), 77–114.

7. The German case has been of special interest to observers of different economic systems in that during the command era, many of the nonsystem factors such as cultural and historical differences were in fact similar in the GDR and the FRG. Moreover, the same argument could be made during the transition era. In this sense, the transition era in Germany has been a special case. However, unlike the case of Czechoslovakia, where there was a split, in the German case there was unification, making it difficult to track the elements of transition during the 1990s.

8. Prior to the disintegration of Yugoslavia as a single political and economic entity, this case was also of special interest to economists because of the very different Yugoslav interpretation of socialism, most notably the system of worker management.

9. Prior to the death of Tito and the political collapse of Yugoslavia, the economy of that country was of great interest as an example of worker management, a variant of the cooperative model. Under this model, one would expect outcomes different from those experienced

under the command model. Thus one might expect different initial conditions in those countries emerging from the experience in Yugoslavia. For a discussion of market socialism, see Chapter 4.

10. Recall that in the Soviet Union, for example, the conduct of foreign trade was centralized in the Ministry of Foreign Trade and the Foreign Trade Organizations (FTOs). Thus the impact of foreign trade on a Soviet republic was arguably quite small; centralized state organs handled the trade of each republic.

11. It is perhaps useful to note that in recent years, the fields of comparative economic systems and economic development have become much more closely identified with each other. Thus many important components of transition—for example, privatization—have been important policy imperatives in nontransition but developing economies in various regions of the world—for example, Asia and Latin America.

12. The issue of data availability and interpretation is fundamental to our examination of transition. During the command era, there were different accounting systems, and both falsification and simple lack of data on many critical issues made empirical analysis very difficult. Much of the data and the analysis of these data during the command era necessarily bore little relation to similar exercises in market economies. During the transition era, transition economies have generally converted to standard world accounting systems, but data availability remains a problem, especially for the early turbulent years of the transition era. Moreover, important contemporary issues, such as restructuring, are much more amenable to analysis in market economies where concepts and data are more unified. Throughout this book we pay special attention to data issues, providing references as appropriate.

13. These differences are emphasized in Janos Kornai and Karen Eggleston, *Welfare, Choice, and Solidarity in Transition: Reforming the Health Sector in Eastern Europe* (Cambridge: Cambridge University Press, 2001).

14. The concept of the shadow economy is important. Although it is difficult to define and to measure with precision, estimates of the importance of the shadow economy suggest that there are systematic differences across different countries. The shadow economy is generally smaller in Eastern Europe than it is in the countries of the former Soviet Union. At the same time, there is evidence of important changes in the magnitude of the shadow economy during transition.

15. A major and complex issue facing analysts of the transition economies is the establishment of output levels at the time of the collapse of the command economies. Obviously, this issue is of central importance if we are to measure changes during transition with accuracy. However, because of the well-known problems of accurately measuring output and output per capita in the command economies, determining exact starting points is difficult.

16. For a recent discussion of these issues, see Nauro F. Campos and Fabrizio Coricelli, "Growth in Transition: What We Know, What We Don't, and What We Should," *Journal of Economic Literature* 40, 3 (September 2002), 793–736.

Recommended Readings

General References

Oliver Blanchard, *The Economics of Post-Communist Transition* (New York: Oxford University Press, 1997).

Christopher Clague and Gordon C. Rausser, eds., *The Emergence of Market Economies in Eastern Europe* (Cambridge, Mass.: Blackwell, 1992).

European Bank for Reconstruction and Development, *Transition Report 2000: Employment, Skills and Transition* (London: EBRD, 2000).

————, *Transition Report 2002* (London: EBRD, 2002).

Philip Hanson and Michael Bradshaw, eds., *Regional Economic Change in Russia* (Northampton, Mass.: Edward Elgar, 2000).

Lucjan T. Orlowski, ed., *Transition and Growth in Post-Communist Countries* (Northampton, Mass.: Edward Elgar, 2001).

Martha de Melo, Cevdet Denizer, and Alan Gelb, "Patterns of Transition from Plan to Market," *World Bank Economic Review* 10, 3 (September 1996), 397–424.

J. L. Porket, *Modern Economic Systems and Their Transformation* (New York: St. Martin's, 1998).

Sheila M. Puffer, Daniel J. McCarthy, and Alexander I. Naumov, eds., *The Russian Capitalist Experiment* (Northampton, Mass.: Edward Elgar, 2000).

Gerard Roland, *Transition and Economics: Politics, Markets, and Firms* (Cambridge, Mass.: MIT Press, 2000).

Andrei Schleifer and Daniel Triesman, *Without a Map* (Cambridge, Mass.: MIT Press, 2000).

Paul Seabright, ed., *The Vanishing Rouble: Barter Networks and Non-Monetary Transactions in Post-Soviet Societies* (Cambridge: Cambridge University Press, 2000).

Nicolas Spulber, *Redefining the State* (Cambridge: Cambridge University Press, 1997).

Kitty Stewart, *Fiscal Federalism in Russia* (Northampton, Mass.: Edward Elgar, 2000).

"Symposium of Economic Transition in the Soviet Union and Eastern Europe," *Journal of Economic Perspectives* 5, 4 (Fall 1991), 3–217.

World Bank, *From Plan to Market: World Development Report 1996* (Washington, D.C.: World Bank, 1996).

OECD, *Russian Federation* (Paris: OECD, 2000).

Salvatore Zecchini, ed., *Lessons from the Economic Transition* (Boston: Kluwer, 1997).

15

Transition Economies: Output Patterns and Measurement Issues

In Chapter 14 we presented a broad survey of contemporary transition economies and identified 26 economies that would be the focus of attention in this book. As we proceed to discuss the various components of transition, we will find it useful to examine selected examples of the broader set of transition economies identified here and to focus on various subgroups—for example, those emerging from the former Soviet Union. We have emphasized the fact that by almost any standard the transition economies differ significantly from one another, both at the dawn of transition and at the present time. Moreover, we have argued that these differences (be they geographic or economic) have affected the degree to which transition has succeeded in different settings. Some of the differences are quite evident. Russia is very large, has significant petroleum reserves, and is in fact a major world producer of oil. Latvia is very small with limited natural resources and must therefore rely on external sources. Similar contrasts abound. However, as we attempt to measure the success of transition, the variables that are important are usually more complicated. Indeed, we need to define what success in transition means, and then try to model those forces that seem to influence success. For our broader discussion of transition outcomes, we focus on a variety of generally identifiable characteristics of success—for example including elements of the safety net. However, our focus in this chapter is narrower. Here we will examine output patterns during transition.

Explaining Patterns of Growth in Output Transition Economies

Initial Conditions and Distortion

Throughout the 1990s a great deal of attention was paid to assessing the results of transition. As we emphasized in Chapter 14, the dominant pattern is what has been termed the "J curve" (see Figure 14.4).[1] We will look first at the nature of the collapse and subsequent recovery; then we will identify the forces more broadly responsible for the changes in output. Why did the output of the transition economies, almost without exception, collapse suddenly during the early years of transition, and why are there such sharp differences in recovery patterns among the transition economies? For example, depending on the precise measures used, Poland experienced a limited decline and rapid recovery, whereas Russia had a sharp, extended decline and a slow recovery. The reader may wonder why we are addressing these issues before we discuss the transition process, given that outcome is in effect a summary of transition results. Understanding transition performance patterns from the outset will help us ask the right questions as we study the components of transition—and will help us appreciate the difficulties of assessing the transition process.

As we will observe, modeling the patterns of performance during the transition era has proved to be a complex but essential task. Most observers would argue that there are at least three main explanatory forces: the **initial conditions** prevailing at the onset of transition, the **policy measures** chosen during transition, and a variety of **environmental factors** (for example the level of economic development of the economy in question, natural resource and regional issues, and the length of time that the command system was in place). In addition, it is necessary to consider differences among countries, possibly by examining performance in groups of countries, such as the former USSR and Eastern Europe. Much of the literature on transition, especially the literature related to performance, focuses on the transition process in selected groups of transition economies: those performing well in Eastern Europe and those performing less well among the Commonwealth of Independent States (CIS) countries. In part, this is a statistical issue, but we will watch it carefully as we attempt to characterize transition patterns and to understand why there are important differences among transition economies.

Many have argued that one significant factor is different **initial conditions**— that is, differences in resource allocation at the outset of transition. These differences are often characterized as representing **distortion**, simply because in many cases, allocation patterns differed from those typically found in market economies.[2] What do we mean by differences in allocation patterns, and why do we care whether these historical differences existed?

Some of the ways in which command and market economies differ in resource allocation are given in Table 15.1. This table reflects structural differences in the pre-transition era—specifically, differences in the sectoral outcomes of allocation under the command systems. In other words, if we examine the sources of output (for example, industry versus agriculture) and the uses of output (for example, consumption versus investment), it is evident that the outcomes in the former command economies did not reflect market forces. As we have discussed earlier, the command systems used both systemic features (state ownership and control) and policy imperatives (an industry-first policy) to ensure that there would be an emphasis on industry, and on heavy industry in particular. Specifically, if we measure the importance of industry (for example, the share of industrial output in total output) and control for the level of economic development of the countries in question, we find that the command economies tended to exhibit systematically larger shares of industrial output than market economies at similar levels of economic development.[3] There are many such examples of what might be broadly termed **structural distortion**.

TABLE 15.1   Structural Differences Between Command and Market Economies[a]

Target Variable	Command Economies	Market Economies
GDP: *sources*		
Industry	+	normal
Agriculture	–	normal
Services	–	normal
GDP: *uses*		
Consumption	–	normal
Investment	+	normal
Government	+	normal

[a]In this table, we provide a stylized comparison of selected target variables for command and market economies. A plus (+) indicates an above-normal share; a minus (–) indicates a below-normal share. A "normal" share is the share that would occur if a large sample of market economic systems were compared, controlling for the level of economic development measured in terms of per capita GDP. Thus a plus for industry in a command setting indicates an industry share larger than would typically be found in market economies, controlling for the level of GDP per capita. Likewise, a minus for the service share in command systems indicates a service share smaller than would typically be found in a sample of market economies, controlling for the level of GDP per capita. Thus market resource-allocation patterns are assumed to be "normal" as a reference point from which to understand deviations in command systems.

Source: Compiled by the authors.

At the same time, the social contract in the command economies was largely state-determined such that the rate of growth of consumption (especially private consumption) could be constrained and the rate of growth of investment could be enhanced. It seems obvious that in a socialist economy where the means of production are owned by the state, and all enterprises are financed through the state budget, the role of the state (in part measured by G/GDP) would be significantly larger than in market economies where private property rights are dominant. These issues have been important throughout this book, and we will address them again when we examine the components of transition, such as the process of privatization.

Our characterization of systemic distortion in Table 15.1 is simplistic but reflects our earlier discussion of command systems and would generally be supported by statistical analysis. Moreover, deviations from market patterns of resource allocation in command systems emerge on many levels, not just in terms of the sources and uses of output. For example, socialist regional policies could and did dictate the nature of resource allocation on a regional basis. Thus, in the case of the Soviet Union, a region such as Siberia received much more attention than would, for example, northern Canada. Many of the urban centers that emerged during the Soviet era were planned "socialist" cities in terms of their location, their size, and many of their characteristics, such as transportation and housing. One does not have to make a judgment about the merits of these differences in allocation; the point is that market arrangements and policies will not typically sustain socialist patterns. For example, whatever the merits of the Soviet development of Siberia, it is very unlikely that this level of development would be sustained under market arrangements.

Another important example is foreign trade. In the command systems, currencies were not convertible, and trade was conducted by the state. Although the state must respect world market forces, state preferences could and did prevail with regard not only to the overall volume of trade but also to many of the important details, such as the commodity composition and geographic distribution of trade. The latter, for example, was strongly influenced by the socialist trade block The Council for Mutual Economic Assistance (CMEA), which collapsed prior to the onset of transition. The socialist trading mechanisms and policies created a pattern of trade sharply different from patterns that occur under market arrangements. As we will see when we examine trade patterns before and after the collapse of the command economies, major shifts in trade patterns occurred.

Indeed, the impact of the command era was significant in many dimensions. Consider, for example, the case of bias in favor of industry. Not only was there an industry bias in the general sense outlined above, but the structure of industry also differed from the industrial structures found in a market setting. For example, it is well known that Soviet industrial enterprises were, for a variety of reasons, large, capital-intensive, and integrated. Both horizontal and vertical integration were favored to resolve the irregularities of the material supply system. In a market economy, the "make or buy" decision is made on different (cost/benefit) grounds. Thus policies and allocational decisions in the command economies created organizational arrangements different from those found in market economies. The introduction of markets is bound to change these organizational arrangements. We will examine this critical element of corporate governance when we discuss privatization.

There were also important differences in the rules guiding enterprises. For example, in Soviet enterprises, workers could not generally be dismissed. This fact, combined with state budgeting of enterprises, created artificial levels of employment—a condition inconsistent with market arrangements. Thus as privatization occurs and the role of the state is reduced, we would expect significant changes in the use of labor.

Why do these initial conditions, which differ widely from market patterns, matter? They matter because as markets are introduced, one can expect allocation patterns under different systemic arrangements and different policies to revert to more "normal" patterns—that is, patterns that resemble long-term market outcomes. Thus one can argue that the more serious the distortions, the greater the distance that an economy must travel to reach market dimensions, and thus the more difficult the transition process will be. In part, the magnitude of these distortions reflects the length of time that socialist arrangements prevailed, although other factors are also important. For example, one might expect, even under socialist arrangements, that a resource-constrained economy such as Hungary would be more open to foreign trade than a large, resource-rich country such as the Soviet Union. Thus, at the beginning of the transition era, we might expect foreign trade to have had a greater impact on resource allocation in Hungary than in the Soviet Union.

Can the effect of initial conditions—and thus distortions—be measured? The answer is yes, but the task of defining, measuring, and accounting for the impact of these distortions is difficult. In Figure 15.1 we provide a simple scatter diagram and a trend line to demonstrate the relationship between initial conditions and the growth

FIGURE 15.1   Economic Growth and Initial Conditions

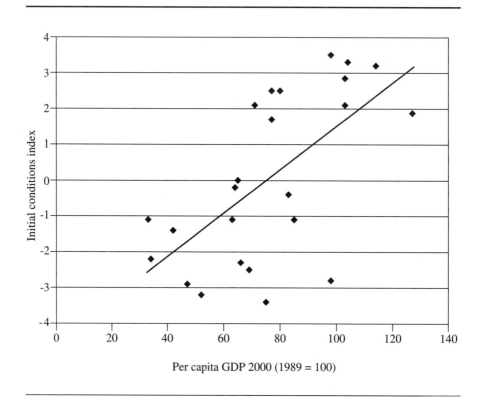

Per capita GDP 2000 (1989 = 100)

Source: EBRD, *Transition Report 2001: Energy in Transition* (Paris: EBRD, 2001), pp. 19 and 59.

of output as captured by EBRD indexes.[4] Larger positive numbers indicate better initial conditions; larger negative numbers indicate inferior initial conditions. Although there is considerable variation around the trend line, nevertheless there is a positive relationship between growth and initial conditions as characterized by these indexes. Indeed, the trend line that we have drawn illustrates the basic nature of this relationship, even though there are interesting outliers. This relationship is interesting and informative, but it turns out that more complex relationships have emerged. We turn our attention to them next.

Assessing Transition Patterns

To understand how we might assess the patterns of performance exhibited by different transition economies, we begin with a simple illustrative approach, working with some of the variables (forces) discussed above. Let's assume that the performance of transition economies is determined by just one variable: the extent to which **liberalization** (the movement toward markets) has taken place. This view, though simplistic, has been popular in the literature, especially among those who favor significant reliance on markets. We formalize this idea in the following simple functional relationship (omitting the error term):

$$Gr_i = f(Lib_i) \tag{15.1}$$

where

Gr_i = an index of growth, 1989–1999 with 1989 = 100
Lib_i = an index of liberalization

Rather than estimating this simple relationship, in Figure 15.2 we provide a scatter diagram relating liberalization and economic growth based upon EBRD indicators[5] The trend line indicates that there is a positive relationship between increases in per capita GDP and liberalization as assessed by the EBRD index. This index characterizes greater liberalization with a positive number, less liberalization with a negative number. It is evident from Figure 15.2 that there is considerable variation around the trend line. However, as a group, the countries of the former Soviet Union have done less well than the countries of Eastern Europe. However, there is much more that we can do in the measurement of these patterns of transition performance.[6]

FIGURE 15.2   Economic Growth and Liberalization

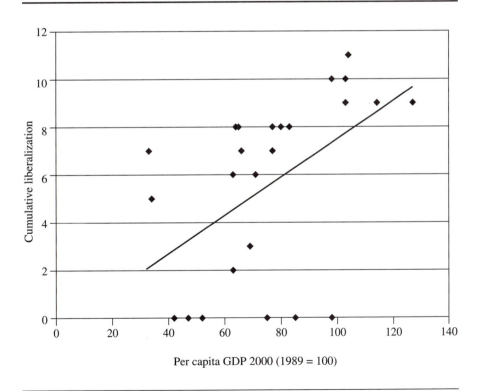

Per capita GDP 2000 (1989 = 100)

Source: EBRD, *Transition Report 2001: Energy in Transition* (Paris: EBRD, 2001), pp. 19 and 59.

We turn to a more complex (yet still relatively simple) model of the transition process. We examine the impact of initial conditions, policies (for example, liberalization), and environmental factors on growth. We specify the following basic relationship:

$$Gr_i = (IC_i, Lib_i, Env_i) \qquad (15.2)$$

where

Gr_i = an index of growth, 1989–1999 with 1989 = 100
IC_i = an index measuring initial conditions
Lib_i = an index of liberalization
Env_i = a measure of environmental factors

We now have a relationship that cannot be readily examined in graphical terms, and we have some variables rather more complicated than those in equation 15.1. However, as we shall see, this model provides us a mechanism to observe the important yet complicated issues involved in understanding the J curve. Obviously, this model could be more carefully specified and estimated using basic econometric techniques. We do not take this step (although we do examine the available empirical evidence on these issues)—hence the importance of understanding the variables used in this type of model and the difficulties encountered in determining actual empirical results.

Typically, in equation 15.2, we would measure growth and our policy variable (liberalization) in the same manner as in equation 15.1. The variable capturing initial conditions is also an index—for example, one of the sort provided by the European Bank for Reconstruction and Development (EBRD). Finally, as an environmental variable, we use per capita GDP of the transition economies. This variable requires additional explanation.

Many have argued that, apart from the issue of distortions left behind from the command era, transition experiences are likely to differ depending on the level of economic development of the transition economy.[7] As noted in Table 14.1, the transition economies that we examine began the process from very different levels of economic development. One could argue that a country with a per capita GDP of U.S.$1,000 is very different from a transition economy with a GDP of U.S.$10,000. Indeed, the former might be characterized as an economy in need of a policy framework for economic development, not transition. Having said this, however, per capita income is difficult to interpret because it presumably captures a variety of past and present economic and noneconomic forces.

In a model such as this, it is important to provide some theoretical underpinning for our expected results. We would expect that better initial conditions (less distortion) would make the transition process easier, and thus there would be a positive relationship between these two variables. Note that in equation 15.2, our measure of initial conditions indicates better conditions with a higher index number, and hence an expected positive relationship in this example (see Figure 15.1).

We would expect that economic growth would be better with more aggressive liberalization (the argument made in equation 15.1 and illustrated in Figure 15.2). Hence, again, we would expect a positive relationship between these two variables. Finally, the potential impact of our environmental variable—per capita output—is less clear. We have already noted that this sort of variable captures a variety of influences. It is, in a sense, an overall measure of the achieved level of economic development, including the development of institutions. At the same time, our argument that economies at higher levels of economic development should be better able to handle transition implies the existence of a positive relationship.

If the relationship suggested here can be specified and estimated, why not do so? In fact, as we have emphasized, this type of model is appealing as a means of understanding transition patterns. However, statistical problems associated with this approach make both specification and estimation difficult if meaningful results are to be obtained. We will briefly discuss these issues and then turn to the available empirical evidence.

Problems of Specification and Estimation[8]

The most serious problem is that of **specification**. How were the variables chosen, and why do we believe that equation 15.2 as we have specified it actually captures the forces that we believe are important? For example, an important omission is that of country differences, which are only partially captured by a variable such as per capita GDP. What might be helpful in this case would be to used a fixed-effects model—that is, a model that captures country differences directly. In this case we might well isolate the countries of the former Soviet Union and those of Eastern Europe, arguing that in transition, these two groups of countries are structurally different. These differences could be examined statistically.

A second major problem with this model is **endogeneity**. Simply put, this model assumes that the variables on the right-hand side are **exogenous**—that is, determined outside the model. By contrast, the variable on the left-hand side—in our case a measure of economic growth—is an **endogenous** variable, to be explained by estimating this model. This is an important and a strong assumption in this model. Thus in equation 15.2, we make the (probably incorrect) assumption that liberalization is an exogenous variable unrelated to our measure of economic growth. Moreover, we assume that the independent variables on the right-hand side are themselves not related to each other—a different issue, but an important assumption here. Why do these assumptions matter in our case? If a variable such as liberalization is not exogenous but rather is endogenous, then there is the possibility of simultaneity between liberalization and the growth of output, and that would require a different specification from the one proposed here.

There is a third problem in our specification, namely **time lags**. Equation 15.2 assumes that there are no time lags. Put differently, liberalization (for example) influences economic growth without any time lag. If liberalization affects growth, the impact is presumed to be simultaneous. Clearly this assumption may be inappropriate, but introducing lags would complicate our analysis. Again, if time lags are thought to be important, then a different specification would be suggested.

A final problem with this type of model is selecting the dependent variable (in our case, the rate of growth over the transition era). If one wishes to assess the results of transition, a variety of possible variables come to mind. Is the rate of inflation, or perhaps the rate of unemployment, an important outcome of transition? The question to be considered is whether the rate of inflation (for example) is a variable that explains the rate of growth, or whether, instead, the rate of economic growth explains (in part) the rate of inflation? These issues are important to our modeling effort, especially when the variables themselves are often difficult to characterize with precision.

During the 1990s, the empirical literature examining the results of transition (the J curve) has wrestled with the complications we have noted. In this sense, the results of empirical investigation are not always robust. Can we, in this setting, provide a useful summary of these results?

The Empirical Evidence

The approach suggested above is not new. Indeed, there is a significant empirical literature related to these issues. Although the approach is subject to the problems generally associated with the use of simple models and aggregated data, it is nevertheless appealing because many observers of transition economies argue that these models attempt to capture the influence of important forces such as differing initial conditions.

A recent study by Krueger and Ciolko both reviews the literature, especially contributions by Sachs (1996), de Melo, Denizer, and Gelb (1996), de Melo and Gelb (1996), Fischer, Sahay, and Vegh (1996), and Aslund, Boone, and Johnson (1996) and also provides additional estimates.[9] These studies raise some of the issues noted above and yield several interesting results.

First, there is debate about what dependent variable or measure of the outcome of performance is appropriate. This is an important issue. Most studies have focused on some measure of growth across the transition economies, but others have focused on outcomes such as unemployment or inflation.

Second, much of the literature on transition attempts to capture the impact of systemic change—specifically, the replacement of command mechanisms with market-type mechanisms. Typically, an index of liberalization has been used, although this index and precisely what it captures and how it is assembled are subjects of controversy.

Third, a major issue in the discussion of transition performance has been the matter of the external balance. Clearly, one would expect transition patterns to vary depending on both initial and evolving interaction with the global economy. This issue is difficult to capture in a single variable, although some measure of trade importance is usually attractive.

Fourth, beyond the theoretical modeling of transition performance and the data used to measure the various transition indicators, there are serious econometric issues. Indeed, a review of the literature already cited (Campos and Coricelli) will reveal that these issues are important and, as suggested earlier, may reflect the difficulties associated with broad indicators such as liberalization.

Data on Transition: What's in the Numbers?

In our discussion thus far, we have assumed that we can look at the data and provide a reasonable assessment of transition issues, especially performance, from simple indicators such as changes in output over time. Although the conclusions we present from the available empirical evidence are probably reasonable, there is more to the story.

Any observer of the command economies knows that measurement problems are serious. Indeed, our earlier discussions of these economies, and of their collapse, focused on critical measurement issues. Basic data series such as those pertaining to national income were fundamentally different from those generated and used in Western market economies. Obviously, these issues have not disappeared, but transition economies have largely shifted to widely accepted national accounting procedures, and, depending on the issues being investigated, we can now have greater confidence in the comparability of data for transition and Western market economies. This confidence does not extend uniformly to all issues, however.

Consider the critical matter of measuring changes from the command era through the transition era, whether we focus on structural issues (for example, how important was heavy industry in the command economies?) or general performance (what was the level of output in Russia in 2000 compared to 1988?). Obviously, to investigate these sorts of issues, one needs output for both the pretransition and the transition eras measured in a comparable manner—in terms of basic definitions, price weights, or the like. These types of estimates are tenuous, and the observer should expect the evidence to vary as a consequence of different, though quite reasonable, assumptions about such things as price weights.

A second issue has been the important changes that have occurred in basic statistical indicators. Consider, for example, the issue of inflation. Any long-time observer of the transition experience is aware that the nature of inflation was very different in the early years of transition, when formerly fixed prices were released, than during the middle and latter years of the decade. These issues present a challenge to the observer of transition who wants to characterize inflation from the late 1980s through the present.

In light of these types of difficulties, it is not unreasonable to "periodize" our assessment of transition, and this is often done in the empirical literature. Thus we might think in terms of a simple threefold classification consisting of the initial period of collapse and attempted stabilization, the beginning of institutional change and policy discussion, and, finally, a period of attempted "transition normalization." This type of classification is useful, although, as always, there are important differences from case to case.

A third problem with transition data is the important qualitative differences among data series—an issue that of course also matters in market economies. For example, measures of unemployment or poverty are likely to be much less reliable than measures of electricity output. One must be concerned about definitional issues, how data are collected, and, if data are aggregated, how this aggregation is accomplished.

A fourth problem with data from transition economies is the issue of "nonstandard" components and influences. For example, a number of transition economies have informal or underground economies that are significant but very difficult to measure. We know that the informal economy is important—indeed, in some cases and at some times it is critical—yet its impact on "traditional" economic variables can be difficult to capture.

In sum, those who study transition economies can access vast amounts of empirical evidence that was not generally available for these economies during the command era. At the same time, the special circumstances of the transition era suggest the need for caution when accessing and interpreting transition data.

Can We Account for the Early Collapse?

Thus far we have focused on overall explanations of transition performance—the J curve, or the collapse followed by recovery.[10] It is important to emphasize that the complete characterization of the J curve as a cycle is difficult. Moreover, variations in the pattern are important. For example, there are cases of a steep decline and a speedy recovery, and there are other cases of a shallow decline and a very slow recovery. Interest has focused on the depth and length of the decline. Why did output collapse in so many transition economies, and what caused that collapse to be severe in some cases?

At first glance, this question might seem simplistic. After all, if an economy "collapses," wouldn't it be reasonable for output to collapse? In the transition economies (unlike market economies in recession), no failure of monetary and fiscal policies was responsible, and (unlike a case of war) all of the production capacity remained fully in existence. What, then, explains the collapse? In fact, there are a variety of explanations, all of which help us to understand the transition process.

First, there is the possibility that the collapse is explained by differences in accounting methods, notably the calculation of net material product (NMP) used during the command era and that of gross domestic product (GDP) used during the transition era. Consider, for example, the issue of the service sector. It was widely argued during the command era that the accounting methods used to determine NMP underestimated the growth and size of the service sector. Thus, as the output of an economy measured in NMP standards is recomputed in GDP standards, the result could be an increase in output even though output calibrated in physical terms has not changed.

Consider a different example, namely agriculture. It has been observed that during the transition era, agricultural output has, on balance, declined less than industrial output. Therefore, an economy with a larger share of agricultural output would decline less, even though it might be (in fact, typically would be) at a lower level of economic development. One suspects that in the agricultural economy, daily decisions and actions are guided much more by tradition than is the case in an industrial economy, where the guidance rules have essentially disappeared. One could also argue that in-kind exchanges in the rural economy would be less likely to be disrupted than those taking place under plan directives in the industrial economy.

It is interesting to note that issues related to the shadow economy, or second economy, could affect our assessment of transition. Is it likely that the shadow economy will be measured differently as the command system collapses and markets emerge? The empirical evidence on this issue is intriguing. The magnitude of the shadow economy in Eastern Europe during the transition era of the 1990s has been relatively small, whereas its magnitude in the states of the former Soviet Union has been relatively large. In the Russian case, the magnitude of the shadow economy increased significantly in the latter half of the 1990s, a puzzling outcome because it is in this period that one would expect market arrangements to have emerged. The issue of the shadow economy thus complicates the task of measuring transition performance, and yet it is less clear that transition differences have been systematically affected by levels and changes in the levels of shadow economies.

A second approach to understanding the magnitude of the collapse is more directly related to the nature of the command economy. This approach focuses on the fact that during the command era, enterprises were governed by directives from planners. What happened when these directives ceased as the command economy collapsed? One could argue that the answer depended on the nature of the relations between a firm and its suppliers and the firm and its customers. Without directives, "market" arrangements, such as prices and information, would become increasingly important, and yet in many transition settings, these signals have been weak. Under these circumstances, it is not surprising that it grew difficult to sustain supplies and, on the demand side, to maintain customers.

Third, it has been popular to blame the policy makers and claim that output fell because policy makers "got it wrong." Although it is difficult to isolate policy issues, the emergence of the "Washington Consensus" (an issue we examine in Chapter 16) has remained controversial in the policy arena. There are probably as many variants of this criticism as there are countries, but the focal point is frequently the problem of the speed and sequencing of transition components. For example, it is argued that privatization cannot be implemented before **corporatization**; banks cannot be privatized before the development of bank supervision and bank insurance arrangements; and the pressure to sustain real interest rates should not result in a severe credit crunch. The criticisms of policy tend to be country-specific, but they are still important to our understanding of transition.

Finally, a major (and original) approach to understanding the collapse of transition economies has focused on the supply and demand components of output. For example, we have already noted that in the transition economies, output of agricultural sectors has generally shown less cyclical fluctuation. Thus an economy with a larger agricultural sector is likely to show a lesser decline than an economy with a smaller agricultural sector. There are other examples. In most transition economies, there has been a sharp decline in investment. This decline is understandable, given the fundamental change in investment arrangements. This initial decline in investment was also accompanied by changes in the other components of aggregate demand.

Is the Transition Economy Real?

An important issue in the assessment of transition economies is the existence of an informal (shadow) or **nonmonetary sector**. Although this issue is of much greater importance in Russia than in most other cases, it nevertheless warrants attention. Indeed, we will note the importance of this issue in subsequent chapters when we investigate the policy framework in transition economies.

Empirical evidence suggests that in many of the transition economies, there is an important nonmonetary component, one that is often difficult to characterize and is more than simply a barter arrangement or exchange of goods. The presence of nonmonetary transactions is greater in the CIS states (especially Russia) than in the transition economies of Eastern Europe.[11] It occurs among households, enterprises, and issues related to government—for example, the payment of taxes in kind. Moreover, there are a variety of explanations for the existence of these arrangements. Although factors such as high rates of inflation tend to encourage barter arrangements, there is evidence that in the transition economies, nonmonetary arrangements are complex and pervasive, involve both state and nonstate activities, and often result from the general weakness or absence of financial markets.

Summary

- We have focused in this chapter on the changing output patterns in the transition economies, specifically the J curve, and on the various explanations for the very different patterns observed across the transition economies.
- The measurement of performance frequently identifies those forces thought to affect the growth of output: differences in starting positions (initial conditions and distortions inherited from the command era), policy differences, and country effects.
- It is hard to characterize these variables—initial conditions, policy variables, and country effects—in such a way that a more formal statistical investigation can be conducted. In addition to both theoretical and econometric issues, we have emphasized the difficulties of working with data from the transition era, and especially the issues related to the assessment of transition performance over time.
- We have examined the forces leading to the decline of output in transition economies, emphasizing both supply and demand forces and other factors, such as the collapse of command instructions and the absence or slow emergence of price and other market-type information signals.
- Assessment of transition results is complicated by the presence in many cases of a nonmonetary barter economy. Empirical evidence suggests that this presence of a nonmonetary economy is greater in the CIS countries, especially Russia, and can be explained by the absence of appropriate market-type organizational arrangements, the limited role of financial markets, and the holdover of patterns of exchange that prevailed during the command era.

Key Terms

initial conditions	structural distortion	endogenous variables
policy measures	liberalization	time lags
environmental factors	specification	corporatization
initial conditions	endogeneity	nonmonetary sector
distortion	exogenous variables	

Notes

1. The concept of the J curve derives from international trade but has been used to characterize the pattern of output decline in transition economies. See Josef Brada and Arthur King, "Is There a 'J' Curve for the Economic Transition from Socialism to Capitalism?" *Economics of Planning* 25, 1(1992), 37–42. For a broad perspective, see Vladimir Popov, "Shock Therapy versus Gradualism: The End of the Debate (Explaining the Magnitude of the Transformational Recession)," *Comparative Economic Studies* 42, 1 (Spring 2000), 1–57.

2. The concept of distortion is often difficult to characterize in a simple fashion. Note that we are not really arguing that there is only one pattern of resource allocation that is "good" but, rather, that under command arrangements, allocation patterns differed sharply from those typically found in market economies. Obviously, this means that as market arrangements replace command arrangements, the allocation of resources will change, and the command economies will in the end come to resemble market economies more closely. As we will note later, such a characterization might be useful for understanding when the process of transition comes to an end.

3. Sectoral shares are frequently characterized in terms of output, although other measures such as labor inputs can be used. Conceptually, these measures ought to be straightforward, but in reality there are many measurement difficulties associated with the national income accounting procedures used in the command economies.

4. The data are from EBRD, *Transition Report 2001: Energy in Transition* (Paris: EBRD, 2001), pp. 19 and 59. The index of initial conditions is "derived from factor analysis and represents a weighted average of measures of the level of development, trade dependence on CMEA, macroeconomic disequilibria, distance to the EU, natural resource endowments, market memory and state capacity."

5. The data are from EBRD, *Transition Report 2001: Energy in Transition* (Paris: EBRD, 2001), pp. 19 and 59. The index of liberalization is based on the number of years that a country achieved a liberalization score of at least 3 on price liberalization and at least 4 on trade and foreign exchange liberalization, as computed by the EBRD. These scales vary from 0 to 4+ for increasing price and foreign exchange liberalization.

6. For a recent assessment, see Nauro F. Campos and Fabrizio Coricelli, "Growth in Transition: What We Know, What We Don't, and What We Should," *Journal of Economic Literature* 40, 3 (September 2002), 793–836.

7. The relationship between the level of development and what we have termed initial conditions is in fact a complex but interesting issue. For example, Uzbekistan was for many years under Soviet (command) governance, and yet we know that at the beginning of transition, there were important differences between Uzbekistan and Russia, not only in the level of output per capita but also in the extent to which distortions could be found in each case. These differences are potentially important to our understanding of transition differences.

8. This section can be skipped without loss of continuity.

9. See Gary Krueger and Marek Ciolko, "A Note on Initial Conditions and Liberalization During Transition," *Journal of Comparative Economics* 26 (1998), 718–734.

10. There is a considerable body of literature devoted to the collapse. See, for example, Robert Holzmann, Janos Gacs, and Georg Winckler, eds., *Output Decline in Eastern Europe* (Boston: Kluwer Academic, 1995). For a theoretical discussion, see Gerard Roland, *Transition and Economics: Politics, Markets, Firms* (Boston, Mass.: MIT Press, 2000), Ch. 7. For an interesting comparison, see Jacek Rostowski, "Comparing Two Great

Depressions: 1929–33 to 1989–93," in Salvatore Zecchini, ed., *Lessons from the Economic Transition* (Boston: Kluwer Academic, 1997), pp. 225–239.

11. See, for example, the discussion in Paul Seabright, ed., *The Vanishing Rouble: Barter Networks and Non-Monetary Transactions in Post-Soviet Societies* (Cambridge: Cambridge University Press, 2000); Wendy Carlin, Steven Fries, Mark Schaffer, and Paul Seabright, "Barter and Non-Monetary Transactions in Transition Economies: Evidence from a Cross-Country Survey," EBRD Working Paper No. 50, June 2000; Eric Friedman, Simon Johnson, Daniel Kaufmann, and Pablo Zoido-Lobaton, "Dodging the Grabbing Hand: The Determinants of Unofficial Activity in 69 Countries," *Journal of Public Economics* 76 (2000), 459–493; Friedrich Schneider and Dominik H. Enste, "Shadow Economies: Size, Causes, and Consequences." *Journal of Economic Literature* 38, 1 (March 2000), 77–114.

Recommended Readings

George T. Abed and Hamid R. Davoodi, "Corruption, Structural Reforms, and Economic Performance in the Transition Economies," IMF Working Paper WP/00/132, July 2000.

A. Aslund, P. Boone, and S. Johnson, "How to Stabilize: Lessons from Post-Communist Countries," *Brookings Papers on Economic Activity* 81, 1, 217–234.

Oliver Blanchard and Michael Kremer, "Disorganization," *Quarterly Journal of Economics* 112, 4 (1997), 1091–1126.

Josef Brada and Arthur King, "Is There a 'J' Curve for the Transition from Socialism to Capitalism?" *Economics of Planning* 25, 1 (1992), 37–52.

Nauro F. Campos and Fabrizio Coricelli, "Growth in Transition: What We Know, What We Don't, and What We Should," *Journal of Economic Literature* 40, 3 (September 2002), 793–836.

Wendy Carlin, Steven Fries, Mark Schaffer, and Paul Seabright, "Barter and Non-Monetary Transactions in Transition Economies: Evidence from a Cross-Country Survey," EBRD Working Paper No. 50, June 2000.

Simon Commander and Christian Mumssem, "Understanding Barter in Russia," EBRD Working Paper No. 37, December 1998.

Mark De Broeck and Vincent Koen, "The Great Contractions in Russia, the Baltics and Other Countries of the Former Soviet Union: A View from the Supply Side," IMF Working Paper QW/00/32, March 2000.

Martha de Melo and Alan Gelb, "A Comparative Analysis of Twenty-Eight Transition Economies in Europe and Asia," *Post-Soviet Geography and Economics* 37, 5 (May 1996), 265–285.

Martha de Melo, Cevdet Denizer, and Alan Gelb, "From Plan to Market: Patterns of Transition," *World Bank Economic Review* 10, 3 (1996), 397–424.

EBRD, *Transition Report 2000* (Paris: EBRD, 2000).

———, *Transition Report 2001: Energy in Transition* (Paris: EBRD, 2001).

———, *Transition Report Update* (Paris: EBRD, 2002).

Maurice Ernst, Michael Alexeev, and Paul Marer, *Transforming the Core* (Boulder, Colo.: Westview Press, 1996).

Saul Estrin, Giovanni Urga, and Stepana Lazarova, "Testing for Ongoing Convergence in Transition Economies, 1970–1998" *Journal of Comparative Economics* 29 (2001), 677–691.

Stanley Fischer and Ratna Sahay, "The Transition After Ten Years," IMF Working Paper WP/00/30, 2000.

Stanley Fischer, Ratna Sahay, and Carlos A. Vegh, "Stabilization and Growth in Transition Economies: The Early Experience," *Journal of Economic Perspective* 10, 2 (Spring 1996), 45–66.

Eric Friedman, Simon Johnson, Daniel Kaufmann, and Pablo Zoido-Lobaton, "Dodging the Grabbing Hand: The Determinants of Unofficial Activity in 69 Countries," *Journal of Public Economics* 76 (2000), 459–493.

Stanislaw Gomulka, "Output: Causes of Decline and Recovery," in Peter Boone, Stanislaw Gomulka, and Richard Layard, eds., *Emerging from Communism: Lessons from Russia, China and Eastern Europe* (Cambridge, Mass.: MIT Press, 1998), 13–41.

Daniel Gros and Marc Suhrcke, "Ten Years After: What Is Special About Transition Countries?" EBRD Working Paper No. 56, August 2000.

Robert Holzman, Janos Gacs, and George Winckler, *Output Decline in Eastern Europe* (Dordrecht: Kluwer Academic, 1995).

Peter Murrell, "The Transition According to Cambridge, Mass.," *Journal of Economic Literature* 33, 1 (March 1995), 164–178.

Vladimir Popov, "Shock Therapy versus Gradualism: The End of the Debate (Explaining the Magnitude of the Transformational Recession)," *Comparative Economic Studies* 42, 1 (Spring 2000), 1–57.

Gerard Roland, *Transition and Economics: Politics, Markets, and Firms* (Boston: MIT Press, 2000).

Jeffrey D. Sachs, "The Transition at Mid-Decade," *American Economic Review Papers and Proceedings* 86, 2 (May 1996), 128–133.

Paul Seabright, ed., *The Vanishing Rouble: Barter Networks and Non-Monetary Transactions in Post-Soviet Societies* (Cambridge: Cambridge University Press, 2000).

Hans van Ees and Harry Garretsen, "The Theoretical Foundations of Reform in Eastern Europe: Big Bang versus Gradualism and the Limitations of Neo-Classical Theory," *Economic Systems* 18, 1 (March 1994), 1–13.

16

Transition: Models, Policies, and Approaches

Thus far we have introduced the idea of transition characterizing those countries that are in transition, and analyzing important measurement issues through the transition era of the 1990s. The goal thus far has been to present a simple overview of basic transition issues. We have also emphasized the fact that when the command economies collapsed in the late 1980s, there was little if any historical experience that might serve to define the possible paths of transition. Indeed, among the transition economies, the settings were different, the expectations were different, and while there are important similarities in the transition patterns, the approaches to transition (initial transition models) provided widely differing perspectives on how transition might be implemented. We have also observed that within individual transition cases, the patterns of change have varied considerably making our analysis of early changes often quite different from our analysis of recent changes. Put differently, our assessment of transition in the new century is now very different than it was during the emergence of the transition process in the late 1980s and early 1990s. As we will see, these differences have sparked a lively debate about the nature of transition and especially the nature of policies that ought to be followed to achieve transition successes, especially economic growth and population well-being.

Transition: The Early Years

The focus here is not initial conditions, but rather the policy choices that were available to guide the transition process given the existence of known initial conditions, and absent significant economic theorizing about the process of transition. To organize our thinking about these issues, it is useful if artificial to categorize transition as occurring in three important stages.

First, as the old order collapsed, it was necessary to think about the new order and how this new order would evolve. This involved very complicated issues, especially in countries such as Russia where the socialist experience had been lengthy and significant. Charting a path through the emergence of markets was constrained by lack of knowledge about markets and by early assumptions that a mixed system might be both desirable and feasible. Bear in mind that transition was occurring in systems where the role of government and the safety net had been large if controversial. Moreover, transition is inherently both a political and an economic phenomenon, a mix often difficult to understand in newly emerging economic and political systems. Next, a particular transition strategy having been decided on, it was necessary to stabilize the economy and try to limit the decline of economic activity, although this decline was not clearly envisioned in the 1980s. Again, the nature and extent of stabilization measures differed in different transition cases. There were no simple prescriptions to be followed.

Second, during the early 1990s, there was a significant period in all transition economies when the rules of the new order were developed in the political sphere. This was an awkward phase—a mix of old and new. It was, however, a period in which the simplistic character of models such as the big push versus the evolutionary approach would quickly become evident and would dominate the literature on transition. This was the period during which the legislative base of transition began to evolve. The need for careful attention to sequencing became apparent, although practical guidelines were not always at hand.

Finally, in the latter half of the 1990s, transition economies began to experience, though to very different degrees, a period of "transition normalization," or the implementation of new policies moving the economies toward market institutions, arrangements, and outcomes.

Transition Models

Most early observers of the transition experience agree that there are two major models of transition: the "big push" and the gradualist, or evolutionary, approach. Both are products of the early years of transition, and both have been replaced by a more subtle and meaningful approach to transition with the stylized models now viewed as simplistic. But both have a lot to tell us.

The characterization of these simplistic transition models is really an outgrowth of early differences in the transition experience, set against a backdrop of what has been termed the Washington Consensus.[1] As international organizations became involved in assisting the transition economies, as market specialists gave advice, and as countries like Poland moved ahead rapidly from relatively favorable initial conditions, a picture of transition policies emerged. The **"big push"** strategy centered on the concept of the rapid development of markets, along with the decline of the state's role in the economy guided by consensus on key policy targets—fiscal discipline, prioritization of public expenditures, tax reform, financial liberalization, trade liberalization, enhancement of foreign direct investment (FDI) flows, privatization, and deregulation. All were a part of the Washington Consensus.

The initial concept of the big push revolved around the idea that transition policies, such as privatization and the introduction of markets, could be implemented rapidly, creating new arrangements in a short period of time. It was often thought that markets would emerge through decentralization, as the state exited from its former dominant role. In addition to minimizing the downside pain associated with disruption, this model had the political appeal of lessening the likelihood of reversal—that is, the abandonment of transition and the possible resurrection of the old order.

Although many would argue that the main components of the Washington Consensus (for example, budgetary balance and the development of financial markets) are appropriate policy objectives, in recent years these policies as applied in the real world have been the subject of considerable criticism, especially that emanating from the former chief economist of the World Bank, Nobel laureate Joseph E. Stiglitz. Stiglitz has suggested the existence of a "Post-Washington Consensus," arguing that we now have a better understanding of markets, that they cannot be applied uniformly across very different economic systems and country settings, and that our objectives have broadened beyond mere economic growth to include, for example, sustainable development and limitations on inequality.[2] Much of this argument is based on the outcomes of applying the Washington Consensus in the transition economies, although it is also based on these prescriptions in other important settings, such as Asia.

The **gradualist approach**, or evolutionary approach, drew on the analogy of how markets and related organizational arrangements and policies emerged in Western industrialized economies, typically over extended periods of time. Fundamentally, the evolutionary argument characterizes institutional change as iterative and path-dependent, such that it is not possible, at any time, to envision sudden changes, especially those dictated by policy makers.

This initial dichotomy of transition models quickly became outmoded for a variety of reasons. First, as we have already emphasized, it was evident that initial conditions differed significantly and that these differences would matter in many ways. For example, countries such as Poland and Hungary that had experienced prereform political and economic change would be much better prepared for transition than Ukraine, where little political or economic change had taken place. Second, it was soon realized that transition was a more complicated process than first envisioned and that any stylized model was likely to be too simplistic. For example, the issues of sequencing and complementarities relating to the components of transition would be important in the design of a transition program.[3] Indeed, even if transition was proceeding rapidly these issues would be important. As an example of **sequencing**, the privatization of banks should not take place until a central monetary authority is in place and banking regulations have been established. Much of the criticism of transition policies, regardless of the speed of transition, rests upon these sorts of considerations. What are **complementarities**? The notion here is that elements of transition cannot be implemented in isolation from one another. For example, if firms are to be privatized and required to seek capital from financial markets, then as privatization takes place, financial markets must be developed simultaneously.

Apart from being a model of transition, however, the evolutionary approach has been a major component of the transition literature. It is, in effect, a contemporary body of economic thought the boundaries of which extend far beyond the transition experience. Accordingly, it bears closer scrutiny in this chapter.

The Evolutionary Approach

The **evolutionary approach** can be characterized as presenting a view of systemic change rather different from that of traditional neoclassical economic theory.[4] Although contemporary neoclassical theory is much richer now than it was, say, twenty years ago, it traditionally viewed organizations as "black boxes" whose behavior could be captured reasonably well by simple models of maximization under constraints. Differences in the scale of the organization or its internal arrangements did not fundamentally change this approach. These differences were assumed to be explained by market forces, technological change, and the like.

The evolutionary perspective takes a much different approach to organizations—and especially to organizational change. The evolutionary approach to organizational change is important on two levels. First, it is useful as we attempt to characterize the nature of an economic system. Second, it is important as we attempt to understand change during transition, both at the system level and at the level of the individual organization. The latter is especially important as we examine changes in corporate governance accompanying the process of privatization.

Fundamentally, organizations are viewed as complex hierarchies within which participants pursue objectives while guided by incentives but subject to bounded rationality. The existence of a **hierarchy** implies an architecture in which there are superiors and subordinates. The superiors define the objectives, and the subordinates are induced by appropriate incentives to achieve these objectives. The limitations faced by decision makers in organizations are often characterized as **bounded rationality**. Bounded rationality might consist of personal limitations (inadequate education, for example) or of limitations imposed by inadequate or inappropriate information upon which to base decisions in pursuit of objectives.

The hierarchical structure of an organization is important and is defined largely by how tasks are assigned, the nature of superior–subordinate relationships, how monitoring will take place, and what information flows are available. This in essence is the "agency problem" that emerges when a superior (principal) assigns tasks and a subordinate (an agent), whose interests may diverge somewhat from those of the principal, carries them out. Notice that in this setting, one does not have to assume that an agent consciously deviates from the achievement of the principal's objectives. Inappropriate incentive arrangements and/or information asymmetries may lead to this result.

How, then, can an organization be designed to perform specified tasks, and over time, how will this design change? Remember that in this approach, organizations are construed as capable of learning and changing. Thus the process of organizational change (during transition, for example) is much more complicated than has generally been imagined. In particular, organizational change is sequential, path-dependent, and evolutionary through a process of organizational learning and adaptation. This implies that an optimal set of organizational arrangements can be found for the achievement of specified objectives under prevailing conditions.

Issues of Speed and Sequencing

We have implied that the simple models of transition developed during the early 1990s have been largely superseded. What has replaced these models? Speed, timing, and sequencing are still important, but it is now recognized that they vary so widely in different transition settings that no single model can capture all the observed differences. This is a fundamental tenet of the Post-Washington Consensus. Moreover, the issue of the optimal speed of transition has focused on sectoral allocation patterns—for example, changes in the allocation of capital and labor. Sectoral modeling of transition paths is very different from the earlier aggregative framework. In the contemporary disaggregated framework, it is possible to model transition paths of critical sectors, as well as to consider both an optimal speed of transition and deviations from that optimal path.[5]

Is There a Common Path?

When we examine the approaches to, and the results of, transition during the 1990s, we observe significant differences from case to case and yet also note many common features. The dominant initial focus in all cases was a reduction of the role of the state and the introduction of markets. As enterprises were privatized, their interaction among themselves and with households was increasingly conducted through emerging markets, although nonmarket arrangements have persisted in some cases. The process of privatization and the development of both product and factor markets necessitated an emerging role for money and money mechanisms, especially banks and a central monetary authority to guide the new system. Thus the role of the state in the real economy decreased, to be replaced by money mechanisms, at least in most transition economies. While these changes were being made in the domestic economy, the need to benefit from foreign trade dictated significant changes in trading arrangements and polices—most notably the relaxing of trade restrictions and the introduction of a convertible currency.

Having characterized these similarities among transition economies, we must also note that important differences remain, and that debate continues about the long-term **convergence** of the transition economies with their market brethren.[6] The concept of convergence has long been subject to a variety of interpretations in the field of comparative economic systems. In the past, emphasis was placed on the idea that in the long term, because of the importance of fundamental development imperatives, capitalist and socialist systems would become increasingly similar in such features as the role of the state, sectoral proportions, and the like. However, the contemporary literature on convergence focuses on a different set of issues, namely growth convergence. What is growth convergence and how is it related to our assessment of transition patterns?

Measuring economic growth is a keystone of economics, of course, but since the early 1990s, there has been a special interest in **growth convergence**, the concept of testing to see whether the growth paths of differing economies in fact tend to converge over time. A variety of measures can be used to test for convergence. An especially interesting one is that proposed by Barro and Sala-I-Martin.[7] Obviously, for our purposes in this book, we focus on the implications of growth convergence theories for transition compared to nontransition economies.

A recent study by Estrin, Urga, and Lazarova focuses on the concept of growth convergence among communist bloc countries after 1970 and between the bloc countries during transition and Western market economies.[8] The authors generally do not find evidence of growth convergence, a fact that raises interesting questions about both the allocational efforts of the socialist era and the effectiveness of the transition era in moving toward market structures and outcomes.

A study by Nauro F. Campos addresses the same issue.[9] This study provides a useful survey of the literature and additional estimates of growth in the transition economies. Campos concludes that "almost a decade after the transition began, the centrally planned economies are still structurally different from market economies at similar levels of per capita income."[10] Perhaps the legacy of the command economic system is greater than generally imagined.

Finally, recent research has attempted to capture the role of institutions in the growth patterns of transition economies. The work of Oleh Havrylyshyn and Ron van Rooden and Fyodor Kushnirsky attempts to include institutional variables, although their results seem to suggest that other variables, specifically initial conditions and structural reform, remain dominant.[11] The recent literature on these issues is summarized by Campos and Coricelli.[12]

We have spent a considerable amount of time discussing the general features of the transition economies and the transition process during the 1990s. We have not yet addressed the components of transition, especially the process of privatization, the development of financial arrangements, and the role of the transition economy in a global setting. We turn to these issues in the remaining chapters.

Summary

- The concept of transition *models,* for example, the big push and gradualist approaches, is substantially based upon the early conceptions of transition paradigms and the attempt to characterize transition in a simple two dimensional manner.
- Many observers believe that stylized models are inappropriate, arguing that approaches to transition can and should vary depending on many factors such as initial conditions. Thus, although the underlying factors remain important for our understanding of transition, the use of stylized models has been superseded by more fundamental analysis. One might interpret this as a movement beyond the Washington Consensus.
- Issues such as sequencing and complementarities are important as the components of transition are developed and implemented. The development of banking institutions, for example, requires a monetary authority in place and established banking regulations. Other components of transition need to be implemented together.
- In spite of the inadequacy of stylized models, the elements of transition have a certain commonality across transition economies. Markets are introduced through privatization and a reduced role for the state. Money and money mechanisms and institutions acquire new importance. Finally, to the extent that the transition economies are to reap the benefits of expanded foreign trade, trading institutions and policies must conform to the demands of the global economy.
- Studies of growth convergence suggest that the growth patterns of transition and nontransition economies have not converged, although much work remains to be done on these issues.

Key Terms

big push	complementarities	bounded rationality
gradualist approach	evolutionary approach	convergence
sequencing	hierarchy	growth convergence

Notes

1. For a discussion of the Washington Consensus, see Marie Lavigne, *The Economics of Transition,* 2nd ed. (New York: St. Martin's, 1999), 158–161.
2. This set of views can be found in Joseph Stiglitz, "More Instruments and Broader Goals: Moving Toward the Post-Washington Consensus" (Helsinki, Finland: 1998 Wider Annual Lecture, January 7, 1998). For a broader and contemporary view, see Joseph E. Stiglitz, *Globalization and Its Discontents* (New York: Norton, 2002).
3. The issue of complementarities in transition has moved beyond the discussion of simple approaches that suggest either a fast or a slow approach. There is also a growing theoretical literature that looks at optimal speed and sectoral and other differences. For a discussion of this literature, see Gerard Roland, *Transition and Economics* (Cambridge, Mass.: MIT Press, 2000), Chs. 5 and 6.
4. For a basic survey of issues related to evolutionary economics, see R. Nelson and S. G. Winter, *An Evolutionary Theory of Economic Change* (Cambridge, Mass.: Harvard University Press, 1982); for a recent discussion, see Geoffrey M. Hodgson, *Evolution and Institutions: On Evolutionary Economics and the Evolution of Economics* (Northampton, Mass.: Edward Elgar, 2000); and Oliver E. Williamson, "The New Institutional Economics: Taking Stock, Looking Ahead," *Journal of Economic Literature* 38, 3 (September 2000), 595–613.
5. See, for example, the discussion in Gerard Roland, *Transition and Economics: Politics, Markets, and Firms* (Cambridge, Mass.: MIT Press, 2000), Ch. 5.
6. The differences are noted in Daniel Gros and Marc Suhrcke, "Ten Years After: What Is Special About the Transition Economies?" EBRD, Working Paper No. 56, August 2000.
7. Robert J. Barro and Sala-I-Martin, "Convergence Across States and Regions," *Brookings Papers on Economic Activity* 0, 1 (January–March 1991), 107–158; Robert J. Barro and Sala-I-Martin, "Convergence." *Journal of Political Economy* 100, 2 (April 1992), 223–151.
8. The interest in testing for growth convergence during the communist era centers on the argument that these countries followed a policy of regional redistribution to limit regional differences, a fundamental element of socialist economic thought. See Saul Estrin, Giovanni Urga, and Stepana Lazarova, "Testing for Ongoing Convergence in Transition Economies, 1970–1988," *Journal of Comparative Economics* 29 (2001), 677–191.
9. Nauro F. Campos, "Will the Future Be Better Tomorrow? The Growth Prospects of Transition Economies Revisited," *Journal of Comparative Economics* 29, 4 (December 2001), 663–676.
10. *Ibid.,* p. 663.
11. Oleh Havrylyshyn and Ron van Rooden, "Institutions Matter in Transition, But So Do Policies," IMF working paper 00/70, 2000; Oleh Havrylyshyn *et al.,* "Growth Experience in Transition Countries: 1990–98," IMF Occasional Paper 184, 1999; and Fyodor I. Kushnirsky, "A Modification of the Production Function for Transition Economies Reflecting the Role of Institutional Factors," *Comparative Economic Studies* 43, 1 (Spring 2001), 1–30.
12. See Nauro F. Campos and Fabrizio Coricelli, "Growth in Transition: What We Know, What We Don't, and What We Should," *Journal of Economic Literature* 40, 3 (September 2002),

793–836; and Nauro F. Campos and Fabrizio Coricelli, "A Tale of Two Peripheries: An Empirical Analysis of Growth in Transition Economies," in Randall K. Filer and Gur Ofer, eds., *Growth in Transition* (New York: Oxford University Press, 2003).

Recommended Readings

Robert J. Barro and Sala-I-Martin, "Convergence Across States and Regions," *Brookings Paper on Economic Activity* 0, 1 (January–March 1991), 107–158.

———, "Convergence," *Journal of Political Economy* 100, 2 (April 1992), 223–151.

Oliver Jean Blanchard, Kenneth A. Froot, and Jeffrey D. Sachs, eds., *The Transition in Eastern Europe,* Vol. 2 (Chicago: University of Chicago Press, 1994).

———, *The Transition in Eastern Europe,* vol. 1 (Chicago: University of Chicago Press, 1994).

Michael Cox, ed., *Rethinking the Soviet Collapse* (New York: Pinter 1998).

Saul Estrin, Giovanni Urga, and Stepana Lazarova, "Testing for Ongoing Convergence in Transition Economies," *Journal of Comparative Economics* 29 (2001), 677–691.

Paul Evans and Georgios Karras, "Convergence Revisited," *Journal of Monetary Economics* 37, 2 (April 1996), 249–265.

Josef Brada, "The Transformation from Communism to Capitalism: How Far, How Fast?" *Post-Soviet Affairs* 9, 2 (1993), 87–110.

Stanley Fischer and Ratna Sahay, "The Transition After Ten Years," IMF Working Paper Wp/00/03, 2000.

John Foster and J. Stanley Metcalfe, *Frontiers of Evolutionary Economics* (Northampton, Mass.: Edward Elgar, 2001).

Norbert Funke, "Timing and Sequencing of Reforms: Competing Views and the Role of Credibility," *Kyklos* 3 (1993), 337–362.

Daniel Gros and Marc Suhrcke, "Ten Years After: What Is Special About Transition Economies?" World Bank Working Paper No. 56, August 2000.

Paul Hare and Tamas Revesz, "Hungary's Transition to the Market: The Case Against a Big-Bang," *Economic Policy* 14 (1992).

Geoffrey M. Hodgson, *Evolution and Institutions: On Evolutionary Economics and the Evolution of Economics* (Northampton, Mass.: Edward Elgar, 2000).

Herman W. Hoen, "Shock versus Gradualism in Central Europe Reconsidered," *Comparative Economic Studies* 38, 1 (Spring 1996), 1–20.

Peter Murrell, "Can Neoclassical Economics Underpin the Reform of Centrally Planned Economies?" *Journal of Economic Perspectives* 5, 4 (Fall 1991), 59–76.

———, "Evolution in Economics and in the Economic Reform of the Centrally Planned Economies," in Christopher C. Clague and Gordon Rausser, eds., *The Emergence of Market Economies in Eastern Europe* (Cambridge, Mass.: Blackwell, 1992), 35–53.

———, "What Is Shock Therapy? What Did It Do in Poland and Russia?" *Post-Soviet Affairs* 9, 2 (April–June 1993), 11–40.

———, "The Transition According to Cambridge, Mass." *Journal of Economic Literature* 33, 1 (March 1995), 164–178.

———, "Evolutionary and Radical Approaches to Economic Reform," *Economics of Planning* 25, 1 (1992), 79–95.

——— and Mancur Olson, "The Devolution of Centrally Planned Economies," *Journal of Comparative Economics,* 15 (1991), 239–65.

R. Nelson and S. G. Winter, *An Evolutionary Theory of Economic Change* (Cambridge, Mass.: Harvard University Press, 1982).

Douglass C. North, *Institutions, Institutional Change, and Economic Performance* (Cambridge: Cambridge University Press, 1990).

Keith Pavitt, "Knowledge About Knowledge Since Nelson and Winter: A Mixed Record," SPRU Science and Technology Policy Research, Electronic Working Paper Series, Paper No. 83, June 2002.

Vladimir Popov, "Shock Therapy versus Gradualism: The End of the Debate (Explaining the Magnitude of the Transformational Recession)," *Comparative Economic Studies* 42, 1 (Spring 2000), 1–58.

Gerard Roland, *Transition and Economics* (Cambridge, Mass.: MIT Press, 2000).

Joseph E. Stiglitz, *Whither Socialism?* (Cambridge, Mass.: MIT Press, 1991).

———, "More Instruments and Broader Goals: Moving Toward the Post-Washington Consensus," (Helsinki, Finland: 1998 WIDER Annual Lecture, January 7, 1998).

———, *Globalization and Its Discontents* (New York: Norton, 2002).

Jozef van Brabant, "Lessons from the Wholesale Transformation in the East," *Comparative Economic Studies* 35, 4 (1993), 73–102.

Hans Van Ees and Harry Garretsen, "The Theoretical Foundations of the Reforms in Eastern Europe: Big Bang versus Gradualism and the Limitations of Neo-Classical Theory," *Economic Systems* 18, 1 (1994).

Oliver E. Williamson, "The New Institutional Economics: Taking Stock, Looking Ahead," *Journal of Economic Literature* 38, 3 (September 2000), 595–613.

World Bank, *From Plan to Market: the World Development Report 1996* (Washington, D.C.: World Bank, 1996).

PART V

Transition in Practice: The Components

17

Introducing Markets: Privatization and the Decline of Government

The most fundamental element in the identification of differing economic systems is property rights. The cornerstone of a market economy is private property, based on clearly identified **property rights**, and a system of markets and exchange resulting in prices that appropriately reflect relative scarcities in both factor and product markets. These prices serve as the most basic mechanism of resource allocation in a market economy. Given the almost complete absence of private property in the command economies, the ill-defined nature of state property rights, and the minimal use of prices (set administratively) for resource allocation, it is not surprising that the initial policy focus of transition was the creation of markets through a process of privatization along with the abandonment of state-set prices.[1]

Beyond these general observations, however, both the theory and the practice of privatization have proved to be complex and controversial, and privatization has become a contemporary policy issue that extends well beyond the transition economies. Indeed, although our focus in this chapter is the nature of privatization in the transition economies, we will see that privatization is a worldwide phenomenon. We begin this chapter with a discussion of the background of privatization. Then we will address theory, policy, real-world applications, and finally results. The outcomes of privatization worldwide are relevant to our analysis, but we will focus mainly on the transition economies.

Privatization in Transition

The Background

The story of privatization is much more significant than one might suspect from the contemporary transition setting. As we have emphasized before, the role of the state in the process of economic development is of great importance. This is especially clear to systems analysts, because differing roles of the state imply very different organizational arrangements and hence different economic systems. Traditionally, the role of government in an economy has been a key element in system classification. A socialist economic system would be likely to have a larger role for government (measured in terms of government spending as a portion of total output) than a capitalist system. Also, in any economic system we characterize as a "welfare state," the role of government is typically important as a mechanism for production and redistribution.

Even judged within a narrow framework of privatization, where **state-owned enterprises (SOEs)** are replaced by private firms, the contemporary setting of privatization extends far beyond the transition economies. Indeed, the onset of a declining role for SOEs pre-dates the transition era. In both developed and developing market and mixed economies, reducing the role of the state through privatization has been a major policy thrust since the early 1980s. One can argue that this choice fundamentally defines the nature of the **social contract** and thus will differ in different cultural and historical settings.

In the field of comparative economic systems, the role of government in an economy, measured in various ways, has been studied extensively.[2] However, before the contemporary era of privatization, there had been only modest theorizing about why the importance of government differs significantly from one case (country) to another as well as varying over time. Moreover, there has been considerable controversy over how best to measure the role of government in different economies. Although this issue has already been discussed in Chapters 3 and 4, it is useful to return to the subject as we assess the nature and meaning of privatization in the 1990s.

In Figure 17.1, we present a picture of the role of government in a number of very different economies, characterizing the importance of government in terms of the ratio of government spending to total output—in this case, for the year 1997. Several

FIGURE 17.1   G/GDP for Selected Countries, 1997

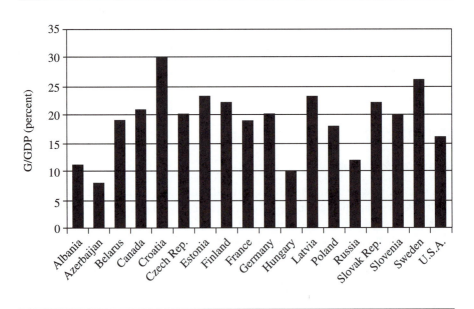

Source: World Bank, *World Development Indicators 1999* (Washington, D.C.: World Bank, 1999), Table 4.9.

conclusions can be drawn from this simple comparison. First, even a quick glance suggests that the role of government as measured here is quite different in different economies, varying from a low of 8 percent in Azerbaijan to a high of 30 percent in Croatia. In spite of the fact that conceptual and measurement issues make comparison difficult; these are clearly important differences. Second, some of the evidence in Figure 17.1 seems to conform to our expectations, even though simple explanations for the observed outcomes are not always available. For example, we would probably expect Sweden (often characterized as a welfare state) to have a large government role, whereas the United States, at the other end of the spectrum, should have a much smaller role for government. The data broadly conform to these expectations. But why is the role of government fully 10 points greater in Croatia than in the Czech Republic, two countries that were part of a larger single country until 1993? And why is the role of government apparently so small (just over 10 percent) in Russia, when many view the role of the state as traditionally very important there? To some degree, differences may be explained by measurement problems. One could argue that the higher the level of development of an economy, the more accurate it is to use government spending as a measure of the government's role in the economy. Thus comparing Canada and the United States in these terms is more meaningful than comparing Croatia and Canada. However, the more fundamental concern is probably how we measure the role of government in a mixed economy and the extent to which government spending actually captures the impact of government. This is a different issue, though an important one in our assessment of transition economies.

Figure 17.2 provides a summary of the role of government from 1950 through 2000 (at five-year intervals) for the United States. The picture that emerges here can be readily explained by reference to historical facts. For example, the growth of the government sector during the era of the "Great Society" (the 1960s) is evident, as is its decline during the era of privatization (the 1980s and thereafter). Even during this relatively short time, the changes in the importance of government in this context are quite significant. These changes can be explained in part by privatization implemented before the beginning of the transition era.

What are the traditional explanations for the varying roles of government in the economic systems of different nations? Traditionally, government involvement has been justified on the grounds of either **equity** or **efficiency**. From an equity viewpoint, government is involved in redistribution, usually sanctioned by society through a voting process. From an efficiency standpoint, much of the contemporary literature on privatization argues that, other things being equal, production can be conducted more efficiently by private than by nonprivate enterprise.[3] However, from both equity and efficiency standpoints, the case in support of government activity has been rather broader. For example, there are traditional public good and/or externality arguments justifying a role for government. And there are regulatory arguments, although these can extend to equity issues in different national settings. Thus on one end of the spectrum, our views of government as a regulatory mechanism in a market economy have changed significantly over time, while at the other end of the spectrum, so have our views on government as a component of financing the welfare state.[4] These issues are just as important in the Western European economic systems as they have been (and still are) in the East European transition settings.

FIGURE 17.2   G/GDP for the United States, 1950–2000

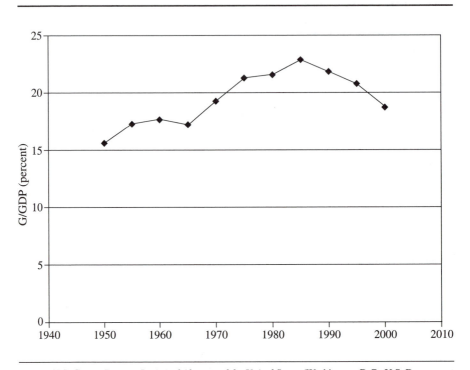

Source: U.S. Census Bureau, *Statistical Abstract of the United States* (Washington, D.C.: U.S. Department of Commerce, various issues).

Finally, we have argued that before the contemporary era in which privatization has been emphasized, theoretical explanations for the growth of government have generally been sparse. One might expect some degree of cyclical variation, but explanations for long-term change tend to focus on issues such as wars and the idea of displacement, in part fueled by a self-aggrandizing bureaucracy. Thus it is common to argue that when the role of government increases (for example, as a consequence of war), that role will decline after the war is over, but not to prewar levels.[5]

To put it differently, the sense that a strong role for government in an economy is important has declined sharply, especially in the latter decades of the twentieth century, to be replaced in both East and West by a view that the unfettered market is superior. Thus, beginning in the 1980s and continuing into a new century, privatization has become a front-burner issue, often described in the transition setting as **mass privatization**. As we shall see, privatization in existing market economies, both developed and less developed, is very different from privatization in the transition setting. It is for these reasons that interest in privatization in the postcommand economies is so intense. Moreover, many would argue that the Western degree of reliance on privatization and markets is inappropriate for many transition economies, where a long-term trajectory is much more likely to be based on a mixed system.

The Context

Although state ownership was not, technically, universal in the command economies, nevertheless in most cases there was very limited private property, limited private economic activity, and for the most part an absence of markets. If a state-dominated command economy is to become a market economy dominated by the private market-place, then state-owned property must be conveyed into an emerging private sector. Such a process implies that it will be possible to identify property rights and, through a process of sale or distribution, to convey these rights to new owners. Unfortunately, these preconditions were seldom met in the transition economies. Property rights were difficult to identify and hence difficult to convey. Without purchasing power and markets through which demand could be exercised, it was not clear how the property rights would be conveyed (in most cases sold) to new owners. The initial absence of financial intermediation meant that investment funds would generally not be available as a mechanism to create investment from savings. Moreover, because state claims to property were largely a result of confiscation during the command era, the issue of **restitution** (to the original owners) arose during the transition era, especially in those countries where confiscation had been relatively recent (Eastern Europe as opposed to the former USSR).[6] These and related considerations have sharply delineated the process of privatization as it has unfolded in the transition economies and in the Western market economies.

The initial conditions that existed in the planned economies at the onset of transition were also important in other respects for the process of privatization. For example, the absence of a legal framework made it hard to define initial property rights—and thus especially hard to change ownership arrangements so that private property rights could be clearly delineated. Much of the legal infrastructure that we take for granted in a market economy, such as the ability to develop, sign, and enforce **contracts**, was largely absent at the onset of transition. At the very least, significant modification of these arrangement was necessary to suit new and very different circumstances. Moreover, the assets that were to be privatized—especially industrial firms—bore little relation to their brethren in market economies, a matter we emphasized during our discussion of initial conditions in Chapter 15.[7] In many cases, there was a **soft budget constraint**, staffing levels were inordinately high to sustain a state-supported **full-employment policy**, and, most important, **scale** issues were often dominant. We have already emphasized the extent to which both vertical and horizontal integration were used to resolve difficulties in the command era—for example, irregular availability of supply (inputs) from sources external to the firm. In many cases, the impact of foreign trade had been minor, and enterprises were overly large, with significant but technologically dated capital structures. In these settings, privatization would prove difficult, and various approaches were used.

Although our emphasis here is privatization in the transition economies, the privatization experience in market economies (both industrialized economies and emerging market economies) offers us a sharp contrast with which to assess the transition experience.

In a market economy, privatization is conceptually feasible, and easier to achieve, under a variety of conditions. First, most privatization in market economies is not mass privatization but rather selective privatization, sometimes related to production but often related to services, regulation, and other government activities. Second, the product or service to be privatized can often be clearly identified. Thus it is not surprising that in the early stages of privatization in market economies, services such as trash collection, janitorial duties, security services, and the like can be readily privatized. In such cases, the product or service is known and most often homogeneous. Third, in the market setting, the legal infrastructure is critical in that a contract can be written, and performance in the fulfillment of the contract can be monitored and ultimately enforced. Note, then, that even in cases where the provision of a service is being privatized, rather than an asset's (such as a firm) being sold, the process is relatively clear. Fourth, markets and financial arrangements exist, so it is possible to make reasonable decisions based on cost/benefit analysis, including some assessment of both private and social costs and benefits.

Finally, it is possible to assess the outcomes of privatization, largely within the framework of efficiency. For example, indicators of firm-level behavior (for example, profitability, dividend payout, and labor productivity) can be measured to examine changes in performance. Thus at the firm level in a market economy, we can examine the results of economic activity before and after privatization to arrive at an assessment of outcomes. In the transition economy where markets are imperfect, obtaining and assessing this type of evidence is difficult. Moreover, we will discover that assessing the results of privatization is not a simple task, especially when we move away from the firm toward a higher level of (societal) aggregation. It is this theme that in the end returns us to the role of the state as a purveyor of regulatory and well-being components in what may become mixed economic systems. These are important issues, especially in different national and historical settings, and they are a fundamental reason why, even among Western market economies, the roles played by the government sector have been and will probably remain very different.

The Transition Setting

The Stages of Privatization

Thus far we have emphasized that the contemporary era of privatization pre-dates, and is much more significant historically than, the privatization taking place under the rubric of transition. At the same time, it is well to note the immense magnitude and difficult circumstances of mass privatization in the transition setting. We will see that although national differences are significant, mass privatization nevertheless exhibited broad similarities in different settings as the need to proceed rapidly took center stage.

It is useful to characterize mass privatization as taking place in the four stages outlined in Table 17.1. These four stages have generally been developed and implemented under some form of **state privatization agency** (the Truehandstalt in Germany, Gosimushchestvo in Russia, and so on). These agencies were conceptually the holders of state property rights and would, under rules and regulations promulgated

TABLE 17.1 Stages of Privatization in the Transition Setting

Develop a legal framework.	Identify properties to privatize.	Create a corporate structure.	Distribute corporate shares.	Restructure enterprises.

Source: Compiled by the authors.

by the government, have the responsibility of shifting the economy from a state-property base to a private-property base.[8]

Before we deal with these stages in greater detail, it is important to appreciate the fact that the rules governing these stages were themselves a matter of controversy. For example, in the case of Russia, it was the Duma that had to define the role of the state sector in a new, privatized economy. This proved to be—and indeed remains—a difficult task. Nevertheless, some boundaries were established; for example, sustaining natural resources and providing for national defense remained responsibilities of the state sector for a variety of traditional reasons. Issues such as common property and the privatization of sectors other than production (housing, for example) involved special problems. These sorts of issues tended to make privatization more appealing for small-scale enterprises, such as those in the service sector.

Carrying out the steps identified in Table 17.1 has turned out to be very problematic in some cases, less so in others. Although the identification of properties to privatize is in theory a reasonable task, in many cases the nature of existing SOEs (large or very large scale, vertical integration, capital-intensiveness) made the process of privatization difficult. Obviously, creating a share structure (often termed **corporatization**) implied a means of control, although sale would be difficult without standard mechanisms for the valuation of shares. Indeed, the issue of **valuation** assumed great importance during the early years of transition.

For example, if a firm is to be sold in a market economy, there are standard mechanisms for establishing some concept of market value. Where a share structure exists, this is an obvious mechanism for valuation. Moreover, even in the absence of a share structure, accounting approaches or some variant of the **present value** of expected future profit streams can provide an assessment of value at a particular time. In the transition setting, however, there were no markets, legal and accounting rules were typically weak and inadequate, and as a consequence, **transparency** in valuation would be impossible to achieve.

Perhaps the most important constraints on privatization in the transition economies have been the absence of purchasing power, limited foreign interest, and the fact that entrepreneurial spirit had so long been stifled in countries with state-controlled systems. This may be why privatization vouchers were widely used to distribute shares to the population. Vouchers seemed to make sense in the transition setting, although, as we will see, they were subject to significant abuse and limitations.

Before we turn to a discussion of the mechanics of privatization and then attempt to assess the results, it is important to note that restructuring, the final stage of the process outlined in Table 17.1, is in many ways the most critical stage of the privatization process. Restructuring is a key focal point as we examine the results of mass privatization in a new century. Many have argued that, whether privatization is based on equity, efficiency, or more general concepts of a role for the state, the transfer of a state-owned enterprise to private owners is not meaningful unless the new owners change the way the property rights are exercised. That is, the fundamental purpose of privatization is to change the nature of resource allocation. This restructuring implies that decision-making arrangements within the firm will change, and when they do change, the results of the firm's operation will be different. This process has been described as making changes in **corporate governance**. And such restructuring has been very difficult.

The Privatization Process

As transition began in the late 1980s and early 1990s, there were no simple road maps for the privatization process. Moreover, important differences in the conditions that prevailed when the transition began were to influence the approach to privatization in various settings. Finally, although economic theory would provide some guidelines, political issues also affected the policy process. Much of the early literature devoted to privatization in the transition economies focused on "strategies" of transition—specifically the speed and sequencing of change, issues that we examined in Chapter 16. From the perspective of privatization, however, the issue was one of guarding against **reversibility** by finding the optimal pace at which privatization should take place to ensure completion of the movement toward a market economy. As privatization proceeded, the issue of cost, and especially social cost (growing levels of unemployment, for example), became a crucial theme in policy discussions.

Finally, it is important to understand that the implementation of privatization *by sector* and *by industry* has been uneven. In all cases, certain sectors (such as defense and energy) were to be retained, at least for some time, by the state. In addition, although Western attention had focused on agriculture, especially in the Soviet case, privatization in agriculture has been uneven and for the most part unsuccessful in the Russian case. Privatization *by region* has also been uneven in large countries such as Russia, partly because of differences in the emerging regional administrative structures and also because of regional differences inherited from the past.

The scale of the industrial establishment also turned out to be important in the process of privatization. Understandably, much of the policy focus centered on medium-sized and large industrial establishments. However, for a variety of reasons, privatization has proved to be more difficult when the largest enterprises are the targets—a problem evident in the contemporary evolution of the Chinese economy. At the other end of the spectrum, privatization has proved to be much easier for the service sector and especially for small-scale, often newly emerging establishments (usually termed **de novo privatization**).

Although the process of privatization has varied from one transition setting to another, two major approaches (or combinations of these approaches) dominated. In **direct sale** of enterprises to buyers, sale could take place either to people not associated with the enterprise being privatized (**outsider privatization**) or to those working in the particular enterprise (**insider privatization**). The actual method of sale could vary from a direct negotiation between buyer and seller to an auction or other indirect method.

A second major approach to privatization was the use of **vouchers**, or financial instruments distributed to the population to be used for the purchase of enterprise shares. Note that these approaches might overlap in that vouchers could be used by "insiders" to gain control of enterprises in which they were employed.[9] Also, depending on the rules established, an employee of one firm who possessed a voucher could use this mechanism to purchase shares in a different firm. In the Russian case, with financial markets very limited, the intent of the voucher program was to pass equity to workers and others within the firm and to do so reasonably quickly. However, voucher privatization did not raise funds, and this was a major problem in a setting where enterprises needed access to new capital.

The approaches were, however, different. Vouchers were appealing because there was little purchasing power available to buy shares of stock. The population did not have sufficient funds, and hence buyers (except perhaps external buyers) could not be found. At the same time, it was argued that the use of vouchers would not provide working capital for the enterprise, a critical issue given that the state was withdrawing from this function, a hard budget constraint would be imposed, and both events would occur largely in the absence of traditional capital markets. This aspect of privatization has been viewed as especially important, because significant capital investment would be necessary for restructuring. Finally, a major focus of early privatization discussions was the issue of restructuring—specifically, what would the different approaches to privatization imply for desired changes in decision making? Would external buyers be more likely to make changes, or would the knowledge of internal buyers be required?

During the early stages of transition, the voucher approach (used, for example, in Russia and the Czech Republic) was proposed as a means to achieve mass privatization very quickly. Note that during the early years, both theoretical and practical arguments were advanced for pursuing privatization at a rapid pace. These arguments were based in part on the simultaneous privatization of SOE components and on the political sense of creating and setting in motion an irreversible process.[10] The threat of reversibility arose from fear that the long-term economic gains to be derived from privatization might well be offset by short-term costs, hence eroding popular support for privatization programs.

In the Russian case (one of the most important), the Russian government distributed to every person, in 1993, a voucher with a face value of 10,000 rubles. These vouchers could then be exchanged for shares of stock at a place of work, exchanged elsewhere through financial intermediaries, or, as a last resort, sold in a secondary (street) market. Direct sale of an enterprise or organization, sometimes through an auction, was one transaction in which these vouchers could be used, along with ruble cash and/or credit, where the latter was available.[11]

The difficulties with the voucher process immediately became evident. Judged in terms of the importance of the private sector (for example, private sector output as a share of total output), the private sector grew rapidly in many transition economies.

But such measurements, though clearly necessary, were inadequate as indicators of the effectiveness of changes in the allocation of resources.

In the Russian case, share structures were defined, and yet "insider privatization" emerged, in which small numbers of influential individuals (former managers, party members, and the like) in effect gained control of the enterprises being privatized. The result was a growing concentration of wealth and what became known as **asset stripping**—the attack on assets of value and the abandonment of other assets. Ironically, in earlier years it was generally thought that creating owners out of workers would be an effective route to privatization and revisions of corporate governance by those who knew the organization best. Evidence has shown, however, that the emerging internal coalitions did not always have the best interests of the organization at heart, resulting in a negative view of insider privatization.

Privatization: Assessing the Results

During the early stages of the transition era (the early 1990s) it was popular to assess privatization by examining the extent to which economic activity had in fact been privatized. For example, in Table 17.2 we present estimates of the percentages of economic activity privatized in various transition economies during the 1990s.

Table 17.2 illustrates several points. First, judging from the evidence for the year 2000, in all of the economies there has been a very significant degree of privatization of output. Second, the starting positions were very different. In some countries, such as Ukraine, there was little private activity in the early 1990s, whereas in other cases, such as Poland, almost half of the output in the early 1990s was derived from the private sector. These two facts suggest that the pace of privatization has differed widely among the transition economies.

A useful way to assess the nature of privatization is the EBRD privatization index. This index, which ranges from 1 (little private ownership) to 4+ (standards typical of

TABLE 17.2   Private-Sector Output as a Share of GDP (percent)

	1992	1996	2000
Russia	25	60	70
Kazakhstan	10	40	60
Ukraine	10	50	60
Poland	45	60	70
Estonia	25	70	75
Hungary	40	70	80
Czech Republic	30	75	80

Source: EBRD, *Transition Report 2001: Energy in Transition* (London: EBRD, 2001), country assessments.

advanced industrial economies with at least 75 percent of enterprise assets in private ownership) is summarized in Table 17.3.

The data in Table 17.3 tell a similar story about privatization, with one important exception. In those countries that have pursued privatization less aggressively (like Ukraine), there is a tendency for the privatization of large-scale enterprises to lag behind. We noted earlier in this chapter that privatizing small-scale enterprises is easier.

Although this sort of evidence has been important for assessing the pace of transition and understanding sectoral differences, there is more to the story. Much of the contemporary literature on privatization quite correctly focuses on what we broadly term **restructuring**. What is restructuring? Why is it important? And why is it so difficult to measure and to assess?

The fundamental objective of creating new property rights is to change the nature of the decision-making arrangements in the newly privatized enterprises and organizations and, by so doing, to change the allocation of resources to improve efficiency. Restructuring is therefore the changing of decision-making arrangements (corporate governance) within an organization, predominantly, though not exclusively, in enterprises in the producing sector of the economy. In the end, restructuring is the critical outcome of the privatization process. Can we judge the success of restructuring?

Although the measures of private-sector shares that we have examined suffer from measurement problems, they are much simpler to gauge than restructuring. The latter would typically be judged by a wide variety of indicators—for example, efficiency indicators (real sales per employee), indicators of the effectiveness of financial markets (percentage of working capital raised in financial markets), and such performance indicators as profitability and dividends per share. An important indicator of restructuring is changes in levels of employment. This variable is often emphasized in the

TABLE **17.3**   The EBRD Index of Privatization in Selected Transition Economies[a]

	1992	1996	2000
Russia	2.0 (2.0)[b]	4.0 (3.0)	4.0 (3.3)
Kazakhstan	2.0 (1.0)	3.3 (3.0)	4.0 (3.0)
Ukraine	1.0 (1.0)	3.0 (2.0)	3.3 (2.7)
Poland	4.0 (2.0)	4.3 (3.0)	4.3 (3.3)
Estonia	2.0 (1.0)	4.3 (4.0)	4.3 (4.0)
Hungary	2.0 (2.0)	4.0 (4.0)	4.3 (4.0)
Czech Republic	4.0 (2.0)	4.3 (4.0)	4.3 (4.0)

[a]The data in parentheses refer to large-scale privatization; the remaining data refer to small-scale privatization.

[b]The scale for privatization ranges from 1, indicating little progress, to 4+, indicating the degree of private economic activity found in advanced industrial economies.

Source: EBRD, *Transition Report 2001: Energy in Transition* (London: EBRD, 2001), country assessments.

analysis of privatized enterprises on the theory that state firms might be expected to shed excess labor to become more attractive to potential purchasers. Unfortunately, although studies that examine key operating variables both before and after privatization are readily available for an assessment of restructuring in Western market economies, these types of studies are hard to come by for transition economies.

There are a great many studies on privatization and restructuring and, fortunately, some good surveys of these studies.[12] The studies of privatization in Western market economies generally suggest that restructuring does in fact occur, improving indicators of operating and financial performance. Privatized firms generally seem to show better performance than nonprivate firms, although the evidence on employment effects and issues pertaining to equity are less clear. However, studies reveal that more than privatization per se is necessary. Also essential are the emergence of new institutions, the existence of a legal infrastructure, and progress in the hardening of budgets. Most studies of privatization have been less successful in identifying the sources of improvement, but outside ownership and changes in management, along with the sorts of institutional changes noted, are all important in these studies.

Compared to studies done on privatization in Western market economies, studies on privatization and restructuring in the transition economies are generally survey-based and limited in scope.[13] Transition studies have focused on differences in ownership arrangements (for example, insider versus outsider ownership), the role of managers, the issue of soft budgets (an important holdover from the command era), product market competition, and the nature of the legal framework. Broadly speaking, the literature supports the view that enterprise restructuring has been less successful in the CIS countries than in the transition economies of Eastern Europe. Whereas this contrast is evident in many transition indicators, there is less agreement on why the CIS countries have performed less well on restructuring. A common theme is the argument that in these cases, the institutions of the command era had been in place much longer and thus were harder to modify.[14] Again, we see the key influence that initial conditions had on progress in the transition era.

Studies of restructuring in the transition economies generally agree on several basic issues, although there are important differences by sector, region, method of privatization, and the like. First, performance improvements are generally better where there is some measure of outsider privatization—either new domestic owners external to the firm or (preferably) foreign owners. (Of course, it is possible that foreigners are simply more likely to be attracted to involvement in better-performing enterprises.) Second, most studies confirm the importance of management and (especially) managerial turnover—that is, the replacement of command era managers by new managers. Third, the development of hard budgets has been a critical factor, and empirical studies show that it is more likely to be achieved in Eastern European than in the CIS countries. Problems in this area doubtless result from a lengthy command era experience and also, in cases such as Russia, from the emergence of an important shadow economy.[15] Finally, recent studies have emphasized the importance of privatization and restructuring in sectors where competitive product markets exist, representing either domestic or foreign competition. Again, regional experiences differ. There is also growing emphasis on the emergence of new institutions, although the empirical evidence on this issue is recent and much research remains to be done.

Another approach to improving our understanding of mass privatization and restructuring in transition economies is to focus on indexes developed by various international organizations, such as the EBRD. Table 17.4 gives the recent scores of several transition economies on indexes of changes in corporate governance and commercial law.

From the evidence presented in Table 17.4 it is clear that there have been significant improvements in corporate governance and the legal infrastructure surrounding the enterprise.[16] At the same time, there are important variations among the transition economies.

On balance, the evidence suggests that privatization has proceeded quite rapidly in the transition economies, although assessing the progress of restructuring has been difficult, and the experiences of individual transition economies have differed significantly from one another. Moreover, as the research literature is beginning to emphasize, there is more to the story of privatization than reduction of the state sector and gains in industrial efficiency. There is an important relationship between privatization and the emergence of financial markets, an issue of critical importance in all the transition economies—and especially in the CIS states, where financial markets are limited in scope and depth. The development of an appropriate legal infrastructure is also critical and will affect the distribution of ownership that ultimately emerges in the transition economies.[17]

Summary

- Privatization is much more than a process to change property-holding arrangements. Privatization implies fundamental changes in the role of the state in the economy.

TABLE 17.4   Changes in Corporate Governance and Commercial Law

Country	Corporate Governance and Restructuring[a]	Overall: Effectiveness and Extensiveness of Commercial Law, 2001[b]
Russia	2+	3+
Kazakhstan	2	4
Ukraine	2	3
Poland	3+	3+
Estonia	3+	4−
Hungary	3+	4

[a]Scale from 1 to 4+, where 1 indicates soft budget constraints and limited changes in corporate governance, and 4+ indicates performance standards of advanced industrial economies.
[b]Scale from 1 to 4+ indicating extensiveness and effectiveness of commercial law—pledge, bankruptcy, and company law.
Source: EBRD, *Transition Report 2001: Energy in Transition* (Paris: EBRD, 2001), Tables 2.2 and 2.1.1.

- Privatization has occurred worldwide, in both industrialized and emerging market economies, but mass privatization in the transition economies has been the major focus of this chapter.
- Although there have been significant country differences in privatization, the process has generally involved a series of stages: development of a legal framework, identification of properties to be privatized, creation of a joint stock framework, and, finally, sale of the properties.
- The mechanisms for transference of property rights from the state to the private sector have varied from some form of direct sale (including the auction process) to a voucher arrangement used in Russia and the Czech Republic. The latter involves the distribution of vouchers (with a specified face value) that can be used to redeem shares in, for example, an enterprise.
- Early research interest focused on an overall assessment of the growth of the private sector in transition economies, whereas the contemporary literature focuses on restructuring, or changes in corporate governance (that is, changing resource allocation and decision making in the enterprise) with the objective of improving efficiency.
- Privatization has been broadly achievable, though controversial, and the impact and results of privatization have been much more evident in industrialized and emerging market economies than in transition economies.
- There is general agreement that among the transition economies, privatization and restructuring have been less successful in the CIS countries than in Eastern Europe, although the degree of variation from one case to another can be significant.
- The extent of privatization has been significant in many of the transition economies; assessing the extent and meaning of restructuring has been more difficult. In the transition economies, new (outsider) ownership enhances privatization, as does devoting attention to management and to the necessary financial and legal arrangements.
- In recent years, the emphasis has been on the development of competitive product markets and on the emergence of new institutions, such as financial markets capable of providing capital to restructuring enterprises. The development of a commercial legal framework is an important element in the transition settings. There remain, as always, important differences among countries, regions, and industrial sectors.

Key Terms

property rights	full-employment policy
state-owned enterprises (SOEs)	scale
social contract	state privatization agency
equity	corporatization
efficiency	valuation
mass privatization	present value
restitution	transparency
contracts	corporate governance
soft budget constraint	reversibility

de novo privatization
direct sale
outsider privatization
insider privatization

vouchers
asset stripping
restructuring

Notes

1. In most of the transition economies of Eastern Europe and the former Soviet Union, prices were released from state control during the early 1990s. Although the release of prices was selective, there was in nearly all countries a sharp spike of inflation, as expected.

2. There is a growing literature on the more general issues relating to the role of the state in differing economic systems. For a useful discussion, see Pier Angelo Toninelli, ed., *The Rise and Fall of State-Owned Enterprise in the Western World* (Cambridge: Cambridge University Press, 2000); and Nicolas Spulber, *Redefining the State: Privatization and Welfare Reform in Industrial and Transitional Economies* (Cambridge: Cambridge University Press, 1997). Political issues are addressed in Harvey Feigenbaum, Jeffrey Henig, and Chris Hamnett, *Shrinking the State: The Political Underpinnings of Privatization* (Cambridge: Cambridge University Press, 1997).

3. Although this broad distinction between state and nonstate (private) ownership is reasonable for our examination of mass privatization in the transition economies, classifying differing equity arrangements is a complex and important issue. Moreover, as transition economies tend to converge toward allocational arrangements found in long-standing market economic systems, simplistic classification in terms of state and nonstate property rights will become less meaningful.

4. The changing role of the state in the provision of social services is an important issue in any economy—and especially in the transition economies, where state involvement was formerly dominant. We will discuss this in greater detail in Chapter 18 when we address issues related to the provision of a safety net.

5. A common interpretation of the apparently expanding role of government in Western industrial economies was provided by displacement theory. This view was also expressed in popular writings on Marxism–Leninism in support of the argument that an expanding state sector (fueled by imperialism, military interactions, and the like) was an essential element of capitalist economic development.

6. The statistical importance of restitution (that is, restitution as a percentage of all forms of privatization) has been small in the transition economies (seldom over 10 percent of privatization). However, the issues involved in cases of restitution are interesting and important.

7. There is a tendency (evident in our discussion here) to emphasize initial conditions in transition economies as those "left over" from the command era, generally organizational arrangements, policies, and structural outcomes that will have an impact on transition policies—in this case, privatization. In addition, however, it is important to note that in the Western literature on privatization, a great deal of emphasis is placed on what steps might be taken, prior to privatization, to facilitate the process. These issues are important in transition economies because they affect the policy mix (the nature of privatization arrangements) and thus the patterns of privatization by region, by sector, and over time.

8. Note that it is useful to distinguish two sorts of rules related to privatization. First, transition economies had to decide, through the political process, what state property rights should be transferred to nonstate ownership. In a sense, these emerging rules came to define the public sector (defense, transportation infrastructure, energy, etc.) in these economies. Second,

it was necessary to establish a set of rules pertaining to privatization arrangements, such as any limits on the distribution of enterprise shares to various groups, such as insiders, outsiders, and managers. Both concepts obviously had an important impact on the outcomes of privatization in differing transition economies during the 1990s.

9. The Russian case is instructive in this respect. Rules governed the distribution of shares to various groups, but it was easy to bypass the rules.

10. As we have emphasized, a common argument in favor of rapid privatization focused on the possibility that privatization (and transition in general) could be reversible if the process moved slowly and the immediate negative impact (for example, the reduction of output) was significant. A second important argument, however, involves theoretical issues. For example, it has been shown that complementarities are critical in transition in general and privatization in particular. For example, if a firm uses two inputs and the sources of these inputs are private and nonprivate, the progress of privatization may be slowed.

11. Manipulation of ownership arrangements and avoidance of legal requirements have been a problem. In the Russian case, the "loans for shares" scandal provides an important example. In the mid-1990s, Russian banks provided loans to the state in return for shares in large state-owned enterprises. Banks, through auctions of shares and the provision of loans, were able to acquire significant holdings. For a discussion, see Juliet Johnson. *A Fistful of Rubles: The Rise and Fall of the Russian Banking System* (Ithaca and London: Cornell University Press, 2000), pp. 184 ff.

12. The literature on privatization and restructuring is now very large. A major source on the transition economies is Simeon Djankov and Peter Murrell, "Enterprise Restructuring in Transition: A Quantitative Survey," *Journal of Economic Literature* (forthcoming). A major survey of privatization and restructuring in both transition and Western economies is William Megginson and Jeffrey Netter, "From State to Market: A Survey of Empirical Studies on Privatization," *Journal of Economic Literature* 39, 2 (2001), 321–389. A useful survey of the Russian case is Carsten Sprenger, "Ownership and Corporate Governance in Russian Industry: A Survey," EBRD, Working Paper No. 70, January 2002. See also Saul Estrin and Mike Wright, eds., "Corporate Governance in the Soviet Union," *Journal of Comparative Economics* 27, 3 (September 1999), 395–474.

13. This is not to be critical of these studies, but rather to make the reader aware that hard data on restructuring indicators such as profitability, sales, product development, capital structure, dividend payouts, and the like are much less likely to be available for the transition economies.

14. This is a theme that was emphasized in Chapters 14 through 16. It remains important in our assessment of privatization and restructuring, suggesting that both privatization and restructuring have been significantly more difficult in those transition economies whose history included a longer time span under the influence of command institutions and policies.

15. It is not easy to characterize and measure the shadow economy with precision. However, as we will emphasize in Chapter 18, the apparent size and nature of the shadow (informal) economy varies considerably from one transition economy to another. It was especially large in the Russian case during the latter half of the 1990s and thus complicates measurement issues.

16. For a discussion of these indicators, specifically their compilation and meaning, see EBRD, Transition Report 2001: Energy in Transition (Paris: EBRD, 2001), Annex 2.1

17. As emphasized in earlier chapters, the broad concept of liberalization, though difficult to characterize and to measure with precision, is nevertheless viewed as an important mechanism for success in the transition experience. Just as the length of time under the command experience can be viewed as important in explaining transition outcomes, so too can the

extent to which liberalization has taken place during the 1990s. By most indicators, those economies that have experienced greater degrees of liberalization have generally performed better in transition.

Recommended Readings

General Works

Joan W. Allen *et al., The Private Sector in State Service Delivery: Examples of Innovative Practices* (Washington, D.C.: Urban Institute, 1989).

William J. Baumol, "On the Perils of Privatization," *Eastern Economic Journal* 19 (Fall 1993), 419–440.

Matthew Bishop, John Kay, and Colin Mayer, *Privatization and Economic Performance* (New York: Oxford University Press, 1994).

Deiter Bos, *Privatization: A Theoretical Treatment* (Cambridge, Mass.: Blackwell, 1992).

Maxim Boycko, Andrei Shleifer, and Robert W. Vishny, "A Theory of Privatization," *Economic Journal* 106 (March 1996), 309–319.

John B. Donahue, *The Privatization Decision* (New York: Basic Books, 1989).

Ahmed Galal, Leroy Jones, Pankaj Tandon, and Ingo Vogelsgand, *Welfare Consequences of Selling Public Enterprises: An Empirical Analysis* (New York: Oxford University Press, 1994).

Leroy P. Jones, Tankaj Tandon, and Ingo Vogelsgang, *Selling Public Enterprises: A Cost-Benefit Methodology* (Cambridge, Mass.: MIT Press, 1990).

J. A. Kay and D. J. Thompson, "Privatization: A Policy in Search of a Rationale," *Economic Journal* 96 (March 1986), 18–32.

Sunita Kikeri, John Nellis, and Mary Shirley, *Privatization: The Lessons of Experience* (Washington, D.C.: World Bank, 1992).

V. V. Ramanad Lam, ed., *Privatization and Equity* (New York: Routledge, 1995).

William C. Megginson, Robert C. Nash, and Matthias van Radenborgh, "The Financial and Operating Performance of Newly Privatized Firms: An International Empirical Analysis," *Journal of Finance* 49 (June 1994), 403–452.

Philip Morgan, ed., *Privatization and the Welfare State: Implications for Consumers and the Workforce* (Brookfield, Vt.: Dartmouth, 1995).

OECD, *Methods of Privatizing Large Enterprises* (Paris: OECD, 1993).

———, *Valuation and Privatization* (Paris: OECD, 1993).

Janet Rothenberg Pack, "Privatization and Public-Sector Services in Theory and Practice," *Journal of Policy Analysis and Management* 6 (1987), 523–540.

Andrew Pendleton and Jonathan Winterton, eds., *Public Enterprise in Transition* (London and New York: Routledge, 1993).

E. S. Savas, *Privatization: The Key to Better Government* (Chatham, N.J.: Chatham House, 1987).

Horst Seibert, ed., *Privatization: A Symposium in Honor of Herbert Giersch* (Tubingen, Germany: Institut fur Weltwirtschaft an der Universitat Kiel, 1992).

E. E. Suleiman and J. Waterbury, T*he Political Economy of Public Sector Reform and Privatization* (Boulder, Colo.: Westview Press, 1990).

John Vickers and George Yarrow, *Privatization: An Economic Analysis* (Cambridge, Mass.: MIT Press, 1988).

Charles Wolf, Jr., Markets or Governments: Choosing Between Imperfect Alternatives (Cambridge, Mass.: MIT Press, 1988).

Regional Literature

Joseph R. Blasi, Maya Kroumova, and Douglas Kruse, *Kremlin Capitalism: Privatizing the Russian Economy* (Ithaca: Cornell University Press, 1997).

Dieter Bos, "Privatization in Europe: A Comparison of Approaches," *Oxford Review of Economic Policy* 9, 1 (1993), 95–110.

Maxim Boycko, Andrei Shleifer, and Robert Vishny, *Privatizing Russia* (Cambridge, Mass.: MIT Press, 1996).

Trevor Buck, Igor Filatotchev, and Mike Wright, "Employee Buyouts and the Transformation of Russian Industry," *Comparative Economic Studies* 36 (Summer 1994), 1–16.

Saul Estrin, "Privatization in Central and Eastern Europe: What Lessons Can Be Learnt from Western Experience," *Annals of Public and Cooperative Economy* 62, 2 (April–June, 1991), 159–182.

Saul Estrin and Xavier Richet, "Industrial Restructuring and Microeconomic Adjustment in Poland: A Cross-Sectional Approach," *Comparative Economic Studies* 35, 4 (Winter 1993), 1–19.

Wendy Carlin and Colin Mayer, "The Truhandanstalt: Privatization by State and Market," in Oliver Jean Blanchard, Kenneth A. Froot, and Jeffrey D. Sachs, eds., *The Transition in Eastern Europe,* Vol. 2 (Chicago: University of Chicago Press, 1994), 189–207.

Simeon Djankov and Peter Murrell, "Enterprise Restructuring in Transition: A Quantitative Survey," *Journal of Economic Literature,* forthcoming.

Maurice Ernst, Michael Alexeev, and Paul Marer, *Transforming the Core* (Boulder, Colo.: Westview Press, 1993).

Roman Frydman and Andrzej Rapaczynski, *Privatization in Eastern Europe: Is the State Withering Away?* (Budapest: Central European University Press, 1994).

Eva Marikova Leeds, "Voucher Privatization in Czechoslovakia," *Comparative Economic Studies* 35, 3 (Fall 1993), 19–38.

Susan J. Linz and Gary Krueger, "Enterprise Restructuring in Russia's Transition Economy: Formal and Informal Mechanisms," *Comparative Economic Studies* 40, 2 (Summer 1998), 5–52.

Susan J. Linz, "Russian Firms in Transition: Champions, Challengers, and Chaff," *Comparative Economic Studies* 39, 2 (Summer 1997), 1036.

Ivan Major, *Privatization and Economic Performance in Central and Eastern Europe* (Northampton, Mass.: Edward Elgar, 1999).

William L. Megginson and Jeffrey M. Netter, "From State to Market: A Survey of Empirical Studies on Privatization," *Journal of Economic Literature* XXXIX, 2 (June 2001), 321–389.

Lynn D. Nelson and Irina Y. Kuzes, "Evaluating the Russian Voucher Privatization Program," *Comparative Economic Studies* 36 (Spring 1994), 55–68.

Marsha Pripstein Posusney and Linda J. Cook, eds., *Privatization and Labor* (Northampton, Mass.: Edward Elgar, 2000).

Clemens Schutte, *Privatization and Corporate Control in the Czech Republic* (Northampton, Mass.: Edward Elgar, 2000).

Marko Simoneti, Saul Estrin, and Andreja Bohm, eds., *The Governance of Privatization Funds* (Northampton, Mass.: Edward Elgar, 1999).

Darrell Slider, "Privatization in Russia's Regions," *Post-Soviet Affairs* 10, 4 (October–December 1994), 367–396.

Carsten Sprenger, "Ownership and Corporate Governance in Russian Industry: A Survey," EBRD, Working Paper No. 70, January 2002.

Pier Angelo Toninelli, ed., *The Rise and Fall of State-Owned Enterprise in the Western World* (Cambridge: Cambridge University Press, 2000).

Milica Uvalic and Daniel Vaughan-Whitehead, eds., *Privatization Surprises in Transition Economies* (Lyme, N.H.: Edward Elgar, 1997).

Western and Developing Countries

Paul Cook and Colin Kirkpatrick, eds., *Privatisation in Less Developed Countries* (New York: St. Martin's, 1988).

Harvey Feigenbaum, Jeffrey Henig, and Chris Hamnett, *Shrinking the State: The Political Underpinnings of Privatization* (Cambridge: Cambridge University Press, 1998).

Dominique Hachette and Rolf Luders, *Privatization in Chile* (San Francisco: ICS Press, 1993).

Steve H. Hanke, ed., *Privatization and Development* (San Francisco: Institute for Contemporary Studies, 1987).

Attiat F. Ott and Keith Hartley, eds., *Privatization and Economic Efficiency: A Comparative Analysis of Developed and Developing Countries* (Brookfield, Vt.: Edward Elgar, 1991).

Jonas Prager, "Is Privatization a Panacea for LDC's? Market Failure versus Public-Sector Failure," *Journal of Developing Areas* 26 (April 1992), 301–322.

Jeremy Richardson, ed., *Privatization and Deregulation in Canada and Britain* (Brookfield, Vt.: Aldershot, 1990).

Gabriel Roth, *The Private Provision of Public Services in Developing Countries* (Oxford: Oxford University Press, 1987).

Nicolas Spulber, *Redefining the State: Privatization and Welfare Reform in Industrial and Transitional Economies* (Cambridge: Cambridge University Press, 1997).

Pier Angelo Toninelli, ed., *The Rise and Fall of State-Owned Enterprises in the Western World* (Cambridge: Cambridge University Press, 2000).

18

The Macroeconomy:
Fiscal and Monetary Issues

One of the fascinating aspects of the transition era has been the development of macroeconomic arrangements in settings where such arrangements typically did not exist in a traditional (market) form during the command era. During the era of classical socialism, the role of the state sector was dominant, and state access to resources was achieved directly through state enterprises and other state organizations, obviating the need for an indirect **"Western-style" tax system**. As we have seen, the banking systems in the command economies were primitive, playing largely a formal role in a system driven by real rather than monetary forces. In many instances, the money supply was a state secret, and the role of money was viewed as passive from the perspective of influencing resource allocation. There were no financial markets (and therefore effectively no financial intermediation), state enterprises being funded directly from the state (consolidated) budget. Foreign trade was directly under state control, with both exports and imports controlled by the state. The currency was not convertible, so the balance of payments was not a function of (external) market forces and commodity and financial flows. And at least in theory, external financial forces had very little impact on the domestic monetary arrangements. This is a situation that was destined to change dramatically during transition.

It may be that the foregoing view of the macroeconomy in the command setting is simplistic. Certainly, as the Soviet economy faltered under Perestroika in the late 1980s, **monetary overhang**, or excess monetary emissions in an otherwise state-controlled economy, was viewed as a growing problem. The macro balance, however, was traditionally viewed in terms of a simple balance between aggregate demand and aggregate supply, and within reason, the state could exercise considerable control over both sides of the equation.

It is not surprising, given the almost complete absence of a macroeconomic system as we understand it in a market economy, that the initial collapse of the old order and the early years of transition to market arrangements were difficult for the command economies. Moreover, as we emphasized in our discussion of the microeconomy, the initial conditions differed significantly from one country to another. A similar set of arguments could be made for the macroeconomy, where the potentially important initial conditions in transition economies included the existence of macroeconomic distortions (for example, the possibility of excess demand in a shortage economy where price controls were pervasive). These are issues that have already been addressed, although the specifics of the macroeconomic environment remain to be investigated.

Creating the Macroeconomy: The Early Years of Transition

As we have already emphasized, the early years of transition unfolded largely in the absence of models or obvious alternatives for the policy makers in charge of the transition processes. As the old order began to collapse, state control of economic activity collapsed with it, and the decentralization of decision making often occurred in an institutional and legal vacuum. In this setting, both the actors and the setting in which these actors would function changed quickly, often with limited policy guidance. During the early years of transition, the emphasis understandably fell on **stabilization,** or the adoption of policies that would limit the downslide of economic activity. Even so the downslide of economic activity was significant—though very different in both pattern and magnitude from one country to another.[1]

In many transition economies, the introduction of familiar institutional underpinnings (financial markets, banking arrangements, and the like) created the appearance of market-type arrangements, but the financial institutions did not always work like their counterparts in established market economies. Financial markets were generally shallow and nontransparent. Moreover, the existence of financial institutions that played only a limited role in the macroeconomy made policy choices especially difficult.

In a market economy, the debate over the nature and effectiveness of various macro policy instruments continues unabated. However, the policy environment of the semireformed transition economies is much more complex than that of developed market economies, especially during the early years of the transition process.

Indeed, policy formulation and execution has been much more complex in the transition economies for several basic reasons, some of which we have addressed in earlier chapters. First, in semireformed economic systems, an optimal policy mix is not generally obvious. Can a policy on interest rates be implemented in a system that has a limited emerging banking system and limited (if any) financial markets? For example, if enterprises do not and cannot obtain funds from financial intermediaries, of what relevance is a policy designed to change investment patterns through these intermediaries (for example, by the manipulation of interest rates)?

Second, in a market economy, the channels through which policies affect economic outcomes are generally understood. Thus the impact of policy variants can be predicted, and intelligent policy judgments can be made.[2] For example, it is well known that interest rates have a significant impact on the purchase of durable goods in market economies. If it is thought desirable to stimulate the sectors that produce and sell these durable goods, then one obvious mechanism to do so is adjustments to interest rates. In the transition economies, especially during the early stages of transition, the policy channels were generally unknown, and thus the potential impact of policy variants could not be predicted. Credit for the purchasing of consumer durables was generally not available, so varying the charges made for the use of credit would have little if any impact on the consumption of durables.

Third, although there is continuing debate about policy objectives even in developed market economies, these issues arguably have been more serious in the transition economies. For example, beyond the basic policy issues raised above, the macroeconomic policy framework is especially fragile in the transition setting, where the external economy will have a major impact on the domestic economy, but under emerging and fragile financial arrangements, especially the exchange rate.[3] Specifically, it is possible—indeed likely—that there will be conflicts between internal and external balance. In most transition economies, the conflict between alternative yet attractive policy objectives made the policy mix especially difficult to determine.

Fourth, the impact of policy choices is an issue in any economic system. And in some transition economies, there is yet another critical dimension: the presence of an important **shadow economy**. In Russia, for example, informal arrangements for resource allocation, dating from the command era, have been sustained. In addition, the shadow economy assumed a variety of new forms in the semireformed Russian economy of the 1990s.[4] Worse, however, is the fact that money surrogates were of major importance by the second half of the 1990s, in some cases replacing traditional mechanisms and channels and thus necessitating very different policy variants. For example, a considerable share of enterprise activity—for example, the payment of taxes to local and higher-level governments—has been conducted in kind. Whatever the reasons for this turn of events, the policy environment in a barter economy is clearly very different from the policy environment in a functioning market economy.

A Macroeconomic Framework

What challenges face the policy makers as they ponder the macroeconomic balance in the transition economies? Perhaps the best way to organize our thinking on these issues is to return to a simple macroeconomic framework (balance) of the sort presented in equation 18.1.

$$I = S + (T - G) + (M - X) \qquad (18.1)$$

where

$$I = \text{investment}$$
$$S = \text{private savings}$$
$$T - G = \text{government balance}$$
$$M - X = \text{foreign balance}$$

An understanding of each of the components of this balance will provide us with an overview of the macroeconomic problems of the transition economies.

Investment

Command economies typically devoted a relatively large share of output to investment. Moreover, the state was the dominant mechanism through which accumulation and investment took place, facilitating its concentration in the industrial sector, as opposed to the service and other sectors. As the command economies collapsed, two major changes occurred. First, the state apparatus through which the investment process took place began to crumble, and it was generally not quickly replaced by alternative (market) arrangements. As we have seen, however, there were considerable differences among transition economies as a consequence of initial conditions, level of development, precollapse reform in countries such as Hungary and Poland, and so on. Second, in the absence of the organizational arrangements to facilitate it, investment might be expected to fall. There were important differences in the evolution of banking systems, for example. In cases such as Russia, banks did not generally perform the usual functions of banks (attracting deposits and making loans), and this denied the system a major channel through which savings might be converted into investment. Moreover, the emergence of financial markets was slow and uneven, usually resulting in limited and very shallow markets.

The absence of adequate sources of enterprise investment was an important aspect of the initial collapse of output, an issue that we have examined.[5] Equally important as the transition era evolved, limitations on investment had a negative impact on the nature and the pace of enterprise restructuring. It is difficult to assemble accurate data for the early and tumultuous years of transition, but let's examine what evidence is available.

During the early years of transition, investment collapsed in many of the transition economies, although there was significant recovery during the 1990s. However, the collapse was generally less, and the recovery stronger, in Eastern Europe than to the CIS states. Figure 18.1 shows the year-to-year percentage change in real gross fixed investment through the mid- and late 1990s for selected transition economies. The patterns here generally conform to the general pattern outlined, although there are important differences among countries and some surprising outcomes, such as the improvement in Russia. On balance, these changes through the 1990s have led to changes in the command era pattern of sustaining a very high investment share relative to the patterns typical in market economies. Figure 18.2 shows investment shares for a sample of transition economies. Both the Czech Republic and Estonia have sustained high investment shares, but the other countries examined here have generally moved toward more modest shares.

Private Savings

As we have emphasized, the mechanism of accumulation in the command economies was fundamentally different from that found in most market economies. Under a system where control of resources and production is in the hands of the state, and returns to factors (wage payments to labor in the socialist economy) are set by the state, there is no need for indirect systems of taxation for the purpose of accumulation. The state has direct access to the product generated in the economy and can, within reason, determine the magnitude of accumulation, assuming that this burden will be tolerated by the population. No wonder that under these arrangements, accumulation and investment could be high by international standards.

FIGURE 18.1   Percentage Change in Real Gross Fixed Investment:
Selected Transition Economies

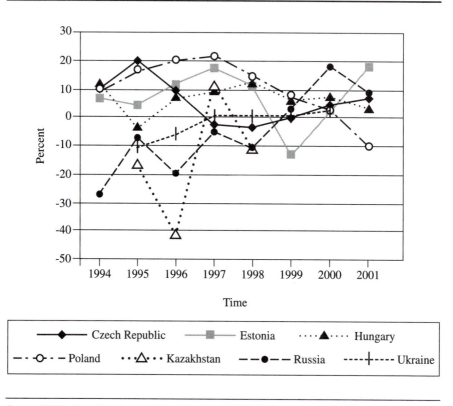

Source: EBRD, *Transition Report Update* (London: EBRD, 2001), Country assessments.

Command systems did, however, facilitate savings in savings accounts or in cash hoards where savings banks were not viewed by citizens as trustworthy. It is perhaps not surprising that as the command system collapsed, patterns of household savings changed, and not always in fully predictable ways. Although data on household savings during the early years of transition are often questionable, overall there was a tendency for savings rates to fall, arguably from roughly 30 percent of household income to some 15 percent or less.[6] Then, somewhat surprisingly, savings rates increased somewhat (from their lowest levels) during the transition era. The Russian pattern is instructive.[7] There was an initial collapse, but more important, Russian households moved away from making deposits in Sberbank (the Russian savings bank) and toward simply holding rubles in cash. Thereafter, there was a sharp movement out of rubles toward dollars as ruble convertibility was introduced. Although Russians initially defected from Sberbank, commercial banks did not pick up the slack, so household savings were not generally available to investors through financial intermediaries.

FIGURE 18.2   Investment as a Percent of GDP: Selected Transition Economies

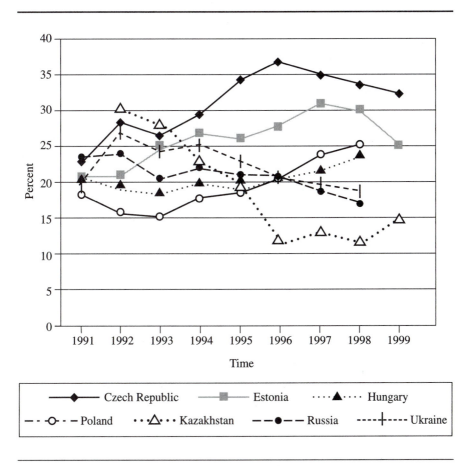

Source: EBRD, *Transition Report 2000* (London: EBRD, 2000), country assessments.

The Government Balance

In equation 18.1, $(T - G)$ represents the government balance—that is, the difference between government revenues (T) and government expenditure (G). During the command era, both elements of the government balance were directly under the control of the state. There was therefore no need to incur either a surplus or a deficit, although this issue has been the subject of controversy, especially during the latter years of the command era.

During the early years of transition, as the command arrangements collapsed, two major changes occurred. First, government enterprises, with no plan directives to guide them, reduced output and thus were unable to pay their expenses (such as wages and materials outlays), let alone accumulate a surplus to be used for financing government expenditure. In the absence of a tax system, government revenues inevitably declined, though again with considerable variation from case to case and over time.

Second, although government expenditure could be shrunk, this alternative proved to be very difficult. In most cases, there was a reluctance to close enterprises because unemployment would result. Moreover, there was continuing pressure to sustain major components of government spending—for example, the social safety net, which was viewed as necessary for maintaining popular support for new political regimes and associated transition programs.

The result of the pressures on both T and G was a budget deficit. Figure 18.3 presents the government balance for the transition economies of Central and Eastern Europe, Southeastern Europe, and the Commonwealth of Independent States. It is evident that during the early years of the transition there were serious imbalances, especially in Southeastern Europe and the CIS.[8] These imbalances were a major element of the Washington Consensus. Second, although the budgetary story improves considerably by the mid- and late 1990s, there remain persistent deficits that vary in magnitude among the individual transition economies. It is clear that these deficits occurred because of pressure to sustain government spending in an environment where old sources of revenue were shrinking and were only slowing being replaced by new sources. But why should we be concerned with these deficits?

FIGURE 18.3   Government Balance: Transition Economies

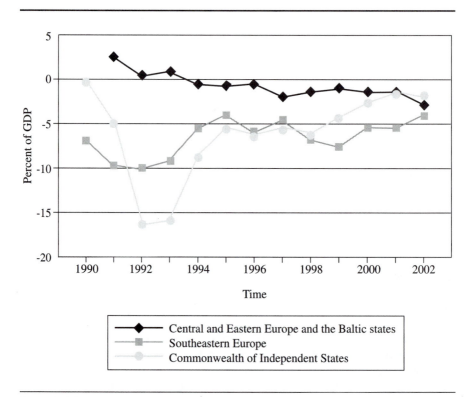

Source: EBRD, *Transition Report 2001* (London: EBRD, 2001), Table A.3.4.

The major problem with the existence of a budget deficit has been the issue of monetizing the deficit, or the impact of financing mechanisms. In the absence of significant financial markets, how could a budget deficit be sustained unless obviously inflationary measures (such as printing money) were used? The issue of the budget deficit took center stage in policy debates for several important reasons. First, during the early years of transition, prices were (more or less) released. This markedly boosted inflation in many transition economies and, of course, the potential for continuing inflation resulting from the macroeconomic imbalance. Second, domestic financial markets were generally not available as a source of finance. This led to the emergence of various other (often controversial) financial instruments, such as Treasury bills in the Russian case. The extent to which domestic borrowing could be contemplated was limited in many of the transition economies. Third, the budget deficit had an immediate and obvious connection to the external economy. This resulted in the emergence of serious policy issues related to the introduction of a convertible currency and the closely related matter of external financial balance. Given the very different transition experiences with the foreign sector, it is not surprising that in many cases the foreign sector did not provide a simple solution to the domestic budget crisis. Finally, since the budget balance was an observable indicator of macrobalance or lack of macrobalance, it became a key and controversial indicator that would be used (for example, by the IMF) to gauge the effectiveness of transition measures and thus eligibility for bank support. These issues, as we have noted earlier, became the focus of the Washington Consensus.

Inflation and Emerging Markets

During the early years of transition, a critical issue was the development of domestic monetary policy and the closely related matter of inflation. Recall that during the command era, prices were set by the state and bore no necessary relation to basic demand and supply conditions. In most of the transition economies, prices were released from state control during the early 1990s. The process was uneven and occurred under political directives that dictated which prices would be released and which would remain subject to state control. Understandably, in a disequilibrium setting, prices generally increased sharply. Figure 18.4 offers an overview of inflation for the period 1990–2002, using the annual mean value of inflation. Two observations are important: The magnitude of inflation in the CIS and Southeastern European states was dramatic as price controls were removed. And the differences in the spike in inflation, especially comparing these cases to the Central and Eastern European states, are striking. The inflation spikes in Central and Eastern Europe were important within these countries but very modest in comparison to the other transition settings.

It is important to appreciate the fact that inflation in the transition economies has been caused by two very different sets of forces. The first set of forces, the release of formerly state-controlled prices, is evident in Figure 18.4: Inflation in the early 1990s exceeded 2,000 percent in Southeastern Europe and the CIS. Figure 18.5 shows that the average annual rate of inflation (using an unweighted mean value) for the latter part of the decade is on a very different scale. In one sense, the rate of inflation came

FIGURE 18.4   Average Annual Inflation in Transition Economies, 1990–2002[a]

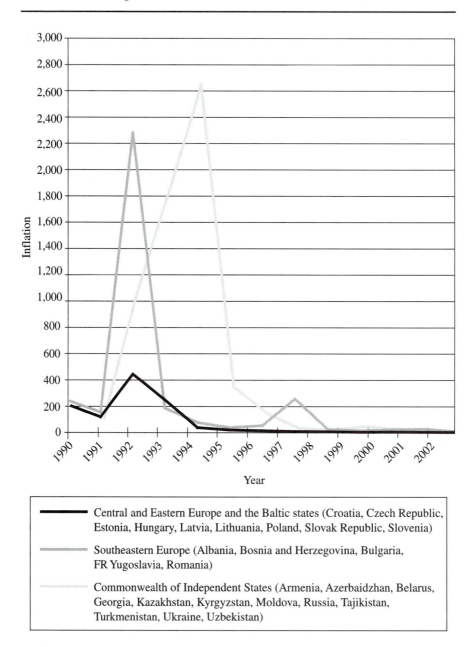

Central and Eastern Europe and the Baltic states (Croatia, Czech Republic, Estonia, Hungary, Latvia, Lithuania, Poland, Slovak Republic, Slovenia)

Southeastern Europe (Albania, Bosnia and Herzegovina, Bulgaria, FR Yugoslavia, Romania)

Commonwealth of Independent States (Armenia, Azerbaidzhan, Belarus, Georgia, Kazakhstan, Kyrgyzstan, Moldova, Russia, Tajikistan, Turkmenistan, Ukraine, Uzbekistan)

[a]Data for 2001 are preliminary; data for 2002 are projections.

Source: EBRD, *Transition Report Update* (London: EBRD, May 2002), Table A-2.

FIGURE 18.5   Transition Economies: Average Annual Inflation

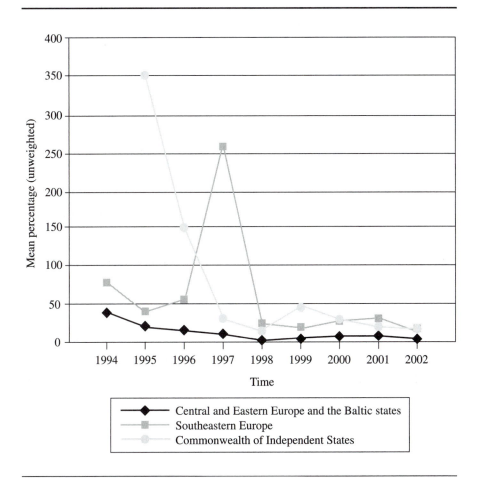

Source: EBRD, *Transition Report Update* (London: EBRD, 2002), Table A.2.

under control, especially in the latter years of the decade, across most transition economies. What has caused a sustained (if much more modest) rate of inflation in recent years in transition economies?

During the early years of transition, stabilization was a difficult task from both a fiscal and a monetary standpoint. As prices increased, a major effort was made to bring both monetary and fiscal variables under control, with the goal of achieving a positive real rate of interest. In Figure 18.6 it is evident that during the initial years of transition in some of the transition economies, the growth of broad money (M2) was rapid, though much more modest rates of growth (in money terms) occurred during the latter half of the 1990s. What are the current prospects for inflation?

FIGURE 18.6   Broad Money (end-year M2): Percentage Change in
Selected Transition Economies

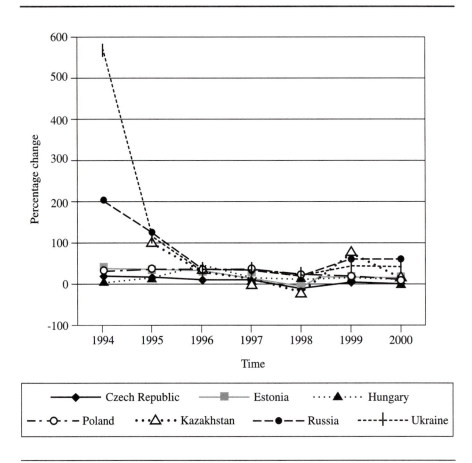

Source: EBRD, *Transition Report 2001* (London: EBRD, 2001), country assessments.

The EBRD in its *Transition Report Update* provides a summary of inflation fore-casts for 2002.[9] The average inflation rates for 2002 have been forecast to be a mod-est 4.3 percent in Central and Eastern Europe and the Baltic states, 13.0 percent in the transition economies of Southeastern Europe, and 13.7 percent in the CIS states.[10]

The External Balance

Possibly the most complex aspect of the macroeconomic balance in transition econo-mies during the 1990s was the external balance. Although we devote Chapter 19 to trade and payments, it is important to relate these issues to the domestic macroeconomy and the developments of the early transition years.

As is well known in the economic literature, an imbalance between the export and import of goods and services implies the movement of capital, which, along with investment flows (either through portfolio investment, loans and grants, or direct foreign investment), implies that an external mechanism may be available for assisting with the budget deficit. Specifically, during the early years of transition, the devaluation of transition currencies led to an increase in exports and financial inflows in the form of loans and grants and direct foreign investment. These flows expand the monetary base and can fuel domestic inflation. Thus, although capital inflows are attractive, they expand the domestic money supply and thus must be controlled by some **sterilization** policy—for example, the sale of state securities by the central bank to shrink the money supply. To the extent that these capital inflows are shortterm, creating instability, they can be the focus of attacks on the domestic currency. It is these issues that came to the forefront in the Czech financial crisis of 1997 and the Russian financial crisis of August 1998.

The Macroeconomic Agenda and Its Evolution

Thus far we have focused on the basics of the macroeconomic balance and the initial problems unfolding in the transition economies. Their responses to these problems were quite different, as were the outcomes.[11] As we have emphasized, the focus of the early transition years was on stabilization, as the old order collapsed and new institutions were yet to be established. Table 18.1 lists some of the formal stabilization programs enacted in the various transition economies. All included the introduction of banking arrangements and related laws, the introduction of stock exchanges, and a myriad of legal regulations governing financial institutions, markets, pensions, and the like. In most transition economies, there has been continuing modification of these arrangements.

Banking in Transition Economies

One of the most controversial aspects of the transition process has been the emergence of new market-type banking arrangements.[12] Conceptually, the agenda for banking is, at least in hindsight, quite clear. It is necessary to create a central bank, as well as distinct and separate commercial banks, and to establish the liberalization of interest rates and the convertibility of the currency such that the banking system can serve the usual functions that it performs in market economies. It is also necessary to create the appropriate legal structure governing the operation of banks. An assessment of banking arrangements should focus on the extent to which they develop as commercially viable operations by attracting a deposit base and contributing to investment through financial markets. What has been the experience in transition economies?

Figure 18.7 offers evidence on the development of banks and nonbank financial institutions, using the index of liberalization of the European Bank for Reconstruction

TABLE **18.1**   The Macroeconomic Agenda: Organizational and Policy Changes

The Czech Republic   1990, two-tier banking system introduced; 1991, bankruptcy law; 1992, initial bank privatization; 1993, beginning of stock exchange trading; 1993–1998, changes in bankruptcy laws; 2001, completion of bank privatization

Estonia   1991, foreign investment law; 1992, bankruptcy law; 1993, securities laws and new banking regulations; 1995, initial bank privatization; 1996, stock exchange established; 1998, pension reform, and deposit insurance becomes effective

Hungary   1990, securities laws introduced, stock exchange established, and banking laws adopted; 1991–1993, bankruptcy laws introduced; 1994, first state bank privatization; 1995, securities and exchange commission established; 1997, pension laws and banking reform; 2001, new central banking act

Poland   1991, banking laws introduced and stock exchange opens; 1992–1993, changes in banking laws and first bank privatization; 1998, changes in banking and bankruptcy laws; 1999, pension reform

Kazakhstan   1991, securities and stock exchange laws passed; 1993, initial banking laws introduced; 1995, decree on bankruptcy, bank and enterprise restructuring agency developed; 1997, bankruptcy law and pension reform; 1999, first domestic bond issues; 2001, national development bank established

Russia   1990, initial banking laws and central bank initiative; 1993, bankruptcy law established; 1995, federal securities commission established; 1998, new bankruptcy laws; 1999, laws on bank insolvency, restructuring, and foreign investment; 2001, banking laws amended

Ukraine   1991, central bank law, securities and stock exchange law; 1992, stock exchange opens, bankruptcy laws; 1995, securities and exchange commission established; 1998, foreign ownership of banks permitted; 2000, new bankruptcy law and new laws on banking

Source: EBRD, *Transition Report 2001* (London: EBRD, 2001), country assessments.

and Development. These ratings fall on a scale of 1 to 4+, where 1 indicates little progress, and 4+ indicates standards of advanced industrial economies. The ratings here suggest a mixed record of banking reform. Some improvements made during the first half of the 1990s were sustained during the latter half of the decade (in the Czech Republic and Estonia, for example), whereas there were declines in the index for Russia and little change for Ukraine and Kazakhstan. Figure 18.8 shows that the development of nonbank financial institutions exhibited a similar pattern. If the emergence of the financial infrastructure has been a mixed experience, what can be said about the abilities of these institutions to provide appropriate intermediation in the transition economies?

Figure 18.9 confirms the importance of "domestic credit to enterprises as a percent of GDP," a ratio discussed earlier in this chapter. With the decline of state budgetary subsidies for enterprises, one would expect other sources to replace the state role. The Czech Republic is a distinct case among the transition economies examined in Figure 18.9, but the levels of domestic credit to enterprises have generally been modest, though gradually increasing, in the latter half of the 1990s. However, there is

FIGURE 18.7   EBRD Index of Banking Sector Reform:
Selected Transition Economies

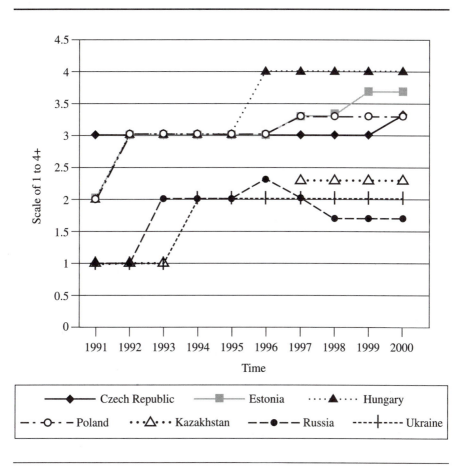

Source: EBRD, *Transition Report 2001* (London: EBRD, 2001), Table 2.2.

another side to the story. To the extent that the banking sector has emerged slowly, and in many cases has been only a modest source of financing, financial difficulties might be expected. These difficulties are illustrated by the importance of bad loans as a share of all loans (see Figure 18.10).

The macroeconomic experience of the transition economies has been a challenging one. Most of these economies began the transition experience with an attempt to stabilize their economies through a combination of emerging fiscal and monetary policies for both domestic and foreign economic activities. As new legislation was drafted to govern the emergence of new institutional arrangements and related policy measures, progress was in many cases modest, and financial markets remained shallow (see Figure 18.11) and nontransparent. The net result, by the late 1990s, was a fragile

FIGURE 18.8   EBRD Index of Reform of Nonbank Financial Institutions:
Selected Transition Economies

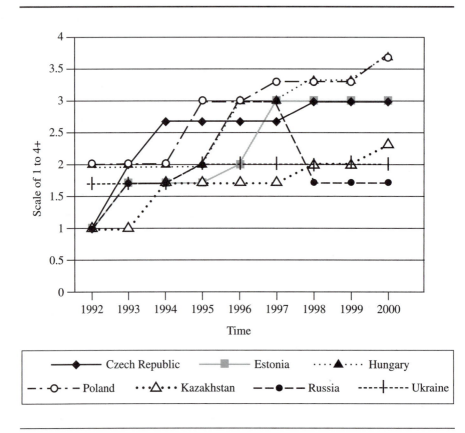

Source: EBRD, *Transition Report 2001* (London: EBRD, 2001), Table 2.2.

macroeconomic setting that varied considerably among the transition economies. In this context, macroeconomic prospects for the new century are difficult to predict with any degree of certainty.

Summary

- Investment initially collapses in the early years of transition, subsequently recovering somewhat, though not generally to levels sustained during the command era.
- Household savings rates (savings as a proportion of household income) declined significantly during the early years of transition, with some recovery in the latter part of the 1990s. The composition of savings changed, and there was a tendency to hold hard currency following the introduction of convertibility.

FIGURE 18.9   Domestic Credit to Enterprises as a Percent of GDP:
Selected Transition Economies

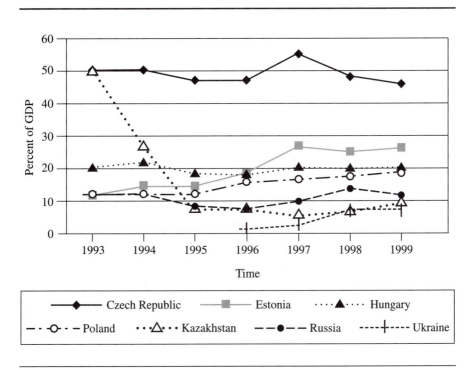

Source: EBRD, *Transition Report 2001* (London: EBRD, 2001), Table 2.2.

- The government balance typically ran a deficit, as government revenues declined but pressure for sustained government spending proved difficult to resist. From initially high levels, the budget deficit has generally become more modest throughout the transition era.
- Inflation has been a major problem in transition economies. As prices were released from state control in the early 1990s, they increased dramatically in many cases. Thereafter, price increases were more modest.
- The macroeconomic agenda has been similar in the various transition economies but has had differing outcomes. Beginning in the early 1990s, the nature of banking arrangements changed significantly, along with the emergence of stock markets, the development of the safety net, and an emergent legal environment.

Key Terms

"Western-style" tax system	stabilization	"Washington Consensus"
monetary overhang	shadow economy	sterilization

FIGURE **18.10**   Bad Loans as a Percent of All Loans:
Selected Transition Economies

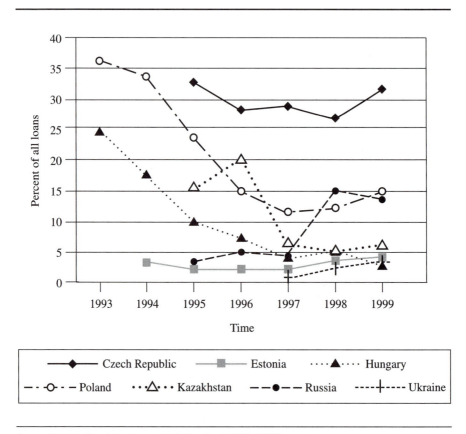

Source: EBRD, *Transition Report 2000* (London: EBRD, 2000), country assessments.

Notes

1. A useful discussion of the early years of transition can be found in "Symposium on Economic Transition in the Soviet Union and Eastern Europe," *Journal of Economic Perspectives* 5, 4 (Fall 1991), 3–236; Christopher Clague and Gordon C. Rausser, eds., *The Emergence of Market Economies in Eastern Europe* (Cambridge: Blackwell, 1992), Part II.

2. Specifically, policy targets can be known, and the leads and lags associated with policy variants can be known, at least within reasonable ranges.

3. There is considerable controversy surrounding the movement from a nonconvertible to a convertible currency in the transition economies. These issues are discussed in Chapter 19.

4. The magnitude of the shadow economy differs considerably among the transition economies, and arguably it is much smaller in Eastern Europe than in the CIS countries. A case of special interest is Russia, where the shadow economy has been very large. See, for example OECD, *Russian Federation* (Paris: OECD, 2000); for a more general discussion, see Eric Friedman, Simon Johnson, Daniel Kaufmann, and Pablo Zoido-Lobaton, "Dodging

FIGURE 18.11   Stock Market Capitalization as a Percent of GDP:
Selected Transition Economies

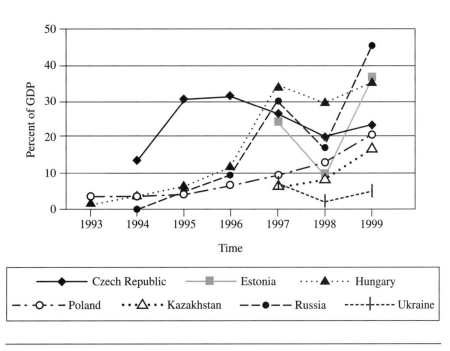

Source: EBRD, *Transition Report 2001* (London: EBRD, 2001), Table 2.2.

the Grabbing Hand: The Determinants of Unofficial Activity in 69 Countries," *Journal of Public Economics* 76 (2000), 459–493; Simon Commander and Christian Mumssen, "Understanding Barter in Russia," EBRD Working Paper No. 37, December 1998; Wendy Carlin, Steven Fries, Mark Schaffer, and Paul Seabright, "Barter and Non-Monetary Transactions in Transition Economies: Evidence from a Cross-Country Survey," EBRD Working Paper No. 50, June 2000.

5. The theoretical underpinnings of these issues are developed in Gerard Roland, *Transition and Economics* (Cambridge, Mass.: MIT Press, 2000), Ch. 12.

6. For a discussion of savings rates during transition, see Cevdet Denizer and Holger C. Wolf, "The Savings Collapse During the Transition in Eastern Europe," a part of the World Bank project entitled "Saving Across the World," EBRD, *Transition Report 1996* (London: EBRD, 1996). Note also that comparison of savings rates before and during transition is difficult in part because of conceptual and definitional differences and the controversy surrounding the magnitude of savings during the command era.

7. For a discussion of the Russian case, see Juliet Johnson, *A Fistful of Rubles* (Ithaca: Cornell University Press, 2000); Michael S. Bernstam and Alvin Rabushka, *Fixing Russia's Banks: A Proposal for Growth* (Stanford: Hoover Institution Press, 1998).

8. It is important to note that during the early years of transition, there were a number of estimates of the size of the budget deficits. These estimates differed considerably one from another, thus further fueling the debate over actual magnitude of deficits.

9. EBRD, *Transition Report Update* (London: EBRD, May 2001), p. 6, Table 1.2.
10. These numbers are mean values of averages, the latter for a series of forecasts.
11. For a useful summary, see Marie Lavigne, *The Economics of Transition,* 2nd. ed. (London: St. Martin's, 1999), Ch. 7.
12. For a discussion, see Steven Fries and Anita Taci, "Banking Reform and Development in Transition Economies," EBRD Working Paper No. 71, June 2002; Charles Enoch, Anne-Marie Gulde, and Daniel Hardy, "Banking Crises and Bank Resolution: Experiences in Some Transition Economies," IMF Working Paper WP/02/56, March 2002.

Recommended Readings

P. Aghion, P. Bolton, and S. Fries, "Optimal Design of Bank Bailouts: The Case of Transition Economies," *Journal of Institutional and Theoretical Economics* 155, 1 (1999), 51–79.

Lorand Ambrus-Lakatos and Mark E. Schaffer, eds., *Fiscal Policy in Transition* (New York: Institute for East–West Studies, 1997).

————, *Monetary and Exchange Rate Policies, EMU and Central and Eastern Europe* (New York: Institute for East–West Studies, 1999).

Michael S. Bernstam and Alvin Rabushka, *Fixing Russia's Banks: A Proposal for Growth* (Stanford: The Hoover Institution Press, 1998).

John Bonin and Istvan P. Szekely, eds., *The Development and Reform of Financial Systems in Central and Eastern Europe* (London: Edward Elgar, 1994).

Frank Bonker, *The Political Economy of Fiscal Reform in Eastern Europe* (Northampton, Mass.: Edward Elgar, 2002).

G. Caprio and R. Levine, "Reforming Finance in Transitional Socialist Economies," *World Bank Research Observer* 9, 1 (1994), 1–24.

Cevdet Denizer and Holger C. Wolf, "Household Savings in Transition Economies," National Bureau of Economic Research, Working Paper No. 6457, 1998.

EBRD, *Transition Report 2000* (London, EBRD, 2000).

————, *Transition Report 2001* (London: EBRD, 2001).

————, *Transition Report Update* (London: EBRD, 2001).

Steven Fries and Anita Taci, "Banking Reform and Development in Transition Economies," The European Bank for Reconstruction and Development, Working Paper No. 71, June 2002.

David M. A. Green and Karl Petrick, eds., *Banking and Financial Stability in Central Europe* (Northampton, Mass.: Edward Elgar, 2002).

Steve H. Hanke, Lars Jonung, and Kurt Schuler, *Russian Currency and Finance: A Currency Board Approach to Reform* (New York: Routledge, 1993).

Hansjorg Herr, ed., *Macroeconomic Problems of Transformation: Stabilization Policies and Economic Restructuring* (Cheltenham, England: Edward Elgar, 1994).

Grzegorz W. Kolodko, *From Shock to Therapy: The Political Economy of Postsocialist Transformation* (Oxford: Oxford University Press, 2000).

David Lane, ed., *Russian Banking: Evolution, Problems and Prospects* (Northampton, Mass.: Edward Elgar, 2002).

Ronald I. McKinnon, "Financial Control in the Transition from Classical Socialism to a Market Economy," *Journal of Economic Perspectives* 5, 4 (Fall 1991), 107–122.

————, *The Order of Economic Liberalization: Financial Controls in the Transition to a Market Economy* (Baltimore: Johns Hopkins University Press, 1991).

Anna Meyendorff, "Transactional Structures of Bank Privatizations in Central Europe and Russia," *Journal of Comparative Economics* 25 (1997), 5–30.

Anna Meyendorff and Anjan Thakor, D*esigning Financial Systems in Transition Economies: Strategies for Reform in Central and Eastern Europe* (Ann Arbor, Mich.: Davidson Institute, 2002).

Janet Mitchell, "Managerial Discipline, Productivity and Bankruptcy in Capitalist and Socialist Economies," *Comparative Economic Studies* 32 (Fall 1990), 93–137.

OECD, *Transformation of the Banking System: Portfolio Restructuring, Privatization, and the Payment System* (Paris: OECD, 1993).

World Bank, *Russia: The Banking System During Transition* (Washington, D.C.: World Bank, 1993).

———, *The World Development Report 1996* (Washington, D.C.: World Bank, 1996).

19

Transition and the Global Economy: International Trade and Finance

Throughout this book we have emphasized the unique organizational arrangements, policies, and outcomes of the command economic systems. A striking example of these differences can be found in the arena of international trade—both the organizational arrangements and policy imperatives for the trading of goods and services, and the financial arrangements associated with the state trading systems of the command era. Although there were significant differences from country to country at the end of the command era, generally speaking the peculiarities of the command era made the transition era difficult, in some cases very difficult. The absence of a **convertible currency** during the command era, and the resulting dominance of **barter** arrangements functioning through state trading organizations, created significant complications that have persisted in many cases during the transition era. As the old order collapsed, it was essential to shrink the role of the state, to create new institutions (in both trade and finance), and to pursue the establishment of a convertible currency. As we will see, the trading arrangements and exchange rate regimes that were chosen varied considerably from one economy to another and have been subject to considerable change during the transition era. As the new trading arrangements emerged during the early transition years, patterns of trade and the financial outcomes of trade changed fundamentally and, for the most part, quite quickly. These ongoing adjustments and differing outcomes have been the subject of a growing volume of scholarly literature. The difficulties of implementing major changes during the transition era now provide us with a base from which we can assess the prospects for the transition economies in a global setting in the twenty-first century.

Collapse and the Early Years of Transition

We have emphasized the fact that during the command era, foreign trade was conducted largely by the state with a nonconvertible currency and no arrangements for multilateral clearing. Although attempts were made to achieve the latter—for example, through the **Council for Mutual Economic Assistance (CMEA)**—these attempts largely failed, and integration was not achieved.[1] In addition, given the lack of financial markets in the command economies, there were no mechanisms for the inflow of foreign capital, whether through **portfolio investment** or through **foreign direct**

investment (FDI). The impact of these command era arrangements has been widely debated in the literature, but basic distortions were evident. It was generally argued that the complexities of these arrangements tended to limit the volume of foreign trade—and thus to limit the extent of integration. Moreover, both the commodity composition of trade and its geographic distribution differed from what might be expected under market arrangements, though again, as we have emphasized, there were significant differences from country to country. Finally, it was often argued that the absence of scarcity-based domestic prices and of a meaningful exchange rate made the foreign trade decision itself exceedingly difficult. Thus, in the measurement of transition performance during the 1990s, foreign-trade distortions have become a critical element of initial conditions, an issue we discussed in Chapter 15. Indeed, the extent to which these initial conditions have been modified over time is itself a matter of dispute, as we noted when we discussed the issue of growth convergence in transition economies.

Beyond the obvious distortions and the possibility that the volume of trade was limited, however, the lack of integration meant that the development trajectories of the command economies were not dictated by external market forces to any degree, and critical benefits often derived through the foreign sector (for example, the importation of foreign technology) were largely absent. Thus, as transition began in the early 1990s, attention focused on the appropriate organizational changes and associated policy measures that would lead to liberalization of foreign trade, or the opening of largely "closed" economies, to pursue integration with Western market economies. Thus it was expected that during the transition era, patterns of foreign trade would undergo significant change, and the financial aspects of trade would take on added importance. The latter would of course be fundamental to the closely related emergence of new domestic macroeconomic arrangements in a transition setting.

It is important to emphasize that there is a close relationship between the foreign sector and the domestic sector and that this relationship is especially fragile in the transition economies. Specifically, financial flows and domestic monetary creation are typically closely related, especially in cases where balance-of-payments flows are of a significant magnitude. This means that domestic monetary and fiscal policies must both be coordinated with the financial arrangements in the foreign-trade sector. What will be the nature of this coordination?

The exchange rate regime is the fundamental link between the domestic economy and the external economy, the goal being "to provide a nominal anchor, to ensure adequate competitiveness, and to insulate the economy from shocks."[2] Having said this, however, it is important to recognize that because of the isolation of the transition economies from the global economy during the command era, in many cases it was at first difficult, if not impossible, to assess differences in real levels of economic activity between transition economies and their possible market-oriented trading partners in a new era. Thus choosing an exchange rate regime became a very difficult task. In addition to the problems of choosing and implementing a new exchange rate regime, the transition economies were experiencing continuing deflation, which suggested that any regime established during the early years of transition would be subject to continuing, possibly major change. It is for this reason that there was a serious search for a nominal anchor, or a mechanism to understand differing real levels of economic activity among the transition economies vis-à-vis trading partners.[3] The nature of price setting in the command economies significantly distorted any comparisons between command and market economies. If a real anchor could be found, the real differences could be understood, facilitating the establishment of an appropriate exchange rate between, for example, a former command economy in transition and a market economy.

As the foreign exchange regimes were established in the transition economies, another important set of issues emerged—specifically, the matter of policy targets and instruments, both in the macroeconomy and in the foreign sector. Although there is a large literature on the relationship among exchange rate regimes, associated policies, and economic performance, there is unfortunately no real consensus on, for example, the nature of the relationship between the exchange rate and the rate of economic growth. Although this greatly complicates planning, it is understandable because many forces beyond the exchange rate influence the rate of economic growth. Nevertheless, it is still necessary to decide on appropriate targets—for example, a particular rate of inflation or a balanced budget—and to define the nature of the policy instruments that will be used to achieve these policy targets. This effort is further complicated in the transition economies because the policy channels—that is, the routes through which policy targets can be achieved by the manipulation of policy instruments—are not always known and are always subject to change. Consider, for example, the case of the macroeconomy in Russia, and the use of interest rates to influence levels of economic activity. If there is a very limited domestic financial market from which firms may borrow, and if the magnitude of the shadow economy is significant, one can argue that changes in interest rates will have little if any impact on the level of economic activity. Indeed, it may be difficult to know the potential impact of any policy variable, an impossible situation.

If changes in the foreign-trade regimes of the newly emerging transition economies were anticipated, what were these changes, and what factors would influence their nature? First and foremost, as the state exited from the active management of these economies, liberalization would imply the replacement of state trading organizations by private organizations, including banking and financial organizations. But liberalization would imply much more as well. These economies would move toward the establishment of trading arrangements patterned after those found in market economies. Thus there would be an effort to reduce restrictions on foreign trade—both quantitative restrictions (import and export quotas, for example) and financial restrictions (such as import and export tariffs).

Along with trade liberalization, the major issue that arose in the early days of the transition economies was the establishment of a convertible currency and of an exchange rate regime that could sustain **external balance** and **internal balance** under very difficult and volatile circumstances. As we can see in Table 19.1, the steps taken in the economies that we examine varied considerably from one case to another. However, most transition economies pursued the introduction of a convertible currency quickly but sequentially and on a piecemeal basis. The initial step was typically the introduction of **current-account convertibility**, followed later by **capital-account convertibility**. These changes, as we will see, had important implications for the

TABLE 19.1   Changing Foreign Trade Regimes: Selected Transition Economies

---

The Czech Republic: 1991, fixed exchange rate adopted; 1993, new currency (koruna) adopted; 1995, full convertibility (current account); 1998, exchange rate band widened; 1998, managed float exchange rate adopted.

Estonia: 1990, state trading eliminated; 1992, new currency (kroon) and currency board adopted; 1994, full current-account convertibility introduced and nontariff trade restrictions removed; 1994, WTO membership; 2000, capital account fully liberalized.

Hungary: 1995, WTO membership; 1996, full current-account convertibility; 1997, currency basket changed, import surcharge abolished; 2000, currency basket changed; 2001, full convertibility (forint) with a fixed band and a euro peg.

Poland: 1990, trade controls removed and nontariff restrictions removed, fixed exchange rate introduced; 1991, crawling peg introduced; 1992, EFTA and CETA arrangements; 1995, managed float with a fluctuation band, current account convertible, WTO membership; 1999, new foreign exchange laws; 2000, exchange rate floated.

Kazakhstan: 1993, custom union with Belarus and Russia introduced; foreign exchange surrender abolished; 1996, full current-account convertibility; 1999, reintroduction of some trade restrictions.

Russia: 1992, state trade monopoly abolished, exchange rate unified; 1993, ruble zone collapses; 1995, currency corridor introduced; 1996, trade liberalization and full current-account convertibility introduced; 1999, dual exchange rate regime.

Ukraine: 1993, multiple exchange rates introduced; 1994, exchange rates unified, reduction of exchange rate quotas; 1996, new currency (hryvnia) introduced; 1997, full current-account convertibility; 1998, trade restrictions (autos) introduced; currency band widened; 1999, currency band further widened; 2000, floating exchange rate introduced.

Source: IBRD, *Transition Report 2000* (Paris: EBRD. 2000), country assessments; Padma Desai, *Going Global: Transition from Plan to Market in the World Economy* (Cambridge, Mass.: MIT Press, 1997).

overall macroeconomy and for the continuing effort to sustain economic growth with reasonable levels of unemployment and inflation.

Later in this chapter we will examine the changes in trading patterns brought about by these new regimes. However, the changes that occurred were obviously a function of the sorts of new trading regimes that were established. Moreover, basic issues such as factor endowments and the legacies of the command era—that is, the initial conditions—were influential. Thus, in general, those economies that were more "open" during the command era (for example, the economies of Eastern Europe) were likely to find the changes more comfortable than those economies that were less "open" (for example, the countries emerging from the former Soviet Union). Indeed, the collapse of the Soviet Union and the emergence of fifteen separate and independent nations, which had been one nation for many years, presented a unique setting.[4] In this setting, political issues and past arrangements were important and would shape the nature of trading systems in the emerging transition economies—a matter that warrants further discussion.

Emerging Trading Arrangements: Regional and Political Issues

Throughout our discussion of transition, we have emphasized that both temporal and spatial issues are important. Transition was clearly different in the early 1990s than in the mid- and late 1990s. This fact helps us to analyze transition patterns. However, we have also emphasized that spatial and related political issues are important. Hence our emphasis on differentiating between the transition economies that are often described as "winners" and those that are often described as "losers." Although the dichotomy is far too simplistic, we emphasize again that the countries that emerged from the former Soviet Union seemed to have a much more difficult transition path during the 1990s than the countries of Eastern Europe. These differences are potentially of great importance for other economies that we have not directly classified as transition economies—for example, in Asia.

When the Soviet Union collapsed as a political and economic entity, fifteen separate countries emerged (often termed the **newly independent states, NIS**), all of which (along with other command economies) had been members of the CMEA. Although the CMEA may not have been a particularly effective organization, nevertheless, when the USSR ceased to exist, there was an immediate attempt to develop and sustain a political and economic union, absent the Baltic states of Latvia, Lithuania, and Estonia, specifically the **Commonwealth of Independent States (CIS)**. The motivation for such an organization was strong, inasmuch as the republics of the former USSR were integrated to a significant degree, and their dawning independence would result in benefits but also costs. Indeed, the latter could be significant, especially during the time before new arrangements and trading patterns could emerge. According to economic theory, integration could take a variety of forms, such as a **monetary union** (essentially the use of a single currency—in this case, a ruble zone) or a **customs union**, in which a group of countries form to lower trade barriers among themselves and establish a common policy regarding barriers between themselves and nonmember countries.[5]

Following the breakup of the Soviet Union in 1991, the CIS was formed, absent the Baltic states of Latvia, Lithuania, and Estonia. During the initial period of transition, the remaining countries of the CIS continued to use the ruble as a national currency, so foreign trade among the CIS states was conducted in rubles. However, because Russia was the sole producer of rubles, these arrangements immediately created problems, and by the mid-1990s, all of the CIS states had introduced their own national currencies. Understandably, patterns of trade among the CIS countries changed, an issue we address later in this chapter. Also, during the first half of the 1990s, there were numerous attempts among the former Soviet republics to integrate in various ways, but the impact of these arrangements was arguably quite limited.[6] The assets of the USSR were largely disbursed according to location, although in the case of military assets (for example in Ukraine), ultimate ownership was a matter of controversy. The foreign debt of the USSR was officially assumed by Russia in 1993, an issue that grew in importance throughout the 1990s until a major agreement on debt restructuring was achieved with the London Club in 2000.

The situation in Eastern Europe was quite different from that of the newly independent states. Beginning in 1991, the countries of Central Europe (Poland, Hungary, and at the time Czechoslovakia) edged toward the abolition of trade restrictions and toward the free movement of capital and labor. By 1992, the **Central European Free Trade Area (CEFTA)** began to expand. Although trade patterns changed under the emerging arrangements, the impact of CEFTA has generally been viewed as modest, with **European Union (EU)** membership the critical issue through the process of accession.

What is accession and why is membership in the EU important for the transition economies? **Accession** is the process of becoming a member of the European Union.[7] For both political and economic reasons, joining the EU has been an important goal for the transition economies of Central and Eastern Europe. Membership, however, requires that countries meet a variety of both economic and political criteria that are often difficult to achieve in the transition setting. These criteria involve political democracy and the liberalization of trade, capital flows, and migration.

Between 1991 and 1996, ten countries (see Table 19.2) became candidate members.[8] By 1996, all had become members of the **World Trade Organization (WTO)** and the **General Agreement on Tariffs and Trade (GATT)**—both requirements for accession to the EU. Toward the end of the decade, discussions about accession were begun with five additional countries (see Table 19.2). This pattern of integration has been much more aggressive than that exhibited by the CIS states. The latter have been slow to pursue GATT/WTO membership, although they have signed partnership agreements with most other CIS countries.

TABLE 19.2 Transition Economies: Membership Commitments

	GATT/WTO Membership	IMF Article VIII Status	EU Association Agreement
Albania	July 2000	—	—
Bulgaria[a]	December 1996	September 1998	March 1993
Croatia	July 2000	May 1995	—
Czech Republic[a]	January 1995	October 1995	October 1993
FYR Macedonia	—	June 1998	—
Hungary[a]	January 1995	January 1996	December 1991
Poland[a]	July 1995	June 1995	December 1991
Romania[a]	January 1995	March 1998	February 1993
Slovak Republic[a]	January 1995	October 1995	October 1993
Slovenia[a]	July 1995	September 1995	June 1996
Estonia[a]	November 1999	August 1994	June 1995
Latvia[a]	February 1999	June 1994	June 1995
Lithuania[a]	—	May 1994	June 1995

[a]EU accession countries.

Source: EBRD, *Transition Report 2000* (London: EBRD, 2000), p. 22, Table 2.3; EBRD, *Transition Report 2001* (London: EBRD, 2001), sec. 2.7

Many of the changing trade patterns and the resulting integration stem from the liberalization of trade or the changing of organizational arrangements and policies. We now turn to a discussion of the changes that have been made. Then we will attempt to assess the impact of these changes.

Transition and Emerging Outcomes in the Foreign Sector

The monetary regimes adopted in the transition economies varied considerably, as did the nature of the policy framework. Thus, although it is possible to generalize about outcomes, there are also important distinctions from case to case. If a flexible exchange rate is used, then the exchange rate adjusts to bring equilibrium to the balance of payments—that is, the inflows and outflows of capital. On the other hand, if a fixed exchange rate is used, then the adjustment takes place though changes in the domestic money supply. The issue of choosing a fixed versus (some form of) flexible exchange rate regime continues to be of interest in the assessment of trade regimes in varying settings. What has happened in the transition economies?

The extent of change in the trade and foreign exchange arrangements of transition economies can be judged to some degree by the evidence presented in Table 19.1. However, there are other useful indicators. For example, the EBRD compiles a system of transition indicators, including an indicator of the degree of liberalization of the foreign trade and exchange system. These indicators range from 1 (little change) to 4+ (standards of advanced industrial economies, including enforcement of policy on competition). In their *Transition Report 2001,* the EBRD identifies fully thirteen countries (Albania, Bulgaria, Croatia, the Czech Republic, Georgia, Hungary, Latvia, Lithuania, Moldova, Poland, the Slovak Republic, and Slovenia) that achieve a score of 4+.[9] There are four other countries that come close, with a score of 4 (Armenia, FYR Macedonia, Kyrgyzstan, and Romania). The lagging countries are Azerbaidjan, Belarus, Bosnia and Herzegovina, FR Yugoslavia, Kazakhstan, Russia, Tajikistan, Turkmenistan, Ukraine, and Uzbekistan.

The EBRD also provides, for selected transition economies, indicators of competitiveness (for example, changes in industrial productivity and measures of competitiveness based on changes in the real manufacturing wage and changes in unit labor costs measured using the deutsche mark). These indicators show important differences in competitiveness among the selected transition countries.[10] For example, deutsche-mark-denominated unit labor costs between 1996 and 2000 increased by 98 percent in Lithuania and increased by only 0.1 percent in Croatia, and 6.7 percent in Slovenia.

An important indicator of change in the foreign sector is the real exchange rate. The pattern in the transition economies has generally been a decline (in some cases a significant decline) in the real exchange rate during the early years of transition, followed by an increase in the real exchange rate during the later half of the 1990s. What explains these changes in real exchange rates? Although a potentially important issue is the nature of initial conditions and the difficulty of implementing a new exchange rate regime during the early years of transition, a popular explanation is changes in the fundamentals underlying determination of the exchange rate—notably, changes in productivity and the real wage relative to changes experienced by trading partners. This hypothesis has been tested by examining the pattern observed in many of the transition economies.[11] A recent examination of this issue, using panel data, seems to confirm the view that appreciation in real exchange rate is productivity-based.[12]

The balance of payments involves the current account and the capital account. If the sum of current-account and capital-account transactions is zero, then the quantity of foreign exchange being demanded is equal to the quantity of foreign exchange being supplied. An imbalance implies an adjustment process, typically a change in the exchange rate, assuming that a flexible exchange rate regime is in place. What is the evidence pertaining to the balance of payments? Figure 19.1 shows the current-account balance for transition economies from the beginning of the transition era through the beginning of the new century. The pattern of decline and limited recovery during the latter part of the 1990s is striking, as is the fact that the outflows are of significant size compared with GDP. What is the nature of capital flows?

Capital Flows: Aid and Foreign Direct Investment

A major component of the opening up of the transition economies has been the integration of these economies with the global economy, and especially with global financial markets. To the extent that cross-border capital flows are increased, from an allocative standpoint the outcome is likely to be positive. However, increased financial flows present important challenges to domestic policy makers, because the domestic (host country) monetary and fiscal regime is no longer fully under domestic control, as we have noted. Thus, in the case of Russia in 1998 and the Czech Republic in 1997, for example, the financial crisis led to a search for both signals and cures. Financial (capital) flows typically take the form of aid, portfolio investment, or foreign direct investment.

Aid and foreign direct investment are very different. For the transition economies during the 1990s, aid was provided mainly by the **International Monetary Fund (IMF)** and the **World Bank**. Both organizations have been involved with transition economies, though largely on a country-by-country basis rather than under any general umbrella. The IMF has been largely concerned with domestic stabilization, whereas the World Bank has been more concerned with loans to stimulate long-term economic growth. Both have functioned under guidelines that proved controversial but were important barometers of achievement in the transition economies.

Figure 19.2 offers evidence on total capital flows for all transition economies (including a linear trend line) and for selected transition economies. The size and growth of capital flows to the transition economies are impressive, although there are important differences among the transition economies and significant fluctuations over time.[13] Portfolio investment in transition economies has increased (irregularly)

FIGURE 19.1   Transition Economies: Current-Account Balance,
1989–2001

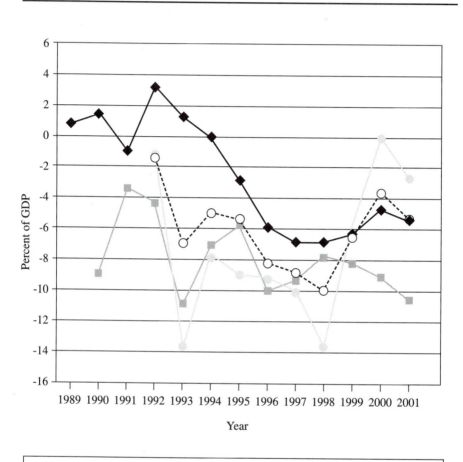

Central and Eastern Europe and the Baltic states (Croatia, Czech Republic, Estonia, Hungary, Latvia, Lithuania, Poland, Slovak Republic, Slovenia)

Southeastern Europe (Albania, Bosnia and Herzegovina, Bulgaria, FR Yugoslavia, FYR Macedonia, Romania)

Commonwealth of Independent States (Armenia, Azerbaidzhan, Belarus, Georgia, Kazakhstan, Kyrgyzstan, Moldova, Russia, Tajikistan, Turkmenistan, Ukraine, Uzbekistan)

----O---- Region

Source: EBRD, *Transition Report Update* (London: EBRD, May 2002), p. 20, Table A.4.

FIGURE 19.2   Transition Economies: Total Capital Flows, 1992–1999

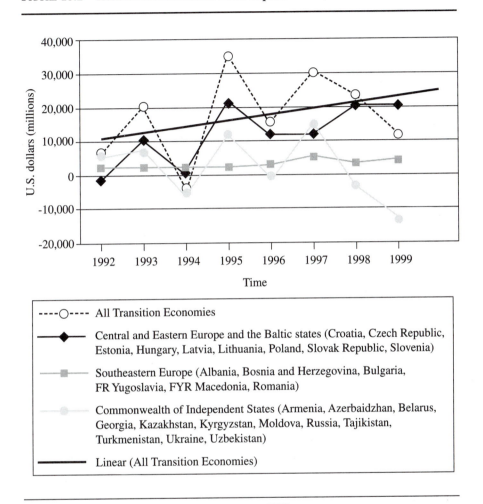

Source: EBRD, *Transition Report 2000* (London: EBRD, 2000).

over time, but foreign direct investment deserves special attention as a major component of capital flows (see Figure 19.3).

Issues surrounding FDI in the transition economies have been controversial. The size and growth of FDI in Central and Eastern Europe has been significant, whereas the opposite has been true for countries of the CIS. How big are these investment flows and what accounts for these significant regional differences?[14] Table 19.3 presents a more detailed picture of FDI by country. Note that as a group, the CIS countries have fared poorly in attracting FDI, and for some cases, such as Russia, the importance of FDI is strikingly small and much less understandable than in cases such as Belarus,

FIGURE 19.3   Foreign Direct Investment: 1990–2002[a]

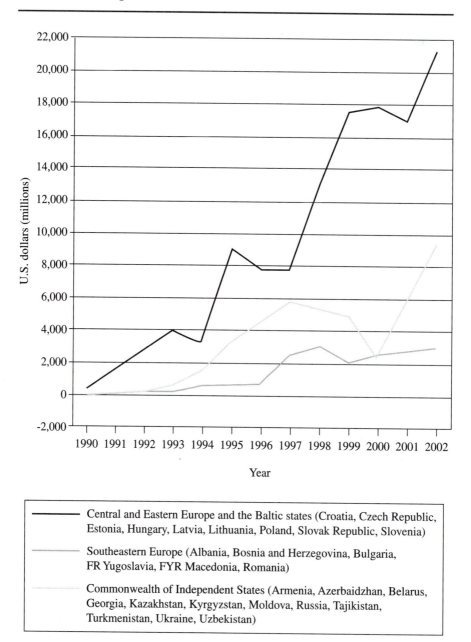

Central and Eastern Europe and the Baltic states (Croatia, Czech Republic, Estonia, Hungary, Latvia, Lithuania, Poland, Slovak Republic, Slovenia)

Southeastern Europe (Albania, Bosnia and Herzegovina, Bulgaria, FR Yugoslavia, FYR Macedonia, Romania)

Commonwealth of Independent States (Armenia, Azerbaidzhan, Belarus, Georgia, Kazakhstan, Kyrgyzstan, Moldova, Russia, Tajikistan, Turkmenistan, Ukraine, Uzbekistan)

[a]Data for 2001 are preliminary; data for 2002 are projections.

Source: EBRD, *Transition Report Update* (London: EBRD, May 2002), Table 2.1.

TABLE 19.3   Foreign Direct Investment in Transition Economies:
             Selected Indicators

	Cumulative FDI, 1989–2001 (million U.S.$)	Cumulative FDI per Capita, 1989–2001 (U.S.$)	FDI as a Percent of GDP, 2001
Czech Republic	26,493	2,570	8.5
Estonia	2,358	1,637	6.4
Hungary	21,869	2,177	4.3
Poland	34,426	890	3.6
Bulgaria	815	241	5.3
Armenia	642	213	4.3
Belarus	1,315	132	0.7
Russia	9,702	67	0.6
Ukraine	3,866	79	1.4
Central and Eastern Europe	98,297	1,365	4.7
Southeastern Europe	15,206	296	5.1
CIS	34,368	196	3.3

Source: EBRD, *Transition Report Update* (Paris: EBRD, May 2002), Table 2.1.

where there has been only very limited economic change during the 1990s.[15] There are other cases, such as Bulgaria and Armenia, where FDI, judged as a share of GDP, is important, though not comparable to that in the front-running countries such as Hungary and the Czech Republic. What accounts for these differences?

There is a large literature devoted to FDI, and especially to the determinants of FDI. Typically, a host country is attractive if it has a reasonable combination of features, including a low country risk assessment, a functional and effective legal framework, a reasonable resource base (for example, available human capital), and an infrastructure appropriate to the sort of investment being contemplated. At the same time, there are a variety of motives for engaging in investment abroad, much of which in recent years has occurred within the framework of **multinational enterprises**. As a portion of financial inflows to the transition economies, FDI has been important, although there are sharp differences among countries and also over time. Variations in level of FDI may result from traditional cyclical factors or from changing patterns of privatization. For example, in the Eastern European economies, substantial portions of FDI inflows during the late 1990s have been from the sale of major enterprises, in effect a one-time source of financial inflows. At the same time, the transition economies' access to Western financial markets has increased, and this access can change the exposure to financial risk through diversification. Finally, capital flows and the FDI component of these flows can be very sensitive to country differences, notably the extent to which there may be natural resources (for example, in the case of Russia) that attract foreign investment.

The Integration of Transition Economies

The foreign trade and payments regimes of the transition economies have been a focal point of attention for a variety of reasons. These regimes were difficult to establish in a new setting, requiring important changes and adjustments throughout the 1990s and reacting to changes that have differed considerably among the transition economies. Although it is difficult to make an overall assessment, several observations are appropriate. First, given the very different transition settings and the difficulties of establishing new trade and payments regimes in these settings, there has been impressive forward movement in many countries. Second, the differences in this forward movement are, on balance, what we would expect from our examination of other transition indicators. The changes in the Eastern and Central European transition economies have generally been much more progressive than those in the countries of the former Soviet Union.

Third, patterns of integration have changed fundamentally during the transition era. Generally speaking, trade among the CIS countries declined as trade was reoriented toward the West. The same has been true for the Eastern European transition economies, although there have been important country-to-country differences.[16]

Summary

- The arrangements of the command era (state control of foreign trade, a nonconvertible currency, and barter trade) caused significant distortions in both trading arrangements and outcomes, creating major problems for the transition era.
- The major emphasis in the early years of transition has been on a sharply reduced role for the state in the conduct of foreign trade and on the creation of financial arrangements for the conduct of trade, especially the introduction of a convertible currency for both the current account and the capital account.
- The emergence of new trading arrangements opened an ongoing discussion about the appropriate policy targets and instruments for the conduct of foreign trade in a new setting.
- Most transition economies pursued the reduction of state involvement in foreign trade and the introduction of a convertible currency.
- The pursuit of integration and membership in world trading organizations has differed considerably among the transition economies. Generally speaking, the countries of the CIS have moved more slowly than those of Eastern and Central Europe.
- Throughout the transition economies, real exchange rates declined during the early years of transition and thereafter increased. Trade patterns have changed, with a reduction of intra-transition trade and an increase in the degree of integration with Western market economies. Capital flows have increased, significantly in Eastern Europe and more slowly in the CIS states. Foreign direct investment (FDI) has been an important component of capital flows, especially in Eastern Europe.

Key Terms

convertible currency

barter

Council for Mutual Economic
    Assistance (CMEA)

portfolio investment

foreign direct investment (FDI)

external balance

internal balance

current account convertibility

capital account convertibility

newly independent states (NIS)

Commonwealth of Independent
    States (CIS)

monetary union

customs union

Central European Free Trade Area
    (CEFTA)

European Union (EU)

accession

World Trade Organization (WTO)

General Agreement on Tariffs and
    Trade (GATT)

International Monetary Fund (IMF)

World Bank

multinational enterprises

Notes

1. The issues pertaining to foreign trade in the command economies were discussed in Chapters 6 and 11. For additional discussion and references to the literature, see Paul R. Gregory and Robert C. Stuart, *Russian and Soviet Economic Structure and Performance,* 7th ed. (New York: Addison-Wesley, 2001).

2. Lorand Ambrus-Lakatos and Mark E. Schaffer, eds., *Monetary and Exchange Rate Policies, EMU and Central Eastern Europe* (New York: East–West Institute, 1999), p. 1.

3. For a discussion of these issues and the nature of the dollar wage as a nominal anchor, see Ambrus-Lakatos and Schaffer, Ch. 2.

4. For an excellent discussion of the Soviet breakup, see Bert van Selm, *The Economics of the Soviet Breakup* (New York: Routledge, 1997). For a discussion of the impact of the demise of the CMEA, see Dariusz K. Rosati, "The Impact of the Soviet Trade Shock on Central and East European Economies," in Robert Holzmann, Janos Gacs, and Georg Winckler, eds., *Output Decline in Eastern Europe* (Boston: Kluwer Academic, 1995), Ch. 6.

5. These issues vis-à-vis the collapse of the Soviet Union are discussed in Bert van Selm. For a background discussion on differing forms of integration, see Beth V. Yarbrough and Robert M. Yarbrough, *The World Economy,* 5th ed. (New York: South Western, 2000), Ch. 9.4.

6. See van Selm, *The Economics of the Soviet Breakup.*

7. For a summary of these issues, see Lorand Ambrus-Lakatos and Mark E. Schaffer, eds., *Coming to Terms with Accession* (New York: East–West Institute), 1996.

8. For a summary of recent trends, see EBRD, *Transition Report 2001* (London: EBRD, 2001), sec. 2.7

9. See EBRD, *Transition Report 2001* (London: EBRD, 2001), p. 12, Table 2.1. See also Constantine Michalopoulos, "The Integration of Transition Economies into the World Trading System," paper presented at the Fifth Dubrovnik Conference on Transition Economies, Dubrovnik, Croatia, June 23–25, 1999.

10. See EBRD, *Transition Report 2001* (London: EBRD, 2001), pages 66–67, Table A.3.8.

11. See Laszlo Halpern and Charles Wyplosz, "Equilibrium Exchange Rates in Transition Economies," *IMF Staff Papers* 44 (December 1997), 430–461; Lorand Ambrus-Lakatos and Mark E. Schaffer, eds., *Monetary and Exchange Rate Policies, EMU and Central and Eastern Europe* (New York: East–West Institute, 1999).

12. Mark De Broeck and Torsten Slok, "Interpreting Real Exchange Rate Movements in Transition Countries," IMF Working Paper WP/01/56 (Washington, D.C.: IMF, May 2001).

13. For a discussion of recent patterns, see EBRD, *Transition Report Update* (London: EBRD, May 2002), Part 1, Ch. 2.

14. See, for example, Pietro Garibaldi, Nada Mora, Ratna Sahay, and Jeromin Zettelmeyer, "What Moves Capital to Transition Economies?" IMF Working Paper WP/02/64 (Washington, D.C.: IMF, April 2002).

15. The Russian case is especially instructive. Although capital flight is difficult to measure accurately, it was arguably a problem in the Russian case during the mid-1990s.

16. For a summary of changing trade patterns, see Constantine Michalopoulos, "The Integration of Transition Economies into the World Trading System," paper presented at the Fifth Dubrovnik Conference on Transition Economies, Dubrovnik, Croatia, June 23–25, 1999.

Recommended Readings

Lorand Ambrus-Lakatos and Mark E. Schaffer, eds., *Monetary and Exchange Rate Policies, EMU and Central and Eastern Europe* (New York: East–West Institute, 1999).

———, Coming to Terms with Accession (New York: East–West Institute, 1996).

Patrick Artisien-Maksimento and Yuri Adjubei, eds., *Foreign Investment in Russia and Other Successor States* (New York: St. Martin's, 1996).

Richard N. Cooper and Janos Gacs, eds., *Trade Growth in Transition Economies* (Cheltenham, England: Edward Elgar, 1997).

Martin Dangerfield. *Subregional Cooperation in Central and Eastern Europe* (Northampton, Mass.: Edward Elgar, 2001).

Padma Desai, ed., *Going Global* (Cambridge, Mass.: MIT Press, 1997).

David G. Dickinson and Andrew W. Mullineux, eds., *Financial and Monetary Integration in the New Europe* (Northampton, Mass.: Edward Elgar, 2002).

Hubert Gabrisch and Klaus Werner, "Advantages and Drawbacks of EU Membership—The Structural Dimension," *Comparative Economic Studies* 40, 3 (Fall 1998), 79–103.

Janos Gacs, Robert Holzmann, and Michael L. Wyzan, eds., *The Mixed Blessing of Financial Inflows* (Northampton, Mass.: Edward Elgar, 1999).

Gabor Hunya, ed., *Integration Through Direct Foreign Investment* (Northampton, Mass: Edward Elgar, 2000).

Hilary Ingham and Mike Ingham, eds., *EU Expansion to the East* (Northampton, Mass.: Edward Elgar 2002).

Marie Lavigne, "Conditions for Accession to the EU," *Comparative Economic Studies* 40, 3 (Fall 1998), 38–57.

John McCormick, *Understanding the European Union: A Concise Introduction* (New York: Palgrave, 2002).

G. Michalopoulos and D. Tarr, eds., *Trade Performance and Policy in the Newly Independent States* (Washington, D.C.: World Bank, 1996).

OECD, *Barriers to Trade with the Economies in Transition* (Paris: OECD, 1994).

———, *Trade Policy and the Transition Process* (Paris: OECD, 1996).

Lucjan T. Orlowski, "Exchange-Rate Policies in Central Europe and Monetary Union," *Comparative Economic Studies* 40, 3 (Fall 1998), 58–78.

Eric J. Pentecost and Andre Van Poeck, eds., *European Monetary Integration* (Northampton, Mass.: Edward Elgar 2002).

Jozef van Brabant, *Centrally Planned Economies and International Economic Organizations* (New York: Cambridge University Press, 1991).

———, *Integrating Europe—The Transition Economies at Stake* (Boston, Mass.: Kluwer Academic, 1996).

———, "On the Relationship Between the East's Transitions and European Integration," *Comparative Economic Studies* 40, 3 (Fall 1998), 6–37.

Bert van Selm, *The Economics of the Soviet Breakup* (London: Routledge, 1997).

Christian von Hirschhausen and Jurgen Bitzer, eds., *The Globalization of Industry and Innovation in Eastern Europe* (Northampton, Mass.: Edward Elgar, 2000).

Jan Winiecki, *Transition Economies and Foreign Trade* (New York: Routledge, 2002).

Zloch-Christy, Iliana, ed., *Eastern Europe and the World Economy* (Northampton, Mass.: Edward Elgar, 1998).

20

Transition and the Safety Net

One of the most striking features of the command era was the dominant role of the state in the development and implementation of **social policies**—which has often been termed the provision of a **safety net**. Whatever the availability and quality of the various components of the safety net during the command era, most elements—unemployment benefits, medical care, and pensions for the elderly, were provided by the state in most command economies. Moreover, although it was widely argued that differences in achievement should be rewarded, the constraints of ideology often led to "leveling," or the elimination of significant differences in rewards. The incentive effects of social benefits provided by the state have always been a matter of controversy, whether in the command economies or (on a smaller scale) in the market economies. Thus it might be reasonable to characterize command economies as systems in which it was very difficult, even through hard work and education, to extract a significantly larger share of the economic pie. At the same time, those who shared in the economic pie seem to have done so more evenly than in market economies.[1]

As the state structure collapsed in the command economies, inevitably it became difficult to sustain the social services. Nonstate variants of social services were slow to emerge, yet many citizens were not able or prepared to make other arrangements. Moreover, states were ill prepared, in the absence of adequate revenue sources and growing budget deficits, to sustain the benefit programs of the command era. The inevitable result has been, by almost any measure, a significant decline in well-being for many citizens, though there have been important variations from one country to another, and, within countries, important variations among various geographic regions and subgroups of the population.

Of course, safety-net issues are a component of any overall assessment of performance in the transition economies (which we discussed in Chapter 15), but there is more to the story—and hence a separate chapter on these issues. Indeed, although economists usually assess the well-being of human populations through basic indicators such as per capita output and quality-of-life indexes, we know that the issues are complex, especially in countries undergoing rapid systemic change. Ultimately, the well-being of the population must be assessed by examining a broad array of indicators, such as access to education, employment, and (for those who need them) support services.

A major component of transition has inevitably centered on population issues—specifically, the reallocation of labor, the dramatic readjustment of the uses of human capital, and the uses of the significant volume of human capital accumulated during the command era. In this chapter, we explore issues broadly related to population and the labor force, in effect examining the winners and losers in the transition era, the changes in the safety net, and the adjustment patterns that led to new outcomes.

Throughout this book we have emphasized the unique nature of transition and its impact on a large number of very different countries. There is another dimension worthy of comment. In Chapter 17 we noted that privatization in the transition era has unfolded in a very broad context: The past twenty years have been an era of privatization and reduction of the role for government in resource allocation worldwide, not just in the transition economies. Precisely the same argument applies to changes in the welfare state, an important set of conditioning factors for policy makers in the transition economies.

In recent years, there has been widespread questioning of welfare programs and their impact on performance (often economic growth) in Western market economies.[2] Although the evidence on these issues is mixed, it has been argued that even in countries not normally identified as "welfare states," welfare programs constrain rates of economic growth and thus ultimately inhibit the long-term growth of well-being. We leave these arguments for others, although it is important to note that the development of new, market-based social welfare programs in transition economies occurs from a unique base (programs during the command era) and in a unique time frame, when such programs are under increasing scrutiny in market systems.

Finally, we would be remiss not to note the critical interaction between social welfare programs and the support for new regimes and new market-type policies in the transition economies. Inasmuch as political support is essential, we should not be surprised to discover that transition economies have faced very difficult policy choices. For example, in a setting where labor-market adjustment is essential but where widespread (even short-term) unemployment was historically unacceptable, what is the optimal tradeoff between unemployment and adjustment in the new transition setting, and how will it be sustained? For social policies used to provide an economic floor for the population, what is the tradeoff between the nature and the size of these benefits and any possible negative work incentives? Labor-market adjustments and the costs of these adjustments are key issues because the command economies lacked adjustment mechanisms over long periods of time. We begin with a discussion of labor markets, after which we turn to the matter of compensation for those unable to adjust to new arrangements.

The Labor Force in the Command Era

We have already devoted a considerable amount of attention to labor-force issues in the command era. We have emphasized several important elements of labor allocation under very different organizational arrangements. First, a major element of the command era was education, especially technical training as opposed to broader liberal arts education. Most transition economies began their passage through the transition era with major stocks of human capital. It is striking to note that, compared to economies at similar levels of economic development, the stock of human capital achieved in the command economies was impressive. This human capital would be available in the transition era, and yet issues related to the use of this human capital in very different settings have been of central importance. Could the stock of human capital available from the command era be readily deployed under emerging market arrangements?

Second, most command economies pursued a policy of what has been termed a **job right constraint**, or full employment.[3] Such policies bore little relation to the Western "full-employment" policies implemented as part of fiscal and monetary policies in a market economy. In the command economies, there was underemployment in a setting where the dismissal of workers, whether productive or not, was generally difficult. However one may assess this type of arrangement, unemployment was not a major issue in the command economies, and making adjustments to the allocation of labor (by field or sector) was difficult. In effect, the unemployment "problem" was incorporated into the enterprise system (in part through a soft budget), at the major cost of unproductive labor and a very ineffective system of labor allocation and reallocation. Be that as it may, many people thought they had jobs, and few were accustomed to the idea of unemployment.

Third, although the command economies did not pursue absolute equality, empirical evidence suggests that income differentials in the command economies were significantly less than would be the case in market economies. Wage differentials were used to reward differential inputs and to motivate effort, but even so, the outcome was generally egalitarian, compared with market economies. This has been an important legacy of the command era, but its impact during transition has been difficult to assess. Inevitably, the distribution of income changed sharply in many transition economies as market arrangements were introduced during the 1990s.

Labor in the Transition Era

During the transition era, a central issue has been the movement of labor from the former state sector to the newly emerging private sector. A prominent model with which to analyze this process is the Aghion–Blanchard model.[4] This model focuses on (1) the speed with which production (and hence inputs) will be transferred from the state to the emerging private sector, and (2) the nature of the mechanisms involved—specifically, changes in the wage level in the declining state sector and in the emerging private sector, and the level of unemployment. The speed and ease with which labor can be released from the state sector and absorbed into the emerging private sector depends in part on wage levels in both sectors. However, these wage levels are increasingly a function of market forces as state wage-setting procedures of an earlier era are dismantled. Unemployment may lead to lower wage levels and thus enhance the demand for labor in the private sector. At the same time, there are significant fiscal and social costs associated with unemployment. Interest in this adjustment process has generated a considerable body of literature on the optimal speed of transition in general and especially in labor markets. How rapidly has labor moved from the public to the private sector? The evidence presented in Table 20.1 suggests considerable variation among

TABLE 20.1   Employment in the Private Sector
as a Percentage of Total Employment

	1992	1996	2000
Albania	3.8	78.6	82.2
Azerbaidzhan	35.6	48.5	63.7[a]
Belarus	n.a.	9.3	18.6[a]
Bulgaria	18.0	47.0	65.0[a]
Czech Republic	31.1	58.9	65.0
Hungary	n.a.	76.8	81.4[b]
Poland	54.0	63.0	72.0
Romania	41.0	52.0	n.a.

n.a. = not available.
[a]1999.
[b]1998.

Source: EBRD, *Transition Report 2001: Energy in Transition* (London: EBRD, 2001).

the transition economies listed. Private-sector employment at the onset of transition differed significantly from one country to another; for example, it was very low in Albania and very high in Poland.[5] These differences are not surprising, given what we know about the initial conditions in these cases. We also note that the growth of private-sector employment has generally been very rapid. Once again, the differences that we observe (for example, the slow emergence of private-sector employment in Belarus) conform closely to our knowledge of the countries (of Belarus as a country) with limited emphasis on transition.

Empirical research on the labor-adjustment process has extended the basic Aghion–Blanchard model. Generally speaking, the reallocation has had results somewhat different from what was commonly anticipated. Unemployment was expected to result from the closure of state enterprises, but was generally of greater magnitude than expected, and often with important sectoral and regional differences. Unemployment has indeed risen—the result of job quitters' entry into unemployment, closure of both state and private enterprises, and limited exit from unemployment back into employment; on balance, adjusting to unemployment has been less successful than might have been expected. As we will see, there have often been unusual forms of adjustment such as the emergence of family safety nets. Moreover, the evidence suggests that sectoral and regional adjustment (for example, in Russia) has been limited, with important differences by age and sex.[6]

Along with the shift of employment by sector, there have been marked changes in aggregate employment levels and in the extent and nature of unemployment. Employment levels declined significantly in the transition economies during the early 1990s. There were, however, marked differences among the various countries. Throughout the decade of the 1990s, the level of total employment in the CIS countries declined steadily, from roughly 11.8 million in 1990 to 10.2 million in 1998. At the same time, in Central and Eastern Europe and the Baltic States and in South-eastern Europe, employment levels initially declined. They began to recover in the mid-1990s, though with only limited gains made toward the end of the decade. During these years, the level of unemployment also increased.

In Table 20.2 we present a summary of unemployment levels for a selected group of transition economies.

Unemployment data for transition economies need to be interpreted with caution. First, it is troubling for the observer to note that evidence about unemployment differs considerably from one source to another and has been subject to major revisions over time. Second, although they are not unreasonable, levels of unemployment are generally high in the transition economies. The increases in unemployment through the transition era have been the result of various factors that we have noted, but adjusting to them has been difficult for populations generally not accustomed to unemployment of the sort experienced in market economies. In other words, both the decline in employment levels and the increase in unemployment levels hide patterns of adjustment in the transition economies.

Unfortunately, in spite of significant differences among countries, labor-market adjustments in transition economies have not generally been significant. There has been only limited adjustment by sector and by region. Moreover, the movement out of unemployment has generally been slow, in spite of a major policy effort to create appropriate components of a safety net while at the same time encouraging mobility. Understandably, mobility has generally been greater into and also out of the emerging private sector.

Employment, Earnings, and the Safety Net

Adjustment in labor markets of the transition economies has varied significantly from country to country. Typically, and especially in the CIS countries, many who are employed are not employed full-time. One adjustment strategy is holding multiple jobs. A second strategy is sometimes termed a "subsistence" approach, such as informal

TABLE 20.2   Unemployment Levels in Transition Economies, Selected Years

Country	1994	1996	1998	2000	2001
Russia	7.8	9.6	11.9	10.5	9.0
Kazakhstan	8.1	8.6	6.6	12.2	11.0
Ukraine	0.3	1.3	3.7	4.2	3.7
Poland	16.0	13.2	10.4	15.1	17.3
Estonia	7.6	10.0	9.9	13.8	12.7
Hungary	12.4	11.8	10.1	9.1	8.4
Czech Republic	3.2	3.5	7.5	8.8	8.9

Source: EBRD, *Transition Report Update* (London: EBRD, May 2002), country assessment.

employment or family activities. According to a recent EBRD report, "family helpers," measured as a percentage of the population over 16, varied from a low of 4 percent in Poland in 1998 to a high of 31.16 percent in Russia in 1998.[7] For the most part, males dominate the "multiple employment" category, females the "family helper" category.

To the extent that unemployment has been a serious problem that has persisted at relatively high levels, unemployment benefits and the possibility of entry into poverty are important issues in the transition setting. The transition economies have generally developed systems of unemployment compensation. These programs differ from country to country and have typically been more generous in Eastern Europe than in the CIS, although the level of generosity has declined over time. In Poland and Hungary, these programs accounted for 2.4 and 2.0 percent of GDP, respectively, in 1994; in Russia they accounted for just 0.4 percent of GDP. The percentage of registered unemployed who were receiving benefits has been high in some cases (77.1 percent in Russia in 1995) and quite low in other cases (23.6 percent in Slovakia in 1992 and 31.2 percent in Bulgaria in 1995).[8]

The budgetary impact of unemployment benefits has been a matter of concern, though it is arguably not large. However, the empirical evidence seems to suggest that these programs do not have a significant impact. Thus with sustained high unemployment (especially for particular segments of the population, such as women and older men), poverty becomes a greater threat. There is also the likelihood of increasing income inequality, an issue to which we return below.

The concept of poverty always involves cultural, regional, and historical characteristics.[9] Two main issues arise in the process of identifying poverty: definition and measurement. In terms of *definition,* it is necessary to establish a poverty line in terms of an appropriate variable, such as income, health conditions, or the availability of basic consumption items such as housing. What does a society deem to be a reasonable minimum level of income? *Measurement,* in this context, means determining what portion of the population is in poverty and thus falls below the established minimum. Thus it is necessary to analyze income levels—a critical issue in transition economies because the composition of household income (reported and unreported) has changed significantly (from earlier socialist patterns) during the transition era. Finally, having identified a poverty line and counted those who are statistically below this line, it is important both to analyze poverty's incidence (how widespread and how deep it is) and to understand who is in poverty, identifying causal factors.

How widespread is poverty in the transition economies? Although there are always measurement difficulties, there is considerable agreement on the magnitude and depth of poverty in the transition economies (see Table 20.3).

A number of observations emerge from the data in Table 20.3 First, there are important differences in the incidence of poverty, which is significant in the CIS states (for example, Russia and Ukraine) and much less significant in the Eastern European cases (for example, Hungary and the Czech Republic). Second, understandably, the **poverty deficit** also differs considerably among the transition economies.[10] Third, although different approaches to measurement yield provide broadly comparable results for the incidence of poverty, there are nevertheless cases where measurement issues are important. In the case of Ukraine, the importance of the poverty deficit

TABLE 20.3   Poverty in Selected Transition Economies, 1993–1995

	Poverty Head Count (HBS)[a]	Poverty Deficit as a Percent of GDP	Poverty Head Count (Macro)[b]	Poverty Deficit as a Percent of GDP[c]
Russia	44	3.3	39	3.7
Kazakhstan	62	8.2	n.a.	n.a.
Ukraine	63	6.9	26	2.3
Poland	14	0.9	10	0.5
Estonia	37	4.2	34	2.9
Hungary	2	0.1	7	0.3
Czech Republic	Less than 1	0.0	n.a.	n.a.

[a]Based on income as measured by (HBS) household budget surveys.
[b]Based on macroeconomic (income) data.
[c]Based on estimates of household expenditures.

Source: Compiled from Branko Milanovic, *Income, Inequality, and Poverty During the Transition from Planned to Market Economy* (Washington, D.C.: World Bank, 1998), Tables 5.2 and 5.3.

varies considerably, depending on the manner in which it is measured. It has been argued that poverty is generally a more serious problem in the CIS countries than in the transition economies of Eastern Europe, although even where the incidence of poverty seems high, the depth of poverty is generally not great.

Thus far we have focused on the safety-net issues related to labor-market adjustments, earnings, unemployment, and the possibility of poverty. Earnings, however, are a function of a wide variety of factors, such as schooling, work experience, length of employment, and a bevy of important personal characteristics such as age, sex, and health status. All are important for our understanding of transition and especially of the critical bottom line: the overall well-being of the population. In this section, we examine the relationship among basic demographic issues, population well-being, and the health care and other support mechanisms.

Demographic Issues and the Safety Net

Many would argue that basic demographic patterns—including birth rates, death rates, and the rate of growth of the population—are typically stable over the long term, barring a catastrophe such as war. An examination of basic data on life expectancy (and birth rates and death rates) in the transition economies reveals two important patterns. First, in some transition economies (notably the CIS countries), a significant decline and then a modest recovery in life expectancy occurred during the early years of the transition era. The pattern is especially striking when compared to similar data from the pretransition era and to data from other countries. Second, an analysis of these patterns of life expectancy suggests that they have been much more severe in the CIS countries and much less severe or virtually nonexistent in Eastern Europe, although in general, the impact on males has been greater than the impact on females. What has accounted for these patterns, and what policy implications emerge?

Studies have shown that the reduction of life expectancy has been primarily a result of rising mortality rates, especially for males. Mortality rates have seemingly risen for identifiable reasons (cancer and cardiovascular disease, for example), but this change is serious and cannot be attributed to possible measurement problems. Specifically, these adverse demographic developments have been in part the result of changing income patterns and an inability to access adequate health care. Consider, for example, the case of Russia.[11]

Figure 20.1 shows crude birth and death rates for Russia from 1970 through 1999. The pattern here is striking and has received a great deal of attention as a "demographic crisis." What is the essence of this crisis, and how is it related to transition and the safety net? An analysis of death rates in the Russian case indicates that especially among males, age-specific death rates from some historically common causes (cancer

FIGURE 20.1   Russia: Birth Rates and Death Rates

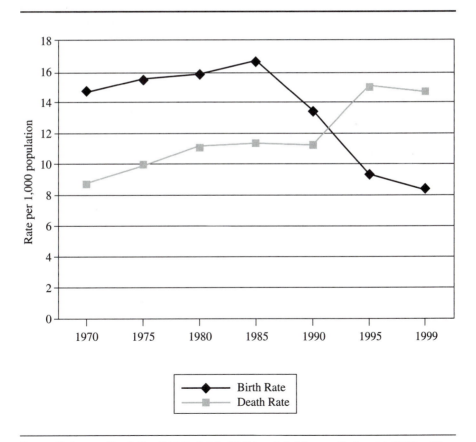

Source: Goskomstat Rossii, *Rossiiskii Statisticheskii Ezhegodnik* (Moscow: Goskomstat, 2000), p. 77.

and cardiovascular disease) increased significantly during the early years of transition. Deaths from these diseases, along with a continuing alcohol problem and increasing crime rates, were associated with the sharp declines in income and the general disruption in the provision of social services that accompanied the end of the command era. The latter issue is not easy to chronicle. However, there is now considerable debate over the demographic issues: Are they directly related to transition, or are they in part related to longer term demographic changes? The data in Table 20.4 indicate significant and sustained expenditure on health and education (as a portion of GDP), but in cases like Russia, there are significant regional differences in the level at which such services are provided, financed, and delivered and in how much disruption of services occurred.

Transition and the Social Sector

Thus far we have observed that changing employment conditions, along with declining income and demographic changes, have led to the emergence of social problems in the transition economies and that these problems have been more serious in the CIS economies than in the transition economies of Eastern Europe. What has been done to address these difficulties? A number of generalizations can be made.

First, it is well known that the command economies provided significant (if controversial) social programs.[12] During transition, however, the arrangements made in the command era were eroded and often could not serve the needs of a new era. For example, unemployment was theoretically nonexistent during the command era but became an important problem during transition. Second, the modes of adjustment (for example, increasing unemployment, severe inflationary pressures, and increases in retirement prompted by inability to adjust to a new employment setting) created pressure on available benefit programs, financial distress, and inevitably worsening standards of living for many. Third, there have been significant policy differences among the transition economies. In advanced cases such as Poland, the typical pattern is a combination of both state and private funding for pensions, partly on a pay-as-you-go

TABLE 20.4   Expenditures on Health and Education as a Percentage of GDP

	1992	1994	1996	1998	2000
Russia	6.0	7.7	7.4	7.4	5.9
Kazakhstan	6.1	5.3	7.2	6.2	6.1[a]
Ukraine	8.6	10.1	8.7	7.9	7.0
Poland	10.8	10.7	10.8	9.9	n.a.
Estonia	12.1	13.4	12.2	12.0	n.a.
Czech Republic	10.1	11.9	11.7	10.8	n.a.

n.a. = not available.
[a] 1999.

Source: EBRD, *Transition Report 2001: Energy in Transition* (London: EBRD, 2001), country assessments.

basis. Health insurance (again both public and private) has been introduced, along with financial reform, to bring contributions and tax levels in line with expenditures for fiscal solvency. These countries have achieved a reduction in the widespread benefits carried over from the command era and their replacement with targeted programs directed specifically at the most needy groups of the population. Indeed, throughout the transition economies, the issue of targeting has assumed major importance.

In other countries, such as the Czech Republic, Albania, and Russia, less has been accomplished. For example, Albania faces serious financial problems in sustaining pensions, and in the Czech Republic these problems are related to longer-term demographic changes—specifically, the aging of the population.

As the transition economies move toward market arrangements, the problems they face become increasingly similar to those debated in the developed market economies. Expenditures on both health care and education are major budget items and must be approached in such a way as to ensure fiscal responsibility. Pension arrangements must account for the increasing dependency ratio, and unemployment schemes must strike an appropriate balance between providing essential benefits and sustaining incentives that lead to critical adjustments in labor markets.

Transition, Inequality, and Levels of Well-Being

Throughout this book we have emphasized the importance of the initial conditions, or factors from the past, that influence development during the transition era. In this chapter we have stressed the fact that dramatic changes have occurred in standards of living during transition, partly because of the erosion of social-sector programs. These programs, significant during the command era, have undergone important changes, which have had rather different results in different transition economies. What can we expect in a new century?

Empirical evidence suggests two conclusions regarding inequality.[13] First, the populations of transition economies generally prefer a more egalitarian distribution of income than would be the case in Western economies. Second, these views are not necessarily generated from the sometimes sharp changes in the distribution of income that occurred during transition but, rather, are based on long-standing views about the nature of the social contract. Understanding this evidence is important, because during transition there have been significant changes in the distribution of income—changes that are having, and will continue to have, important social and economic consequences.

In nearly all transition economies, inequality (measured by the **Gini coefficient**) increased during the early years of transition (see Table 20.5)—in some cases significantly.[14] In part, these changes are the result of changes in the composition of income, but these changes have themselves had a disproportionate impact on certain social groups. Specifically, the burden of inequality has been borne by the elderly, farmers, those not fully employed, and (to some degree) women.

It is important to appreciate that these changes in the Gini coefficient, especially in cases such as Russia, are very large, especially in a setting accustomed to a more

TABLE 20.5   Inequality in the Early Years of Transition:
Annual Gini Coefficient

	1987–1988	1993–1995
Russia	24	48[a]
Kazakhstan	26	33
Ukraine	23	47[b]
Poland	26	28[c]
Estonia	23	35[a]
Hungary	21	23
Czech Republic	19	27[b]

Note: In most cases, income in 1987–1988 is gross income and in 1993–1995
is disposable income.
[a]Quarterly.
[b]Monthly.
[c]Semiannual.

Source: Compiled from Branko Milanovic, *Income, Inequality, and Poverty
During the Transition from Planned to Market Economy* (Washington,
D.C.: World Bank, 1998), p. 41, Table 4.1.

egalitarian distribution of income. This outcome conforms to a popular view in Russia—
namely, that the benefits of transition, broadly defined, have been very unevenly distributed. These issues are important for our overall assessment of transition and of the
mechanisms and policies that have been used in the various transition economies.

Summary

- During the command era, the safety net was provided by the state. During transition, it has been difficult for the state to sustain the safety net, private-sector alternatives have been slow to emerge, and state budgets have lacked an adequate
  revenue base. However, safety-net benefits such as reduction of poverty and the
  provision of pensions, medical care, and unemployment benefits are all important
  elements for our assessment of transition. They also influence the extent to which
  there is popular support for transition programs.
- Our analysis of safety-net issues begins with a discussion of the allocation of
  labor, the end of state employment, and the entry into private-sector employment.
  To the extent that this process is uneven, the ineffective use of a significant stock
  of human capital in the transition economies has important implications for economic growth, and the resulting growth of unemployment boosts the demands
  placed on the safety-net programs.
- We emphasize the fact that while transition economies are struggling with safety-
  net issues in countries not accustomed to widespread unemployment, the debate
  over these programs and their potential impact on economic growth is also a
  major issue in Western industrialized economies.

- Although the labor-allocation adjustment in the transition economies has generally entailed a decline in state-sector employment and an increase in private-sector employment, the process has grown more complicated as the structure of household incomes has changed and aggregate levels of unemployment have risen significantly.
- One major outcome of these difficult labor-market changes has been significant increases in the levels of poverty in transition economies. However, studies suggest that there are significant differences in the incidence of poverty (aggregate levels of poverty and its impact on different population groups by region, age, and gender). As with other indicators of transition, there are important differences between the transition economies of Eastern Europe and the CIS states.
- Considerable attention has been paid to the broad relationships between safety-net issues and the emerging demographic patterns in transition economies. Although the evidence suggests that expenditures on health have largely been sustained (measured as a portion of state spending), nevertheless difficulties in the delivery of health services have contributed to what in some countries (such as Russia) has been termed a "demographic crisis": increases in death rates and reductions in birth rates. Again, there are significant differences between the patterns observed in the CIS states and those observed in Eastern Europe.
- An important and controversial outcome of the transition era has been changes—sometimes sharp changes—in the extent of income inequality, measured by the Gini coefficient.

Key Terms

social policies   poverty deficit
safety net   Gini coefficient
job right constraint

Notes

1. Inequality varied regionally in command economies such as the Soviet Union and generally increased during the 1980s, when the gini coefficient ranged from the mid- to upper twenties. For a discussion of inequality during the command era, see Paul R. Gregory and Robert C. Stuart, *Russian and Soviet Economic Performance and Structure* (New York: Addison Wesley Longman, 2001), Ch. 7.
2. For a useful discussion of these issues, see A. B. Atkinson, *The Economic Consequences of Rolling Back the Welfare State* (Cambridge, Mass.: MIT Press, 1999).
3. The classic work is David Granick, *Job Rights in the Soviet Union: Their Consequences* (New York: Cambridge University Press, 1987).
4. See the discussion in Oliver Blanchard, *The Economics of Post-Communist Transition* (Oxford: Clarendon Press, 1997), Ch. 2; and P. Aghion and O. Blanchard, "On the Speed of Transition in Central Europe" *National Bureau of Economic Research Macroeconomics Annual,* 1994, pp. 283–320.

5. Again, as we have emphasized, some of the command economies (for example, Poland and Hungary) experienced considerable economic reform and change during the latter years of the command era. These experiences are in sharp contrast to cases like the Czech Republic (then Czechoslovakia), where there was little economic reform in the post-1968 period.

6. There is a large literature on employment policies in transition countries. For a survey, see Tito Boeri and Hartmut Lehmann, eds., "Unemployment and Labor Market Policies in Transition Countries," *Journal of Comparative Economics* 27, 1 (March 1999), 1–130; for a discussion of the Russian case, see J. David Brown and John S. Earle, "Gross Job Flows in Russian Industry Before and After Reforms: Has Destruction Become More Creative?" IZA, Discussion Paper No. 351, August 2001; for a discussion of the Polish case, see Andrew Newell and Francesco Pastore, "Regional Unemployment and Industrial Restructuring in Poland," IZA, Discussion Paper No. 194, August 2000. See also Hartmut Lehmann and Jonathan Wadsworth, "Tenures That Shook the World: Worker Turnover in Russia, Poland, and Britain," *Journal of Comparative Economics* 28, 4 (December 2000), 639–664; Elizabeth Brainerd, "Winners and Losers in Russia's Economic Transition," *American Economic Review* 88, 5 (December 1998), 1094–1116; EBRD, *Transition Report 2000* (London: EBRD, 2000), Ch. 5.

7. For a discussion of these issues, see EBRD, *Transition Report 2000,* Ch. 5.

8. These data are from *ibid.*

9. There is a large literature on poverty in the transition economies. See, for example, Sandra Hutton and Gerry Redmond, eds., *Poverty in Transition Economies* (London: Routledge, 2000); Branko Milanovic, *Income, Inequality, and Poverty During the Transition from Planned to Market Economy* (Washington, D.C.: World Bank, 1998); World Bank, *From Plan to Market: World Development Report 1996* (Washington, D.C.: World Bank, 1996); Janos Kornai and Karen Eggleston, *Welfare, Choice and Solidarity in Transition* (Cambridge: Cambridge University Press, 2001); Ethan B. Kapstein and Michael Mandelbaum, eds., *Sustaining the Transition: The Social Safety Net in Postcommunist Europe* (New York: Council on Foreign Relations, 1997).

10. The poverty deficit, or poverty gap, is the amount of funding that would be necessary to eliminate poverty—that is, to raise all who are below the established poverty line up to that line.

11. See, for example, the discussion in Julie DaVanzo and David Adamson, "Russia's Demographic 'Crisis': How Real Is It?" Rand Corporation, Center for Russian and European Studies, Labor and Population Program, July 1997; Mark G. Field, "The Health Crisis in the Fortmer Soviet Union: A Report from the 'Post-War' Zone," *Social Science Medicine* 41, 11 (1995), 1469–1478; Elizabeth Brainerd, "Death and the Market," Department of Economics, Williams College, typescript. A useful set of articles on population in Russia can be found in *The World Development Report* 26, 11 (1998).

12. A useful survey of basic issues is Peter S. Heller and Christian Keller, "Social Sector Reform in Transition Economies," IMF Working Paper WP/01/35.

13. See the discussion in Marc Suhrcke, "Preferences for Inequality: East vs. West," UNICEF, Innocenti Working Paper No. 89, October 2001.

14. There is a significant body of literature addressing issues of inequality in transition economies. See, for example, Branko Milanovic, *Income, Inequality, and Poverty During the Transition from Planned to Market Economy* (Washington, D.C.: World Bank, 1998); John Flemming and John Micklewright, "Income Distribution, Economic Systems and Transition," UNICEF, Innocenti Working Paper, No. 70, May 1999.

Recommended Readings

Joachim Ahrens, *Governance and Economic Development* (Northampton, Mass.: Edward Elgar, 2002).

Annette N. Brown. ed., *When is Transition Over?* (Kalamazoo, Mich.: Upjohn Institute, 1999).

Michael Cuddy and Ruvin Gekker, eds., *Institutional Change in Transition Economies* (Burlington, Vt.: Ashgate, 2002).

Patricia Dillon and Frank C. Wykoff, *Creating Capitalism* (Northampton, Mass.: Edward Elgar, 2002).

Robert Gilpin, *The Challenge of Global Capitalism* (Princeton, N.J.: Princeton University Press, 2000).

Louis Haddad, *Towards a Well-Functioning Economy* (Northampton, Mass.: Edward Elgar, 2003).

Christian von Hirschhausen, *Modernizing Infrastructure in Transformation Economies* (Northampton, Mass.: Edward Elgar, 2002).

Jay H. Levin, *A Guide to the Euro* (Boston: Houghton Mifflin, 2002).

Richard Pomfret, *Constructing a Market Economy* (Northampton, Mass.: Edward Elgar, 2002).

Linda M. Randall, *Reluctant Capitalists* (New York: Routledge, 2001).

James N. Rosenau, *Distant Proximities: Dynamics beyond Globalization* (Princeton, N.J.: Princeton University Press, 2003).

Andrei Shleifer and Robert W. Vishny, *The Grabbing Hand* (Cambridge, Mass.: Harvard University Press, 1998).

Horst Seibert, *The World Economy,* 2nd ed. (London and New York: 2002).

Gertrude Tumpel-Gugerell and Peter Mooslechner, eds., *Economic Convergence and Divergence in Europe* (Northampton, Mass.: Edward Elgar, 2003).

World Bank, *The World Development Report 2003* (Washington, D.C.: World Bank, 2003).

21

Perspectives on Transition Performance Since the 1980s

The concept of transition implies a shift from one state to another and thus, implicitly, the end of the process as the end state is reached. In the case of the contemporary transition economies, the concept of completion is difficult to define with precision, although conceptually, as markets replace the organizational arrangements of the command era, transition should come to an end. Is the Czech Republic a transition economy or is it a small, open Eastern European economy at a middle level of economic development? Does the distinction matter? Will the concept of transition largely disappear as Eastern European economies become members of the European Union? In this chapter we present some appropriate signposts to guide the reader in an assessment of the transition economies into the new century. Specifically, we examine contemporary estimates of economic growth and discuss the likelihood of continuing systemic change. Finally, in Chapter 22, we will draw broad conclusions about the nature of differing economic systems in the twenty-first century.

Throughout this book we have emphasized that it is convenient, for purposes of analysis to classify different economic systems and their real-world country outcomes in various groups. We have also emphasized, however, that many of the components of transition (for example, privatization) occur in a variety of countries and under varying economic systems that bear no resemblance to transition economies. Systemic change exhibits patterns that differ widely among both the transition and the nontransition economies. In this sense, as we examine the former command economies and classify most of them as transition economies, the historical legacy is important, just as are the contemporary differences from other economic systems. A careful observer of the contemporary literature in economics will find it difficult to arrive at decisive answers to questions about the end of transition. Moreover, it may not be useful to be very concerned with the issue, because our analyses of differing economic systems must always take into account (1) historical and other experiences that are relevant to the specific cases being examined and (2) the differing objectives of various analysts. Thus, in the end, the issue of initial conditions (to which we have devoted a great deal of attention) may be less relevant for our analysis of the Czech economy than it is for our analysis of the Russian economy.

500

Growth Patterns in Transition Economies

There is now a considerable measure of agreement on transition outcomes, and yet there are also many controversies and numerous issues yet to be researched and fully understood. Few would disagree with the observations that follow. First, if we characterize a successful transition as one where underlying organizational and allocational arrangements have changed, producing sustained positive economic growth, then clearly there are marked differences among the transition economies. Generally speaking, the transition economies emerging from the Soviet Union have done least well, whereas those of Central and Eastern Europe have done the best. Again, as we have repeatedly emphasized, there are interesting and important differences even within subgroups. On balance, those transition economies that have been able to sustain liberalization have done best, although this observation still leaves open the question of the appropriate speed and pattern of reform.

Second, the best-performing transition economies have been those that have achieved the most organizational change and have developed a new market infrastructure. Although it is not easy to measure the degree of liberalization of the economic and political arena, economic growth has generally been closely associated with liberalization of the economic environment, typically measured by a variety of indicators, such as a reduction of state controls, limitation of policy constraints, and the emergence of a legal infrastructure.[1]

Third, most observers would argue that the policy agenda for transition economies is critical, and yet the policy choices are often difficult and associated with unattractive tradeoffs. For example, most would agree that liberalization has enhanced the shift of resources away from less productive toward more productive sectors, leading to improvements in allocative efficiency. At the same time, the result has often been unemployment and/or fiscal burdens that have themselves resulted in unacceptable rates of inflation. Striking a balance in such cases presents unusual challenges.

Fourth, a major change in the former command economies has been the gradual integration of these economies into the global arena of world financial markets.

Economic Growth in Transition and Nontransition Economies

Especially after the downturn of transition economies during the early years of transition, economic growth became an obvious success indicator for the transition economies. As we emphasized in Chapters 14 through 16, the initial decline in output in most transition economies was followed by a generally improving pattern of growth performance, although the more substantive issue of growth convergence remains controversial. One way to assess the long-term patterns of change in transition economies is to compare their rates of growth with those in other market economies within the framework of convergence.

In Chapter 16 we examined the concept of growth convergence, in which long-term rates of economic growth for transition and nontransition economies are compared, after controlling for variations in income levels using cross-sectional differences across countries. Recent studies have examined the possibility of growth convergence both within the transition economies as a group and between the transition economies and Western economies. Interestingly enough, initial studies indicate that there has not been convergence either among the transition economies or between this group and Western (typically OECD) countries.

This research will undoubtedly continue, especially as longer data series become available for the transition era, but preliminary results seem to deny convergence and thus to deny the existence of an important indicator by which the end of transition might be judged.[2]

Economic Growth in a New Century

In Figure 21.1 we summarize the growth patterns of the Eastern and Central European transition economies and the CIS countries. These results present a familiar pattern of collapse and improvement. The improvements in recent years differ among the country groupings but are generally of significant magnitude. Growth performance in recent years has been mixed, although it is difficult to draw strong conclusions with such a limited time frame.

There is a great deal of interest in the nature and rates of economic growth in the transition economies. In the *Transition Update* for 2001 published by the EBRD, there are no fewer than thirteen separate forecasts of projected growth rates for transition economies for the year 2002. Table 21.1 offers a summary of these forecasts. In this table, the projected growth weight is an average of the various forecasts presented by EBRD, and the range is the spread between the lowest and the highest forecasted rates of growth for each country.[3]

Several observations are suggested by these forecasts. First, there are many forecasts for which the range is quite small, indicating a considerable measure of agreement among different observers. There are, however, a number of cases where the extent of disagreement is quite significant. In one extreme case (Tajikistan), the estimates range from a low of 4 percent to a high of 7.5 percent. In general, the differences among the growth estimates are greatest for the CIS countries and much less for the central Eastern European and the Baltic states.

Second, although there are understandably market differences from country to country, it is striking that all of the estimates are positive and of reasonable magnitude. The unweighted average for the CIS states is 4.4 percent; for the central Eastern European, and the Baltic States it is 3.5 percent; and finally, for the states of Southeastern Europe, the average is 4.5 percent. The overall unweighted average is 4.4 percent, and the overall weighted average (weighted by $US GDP in 2000) is 3.3 percent.

What are the growth prospects for the future? It is difficult to provide serious growth forecasts for transition economies. Recent year-to-year growth rates have

FIGURE 21.1   GDP: Percentage Change (year to year in constant prices) for
Selected Transition Economies, 1990–2002[a]

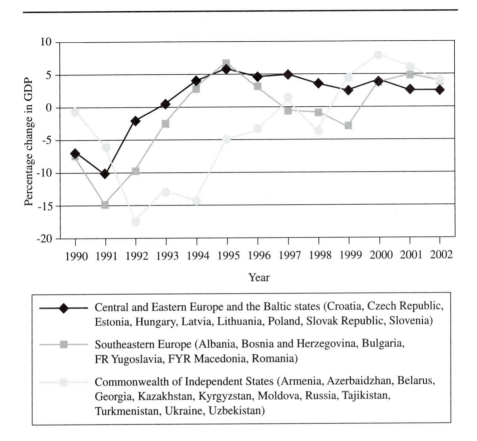

---

[a]Data for 2001 are preliminary; data for 2002 are projections.

Source: EBRD, *Transition Report Update* (London: EBRD, May 2002), Annex 1.1.

---

been generally good, and the forecasts generally optimistic. At the same time, there
are a variety of underlying forces that make a summary judgment difficult. The recent growth performance of Belarus, for example, has been solid, and yet this is an
economy that has undergone very little transition. In effect, we are seeing economic
growth based on the old order—a setting very difficult to extrapolate into the future.
There are, however, a number of factors that are important.

First, for those economies preparing for accession to the EU, the economic climate of the EU and the adjustments being made will clearly have an important—and
arguably a positive—influence on economic growth.

TABLE 21.1   Economic Growth in Transition Economies:
Projections for 2002

Country	Average Projected Rate of Growth	Range
Croatia	3.4	1.8
Czech Republic	3.4	1.2
Estonia	4.4	2.6
Hungary	3.6	1.1
Latvia	4.9	1.0
Lithuania	4.0	1.4
Poland	1.5	2.2
Slovak Republic	3.3	1.6
Slovenia	3.2	1.0
Albania	6.5	1.6
Bosnia and Herzegovina	5.4	2.1
Bulgaria	3.7	1.1
FR Yugoslavia	4.7	1.5
FYR Macedonia	2.7	5.0
Romania	4.0	2.9
Armenia	5.8	1.5
Azerbaidzhan	7.5	2.0
Belarus	2.1	1.0
Georgia	4.0	2.0
Kazakhstan	7.4	2.4
Kyrgyzstan	4.7	1.6
Moldova	3.8	2.1
Russia	3.5	1.4
Tajikistan	6.1	3.5
Turkmenistan	8.4	6.5
Ukraine	4.5	2.5
Uzbekistan	2.7	1.9

Source: EBRD, *Transition Report Update* (London: EBRD, May 2002), Table 1.1.

Second, the transition economies have generally moved sharply toward integration with the global economy, and the nature of this integration is very different from that which existed during the command era. Thus economic trends in Western countries—and especially economic trends among the trading partners of the transition economies—will be important.

Third, there are a number of countries for whom specific identifiable factors are at work. For example, oil prices will be of major importance to the future growth of the Russian economy.

More broadly, both events at home and events in the global economy will affect the determination of capital flows, especially the continuation of foreign direct investment. In addition, such related factors as the development of a stable legal infrastructure will be important both for continuing domestic development in the transition economies and for integration with Western partners.

Finally, it is obvious that the nature of liberalization at home will affect the performance of the transition economies. We have emphasized the important differences among the policy and organizational changes of the various transition economies. These factors will remain important in future years.

Beyond Growth: Perspectives on Systemic Change

Throughout this book, we have generally assumed that the transition economies have abandoned or will abandon the command model and will move in varying degrees toward market arrangements. This assumption is reasonable, but it leaves unanswered questions about the possible emergence of mixed systems that are neither command nor market but differ in varying degrees from both. It is difficult to speculate on future outcomes of this sort, although an understanding of the past would certainly suggest that there are likely to be important systemic variations among the transition economies. To the extent that these differences emerge, we should not be surprised if the issue of convergence examined in Chapter 16 remains controversial and important. What directions might we expect change to take?

Recall that when the command economies (both the economic and the political systems) collapsed in the late 1980s, the nature of this collapse and the settings in which it occurred varied considerably from case to case. Moreover, the initial discussions about transition alternatives also differed, as did the actual transition experiences during the 1990s.

Even so, we may be able to speculate about systemic variations that may be likely given these differences. In broad terms, we might expect the social contract to be different across the transition economies, and there will probably be differences in the systemic arrangements and associated policies that support variations in the social contract.

Although the old order as we knew it is unlikely to reemerge, it is important to emphasize that there are some transition economies (for example, Belarus) where much of the old order remains in place. Moreover, there are other transition economies (for example, those in central Asia) where the extent of liberalization has been limited, and state controls remain important. More generally, we might anticipate a greater role for the state in these systems, along with policy imperatives that reflect the old order. An example of these are the safety net and the role of the state in providing public goods. Finally, we may anticipate a continuing role for the state in the management of important sectors in the economy— for example, energy and natural resources.

To the extent that mixed systems emerge, we may anticipate a lesser degree of convergence, and sustained differences among the transition economies and between the transition economies and other market systems of Western Europe.

Summary

- Clearly, the rate of growth of output in the transition economies has improved considerably in recent years, although there are important variations in the growth rates observed in the various economies.
- Rates of economic growth have generally been quite good in recent years, but the time frame in which we have been able to observe these rates of growth is short, and thus extrapolation of these rates into the future is difficult.
- Although much remains to be done, early studies that have examined convergence in general and growth convergence in particular suggest that convergence has been limited, indicating that differences among the transition and the nontransition economies may remain important.
- If the outcomes of the transition economies remain even modestly distinctive, it will be important to continue to examine the long-term nature of systemic change in the transition economies and to appreciate the possibility that mixed systems will emerge.
- If mixed systems emerge in the transition economies, the impact of the past will be one of many influential factors that may encourage an important role for the state in the achievement of social and economic objectives somewhat different from those pursued in nontransition economies at similar levels of economic development.

Notes

1. As we have emphasized, the various transition reports of the European Bank for Reconstruction and Development (EBRD) are useful for assessing the process of liberalization in the transition economies.
2. Both the importance and the complexity of these issues are addressed in Nauro F. Campos and Fabrizio Coricelli, "Growth in Transition: What We Know, What We Don't, and What We Should," *Journal of Economic Literature* 40, 3 (September 2002), 793–836.
3. For the details of various estimates, see EBRD, *Transition Report Update* (London: EBRD, May 2002), Table 1.1.

Recommended Readings

Erik Berglof and Romesh Vaitilingam, *Stuck in Transit: Re-Thinking Russian Economic Reform* (Stockholm: CEPR, 1999).

Oliver Blanchard, *The Economics of Post-Communist Transition* (New York: Oxford University Press, 1997).

Christopher Clague and Gordon C. Rausser, eds., *The Emergence of Market Economies in Eastern Europe* (Cambridge, Mass.: Blackwell, 1992).

Martha de Melo, Cevdet Denizer, and Alan Gelb, "Patterns of Transition from Plan to Market," *The World Bank Economic Review* 10, 3 (September 1996), 397–424.

European Bank for Reconstruction and Development, *Transition Report 2000: Employment, Skills and Transition* (London: EBRD, 2000).

————, *Transition Report 2001* (London: EBRD, 2001).

————, *Transition Report Update* (London: EBRD, 2002).

Philip Hanson and Michael Bradshaw, eds., *Regional Economic Change in Russia* (Northampton, Mass.: Edward Elgar, 2000).

OECD, *Russian Federation* (Paris: OECD, 2000).

Lucjan T. Orlowski, ed., *Transition and Growth in Post-Communist Countries* (Northampton, Mass.: Edward Elgar, 2001).

J. L. Porket, *Modern Economic Systems and Their Transformation* (New York: St. Martin's, 1998).

Sheila M. Puffer, Daniel J. McCarthy, and Alexander I. Naumov, eds., *The Russian Capitalist Experiment* (Northampton, Mass.: Edward Elgar, 2000).

Gerard Roland, *Transition and Economics: Politics, Markets, and Firms* (Cambridge, Mass.: MIT Press, 2000).

Paul Seabright, ed., *The Vanishing Rouble: Barter Networks and Non-Monetary Transactions in Post-Soviet Societies* (Cambridge: Cambridge University Press, 2000).

Andrei Schleifer and Daniel Triesman, *Without a Map* (Cambridge, Mass.: MIT Press, 2000).

Nicolas Spulber, *Redefining the State* (Cambridge: Cambridge University Press, 1997).

Kitty Stewart, *Fiscal Federalism in Russia* (Northampton, Mass.: Edward Elgar, 2000).

"Symposium on Economic Transition in the Soviet Union and Eastern Europe," *Journal of Economic Perspectives* 5, 4 (Fall 1991) 3–236.

World Bank, *From Plan to Market: World Development Report 1996* (Washington, D.C.: World Bank, 1996).

Salvatore Zecchini, ed., *Lessons from the Economic Transition* (Boston: Kluwer Academic, 1997).

22

Prospects for 2050

The economic system does matter. The Soviet planned socialist economic system was abandoned when it failed to produce satisfactory economic performance. The economic system adopted by the Four Tigers of Southeast Asia—low taxation, promotion of exports, and human capital enhancement—led to remarkable economic results. The Four Tigers, which began the postwar era as poor economies, either have joined or are on their way to joining the ranks of the affluent countries. Other countries, such as Pakistan and Bangladesh, which had as much promise as the Four Tigers, have failed to generate economic growth. China, after decades of political turmoil, adopted market-oriented reforms that generated rates of growth among the highest in the world for more than two decades. Whereas in the 1960s there was talk that the Soviet Union would become a dominant power in the world economy, this is now said of China. India, which opened its economy to trade and a larger role for the private sector, including foreign investment, has been among the world's fastest-growing economies since 1991.

The economies of the European Union have failed since the 1970s to generate economic growth on a par with the Unites States and Asia. They have settled into consensus models based on heavy social protection, employee rights, worker representation, and high taxation. They are testing the limits of the welfare state to determine whether consensus and worker protection are consistent with economic growth and full employment. Whether they can change their system in the face of powerful vested interests remains an open question. There are European exceptions. Great Britain, the traditional economic laggard of Europe, revived its economic growth under policies initiated by Margaret Thatcher, and the United Kingdom's per capita GDP has begun to rise again relative to the other European nations. Ireland is now one of the fastest-growing European nations since adopting market liberalizing reforms in the 1990s. After more than a century, the Irish as a whole are either remaining in Ireland or emigrating back to Ireland to take advantage of its economic prosperity.

The most fascinating open question is the outcome of the transition from planned socialism to market capitalism that is under way in the former Soviet Union and in Central and Southeastern Europe. The answer is far from clear from the vantage point of the beginning of the twenty-first century. Some countries have navigated the treacherous waters of transition; they include Poland, the Czech Republic, Hungary, the Baltic States, and Slovenia. However, even in the case of these apparent successes, the costs of transition have been high and the political consequences brutal. Another case of "successful" transition occurred in the eastern part of the now-reunified Germany, which began its transition from a planned to a market economy in 1990. Again the economic costs have been substantial, although they have been borne largely by German taxpayers.

The outcome of transition in the rest of Eastern Europe and the former Soviet Union is far from clear even though transition is more than a decade old. The most important economy of the region, Russia, has made significant changes in its fiscal and monetary systems, has initiated structural reforms, and has completed privatization. However, the privatization process put nomenklatura (or insider) capitalists in charge of Russian industry—managers whose interests are different from those of the economy at large. It remains to be seen whether Russia, under its relatively young president, Vladimir Putin, can overcome the challenges of this period of "wild" or "frontier" capitalism, effect major restructuring, and settle down to a more productive form of capitalism.

Changing Views of Economic Systems

John Maynard Keynes remarked in his *General Theory,* published in 1936, that we are all captives of the economic ideas and philosophies of the past. Just in the postwar period, we have seen a number of economic ideas and philosophies come and go. In the 1950s, economists naively believed in state planning. The Soviet Union appeared to be growing rapidly; the Soviets, not the Americans, were the first in space, and the Soviet premier, Nikita Khrushchev, threatened to "bury" capitalism beneath the wheels of the communist economic machine. A different form of planning, indicative planning, was being carried out in France, which was experiencing rapid growth. The fact that the Soviet Union appeared to overcome the consequences of backwardness in less than a decade in the 1930s had enormous appeal for the countries of the developing world. India wholeheartedly adopted the Soviet planning philosophy, although political and other constraints prevented India from adopting the Soviet economic system in its entirety.

The 1960s was the period of the European economic miracle, the "Golden Age" of growth not only in Europe but also in other parts of the globe. The world's wealthiest country, the United States, appeared to be losing ground and even sent emissaries to Europe to study the European model. Germany grew at such rapid rates in the 1950s and 1960s that the term *Wirtschaftswunder* was coined to describe its success. Europe appeared able in the 1960s to combine rapid economic growth with a burgeoning welfare state in which workers were protected from all risks.

Events of the 1970s diverted attention from Europe to Japan. The Japanese economy was experiencing accelerating growth, despite a world energy crisis that should have devastated the resource-poor Japanese economy. Japan's success focused attention on its system of lifetime worker tenure and its industrial policy. Japan's powerful Ministry for Industry and Trade appeared to pick the industrial winners of the future. The close alliance between business and the state seemed to be the key to Japan's economic success.

The 1980s and 1990s were decades of deregulation and free enterprise. Two of the world's major economies, the United States and the United Kingdom, elected conservative governments that deregulated industry, communications, finance, and transportation and lowered marginal tax rates. U.S. economic performance was superior to hat of Europe. Great Britain's long affliction with the "British Disease" ended, and England began slowly to catch up with the other countries of Europe. The other impetus to free enterprise and open economies emanated from the Four Tigers of Southeast Asia, whose rates of growth over two decades were sufficient to transform them from poor to relatively wealthy economies. In the face of this exceptional performance, China embarked on ambitious marketization reforms that have given China more than two decades of rapid growth.

The transition of the former planned socialist economies in the 1990s required economists to consider how economies make the transition from central planning to market resource allocation. Whereas earlier, only a few specialists had studied this issue, now the best economists and the major international economic institutions sought to provide programs for a successful transition.

We do not know what ideas and philosophies will govern the first few decades of the twenty-first century. We will probably be in for a number of surprises. We may hear renewed arguments that the socialist planned economy is sound in principle and that if the leaders of these economies had done a better job, the experiment with planned socialism would have been a success.

One of the major intellectual changes of the last two decades of the twentieth century was a rethinking of the role of the state in economic life. We began the postwar period with a view of the state as a benign instrument for good that could overcome problems of underdevelopment and inequity. But we began the twenty-first century with a less benign view that recognizes the state as a potential problem, not a solution.

Rising and Falling Economic Fortunes

In earlier chapters, we have cited the work of Angus Maddison, whose empirical studies identify countries and periods in which economic growth has been rapid or slow.[1] Economic growth has been uneven among the different regions of the world. Africa and Latin America have grown relatively slowly or not at all over the past half-century; the industrialized core countries of Europe and North America have experienced sustained growth for nearly two centuries. The past century has witnessed two major changes of economic fortunes. One was the rapid growth of Asian countries (starting with Japan and then spreading to Southeast Asia) from the 1930s on; the second was the rise and decline of the European periphery, consisting primarily of the former Soviet Union and Eastern Europe. For a brief period of time, the European periphery of planned socialist economies appeared to outgrow the industrialized core, but their growth faltered after 1970. Their failure to make further progress vis-à-vis the industrialized core explains why the system of planned socialism was abandoned. Figure 22.1 captures the dramatic rise of Asia and collapse of the Soviet Empire over the past twenty years.

What are the prospects for further reversals—that is, the prospects for a region that has typically grown slowly to move to a posture of fast economic growth sufficient to overcome part or all of the income gap?

First, it should be emphasized that as of the start of the twenty-first century, underdevelopment and low incomes are more typical than development and high incomes.

FIGURE 22.1   Shares of World Output, 1980 and 2000

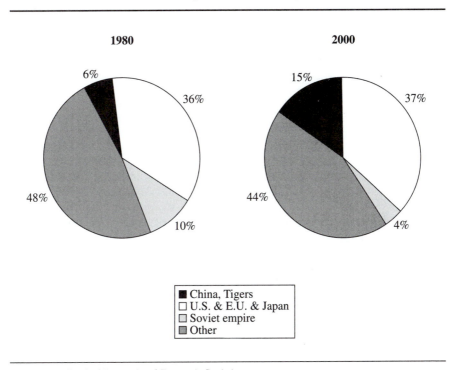

Source: Handbook of International Economic Statistics.

In 2000 the population of the world was near six billion persons, with a world GDP of nearly 40 trillion dollars.[2] As Table 22.1 shows, the distribution of product is uneven. More than three-quarters of the world's people still live in developing economies, where they receive less than two-fifths of the world's total product and subsist at low levels of income and wealth, with minimal education, and in poor health. Less than 20 percent of the world's population lives in high-income countries. Underdevelopment remains a fact of life.

Second, these figures can be changed by one or two significant events. One of these events would be the continued rapid economic growth of China and India, countries that account for two billion of the world's five billion inhabitants. The second factor would be the growth of those few Central and Latin American countries that for the first time appear to be growing rapidly.

Starting with Chile under Augusto Pinochet in 1981, and then spreading to six other countries in Latin America (Argentina, Bolivia, Colombia, Mexico, Peru, and Uruguay), a Latin American model of reform has been created. This Latin model uses privatization, strengthening of private-property rights, pension reform, and deregulation—combined with monetary and fiscal austerity—to create a favorable climate for growth and foreign investment.[3] As a consequence of these actions, Latin American government deficits fell from 5.5 percent of GDP in 1988 to 1.8 percent

TABLE 22.1   World Gross Domestic Product and Population in 2000

	Gross Domestic Product (percent)	Population (percent)
Developing countries	38	76
Eastern Europe and the former USSR	6	7
United States	22	5
European Union	20	6
Japan	8	2
Total: World	100	100

Source: Central Intelligence Agency, *Handbook of International Economic Statistics,* updated by authors.

in 1995. Average tariff rates have fallen to the level of those of the United States. Since 1991 the Latin American economies have achieved an average annual rate of growth of 3.1 percent, a rate not deemed a sufficient reward for the difficult reforms that have been undertaken. However, if the reforms ultimately prove sufficient to create a climate for growth, their payoff should be felt during the first decades of the twenty-first century.[4] Latin America's problem, however, has been sustaining reforms. Reforms are announced, some initial successes are achieved, but then a "crisis" ensues and convinces people that reform has failed. Latin American crises, such as in Argentina in 2001–2002, tend to be the result of poor policy or even the natural cycles of market economies.

Golden Ages

World economic growth appears to go through cyclical or longer swings, which have been studied in the past by such eminent students of the business cycle as N. D. Kondratiev,[5] Simon Kuznets, and W. C. Mitchell. Figure 22.2 shows that the 1970s was a period of low growth, largely as a consequence of the energy crises of that period. The 1980s was generally a period of rising growth. The 1990s was a period of rising world economic growth—a development that economist Jeffrey Sachs described as "an important historical event. The positive side is spectacular."[6] Several factors have been offered to explain the upsurge in economic growth in the 1990s: the vast expansion of economic freedom and property rights, the reduction in the scope of government, and an explosion in trade and private investment. Whole new industries have sprung up in computer networking and biotechnology. Even the secretary general of the United Nations saw the world as "entering a new golden age" fostered by soaring private investment and technical advances that will enable poorer nations to avoid some of the growing pains that others had to go through to develop. The new "golden age" of growth may have come to an end with the Asian crisis of summer 1997, the stagnation of growth in Europe and Japan, and then the stagnation

FIGURE 22.2   World Economic Growth

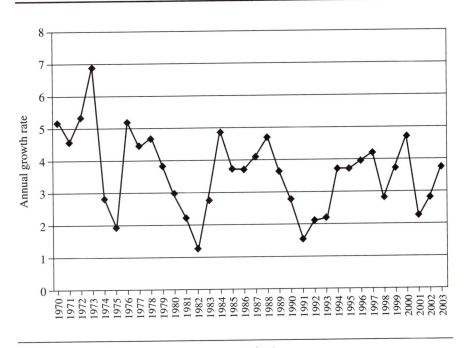

Source: International Monetary Fund, database (*www.imf.org*).

of U.S. growth in 2001. We do not know whether these events represent a brief interruption, a long-term trend in world growth, or a fundamental long-term trend.

Figure 22.3 shows the distribution of economic growth among the major regions of the globe. The two outliers are the exceptionally rapid growth of the industrializing Asian economies and the collapse of the output of the transition economies in the former Soviet Union and Eastern and Southeastern Europe. In the 1970s, U.S. and European growth were similar, but since 1980, U.S. growth has been generally above Europe's. African growth has been either below or, at best, on a par with that of other countries, suggesting that Africa is not overcoming its relative backwardness. Figure 22.3 also shows that the advanced industrialized countries are not immune to business cycles or "crises." Since 1970, the U.S. economy has experienced six years of stagnant or negative growth (more, in fact, than the European Union). The industrialized Asian economies suffered one major episode of negative growth in 1998, following the Asian crisis of the summer of 1997. Although the transition economies have been robust in the latter half of the 1990s, there remain important performance differences, especially between the transition economies of Eastern Europe and those of the former Soviet Union.

The world has in fact experienced a number of **golden ages of growth**. The first was the 40-year period before World War I. During this period, world economic growth

FIGURE 22.3   World Economic Growth by Regions

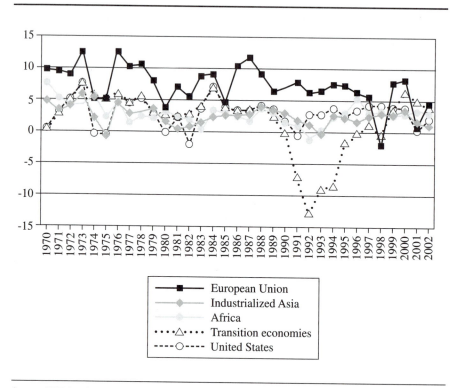

Source: IMF data bank.

averaged 2.1 percent per annum—relatively slow growth by today's standards but more than double the rate of the previous half-century. The second golden age ran from 1950 to the oil shock of 1973. During this second golden age, world economic growth averaged 4.9 percent per year. The first golden age was a consequence of the spread of the Industrial Revolution. The second golden age resulted from the release of bottled up technology that had been restrained by the Great Depression and World War II and by the wartime devastation in Europe and Japan that wiped out entrenched interests and outmoded infrastructure. The third golden age of growth may be the period of the 1990s, or even starting in the early 1980s. It is associated with the computer and information revolutions in the West with the rise of Asia.

A major factor in worldwide growth has been the ongoing process of economic integration and the elimination of controls on international capital flows. Most of the world's governments are now convinced that economic liberalization is the surest path to economic growth. To quote a Mexican specialist, "Governments all over the world are moving in the same direction—deregulating, cutting their deficits and vying for foreign investment."[7] Economist Steve Hancke has studied the relationship between economic freedom and economic growth, where economic freedom is defined in terms of strong property rights, absence of currency controls, and lack of official corruption and bribes. He finds that for every 10 percent increase in economic freedom, GDP per capita rises between 7 and 14 percent.[8]

Poorer countries are in a position to play rapid catch-up in today's world, because relatively backward countries are not saddled with old capital. They can use the latest equipment, which operates at lower cost and more efficiently. In prior eras, the relatively backward countries had to make do with older technology, but now new Pentium chips are manufactured in China using the latest Intel technology.

Foreign direct investment between the developed and the developing countries quintupled between 1990 and 2000 to $238 billion.

Technology and know-how are transferred from industrialized to developing countries most immediately through foreign direct investment (FDI), in which a business of one country takes a direct and significant stake in a company located in another country. FDI from industrialized to developing economies takes place when investments yield higher rates of return in the developing world, which have low-priced but skilled labor and unexploited investment opportunities. In this fashion, FDI transfers technology and creates a better distribution of world capital. Table 22.2 shows the amount of FDI in developing countries between 1998 and 2001. It shows that about 70

TABLE 22.2   Foreign Direct Investment Inflows, in Country Groups ($ millions)

Group	1998	1999	2000	2001
TOTAL WORLD	694,457.3	1,088,263.0	1,491,934.0	735,145.7
Developed countries	484,239.0	837,760.7	1,227,476.0	503,144.0
Western Europe	274,738.8	507,221.7	832,067.4	336,210.0
North America	197,243.3	307,811.3	367,529.3	151,899.9
Least-developed countries	3,947.6	5,428.3	3,704.3	3,837.6
Developing countries	187,610.6	225,140.0	237,894.4	204,801.3
Africa	9,020.9	12,821.2	8,694.0	17,164.5
North Africa	2,788.1	4,896.3	2,903.7	5,323.4
Other Africa	6,232.8	7,924.9	5,790.3	11,841.1
Latin America and the Caribbean	82,203.3	109,310.8	95,405.4	85,372.6
South America	51,885.6	70,879.6	56,837.1	40,111.4
Other Latin America and Caribbean	30,317.7	38,431.2	38,568.4	45,261.2
Asia	96,386.5	103,008.0	133,795.0	102,264.2
Central and Eastern Europe	22,607.7	25,362.8	26,563.1	27,200.4
All developing countries minus China	143,859.6	184,821.0	197,122.4	157,955.3

Source: UNCTAD World Investment Report 2002 at *http://www.unctad.org/Templates/WebFlyer.asp? intItemID=2111&lang=1&print=1*

percent of the direct investment of the firms of one country in firms of other countries takes place among developed countries. But 27 percent represents direct investments of developed countries in companies located in developing countries. In 2001, for example, developing countries received direct investments of 204 billion dollars, of which 50 billion dollars went to China alone. With the possible exception of Hungary, the transition economies have had mixed results attracting FDI, although the latter years of the 1990s witnessed improvement.

Convergence of Incomes

When comparative economics focused primarily on the differences between capitalism and socialism, there was much discussion of the notion of **convergence**. Convergence was then construed as the process of socialist and capitalist economies becoming more alike, whether a socialist economy becoming more like a capitalist economy or vice versa. With the transition of the socialist planned economies to capitalist market economies, it is clear that this type of convergence is taking place. However, the nature of the convergence process has turned out to be very different from what was once expected.

Another way to look at convergence is as the lessening of income or earnings differentials among economies. In other words, instead of looking for a lessening of institutional differences among economies, we look instead for a lessening of differentials in outcomes.

The world economy has experienced periods of convergence and divergence. If we restrict our field of vision to the industrialized core of countries, we find that there was considerable convergence between the 1870s and the outbreak of World War I.[9] The interwar period was one of deconvergence. Income and wage differentials among countries increased as reversion to protectionism restricted the flow of labor and capital among countries. The postwar period has been one of convergence, as income differentials have diminished—not only among the industrialized core of countries but also between the industrialized core and Southeast Asia.

The sources of convergence have been identified by economic historians. Convergence occurs when labor and capital are free to move from country to country and when there is free trade in goods and services. The sources of convergence before World War I and then after World War II are therefore apparent. Both were periods of rapid expansion of trade and of the relatively free flow of labor and capital.

The postwar period has seen the creation of institutions that promote convergence. First GATT and then the **World Trade Organization** have worked through international negotiations to lower trade barriers among countries. There also has been a tendency to create regional free-trade zones, such as the **European Union** and the North American Free Trade Agreement. The ultimate stimulus for convergence among the European nations is the complete integration of the European Union countries into one economic zone with a common currency. Not only are the major European economies part of one common market; they are also scheduling the admission of new countries, such as Poland, Hungary, the Czech Republic, the Slovak Republic, Slovenia, the Baltic states, Bulgaria, and Romania. Once admitted to a common market we would expect further convergence in terms of institutions and income levels.

Resolving Economic Problems in the Twenty-First Century

We entered the twenty-first century with some economies performing well in terms of economic growth, employment, and inflation. The U.S. economy was said to be a "new economy" that would grow rapidly for the foreseeable future because it was tapping into the fruits of the vast scientific and technical revolutions associated with personal computers and new information technologies. Scientists and engineers cited Moore's Law, which predicted exponential advances in science and technology. These new innovations were said to overshadow past technological revolutions, such as the steam engine, the telephone, and the railroad. Faith in the "new economy" of the United States was somewhat dashed with the slowdown of growth at the start of 2001. Despite this cyclical setback, there is no reason to doubt that the U.S. economy is basically sound and will continue to perform as well in the future as it has in the past.

There is more skepticism concerning two other major economic regions—the European Union and Japan, both of which entered the twenty-first century with apparent economic weaknesses. Japan, so recently one of the world's most dynamic economies, was mired in almost a decade of economic stagnation. The European Union was plagued by slow growth and by high unemployment.

Growth or Eurosclerosis for Europe?

The European economies all have extensive safety nets that provide income and employment security as a part of a comprehensive welfare state. The role and size of the state, as measured by the state's share of resources and the state's intrusion into economic life, are great. There has been a tendency to protect vested interests from economic change, through subsidization and protective legislation. These societies have been stable for more than a half-century, so powerful vested-interest groups have formed, such as strong trade unions, craft groups, and employer organizations.

Mancur Olson, beginning with his study of the decline of Great Britain in the early part of the twentieth century, raised the question of whether the mature industrialized European economies would succumb to what he called Eurosclerosis.[10] If Eurosclerosis were allowed to proceed, European growth would stagnate over the long term as a consequence of paralysis imposed by special vested interests. Olson warned that in stable mature economies, distributional coalitions form that engage in monopoly rent seeking. Stable mature economies can therefore be dominated by monopolies, cartels, powerful labor unions, and the like, which are interested in maximizing their share of economic output at the expense of others.

Europe in the early twenty-first century bears a striking resemblance to Olson's Eurosclerotic states: Vested interests support the status quo of a heavy tax burden, the continuation of subsidies, the imposition of rigid work rules, and the perquisites of the welfare state. Vested interests continue to dominate industrial life, the old guard being awarded management of newly privatized enterprises. One of the most powerful interest groups—the employed—continue to demand rules that prevent them from becoming unemployed and keep their wages and benefits high, thereby reducing the flexibility of managers to restructure their businesses.

Figure 22.4 shows Europe's rising problem of unemployment. In the 1960s, the two major European economies—France and Germany—had equal or lower unemployment than the United States and the United Kingdom. For the period 1995–2002, France and Germany's unemployment rate has been double that of the United States and well above that of the United Kingdom. The major European economies, ranging from Scandinavia in the north to Spain and Italy in the south, are grappling for solutions to high unemployment. Figure 22.5 shows the decline in European growth rates after 1973. In the period 1950 to 1973, the major European countries outgrew the United States and the United Kingdom. After 1973, European growth declined to an average close to 2 percent, while the U.S. economy recorded average growth rates of 3 percent. Unless Europe is to fall further behind the United States, it must introduce policies that reduce unemployment and raise economic growth.

Can Europe's declining growth be reversed? The example of the United Kingdom under Thatcher was an attack on Eurosclerosis—at least an attack on trade union vested interests. Britain's recovery after 1979, therefore, was at least partially also the result of Thatcher's assault on high marginal tax rates, irresponsible monetary policy, and the power of trade unions.

A powerful force against Eurosclerosis may be Europe's decision, made in Maastricht in 1991, to reduce and even eliminate differences among national markets by making the entirety of Europe one common market with one common currency. Europe now has a single currency, the euro, and trade barriers have been eliminated, common monetary and fiscal policies have been enacted, and uniform policies of competition are supposed to be observed. Open access to national markets of enterprises from all member nations in air transport, telecommunications, and utilities is supposed to prevail.

With a single market, powerful forces should be set in motion to combat special interests within any particular nation. France and Germany will no longer be able to subsidize their state enterprises; inefficient companies from one country will not be able to survive competition with more efficient enterprises from other countries. Germany's and Italy's restrictive work rules will simply cause jobs to go to other European countries.

The European Union is still in its infancy. It is unclear how power will be shared between the member countries and the union, whether the nonelected European Commission made up of technocrats will be more powerful than the elected European Parliament, whether the European Union can agree on acceptable rules that treat large and small, new and old members fairly. The European Union still lacks a constitution, which will create either a "United States of Europe" or a looser federation of member countries. The proposed draft constitution, prepared by the former

FIGURE 22.4   Inflation and Unemployment in the United States and Europe,
1960–1970 and 1995–2000

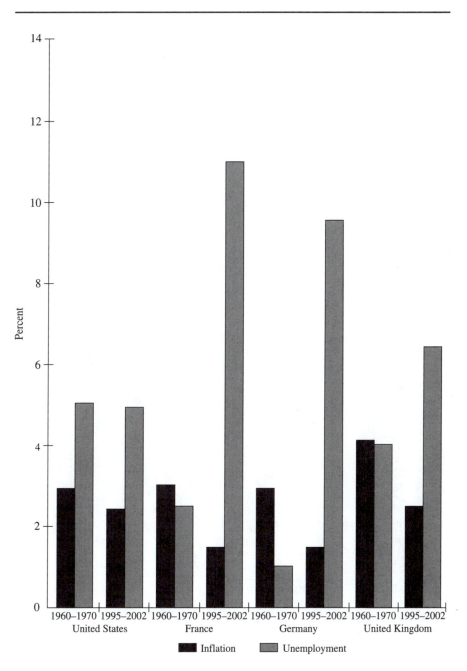

Source: Economic Report of the President (selected years) and OECD Standardized Unemployment Rates
(*www.oecd.org*).

FIGURE 22.5   Long-term Growth Rates in Europe Compared to the United States

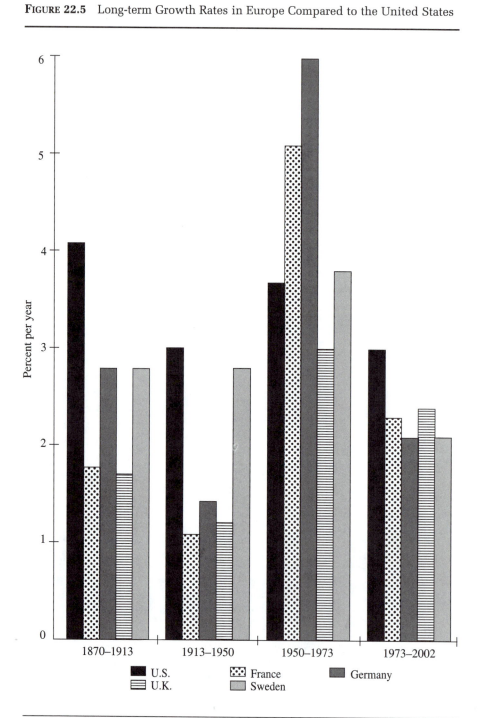

French prime minister Valéry Giscard d'Estaing, describes the EU as a "Union of European States" that closely coordinate their policies and administer certain common policies on a federal basis, while retaining their national identities.[11] The constitution must establish voting procedures, such as which measures must be approved by national parliaments and under which voting rules (majority rule or veto rights). Whether the European Commission will have the power to enforce common economic rules, such as harmonized tax regimes and fiscal policy rules, remains undecided. How, for example, will both France's and Germany's exceeding budget deficit limits established by the European Union's stabilization pact in 2003 be addressed. As new member states are admitted, the number of member countries will become so large that decision making will be quite complicated.

The European Union will have to confront the same issues that the United States and its fifty states have struggled with since ratification of the U.S. Constitution. This struggle will determine whether Europe becomes, in effect, a single state with common laws and economic policies or whether it remains as is—a loose federation of states that make their own policies.

The European Union was created for two reasons: First, the creation of a single market larger than that of the United States was expected to promote the growth of trade, capital flows, and overall economic growth. The exposure of domestic companies, even those that had been traditionally protected (such as the national telephone company and the national airline), to new competition was expected to improve their economic performance. Second, the founders of the European Union hoped to create, for companies in all member countries, a "level playing field" that would promote competitiveness and efficiency. This second outcome is far from guaranteed. The level playing field may become overrun by restrictive rules and regulations that enable the least competitive to survive. For example, if the restrictive work rules of Germany, France, and Italy are imposed on new entrants such as Poland and the Czech Republic, the EU as a whole will become less able to compete with the outside world. Similarly, if the European Commission makes economic decisions such as denying mergers that lower costs, the EU will become less competitive. And if it does not allow for experimentation among member countries, such as Ireland's current market liberalization reforms, the EU will become an ossified economic structure. Finally, the process of accession for the transition economies presents new problems as these economies depart from the command experience and attempt to pursue a market trajectory.

An End to the Asian Miracle?

The Four Asian Tigers recorded rates of growth more than double those of the industrialized world from 1970 to the present. It is this rapid growth over two decades that made the Four Tigers either "rich" countries or "future rich" countries. As Chapter 11 showed, the success of the Four Tigers spread to other parts of Southeast Asia (the ASEAN region—Association for Southeast Asian Nations)—to Malaysia, Thailand, and Indonesia and, to some extent, to the Philippines. These countries also began to achieve rapid growth by adopting some of the policies of the Four Tigers.

Perhaps more important, the Four Tigers themselves began to invest in the region. This investment was funded by the growing difference between domestic savings and domestic investment.

Never before has a region sustained economic growth in the neighborhood of 8 percent per annum for more than three decades, as have the economies of East Asia. The original Four Tigers—Hong Kong, South Korea, Singapore, and Taiwan—have joined the ranks of the developed countries in terms of per capita income. Hong Kong and Singapore are now richer than the United Kingdom. In the last two decades, the poorer countries of East Asia—Indonesia, Malaysia, and Thailand—have grown rapidly and have started to chase the leaders of East Asia, even though they started from a much lower level of income.

In 1996 and 1997, the growth of the ASEAN countries slowed; they logged export growth of only 5 percent per year. There were other signs of trouble: Malaysia, South Korea, and Thailand ran current-account deficits; South Korea was beset by labor unrest and political crisis. The Korean and Thai stock markets fell, and growth for the region slowed from 9 percent in 1995 to 7 percent in 1996. Growth slowed even more for the richest three tigers—to 5 percent for the year. The declining growth was ominous because international investors had invested in the region on account of its reputation for rapid growth.

During the second half of 1997, the Asian miracle appeared to collapse, beginning with Thailand and spreading to Indonesia, Malaysia, South Korea, and Japan. Although the reasons for collapse vary, a common thread appeared to be a loss of confidence in the currency, followed by drastic devaluations of the currency. In many cases, Asian countries had tied their own currency to the U.S. dollar. As they experienced higher inflation than the United States, their currencies became overvalued, prompting attacks on their currencies by speculators. As their currencies fell in value, these countries were unable to service their large external debts, and they had to petition their foreign creditors for debt relief. Given the magnitude of the debt problem, they had to negotiate with the International Monetary Fund for stand-by credits.

The currency collapse also exposed the weakness of the banking system, which had made too many real estate loans backed by office buildings and other real estates whose values had also collapsed. The collapse also revealed the extent of corruption, whereby low-interest loans had been granted to well-connected families and business groups.

Countries particularly hard-hit by the Asian Crisis were Thailand, Indonesia, and South Korea. Figure 22.6 illustrates the impact of the Asian crisis and its immediate aftermath. The poorer ASEAN countries, such as Thailand, Indonesia, and Malaysia, were hit the hardest. The figure shows that average growth for the period 1996 to 2002 remained low compared to earlier periods, although South Korea, Taiwan, and Singapore grew at almost 5 percent—a rapid rate by international standards.

It is clearly too early to determine whether the Four Tigers' economies can resume their exceptional growth. Analysts fall into two groups, the optimists and the pessimists, who debate the original sources of rapid growth in East Asia and hence its sustainability.[12] The pessimist case was advanced by Paul Krugman, who argued that East Asia's growth was achieved primarily through the rapid growth of the capital

FIGURE 22.6   The Impact of the Asian Crisis and Its Aftermath:
Growth Rates of GDP

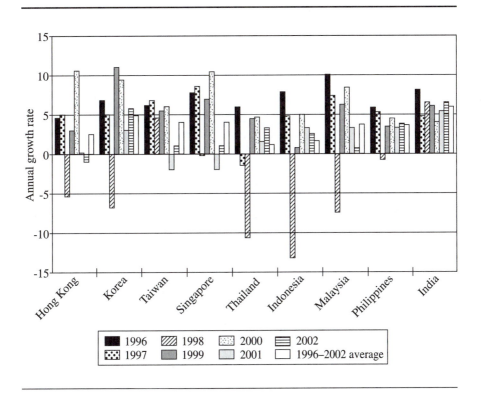

stock and through shifts in resources from agriculture to industry. Thus East Asian growth was similar to that of the Soviet Union: It was primarily extensive in nature. Although a rapid expansion in resources can lead to higher growth, as it did in the Soviet Union, such growth cannot be sustained, because a country cannot indefinitely expand its resources without exhausting the resource-generating ability of the population. According to Krugman, growth based on the expansion of inputs is self-limiting. His statistics suggest that very little of East Asia's growth has been based on the growth of the residual—the growth of total factor productivity.

Krugman based his conclusions on the empirical work of Alwyn Young, who analyzed the growth experiences of 118 countries from 1970 to 1985, splitting GDP growth into growth due to the expansion of inputs and growth due to the more productive use of these inputs.[13] Young found that the growth of total factor productivity was no higher in the East Asian countries than in the industrialized countries. Arnold Harberger, on the other hand, argues that the ASEAN countries experienced both high GDP growth and high factor productivity growth. The rates of growth of output per unit of labor and capital input ranged from a low of 2.2 percent per year

(Malaysia) to a high of 4.2 percent per year (Taiwan). Industrialized countries would be quite content to achieve even the lower rate.[14]

Whether the Asian countries of Southeast Asia resume their unprecedented growth or not will have a major impact on the shape of the first half of the twenty-first century. Although the Asian miracle took on different forms in different countries, it was fundamentally based on the notion of trade expansion and integration into the world economy. This formula permitted a few Asian countries to join the ranks of the affluent countries. If the Asian miracle continues, a larger number of countries will become relatively affluent: Thailand, Vietnam, Malaysia, Indonesia, and the Philippines. As affluent countries integrate into the world economy, they will be positive forces for political and economic stability. If they fail to resume their earlier growth, however, political instability will increase, and the citizenry will become disaffected and vulnerable to anti-Western messages. The relative political stability of Southeast Asia played a major role in attracting foreign capital to the region.[15] In the aftermath of the Asian crisis, political instability increased in Malaysia, Indonesia, and the Philippines, and the appeal of Muslim fundamentalism became stronger. Thus resumption of the Asian miracle and political stability in the region are intimately linked.[16]

Japan launched the Asian miracle with its rapid and accelerating growth in the late nineteenth and twentieth centuries. At the turn of the twenty-first century, Japan's per capita GDP was on a par with Western Europe's. Although the levels of affluence of the two island economies of Southeast Asia—Hong Kong and Singapore—also compare with those of Western Europe, the other rapidly growing Asian economies, such as South Korea and Taiwan, are still relatively poor, having about half of Japan's per capita income. The poorer ASEAN countries, such as Thailand, Malaysia, and Indonesia, log in at below 30 percent of Japan; they must undergo further decades of growth before they can approach Japan's level of affluence. Unlike its Asian neighbors, Japan has experienced virtually zero growth from 1990 to the present. Does Japan represent the eventual future of the Asian economy at large? Or can the other Asian economies continue to grow rapidly? In the 1970s and 1980s, Asian economists referred to a "flying geese" model of development, with the more affluent Asian economies, spearheaded by Japan, leading the way for the less affluent Asian economies. It was assumed that the follower Asian countries needed only to emulate what their more advanced neighbors had been doing a decade earlier. With the collapse of its growth, however, Japan is no longer able to be the leader in this "flying geese" model.

The debate over the causes of Japan's decade-long decline in growth has focused on Keynesian policies versus structural reform. Proponents of the Keynesian solution argued that growth would resume if the government and the central bank pursued expansionary policies. The Keynesian approach was tried, and Japan achieved exceptionally large budget deficits and zero interest rates, but growth did not resume. Structural reform remains in its infancy in Japan because it can be blocked easily by vested interests. The major structural change needed apparently is widespread reform of the banking system. As we noted in the Chapter 10, Japanese companies enjoy a close relationship with their lending banks, which usually participate in an interlocking directorate with their client customers. As the Japanese economy grew weak, the business assets that secured bank loans declined in value, and banks were left with trillions of dollars of bad loans. The long-term solution to this problem is to write off bad debts and refuse to make additional loans to ailing companies, forcing them into bankruptcy. However, massive bankruptcies would threaten the traditional Japanese system of guaranteed employment and bank support of failing companies. Despite the election of a reform-minded prime minister, the Japanese economy has yet to address its structural economic problems, primarily because of political inertia.

Figure 22.7 shows the ominous side of Japan's disappearing growth: Despite high rates of national savings and investment, which peaked in the late 1960s but have remained high ever since, Japan has achieved only slow growth. High rates of investment should produce growth, but in Japan's case they have not. The reasons include Japan's inefficient capital market, which is dominated by bank lending among related firms; the lack of bankruptcy; and simply diminishing returns to capital investment. It may be that countries cannot grow forever on the basis of extensive growth through capital formation. Inasmuch as the other Asian countries have based their growth on capital formation, Japan's experience may portend an ominous future for them.

FIGURE 22.7   National Savings and Gross Investment Rates in Japan, 1887–2000 (percent)

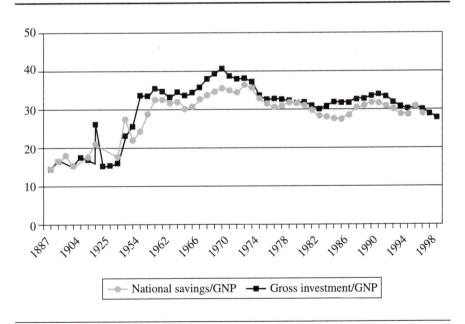

Sources: K. Ohkawa and M. Shinohara, eds., *Patterns of Japanese Economic Development: A Quantitative Appraisal* (New Haven: Yale University Press, 1979); Global Development Finance and World Development Indicators; IMF's International Financial Statistics.

China and India

China and India are home to some 40 percent of the world's population. As long as they remain poor, the world will remain poor also. Chapter 12 related the rapid growth that China has experienced since modernization reforms were introduced in 1979. Since then, China has been one of the world's fastest-growing economies and has attracted more foreign direct investment than any other developing country. The Chinese leadership chose to retain the monopoly of the Communist party as the sole source of political power in China, unlike Russia, which opted for democracy and discredited its Communist party. However, the Chinese Communist party has overseen the modernization reforms, and its commitment to reforms was reconfirmed with the changing of the party leadership determined in late 2002. China, like the other rapidly growing Asian economies, has based its growth on high rates of capital formation and an economy open to foreign trade and investment.

Figure 22.8 shows that despite China's rapid growth, it remains a very poor country with a per capita income of only $1,000. If it is to join the ranks of prosperous countries, it must continue to grow rapidly for decades. China's future growth will depend on its political stability, on its continued openness to trade and capital flows, and on its willingness to continue marketization reforms. To date, China's growth has been based on agricultural growth and on the formation of new businesses, which manufacture toys, electronic products, clothing, and other consumer

FIGURE 22.8   GDP per Capita for China and India ($US)

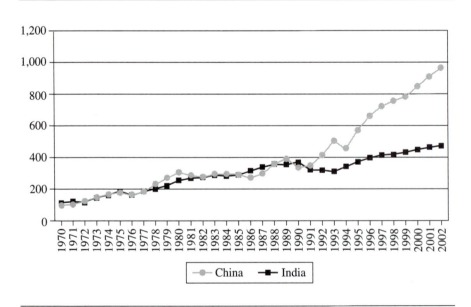

Source: IMF Database.

goods. The huge companies that produce China's heavy-industry goods remain largely owned by the state and are, by and large, unprofitable. They also account for a substantial portion of urban employment. China began the restructuring of the state-owned-enterprise sector rather late, and as this restructuring proceeds, many of these companies will go under and their employees will have to be let go. Whether China will be willing to tolerate the massive unemployment associated with the restructuring of large enterprises remains to be seen. Another major unknown is the future of the Communist party. Although its leadership recently agreed to admit entrepreneurs into the party, that body is still largely an organization of professional party officials. If it remains aloof, the party will increasingly grow out of touch with the business community, which eventually will become a powerful political lobby. The potential clash between party and business interests, therefore, could threaten the party's monopoly position, and the outcome could be repression, political democracy, or a growing democratization of the party itself.

Figure 22.8 shows that India also remains a very poor country. Its per capita income was essentially equal to that of China through the 1980s, but in the 1990s China's growth soared, and its level of affluence roughly doubled that of India.

India is the world's largest democracy. Its government is patterned on the English parliamentary system, and over the years Indian politics has been dominated by the Congress party. India comprises a multiplicity of ethnic groups, who speak different languages, and has suffered over the years from ethnic and regional strife. Indeed, this strife remains important in the twenty-first century, such as the continuing conflict between India and Pakistan over Kashmir. The Indian economy prior to independence from Britain in 1947 was a traditional society with a long history of colonial domination.[17] Prior to British rule, the Indian **moghul economy** (so called because a Muslim minority was the ruling elite) operated according to long-standing traditional rules. Society was divided into castes. Place in society and occupation were determined at birth.

Economic progress under the moghul economy was limited. Population did not increase for two thousand years. In the sixteenth century, per capita income in India was on a par with that of Western Europe, and contemporary European visitors even felt that average living standards were higher in India than at home. By the time of British rule, however, per capita income in India was very low compared with that of Western Europe. The reasons for India's declining economic position were the rigid caste system, religious restrictions, uncertain property rights, barriers against productive investment and civil strife.

The modern Indian economy was the creation of the Congress party and its leaders, Mahatma Gandhi and Jawaharlal Nehru, who referred to India as a socialist economy. Gandhi extolled the traditional village community, whereas Nehru favored industrialization and emphasized heavy industry. After independence, only limited progress was made in land reform. Land remained unequally distributed.[18] Rather than seeking to achieve "socialist" objectives through income redistribution, the architects of the Indian economy emphasized state ownership in industry. State promotion of heavy industry was to lead to economic development. In the early postwar period, the Indians adopted one basic feature of the Soviet development model: the priority of heavy industry over light industry and agriculture. The creation of a domestic heavy-industry base would lead to more rapid development, would promote domestic savings, and would make India less dependent on the outside world.[19] Steel, heavy machinery, chemicals, power, fuel, communication, transportation, and life insurance were nationalized in the early 1950s. In the 1970s the state moved to enlarge the public sector by nationalizing the large banks, the copper industry, the wholesale grain and jute trade, and a number of coal mines and textile mills. Nationalization was usually accomplished by compensation of previous owners (rather than expropriation), and an increasing "Indianization" of industry ownership evolved as foreign owners were displaced.

Governmental controls over resource allocation were extensive in India.[20] In addition to planning, a whole range of extramarket controls were utilized. The rationale was the widespread belief that the free market cannot be trusted. The Industries Act of 1951 gave the government authority to grant licenses for expanding capacity and to control the allocation and prices of raw materials and, in some instances, the prices of finished products. The prices of basic agricultural products were controlled according to a complex zonal pricing system. The state also regulated foreign exchange and imports. Imported capital equipment was regulated by industrial licensing. In order to justify an import, the domestic user had to demonstrate that the commodity was essential and that it could not be purchased at home.[21]

India began introducing serious reforms in 1991 and achieved an average annual growth rate of 6 percent between 1992 and 2002. India had experimented with reforms in the 1980s, but these reform efforts were not sustained. The Indian reforms focused on dismantling the extensive system of industrial policies and controls practiced by the central and state governments, reducing federal government deficits, reducing trade barriers, and limiting state controls on the capital market, such as interest-rate controls and government approval of large bank loans. In the late 1990s, the Indian government embarked on a privatization program designed to sell off key government-owned businesses to private buyers.[22] Probably the most effective part of India's reform program was its elimination of intrusive state controls and rules that reduced economic efficiency. Industries that had previously been reserved for the public sector—including iron and steel, telecommunications, oil, mining, and transportation services—were opened to private owners. Surprisingly, the policy of reserving certain items for the small-scale sector has been preserved, which has meant that larger companies cannot manufacture, for example, toys. These liberalization policies at the federal level must be accompanied by liberalization at the state level as well, because state governments can require licenses. To date, there has been considerable variation among state governments in licensing procedures. Prior to its reforms, India had high protective tariffs. In 1991 the average import duty was 73 percent. By 2002 the average duty had dropped to 29 percent, a rate that is still high by international standards. These high import duties have impeded Indian industrial growth because they raise the costs of production.

India, like other Asian countries, has a high savings and investment rate. Private-sector savings equaled 25 percent of GDP in 2002, slightly up from 22 percent in 1991. The major change has been the increased share of the private sector in investment at the expense of public-sector investment. Whereas private-sector investment accounted for 60 percent of the total in 1991, it made up 72 percent in 2002.

India's growth prospects over the next few decades will depend on the continuation of reforms. India is still a relatively closed economy and stands to benefit from greater opening up. India has just begun to attract foreign direct investment. If India could attract foreign direct investment on the magnitude of China, its growth would be considerable. Unlike China, whose political future is in doubt, India is a long-standing democracy.

Corruption and Dictatorship

A large number of economies either do not grow or experience negative growth, especially on a per capita basis. Of the approximately 120 countries for which per capita real GDP growth records are available, some 35 countries experienced negative growth of per capita income either in one or both decades from 1980 to the present.[23] These countries are primarily located in Africa and Latin America; some, such as Nigeria and Argentina, possess rich natural resources. Such failure to grow over extended periods is usually a product of corruption. Corruption stifles economic growth when ruling groups engage in such pervasive rent seeking that resources are diverted from productive uses. Although democratic societies are not immune to corruption, dictatorships are more fertile ground for corruption in that dictators either appropriate the economic rents for themselves and their immediate families or award such rents to politically loyal patrons. Some dictators, such as Robert Mugawe in Zimbabwe, sacrificed the property rights of white land owners (and hence ensured the destruction of Zimbabwe agriculture) to retain political power.

Transition in a New Century

The transition experience of the 1990s has received a great deal of attention as the command systems have been replaced by market economic systems. Perhaps more striking is the fact that much of the transition experience has been "learning by doing," although many of the components of the transition experience, such as privatization, have also been components of change in Western economies, both industrialized and developing. A major result has been a significant growth of interest in differing economic systems as a critical component of neoclassical economics—an integration that for the most part did not occur during the command era. Can we generalize about the results of transition and the prospects for the transition economies in a new century?

As we have emphasized, there is now a large body of both theoretical and empirical literature pertaining to the transition experience. The decade of the 1990s clearly demonstrated that the declining output of earlier years could be reversed and significant positive economic growth achieved. At the same time, general indicators of economic performance can be deceptive, as those living in the transition economies would testify. There have been significant differences in performance among the transition economies, and results have generally been better in Eastern Europe than among the countries that emerged from the former Soviet Union. In many cases, the social contract has changed significantly, and the pressure of inequality, unemployment, and poverty places a strain on the emerging democratic political systems.

As our knowledge of transition economies has increased, our approach to assessing these emerging systems has changed, promising a better understanding, but in a much more complex setting. Financial markets are often shallow and nontransparent, functioning in combination with a significant shadow economy. These characteristics make the interpretation of macroeconomic indicators difficult. Privatization no longer simply entails implementation and outcomes but also involves changes in corporate governance, which are much more difficult to assess in the transition setting than in Western market economies. The impact of privatization on efficiency has attracted much more attention than equity issues.

Do the successes of transition imply that transition is over? The question is important and the evidence mixed. Clearly, there are cases where one could argue that transition has been substantially completed. The Czech economy, for instance, is a small, open, relatively developed economy. But transition has barely started in Belarus and has been a very mixed experience, at best, in Ukraine. Comparison in terms of almost any basic performance indicator suggests marked differences among the transition economies. How should we judge whether transition is over?

A more fundamental approach might be to examine the extent to which the new systemic arrangements and policies of the transition era have eradicated the features of the command era, whether these features are structural (sector shares, for example) or pertain to patterns of economic growth. Although much remains to be done in this sphere, the early empirical evidence seems to suggest that many of the transition economies have retained elements of the past and that their growth paths have yet to conform to those of market economic systems.

The transition era of the 1990s was remarkable. What we have learned about economic systems by studying this era, and what we will learn in the future, promise to provide a major new foundation for our understanding of economic growth and development, not just in a transition setting but from a much broader perspective as well.

Summary

- There have been major changes in the economic fortunes of the world's regions. In the past half-century, the economic fortunes of Japan and the former Soviet empire have declined, while Southeast Asia has grown rapidly. In the past two decades, the United States has outperformed Europe.
- There have been several "golden ages of growth" such as the early postwar period and the period of the 1990s in the United States.
- As the world economy becomes more integrated, we expect convergence of per capita income. New entrants into common markets, such as the relatively poor countries that are entering the European Union, should experience rising income relative to the more affluent European countries.

- Europe's and Japan's stagnations have been explained by the notion of Eurosclerosis, caused by t`he growing domination of interest groups. The European Union was intended to break this Eurosclerosis.
- The world economy's prospects over the next few decades will depend upon a resumption of the Asian miracle and the continued growth of the world's two most populous countries, China and India.

Key Terms

golden age of growth   Eurosclerosis
convergence   moghul economy
World Trade Organization   corruption
European Union

Notes

1. Angus Maddison, *Explaining the Economic Performance of Nations* (Cambridge: Cambridge University Press, 1995); *Economic Growth in the West* (London: George Allen & Unwin, 1964).
2. Central Intelligence Agency, *Handbook of International Economic Statistics,* 1996 (Washington, D.C.: CIA, 1996), Figure 4.
3. "Lure of the Latin Model," *Financial Times,* April 9, 1997; *Financial Times Survey, Latin America,* March 14, 1997.
4. Union Bank of Switzerland, *Global Economic Outlook,* First Quarter 1997, p. 41.
5. L. A. Nefiodow, *Der Sechste Kondratieff* (Frankfurt: Rhein-Sieg Verlag, 1996).
6. "Global Growth Attains a New, Higher Level That Could Be Lasting," *Wall Street Journal,* March 13, 1997.
7. *Ibid.*
8. *Ibid.*
9. Jeffrey Williamson, "Globalization, Convergence, and History," *Journal of Economic History* 56, 2 (June 1996), 277–305.
10. Mancur Olson, *Rise and Decline of Nations* (New Haven: Yale University Press, 1982).
11. "Skeleton Gives Bare Bones of the Future EU Constitution," *Financial Times,* October 29, 2002.
12. "The Asian Miracle: Is It Over?" *The Economist,* March 1, 1997, 23–25; Paul Krugman, "The Myth of the Asian Miracle," *Foreign Affairs* 73, 6; "The Asian Miracle," *UBS International Finance* 29 (1996); IMF Conference, "Growth and Productivity in the ASEAN Economies," Jakarta, Indonesia, November 1996.
13. Alwyn Young, "The Tyranny of Numbers: Confronting the Statistical Realities of the East Asian Growth Experience," *Quarterly Journal of Economics* 110, 3 (August 1995), 64–68.
14. Arnold Harberger, "Evaluating Development Experiences in Latin America and East Asia," Third Senior Policy Forum, East–West Center, Honolulu, May 1997.
15. Seiji Naya, *The Asian Development Experience: Overcoming Crises and Adjusting to Change* (Hong Kong: Asian Development Bank, 2002), Ch. 1.

16. For a survey of the aftermath of the Asian crisis, see *Journal of Asian Economics* 13 (2002), 573–575.

17. This historical overview is from Angus Maddison, *Class Structure and Economic Growth: India and Pakistan Since the Moghuls* (New York: Norton, 1971), Chs. 2–4.

18. Raj Krishna and G. S. Raychaudhuri, "Trends in Rural Savings and Capital Formation in India, 1950–1951 to 1973–1974," *Economic Development and Cultural Change* 30 (January 1982), 289–294.

19. For a discussion of the Indian controversy over planning priorities, see Jagdish Bhagwati and Sukhamoy Chakravaty, "Contributions to Indian Economic Analysis: A Survey," *American Economic Growth* 59 (September 1969), 4–29; and V. V. Bhatt, "Development Problem, Strategy, and Technology of Choice: Sarvadaya and Socialist Approaches in India," *Economic Development and Cultural Change* 21 (October 1982), 85–100.

20. This discussion is based on Maddison, *Class Structure and Economic Growth,* pp. 120–125.

21. Bhagwati and Chakravaty, "Contributions to Indian Economic Analysis," pp. 60–66.

22. This section is based on Montek Ahluwalia, "Economic Reforms in India Since 1991: Has Gradualism Worked?" *Journal of Economic Perspectives* 16, 2 (Summer 2002), 67–88.

23. World Bank, *World Development Report,* selected years.

Glossary

accession Process through which states become members of the European Union.

administrative command economy Economic system that involves minimal use of markets for resource allocation. Such a system operated in the former Soviet Union.

adverse selection The concealing of information from principals by agents.

adjusted factor cost concept Method of adjusting output series from the planned socialist systems to account for difficulties such as the non-scarcity-based prices used in those systems.

agency-managerial problems Conflicts between organizational objectives and the personal self-interest of a principal in the organization. Also called principal agent problem.

agent Party that acts as a representative of a principal.

allocative efficiency Effectiveness with which resources are used across sectors—for example, capital used in industry versus agriculture.

Anglo-Saxon model Model patterned after the classic liberal ideas of Adam Smith, with historical origins in Great Britain.

Asian model Model based on family-owned conglomerates and low welfare spending. Focuses on high rates of capital formation.

asset stripping Removing valuable assets from an organization without making appropriate payment for those assets.

Austrian School Ludwig Mises and Frederick Hayek argued that the planning task in a planned socialist economy is too complex and that decentralized decisionmaking is an inefficient means of allocating resources in the absence of private-property rights.

balance of the national economy Forerunner of Leontief's input-output analysis.

barter Exchange of goods and services between two parties when money is not involved as an intermediary.

"big push" Early approach to transition that involves moving quickly to eliminate the old order and to replace it with new organizational and policy arrangements—specifically, markets.

Bolshevik Revolution Political and social upheaval through which state ownership, national economic planning and collectivism in agriculture became the dominate economic themes after 1917 in the Soviet Union.

bounded rationality Guidelines or rules established to enhance decisionmaking in situations where there is a lack of perfect information.

calendar time Examination of transition dated from a general starting point, for example 1989.

capital account Borrowing and lending among nations, and the sale and purchase of assets among nations.

capital account convertibility Exists when a currency can be purchased and sold in a market for the purpose of engaging in transactions pertaining to assets.

capitalism Economic system characterized by private ownership of the factors of production.

capitalist breakdown Conditions such as overproduction, underconsumption, and the exploitation of workers that, according to Marx, induce violent overthrow of capitalism.

capital market   Market for trading long-term securities (stocks and bonds) where a company raises capital.

capital productivity   Output per unit of capital input.

Central European Free Trade Area (CEFTA)   Free trade area (common market) formed in 1992 by Poland, Hungary, and Czechoslovakia.

centralized organizations   Organization in which decisions are made by upper management.

closed economy   Economy wherein trade barriers are high and trade does not flow freely.

coefficient of relative effectiveness   Soviet approach to comparing investment projects.

command economy   Economic system in which a principal (planner) develops economic plans and disseminates commands to agents (enterprise managers) absent markets and the use of prices and related money variables are not used to regulate the economy.

Commonwealth of Independent States (CIS)   Organization that comprises those states emerging from the former Soviet Union except the Baltic states of Latvia, Lithuania and Estonia.

comparative economic systems   Study of economic systems and their impact on resource allocation in various institutional, geographic, and political settings.

contract   Document spelling out the terms and conditions of an agreement between two (contracting) parties. For example, a state government may enter into a contract with a private company to provide a particular service to the population.

convergence   The idea, important in the comparison of economic systems, that differing economic systems will become more similar over time because of the fundamental imperatives of economic growth and economic development.

convertible currency   Currency for which there is a market (supply and demand), and thus a market-determined rate of exchange, available to participants within and beyond the borders of a country.

cooperative economy   Variation of market socialism that emphasizes worker participation in the decisionmaking that affects their well-being. Also called labor-managed economy or producer cooperative.

consumer sovereignty   Prevails when the decision of what to produce is driven by consumers.

corporate governance   Internal decision making arrangements in a corporation. Changes are often called restructuring.

corporate raiders   Individuals or institutions with substantial funds who engage in hostile takeovers of corporations that are underperforming.

corporation   Enterprise set up as a legal entity owned by the shareowners.

corporatized firms   State-owned enterprises where the state maintains majority ownership but management is independent.

corruption   The extraction of economic rents granted by government by opportunistic agents.

Council for Mutual Economic Assistance (CMEA)   Trade bloc established by the former administrative command economies in 1949 to promote integration of the command economies through coordinated national economic planning and trade. Abolished in 1989.

counterfactual information   Indication of what would have happened in the absence of a particular event.

creative destruction   Schumpeter's process of innovation whereby companies develop new products and new production techniques.

cross section   Sample that is taken at a particular point in time and differs in one or more features from samples taken at other times.

customs union   One of a variety of forms of economic integration that involves the elimination of trade barriers among member countries and the imposition of a common external tariff on nonmember countries.

current account   Imports and exports of goods and services, along with income generated from investments and transfers.

current-account convertibility   Exists when a currency can be purchased and sold in a market for the purpose of engaging in transactions pertaining to the current account.

decentralized organization   Organization in which decisions are made at low levels of the organization.

decision-making levels   Vertical hierarchical approach used in the Soviet economic system.

de novo privatization   Privatization that occurs through the introduction of new (usually small) firms, possibly in the service sector, where entry constraints are limited and capital requirements are modest.

dictators   Group or individual making key political decisions in a nondemocratic society.

direct sale   Privatization in which the owner of an enterprise (such as the state or state privatization agency) sells the enterprise directly to a new owner.

distortion   The concept that initial conditions created by the command experience differ from conditions that would have resulted from market arrangements. Thus market outcomes are argued as being "normal" in the sense that under transition, markets will emerge and change the allocation of resources.

dynamic efficiency   Ability of an economic system to enhance its capacity to produce goods and services over time without an increase in capital and labor inputs.

economic growth   Increase in, for example, national output over time; a dominant indicator for measuring economic achievement in a national economy.

economic institutions   Manner in which economic activities are organized.

economic levers   Prices, costs, and profits in a decentralized system.

economic system   Hierarchial structure and internal rules that govern the allocation of resources in a national (country) setting.

efficiency   Cost-effectiveness with which an economic system uses its resources at a point in time (static efficiency) or through time (dynamic efficiency).

efficiency of market allocation   May be achieved in markets characterized by a large number of buyers and sellers competing in a market, along with information efficiency.

emerging market economies   Countries that are actively pursuing economic growth and development through strengthening market forces but not via the route of transition.

endogenous variables   Variables on the left-hand side of the regression equation, the values of which are determined by solving the model, in an effort to understand the impact of variables on the right-hand side.

enterprise (technical) efficiency   Output per unit of input in an enterprise.

equilibrium   Equality of quantity demanded and quantity supplied.

equity   Fairness, though what is considered to be fair can vary from one issue and setting to another. An example is rewards to individuals commensurate with their contribution.

European model   Model based on economic principles developed in Germany and France in the nineteenth century that place less emphasis on the invisible hand and more emphasis on state intervention in the economy.

European Union (EU)   Group of European nations making up a single economic community.

Eurosclerosis   Term coined by Mancur Olson to describe the reasons for the stagnation of Europe in the past two decades.

exogenous variables   Variables on the right-hand side of a regression equation, the values of which are determined outside the model.

extensive growth   Growth of output generally achieved by expanding the use of inputs such as labor and capital.

external balance   When the demand for an supply of foreign exchange is equalized—in other words, the market for foreign exchange is in equilibrium.

external effects   Effects that the actions of one consumer or producer have on the cost or utility of other producers or consumers. Negative effects such as pollution are external diseconomies, whereas positive effects are external economies.

flexible labor market   Labor market wherein wage rates and employment can be varied in the short run.

foreign direct investment (FDI)   Investment flows from one country to another that occur directly—for example, through the construction of plant and equipment by a donor country in a host country, rather than through financial instruments such as stocks.

final demand   Output that is used for final consumption.

fiscal policy   Use of government spending and taxation in an effort to achieve macroeconomic goals.

full employment policy   In command economies, the existence of a "job right constraint" in enterprises in command economies such that full employment could exist even if unnecessary labor was sustained in an enterprise with low productivity.

funded commodities   In the Soviet economic system, major commodities such as steel and machinery that are centrally allocated. Also called limited commodities.

"Gang of Four"   Representatives of the revolutionary left in China who espoused continued use of the Stalinist model of industrialization.

General Agreement on Tariffs and Trade (GATT)   Predecessor to the World Trade Organization, established as a framework for world trade policy discussions and negotiations.

Gini coefficient   Standard measure of income inequality that usually expresses the gap between low-income earners (say, the bottom 10 percent of earners) and high-income earners (say, the top 10 percent of earners).

golden age   Periods of extended and rapid economic growth such as the rapid world growth after World War II.

golden parachute   Generous severance bonuses awarded to certain top executives if the company is taken over by a new management team.

gosplan   Soviet state planning agency which converted directives into operative plans.

gradualist approach   Approach to transition based on encouraging the slow and sequential emergence of new institutions, paying special attention to timing and complementarities.

Great Leap Forward   China, 1958–1960, An ideaology, launched by Mao, which replaced rationality. Emphasis was placed on communes and small scale enterprises

growth convergence   The concept that the growth patterns of transition and nontransition economies should become increasingly similar over time.

hard budget constraint   Principle whereby, under capitalism, firms must cover costs and earn an acceptable rate of return to remain in business.

hierarchy   Principle of vertical organization based on the establishment of objectives by principals and the completion of assigned tasks by agents (subordinates).

horizontal transaction   transaction among subordinates at the same level of the administrative structure without the approval of administrative superiors.

Hundred Flowers Campaign   In China, a relatively liberal period of open discussion of the economic and political system. (1956–1975)

implicit contracts   Unwritten rules of hiring and layoffs, among other things.

income distribution   Manner in which income generated in an economy is divided among the participants (population); often analyzed in terms of groups of the population and the share of income, from high to low, that each group receives.

Industrial Revolution   Nineteenth century period of vigorous economic growth in Europe and North America, which began in England.

indicative planning   Economic system in which, although the market is the primary means of resource allocation, a plan is devised to guide decisions.

industrial policy   Role of the state in promoting, subsidizing, and managing economic growth.

initial conditions   Conditions prevailing at the beginning of transition—for example, structural imbalances (such as the inappropriately large share of heavy industry) existing in former command economies and subject to change as market forces and institutions emerge.

initial public offering   Issuance of stocks or bonds for sale in a primary market.

insider privatization   Privatization in which the new owners are those participating within the organization, such as employees or managers.

insider trading   Illegal trading by managers, board members, or other parties on the basis of information not available to public shareowners.

intensive growth   Growth of output generally achieved by the improved use of available inputs such as labor and capital.

interindustry demand   Exists when the output of one industry is used as an input into another.

intermediate inputs   non-primary inputs such as iron or fuel used to produce other goods.

internal balance   Equilibrium of the domestic economy, usually characterized by full employment of resources and absence of inflation.

International Monetary Fund (IMF)   World organization helping member nations to manage international financial transactions.

invisible hand   Adam Smith's theory that individuals acting in their own self-interest would behave in a socially responsible manner in competitive markets.

job right constraint   Policy, prevalent in command economies, in which full employment would in effect be guaranteed through limitations on the firing of unneeded workers and the provision of budgetary funds to sustain unneeded workers.

Keynesian revolution   Keynesian notion that government activism was necessary to stabilize capitalist economies.

labor day   Soviet measure of work input on an arbitrary basis in collective farms.

labor income   Income generated by labor.

labor productivity   Output per unit of labor input.

labor union   Organization of workers in a company that forms for the purpose of negotiating for better wages, hours, and working conditions. Also called trade unions.

Lange model   Variation on market socialism wherein markets are employed only indirectly.

leveraged   Said of a company with a heavy debt burden that requires interest and principal payments.

liberalization   Replacement of command elements of an economic system by decentralized market -type elements through privatization and reduction of government intervention.

managerial capitalism   System of corporate governance that puts the interests of the stakeholders above those of the shareowners.

managerial success indicator problem   Soviet managers' efforts to fulfill a plan were often assessed by a series of vague or contradictory indicators.

marginal productivity theory of income distribution   Private owners of resources and factors of production are paid the marginal revenue product of their factors.

market-based contracting   Informal means of contracting based on formal contracts under the rule of law.

market capitalization   Product of the number of outstanding shares of a company and the price per share of the stock.

market economy   Economy in which fundamentals of supply and demand provide signals regarding resource utilization.

market for corporate control   Setting wherein rival management reams have the opportunity to buy control of a corporation from its owners.

market power   In product markets, the concentration ratio, or percentage of industry sales accounted for by the largest four, eight, or twenty firms.

market socialism   Economic system characterized by public ownership of the factors of production. Decisions are decentralized.

Marxist–Leninist framework   Framework developed by Karl Marx and elaborated by Vladimir Lenin for the dynamics of socioeconomic change.

Marx's theory of capitalism   Theory that economic forces determine how production, markets, and society are organized.

mass privatization   Privatization in which the goal is privatization of a large number of properties rather than the selective sale of state assets in an existing market setting.

material balances   Planning system used in planned socialist economies to balance aggregate demand and supply for industrial commodities.

material incentives   Incentives that promote desirable behavior by giving the recipient greater claims over goods.

mercantilism   View that a strong state is necessary to regulate and control the economy in order to enhance the political and economic strength of a country relative to other countries.

merger   One company's acquisition of another via exchange of stock, purchase, borrowing, or corporate debt.

ministries   Soviet hierarchical organized developed by production type (such as steel).

Ministry of Foreign Trade   Soviet ministry concerned with planning foreign trade.

moghul economy   The traditional caste-bound economic system that prevailed in India prior to British colonial rule.

monetary overhang   In the command economies, states "printing money" to finance hidden budget deficits, thus placing large sums of money in the hands of the population, in the absence of consumer goods that might be purchased with these monies.

monetary union   One of a variety of forms of economic integration in which member countries agree to use a common currency.

monopoly   Single producer (firm) in a given market.

moral hazard   Occurs when a lower-level unit uses an information advantage against an upper-level unit.

moral incentives   Incentives that promote desirable behavior by appealing to the recipient's responsibility to society (or to the company).

multinational enterprises   Firms that function in two or more different countries.

nationalization   Acquisition of private property is acquired by the state.

New Economic Policy (NEP)   Partial return to private ownership, introduced in the Soviet Union in 1921.

newly independent states (NIS)   States (countries) emerging from the former Soviet Union; these states are sometimes known in Russia as the "near abroad."

nomenklatura appointments   Soviet system of appointing party members to all responsible managerial positions.

nonmonetary sector   Exchange arrangements that lie outside the traditional price/money channels——for example, barter, wherein one good or service is exchanged for another good or service.

nonperforming loans (NPLs)   Bank loans that are not being serviced with interest and principal payments.

nonpublic information   Information from enterprise planning ministries about production shortfalls and material shortages.

objectives   Goals established by an organization.

objective function   Mathematical formula that summarizes the planner's economic objectives in a precise relationship.

open economy   Economy where trade barriers, such as tariffs, are low.

organizations   Firms organized to conduct business, as well as churches, charitable bodies, governmental agencies, and clubs.

opportunistic behavior   A lower-level unit's use of its information advantage against the interests of superiors.

optimality   Selection of the best plan of all consistent plans with which it would be possible to achieve a balance of supplies and demands.

partnership   Business owned by two or more partners, who make all decisions and receive all profits (losses).

perestroika   Failed effort, under Gorbachev, to restructure and reform the Soviet economy.

plan   Set of objectives and the means to achieve the objectives.

planned economy   Economy in which instructions are formulated by a planning board and disseminated through a planning directive.

planned socialism   Economic system characterized by public ownership of the factors of production. Decisions are centralized.

planners' preferences   Prevail when the decision of what to produce is made by planners.

policy   Factor that can be changed without changing the underlying economic system.

policy activism   Discretionary use of fiscal policy and monetary policy in an effort to limit the volatility of the business cycle.

policy measures   Directives, usually promulgated in the political sphere, that guide and influence decision makers in the economy.

portfolio investment   Investment flows from one country to another that occur through the purchase of financial instruments such as stocks and bonds rather than as foreign direct investment (FDI).

poverty deficit   Amount of funding that would be necessary to raise all those below an established poverty line up to that line.

present value   Present worth of a series of future returns that will be generated through time; often used to assess the value or price of an enterprise during privatization.

primary inputs   Land, labor, and capital.

primary market   Market for new offerings of stock or bonds (initial public offerings).

primitive capitalist accumulation   According to Marx, initial accumulation of capital by an emerging capitalist class.

principal   Individual with controlling authority.

privatization   Shift of economic activity from the public sector to the private sector.

production relations   Arrangement for producing goods and services.

progressive tax   Tax that has the effect of redistributing income from high-income earners to lower-income earners.

production team   In China, numerous households within a village.

property ownership   The three forms of property ownership are private, public, and collective (cooperative).

property rights   Ownership of assets that conveys the right to either use or dispose of those assets.

public choice   The public making political decisions on taxation and government spending. Public-choice theorists believe that public choices in a democratic society cannot be made efficiently.

public goods   Government-produced goods and services such as national defense, police protection, and fire protection.

pure democracy   System wherein every public choice is based on majority vote.

rational expectations theory   Theory that activist policy will have the desired effect only if it catches people off guard.

reform   Effort to improve an economic system without changing its fundamental character.

regressive tax   Tax that has the effect of redistributing income from low-income earners to high-income earners.

regulation   Agency or legislative effort to ensure that monopolies produce efficiently.

relational contracting   Contracting based on personal relationships and trust rather than on the rule of law.

relative backwardness   A country's gross underutilization of its potential.

representative democracy   Political system wherein voters elect representatives to make public choices on their behalf.

representative economic system   Concept that one can isolate a single economic system that accurately represents a broader system category—for example, taking the Soviet Union as representative of planned socialist economic systems.

repressed inflation   Soviet imbalance in aggregate supply and aggregate demand.

resource base   The resources, broadly defined, available in a given national (country) setting— for example, natural resources (timber, oil, etc) and human resources (levels of education).

resource managers   Individuals who allocated resources in the Soviet Union.

restitution   Return, of property rights that had been confiscated by the state.

restructructuring   Changing decision-making arrangements (corporate governance) and rules in organizations such that there is an improvement in efficiency.

reversibility   Concept that privatization, if deemed unworkable, might be reversed and state ownership reinstated.

ruble control   Soviet assumption that all physical transactions must have a parallel financial transaction.

Rural Peoples Commune   In China, bodies set up to combine collectives in order to produce agricultural and other goods and to serve as local governments.

safety net   Policies to sustain some minimum standard of living for the population. Examples include unemployment insurance programs, pensions for the elderly.

Say's law   Notion that there can be no lasting deficiency of aggregate demand because producing a given level of output also produces an equivalent level of income, which must be either spent or saved.

scatter diagram   Diagram which plots two or more variables taken from the same point in time for different countries to show the relationships between the two variables.

second economy   Soviet market based activities which allowed unplanned exchanges among producers and consumers.

sectors   Those that produce outputs and those that use final output.

self-interest   Maximization of some utility function subject to the constraints of human limitations.

shadow economy   That part of an economy that is often outside official channels and is generally conducted in nonmonetary terms but not necessarily in violation of laws.

shareowner value   Stock market value of a corporation as measured by market capitalization.

social contract   Implicit agreement between a government and its citizens characterizing the responsibilities of each.

socialist controversy   Issue of whether planners can make rational decisions about the use of scarce resources.

social policies   A broad concept referring to policies adopted for sustaining the well being of society, for example income maintenance programs, unemployment benefits and the like.

soft budget constraint   Soviet process whereby enterprises that failed to cover their costs receive subsidies from ministries or government.

sole proprietorship   Enterprise with a single owner who makes all decisions and absorbs all profits (losses) of the business.

specification   Form taken by a model that relates a result (for example, economic growth) to a series of variables (for example, initial conditions) thought to explain the observed growth pattern.

stability   Absence of significant fluctuations in economic growth rates.

stabilization   During the early years of transition, arresting the decline of the economies rather than focusing longer-term issues such as economic growth.

stakeholders   All who participate in the operation of a corporation as employees, managers, workers, customers, or suppliers.

state farms (sovkhozy)   Soviet farms in which the farmers were paid like industrial workers.

state intervention   Government regulation of resource allocation, required because of monopoly, externalities, and other problems, according to critics of the harmonious model of capitalism.

state-owned enterprises (SOEs)   Enterprises owned by the state in the command and subsequent transition economies. Many are large enterprises that have been difficult to privatize.

state privatization agency   Agency established in a command economy to manage the process of privatization by identifying properties and preparing them for sale.

static efficiency   Effectiveness with which a system uses its available resources at a particular time.

sterilization   Policy designed to prevent the loss of foreign exchange reserves from affecting the domestic money stock.

stock option   Right granted executives of a company to buy a certain number of shares of stock in that company at a specific price.

structural distortion   Specific type of distortion related to sectoral shares—for example, the importance of the industrial sectors, typically measured by the ratio of industrial output to total output of the economy.

system objectives   Goals, adopted by those directing the economic system, for economic growth, income distribution, regional income differentials and so on.

superstructure   Organization of society, according to Marx.

surplus value   Marxian view of exploitation of labor as the source of profits.

techpromfinplans   Soviet technical, industrial, and administrative plans.

technical–administrative problems   Difficulties derived from individuals whose decision-making ability is impaired by such limitations as incomplete information.

time lags   In a formal model, a time delay between changes in the explanatory variable(s) and changes in the dependent variable such as economic growth.

total factor productivity   Output per unit of combined (capital and labor) inputs. The inputs are usually weighted by their respective contribution to total output.

total income   Aggregate income of a unit such as an economy.

transaction costs   Costs associated with searching for information, bargaining, policing, and enforcement.

transition　Movement from one economic system to another and different economic system. During the 1990s, the replacement of the command economy with the market economy.

transition time　Examination of transition dated from the actual beginning of the transition process.

transparency　Openness in financial and contractual dealings such that all elements of transactions are readily apparent to the participants.

trial-and-error model　Problem-solving method proposed by Oscar Lange that focuses on the use of a general equilibrium framework to find equilibrium prices through a number of sequential stages.

unfunded liability　Shortfall in funds currently available to meet the future obligations of a retirement program.

underemployment　Utilization of labor in a less than fully productive fashion; in planned economies, the outcome of a full-employment policy imposed even in those cases where there was excess labor vis-à-vis the tasks to be done, for example, in an enterprise.

universal banks　European banks that are engaged in traditional banking services, such as deposit taking and lending, but also in risk taking, investment banking, and merchant banking.

universal coverage　Such as in Sweden, cradle-to-grave welfare system that allowed anyone to receive benefits regardless of work situation or other criteria.

valuation　Assessment of the value or potential price of an enterprise for purposes of privatization; in market economies, this is generally done through stock valuation, accounting methods, or present-value calculations.

vertical planning structure　Administrative structure in which orders are issued by superiors to subordinates.

voucher privatization　Privatization via issuance, to the population in a transition economy, the use of vouchers that can be redeemed for shares in an organization.

war Communism　Introduction of substantial state ownership within the Soviet Union (1917–1921) to eliminate market relationships in industry and trade, and to institute the forced requisition of agricultural goods.

"Washington Consensus"　Set of guidelines developed and implemented by the IMF to promote economic growth through macroeconomic stabilization and privatization.

"Western-style" tax systems　Tax systems used in market economies (such as sales and income taxes, VAT taxes, and user charges), in contrast to the types of taxes used in command economies (such as the turnover tax and enterprise profit taxes).

work councils　Mechanism through which employers must consult with employees regarding decisions that affect their jobs. Established by the European Works Council Directive in 1994.

World Bank　An international organization providing loans to member countries for the purpose of promoting economic growth and development. Founded in 1944, located in Washington, D.C., and closely associated with the International Monetary Fund.

World Trade Organization (WTO)　Successor to the GATT that provides a forum for the discussion of trade issues.

Index